FOR LESBIANS ONLY:
a separatist anthology

Published by Radical Feminist Lesbian publishers,
Onlywomen Press, Ltd.
38 Mount Pleasant, London WC1X 0AP.
1988, re-issued 1991.

Cover design © Nett Hart (1991)

Typeset by Columns, Reading, U.K.
Printed and bound by Billing & Sons, Worcester, U.K.

British Library Cataloguing in Publication Data

For Lesbians Only
  1. Lesbianism
  I. Hoagland, Sarah Lucia II. Penelope, Julia
     306. 7' 663

    ISBN 0-906500-28-1

FOR LESBIANS ONLY:
a separatist anthology

Contents

Contents

ACKNOWLEDGMENTS

No one will be surprised if we acknowledge immediately that it is impossible to mention each of the many Lesbians who has helped with this anthology. It goes without saying that we would not have undertaken this project were it not for the persistent attacks on separatism by feminists and lesbian-feminists who have tried to discredit it as a political analysis by claiming that it is racist, classist, and elitist, and who have tried to trivialize separatists by calling us unrealistic, divisive, and ahistorical. Our anger, frustration, and commitment combined to impel us to compile an anthology of separatist writing. But the anthology would not have been completed without the support and enthusiasm of the many Lesbians who have encouraged us when we despaired and made us laugh when we were ready to give up.

Two Lesbians in particular have been resourceful, creative, and consistent in their help and support, Sidney Spinster and Ariane Brunet. Both Sidney and Ariane actively sought contributors for the anthology, here in the U.S. and internationally. It was Sidney who finally came up with the title for the anthology, after compiling a list of suggestions on her way from Lincoln, Nebraska to Lawrence, Kansas, and Ariane who challenged us when we were ready to quit, encouraged us in our lesbian focus, and argued with us unceasingly about the kind of political statement this anthology should make. We would also like to thank Kate Lavender for putting us in touch with Australian Separatists, Claudie Lesselier for helping us to contact European Lesbian Radicals, Diana Solis for helping us to find contacts in Central and South America, Elana Dykewomon for connecting us with 'lost' Separatists, and the Editors of *Connexions* for their issue on Global Lesbianism #3 (Winter, 1982), for the contacts their efforts produced. Roma Rector, of the Department of English at the University of Nebraska, deserves more credit than we can give her for typing and retyping most of the manuscripts and bringing our editorial errors to our attention.

Several Lesbians read the entire manuscript (or parts of it) and offered criticism, suggestions, and encouragement; their enthusiasm and belief in the importance of this anthology came at critical points: Nett Hart, Lee Lanning, the Bloodroot Collective (Selma Miriam, Betsey Beven, and Noel Giordano), Anna Lee, Anne Throop Leighton, Bette Tallen, Nell Wagonaar (of Labrys: a Women's Wilderness Resort) and most important, the Onlywomen Press Collective.

We also want to thank Sheila Jeffreys who, upon hearing about

Acknowledgments

the anthology from Marilyn Frye, contacted Sarah and carried the manuscript back to England with her; Lee Evans who put special care into bringing separatists from all over the country to the National Radical Thought Conference for Women in Cleveland, May, 1987; and Barbara Grier who has consistently offered her advice, help, and enthusiasm.

Finally, of course, we must thank our contributors, who have been patient when we were slow, open to our editorial suggestions and requests for revisions, A-mazing in their diversity, and inspiring in their creativity. We send special thanks to Meg Jochild, Amber, Jacqueline Elizabeth, Rebecca Lewin, Linnea Johnson, J.E.B., Giovanna Tató, Kimberly O'Sullivan, Susan Hawthorne, and Chiyuki Tada, whose work we were unable to include. Without all of our contributors there would be no Separatist anthology at all, and its strength and vitality spring from their combined gynergies. Omissions and shortcomings are ours.

Grateful acknowledgement of first publication and permission to reprint is made for the following:

'Over the Walls', 'Separatism', 'Directions', 'Lesbian Mothers', 'Addition' and 'Problems of our Movement' by Alice, Gordon, Debbie and Mary, *Lesbian Separatism: An Amazon Analysis*, July 1973, Seattle. (The collective grants others in the movement the right to reprint any portions of the document provided each section is reprinted in its entirety.); 'Why Be Separatist? Exploring Women-only Energy' by Alix Dobkin, *Womanews*, Vol. 4, No. 4, April 1983; An earlier version of 'A Black Separatist' by Anna Lee was published as 'One Black Separatist', *Innerviews*, Vol. 5, No. 3, Aradia, 1981; 'The Tired Old Question of Male Children' by Anna Lee, *Lesbian Ethics*, Vol. 1, No. 2; 'Separatism and Radicalism' by Ariane Brunet and Louise Turcotte, first published as a report entitled 'Rapport des ateliers', *Amazones d'hier, Lesbiennes d'aujourd'hui*, Vol. 1, No. 2–3, 1982; 'We Have To Ask The Question: What is Happening?' by Baba Copper, *Common Lives/Lesbian Lives*, Fall, No. 9, 1983; 'Lesbian Separatism: A Historical and Comparative Perspective' by Bette S. Tallen, was prepared for delivery at the National Women's Studies Association Conference in Columbus, Ohio, 1983; 'For Women Who Call Themselves Lesbians – Are You Thinking of Getting Pregnant?' by Bev Jo, is a shortened version of an essay which first appeared in *Furie Lesbienne/Lesbian Fury*, Vol. 3, No. 1, Spring, 1986, *Hag Rag* 4, Winter, 1987, and *Amazones d'hier, Lesbiennes D'aujourd'hui*, Spring, 1988; 'Owning Jewish Separatism and Lesbian Separatism' by Billie Potts, *The Lesbian Insider/Insighter/Inciter*, No. 9, December 1982; 'Separatist' by Caryatis Cardea, *Common Lives/Lesbian Lives*, No. 13, Autumn, 1984; 'Warning: Heterosexuality May Damage Your Health' by Vanilla-Strawberry, *Clit 007*, Geneva, February, 1982;

'Bibliography on Lesbian Separatism' by Clare Potter, *Lesbian Periodicals Index*, Naiad, 1986; 'Motherhood' by Claudie Lesselier, and 'Feminism and Radical Lesbianism' by Claudie, Graziella, Irene, Martine and Françoise, were first published as 'A Propos de la Maternite' and 'Feminisme et Lesbianisme radical', Front Des Lesbiennes Radicales, Textes de la rencontre des 14 et 15 novembre, 1981; 'CLIT Statement No. 2', 'The Agent Within' and 'Trying Hard to Forfeit All I've Known' are part of the CLIT Statement No. 2, collection 1, *off our backs*; Part of the essay 'x-tra insight' by flyin thunda cloud, first appeared as a letter to the editors, *The Lesbian Insider/Insighter/Inciter*, No. 7, April, 1982; 'The Furies' by Ginny Berson, *The Furies*, No. 1, January 1972 and *Lesbianism and the Women's Movement*, ed. Nancy Myron & Charlotte Bunch, Diana Press, Baltimore, 1975; 'Response' by The Gorgons, was part of 'Separatist Symposium', *DYKE, A QUARTERLY*, No. 6 (Summer 1978), Tomato Publications; 'Over The Walls', 'Separatism', 'Finally Out of Drag', 'Gut Feeling' and 'This is the Year to Stamp out the Y Chromosome' by Gutter Dyke Collective, *Dykes and Gorgons*, May/June 1973; 'In Defence of Lesbian-Separatism: A Response to the Combahee River Collective Statement' by Isabel Andrews and Doreen Worden, *Voices: A Survival Manual for Wimmin*, No. 6, December 1981; 'How Gay to be Different' and the abortion demonstration leaflet by Isabel Dargent, *Le Feminaire*, No. 4; 'Lesbian Separatist Basics' and 'Comparative Separatism' by Jean Langford, Kathy Ross and K. Hess, *Feminism First/Feminismo Primero*, Tsunami Press, 1981; 'Remembering: A Time I will Be My Own Beginning' by Jeffner Allen, *Lesbian Philosophy: Explorations*, Institute of Lesbian Studies, 1986; 'A Cursory and Precursory History of Language and the Telling of It,' by Julia Penelope first appeared in Sinister Wisdom 1 (December 1976); 'Lesbian Separatism: The Linguistic and Social Sources of Separatist Politics' by Julia Penelope, was originally prepared for a workshop on Lesbian Separatism for the Fourth Annual Congress of the Rutgers Student Homophile League, 1974, published in *The Gay Advocate*, ed. Louie Crew, ETC Publications, Palm Springs, 1978. A longer version of 'The Mystery of Lesbians' by Julia Penelope first appeared in *Lesbian Ethics*, Vol. 1, Nos 1, 2 and 3, 1984–1985; 'Separatist Symposium' by Liza Cowan, *DYKE, A QUARTERLY*, No. 6 (Summer 1978), Tomato Publications; 'The Awakening' by Lee Lynch, *Old Dyke Tales*, Naiad Press, 1984; 'Album Liner Notes From a Lesbian Portrait' and 'Family of Woman' by Linda Shear are part of the album, *A Lesbian Portrait*, copyright Old Lady Blue Jeans, 1975, 1977 a/b/a Linda Shear, October 1977; 'The Issue is Woman-identification' by Margaret Sloan-Hunter, *Plexus: West Coast Women's Press*, Vol. 3, No. 4, June 1976; 'Some Reflections on Separatism and Power' by Marilyn Frye, was first presented at a meeting of the Society for Women in Philosophy, Eastern Division, December 1977 and published in *Sinister Wisdom*, No. 6, Summer 1978 and in *The Politics of Reality: Essays in Feminist Theory*, The Crossing Press, 1983; 'Separation: Room of One's Own' by Mary Daly excerpted from *Gyn/Ecology*, Beacon Press, Boston, 1978 and The Women's Press, London, 1979; 'Be-Friending: the Lust to Share

Acknowledgments

Happiness' by Mary Daly excerpted from *Pure Lust: Elemental Feminist Philosophy*, Beacon Press, Boston, 1984 and The Women's Press, London, 1984; 'The Mind-Drifting Islands' by Micheline Grimard-Leduc, *'L'Ile des amantes'*, Micheline Grimard-Leduc, Quebec, 1982, forthcoming publication in a Canadian lesbian anthology edited by Sharon D. Stone; 'The Straight Mind' by Monique Wittig, *Feminist Issues*, Vol. 1, No. 1, Summer 1980; 'One is not Born a Woman' by Monique Wittig, *Feminist Issues*, Vol. 1, No. 2, Winter 1981; 'Response' by Penny House was part of 'Separatist Symposium', *DYKE, A QUARTERLY*, No. 6, Summer 1978, Tomato Publications; 'The Woman Identified Woman' by Radicalesbians was first distributed as a leaflet at a New York City conference, *The Ladder*, Vol. 11 & 12, August/September 1970, *Notes From the Third Year: Women's Liberation*, 1971; 'How to Stop Choking to Death or Separatism' by Revolutionary Lesbians, *Spectre: paper of Revolutionary Lesbians*, No. 2, May/June 1971; 'Battle Fatigue' and 'They Tried to Make it Personal' by Revolutionary Lesbians, *Spectre: paper of Revolutionary Lesbians*, No. 4, September/October 1971; 'Some Thoughts on Separatism' by Sarah Grace, *The Lesbian Insider/Insighter/Inciter*, No. 5, November 1981; 'An Invitation' by Sarah Lucia Hoagland, *Lesbian Ethics*, Vol. 1, No. 3, Fall 1985; 'Introduction' by Sarah Lucia Hoagland was first published in a shortened form as 'Lesbian Separatism: An Empowering Reality', *GOSSIP*, No. 6 and *Sinister Wisdom*, No. 34, Spring 1988; 'The Evolution of Lesbian Separatist Consciousness' by Sidney Spinster, *The Lesbian Insider/Insighter/Inciter*, No. 7, April 1982.

INTRODUCTION[1]

For Lesbians Only (FLO) began in the u.s. in january of 1981 as Julia Penelope and I finished our work guest-editing *Sinister Wisdom* 15, the special issue on violence against lesbians. Separately but simultaneously it occurred to us to bring out an anthology on separatism. For the next four years, our work proceeded between busy university schedules and across 500 miles, which at least tripled the project's schedule. Nevertheless, soliciting or finding material, reading and working on the manuscripts, and corresponding with contributors and others excited by the project kept me heartened and struggling. The process was enlivening for me and for Julia.

We began by putting notices in u.s. lesbian and feminist publications soliciting separatist material. Mostly, however, our soliciting occurred by word of mouth. We put a great deal of effort into locating separatists we knew of, tracking down early separatist material, and encouraging separatists to write new material.

There is a story for each contribution. For example, one separatist, whom I had been after to write something for the anthology for over two years, finally did write a poem and read it one night at chicago's mountain moving coffeehouse. Right after the reading I went up to her and snatched her poem, afraid that if I let her go home with it, it would be buried and I might never have another chance to get my hands on it. The next morning it occurred to me that I had taken the poet's only copy of her poem. I immediately copied it and took it back to her, managing to wake her up in the process!

While this is primarily a u.s. anthology, Julia and I sought contributions from separatists in other countries as well. Ariane Brunet and Danielle Charest of amazones d'hier, lesbiennes d'aujourd'hui in québec encouraged us, and out of Ariane's efforts grew our work on the section on radical lesbianism: material from québec, france, belgium, and switzerland – french-speaking areas – which offers an approach distinct from u.s. separatism (which has its own variations) but which nevertheless emerges from a sister spirit.

In addition, we wrote to addresses listed in the global lesbian issue of *Connexions*,[2] receiving many wonderful replies. Again, word of mouth played a significant part. We contacted separatists, other lesbians, and supportive feminists in australia, brasil, india, germany, finland, japan, italy, and mexico. We received material from italy, australia, and japan. In the long run, however, we did not include this material. As Onlywomen suggested, to simply include it among the u.s. material had an homogenizing effect while to include it in a separate section was tokenizing. As we found no way around this problem, we reluctantly agreed to drop the material. We also received material from english-speaking canada which we have included since it is intimately involved in the debates about separatism that have gone on here in the u.s.

From the beginning we encountered resistance in the u.s. to our effort: some feminist periodicals did not print our call for papers and some separatists exhorted others not to contribute. We encountered lesbian publishers who were unwilling to take on the project either because of its size or their politics. Smaller lesbian presses, excited by the project, were simply unable to take it on. Finally, in 1984 with over 75 contributors and much interest in the manuscript, Julia and I put it down for lack of any publishing prospect beyond self-publishing, which neither of us was able to take on.

Then in 1986, Onlywomen Press of england contacted us inquiring about publishing FLO. Because of what had gone on in the past, I could not believe that the Onlywomen Collective was excited about the anthology. Their enthusiasm and concern about the work deeply encouraged both Julia and me. By that time I had taken over the project; Julia subsequently acted as a consultant, and the final work toward publication began.

The material in this anthology was principally written between 1970 and 1984. Some of the contributors have changed their positions (a few no longer consider themselves separatists while others are more firmly separatists and still others have changed their separatist focus). But once Onlywomen asked to publish FLO, rather than open the selections to revision, we decided contributors could specify significant changes in their politics by means of their contributor's note. Julia and I actually made this decision in considering what to do with the 'old' and out of print separatist material. We have chosen selections we were able to get ahold of which we consider significant separatist statements and which each author, regardless of subsequent changes, agrees should be made available. One favorite part of this anthology is the contributors' notes precisely because these notes were written at least four years (and often much longer) after the author's contribution was written. The unexpected treat from this is the sense of change and process that takes place in our lives which the contributors' notes reflects.

Julia and I worked on this anthology because we were tired of so many non-separatists telling us what separatism is, and we felt it time we speak for ourselves. I must emphasize, however, that this work is neither complete nor representative; we gave up that dream somewhere toward the end of 1983.[3] *For Lesbians Only* is simply a collection of writings on separatism primarily by u.s. separatists, each of whom offers something unique and whose work contributes to the ground of lesbian being.

My pleasure in working with lesbians of backgrounds different from my own has been twofold. First, as a result of such work I have realized that my own voice is centered and whole and yet also limited – that is, unique. Secondly, through attending different lesbian voices, I have realized that our voices are not in competition with one another. Instead, together they solidify a lesbian ground of being, making possible the creation and development of lesbian meaning. I find this exciting. Bringing together lesbian perceptions excites me.

This book excites me. Each contributor writes in her own voice, the voice she is comfortable with. Each offers something she found important at this time of her spinning, telling us what she was drawn to and came to understand. Each moves with integrity though no one tells the whole story. And each is operating out of a lesbian context; she is somehow related to the others and yet unique. While there are significant differences within these pages, each contributor makes clear her relationship to the society of dominance. At the time of creating her work, each had made a certain type of ethical choice, a choice to separate, to withdraw.

Yet that choice has been distorted or erased far too often. In developing my work on Lesbian Ethics I realized that traditional ethics does not recognize withdrawal, separation, as a legitimate ethical option. Within the society of dominance, separation is a non-choice. This judgment is reflected among lesbians. Too many lesbians hold the perception that separatism is not active, that separatists are hiding from reality and ignore the 'larger picture.' This judgment is an erasure of the moral and political function of separatism.

Separatism offers a significant type of choice, one which has a different function than that involved in choosing to challenge the system from within. Philosophically, there are at least two ways to challenge a basic statement or idea: we can argue that it is false or we can render it nonsense. Rendering it nonsense is to treat it as unintelligible, as having no sense. Arguing that it is false may bring a certain kind of satisfaction, but it is nevertheless to agree that the statement is possibly true – that it makes enough sense to debate. Thus while challenging it this way we are, at a deeper level, validating it.

3

For example, one idea still basic to university atmospheres is that blacks are genetically inferior to whites. Liberals will come up with a raft of arguments to prove that claim false. But in so doing, they are tacitly agreeing that the claim is intelligible and debatable. In arguing that blacks are not genetically inferior to whites, academic liberals agree that it makes sense to consider whether blacks (but not whites) are genetically inferior (to the norm, namely whites). Another choice is to refuse to engage in debate, to separate from it, to treat the claim as nonsense, to say it makes no sense.[4] Similar situations exist concerning the 'debate' about women's rights, the 'debate' about whether large numbers of jews were murdered during the holocaust, and many other 'debates.'

We live within a system of values, a system which constructs what we perceive as fact – for example, man is rational, woman needs a man's guidance. When we engage in that system, tacitly we agree to its values. When we engage in a system which offers the system's background values as fact, for example white supremacy or male supremacy, we contribute by consensus to its underlying structure even when also challenging it by attempting to reform or deny such values. To withdraw from a system or a particular situation is a different kind of challenge. To withdraw or separate is to refuse to act according to the system's rules and framework and thereby refuse to validate its basic values.[5]

Withdrawal and separation are not perceived as options when the game played appears to be the only game in town and so is taken for reality. In a sense the game is reality, but its continued existence is not a matter of fact, not a matter of nature, so much as it is a matter of agreement: players agree on what will count as reality by what they focus on and attend.

Separatism is not recognized as a moral and political choice because those in power do not want us to perceive participation as a choice. To engage in a situation or a system in order to try to change it is one choice. To withdraw from it, particularly in order to render it meaningless, is another choice.

Within a given situation or at a given moment there are often good reasons for either choice. Further, both choices involve considerable risk; neither one comes with guarantees: while directly challenging something can validate it, withdrawing may allow it to continue essentially unhampered. But what is missing from traditional ethics and often from lesbian community ethics is acknowledgment that there are ethical choices at this level, that participation is one of those choices, and that separation is another. And in assessing those choices, as Anna Lee notes, separatists realize that to participate is to enact the values of a hostile society and so to participate in the attack on women and the erasure of lesbians.[6]

Thus, the perception that separatism is merely a reaction, a running away, and has no integrity of its own, is a failure or refusal of understanding. Separatism is not a retreat in the sense of hiding from reality and refusing to deal with the facts. Nor is separatism a reactionary movement: it does not emerge from a fear of men or an inability to cope or deal with them or because a lesbian either was or was not fucked.

Similarly, separatism is not a phase during which we learn to feel better about ourselves and get rid of negative feelings so we can function better in coalitions. To understand separatism in any of these ways is to invoke a patriarchal context. As Jeffner Allen writes about manhating in her contribution to the anthology, it is not a whim or an aberration. It is a challenge to a context and values which accepts, indeed finds it desirable, that men do what they do.

Separatism is a chosen response, separatists having taken cognizance of our environment, an affirmation of what we hold valuable to our selves. Separatism is a challenge to what counts as fact and the beginning of the creation of new value.

In this respect, separatism is a yes-saying as much as it is a no-saying. No-saying is essential, as Marilyn Frye argues in her contribution to the anthology. But if we perceive separatism only in terms of a no, then, as Nett Hart suggested to me in a conversation about separatism, we have serious conflicts. For example, we have a conflict between being open to creative changes in the universe, on the one hand, and rejecting the direction of 'new-age' or 'sensitive' men, on the other. Or, another example, we have a conflict between perceiving ourselves as caring beings on the one hand and not being willing to deal with little boys on the other. But such conflicts are not necessary; when we perceive separatism as a yes, we perceive ourselves as caring beings who create values possible for lesbians and all women.[7] And we realize we can't do both – give satisfaction to boys' needs as constructed by society, for example, *and* move toward lesbian culture. Significantly, of the organizations I know which have policies restricting or excluding male children, none began its policy on purely theoretical grounds. Each developed its policy as a result of experience.

There's a choice. And separatists focus on what allows us to choose ourselves and lesbians, not always compromising that choice with man-serving. Once we perceive separation as a yes, we can build more and more choice on that initial yes and so create lesbian community for itself, not simply in response to an outside threat.

This brings in focus the question of separatist motivation, particularly decisions around when to work in coalition and when not. It's our impulse towards creating our own communities and values that guides our choices. As Joyce Trebilcot wrote in a letter to *The Women's Review of Books*:

> Lesbianism for me excludes participating in relationships with men for their own sake, but it does not preclude political action that confronts men and their institutions. Sometimes directly facing men is necessary or worthwhile in order for us to establish our rights, to obtain the resources we need, or to defend and support other women. Many separatists are regular organizers of and participants in political actions that involve dealing with men both in confrontation and in coalition. It is a misunderstanding of separatism to suppose that it is always or usually similar to the withdrawal of some Germans into an 'interior life' during the Third Reich.[8]

She goes on to state that rather than valuing woman-only space as a means to a better relationship with men, she will deal with men only as a means to being with women. Sometimes our tactics might seem identical to those of non-separatists and non-lesbians, but separatists are doing something different.[9]

In this respect, as Nett Hart noted in conversation, it is erroneous to regard separatism as coming out of feminism. If we perceive separatism as merely derivative of feminism, we would think of it as an extreme reaction because of what passes for feminism today. Early feminism of this wave (very late 60s, early 70s), in its focus on women, was deeply disturbing to the status quo. In changing their relationship to the world – nature and culture – women were removing themselves from the world men had taken/dominated for their own purposes. Early feminists were separating from patriarchy and its values.

No, separatism does not come out of feminism, rather feminism has developed away from separatism. Reform feminists broke from early feminism by assimilating their goals to the goals patriarchy has for humans (males). That is, they fight to be humans in patriarchal terms. It is not that there was early radical feminism and then separatists broke off as more radical. Rather feminists broke off toward assimilation. Early feminist groups were separatist; there was no place for men.[10] As Bette Tallen comments, lesbian separatists are the only stability the women's movement has known, holding on to basic political analyses developed in the early 70s while other parts of the feminist movement wavered and often abandoned the politics with which they began.[11]

Separatism is not perceived as an ethical choice in part because it is not perceived as active nor separatists as activists. But such a judgment affirms patriarchal values. As Joyce Trebilcot wrote in *Gossip* and *off our backs*:

> To be an activist is to engage in actions intended to make changes in who has what political power. In male-thought, it is assumed that there is a fixed amount of power in a particular situation. Hence, activism is understood by men as aimed at a redistribution of power (as distinct from the creation of new power) and as essentially adversarial. In this context, the essence of activism is to persuade those in power that they morally (i.e., because it is right) or prudentially (i.e., because it is in their interest) ought to change their behaviour. Paradigm cases of activism include demonstrations, letter-writing campaigns, and guerilla actions.
>
> This heteropatriarchal concept of activism excludes two central kinds of feminist activism: separatism and private activism. The activism of separatists is based on the understanding that one way to change the distribution of power is for a hitherto powerless group to separate off and empower themselves. When women separate and hence create power for ourselves, certain men are deprived of power they would otherwise have had, i.e., power over these particular women; but the women's power isn't seized *from* the men, it is created by the women for ourselves. Thus, while separatism doesn't *re*distribute power, it alters, sometimes radically, the over-all distribution of power.[12]

And this brings up the issue of the 'larger picture': Is our separatism the big picture or is it that we separate in order to come back to a big picture? What lesbian separatists have argued is that big political movements and legal reform don't bring the kind of change we're after. Yes, women can vote now, and that is a necessary step; and yes, segregation per se is no longer openly legal; and yes, the nazis were stopped, temporarily; and yes, in russia and china mammon does not reign supreme . . . yet; and yes, the official war in vietnam is over, temporarily; and on and on. But no, these accomplishments have not brought or even encouraged the kind of lesbian values that separatists and radical lesbians are working toward.

At most, large political movements and legal reforms stop crises, and at times we may decide that now is a time to work to stop some crisis or other. But such movements and reforms do nothing to change the fabric of our society, they do not undermine the structure and foundation which feed oppression and which will make it credible again and again in countless different arenas. Further, insofar as these crises force us to play by dominant rules, they reinforce dominant structure and ideology. Others forget or have not figured out that men create crises, when all else fails, to force us to play by their rules and game plan, to force us to stay focused on them. Responding to crises does nothing to deter the direction of a society that thrives on crises.

Those who dismiss separatist politics as hiding from reality tacitly agree with the patriarchy and help to keep us believing that patriarchy is the only reality, that what men call revolution is the only revolution, and that what men call change is the only change. In my opinion, it is separatists who are fighting the 'larger' cause.[13]

Related is the issue of 'widening' feminist politics to include greater numbers. Early radical feminism presented a choice for women. Watering down the politics to make them more palatable undermines that choice. It is more important to make the values and choices clear and allow each woman to choose than it is to lure a woman on false pretenses or worse, to change feminist politics to include those who would reject feminist values. That, of course, is not to 'widen' feminist politics, but shift its locus from those who create its values to those who don't find the values valuable.[14] It is condescending and demeaning to everyone involved. Beyond this, the 'widening' has not resulted in the inclusion of more women, particularly more women of color, but it has resulted in the inclusion of men, particularly white men.

And this raises the question of racism. Separatism is portrayed as racist either because separatists allegedly do not recognize or acknowledge that men of color are oppressed or because it is alleged that the only way to end racism is to work in coalitions or because some women of color don't feel comfortable separating from men of color. Of course, some lesbians/women of color and jewish lesbians/women feel quite comfortable separating from men, and some white, gentile women don't feel comfortable separating from white, gentile men . . .; the issue is, what value is enacted by the choices? As Anna Lee writes: 'The ideology of separating from males is racist only if one accepts that males define ethnic community.'[15]

A more significant and problematic argument is that if lesbians/women of color and/or jewish lesbians/women separate, the separation is not only from the values of white, capitalist patriarchy, but also from the values of black or puerto rican or jewish culture, for example. This second separation involves conforming to the dominant culture's attempt to annihilate the values of mexican and chinese and black culture, for example, and brings up questions of identity and group loyalty which each separating lesbian must answer to her own satisfaction. Nevertheless, the lesbians/women who do make the choice to separate do not totally reject jewish or chicana or quebecoise culture, for example, though there is a separation from masculinist parts of the culture. Lesbian separatists of color and jewish lesbian separatists bring those values of black and seminole and jewish culture, for example, to lesbian community which enrich and develop lesbian values. (In like fashion, non-jewish white lesbians bring those values of non-jewish white culture to lesbian community which enrich and develop lesbian values.)

Lesbian community is a rich source of diversity and offers us concrete access to a multitude and variety of differences virtually not available elsewhere, certainly not to lesbians. As Elana Dykewomon and Anna Lee both commented to me, lesbian community provides us with the ability to really sweat it out together, to understand how our different values operate/engage/distort/contribute/mesh/clash/complement in our various political/cultural work. That others offer what I do not have direct access to is a gift I cherish, and it is part of what makes lesbian community so very special.

Labeling separatism racist *per se* is a way of disagreeing with separatist politics without any real argument or debate over political differences. Merely hurling a label no one of us would want to be accused of is an effective tool to avoid debate of the issues, to censor ideas and silence argument, especially criticism.

For example, there is a difference between concerning ourselves with racism as lesbian separatists and deciding that the only way to *really* work on racism is to stop being separatists and join with men. The latter claim presupposes both that lesbians are not valuable enough to receive our own attention and that lesbians are incapable of accomplishing meaningful work without men. Beyond self-effacement of this kind, there is an unwillingness to learn from herstory. Time after time after time, both in the first wave of feminism and in this wave, when women bring in men, the values of the project, whatever it is, shift to men's values and purposes.

In some respects, I find labeling separatism racist functions to obscure a serious division between socialist and anarchist tendencies among lesbians. In my experience, anti-separatists have more u.s. socialist sensibilities – challenging the system by trying to substitute another one which, while addressing significant economic problems, nevertheless relies heavily on hierarchy (dominance and subordination), manipulation, and institutional control; often sacrificing means to end. Separatists tend to have more anarchist sensibilities – distrusting institutional power of any kind, wanting new value to emerge from small groups engaged in creating new ways of being, and realizing that the means determine the end – that is, how we behave toward each other is the value we enact.

And this leads to what is perhaps the most important aspect of separatism for me, namely its focus on lesbians (or women) and a creation of lesbian meaning, lesbian reality. Perceiving is a process of creation. As we choose what we will attend, we determine what is significant and what is not; we give meaning to, validate, that which we focus on. I am not interested in focusing on men, whether exceptional or normal. Separatism, for me at least, is largely a matter of what Marilyn Frye and Carolyn Shafer term lesbian connectionism and also what french-speaking lesbians call radical lesbianism. By focusing on ourselves and pursuing what we find valuable, we create lesbian meaning.

Each lesbian whose work lies within these pages has made a break and she has chosen to focus on lesbians, or in some cases, on women. Despite the lack of ethical and political acknowledgment and despite all the distortions, each of these contributors, and many others whose work does not appear in this anthology, chose to begin withdrawing her focus from the dominant culture's romance with men and their values. And regardless of whether her focus is lesbians or women, the context is lesbian. These works do not disagree about withdrawing and refocusing. This tacit agreement gives life to a new reality. The point of my separating is to maintain this focus, this ground of being; to develop my own emerging perceptions and encourage development of the emerging perceptions of my peers, perceptions which grow away from the values of the dominant ideology.

Yes, of course, to have chosen to withdraw from – to cease validating – the dominant ideology is not yet to say what will take its place. While we have named the direction and suggested certain parameters of our ideals, we have not yet developed the full set of values which replace those which justify and validate oppression. We are acknowledging the task and setting ourselves to begin the creation of new value. That is precisely why it is crucial we focus on ourselves as lesbians and create lesbian meaning.

And we have begun. We have begun lesbian journeying. We have begun lesbian journeying to touch a rich source of imagination and dreams. We have begun exploring these ideas, living them to find out what works, what doesn't, and why.

Nevertheless, while we have begun, we have also let up in certain respects. I think u.s. separatists have much to gain from the work of both french-speaking radical lesbians and separatists in england. Separatists in the u.s. have retreated from developing our analysis of heterosexualism and affirming the value of lesbianism. Sometimes I describe this as lesbian journeying coming to a halt. To this idea Nett Hart responded:

> I don't think lesbian journeying ever came to a halt. Instead I think our words/actions became less identifiably separatist as they took on complexity, as we adapted our work to a much longer struggle than we anticipated in the early years. Much early separatist theory was developed by dykes (both urban and rural) in communal households/tribes, and in political action and work collectives. As things began to change, separatist theory had a hard time adapting to new circumstances, i.e., the proximity of men. These circumstances changed both our focus and how we named that focus. I think our sense that the movement was coming to a halt emerges from a failure to validate what we have been doing.

She goes on to suggest that there may be more separatists now than at any previous time:

> I think the betrayal of a radical agenda by reform feminists has been significant. Many separatists worked in female environments on straight agendas – abortion, childcare, battered women, welfare reform, sexual harassment and discrimination, rape crises, women's studies – and as the ideology with which we came to these commitments is supplanted by pieces of the 'feminist' pie, we have come to realize how much we were feeding a reform agenda. Both these 'political' movements and feminist therapy have served to help women adjust to the world as created by men. Not every coalescence around women is radical. In choosing to work with women (because 'every woman can be a Lesbian' as Alix Dobkin sings) we accepted the circumstances of their lives and diverted ourselves from

our lesbian focus. I think the realization that these reform measures neither engender nor tolerate Lesbian vision has catapulted many Lesbians into Lesbian separatist self-love.[16]

It is time to come back, to focus on an organic Lesbian journey. Julia Penelope's concern in working on this anthology has been with erasure, mine is with focus. But they are two aspects of one commitment, for when we stop focusing on each other and instead focus on the agendas of the fathers, we engage in our own erasure. When lesbians turn our backs on each other as lesbians, we cease to exist in certain key ways. We can not exist as lesbians in the dominant society, and if we don't exist in each other's attention then we don't exist at all except as isolated beings left to survive and hang on and integrate as best we can into heterosexual concepts, or we are left to be complete loners with no fertile ground on which to grow and develop.

At the national radical thought conference for women in cleveland, may, 1987, about 49 separatists from all over the u.s. came to participate. We found that while we had all come through a period of attack and retrenchment, we had endured; and we found we were moving toward creating lesbian value. It was a powerful time for us.[17] And the conference worked for us because it was made up of self-loving women who, for the most part, were working on issues that directly concern us.

It is time to come back. We have many difficult and complex tasks ahead of us. For example, continuing to address world-wide misogyny, without falling prey to arguments which use cultural relativism to block criticism of the subordination of women and the annihilation of lesbians, while also realizing our own connection to a u.s. imperialist tradition. For example, dealing with the pressure of coalition thinking (vs. actual coalition work at given times for particular reasons) as men parade back and forth with nuclear 'power' and try to transfix us with their existential necrophilia. For example, answering the challenge to lesbian feminism from the various French-speaking radical lesbians which exposes how u.s. lesbian feminists have been remiss in developing analyses of the ideology of heterosexualism.

It is time to come back again to ourselves and our own ground of being with all our differences and ragged edges. It is time we refocus and continue our journey. The breaks we have made from patriarchal thinking come from lesbians daring to try to create something new. Such focus, away from erasure, defensiveness, silence, and mere survival, is important; it is time to move again as lesbians.

Sarah Lucia Hoagland
1984 and 1987

Notes

1.   I received much help in preparing this introduction. In particular Nett Hart, Anne Throop Leighton, Anna Lee, Lee Evans, Elana Dykewomon, Julia Penelope, zana, Michele Gautreaux, Lilian Mohin, Anna Livia, and Kathy Munzer have contributed thoughtful criticisms. The body of this introduction has appeared in both *Gossip* 6 and *Sinister Wisdom* 34 to announce the anthology.
2.   *Connexions: An International Women's Quarterly* 3 (Winter 1982), a special issue on global lesbianism.
3.   For example, there is very little material in this anthology from lesbians on the land. For an anthology of writings by lesbians on the land, note *Lesbian Land*, ed. Joyce Cheney, 1985, Word Weavers, Box 8742, Minneapolis, MN 55408, U.S.A.
4.   Note that the erasure of lesbian choice and existence by the fathers in effect renders the choice nonsense, unintelligible, unthinkable, non-choices within a patriarchal framework.
5.   The next two paragraphs contain arguments presented in my manuscript, *Lesbian Ethics: Toward New Value* (forthcoming, Institute of Lesbian Studies, PO Box 60242, Palo Alto, CA 94306, U.S.A.).

Note that in this respect, separatism has a function different from that of segregation. Segregation is done by a dominant group to a group it wishes to subordinate and control, while separatism involves a person or group withdrawing from a group situation in order to avoid being controlled by the framework of that group. Thus the function of segregation is a dominant group separating off another group in order to keep the group subordinate and to determine the social perception of that group through such methods as stereotyping, thereby engaging in effective erasure. The function of separatism is a group withdrawing from an existing group's framework in order to not be constructed by that group's values – often to exorcise stereotypes, combatting that erasure – and to create its own values, values not attainable within the framework of the initial group.

The erasure is intimately related to choice. Michele Gautreaux, who grew up in a totally black housing project isolated from chicago proper, relates that 'because most had not chosen that environment or that it be all Black, at the time separateness was a perceived disadvantage compared to eatonville of Zora Neal Hurston's childhood which was chosen.' [personal communication]
6.   Anna Lee, paper in progress on the lesbian community.
7.   In fact, as Lee Evans mentioned to me in passing, choosing ourselves

is part of what makes us lesbians, for traditional woman values dictate always choosing others.

8. Joyce Trebilcot, letter, *The Women's Review of Books* IV 2 (November 1986): p. 4.

9. Conversation, Nett Hart.

10. Conversation, Nett Hart. Significantly, as Leslie Levy and Caryatis Cardea noted at the national radical thought conference for women in cleveland, may, 1987, when compromise is called for it is the more radical elements who are expected to compromise toward a lesser politic; the less radical are not expected to compromise by increasing in radicalism.

11. As cited in 'Doing Things Differently,' J. Robbins, *Womanews* 8 6 (June 1987): p. 2.

12. Joyce Trebilcot, 'In Partial Response to Those Who Worry That Separatism May Be a Political Cop-out: An Expanded Definition of Activism,' *Gossip* 3, pp. 82–83; an earlier version appeared in *off our backs* xvi, 5 (May 1986): p. 13.

13. This argument first appeared in my commentary, 'Dear Julia,' *Lesbian Ethics* 1, 2 (Spring 1985): pp. 68–73.

14. In other words, feminism is not for all women, feminism is for all women who choose feminist values. Those concerned with making feminism popularly palatable tend to forget this.

15. Anna Lee, letter, *Womanews*, 8 5 (October, 1987): p. 15.

16. Nett Hart, together with Lee Lanning, runs Word Weavers. Together they have produced *Maize: A Lesbian Country Magazine* as well as *Ripening*, *Dreaming*, and *Awakening*, three almanacs of lesbian lore and vision. (Word Weavers, Box 8742, Minneapolis, MN 55408, U.S.A.)

17. One significant aspect of the conference as a whole is that at the end, separatists and non-separatists gave the organizers a standing ovation. While there were mistakes and problems, what we celebrated at that time were the accomplishments.

BEGINNINGS OF OUR CONSCIOUSNESS: DEFINING LESBIAN SEPARATISM

THE WOMAN IDENTIFIED WOMAN

Radicalesbians
1970

What is a lesbian? A lesbian is the rage of all women condensed to the point of explosion. She is the woman who, often beginning at an extremely early age, acts in accordance with her inner compulsion to be a more complete and freer human being than her society – perhaps then, but certainly later – cares to allow her. These needs and actions, over a period of years, bring her into painful conflict with people, situations, the accepted ways of thinking, feeling and behaving, until she is in a state of continual war with everything around her, and usually with herself. She may not be fully conscious of the political implications of what for her began as personal necessity, but on some level she has not been able to accept the limitations and oppression laid on her by the most basic role of her society – the female role. The turmoil she experiences tends to induce guilt proportional to the degree to which she feels she is not meeting social expectations, and/or eventually drives her to question and analyse what the rest of her society, more or less accepts. She is forced to evolve her own life pattern, often living much of her life alone, learning usually much earlier than her 'straight' (heterosexual) sisters about the essential aloneness of life (which the myth of marriage obscures) and about the reality of illusions. To the extent that she cannot expel the heavy socialization that goes with being female, she can never truly find peace with herself. For she is caught somewhere between accepting society's view of her – in which case she cannot accept herself – and coming to understand what this sexist society has done to her and why it is functional and necessary for it to do so. Those of us who work that through find ourselves on the other side of a tortuous journey through a night that may have been decades long. The perspective gained from that journey, the liberation of self, the inner peace, the real love of self and of all women, is something to be shared with all women – because we are all women.

It should first be understood that lesbianism, like male homosexuality, is a category of behavior possible only in a sexist society characterized by rigid sex roles and dominated by male supremacy. Those sex roles dehumanize women by defining us as a supportive/serving caste in relation to the master caste of men, and emotionally cripple men by demanding that they be alienated

17

from their own bodies and emotions in order to perform their economic/political/military functions effectively. Homosexuality is a by-product of a particular way of setting up roles (or approved patterns of behavior) on the basis of sex; as such it is an inauthentic (not consonant with 'reality') category. In a society in which men do not oppress women, and sexual expression is allowed to follow feelings, the categories of homosexuality and heterosexuality would disappear.

But lesbianism is also different from male homosexuality, and serves a different function in the society. 'Dyke' is a different kind of put-down from 'faggot,' although both imply you are not playing your socially assigned sex role – are not therefore a 'real woman' or a 'real man.' The grudging admiration felt for the tomboy and the queasiness felt around a sissy boy point to the same thing: the contempt in which women – or those who play a female role – are held. And the investment in keeping women in that contemptuous role is very great. Lesbian is the word, the label, the condition that holds women in line. When a woman hears this word tossed her way, she knows she is stepping out of line. She knows that she has crossed the terrible boundary of her sex role. She recoils, she protests, she reshapes her actions to gain approval. Lesbian is a label invented by the man to throw at any woman who dares to be his equal, who dares to challenge his prerogatives (including that of all woman as part of the exchange medium among men), who dares to assert the primacy of her own needs. To have the label applied to people active in women's liberation is just the most recent instance of a long history; other women will recall that not so long ago, any woman who was successful, independent, not orienting her whole life about a man, would hear this word. For in this sexist society, for a woman to be independent means she can't be a woman – she must be a dyke. That in itself should tell us where women are at. It says as clearly as can be said: woman and person are contradictory terms. For a lesbian is not considered a 'real woman.' And yet, in popular thinking, there is really only one essential difference between a lesbian and other women: that of sexual orientation – which is to say, when you strip off all the packaging, you must finally realize that the essence of being a 'woman' is to get fucked by men.

'Lesbian' is one of the sexual categories by which men have divided up humanity. While all women are dehumanized as sex objects, as the objects of men, they are given certain compensations: identification with his power, his ego, his status, his protection (from other males), feeling like a 'real woman,' finding social acceptance by adhering to her role, etc. Should a woman confront herself by confronting another woman, there are fewer rationalizations, fewer buffers by which to avoid the stark horror of her dehumanized condition. Herein we find the overriding fear of many women towards exploring intimate relationships with other women: the fear of her being used as a sexual object by a woman, which not only will bring no male-connected compensations, but also will reveal the void which is woman's real situation. This dehumanization is expressed when a straight woman learns that a sister is a lesbian; she begins to relate to her lesbian sister as her potential sex object, laying a surrogate male role on the lesbian. This reveals her heterosexual conditioning to make herself into an object when sex is potentially involved in a relationship, and it denies the lesbian her full humanity. For women, especially those in the movement, to perceive their lesbian sisters through this male grid of role definitions is to accept this male cultural conditioning and to oppress their sisters much as they themselves have been oppressed by men. Are we going to continue the male classification system of defining all females in sexual relation to some other category of people? Affixing the label lesbian not only to a woman who aspires to be a person, but also to any situation of real love, real solidarity, real primacy among women is a primary form of divisiveness among women: it is the condition which keeps women within the confines of the feminine role, and it is the debunking/scare term that keeps women from forming any primary attachments, groups, or associations among ourselves.

Women in the movement have in most cases gone to great lengths to avoid discussion and confrontation with the issue of lesbianism. It puts people up-tight. They are hostile, evasive, or try to incorporate it into some 'broader issue.' They would rather not talk about it. If they have to, they try to dismiss it as a 'lavender herring.' But it is no side issue. It is absolutely essential to the success and fulfillment of the women's liberation movement that this issue be dealt with. As long as the label 'dyke' can be used to frighten women into a less militant stand, keep her separate from her sisters, keep her from giving primacy to anything other than men and family – then to that extent she is controlled by the male culture. Until women see in each other the possibility of primal commitment which includes sexual love, they will be denying themselves the love and value they readily accord to men, thus affirming their second-class status. As long as male acceptability is primary – both to individual women and to the movement as a whole – the term lesbian will be used effectively against women. Insofar as women want only more privileges within the system, they do not want to antagonize male power. They instead seek acceptability for women's liberation, and the most crucial aspect of the acceptability is to deny lesbianism – i.e., deny any fundamental challenge to the basis of the female role.

It should also be said that some younger, more radical women have honestly begun to discuss lesbianism, but so far it has been primarily as a sexual 'alternative' to men. This, however, is still giving primacy to men, both because the idea of relating more completely to women occurs as a negative reaction to men, and because the lesbian relationship is being characterized simply by sex, which is divisive and sexist. On one level, which is both personal and political, women may withdraw emotional and sexual energies from men, and work out various alternatives for those energies in their own lives. On a different political/psychological level, it must be understood that what is crucial is that women begin disengaging from male-defined response patterns. In the privacy of our own psyches, we must cut those cords to the core. For irrespective of where our love and sexual energies flow, if we are male-identified in our heads, we cannot realize our autonomy as human beings.

But why is it that women have related to and through men? By virtue of having been brought up in a male society, we have internalized the male culture's definition of ourselves. That definition views us as relative beings who exist not for ourselves, but for the servicing, maintenance and comfort of men. That definition consigns us to sexual and family functions, and excludes us from defining and shaping the terms of our lives. In exchange for our psychic servicing and for performing society's non-profit-making functions, the man confers on us just one thing: the slave status which makes us legitimate in the eyes of the society in which we live. This is called 'femininity' or 'being a real woman' in our cultural lingo. We are authentic, legitimate, real to the extent that we are the property of some man whose name we bear. To be a woman who belongs to no man is to be invisible, pathetic, unauthentic, unreal. He confirms his image of us – of what we have to be in order to be – as he defines it, in relation to him – but cannot confirm our personhood, our own selves as absolutes. As long as we are dependent on the male culture for this definition, for this approval, we cannot be free.

The consequence of internalizing this role is an enormous reservoir of self-hate. This is not to say the self-hate is recognized or accepted as such; indeed most women would deny it. It may be experienced as discomfort with her role, as feeling empty, as numbness, as restlessness, a paralyzing anxiety at the center. Alternatively, it may be expressed in shrill defensiveness of the glory and destiny of her role. But it does exist, often beneath the edge of her consciousness, poisoning her existence, keeping her alienated from herself, her own needs, and rendering her a stranger to other women. Women hate both themselves and other women. They try to escape by identifying with the oppressor, living through him, gaining status and identity from his ego, his power, his accomplishments. And by not identifying with other 'empty vessels' like themselves, women resist relating on all levels to other women who will reflect their own oppression, their own secondary status, their own self-hate. For to confront another woman is finally to confront one's self – the self we have gone to such lengths to avoid. And in that mirror we know we cannot really respect and love that which we have been made to be.

As the source of self-hate and the lack of real self are rooted in our male-given identity, we must create a new sense of self. As long as we cling to the idea of 'being a woman,' we will sense some conflict with that incipient self, that sense of I, that sense of a whole person. It is very difficult to realize and accept that being 'feminine' and being a whole person are irreconcilable. Only women can give each other a new sense of self. That identity we have to develop with reference to ourselves, and not in relation to men. This consciousness is the revolutionary force from which all else will follow, for ours is an organic revolution. For this we must be available and supportive to one another, give our commitment and our love, give the emotional support necessary to sustain this movement. Our energies must flow toward our sisters not backwards towards our oppressors. As long as women's liberation tries to free women without facing the basic heterosexual structure that binds us in one-to-one relationship with a man, how to get better sex, how to turn his head around – into trying to make the 'new man' out of him, in the delusion that this will allow us to be the 'new woman.' This obviously splits our energies and commitments, leaving us unable to be committed to the construction of the new patterns which will liberate us.

It is the primacy of women relating to women, of women creating a new consciousness of and with each other which is at the heart of women's liberation, and the basis for the cultural revolution. Together we must find, reinforce and validate our authentic selves. As we do this, we confirm in each other that struggling incipient sense of pride and strength, the divisive barriers begin to melt, we feel this growing solidarity with our sisters. We see ourselves as prime, find our centers inside of ourselves. We find receding the sense of alienation, of being cut off, of being behind a locked window, of being unable to get out what we know is inside. We feel a realness, feel at last we are coinciding with ourselves. With that real self, with that consciousness, we begin a revolution to end the imposition of all coercive identifications, and to achieve maximum autonomy in human expression.

HOW TO STOP CHOKING TO DEATH OR: SEPARATISM

Revolutionary Lesbians
1971

We're constantly asked to explain (actually to justify) our 'vision' of society. Separatism bothers an incredible number of people – or so it seems . . . especially males. Some males are sympathetic – but worried. Others are furiously resentful – and rightly so; they sense the threat to their control.

We see separatism as working directly only with women. Any contact with males (especially male dominated groups) is indirect – primarily through the paper [*Spectre*, eds.]. We do not participate in discussion groups with men. All our energy and time is spent with women and working on things which will further our liberation. To us, separatism has meant that no new relationships with men are formed and that there is a changing – a slow withering away of old male friendships (living friendships demand time and energy).

Separatism is a crucial position to us for many reasons and our experiences have reinforced this position over and over.

We know that women are constantly catering to the 'needs' of men – serving their endless demands. We know that whenever a man is in a group – our growth and feelings are subordinated to the demands of men.

With other women we have more freedom to discover and strengthen our abilities – we are no longer defined by men but by ourselves.

One of the most common problems of women is that we are forced into being defined (or living THROUGH) a family, a boyfriend, a husband. . . .

When a woman finds herself without male 'protection', she is suddenly faced with the realization that she doesn't have any identity. She doesn't know 'who she is'.

Men will continue doing this to women, to keep us dependent financially and emotionally in order to keep women sucking up to men and supporting THEM.

But with other women we can grow stronger and achieve an honest enjoyment of ourselves which is not possible in hetero-sexual relationships.

Two population researchers at Stanford recently 'discovered' that men in crowded conditions (enough room to sit but not to lie down) would become disagreeable, competitive and grow to like each other less. Women in the same crowded conditions would become more lenient, comfortable and grow to like each other more.

The solution suggested by the two male researchers for THE problem? 'Stick a chick in the crowd.'!!

Basic assumption: the problem is men's problem – not why the hell do women have to put up with men and their macho values ... after all, history is MEN; women are here to comfort men – after all the shit they do to each other.

Every time we talk in mixed groups, the women are usually afraid at first of telling the men that we really do feel more comfortable and are able to communicate better with other women. But eventually the women always decide to separate into all women's groups. These groups were almost always exciting and revealing and most women wouldn't even want to return to the original mixed group.

If we did return to talk 'with' the men, we would never be able to say one word. The men will invariably dominate everything. It is always THEIR problems, THEIR 'needs', THEIR egos, THEIR discussion and THEIR LIVES.

In one group (a University of Michigan staff meeting of counselors, shrinks etc. with gay women and men) both the women of the staff and the lesbians were infuriated. When we returned from our woman's group the men couldn't seem to understand why the women needed to be together WITHOUT THEM! After all, *they* didn't like being with only *men*. Even though the women explained that they couldn't talk as long as men were present, the men *continued to do all the talking*.

All the men seemed to care about was keeping 'their' women. They said, 'If we have to change, then YOU have to help us.' But for some reason the women didn't seem as interested in staying with the men as the men were with the women. . . . As for 'helping' men – THAT'S WHAT WE'VE BEEN DOING ALL OUR LIVES!!

The men never seemed to think that they should work with other men – but then again, they really do dislike each other. . . .

But it is men who know the training that they and all men go through; and it is only men and NOT WOMEN who can get inside that male socialization process and begin to break it down. In the end, men have to change the way they act with other men. But as long as men are getting the attention and energy of women they will not face their sexism.

Separatism is not a necessity only for women – it is a necessity for men.

... *REVOLUTIONARY LESBIANS* see their struggle as a total one as a struggle for a non-exploitive communist society. Although we have carved out some space in which we can move, we know that the word 'freedom' is not a meaningful term in this society. We feel that none of us will be able to be free until ALL forms of oppression – ALL exploitive relationships (capitalism, imperialism, racism, sexism, youth oppression ...) are eliminated. We commit ourselves to that total struggle for REAL LIBERATION. ...

THE FURIES

Ginny Berson
1972

The story of the Furies is the story of strong, powerful women, the 'Angry Ones,' the avengers of matricide, the protectors of women. Three Greek Goddesses, they were described (by men) as having snakes for hair, bloodshot eyes, and bats' wings; like Lesbians today, they were cursed and feared. They were born when Heaven ↑ (the male symbol) was castrated by his son at the urging of Earth (the female symbol). The blood from the wound fell on earth and fertilized her, and the Furies were born. Their names were Alecto (Never-ceasing), Tisiphone (Avenger of Blood), and Magaera (Grudger). Once extremely powerful, they represented the supremacy of women and the primacy of mother right.

Their most famous exploit (famous because in it they lost much of their power) involves Orestes in the last episode connected with the cycle of the Trojan War. Orestes, acting on the orders of the Sun God Apollo, killed his mother Clytemnestra, because she had killed his father. Clytemnestra had killed the father because he had sacrificed their daughter Iphigenia, in order to get favorable winds so his fleet could sail to Troy. The Furies tormented Orestes: they literally drove him crazy, putting him under a spell where for days he could not eat or wash his blood-stained hands. He bit off his finger to try to appease them, but to no avail. Finally, in desperation, Orestes went before the court of Athena to plead his case.

The point at issue was whether matricide was justifiable to avenge your father's murder, or in other words whether men or women were to dominate. Apollo defended Orestes and totally denied the importance of motherhood, claiming that women were no more than sperm receptacles for men, and that the father was the only parent worthy of the name. One might have thought that Athena, Goddess of Wisdom, would have condemned Orestes, but Athena was the creation of the male God, Zeus, sprung full-grown from his head, the first token woman. Athena decided for Orestes. Some mythologists say that Zeus, Athena, and Apollo had conspired from the beginning, ordering Orestes to kill his mother in order to put an end, once and for all, to the religious belief that motherhood was more divine than fatherhood. In any case, that was the result.

The Furies were, of course, furious, and threatened to lay waste the city of Athens. But Athena had a direct line to Zeus, King of the Gods; she told the Furies to accept the new male supremacist order or lose everything. Some of the Furies and their followers relented, the rest pursued Orestes until his death.

We call our paper *The Furies* because we are also angry. We are angry because we are oppressed by male supremacy. We have been fucked over all our lives by a system which is based on the domination of men over women, which defines male as good and female as only as good as the man you are with. It is a system in which heterosexuality is rigidly enforced and Lesbianism rigidly suppressed. It is a system which has further divided us by class, race, and nationality.

We are working to change this system which has kept us separate and powerless for so long. We are a collective of twelve Lesbians living and working in Washington, D.C. We are rural and urban; from the Southwest, Midwest, South and Northeast. Our ages range from 18 to 28. We are high school drop-outs and Ph.D. candidates. We are lower class, middle and upper-middle class. We are white. Some of us have been Lesbians for twelve years, others for ten months. We are committed to ending all oppressions by attacking their roots – male supremacy.

We believe *The Furies* will make important contributions to the growing movement to destroy sexism. As a collective, in addition to outside projects, we are spending much time building an ideology which is the basis for action. For too long, women in the Movement have fallen prey to the very male propaganda they seek to refute. They have rejected thought, building an ideology, and all intellectual activity as the realm of men, and tried to build a politics based only on feelings – the area traditionally left to women. The philosophy has been, 'If it feels good, it's O.K. If not, forget it.' But that is like saying that strength, which is a 'male' characteristic, should be left to men, and women should embrace weakness. Most straight women, to say nothing of men, feel afraid or contemptuous of Lesbians. That fear and contempt is similar to the feelings middle class whites have toward Blacks or lower class people. These feelings are the result of our socialization and are hardly worth glorifying. This is not to say that feelings are irrelevant, only that they are derived from our experience which is limited by our class, race, etc. Furthermore, feelings are too often used to excuse inaction and inability to change.

A political movement cannot advance without systematic thought and practical organization. The haphazard, non-strategic, zig-zag tactics of the straight women's movement, the male left, and many other so-called revolutionary groups have led only to frustration and dissolution. We do not want to make those same mistakes; our ideology forms the basis for developing long-range strategies and short-term tactics, projects, and actions.

The base of our ideological thought is: Sexism is the root of all other oppressions, and Lesbian and woman oppression will not end by smashing capitalism, racism, and imperialism. Lesbianism is not a matter of sexual preference, but rather one of political choice which every woman must make if she is to become woman-identified and thereby end male supremacy. Lesbians, as outcasts from every culture but their own have the most to gain by ending class, race, and national supremacy within their own ranks. Lesbians must get out of the straight women's movement and form their own movement in order to be taken seriously, to stop straight women from oppressing us, and to force straight women to deal with their own Lesbianism. Lesbians cannot develop a common politics with women who do not accept Lesbianism as a political issue.

In *The Furies* we will be dealing with these issues and sharing our thoughts with you. We want to build a movement in this country and in the world which can effectively stop the violent, sick, oppressive acts of male supremacy. We want to build a movement which makes all people free.

For the Chinese women whose feet were bound and crippled; for the Ibibos of Africa whose clitori were mutilated; for every woman who has ever been raped, physically, economically, psychologically, we take the name of *The Furies*, Goddesses of Vengeance and protectors of women.

OVER THE WALLS

Gutter Dyke Collective
1973

The politics of this paper are representative of a growing movement of dyke/separatists expanding throughout the country. We come from many and varied backgrounds (a lower East side kid, the Mid-west, North West and the West; lower class, working class and middle class; Puerto Ricans and whites; some of us were dykes before the Women's Movement and some of us dykes came out through the Women's Movement.) But where we are now is what counts and where we are going is what really matters. At this time in history we must learn to band together for our own survival in order that we might consolidate our strengths to fight off the male supremacist society that surrounds us and continues to rape our world. . . .

SEPARATISM

Since we do not relate to men at all and never will, this is not aimed at them but instead towards certain lesbians and women.

SEPARATISM, as a position, is the way in which we relate to other lesbians, women and the enemy.

The only mention I will make of straight women who relate to men on a close sexual level is that it is up to the straight feminists to reform them. Straight/heterosexual women can't be trusted in any real situation because they will sell you out if it gets too heavy for them – men are the focal point of their lives.

Bisexual women have a similar problem with men. Even though they are partly in touch with their feelings in that they are loving women, they have not given up their heterosexual privilege. Male approval and identification is still primary to their existence. By being 'liberated' enough to relate sexually to women, they are giving men an extra amount of titillation. Any woman who has tried to explain her lesbianism to a man realizes how exciting and challenging she becomes to him. This is even more dangerous when women who relate only to women are brought into contact with men through their relating to bisexuals. The lesbian is pressured in one way or another to maintain a façade of friendliness to the prick so that her relationship with the bisexual isn't threatened. Not to mention she is sharing this woman with a man.

As far as straight women are concerned, or those who are celibate now but foresee giving their energies to men after they supposedly have overcome their sexism, we have found that it is very difficult to maintain an equal relationship with them. If they have a strong feminist background and accept the fact that true feminism should ultimately lead to lesbianism, then they view us, the lesbians, as more perfect, stronger persons than themselves. Therefore much weight is laid on our actions and decisions, giving us the greater burden of responsibility. The straight feminist will tell us how much she should want to love women but she's still afraid, etc. In this manner the straight woman is relieving herself of numerous oppressions by not identifying as a lesbian. She usually does not want to hear about our depressions or hassles with other women because that would ruin her lesbian fantasy. So we are left with her sad stories and miseries, but goddess forbid we should comfort her with a warm hug. Anyway we look at it we are expected to maintain an image and live up to it for the sake of lesbianism. We can't be truly honest and real with a straight woman. Casting aside some feminists, most straights still bear the old stereotypes of lesbians. There's something wrong or weird about you. You've got 'problems.'

Another way that straight women treat lesbians is in the role of observer. Rather than partaking in an experience, they sit back and watch. We feel it is essential to develop close, binding relationships with those lesbians whose motivations and feelings are similar to our own.

Although we feel lesbianism is the only natural way for women to interrelate since we are physical as well as emotional beings, we realize that for many women now, in this male supremacist shitpile, intense emotional and sexual relationships are difficult and can be destructive.

Therefore, women who consider themselves celibate, not lesbian, fighting for a loving female world and recognizing that there is no reconciliation with men, are our allies.

Some lesbians feel a separation from the celibate since they see that she will not open herself completely to them. But that is a valid option for each of us. We also tend to be selective in our sexual and emotional relationships, and many of us who call ourselves lesbian do spend the greater part of our lives as actually celibate. If a matriarchal celibate views lesbianism as a good and viable choice for her future, and doesn't feel alienated from us dykes, then we respect her opinion to identify as a celibate and value her friendship.

BECAUSE WE WANT TO BUILD RELATIONSHIPS ON A MUCH MORE INTERPERSONAL LEVEL AND GROW, WE HAVE FOUND IT NECESSARY TO SEPARATE OURSELVES FROM CERTAIN LESBIANS. By separating, we don't mean it in the alienating way it sounds. We usually relate in a friendly manner to most lesbians we know. However, there is no desire to develop close, binding ties with those lesbians whom we have major clashes with. For the most part, we want to withdraw ourselves from very oppressive, negative situations into more positive ones. This is the basis of our politics. When you have little or nothing in common with someone, you tend to argue over what you might consider very obvious and elementary – there is usually not much room left for any other interaction. We would prefer to avoid a lot of fighting and start dealing with the 'fine' lines between us, as well as support each other in our agreements. We are not out to build a mass movement. We have seen the futility and unreality of that dream at this time. There is too much struggling to be done internally before we can deal with other women.

Major differences begin with the extent of one's feminism. Lesbians who do not see all women as a strong, motivating force in creating change are very difficult to build real relationships with. To convince a lesbian that women *are* the 'first sex' and *are* responsible for all of the technology, inventions and structures of the past can be almost impossible, considering most people are skeptical of the few books that lead into these facts. Many lesbians are also fearful of believing that a plot has existed amongst *all* men to subjugate women, continually telling us lies about our heritage and culture, and suppressing our capabilities (talents, skills, and knowledge). Unfortunately, there are also those lesbians who have low opinions of women, in general, and don't see men using us to their own advantage as homemaker, babymaker, and sexmaker. We feel it is also very important to view all men as being part of the conspiracy, since they all obtain privileges from the system and would all fight to maintain it. Therefore, it is also rather trying to be with lesbians who support their 'exceptional' male friendships. Some lesbians even go so far as to inquire about one another through past male acquaintances.

For those lesbians who have stopped relating to all men, this kind of forced interaction creates a dangerous vulnerability.

It is obviously difficult to get together with those lesbians whose political ideologies are concerned with exchanging one male hierarchy for another. *We see sexism as being the basis of all of our oppressions* – all the other 'isms' that continue to perpetuate themselves (capitalism, nationalistic socialism, imperialism, racism, classism, etc.). Just as sexism is the source of all of our other oppressions, maleness is the source of sexism. In order to rid the world of sexism we must first rid the world of men. But obviously we must also begin to deal with the racial and nationalistic and class divisions that men have created between us. We must strike back at the cancerous growth of their male defined structures, specifically the insidious infiltration into our Lesbian communities by their various 'liberation' movements, socialist parties and groups, and socialistically male defined 'revolutionary' *politics*. As feminists, we believe that women are inherently collectively oriented. *True socialism is an integral part of our vision of feminism; 'socialist feminism,' therefore, is redundant.*

Throughout centuries of patriarchal rule, women have been conditioned to react in an acquiescent and supportive way to the multitude of anti-female institutions. Our lives have been wasted by subtle diverting of our energy into male alternatives, such as 'revolutionary' groups designed to alter the hierarchy of male power, but keeping the oppression down on women. Some Lesbians even fall into the trap of the other extreme by joining the female end of the U.S. military core. While seeing a survival alternative to the 'straight' world, they wind up an integral part of this system which is constantly denying us all our rights and privileges. The feminist movement around the world was sold out by the vague and empty 'power' of the vote. Continued hope in male politicians and male power struggles is equally destructive to our lesbian/feminist movement. Even if these groups include intensely oppressed women.

Another real difference that exists is 'class.' If a lesbian is not heavily struggling with her class in a way that doesn't hurt lower and working class lesbians, then I don't want to get too close to her. If judgements are being made on my mannerisms, then I'm gonna start scrutinizing too. Since men in society have set the standards on what's passable and what isn't, I say 'throw it all away and be natural.' It's valid to say that middle and upper class attitudes are an outgrowth of a destructive system that enslaves women of all races and would eliminate lesbianism if it could. Class privilege is a protection in the competitive male world. The lesbian community has no use for it.

Separatism is not an end in itself. It is the means by which we attain a stronger sense of ourselves so that we can eventually work with all lesbians. And then, we would be a forceful unit in attacking the oppressive elements in this society.

SEPARATISM

Alice, Gordon, Debbie, & Mary
1973

Out of our experience, we are developing a new ideology – lesbian separatism – which we feel speaks most truly and directly to the deep needs of all women.[1]

In the past, women have been forced to try to satisfy these needs through the pig-government, the church, jobs, and the home (the nuclear family). Given such little power and such a small sphere for participation, it is no wonder that under patriarchy we are unsatisfied in many ways, all the time.

We chose to be lesbian separatists based on our analysis that male supremacy is the basic oppression of our society, and due to this male system of domination which was established by the patriarchies, the other major forms of oppression – racism, classism, ageism, elitism, capitalism, fascism – were created as ways for some men to divide and conquer us all, as well as gain power over other men. Male supremacy is the system; sexism is the method of persecution and degradation of lesbians and all women.

A lesbian is a woman who loves other women emotionally and spiritually, and desires to express that love and commitment sexually.[2]

Lesbian separatism is inherently linked with feminism, the ideology and practice that considers woman prime. Feminists are women who get their emotional and physical identity and support from other women; women who are committed to struggling against and defeating male supremacy. Men need women for support in countless ways; they built their system on our backs. But lesbians, by loving women and not men, pose a dire threat to the very basis of male supremacy. From this analysis, we conclude that lesbians have the ability and commitment to women that will be necessary to overthrow male supremacy and its attendant forms of oppression. Further, we believe that this political ideology is the only ideology formulated, thus far, that offers us a structure and a plan for action that directs itself toward obtaining our goals, which we also see as goals for all women. Lesbian separatism is feminism carried to its logical conclusion. Other ideologies may recognize that sexism is bad, and should be eliminated. But unless the root, the cause, is recognized and eliminated, the oppressions and problems that men foisted on us all when they overthrew the matriarchal societies can never be truly eliminated.

No other ideology does this; no other ideology speaks to all of our needs; no other ideology will or *can* destroy patriarchy and male supremacy and build an egalitarian matriarchal society.[3]

What we have undertaken is a huge, difficult task. We will need all women to be involved. But, as outlined previously, we have no other choice. Capitalist-patriarchy has polarized things to the point where we must fight and win or die and lose everything. By over-throwing capitalist-patriarchy we will be able to get rid of the actual objective reasons for profit-motive – for oppression – for divisions such as race, class and age. Then we must eliminate the manifestations of sexism, racism, classism, ageism, from all of us and our institutions.

We know, from the past matriarchies, that women can build advanced societies without there being economic classes, without exclusion or prejudice based on race, etc. Our new matriarchy must be even better. It must include every kind of woman; and we will work to make sure that the restoration of the Female Principle does speak to all our needs. Because sex cuts across all lines – race, class, age, all kinds of power and privilege, so must our revolution. But we have a strong model to look back to for inspiration, and we need not be limited by anything in building our new society. Just as the Amazons fought to defend matriarchy, we will develop a new kind of Amazonism to destroy patriarchy and to bring us forward to a new matriarchy.

As lesbian separatists, we believe in directing our energy toward ourselves, and from a foundation of strength, going out from ourselves and giving energy to other lesbians. We see this as our highest priority. We want to continually raise our own consciousness, as well as our physical ability and other skills. We want to be able to fight (in any way) and perform all primary functions ourselves.

In addition to seeing lesbian separatism as a good, positive thing, we also see it as a viable, permanent alternative, which will prepare us for the time when we will be able to reinstate new forms of the old matriarchal societies and when, once again, the

Female Principle will have jurisdiction over the earth.

We trust and welcome any lesbian, and encourage her to join us in defeating male supremacy. We took many different routes to get to where we all are now; however, these differences need not be divisive as long as we are willing to recognize them and struggle around them, and as long as we agree on who we are and what we hope to accomplish.

Coalitions

We can foresee the possibility of allying with other groups over specific issues or projects. These temporary coalitions, however, can never be used to dilute our politics, or be at our expense. Too often we have seen lesbians exploited in coalitions, where it seems all that is profited is the lesbians fighting for someone else's issues. While we do not see straight women as our oppressors or as our enemy, their interests are often opposite to ours, and, as the agents of men, their behavior is sometimes oppressive to us. Therefore, our primary work and group associations will be with other lesbians. To work on certain issues, we may be in coalitions with straight women; as long as our needs and interests are maintained. On the other hand, we cannot see working in such 'offensive' coalitions with any groups of men, but we recognize that in the face of terrible repression, we may form alliances with them in 'defensive' coalitions.

We have dug beneath the façades of many myths perpetrated by the straight women's movement, where all differences were supposed to be ignored under the guise of 'sisterhood.' We have realized that not all women are our sisters, much as we would like to believe that they are. There are many differences among us – race, class, age, life styles, etc., but it is important to see these things as differences, not divisions, to analyze them and provide a framework which leads to understanding and the elimination of these differences being oppressive to any of us.

One of the major differences seems to be how men, and their privilege, is viewed. We no longer believe that we are all just 'people' – just 'human beings.' Either you are a man or a woman; either you have male privilege or you don't; either you get benefits from that privilege as a straight woman, or you don't. Even if you don't want to use or acknowledge your privilege, society does for you. Thus, either you are fighting for an end to male supremacy, or you are responsible for upholding that system which took the world away from women and made us the slaves of men – technologically, economically, spiritually, psychologically, physically and sexually.

More than a question of sexual preference

Lesbianism, therefore, is more than a question of sexual preference. We do, in fact, prefer to sleep with women because we are lesbians; because we love women; because we see women as the only true 'people,' and because our complete identity, and source of support, is from other women. We not only 'prefer' to sleep with women; we love it and we would not ever consider sleeping with men. Not because we hate men, which we do, but because (even if we could be attracted to a man, which is pretty far-fetched) all men are our enemy. Men, as a class, are the oppressors of women; and it is due to all of men's institutions: the nuclear family, marriage and the home, the church, the state, schools, laws, the army, pornography ... that keep lesbians and other women oppressed and exploited every day of our lives for thousands of years since patriarchy conquered the matriarchal societies.

We do not want to fraternize with men, our enemy.

Male children

Just as we believe that no woman should relate to a man, and rob herself of precious time and energy in trying to change one of our millions of male oppressors, we believe that no woman should relate to raising male children. The patriarchal system is crumbling, and men are therefore beginning to wage all-out gynocide against us in a last-ditch effort to hold themselves up. Considering this, it is obvious that no personal solutions can adequately deal with the problem. Women raising male children hope that because of their influence, the child will not grow up to be a pig, or at least, only half as piggy. But this is impossible; societal conditioning and socialization are vastly powerful; and since all men oppress all women, there are no exceptions. Further, this dynamic will only be reversed when we women reinstate new forms of matriarchy.

In the past, women in Amazon societies had several alternatives as to how to relate to male children: they either gave them to the men to raise, killed them at birth, or maimed them to insure that they could never be physically stronger (and be able to fight against the women) or be anything but peripheral to the women's society.

We realize that all of these possibilities seem very extreme; we also realize that third world women, who face a different reality and feel that their families (including males) will be necessary in fighting racism and fascism, may not adhere to our ideas.

We cannot, therefore, make this part of our ideology applicable to all women. We do reiterate, however, based on each woman's situation and choice, that relating to male children is the same thing as relating to men, and we will never defeat supremacy by consorting with men. (See section on lesbian mothers.)

We consider lesbianism to be inherent in a feminist analysis. Further, we see 'straight' feminists, or non-lesbian feminists, to therefore be a contradiction in terms: You cannot be dedicated to eliminating male-supremacy (sexism) and, at the same time, be relating to men, who are the enemy. Lesbianism as we mean it incorporates feminism; however feminism as practiced by straight women, not only does not incorporate lesbianism, but is *opposed* to women *not* being dependent on men in some way.[4] A lesbian movement will encompass all women's needs whereas the straight women's movement not only does not meet the needs of lesbians, but will never be able to overthrow male supremacy, and thus eliminate the basis for all women's oppression.

However, in the Women's Movement, straight women, who are daily living terrible contradictions in their lives, persist in calling themselves feminists, thereby creating a reality gap in terms of what these words mean, and also in terms of who we all are.

As long as straight women continue to give their emotional energy (and sexual energy and love and commitment and thoughts) to men, they cannot truly be fighting against male-supremacy. They are making themselves part of the male-supremacist system and sharing in the privileges men and their women (heterosexuals) get from that system.[5] Furthermore, the most 'straight' feminists can hope to gain is the delusion of equality, a piece of the pie, a more thoughtful oppressor.

There is a solution to this dilemma, fortunately.

If all 'feminists' were lesbians, then this major contradiction would not exist. However, we have some mixed feelings about all women being lesbians. Basically, we believe that all women have the potential to be lesbians; in fact, in past amazon societies and large portions of matriarchal societies, women were lesbians.

Many 'straight' feminists have come to the realization that politically, they *should* be lesbians: that to live their lives any other way is false, and subjects them to much stress and many problems. They are sometimes referred to as 'political lesbians'. However, there is a real danger in women becoming lesbians because they think it is politically correct. Moreover, it will never really work: their commitment to other women will never be true and real unless emotionally and physically they *want* to love other women, unless they feel a true identity with other women and are lesbians in their guts as well as in their minds.

This brings us to the question, then, are lesbians made or born? Some of us feel that we have always been lesbians; some of us were in touch with it from our earliest memories, whereas others of us realize that we repressed it for years, or for most of our lives. We were, regardless of when we *finally* realized it, *always* lesbians.

Others feel that they were not always lesbians, that perhaps if they could have dug underneath all that societal conditioning and socialization that they were not lesbians until a specific point in their life, when circumstances put them in touch with feelings and thoughts and they decided at that point that they were lesbians. This phenomenon happened to many women in the women's movement, although they recognize that they were not lesbians prior to that. Some of these 'nouveau' lesbians are sincere.

Unfortunately, some are not. Some 'nouveau' lesbians have *used* lesbians in order to assuage their guilt and experiment with a 'lesbian experience.' We feel a great deal of hostility toward these women because they have the privilege to experiment with our lives, because they have betrayed us when being a lesbian became no longer fashionable (or politically correct) and they went right back to fucking men, and its attendant male privilege; many of them exploited, used and hurt lesbians in order to have their 'lesbian experiences.'

Just as it is not up to women to 'show' men how not to be pigs, and it is not up to third world women to show whites how not to be racist, it is not up to lesbians to show straight women how not to oppress us. In fact, the simplest way for straight women to not oppress us is to give up their heterosexual privilege and join us.

We do not want to give the impression to women coming out now that they are doomed and have no options. We feel somewhat inadequate to deal with this problem, because it is not within our experience. We hope that lesbians who have come out as a result of political convictions will analyze their experience. We feel that, by doing so, they will aid other women who are attached to men, want to come out, and don't know how to bridge the gap between where they are and where they want to be.

In terms of 'straight' feminists or 'political lesbians' who cannot find it in themselves to deeply, truly love women and want to destroy male supremacy at its roots, we have only one real solution at this time. Women who are celibate or asexual are at least not giving primary support and energy to the Man and are our potential allies. Such women might be called 'asexual' or 'celibate' feminist separatists. At least they would be honest, and they would be resolving the contradiction of consorting with the enemy in a way that is a viable alternative, and one that demands respect. We recognize that good, strong, healthy relationships among women are sometimes difficult now, given the ways our minds, bodies and culture have been repressed, oppressed and depressed by male supremacy.

Our hope for allies lies with other lesbian separatists and other lesbians; also, with these feminist separatists. The most we can hope for from women who persist in remaining straight is communication and occasional support.

We realize, however, that being separatist may be difficult or impossible for certain women or in certain circumstances. If some women are particularly isolated, especially in terms of race, class, age, a rural environment, a very small population (especially with little or no other movement activities), they may not be able to be separatists except at the cost of their sanity or sacrificing certain goals which they feel are essential. One solution would be for separatists to make as many alliances, as necessary, in order to survive and get what they feel is necessary accomplished, as well as maintaining and not losing or diluting their politics within these alliances or coalitions.

Some women have incorrectly perceived lesbian separatists as asserting themselves as the vanguard of the women's movement. We do not believe in vanguards, in which one particular group takes leadership for a whole movement. We do not like vanguardism because of its many pitfalls and unegalitarian and elitist nature, and we do not want to see any group become a vanguard. We see ourselves as working with other lesbians on an equal basis, as part of the lesbian movement. We certainly do not want to have to lead straight women. We want every lesbian to be a leader in her own right, because of her own strengths and knowledge. And we look forward to the day when the women's movement and the lesbian movement are one and the same thing.

> Many women will for a while continue to think they dig men, but as they become accustomed to female society and as they become absorbed in their projects, they will eventually come to see the utter uselessness and banality of the male.
>
> *Valerie Solanas*

NOTES

1. The deeper needs of women:
to be independent and have control over all aspects of our lives
to be self-reliant and confident

to have strength (physical, mental, emotional)
to have acceptance for self
to be needed, loved, appreciated, valued
to love and have sex
to have emotional support – to care
to be productive
to be creative
to have intellectual stimulation and growth
to gain knowledge
to be spiritual – to feel at one with the universe and to have meaning for one's life
to be involved and active
to be just and fair
to not be oppressed and to not be oppressive in any way

2. On bisexual women: Many women who are really lesbians act as bisexuals because they have accepted society's demand that they relate sexually to men though they prefer women. In the past, it has been difficult (for many women impossible) to reject society's demand without the support of other women as now exists in the Lesbian Movement. Earlier, there was usually only the support of a few other lesbians who often saw themselves as sick or deviant, which is no support at all. But bisexual women get energy from other women and then turn around and put that energy into working out their relationships with men. Therefore, bisexual 'feminists' live in the same contradiction as straight 'feminists.' They are still relating to men in a primary way. In addition to this contradiction, bisexual women force lesbians that they relate to to have some sort of contact with and even sometimes compete with men. Bisexuality is not a commitment to women. Bisexual women get male privilege off of the men they associate with, and heterosexual privilege off the relationships with men. They are perhaps trying to have the 'best of both worlds,' but they do not evoke trust from many lesbians since they also sleep with the oppressors. Further, they are refusing to recognize that who you sleep with is a political issue. In this society, if you deviate from the norm you are associated with the deviation, thus bisexual women may be considered lesbians by society; but this 'deviation' is sometimes tolerated or even considered exotic since the bisexual woman still proves that she is a 'real' woman by relating to men. We do not consider bisexual women to be lesbians. To reiterate, you cannot be dedicated to defeating male supremacy by consorting with the enemy. (This issue was further discussed in a section of the treatise on Human Beingism.)

3. Many other political ideologies direct themselves, in one way or another, to the problems of lesbians, women, working people, third world people, etc. The major ideologies, however, (bourgeois democracy, capitalism, individualism, christianity, anarchism, socialism, communism, hippie-ism, straight feminism) clearly do not recognize patriarchy to be the root of all oppression. Some of them realize that men perpetrate sexism on all women (while some do not even go that far); however, none of them speak to the needs of lesbians and none of

them have a structure or plan that will provide a way to do away with ALL the forms of oppression that patriarchy has developed. For, in order to do that, they would have to be anti-patriarchal, and being anti-patriarchal poses a direct threat to men, who play some part in all of them.

For reasons of time and space, we will only present an analysis of why the most popular of these ideologies among feminists – socialism – is not an acceptable theory.

Capitalism developed from patriarchy, from the economic systems men devised to structure their male society. Capitalism is the major method used to exploit people economically in a sexist society. Capitalism is oppressive; but destroying capitalism does not mean destroying sexism (or racism or ageism, etc.) in and of itself. A clear example of this is any socialist country today, where, despite a move toward collectivity economically and otherwise, lesbians and all women are still second-class citizens, still stuck in the stereotyped role of women. Sexism is not some magical, mystical thing. Sexism is practiced by men and their institutions. If you want to get rid of sexism, you'd better do something about male privilege and male power (i.e., men). Not even Cuba, the socialist 'model,' has dealt in any way with male privilege. Men predominate in the government, as in all societal institutions. Women are integrated into the work force, but still play the double role of housewives. Further, socialist ideologies advocate large or mass groups as a means of organizing, at this time. We are in favor of small collective-type groups because we feel that they are more realistic; they function better; they avoid the pitfalls of large groups. From these small collective groups, we will build a larger structure. But we have seen how, when a structure starts with large groups first, there are always large differences, and usually problems with power/control, elitism, etc. Some socialists wonder if the women's movement will die in a few years, after women have made more inroads into male society. But this is indicative of their politics – to even question that the women's movement might die. Our struggle is central to our very existence; at this point in history, the defeat of the women's movement would mean the triumph of gynocide. We cannot allow this to happen to ourselves, to all women. We do not have the privilege of speculating about it; women's interests are our interests and vice-versa. Socialism might provide less alienated labor for men, or a way for men to better share their resources and wealth; it provides little way for women to have a better life, much less does it attack the root of our oppression, male supremacy.

4. Most issues of the straight women's movement relate to those aspects of women's lives that relate to men: i.e. abortion, birth control, the ERA (getting equality with men), consciousness-raising groups that deal with problems women have with their men, such as how a feminist should fuck with a man, who should take out the garbage, how to start including men in women's activities, etc.

5. All men in this patriarchal society have privilege because they are men. Some of this male privilege is extended to straight women because of their willingness to ally themselves with men. Heterosexuality is

considered to be the only 'accepted' sexual behavior. Further, lesbians are persecuted because *we will not suck up to men*, our oppressors. Thus, those with heterosexual privilege oppress those without it.

Many gay men use the argument that they are oppressed and persecuted because they are gay, and do not have heterosexual privilege. But gay men are first and foremost men, and have male privilege. Further, women do not inherently have this privilege; it is only extended to them *by men* when they associate with men. (In this society all women are assumed to be heterosexual, to be associating with men, unless they show otherwise.) While heterosexual couples, in particular, get heterosexual privilege, we reiterate that this comes from the male privilege that all men have.

DIRECTIONS

Alice, Gordon, Debbie, & Mary
1973

In the past, the lesbian/feminists in Seattle have suffered from a lack of an overall plan. We've done many projects, generally with straight women, and in most cases have done the projects with much hard work, energy, and enthusiasm. At best we've had a vague, distant vision of 'lesbian freedom,' the meaning of which varies upon who's using the phrase. At the same time, we've worked on concrete, almost apolitical service projects.

We don't have a comprehensive strategy to offer at this time. In fact, such a strategy would be premature. Some things are not yet clear: what position third world women will take, whether there will actually be men who will become traitors to their sex, etc. Most lesbians are not involved in our movement, and many don't have contact with any kind of a women's movement.

Several things do seem clear to us as far as long-range strategy. The distinction that's currently being made between building a lesbian nation and struggling to overthrow patriarchy and seize power is a naïve one. There is no way that lesbians are going to be permitted to simply withdraw quietly to some area and to begin to take control over our lives and community. Even those lesbians with enough privilege to talk of buying land have no way to make sure that the government will not come in and destroy all they've built.[1]

Lesbians who envision a seize-power strategy see us as working among lesbians to build for the day when we will overthrow the patriarchy and establish a new matriarchal society. The lesbian nation plan is often posed as an alternative. In this plan, lesbians see us as building a large lesbian nation (as opposed to farm) someplace and successfully defending it, thereby defeating patriarchy.

In either plan we must be prepared to struggle to gain our right to determine our own lives and community. Thus the essential difference between the two is the question of a scattered base strategy vs. a liberated zone strategy, a question which is far enough in the future for us to be unable to consider it now.

Right now, we see the lesbian nation as a psychological, spiritual, and emotional entity, as well as a possible physical goal. But the fact that it is not a physical reality right now makes the unity across space and time that lesbians are developing no less real.

It seems clear to us that in order for us to win, almost all the women who are lesbians now, and almost all the women who will become lesbians, must be involved from start to finish. (This includes both rural and urban lesbians working in co-operation in either strategy.) We see several things which must happen before we will be in a position to wage a military struggle to institute matriarchy. They are listed here, not in the order we see them happening (because we believe that most of them will be happening simultaneously), nor is this list by any means complete: Lesbians become conscious of our own oppression and community, realize our identity and oppression as women, and that our oppression is due to patriarchy; straight women realize their oppression, stop sleeping with men and having their children; we define the enemy, deal with other kinds of oppression and other oppressed groups, recognize and develop our lesbian vision, overcome cynicism, develop structures that will meet our needs, develop our own institutions, raise girl children communally, develop individual and group skills, deal with differences in the movement, develop strategy.

Right now, there are very few politically conscious and involved lesbians, even using the broadest possible definitions. Many are involved in such reactionary or futile movements as the MCC, mixed gay groups, and the straight women's movement.

We see the next 3–5 years [1976–1978, eds.] as the period where we can lay the foundations for building the comprehensive lesbian movement that will be necessary to overthrow patriarchy. We see this as the time to consolidate the lesbian community ideologically, politically, organizationally, etc.

Right now, the 'lesbian movement' consists mainly of shifting groups of individuals with fluctuating levels of commitment.

Individuals and groups are constantly dropping in and out of the movement. Often interpersonal problems are allowed to fester until they immobilize all of the lesbians in an entire city. Lesbians become afraid to become too involved in the movement because they are not sure other lesbians will support them.

During the next several years, we should work towards structures that will be more permanent, structures that will provide the security we all need, allow us to work together, to solve survival problems, and to work out our personal, sexual and emotional relationships. These permanent structures should enable us to put more of our energy into the content of what we're doing. They should be collective and small enough for us to relate to, as well as being part of larger structures which can help lend permanence, and can facilitate communication between the smaller groups.

These structures must be the kind we can all live with. It's going to be a long struggle, and we can't afford the kind of frenzied individuality-denying collectivism that in 3–6 months 'burned out' many people in the New Left. The structures should become the bridges between our individual desires, talents, needs, joys, etc., and our collective goals, desires, needs and joys.

Hopefully, these structures will become national and international, enabling us to develop communication and strategy, as well as enabling individuals to move from one place to another on occasion, without disrupting their involvement in the movement.

We think that we should begin to examine all of the structures that have been used to support life-time commitments such as convents, marriage, and some of the communist organizations.

We see the development of these structures as an integral part of the development of the lesbian community as a whole. Some basic structures must be developed before the end of the several years' prelude period.

Finally, since the next five years are years in which we hope to lay the foundation for our movement, we must, in these years, seriously struggle around racism, classism, ageism, sexism and other problems of our movement, so that our foundation will be strong. If this is not done at the beginning of our movement, then we can not be surprised if our movement fails.

Thus, our goals for the next 3–5 years are:

1. to build a sense of community among lesbians and a movement in that community
2. to develop long-term durable structures for that movement
3. to begin the long-term struggles with racism, classism, ageism, etc.

Projects

In this section, we will only discuss projects that we hope will lead to these five-year goals. Basically, our criteria are simple:

1. the project should be anti-racist, anti-classist, anti-ageist, and anti-sexist in its form
2. it should be composed solely of lesbians
3. it should relate to real needs or problems confronting LESBIANS and not be just a straight women's project grafted onto the lesbian community
4. it should attempt to build roots and contacts in the lesbian community and involve lesbians not already politicized

Through the straight women's movement in Seattle, we've had a lot of experience with 'alternative institutions' – women's clinics, abortion referral, day care centers, legal services, etc. We believe that as the lesbian movement grows it will be possible and desirable for the lesbian community to really begin to meet some of our needs and also to begin to create the structures of our new matriarchy.

But right now there are very few politically active lesbians here. It would take all of our energy to just provide the service portion of any such alternative at this time. We have seen the disaster these service projects (devoid of a political base) can turn into – the client/expert split, the drain of energy and the demoralization.

We therefore see that at least right now our projects should be more modest and more directly related to the oppression we are being subjected to right now. There should be a balance between reaction to an immediate situation and taking the offensive to prevent oppression.

Our goals for the immediate future are:

1. to unite with the already politically active lesbians to form an independent lesbian movement
2. to develop ties with lesbians who are not now in the movement

We see the 'study' groups in Seattle as a positive development, but we've quickly come to the realization that unless the study and political discussion is combined with action the groups are in danger of isolation and of falling apart.

We think the idea of small groups being the basic units with regular combined meetings and actions is really good. The distinctions between groups should be based on what the lesbians in the city perceive as real differences (like class, race, ideology). The Friedan action has shown us that these groups can form a good action base for dividing labor, responsibility and leadership.

We see these small groups as being the beginning of the foundation of the lesbian movement. We also see them as the most viable plan for action right now.

Notes

1. This is not to say that we're opposed to setting up lesbian rural communes or farms. Farms are good places to build up skills with machinery, tools and guns, and to build up our bodies, as well as to develop needed agricultural skills and self-reliance. Lesbians on farms can produce some of the food we will need. They can learn the geography of the countryside. They can make contact with other rural lesbians and thus form a rural base. But a lesbian farm is NOT the lesbian nation, because the lesbians on that farm have no real power to control their community in terms of the outside society.

Lesbian Separatism:
The Linguistic and Social Sources of Separatist Politics

Julia Penelope
1974

Separatism as a political stance is certainly not a recent phenomenon, nor is it an issue restricted to the gay liberation movement. For a group of people whose history is one of negative identity, it is probably a necessary first step toward self-respect and self-comprehension. Perhaps because lesbians and gay males have only begun to explore themselves, lesbian separatism has been, and remains, one of the most painful issues within gay liberation organizations. I say 'painful' because it is difficult for a lesbian to put aside her neo-humanistic ideal that 'we're all human beings, after all,' and because gay males have too often interpreted lesbian separatism as a personal rejection rather than seeing it as one part of the generalized anger of women who have to live in a male-dominated culture. In an effort to make clear the political necessity for lesbian separatism, I will present some of the linguistic and personal evidence that moved me into a separatist political position. Comprehension of the sources of separatism may make a painful process less painful for all of us. If we can deal explicitly with the cultural realities that make separatism a necessity, perhaps we can move more quickly to effect social changes.

Lesbian separatism is a subject bound to arouse anger and hostility not only in men but also in women. We are all afraid of it, but for different reasons. Gay men, for some reason, are affronted when lesbians leave their organizations, and I find it unfortunate, though not incomprehensible, that separatism should be taken as singularly antagonistic on the part of lesbians. I've listened to gay men demand 'reasons' for the withdrawal of lesbians from the ranks of gay liberation, and they become more angry when lesbians refuse to respond to their demands. Gay men, like men in general, seem to believe that we *owe* them an explanation, and our refusal to offer elaborate justifications is one aspect of our decision not to put our energies into dealing with men. And, as a consequence, there is anger, frustration, and hostility on all sides. As lesbians realize that 'Gay Liberation' is 'Gay *Male* Liberation,' more and more lesbians will gradually drop out of predominantly male organizations, so it is important for us to understand some of the underlying motivations and tensions that make separatism a logical step for lesbians in terms of our own growth.

The withdrawal of lesbians from predominantly gay male organizations is an act necessary for our survival. No, it goes beyond survival. Withdrawal from gay male organizations is the first, most important step we have to take toward establishing our lesbian identity. Hopefully, it will be our first step toward lesbian *community*. I can't begin to define what I mean by 'lesbian community,' but I want it to come into existence. I cannot conceive what such a sense of community might be like. It's too soon. We are a long way from Lesbian Nation. We don't know *who* we are, and our culture has somehow neglected to provide lesbians with an identity, beyond the traditionally-imposed characteristics of sinfulness, sickness, and illegality. Of course, there are important reasons for this unfortunate oversight on the part of our culture: to name something is to accord it the dignity of recognition. We are 'mere obscenities.' The only names we have are those men have made for us, and even those names are never heard. For example, the *Random House Dictionary* lists the term *woman-hater* but not its antonym, *man-hater*. Such exclusion is one of those unconscious, unplanned 'accidents' that reveal so

45

much. Man-hating is inadmissible in a patriarchal society. Woman-hating is a recognized activity. Since lesbians are, by popular definition, man-haters, and since man-hating does not exist, lesbians don't exist. We are syllogistically reduced to zero. No one wants to believe that lesbians exist; no one wants to believe that it's possible for women to love each other. We are the only people who believe in our existence, and it is up to us to define that existence. No one else has a vested interest in it. For once, perhaps, the silence surrounding our lives is to our advantage.

Because our culture has ignored us, we have the unique opportunity few people have: we can set about constructing our lives and deciding who we are. We know that we exist, but even we aren't sure what that *means*. We can't agree among ourselves on what defines a woman as a lesbian, although we are beginning to talk about it. We agree that being a lesbian involves loving other women, but when we try to define what that love entails, our agreement ends. Can one be a lesbian if she says that her primary love is for other women, or does calling oneself a lesbian depend upon having had *sexual* experience with another woman? We're arguing not just about labels, but about the concepts behind the labels and their application to ourselves and other women. And, to complicate these discussions, the labels aren't even ours. We didn't make them up, so that the original concept that required the label is not our possession either. As women, specifically as the most despised women, we have no identity, no tradition, no history. We have to begin to create our own traditions and, in order to do this, we have to separate ourselves from gay men and their activities. We have been the small, subordinate subclassification of homosexuality for too long. We have to discover our meaning of being a lesbian; we can no longer accept the definitions provided *for* us by men. That much is clear.

There is a myth that we have to destroy. The myth, constructed by psychologists and psychiatrists, asserts that there is such a thing as 'homosexuality.' Those who wish to maintain the myth promote *homosexuality* as a 'generic' term for same-sex love, as though there were no qualitative differences. For example, Sheldon Cashdan, in his book *Abnormal Psychology*, defines the term as follows:

> *Homosexuality* is the generic term used to denote sexual responsiveness to members of the same sex. Although more frequently used to describe erotic attachments among men, it also technically encompasses female-female, or *lesbian*, relationships.
>
> (p. 44)

In the two pages, Cashdan goes on to quote a gay male, he cites Humphries' study of tearoom trade, and then he discusses voyeurs. Once you've talked about tearoom activities, any graceful transitions to lesbian life are difficult. The passage from Cashdan exemplifies the traditional treatment of lesbianism, especially in the social sciences. Lesbians don't want to be 'technically encompassed' by terms that apply to the lives of men. We want our own identity.

Perhaps a similar quotation from a different field will make my objections even clearer. Rictor Norton, in the March, 1974 issue of *College English*, published an article entitled 'The Homosexual Literary Tradition.' From the beginning it is clear that the 'homosexual literary tradition' belongs to gay men. After he has outlined the first two units of a four-unit course, he suggests that the third unit be devoted to lesbian literature. He justifies such a unit in the following way:

> By now some students may become irritated that only
> male homosexual literature has been discussed, so I
> would devote the third unit to lesbian literature.
>
> (p. 689)

Norton's primary reason for including lesbian literature in the course he describes is the possible 'irritation' of students in the class. (Note also that the students would only be 'irritated,' not *angry*.) He then goes on to suggest possible inclusions, such as Sappho, the story of Ruth and Naomi, and Pierre Loüys' *Songs of Bilitis*. Certainly a 'mixed bag.' Norton next mentions more contemporary writers, Ann Aldrich and Judy Grahn, and makes the following comment:

> You may also wish to examine how male writers such
> as Henry James, D. H. Lawrence, and Balzac have
> treated lesbian themes.

Lesbians are reduced to a single unit in a course on the homosexual literary tradition, and our lives become 'lesbian themes' in the works of male writers. In any study that assumes that lesbians are 'encompassed' by 'homosexuality,' we are included only as a subordinate clause at the end of a paragraph, or we are left as something to be handled in one unit or one chapter, always at the end.

The course described by Rictor Norton is not one in which many lesbians would have any interest. Quite frankly, as far as I can see, 'Gay Studies,' should it gain a niche in the academic curriculum, will necessarily remain the preserve of gay men. Whenever lesbians are subsumed under a generic term, whether it is gay or *homosexual*, the subject matter has little or nothing to do with our lives. We are trivial marginalia, digressions.

Thus far, I have cited two authors in support of my contention that lesbians have to actively refuse to be included in any discussion that presupposes that the lives of lesbians are covered by the term *homosexuality*. To continue to subsume ourselves uncomfortably under either umbrella term, *gay* or *homosexual*, is to deny the validity of our separate experiences. Worse, as a lesbian, it requires maintaining an uneasy stance in the shadow of the lives of gay men. I'm no longer interested in being defined by comparison or contrast with men. What I'm suggesting is something that has been obvious to lesbians and gay men of my acquaintance for a long time: lesbianism and homosexuality are not the same thing. We are dealing with two very different phenomena. The two lifestyles are not identical, however one may wish to construe that fact. There are lesbians, and there are homosexuals, and we need the terminological distinction in order to do justice to the two different kinds of experience. We also need to remember that lesbians and homosexuals did not put ourselves in the same category – the law did, the psychiatrists and the psychologists did. That's the way they classify in the heterosexual world, the better to make generalizations and analyze their statistics, the better to blur the real fear that motivates their classifications and judgments.

Have you ever wondered about the source of the taboos against loving someone of the same sex? Have you ever wondered why, if heterosexuality is, in fact, 'natural,' it had to be institutionalized? If *everyone* were naturally heterosexual, would it be necessary to buttress this definition of human sexuality with all of the religious, philosophical, political, and legal sanctions our society has formulated? George Weinberg, in *Society and the Healthy Homosexual*, has suggested that the taboos derive from *homo-phobia*, the fear of homosexuals. But he doesn't ask the next, logical question: What is the source of this fear? I would like to suggest that the fear has a very real cause: If people could be whatever they wanted to be, without all the intense social conditioning, they would be lesbians and homosexuals. *Whoever* set civilization in motion realized something important at an early date: You can't have a society, at least not one like ours, if people are allowed to be whoever they want to be. And if everyone were lesbians and homosexuals, we wouldn't be here, as heterosexuals are fond of reminding us. In short, the taboos against both lesbians and homosexuals are necessary in order to perpetuate society, as *we know it*. From this necessity derive institutionalized heterosexuality, the nuclear family, and the sex-role stereotyping that guarantees the continued existence of our social and economic structure.

I am not concerned here with tracing historical development, chronology, or placing blame. I am not concerned about whether or not it was a patriarchy or a matriarchy that first established the sexual taboos. All of us have to deal with the quality of our life experiences now, today, and tomorrow. We were raised in a society that depends upon sex-role stereotyping for its perpetuation. Because we have all been exposed, are constantly being exposed, to these sex-role stereotypes, lesbianism and homosexuality cannot be the *same* phenomenon. The psychologies of women and men are too different as our society has created them.

In order to make the specific features of the female and male roles more explicit as our culture has defined them, I've copied some definitions of terms from the *Random House Dictionary*. I chose this dictionary as my source because it is recent, and the definitions are those that reflect the cultural belief system with which we were indoctrinated. The terms are *womanly, manly, feminine, masculine, tomboy, sissy*, and the definition of *effeminate* provided under *female*. As you read through these definitions, keep in mind two other terms, *bull-dyke* and *drag queen*, because my later discussion will focus on these terms as representative of the underlying tensions, created by the sex-role stereotypes, that motivate lesbian separatism.

Definitions

manly – having the qualities usually considered desirable in a man; strong, brave; honorable; resolute; virile. Syn. – **Manly** implies possession of the most valuable or desirable qualities a man can have, as dignity, honesty, directness, etc., in opposition to servility, insincerity, underhandedness, etc. It also connotes strength, courage, and fortitude: . . .

mannish – applies to that which resembles man: . . . Applied to a woman, the term is derogatory, suggesting the aberrant possession of masculine characteristics.

(The antonyms listed for *manly* are three: feminine, weak, cowardly.)

womanly – like or befitting a woman; feminine; not masculine or girlish. Syn. – *Womanly* implies resemblance in appropriate, fitting ways, *womanly decorum, modesty. Womanlike*, a neutral synonym, may suggest mild disapproval, or, more rarely, disgust. *Womanlike, she (he) burst into tears. Womanish* usually implies an inappropriate resemblance and suggests weakness or effeminacy: *womanish petulance.*

(Under *female* RHD provides the following statement on *effeminate.*)

Effeminate is applied reproachfully or contemptuously to qualities which, although natural in women, are seldom applied to women and are unmanly and weak when possessed by men: *effeminate gestures*; an *effeminate voice. Feminine*, corresponding to masculine, applies to the attributes particularly appropriate to women, esp. the softer and more delicate qualities. The word is seldom used to denote sex, and, if applied to men, suggests the delicacy and weakness of women: a *feminine figure, point of view, features.*

feminine – 1. pertaining to a woman or girl: *feminine beauty, feminine dress.* 2. like a woman; weak; gentle.

masculine – 1. having the qualities or characteristics of a man: manly; virile; strong; bold; a deep, *masculine voice.* 2. pertaining to or characteristic of a man or men; *masculine attire.*

tomboy – 1. an effeminate boy or man. 2. a timid or cowardly person. 3. a little girl.

If you've read through these definitions carefully, you cannot have missed the reasoning that underlies the exclusion of *man-hater* from this dictionary, the same reasoning that requires the inclusion of *woman-hater*. The existence of these terms in itself demonstrates the basic dichotomy of personality that our culture assumes and perpetuates. The definitions, both in tone and word-choice, reflect the cultural value attached to the roles of women and men, and delineate neatly and unmistakably the sex-role stereotypes with which we grew up. Men can be strong, virile, forthright, honest, and dignified. Woman are 'naturally' weak, gentle, delicate, cowardly, timid, modest. For women to be honest, dignified, forthright, etc., is regarded as 'aberrant.' The role of women as our culture defines it is certainly less than fully human, and loaded with negative values, while the role of men is portrayed as positively valued.

With the features and values attached to the sex-role stereotypes explicit, I can now demonstrate the differences between lesbians and homosexuals that necessitate lesbian separatism. From the time we were born, we have been conditioned in terms of our culture's expectations of us. Our conditioning is determined by our biological sex. Somehow, though, some of us escape *total* conditioning and, in varying degrees, some women decide that they can be strong, and some men decide that they can be weak. (Ultimately, we must abandon such adjectives.) The lesbian rejects the image and definition of herself as a woman, and the homosexual rejects our culture's definition of him as a man. And within this rejection we can find the origins of the bull-dyke and the drag queen, and the basic differences that distinguish lesbians from homosexuals, as we understand those terms today.

The lesbian rejects the definition of herself as weak, passive, timid, dependent, and instead gravitates toward the male role, which permits her that latitude of self-expression and independence denied to women. It is also the male role that makes it possible for the lesbian to take hold of her anger and act politically in terms of that anger. The homosexual, by rejecting the male stereotype moves toward the female role, taking on those qualities regarded as characteristic of women – passivity, timidity, and lack of self-assertiveness. (For empirical support of this observation, see the study published by Fred Myrick, 'Attitudinal Differences between Heterosexually and Homosexually Oriented Males and between Covert and Overt Male Homosexuals,' *Journal of Abnormal Psychology*, 1974, 83, 81–86.) In addition to his conclusion that homosexuals are lower in self-esteem, personal competence, and self-acceptance than heterosexual males, Myrick also found that covert homosexuals have higher self-esteem and self-acceptance than overt homosexuals. (This observation has political implications, which I'll discuss shortly.) The bull-dyke thus represents the lesbian extreme of role-switching, for she may also take on the undesirable features of the male role, violence, woman-hatred (which, for her, involves self-hatred), and a brutal callousness, a refusal to admit to emotions associated with being a woman. In contrast, the drag queen rejects the male role, and acquires the extreme characteristics of the female role, self-trivialization, superficiality, and a refusal to accept responsibility for his actions. The essence of camp is the refusal to take oneself seriously.

As I've indicated, the bull-dyke and the drag queen are extremes, and there are variations in every direction. (For example, the male homosexuals who go to the other extreme with the masculine stereotype.) But I think the consequences of the role dichotomy are evident in all of us to some extent, especially those of us who have been involved in Gay Liberation. Both lesbians and homosexuals are trapped at some point between the female and male roles of our culture. Thus, I may differ only in degree from another woman in the extent to which I can be intimidated by a man. Nevertheless, the tendency to allow myself to be intimidated is always there, and however aggressive and independent I may be I have to constantly monitor my own behavior. Similarly, a gay man differs from a straight man only in the degree of his will to dominate or manipulate others, in particular, women. These are the reasons why it is extremely difficult for lesbians to work politically with gay men. No matter how passive, how inane, how trivialized a gay man has become, he always reserves the right to revert to the male supremacist role. Perhaps an example will demonstrate my point. One night I went with two other lesbians to a gay bar that had a drag show. One of the drag queens, dressed in a tight, red, velvet dress slit up the sides, came out into the audience as part of his performance, doing a 'vamp' routine. He was acting out the seductive image of women so popular in our culture. Unfortunately, he chose me as one of his partners in this role fantasy. When he strutted over to me and leaned against me, doing his 'come-on,' I turned my head and refused to play along. He then leaned over and said, 'Aren't we the snotty butch!' I continued to keep my head turned away, until he actually grabbed my chin and jerked my head around, forcing me to look at him. In reply, I shot a bird at him. He stormed off, returned to the stage, grabbed the microphone, and began to insult me. His insults reveal the barriers promoted by sex-role stereotypes. He informed me that no matter how 'butch' I thought I was, I was still 'just' a woman, and that I would never be 'a man.' At the end of his tirade, he made one classic statement that is worth repeating verbatim: 'Listen, honey! You may think you're as good as a man with those pants on, but let me tell you one thing. Just because I have on a dress and heels doesn't mean I'm not a man, and if you want to find out how much of a man I am, come on outside! We'll see who the man is!'

This was a man who had voluntarily donned women's attire, a man who made some money wearing those clothes that symbolize the female's subordination to the male, the clothes that are designed to make women more available to the male. Of course, he had nothing to lose by wearing women's clothes; biologically, he is still a male and thereby entitled to male prerogatives in our society. This encounter exemplifies the reasons that feminists are opposed to female impersonation. It also foregrounds the psychological differences between homosexuals and lesbians that make political alliances tenuous, at best. Because the female and male roles are polarized in our culture, and because as members of this society we are all thereby polarized, the political goals and the processes leading to self-realization for lesbians and homosexuals cannot be shared.

Many homosexuals have adopted the feminist issue of sex-role stereotyping as a commonly-held problem. They have used this issue to justify female impersonation as a male's way of breaking out of his sex-role. Certainly, in a limited sense, this is true. But as a lesbian, I cannot fight for the right of a man to take on all the features assigned to women, like passivity and triviality. I cannot support homosexuals who would glorify those characteristics of my sex-role that I detest. While I cannot deny to another human being the right to self-degradation and self-immolation, neither can I be expected to endorse it. As I see it, the personal directions for homosexuals and lesbians take separate paths. While the lesbian's struggle is toward self-confidence, self-assertion, independence, and the ability to express her anger outwardly, the homosexual's struggle is toward realizing his potential for tenderness, reclaiming the emotions he has had to deny as a 'man,' relinquishing the political power accorded to his biology, and developing his capacity for compassion. But there are serious problems for all of us as we move toward self-integration. As the lesbian acquires strength, dignity, and self-possession, she cannot fall into the trap of also emulating the violence, brutality, and lack of concern for other people that characterize the male sex-role. Nor can the homosexual make the mistake of becoming weak, ineffectual, and the senseless pawn for other people.

Perhaps an example of the consequences of being trapped between the roles will make the dangers explicit. Recently, I went to a party given by a homosexual collective. I arrived late, and most of the other lesbians had already left, although I met a few who were leaving as I was going in the front door. They advised me not to bother going into the house. Once I was inside, I became aware of tension all around me, barely disguised hostility. I could sense the violence around me. A couple of the women who were still at the party came up to me, and told me some stories that confirmed my own initial impressions of the atmosphere. I will give you one example of the overt violence some of the women experienced. One of the women was wearing a purple hardhat with a feminist symbol painted on the front and 'Sisterhood is powerful!' painted on the back. A man had asked her why she was wearing the hat. Then he hit her over the head, saying 'Isn't *that* why you're wearing it?' After I'd looked around for myself, and seen all the straight men crowding the dance floor, leaning against the walls staring at the women, and grabbing us as we walked by, I went over and talked to one of the gay men, to find out why all of these straight men were at a party I had believed to be for gay people. He told me that they had crashed the party, but that there was nothing he could do to make them leave. Another gay man told me that another gay man had invited them, but he wasn't going to make them leave either. Although the party was in their home, neither of the gay men, as I was told later, wanted to 'get into a macho power trip.' For many gay men, asserting one's rights, taking control of one's surroundings, one's home, is a 'macho power trip.' As all of this translated to me, however, these gay men were saying that they weren't angry about the conduct of these men, they didn't mind the overtly aggressive and hostile behavior, and they weren't going to do anything about it. As one gay man explained to me later: 'We didn't want to discriminate against them because they're heterosexuals.' But another gay man admitted that, in fact, *none* of them had been aware that anything was wrong at the party until I mentioned it. It all boils down to the fact that gay men, through their passivity, condone the behavior of other men rather than challenge them. When some of the lesbians took over the dance floor in an effort to dislodge the straight men, the gay men were 'shocked' at our 'hostile' behavior, and informed me that we had been unduly rude and aggressive. Finally, we decided to leave, and as I was going out the door, one of the gay men came rushing over to me and said, in his thickest back-to-Tara accent: 'Why Julia! Why are you leaving?' For me, that capsulized the whole event. It also captures the basic reason for lesbian separatism. If the gay men were appalled by my self-assertion and aggressiveness, I was equally taken aback by their indifference, their lack of concern, their lack *of anger*. Gay men are not angry as I am angry, and if they are angry, it is not at all for the same reasons, because the sources of our anger are different. As a consequence, so are our political goals.

The psychological distance, and the concomitant political estrangement, between lesbians and homosexuals derives from the sex-role stereotypes kept alive within our culture. While gay men are trying to put aside the male stereotype, they tend to discard some of the good features of it along with the bad. In the process of shedding the privileges of male supremacy, it isn't necessary to surrender control over one's life, independence, and the will to assert one's rights. In discarding the negative characteristics of the female role, it shouldn't be necessary for lesbians to give up positive attributes like gentleness and compassion. These are problems that lesbians and homosexuals will have to work through as distinct, self-identified groups. We aren't coming from the same place, and to ignore the real difficulties that set us apart from each other would be to prolong the existence of those differences. I suspect that the sex-role stereotypes, if put back together, would provide us with some idea of what a whole human being might be like. There is no inherent reason why one cannot be both independent and gentle, intuitive and self-assertive, angry and compassionate. Certainly these personality traits are not mutually exclusive, by definition. But lesbians and homosexuals will have to grow toward wholeness in different ways, and we can best help each other by understanding and confronting our differences instead of minimizing them.

A Cursory and Precursory History of Language, and the Telling of It

Julia Penelope
1976

Today I offer my words to the women who created me in love and in life, in our lives, of whom I am and will be in this life. This is my telling of our history of how I dreamed it, of how we came into our own sayings.

> (the men) say that they have said, this is such or such a thing, they have attached a particular word to an object or a fact and thereby consider themselves to have appropriated it. The women say, so doing the men have bawled shouted with all their might to reduce you to silence. The women say, the language you speak is made up of words that are killing you. They say, the language you speak is made up of signs that rightly speaking designate what men have appropriated. Whatever they have not laid hands on, whatever they have not pounced on like many-eyed birds of prey, does not appear in the language you speak. This is apparent precisely in the intervals that your masters have not been able to fill with their words of proprietors and possessors, this can be found in the gaps, in all that which is not a continuation of their discourse, in the zero, the O, the perfect circle that you invent to imprison them and overthrow them.

> *Monique Wittig, LES GUÉRILLÈRES, p. 114*

Winter Solstice, the year 400 of the Age of Women. The time of processes evolving themselves out of what has been. The women

55

emerging into the light, out of the earth that had sheltered them for 200 years. This is the story of one woman and her going-out, the story of what she knew and carried within her, bringing her past to the future.

The 'feminist solution' had come easily, as things do, when everyone had relaxed and stopped stumbling over themselves. As usual, the solution was the easiest and the most obvious, and had been within reach forever, but no one had seen it. We had been looking off into the distance for so long that the obvious was easy to miss, being obvious. And the analysis of the feminist situation came even easier.

Energy. That simple. Women had energy. Men, *lords and masters of the earth*, as they'd liked to call themselves, with typical presumption, had indeed been 'masters' of a simple trick of manipulation which had given them the control of energy they needed to maintain their 'ego-strength.' During the dark[1] centuries known as the Time of Men, they had learned to tap into energy sources. They had learned to draw the huge quantities of energy they required from the earth, water, fire, sun, and atom. Most importantly, they had learned how to draw energy from women. The major difference, however, between the energy of women and other kinds of energy was that the energy of women, *psychic energy*, couldn't be stored or controlled. So men had put the women in little boxes, which they called 'houses,' restrained the power of female energy with monogamy, channeled that energy into maintaining the nuclear family, and plugged it in a direct line to male supremacy. This insured that every man would have a life-long supply of one woman's psychic energy to support him in his struggles with other men. No man had to earn such support; it was his as a result of what some called 'divine right' and others called 'survival of the fittest.' Fortunately, men didn't live as long as women, so we had a few years to ourselves as we prepared for our dying. Now, without that permanent source of psychic energy, men were about as powerful as dead storage batteries or burnt-out light bulbs. And the analogy will hold if you work it out to its conclusion.

Now, some have insisted on asking *why* women, if they were so strong, even in those days, went on letting men harness them and use them without resisting in some way. Some have even gone so far as to suggest that this *lack of resistance* proves the 'inferiority' of women. After all, how could any person be *stupid* enough to

---

[1] My use of 'dark' in this phrase is clearly racist because 'the Time of Men' is used disparagingly. My apologies to wimmin-of-color readers for this racist use of 'dark'.

remain trapped for so long? Which is only one way of asking a ridiculous question, a pseudo-question. Women did not 'fight back' because they didn't have the energy to construct alternatives for themselves. They had learned to be content with living, breathing, and caring, each in her own way. It was the women, after all, who maintained living, who nurtured, who fed, who clothed, who created the 'home.' They had not yet realized that they could nurture and feed each other, and they rarely begrudged their giving to these weaker creatures who seemed to need nurturing so much more than they did. Consequently, there was no 'battle to be fought.' Women smiled, encouraged, and sometimes wept, and went on being women, although they began to wear themselves out trying to fulfill the needs of men. (Men required tremendous quantities of energy.) You could always spot a woman who was connected to men in those days, especially toward the beginning: they began to age quickly, usually within three or four months after accepting the male. They would develop a harried, haggard look, severe lines around the eyes and mouth, and their eyes would become clouded with pain and frustration. In the latter days, women began to turn to each other, and the effects of living with men became clearer to everyone, because these woman-loving-women, who had as little as possible to do with men and their tiring games, looked fuller, healthier, somehow more alive and self-satisfied.

The men, meanwhile, went on about their 'business,' making more 'business' for themselves, setting traps and springing them, breaking them, putting them back together. Of course, part of the arrangement that pleased the men the most was called 'the double standard,' even back then. Women were taught, usually by their mothers, that they were to love only one man forever, and it usually worked out that way, because the women didn't have the time or the energy for exploration. The men, on the other hand, were free to 'raid' other women of their energy, as long as no one noticed that they were draining more than one woman. In fact, having more than one woman for energy was a great source of pride to them, since it proved that they were 'manlier than other men,' and they loved to boast of their 'conquests.'

At any rate, once women began to love themselves and each other, they awakened and realized what had been happening to their lives, and they started to move together, what they called 'a movement,' a moving in and out of each other's lives, and it was only a question of time until they came to know each other, and the future began to happen. Therein lay the solution, although no one knew it then, looking back on the events that we now see to be inevitable. Energy being energy, it will always flow in the direction of least resistance. You can cut channels for it, as the men had, channels like 'marriage,' to make it move easier, but energy will flow with or without the channels.

What sparked those first feminists was the fact that men had begun to take themselves seriously, actually believing that their pretentions and pomposities were profound and important events! They thought they were NECESSARY! They began to believe that they were self-perpetuating, and it finally reached a point where they had plundered and pillaged, ravaged and raped, not only the women, but the earth, and each other. It became clear that the energy was running low, because men *used* a lot of energy, but they were physically and psychically incapable of *returning* energy to its source. They never put anything back into the resources they were using up so quickly, and things got worse and worse, and the men became dissatisfied and irritable as they had less and less energy with which to propel themselves, and they didn't understand what was happening. They didn't think there was anything to understand.

The feminists, all this time, went on having meetings where everyone disagreed about everything imaginable, talking and arguing with other women, putting out a lot of energy and getting a lot of energy from other women, which they called 'consciousness-raising,' learning to love themselves and each other, and learning to do all the things they had believed they couldn't do. Nothing seemed to make sense, and then all of it made sense, and they continued to become what they were becoming. They were getting ready for what was going to happen, preparing themselves for living in a new world coming around. They had ceased to oppose the ordering of the men, had realized that opposing, the act of opposing, drains energy, creating its opposite, lack of energy. They had learned that opposing a thing merely feeds it and strengthens it, giving it a reason to continue itself. Instead, they withdrew into their centers, forcing the men to oppose them, to drain themselves in the idle activity of battle *against*, while the women began to live *for*. The women, growing toward wholeness, began to understand that opposition is itself: *opposition*. The men, in their appropriation of the world, had defined identity as opposition. The women, in becoming themselves, began to create identities out of themselves, on a new ground. They refused to oppose, for opposition merely validates that which it negates. Now, none of them knew how to live differently, but they came to understand that whatever was coming around would grow out of their lives, and they knew that 'dissent must transcend the status of negative identification.' They had to create the future out of themselves.

The feminists went underground all over the world, moving into the large networks of underground caverns, taking with them their psychic energy, leaving the men to their own violent devices. They took their power into themselves and transformed their lives. Because things that are going to happen, will happen, women gave their energy to each other, which meant there was no depletion among them, and the men destroyed themselves on the 'horns (so to speak) of their own dilemma.'

When the women began to withdraw more and more noticeably, in increasing numbers, the men didn't know what to do. But they tried everything that could come into their one-track minds, and all they could think about was 'how to get the women back.' What is a man without a woman? So they stormed, they threatened, they raged, they killed, and finally, they begged, pleaded, and, yes, even wept. To no avail. We'd heard all the lines before, maybe phrased a little more subtly, but a line is a line!

Things went back and forth for awhile. It took anywhere from three to five years in those times for a woman to be born to herself again, and even today we're still sorting through, getting rid of centuries of bondage and drainage. Those of us alive now will never be whole, but we'll die on the way to regaining our full womanpower. Others, who come after us, will be the women we aspire to be.

Back to our story. The women began to leave the men, singly at first then in twos and threes, often waiting until nightfall to slip away to the nearest underground group. The men couldn't find them, although they tried. Even if they had been able to find them, there was nothing they could do to accomplish their purpose, getting back the women. This was their dilemma: they needed the women in order to continue to do the things they had always done; but all they knew was violence and hatred. In order to get the women out of the caves, they would have had to blow the caves up, thus killing the women, thus destroying the very thing they were after. In their anger, they would have destroyed the women who were the targets of their anger, and the reason for the anger in the first place. All that they knew how to do was fight and coerce and destroy. Even their promises were transparent threats. Therein lay the paradox, the consequences, and the solution. Since men needed women for psychic energy, they couldn't risk destroying them. Without women, they had only their own negative energy, and in one, last desperate rage, they turned their negative energy on themselves, blowing themselves into eternity. Leaving the earth, such as it was, to the women.

And we learned and grew together in the caverns, reclaiming the powers we had put aside and denied, learning much together of joy and wholeness. Learning again to love, creating from our loving a language of feeling, of movement, of growing. The language of women loving became a language of sharing love, a speaking of minute sensualities and flickering tongues, a language that expressed our thoughts and feelings, quick things, languid things, but alive and changing.

The language we had learned in the world of men, the language we had brought with us to the caverns, gradually fell away from our minds. Its rigidity, the inflexibility of its categories, its need for classification, were no longer sufficient for the things we were experiencing. We no longer had space for dichotomies and abstractions, for as we outgrew dichotomies, we found we didn't need abstractions. Our eyes became alive, and our language formed itself out of our perceptions of distinctions evolving within us and around us. We no longer needed that peculiar fusion of opposites in expressing our joy or our disappointment. Words that had once served the dual functions for describing our sexuality and our feelings of rage or disgust began to drop out of usage; we did not need to speak of being fucked, screwed, nailed, or ripped off, nor did we have any use for the strange combination of violence and sex that we had learned from such words. As our understanding of change grew out of our own changes, so our use of time began to change, and we understood how the present was the creative evolution of the past blending with the possibility of the future. And our language gradually developed a time in which our memories of the time before and our hopes for the days to come blended and fused.

In the caverns, we learned to explore silence, both what it had meant to us before and what it might come to mean in our understanding. In the old days, before we had come to know ourselves, we had felt uneasy within our silences, the silences that often come among people. Then, our silences had been painful, uneasy obstacles that we tried to leap with words; but our words were empty, not carrying meanings to ourselves or others, because we were afraid of our meanings, of our feelings. Because our words were empty, we would throw them into our silences, trying to fill our silences with noises, chattering teases, lips and tongues struggling toward meaning, but our throats tensed to strangle any meaning that might slip through our defenses. We had carefully been taught to excise our thoughts and feelings from our spoken words and, in the process, we came to realize how we had falsified our words and our silences, thereby betraying ourselves. We had filled our silences with words that pointed *away* from our center, and the awkward silence into which we had hurled our useless words had remained, full of the strain and tensions of our unexpressed motivations, expectations, and fears. And that jostling crowd of what we did not say became the air we breathed.

As we grew in knowing ourselves, we put aside the language we had once cherished for its ambiguities, although we had called those ambiguities 'subtle nuances.' We had once been proud to speak a language in which we had no means of speaking our meanings clearly, even to ourselves. First, we had to discover our meanings, and out of that discovery grew a language that expressed them clearly. As strength dissolved our need for fear we began to explore our silences, which came to satisfy us as rest and the fulfillment of meaning. We learned to speak only when there is meaning in our words. That was the hardest thing we had to learn, so many of us did not know we had meanings.

The language that evolved out of our learning together was a language of acting in the world, rather than 'events'; it was a speaking of our living, not our 'lives'; of our doing, not our 'deeds'; of our touching, eating, tracing, dancing, of moving, not 'motion,' of dying, not 'death.' The nouns of men became our verbs, what had been 'objects' became doers. The abstraction, the labeling, the classification, the imposing of a fixed, external order was no longer needed. 'Love,' 'death,' 'honor,' 'dignity,' and 'trust' were expressed in our living together; we did not need to speak of such things as though they were unreal, fragile. Through the verb we entered into the world and began to understand the other beings in the world as they lived. We began to learn to participate in the world, to move and grow with it, and so our speaking became our meaning in the life of the world.

There is a story we still tell for the joy of the telling, of a group of women who once gathered together, and some of the women called for words from the other women, and out of these words they wove a chant, and the chant became a singing together. And one woman yelled out the word *anarchism*, which was then woven into the fabric of the chanting, and in the chanting that word became *orgasm*, going on.

Accept this telling of me as it is of you. We belong to ourselves. Feel the power that is yours swell and lift within you. It is yours. It is you. It is all of us. Womanlove self-creating womanpower within us. Take your power into your hands and lift them up, your power living in you. Let us join our hands together in strength and in love, the radiant power of women. Let us speak the language of our living.

Bibliography

Bryant, D. M. *The Comforter: a mystical fantasy.* (Berkeley, California: Evan Press, 1971).

Daly, Mary. 'The Qualitative Leap beyond Patriarchal Religion,' *Quest*, I (Spring 1975), 20–40.
Herbert, Frank. *The Godmakers*.
Wilden, Anthony, *System and Structures: Essays in Communication and Exchange*. (London: Tavistock Publications, Ltd., 1972).

Some Reflections on Separatism and Power[1]

Marilyn Frye
1977

I have been trying to write something about separatism almost since my first dawning of feminist consciousness, but it has always been for me somehow a mercurial topic which, when I tried to grasp it, would softly shatter into many other topics like sexuality, man-hating, so-called reverse discrimination, apocalyptic utopianism, and so on. What I have to share with you today is my latest attempt to get to the heart of the matter.

In my life, and within feminism as I understand it, separatism is not a theory or a doctrine, nor a demand for certain specific behaviors on the part of feminists, though it is undeniably connected with lesbianism. Feminism seems to me to be kaleidoscopic – something whose shapes, structures and patterns alter with every turn of feminist creativity; and one element which is present through all the changes is an element of separation. This element has different roles and relations in different turns of the glass – it assumes different meanings, is variously conspicuous, variously determined or determining, depending on how the pieces fall and who is the beholder. The theme of separation, in its multitudinous variations, is there in everything from divorce to exclusive lesbian separatist communities, from shelter for battered women to witch covens, from women's studies programs to women's bars, from expansions of day-care to abortion on demand. The presence of this theme is vigorously obscured, trivialized, mystified and outright denied by many feminist apologists, who seem to find it embarrassing, while it is embraced, explored, expanded and ramified by most of the more inspiring theorists and activists. The theme of separation is noticeably absent or heavily qualified in most of the things I take to be personal solutions and band-aid projects, like legalization of prostitution, liberal marriage contracts, improvement of the treatment of rape victims and affirmative action. The contrariety of assimilation and separation seems to me to be one of the main things that guides or determines assessments of various theories, actions and practices as reformist or radical, as going to the root of the thing or being relatively superficial. So my topical question comes to this: What is it about separation, in any or all of its many forms and degrees, that makes it so basic and so sinister, so exciting and so repellent?

Feminist separation is, of course, separation of various sorts or modes from men and from institutions, relationships, roles and activities which are male-defined, male-dominated and operating for the benefit of males and the maintenance of male privilege – this separation being initiated or maintained, at will, *by women*. (Masculist separatism is the partial segregation of women from men and male domains *at the will of men*. This difference is crucial.) The feminist separation can take many forms. Breaking up or avoiding close relationships or working relationships, forbidding someone to enter your house; excluding someone from your company, or from your meeting; withdrawal from participation in some activity or institution, or avoidance of participation; avoiding of communications and influence from certain quarters (not listening to music with sexist lyrics, not watching tv); withholding commitment or support; rejection of or rudeness toward obnoxious individuals.[2] Some separations are subtle re-alignments of identification, priorities and commitments, or working with agendas which only incidentally coincide with the agendas of the institution one works in.[3] Ceasing to be loyal to something or someone is a separation; and ceasing to love. The feminist's separations are rarely if ever sought or maintained directly as ultimate personal or political ends. The closest we come to that, I think, is the separation which is the instinctive and self-preserving recoil from the systematic misogyny that surrounds us.[4] Generally, the separations are brought about and maintained for the sake of something else like independence, liberty, growth, invention, sisterhood, safety, health, or the practice of novel or heretical customs.[5] Often the separations in question evolve, unpremeditated, as one goes one's way and finds various persons, institutions, or relationships useless, obstructive or noisome and leaves them aside or behind. Sometimes the separations are consciously planned and cultivated as necessary prerequisites or conditions for getting on with one's business. Sometimes the separations are accomplished or maintained easily, or with a sense

63

of relief, or even joy; sometimes they are accomplished or maintained with difficulty, by dint of constant vigilance or with anxiety, pain or grief.

Most feminists, probably all, practice some separation from males and male-dominated institutions. A separatist practices separation consciously, systematically, and probably more generally than the others, and advocates thorough and 'broad-spectrum' separation as part of the conscious strategy of liberation. And, contrary to the image of the separatist as a cowardly escapist,[6] hers is the life and program which inspires the greatest hostility, disparagement, insult and confrontation and generally she is the one against whom economic sanctions operate most conclusively. The penalty for refusing to work with or for men is usually starvation (or, at the very least, doing without medical insurance[7]); and if one's policy of non-cooperation is more subtle, one's livelihood is still constantly on the line, since one is not a loyal partisan, a proper member of the team, or what have you. The penalties for being a lesbian are ostracism, harassment, and job-insecurity or joblessness. The penalty for rejecting men's sexual advances is often rape, and perhaps even more often forfeit of such things as professional or job opportunities. And the separatist lives with the added burden of being assumed by many to be a morally depraved man-hating bigot. But there is a clue here: if you are doing something that is so strictly forbidden by the patriarchs, you must be doing something right.

There is an idea floating around in both feminist and anti-feminist literature to the effect that females and males generally live in a relation of parasitism,[8] a parasitism of the male on the female ... that it is, generally speaking, the strength, energy, inspiration and nurturance of women that keeps men going, and not the strength, aggression, spirituality and hunting of men that keeps women going.

It is sometimes said that the parasitism goes the other way around, that the female is the parasite. But one can conjure the appearance of the female as parasite only if one takes a very narrow view of human living – historically parochial, narrow with respect to class and race, and limited in conception of what are the necessary goods. Generally, the female's contribution to her material support is and always has been substantial; in many times and places it has been independently sufficient. One can and should distinguish between a partial and contingent material dependence created by a certain sort of money economy and class structure, and the nearly ubiquitous spiritual, emotional and material dependence of males on females. Males presently provide, off and on, a portion of the material support of women, within circumstances apparently designed to make it difficult for women to provide them for themselves. But females provide and generally have provided for males the energy and spirit for living; the males are nurtured by the females. And this the males apparently cannot do for themselves, even partially.

The parasitism of males on females is, as I see it, demonstrated by the panic, rage and hysteria generated in so many of them by the thought of being abandoned by women. But it is demonstrated in a way that is perhaps more generally persuasive by both literary and sociological evidence. Evidence cited in Jesse Bernard's work in *The Future of Marriage* and in George Gilder's *Sexual Suicide* and *Men Alone* convincingly shows that males tend in shockingly significant numbers and in alarming degree to fall into mental illness, petty crime, alcoholism, physical infirmity, chronic unemployment, drug addiction and neurosis when deprived of the care and companionship of a female mate, or keeper. (While on the other hand, women without male mates are significantly healthier and happier than women with male mates.) And masculist literature is abundant with indications of male cannibalism, of males deriving essential sustenance from females. Cannibalistic imagery, visual and verbal, is common in pornography: images likening women to food, and sex to eating. And, as documented in Millett's *Sexual Politics* and many other feminist analyses of masculist literature, the theme of men getting high off beating, raping or killing women (or merely bullying them) is common. These interactions with women, or rather, these actions upon women, make men feel good, walk tall, feel refreshed, in*vigor*ated. Men are drained and depleted by their living by themselves and with and among other men, and are revived and refreshed, re-created, by going home and being served dinner, changing to clean clothes, having sex with the wife ... or by dropping by the apartment of a woman-friend to be served coffee or a drink and stroked in one way or another, or by picking up a prostitute for a quicky or for a dip in favorite sexual escape fantasies, or by raping refugees from their wars (foreign and domestic). The ministrations of women, be they willing or unwilling, free or paid for, are what restore in men the strength, will, and confidence to go on with what they call living.

If it is true that a fundamental aspect of the relations between the sexes is male parasitism, it might help to explain why certain issues are particularly exciting to patriarchal loyalists. For instance, in view of the obvious advantages of easy abortion to population control, to control of welfare rolls, and to ensuring sexual availability of women to men, it is a little surprising that the loyalists are so adamant and riled up in their objection to it. But look . . .

The fetus lives parasitically. It is a distinct animal surviving off the life (the blood) of another animal creature. It is incapable of surviving on its own resources, of independent nutrition; incapable even of symbiosis. If it is true that males live parasitically upon females, it seems reasonable to suppose that many of them and those loyal to them are in some way sensitive to the parallelism between their situation and that of the fetus. They could easily identify with the fetus. The woman who is free to see the fetus as a parasite[9] might be free to see the man as a parasite. The woman's willingness to cut off the life-line to one parasite suggests a willingness to cut off the life-line to another parasite. The woman who is capable (legally, psychologically, physically) of decisively, self-interestedly, independently rejecting the one parasite, is capable of rejecting, with the same decisiveness and independence, the like burden of the other parasite. In the eyes of the other parasite, the image of the wholly self-determined abortion, involving not even a ritual submission to male veto power, is the mirror image of death.

Another clue here is that one line of argument against free and easy abortion is the slippery slope argument that if fetuses are to be freely dispensed with, old people will be next. Old people? Why are old people next? And why the great concern for them? Most old people are women, indeed, and patriarchal loyalists are not generally so solicitous of the welfare of any women. Why old people? Because, I think, in the modern patriarchal divisions of labor, old people too are parasites on women. The anti-abortion folks seem not to worry about wife-beating and wife-murder — there is no broad or emotional popular support for stopping these violences. They do not worry about murder and involuntary sterilization in prisons, nor murder in war, nor murder by pollution and industrial accidents. Either these are not real to them or they cannot identify with the victims; but anyway, killing in general is not what they oppose. They worry about the rejection *by women*, at *women's discretion*, of something which lives parasitically on women. I suspect that they fret not because old people are next, but because men are next.

There are other reasons, of course, why patriarchal loyalists should be disturbed about abortion on demand, a major one being that it would be a significant form of female control of reproduction, and at least from certain angles it looks like the progress of patriarchy *is* the progress toward male control of reproduction, starting with possession of wives and continuing through the invention of obstetrics and the technology of extra-uterine gestation. Giving up that control would be giving up patriarchy. But such an objection to abortion is too abstract, and requires too historical a vision, to generate the hysteria there is now in the reaction against abortion. The hysteria is I think to be accounted for more in terms of a much more immediate and personal presentiment of ejection by the woman-womb.[10]

I discuss abortion here because it seems to me to be the most publicly emotional and most physically dramatic ground on which the theme of separation and male parasitism is presently being played out. But there are other locales for this play. For instance,[11] women with newly raised consciousness tend to leave marriages and families, either completely through divorce, or partially, through unavailability of their cooking, housekeeping and sexual services. And woman academics tend to become alienated from their colleagues and male mentors and no longer serve as sounding-board, ego booster, editor, mistress or proof-reader. Many awakening women become celibate or lesbian, and the others become a very great deal more choosy about when, where and in what relationships they will have sex with men. And the men affected by these separations generally react with defensive hostility, anxiety, and guilt-tripping, not to mention descents into illogical argument which match and exceed their own most fanciful images of female irrationality. My claim is that they are very afraid because they depend very heavily upon the goods they receive from women, and these separations cut them off from those goods.

Male parasitism means that males *must have access* to women; it is the Patriarchal Imperative. But feminist no-saying is more than a substantial removal (re-direction, re-allocation) of goods and services because Access is one of the faces of Power. Female denial of male access to females substantially cuts off a flow of benefits, but it has also the form and full portent of assumption of power.

Differences of power are always manifested in asymmetrical access. The President of the United States has access to almost everybody for almost anything he might want of them, and almost nobody has access to him. The super-rich have access to almost everybody; almost nobody has access to them. The resources of the employee are available to the boss as the resources of the boss are not to the employee. The parent has unconditional access to the child's room; the child does not have similar access to the parent's room. Students adjust to professors' office hours; professors do not adjust to students' conference hours. The child is required not to lie; the parent is free to close out the child with lies at her discretion. The slave is unconditionally accessible to the master. Total power is unconditional access; total powerlessness is being unconditionally accessible. The creation and manipulation of power is constituted of the manipulation and control of access.

All-woman groups, meetings, projects seem to be great things for causing controversy and confrontation. Many women are offended by them; many are afraid to be the one to announce the exclusion of men; it is seen as a device whose use needs much elaborate justification. I think this is because conscious and deliberate exclusion of men by women, from anything, is blatant insubordination, and generates in women fear of punishment and reprisal (fear which is often well-justified). Our own timidity and desire to avoid confrontations generally keeps us from doing very much in the way of all-woman groups and meetings. But when we do, we invariably run into the male champion who challenges our right to do it. Only a small minority of men go crazy when an event is advertised to be for women only – just one man tried to crash our women-only Rape Speak-Out, and only a few hid under the auditorium seats to try to spy on a women-only meeting at a NOW convention in Philadelphia. But these few are onto something their less rabid com-patriots are missing. The woman-only meeting is a fundamental challenge to the structure of power. It is always the privilege of the master to enter the slave's hut. The slave who decides to exclude the master from her hut is declaring herself not a slave. The exclusion of men from the meeting not only deprives them of certain benefits (which they might survive without); it is a controlling of access, hence an assumption of power. It is not only mean, it is arrogant.

It becomes clearer now why there is always an off-putting aura of negativity about separatism – one which offends the feminine Pollyanna in us and smacks of the purely defensive to the political theorist in us. It is this: First: When those who control access have made you totally accessible, your first act of taking control must be denying access, or must have denial of access as one of its aspects. This is not because you are charged up with (unfeminine or politically incorrect) negativity; it is because of the logic of the situation. When we start from a position of total accessibility there *must* be an aspect of no-saying, which is the beginning of control, in *every effective* act and strategy, the effective ones being precisely those which *shift power*, i.e., ones which involve manipulation and control of access. Second: Whether or not one says 'no,' or withholds or closes out or rejects, on this occasion or that, the capacity and ability to say 'no' (with effect) is logically necessary to control. When we *are* in control of access to ourselves there will be some no-saying, and when we are more accustomed to it, when it is more common, an ordinary part of living, it will not seem so prominent, obvious, or strained . . . we will not strike ourselves or others as being particularly negative. In this aspect of ourselves and our lives, we will strike ourselves pleasingly, as active beings with momentum of our own, with sufficient shape and structure, with sufficient integrity, to generate friction. Our experience of our no-saying will be an aspect of our experience of our definition.

When our feminist acts or practices have an aspect of separation we are assuming power by controlling access, and simultaneously by undertaking definition. The slave who excludes the master from her hut thereby declares herself *not a slave*. And *definition* is another face of power.

The powerful normally determine what is said and sayable. When the powerful label something or dub it or baptize it, the thing becomes what they call it. When the Secretary of Defense calls something a peace negotiation, for instance, then whatever it is that he called a peace negotiation is an instance of negotiating peace. If the activity in question is the working out of terms of a trade-off of nuclear reactors and territorial redistributions, complete with arrangements for the resulting refugees, that is peacemaking. People laud it, and the negotiators get Noble Piece Prizes for it. On the other hand, when I call a certain speech act a rape, my 'calling' it does not make it so. At best, I have to explain and justify and make clear exactly what it is about this speech act which is assaultive in just what way, and then the others acquiesce in saying the act was *like* rape or could figuratively be called a rape. My counter-assault will not be counted a simple case of self-defense. And what I called rejection of parasitism, they call the loss of the womanly virtues of compassion and 'caring.' And generally, when renegade women call something one thing and patriarchal loyalists call it another, the loyalists get their way.[12]

Women generally are not the people who do the defining, and we cannot from our isolation and powerlessness simply commence saying different things than others say and make it stick. There is a humpty-dumpty problem in that. But we are able to arrogate definition to ourselves when we re-pattern access. Assuming control of access, we draw new boundaries and create new roles and relationships. This, though it causes some strain, puzzlement and hostility, is to a fair extent within the scope of individuals and small gangs, as outright verbal redefinition is not, at least in the first instance.

One may see access as coming in two sorts, 'natural' and humanly arranged. A grizzly bear has what you might call natural access to the picnic basket of the unarmed human. The access of the boss to the personal services of the secretary is humanly arranged access; the boss exercises institutional power. It looks to me, looking from a certain angle, like institutions *are* humanly designed patterns of access – access to persons and their services. But institutions are artifacts of definition. In the case of intentionally and formally designed institutions, this is very clear, for the relevant definitions are explicitly set forth in by-laws and constitutions, regulations and rules. When one defines the term 'president,' one defines presidents in terms of what they can do and what is owed them by other offices, and 'what they can do' is a matter of their access to the services of others. Similarly, definitions of *dean*, *student*, *judge*, and *cop* set forth patterns of access, and definitions of *writer*, *child*, *owner*, and of course, *husband*, *wife*, and *man* and *girl*. When one changes the pattern of access, one forces new uses of words on those affected. The term 'man' has to shift in meaning when rape is no longer possible. When we take control of sexual access to us, of access to our nurturance and to our reproductive function, access to mothering and sistering, we redefine the word 'woman.' The shift of usage is pressed on others by a change in social reality; it does not await their recognition of our definitional authority.

When women separate (withdraw, break out, re-group, transcend, shove aside, step outside, migrate, say *no*) we are simultaneously controlling access and defining. We are doubly insubordinate, since neither of these is permitted. And access and definition are fundamental ingredients in the alchemy of power, so we are doubly, and radically, insubordinate.

If these, then, are some of the ways in which separation is at the heart of our struggle, it helps to explain why separation is such a hot topic. If there is one thing women are queasy about it is *actually taking power*. As long as one stops just short of that, the patriarchs will for the most part take an indulgent attitude. We are afraid of what will happen to us when we really frighten them. This is not an irrational fear. It is our experience in the movement generally that the defensiveness, nastiness, violence, hostility and irrationality of the reaction to feminism tends to correlate with the blatancy of the element of separation in the strategy or project which triggers the reaction. The separations involved in women leaving homes, marriages and boyfriends, separations from fetuses, and the separation of lesbianism are all pretty dramatic. That is, they are dramatic and blatant when perceived from within the framework provided by the patriarchal world-view and male parasitism. Matters pertaining to marriage and divorce, lesbianism, and abortion touch individual men (and their sympathizers) because they can feel the relevance of these to themselves – they can feel the threat that they might be next. Hence, heterosexuality, marriage, and motherhood, which are the institutions which most obviously and individually maintain female accessibility to males, form the core triad of anti-feminist ideology, and all-woman spaces, all-woman organizations, all-woman meetings, all-woman classes, are outlawed, suppressed, harassed, ridiculed, and punished, in the name of that other fine and enduring patriarchal institution, Sex Equality.

To some of us these issues can almost seem foreign . . . strange ones to be occupying center stage. We are busily engaged in what seem to *us* our blatant insubordinations: living our own lives, taking care of ourselves and one another, doing our work, and in particular, telling it as we see it. Still, the original sin is the separation which these presuppose, and it is that, not our art or philosophy, not our speech-making, nor our 'sexual acts' (or abstinences), for which we will be persecuted, when worse comes to worst.

Notes

1.   Before publication, I received many helpful comments from those who heard or read this paper. I have incorporated some, made notes of others. I got help from Carolyn Shafer in seeing the structure of it all, in particular, the connections among parasitism, access and definition.

2.   *Adrienne Rich: '. . . makes me question the whole of "courtesy" or "rudeness" – surely their constructs, since women become "rude" when we ignore or reject male obnoxiousness, while male "rudeness" is usually punctuated with the "Haven't you a sense of humor" tactic.'* Yes; me too. I embrace rudeness; our compulsive/compulsory politeness so often is what coerces us into their 'fellowship.'

3.   Help from Claudia Card.

4.   *Ti-Grace Atkinson: Should give more attention here to our vulnerability to assault and degradation, and to separation as PROTECTION.* Okay, but then we have to re-emphasize that it has to be separation at *our* behest – we've had enough of their imposed separation for our 'protection.' (There's no denying that in my real-life life, protection and maintenance of places for healing are major motives for separation.)

5.   Help from Chris Pierce and Sara Ann Ketchum. See 'Separatism and Sexual Relationships,' in *A Philosophical Approach to Women's Liberation*, eds. S. Hill and Weinzweig (Wadsworth, Belmont, California, 1978).

6.   Answering Claudia Card.

7.   Levity due to Carolyn Shafer.

8.   I first noticed this when reading *Beyond God the Father*, by Mary Daly (Beacon Press, Boston, 1973). See also *Women's Evolution*, by Evelyn Reed (Pathfinder Press, New York, 1975) for rich hints about male cannibalism and male dependence.

9.   *Caroline Whitbeck: Cross-cultural evidence suggests it's not the fetus that gets rejected in cultures where abortion is common, it is the role of motherhood, the burden, in particular, of 'illegitimacy'; where the*

institution of illegitimacy does not exist, abortion rates are pretty low.
This suggests to me that the woman's rejection of the fetus is even more
directly a rejection of the male and his world than I had thought.
10.   Claudia Card.
11.   The instances mentioned are selected for their relevance to the lives
of the particular women addressed in this talk. There are many other
sorts of instances to be drawn from other sorts of women's lives.
12.   This paragraph and the succeeding one are the passage which has
provoked the most substantial questions from women who read the
paper. One thing that causes trouble here is that I am talking from a
stance or position that is ambiguous – it is located in two different and
non-communicating systems of thought-action. *Re* the patriarchy and the
English language, there is general usage over which I/we do not have the
control that elite males have (with the cooperation of all the ordinary
patriarchal loyalists). *Re* the new being and meaning which are being
created now by lesbianfeminists, we *do* have semantic authority, and,
collectively, can and do define with effect. I think it is only by maintaining
our boundaries through controlling concrete access to us that we can
enforce on those who are not-us our definitions of ourselves, hence force
on them *the fact of our existence* and thence open up the *possibility* of
our having semantic authority with them. (I wrote some stuff that's
relevant to this in the last section of my paper 'Male Chauvinism – A
Conceptual Analysis.') Our unintelligibility to patriarchal loyalists is a
source of pride and delight, in some contexts; but if we don't have an
effect on their usage, while we continue, willy nilly, to be subject to theirs,
being totally unintelligible to them could be fatal. (A friend of mine had a
dream where the women were meeting in a cabin at the edge of town, and
they had a sort of inspiration through the vision of one of them that they
should put a sign on the door which would connect with the patriarchs'
meaning-system, for otherwise the men would be too curious/frightened
about them and would break the door down to get in. They put a picture
of a fish on the door.) Of course, you might say that *being* intelligible to
them might be fatal. Well, perhaps it's best to be in a position to make
tactical decisions about when and how to be intelligible and unintelligible.
13.   In (improbably enough) *Philosophy and Sex*, edited by Robert Baker
& Frederick Elliston (Prometheus Books, Buffalo, New York, 1976).

Lesbian Separatist Basics

K. Hess, Jean Langford, and Kathy Ross
1980

The term lesbian separatism has been used to express many
different politics. To us it means, most importantly, not a way of

promoting exclusively lesbian concerns, or a way of protecting lesbians from heterosexism in political groups, but a possibility of prioritising feminism. We want to distinguish clearly between women's interests and men's interests so that we can act in women's interests. The institution of heterosexuality blocks this process by encouraging women to see our interests as identified with men's instead of opposed to them. Women are not going to be able to persuade men as a group that it is in their best interests to set women free because it isn't. Men get material benefits from women's oppression: better pay, better working conditions, free labor in the household, more status, greater control over sexual relations, et cetera. As one radical feminist wrote:

> I fully recognize that some radical males have on occasion baked a tray of brownies to celebrate May Day. This does not alter the fundamental structure of American life.[1]

Economically and emotionally men's interests are best protected by the oppression of women. It is pure idealism to imagine men *as a group* rising above their interests in order to be charitable to women. Men will make room for women's interests only if and when women are strong enough to force the point. As separatists we choose to oppose men rather than try to reform them, not out of a belief that men can't change but out of a belief that they won't change until they understand that they have to.

We may fight *alongside* (we do not say *with*) men in certain situations like the anti-Nazi and anti-Initiative 13 marches in Seattle in the summer of 1978 but in these situations we insist on our political independence.[2] We will not put it aside in order to emphasize unity. Men are not allies in feminism which is the framework of our political position on any issue. Lesbian separatism is not about asserting lesbianism as a superior lifestyle but about making use of its potential for political independence from men.

The aim of lesbian separatism is feminist revolution. We share this goal with most radical feminists and many socialist feminists but we define it differently. . . .

Notes

1. Olah, Suzie, 'Economic Function of the Oppression of Women,' *Notes from the Third Year: Women's Liberation*, 1971.

2. Initiative 13 was a city-wide initiative designed to severely limit the civil rights of lesbians and gay men. It didn't pass.

Female Only

Bev Jo
1981

Separatism is a dirty word in the 'women's' and lesbian communities. In my experience, of all the many groups of lesbians who exist, separatists are the safest to attack. At this time when fascism and the New Right are on the rise, it is becoming more and more dangerous to be an open lesbian. And separatists are the most out lesbians of all. It would be hard enough to deal with attacks from men and straight women, but it's even more painful when we're also attacked by other lesbians.

Separatism means a lot of different things to different lesbians. Like any lesbians, separatists all have different definitions and disagreements about who we are and what we want to do. I can only speak for myself as a separatist.

Separatism is *not* having no contact with the patriarchy. Even the richest lesbians can't afford to do that, and most separatists I know are *not* rich. We have to work, deal with county, state and federal agencies, go to grocery stores, deal with landlords, etc. We do not relate to males when we don't have to. This is a positive decision: we choose to share our energy and intensity with other lesbians, preferably separatists. Anti-separatists like to act like we're a very privileged group. We aren't. Separatists come from all racial and class backgrounds. Like most lesbians and women, the most privileged are the most visible. Assuming that well-known separatists represent all of us is oppressive to the most oppressed of us. It is a racist, classist assumption, as well as being oppressive in other ways. How would you, as a woman, like to be represented by Gloria Steinem (as spokesperson for all women)?

When I go to a lesbian event the group that I'm most likely to hear being attacked are separatists – more than capitalists, socialists, religious groups, straight women, men, or anyone else. I think the reason that it's open season on separatists is that women who have a connection with men or male institutions, even if they are lesbians, get a lot more respect than we do. Separatists are carrying the idea of lesbianism, women being with women, into all parts of our lives. Attacks on separatists are a subtle attack on lesbians in general, and it's a very self-hating thing for a lesbian to do. But for most lesbians there seems to be more loyalty toward men than toward women.

The one thing that most separatists have in common is wanting women and girls-only space. Why is this such a threat to women and lesbians? When I first came out, it was a relief to find other lesbians. It seemed understood that lesbians were getting together to make spaces separate from men and sometimes also separate from straight women. The 'women's community' was pretty much a lesbian community and most events put on by lesbians, like parties, dances, concerts, readings, workshops, etc., were for women and girls only. It was a rare event that was open to men. This seemed to be true across the country wherever there was a lesbian community big enough to sponsor a 'women's event.' In the last few years, in most places that I've heard of, a women-and-girls-only event is becoming rare. The reason we needed space away from men and boys has not changed. We need to be with each other, where we can feel safe from harassment and not be influenced by the presence of males. Also, boys may be less threatening to women than men, but they are still a threat to girls, and the harassment can be verbal and sometimes physical. Little girls *are* raped and beaten by little boys. Why have so many women forgotten what it feels like to be threatened by boys? Most of us experienced it and girls are still being attacked now.

Even if there is no blatant harassment at an event from males, the entire *feeling* of what is going on changes. When women are talking with each other and a man enters the room, everything still changes, even if the women are all lesbians. The patriarchy has not ended, and men still control our lives. The effects are blatant and they are also subtle.

There are more lesbians than ever and there are more lesbian-owned businesses and 'women's events' than there have ever been before. But there is less women-and-girl-only space than there has been in the past ten years. Why is it such a threat for women and girls to have space separate from men and boys? It's a constant fight for us to not give up our space and identity to men. The pressure is constant, and, as it increases, I'm seeing a lot of lesbians selling out by going straight or trying to pass more. As the general mood of the lesbian community goes toward passing, then lesbians who can't or won't pass are a threat. And separatists are usually the most resistant of all to going back to the closet. When lesbians are invisible again, the patriarchy will have us where it wants us.

Freedom

Redwomon
1981

Except for a brief week of bisexual rhetoric after I came out, separatist ideology has always made sense to me. After 24 years of compulsively giving energy[1] to men, the idea of using my energy for myself and other wimin[2] was a novel, refreshing idea. Certainly we had been deprived of much that was rightfully ours, so separatism as a sort of affirmative action program seemed like just the thing to insure our getting some extra attention. I know I looked forward to being nurtured by wimin, since men hadn't given me anything remotely resembling a good stroke (pun intended).

Because we were raised in a male-centered world to support and take care of male needs, *every* male benefits from patriarchy – personally, economically, and socially. It is appropriate and necessary for wimin to make a special effort to bond with each other for validation and survival, as well as for progress on a global scale.

The most basic definition of a feminist is someone who does not believe that wimin are innately inferior to men; feminists then vary in beliefs from the bourgeois liberationists to radical feminists/lesbians to dyke separatists. Feminism, by definition, implies a withdrawal of energy from men who have long gotten more than their share, and separatism is even more womoncentered than feminism, implying total commitment to wimin. Just as black nationalists realized that, in order to build unity and economic power, they must keep their money and energy from whitey and for themselves, so wimin must in general practice at least some degree of separation from men and even from maleidentified wimin. Separatism gave me permission to be centered and free.

A lot changes when we stop paying attention to The Man: we have more energy for our lives and will truly discover the meaning of freedom. Without him in our lives and minds, we are free to learn to question authority and think for ourselves, to create new structures of cooperation and collectivity, and to discover better ways to feed and heal wimin, make art, and relate. And as we learn new skills and eliminate the weaknesses of mind and body which men bred into us, we will find ways not only to help wimin but also to sabotage patriarchy.

Apathy and withdrawal can be useful tools. Instead of continually confronting men and male-identified wimin (which drains our energy and presupposes a connection – that men are willing and capable of learning), we can disconnect from their system and spin our own webs of relating and culture. Rather than get hooked into fighting them, encouraging them, or making it okay for them, we can avoid them as much as possible so that their judgments and attacks won't interrupt our lives or interfere with our growth and becoming.

When we do have to deal with men in school or jobs, we can go in and take what we need, staying centered. On papers, write 'he thinks that' instead of accepting his value judgments as objective truth. Never forget his heterosexist, racist, classist, able-bodied assumptions which negate the reality of beings unlike himself. When we need a doctor, we can find a female M.D. or chiropractor or herbalist. When a prick tries to converse with me, I can ignore him or walk off because every minute I spend on a male is one less minute (at least!) that I have for myself or other wimin.

If this is 'selfish,' so be it. We are no longer self-sacrificing good girls for big daddy, no longer dependable slaves. Separatists make waves and rock the boat of patriarchy, not to mention drilling holes in its hull! Instead of racking our brains trying to please men or raise their consciousness or get a bigger piece of their rotten capitalist pie, we can actively create new kinds of relationships and organizations egalitarian in power, which heal, not hurt, ourselves and Mother Earth.

Well, it seemed logical to me, but soon I found a lot of wimin quick to trash separatism as negative, man-hating (tsk!), and fascist. Even white lesbians, who accept political separatism for Third World people, continue to put down political separatism for lesbians, although working with men and straight wimin does not strengthen our unity or independence. As noted in *Off Our Backs* in late '77, 'Oppressed groups should not be expected to compromise their struggle by fighting alongside their oppressors or those who directly support their oppressors.' The controversy suggests how very far we have to go, since even a slight rejection of the 'sacred male' (my term) brings out the Uncle Tom in many wimin, who then act as overseer for patriarchy, pushing us back in line via put-downs and ostracism.

Many wimin are leery of spending too much time on wimin, of 'going overboard.' They think they must spend time with pricks and not neglect the poor fellows, yet these same wimin do not hesitate to be unfair to wimin while unhesitatingly going overboard for The Man! These wimin, both straight and lesbian, have not outgrown the conditioning which makes them reluctant to give wimin the first place. They hide behind excuses and have their 'exceptional men,' but what it boils down to is that it's much easier to be a 'good girl' than a 'bad nigger.' (I apologize if the latter term offends anyone, but I feel it is the best synonym to say exactly what is meant, as it refers to people found rebellious and uncooperative by slave owners.) They need male approval in order to feel good about themselves as wimin.

I think a lot of dykes lack a concept of sisterhood which extends outside of their circle of friends. It is a prime contradiction when these male-identified lesbians put considerable energy into maintaining relationships with men, yet will drop a womon friend at the slightest excuse or political difference. Whoever heard of men having 'exceptional dykes?' Men don't need token queers in order to feel okay because so many wimin automatically assume the boyzitos *are* okay, and rush to make excuses *ad nauseam* for men's woman-hating behavior.

To those who recite tired rhetoric that 'men are oppressed too,' I say that men are morally limited by their millenia of murderous actions to wimin, but men certainly aren't *oppressed* because wimin do not have a powerful system with which to oppress any group! Can blacks oppress whites just as much as whites oppress blacks? Hardly. Only men control the world's food supply and weaponry; they have trained us into weakness and they victimize us constantly on the streets. Even at home, many wimin are so brainwashed, overworked and fucked up that none of their time or money is their own; plus they're deprived of their identity and herstory. How could they oppress anyone on a major scale except maybe the children or the dog?

Then liberals make the assumption 'all humans are the same,' discounting the uniqueness of one's race, class, and culture. They also assume (when convenient) that wimin and men are basically alike, whereas a study of facts from every field makes it obvious that we are quite different from men, even without sex-role conditioning. This must be taken into account so we can deal with men's presence and dominance as wisely as possible. Every year, men discover new ways to replace and eliminate us (cloning, sex-selection, robots, sex-change operations, etc.), so we don't dare forget we are still fighting for our lives.

As for the issue of our 'neglecting' men ('reverse sexism'), the solidarity of an oppressed group can hardly be equated with the basic white male position of dominance and death-orientation which limits, controls and kills us. Separatism is a gutsy political choice and strength, not an emotional incapacity. Just as I chose to major in one subject in college (which was labelled focussed or specialized, rather than limited), I also choose to devote my life to my major interest group – wimin. I'm like the black person who escapes the ghetto to get a good job or college education, then goes back to work solely with other blacks and help them. She may respect certain whites but still choose to work with her own people, time and energy being limited.

I would also remind ostrich-headed liberals that the word *humanism* comes from the renaissance, which was actually a period of incredible oppression for wimin, who were burned by the millions by humanist christian men – murdered for healing, for owning land that the church wanted, or for being married to an impotent man. It was our age of obscurity and sorrow, and one should refuse to use the term renaissance on principle, for it is far from being as universal as it pretends to be. Besides, how can anyone truly be a humanist if they lack wide-ranging feminist consciousness? Therefore, the only true humanists, if there is such a thing, are feminists.

For awhile I said I was a 95% separatist, since I attended a male-run school, but now I don't bother to make that distinction since men own the food stores, housing, and everything else including menstrual pad/tampon companies (making money off our blood!), having structured it so that our money flows to them sooner or later. Money is an important part of patriarchal power, and we become a force to be reckoned with when we use what Flo Kennedy calls our body power, our vote power, and our dollar power (such as it is). I urge wimin everywhere to practice pushing the limits even further – to undermine men's businesses by creating and supporting wimin's businesses. We do have lesbians and feminists publishing books and producing concerts and albums so we can say what we want, rather than toning down our message to make it acceptable to men. Or rather, nonseparatists have been doing real good in this department, while separatists continue to be trashed, censored and silenced.

Separatists today are in the same position as were lesbians in the early wimin's movement – shut up and shit upon. I'm tired of being verbally attacked by my so-called sisters and forced into a defensive position. Separatism has become a tainted word, thanks to womon-hating paranoia and misunderstanding. Those who criticize us often make inaccurate assumptions about where we're coming from, and they don't even try to see the useful aspects. It's much easier to lash out with self-righteous, trashing words than to take the time to listen and understand.

And, as we're not perfect, anti-separatists attack our personal failings, as if these have something to do with the validity of our philosophy.

But since a lot of wimin don't have any idea what separatism really is, we have a chance to give them our definition before they become prejudiced by the negative rhetoric against us. Separatism needn't be interpreted as an attack on nonseparatist wimin – it is our attempt to survive. We're not dropouts, we're refugees building a new world – true expatriates from the fatherland. As I read somewhere, 'If we seem a little hardline at times, it's because we have no support anywhere and go a little crazy when we find boys and men at a wimin's concert ogling us.' Lesbians who attack us when we don't nurture men are supporting the patriarchal power which is squashing us.

I was friends (I thought) with one such womon who defined herself as a radical lesbian-feminist and even said she hated men. (I have since learned to beware of mere talk of man-hating since many straight wimin hate men but still continue to live with and be loyal to them; what we want to hear is some awareness of how we benefit once we limit our response to men's continual demands.) Janet was cute and charming, and I trusted her; although I noticed that her lover and all of her friends were male-identified or straight, I was unaware of what that could mean for me. As it turned out, she had never outgrown the good-girl compulsion to please (slave mentality) – to please men and straights, that is. If she shuffled any faster, she'd break her feet!

One day, all her frustrations with her boss and lover came pouring out on me; the only person who'd ever encouraged her writing or taken her seriously. We had gotten together as usual to talk about writing, wimin and ideas, but her lover was there and they wasted hours of my time dragging me all over a hilly section of San Francisco which caused me a week of intense pain (am disabled) and loss of work. Then Janet blew up when I politely but firmly said I didn't want to hear about the man who wanted to be her lover or about the poor little pricklet next door – who will grow up to have more privilege and money than I ever will. Instantly, she threw our friendship aside, calling me a fascist, and went into her usual self-righteous whiny martyr trip with me cast as the ogre. When I tried to discuss it with her, she kept laughing and refused to hear my analogies or feelings. When the crunch came, she reverted to straight lady behavior and chose The Man over a sister.

We can all use more practice in treating other wimin and ourselves well, as important beings with value and potential, who are central to our lives, not peripheral or competitors. It is obviously in men's best interests to keep wimin apart, so the most revolutionary thing we can do is to unite, with the practice of separatism being the strongest counter. When wimin affirm each other, it pierces gaping holes in the fabric of patriarchy. We must seek out progressive wimin and support each other's accomplishments so we will gain the strength to go further. It takes time and effort and loyalty to heal ourselves.

Usually I think that every woman is potentially a lesbian and separatist and that many will eventually join us, so talking to them isn't always a waste of time. A few words from us could clarify their direction and bring them further along; in fact, this outreach is needed to counteract the pro-male propaganda directed at them. It's tempting to see some wimin as hopeless, but we shouldn't make that judgment so readily. For one thing, we may be wrong, and it also limits the way we relate to them and the way they see themselves, like self-fulfilling prophecies. Once I was a born-again x-ian and compulsive heterosexual, dressed like a barbie doll, but now I dress comfortably and am centered and capable, more interested in revolution than in pleasing anyone. So I figure one can at least introduce new wimin to feminist bookstores and coffeehouses/bars, so they will know where to go for more contacts and information; that's a real choice and option that men don't want them to have.

When I envision separatism, ideally I think of well-informed wimin who consistently show each other affection and respect (the least we can do), who help each other overcome internalized oppression and race/class/able-bodied ignorance, and who plot strategy against patriarchy. However, this is not what I have found. I could go on at great length with incidents and names, but I think that an overall look at the forest will be more helpful than a close scrutiny of the trees.

Unfortunately, the sisterhood I've read about and worked for, does not seem to include me. Despite years of commitment and growth, I keep getting messages that I don't fit in and am unwelcome – that I'm too radical, too conservative, too middle-of-the-road, too enthusiastic, too quiet – but nothing tangible I can deal with. I am left with the impression that everything or a mysterious something about me is irrevocably wrong – not merely that I'm mistaken on a subtle political point, but innately and forever doomed.

Seems ridiculous, I know, but it has caused me to grow afraid of lesbians, even separatists who are the only peer group I can possibly have. Such ambivalence is impossible to live with, and one naturally seeks resolution. Shall I accept such poor treatment, ostracism, and lack of appreciation, which is killing me, and stay at the fringes of the movement, unable to put my full intelligence and talent to work on wimin's behalf? Too painful. Or shall I leave – and go where? Some wimin have been treated so unjustly and coldly that in desperation we think about going back to men where we at least had some fun, affection, and conversation. But if a womon can't bring herself to do that, and is unaccepted by 'the wimin's community,' she is left with the choice of isolation or suicide. I care that she survive and have wimin to love and work with. Do you?

Perhaps this isn't so much an isolated personal problem as it is an example of a fatally flawed movement, flawed not in principle but in practice. Several times I've been kicked out of groups (rap, support, and study) for no good reason – along with other workingclass, black or Asian wimin – each time by thin, white, able-bodied, middle-class wimin who always seem to have power and be in charge, even in 'leaderless' groups. I have never heard of a white m-c womon being ejected from anything. The damage done by this elitism is incalculable, both individually and to the movement and community.

Having tried my best, I can no longer doubt myself. Instead, I call upon so-called wimin-loving-wimin to take another look at the racism, classism, looksism, and ableism running rampant among us. We must work out our problems in ways that do not attempt to assimilate poor, non-white or disabled wimin into the white middle-class able ideal of manners and appearance. There must be a way to build on our diversity and create coalitions and a united group.

Although a number of us are rejecting feminism, I favor reclaiming the word to use as a tool of guidance which can give us needed vision and unity so we don't deteriorate further into self-centered fascism. Wimin need to break all patriarchal ties/identification in order to create a womon-loving revolution/evolution which will take us from death to life, from pain to pleasure. One of our primary tasks is to work on living harmoniously with each other, really feeling kinship with other lesbians and separatists. We can only benefit from each other's interest and support; I know I really need some.

We also need long-term perspectives and goals to work toward, as well as immediate advances as we struggle along day-to-day. Learn to think in terms of tactics and strategy like Ti-Grace Atkinson does in *Amazon Odyssey*, of infiltration and fucking up the system (Valerie Solanas in *The SCUM Manifesto*), and of creating alternatives in every field to the man's world. There are daily opportunities when we become more aware and think creatively. We can all be doing more!

Real commitment and solidarity will mean extra effort on each womon's part – going the extra mile for a sister, rather than just coasting along doing what's comfortable for you and your friends. It also means dealing with your own games and prejudices . . . *caring* enough to do so. Responsibility to ourselves and other wimin is the issue. How do we as individuals create true sisterhood with its value of nurturing, sharing, and freedom? It may not come at all, ever, unless each of us works at it – and hard.

Notes

1.   Energy: The power by which anything acts effectively to move or change the other thing or accomplish any result; potential energy is that due to the position of one body relative to another; that property of style by which a thought is forcibly imposed upon the hearer's mind; life, spirit, vigor, potency, strength, fire, ardor, animation, warmth, activation.
2.   Woman: wife of a person (OE), the female part of the human race, a female attendant or servant or kept mistress; effeminate, timid, weak.
   Womon/Wimin: us.

A Black Separatist

Anna Lee
1981

I often read the words 'feminist,' 'womon,' etc. used to designate white only. In this paper, I've used the terms to specify all wimmin. I use the term 'sister' to address black wimmin.

While I am an active feminist, I cannot afford economically to discuss lesbian separatism in print under my own name. As a black womon, I am in 'double jeopardy.'[1] I live on the edge of working or welfare. To publicly embrace my lesbianism would force me onto the welfare rolls.

I became a separatist gradually. Over a period of twelve years, I changed from being celibate in a heterosexual environment to being gay, but accepting heterosexual norms as givens. For example, I spent my money on movies, eating out and entertaining males in my home. I believed and acted on society's dictum that I was the same as straight people, but simply loved wimmin. When I moved from the Midwest, I learned many things and realized how much self-hatred I had internalized. The Midwest did not have a wimmin's community or feminist activities that might have challenged my assumptions. I'm glad that various groups have formed since I left. For me, leaving the Midwest provided access to a variety of opportunities. There were and are sisters talking about feminism and introducing a perspective into white feminism that supported my commitment to a wimmin's movement that included all wimmin.

The diversity of goals and projects was exciting in my new community. Here, at last, was a chance to be challenged by wimmin who had been thinking about theory and acting on their knowledge. I began to re-evaluate some of my assumptions about our possibilities. I began to perceive my lesbianism to include not only what I did in bed and with whom, but also as an analysis of the world.

Presently, I claim and affirm under tremendous pressure all of who I am – black lesbian separatist. To do so puts me in conflict with each of the groups from which I could reasonably expect support, nurturance and sustenance. It's a juggling act to maintain my sanity and to remember who my real enemy is. Remembering who my real enemy is forces me to consider carefully some very critical choices. It is not easy or simple to delineate which acts I commit move us as wimmin forward and which ones do not. It would be simpler to ignore this issue. It would be easier to avoid considering the ramifications of my individual acts. To do so, however, would condemn me and us to failure. To act ethically is difficult, but to grapple with the question may mean that in the struggle I and, perhaps, we will at least learn more than if no struggle had occurred.

For example, the existence of rape brings my often conflicting selves to the forefront, not so much as to the perpetrator of rape, but in terms of my and, really, our response to rape. In part, the questions are, how have white feminists (even separatists) analyzed, discussed and reacted to the occurrence of rape, and what would an ethical response include?

The issue of rape requires wimmin to define our enemy clearly and consider the ramifications of our analysis. The complexity of rape demands our full attention. I support a woman's right to be free of the fear of rape which is used by the fathers to keep all of us in line even if, and sometimes especially if, we do not consort with them.

There are realities that are conveniently omitted from feminist analysis. One is the acknowledgement that all males are potential rapists but some males are consistently selected to bear the punishment for the crime. In psychological studies, the profile of the rapist does not differ from the profile of a 'healthy' white heterosexual male. I hear white feminists express their fears about the black male on the street more often than any indication that their boyfriend, husband or white neighbor might rape them. While it would be easier to say that all males are potential rapists, white feminists conveniently ignore that it is black males that are singled out for punishment.[2] This must be kept in mind if there is a serious commitment by white wimmin to confront our enemy. To do otherwise is to support the same status quo that devalues our worth as wimmin.

White feminists conveniently forget that black males are arrested, prosecuted, and convicted at a higher rate than white males. The Scottsboro trial is part of my indelible memory, but does not seem to be part of theirs. The black males involved in that trial were convicted even though historically more white males have raped wimmin. Today the statistics have not changed. Black males receive stiffer penalties and are recommended for execution in disproportionate numbers. A feminist response to the issue of rape cannot stop with the knowledge that black males are seen as the archetypical rapist.

The fact is black wimmin also bear the burden of rape. Whether we are discussing the rape of black wimmin during slavery or sisters being raped on a Saturday night, the percentage of sisters being raped is disproportionate to our absolute numbers. The convergence of sex and race insures that we face a much greater chance of being raped in our lifetimes than white wimmin.

So far both these factors have been excluded in white feminist analysis. Surely, white wimmin directly benefit from these omissions. The ignorance of racial implications can allow white feminists to pretend that a white analysis of rape transcends the question of black and white. That ignoring also encourages white feminists to deny that rape is anything other than a simple belief that all males are potential rapists. I have no qualms about the statement. My objection is concerned with the refusal to examine the complexity of the issue. That refusal leads ultimately to some harmful effects which I will discuss later in this paper.

As separatists, we are not free of the fear of rape. Any analysis of that issue should have our input. I believe that using the analytical tools we have garnered as separatists will lead us to develop and respond to the issue of rape in a manner that will move us forward as wimmin. Given that the justice system is both class and race conscious while denying both, black males are assured of receiving the harsher punishment. In demanding wider use of that justice system, white feminists encourage by default the penalizing of both black females and males. For a sister raped, the white boy's system will not find her attacker or convict the culprit. For black males, the justice system will convict him even if he is innocent. The outcome for each is different but equally demeaning and oppressive.

While wimmin do not rape, this fact does not eliminate our responsibility and particularly white wimmin's responsibility to discuss and analyze the dimensions of rape in an ethical manner. To do otherwise often leads us to the mistaken belief that more police officers or more female police officers would begin to alleviate the horrors wimmin face in being raped. The single-minded focus of all males as potential rapists encourages rape crisis centers to invite the police to actively participate in their programs and to cooperate in police programs. Eventually, rape crisis centers become subsumed by police goals, no longer challenge the anti-womon philosophy of this society and become so non-threatening that city governments can safely fund them. Of course, this is not the sole reason that crisis centers cease to serve wimmin's interest. Economic crisis forces centers to seek out LEAA grants.[3] I wonder, if white feminists had a clearer understanding of who was hurt and who was helped by their demands, would the money seem as attractive or acceptable?

The accepted analysis of rape has divided black and white wimmin. In doing so, white feminists have chosen to align themselves with white males at the expense of forming coalitions with sisters. It is not just rape crisis centers that have chosen this 'solution.' Later I will discuss this choice in another context. The point is simply that to date white feminist analysis of rape successfully ignores the complexity of the issue, insuring that the choices made exclude sisters while putting white males in the forefront. The analysis precludes ethical choices that would include all wimmin and allow us to move forward.

It seems to me to create our own rape squads to deal with our rapists is a better stop-gap measure than the call for more police protection. In the long run, stopping the rapist mentality is even more important. (I will return to this question.) Any analysis of rape must confront the white males instead of bonding with them to kill black males.

To state all this is to begin to raise necessary considerations concerning ethical stances. For example, I still feel alienated from the black male nationalist community because I am a lesbian, and yet I understand that our struggles are intimately intertwined. At the same time, I often feel alienated by the white feminist community which has the privilege to ignore and to minimize racism. White feminists can demand my support, presence and energy without seeing what it is they are asking of me. They can refuse to acknowledge the price I pay: the losing of my protection as limited and limiting as it is. My blackness is visible and the first line of attack on me. I am also a womon and choose to continue my struggle within the wimmin's community. I have stopped struggling with my brothers around their homophobia and sexism. As I have indicated, merging my seemingly separate identities is not easy, but all of them exist within me. It is very important to me to recognize that racism hurts both my brothers and me. While it may manifest itself differently for each of us, it is the blackness that defines the conditions we live under. I am very clear that my brothers hold the power of the penis. They are not confronted with being women in this world and I am. It is true that any male regardless of class, income, or race holds power in the world. For sure, some males have more control in the world than others. Each has if nothing else a womon or womon-substitute as his slave – wife, mother, girlfriend, etc. This is not true for me. I do know white wimmin who are active in anti-racist struggles and willing to address this issue. Unfortunately, I know of no males of color who are or have been willing to deal with their own sexism or homophobia. My analysis of power, who has power, and who gets what resources allows me to make the distinction between power and revokable privilege. White wimmin have revokable privilege. During slavery white wimmin tortured black wimmin slaves and today act as if privilege is, in fact, power. The reality is that revokable privilege is just that. If the group exercising the privilege decides to use their 'powers' in a way objectionable to those who actually hold power, their privilege is immediately revoked. Too few white feminists realized their privilege was given by white males and can as easily be taken back if not exercised in the interest of white males. Or, perhaps, they do realize this; and making the connection, white wimmin wish to delude sisters regarding this reality. No matter. The result is that the hegemony of white males remains unchallenged by white wimmin who are not willing to acknowledge or to address the ways privilege is used to divide black and white wimmin.

Separatism gave me the analytical tools and, yes, the guts to say out loud that males are the enemy. Do you think I will be struck down by god (good ole white boy that he is)? Not only will I say it out loud but I will also operate as much as possible from a womon-identified context. Becoming a separatist encouraged me to realize that the world can be interpreted through my lesbian eyes. My sexuality gives me fire and peace. It is a way of living that is the basis for reaching out, understanding, and bonding with other wimmin.

Separatism is not withdrawing from the world or denying that what happens in the world affects me. I cannot simply ignore the heterosexist, racist, misogyny of the world. White male hatred of me controls my economic reality. I cannot operate out of wimmin-only space and pretend that I am living independently of boys. I hope wimmin who function or claim to do so at that level are doing so without pretense, and therefore responsibly. I do think it is important that wimmin own and live on land, but the claim that they are totally separate from boys evades the interdependency of the world. For example, electricity can be given up, but the payment of taxes cannot be. Beyond that, what I have heard and read about wimmin claiming to be independent of boys is so incredibly class unconscious that I am furious. For the privilege necessary to maintain the pretense is very transparent and NOT AVAILABLE TO SISTERS. Each time I hear how it is being done, I also see the woman's ability to re-join patriarchal, capitalist society, even if she denies her ability to do so. Do white wimmin expect us to be so dumb as to accept what they say as the final truth? Any sister who survives has taken a crash course on white lies and learned to perceive the reality, not what whites would have us believe to be true. White wimmin's privilege is not mine! I have no white father, no connection who will grease my re-entry. I have already, in fact, been chosen to provide the back on which capitalism can build and prosper.

By focusing on white privilege often manifested in the interest of living in the country, I do not wish to denigrate wimmin-only space. That space is crucial to me and I consistently fight to preserve it. It is a place that we as wimmin, killed and hunted by boys, can go to renew our energy, to remember why we have chosen such a difficult struggle. Some day – even right now we are learning in bits and pieces how to live with and love each other in a very different way – we can make reality finally conform to our own vision.

Separatism is the transition from a bisexual population (female–male) to exclusively female. One in which differences are just that: neither good or bad. I want to be very clear. My vision of the future does not include males. There are those who worry about what is to become of them. I do not share their concern. To me stopping the rape mentality presumes the necessity of eliminating the cause – boys. I will not focus on them or give up my precious energy once again to attend to male needs or well-being. For, I no longer believe that it is possible to re-educate males to give up power. Wimmin delude themselves with the belief that males do not really want to dominate them. If they knew any other way to behave, then the 'poor' boys would willingly choose the alternative and remove their feet from wimmin's necks. That delusion is based on the assumption that domination is the other side of submission. If wimmin continue to hold onto that belief, we perpetuate the conspiracy that no one rapes or batters us. It is the system, not some boy who bloodied our mouths. In fact, it is in the interest of boys to encourage us not to see the perpetuator of our oppression. There is a war going on and most wimmin refuse to acknowledge we are even fighting. A commitment to individual liberalism – different strokes for different folks – precludes them from perceiving each womon raped, battered, killed, or locked up in prison or mental institution as a war casualty. We continue to want to believe that no one, certainly not our brother, father, faggot friend, could possibly hate us that much. Our casualties are, in fact, part and parcel of every male's outlook on the world. It is the submissive and nurturing female that distinguishes his maleness. Each time I hear some boy is nice or gentle I remember Ntozake Shange's poem warning us about seemingly nice boys. She exhorts us to realize that some womon could have been hurt by this gentle boy. Some womon we do not know, may never meet, but one is too many. For I am really clear, the next time it could be me or you.

As male-identified western society leaps to the right (which is somewhat of an inaccurate characterization since it implies it had at one time been progressive), womon-identified wimmin cannot afford to become more conservative. We cannot afford to buckle down, dig in our heels, and lower our heads hoping this reactionary wave will pass leaving us untouched, unmarked by its passing. Now is the time to intensify our struggles, not to retreat!

We need to identify our own goals. *Ms Magazine*, that bastion of acceptability (to males and male-identified women), can feel free to proclaim some boy as a feminist, on its front cover no less. *Ms* ceases to deserve our support. Talking about male feminists should be done in the same breath as discussing white negroes. While Norman Mailer wrote about the white negro, he was also busy stabbing his wife. This is precisely the danger of including those who purport to be supportive of our goals as one of us when who knows what damage or pain he is causing some womon. Even if we do not know the damage, support is not the same as identity. Including boys as feminists only serves to confuse the issue of who our enemy is thereby blurring the distinctions so much so that the strength of the ideology is reduced to the consistency of pablum.

It is becoming apparent many white feminists and some separatists are giving into the politics of the moral majority, accepting these fascists' definition of what are the important issues to be discussed. In short, allowing the right to dictate the lesbian agenda for white wimmin. This is particularly dangerous given the domination of the feminist media and ideology by white wimmin. White wimmin's agenda is, then, put forth as the one for all wimmin. In fact, white feminists are more willing to change their ideology to include white males in their books, concerts, and other projects than to change their ideology to include sisters. A feminist space wants to encourage males to meet there to discuss how they can be supportive to wimmin and at the same time denies access to an Afro-American wimmin's group. Or wimmin scream bloody murder because the SF Women's Building refuses space for a female police officers group to meet there.[4] The males sought are white; the absence of sisters is not noticed. This trend recognizes white males hold power in this society. To get their support, the boys must be catered to and appeased. In holding power, white boys can give or withhold all kinds of goodies, including free rent or ad space or publication of a book. The list is endless.

Underneath the power white boys hold is the unacknowledged bond between white females and males. A bond based on racial similarity. A bond denied when challenged. I recognize the bond exists when I note the results of white wimmin's outreach. This purported outreach is directed to sisters, nevertheless the numbers of white males increase while the numbers of sisters do not in the same projects. Am I really supposed to believe that white wimmin are serious in their claim to desire more participation of sisters? I no longer care if the bond between white females and males is conscious; in fact, it is irrelevant when the same results occur time and time again.

Some white feminists to correct their past error will use black males to avoid the charge they are bonding with white males. *Big Mama Rag* will go to greath lengths to demonstrate their concern about racism in this country but continue to ignore the concerns of sisters as articulated by us.[5] Their discussion becomes an underhanded way to form coalitions with white males claiming the larger issue of racism as their cover. It is not only *Big Mama Rag*; the deception pervades white feminists' projects.

Separatism is a difficult issue. While I believe that white separatists are no more racist than other white feminists, I also know that being a separatist does not automatically exclude the possibility of being a racist. I challenge all separatists particularly white ones to actively participate in the anti-racist struggle in our community and to some extent in the larger society. We must not lose our own goals in this process nor can white separatists forego sisters' input in this struggle.

The non-struggle around racism by white wimmin has created the situation which exists today. Few black lesbian feminists are visible or active in the white wimmin's communities. When separatism is an additional dimension, our numbers are drastically reduced. Given the prevalence of racism in white feminist communities, it becomes easy for them to set up sisters to be at each others' throats. White wimmin too often uphold one sister's opinion as superior to another. I reject this tendency by affirming the right of each of us to participate in the struggle as we deem necessary. I specifically support sisters to do so. With all our emerging and merging identities, sisters have a right to be able to receive support for the choices we make in fighting white patriarchy.

Finally, to all my sisters who perceive separatism as a white ideology, I reject that notion. We have been defined by those who have power over us. We have not been able to define for ourselves or to develop our own ideology. Separatism and blackness are not necessarily contradictory. To bring them together requires acknowledgement of and commitment to addressing concerns for all wimmin and holding onto our particular vision. It is hard for me to integrate the two, yet I believe the reason for the difficulty is not inherent in the theory or analysis but is due to the unhelpful baggage we bring to each other. While boys may not be in our homes, they still reside in our minds. To rid ourselves of them and their agenda requires constant attention. If we are not always aware, we endanger ourselves and our movement for we will continue to fight their battles for them.

This paper is a beginning of a discussion I hope will continue. The issues raised are crucial to our very survival and the quality of that survival. Will those wimmin with more privilege than others bond with white males to maintain white middle-class hegemony as they did during the suffrage movement? Or will wimmin bond with each other finally? Will we recognize that we as a group have a right to our own integrity and ideals? Can we as wimmin afford to, as Naomi Littlebear reminds us, leave any sister behind?

Acknowledgments

I want to thank Bell Hooks for devoting a whole book, *Ain't I a Woman*, to the issue of sisters being excluded from both the black male and white wimmin's movement. Bell, unfortunately, does not recognize the existence of black lesbians. That analysis had to wait for *This Bridge Called My*

Back edited by Cherrié Moraga and Gloria Anzaldúa.

Many wimmin have been instrumental in clarifying my thoughts and assisting me in considering new possibilities including Sarah Hoagland who asked for a longer version of this article which this is. Karlyne Nelson who consistently has given me critical support and reviewed this article as a non-separatist sister providing valuable input. I want to thank Denslow Brown who introduced me to the concept of separatism as an analytical tool which has been so helpful to me. I also want to thank Tara Ayres for pushing and prodding me to write this because she felt it was necessary for all wimmin to know and accept that black separatists do exist.

This paper is a revised version of one that appeared in the Racism issue of *Innerviews*.

Notes

1. Frances M. Beal, 'Double Jeopardy: To be Black and Female,' *Sisterhood is Powerful*, ed. Robin Morgan (New York: Vintage, 1970), pp. 340–53.
2. Deb Friedman, 'Rape, Racism and Reality,' *Quest* 5, 1 (Summer 1979), pp. 40–51.
3. Law Enforcement Administration Assistance was promulgated by Richard Nixon. LEAA provided anti-riot gear to local police forces.
4. Sharon F. Hiller, Letter, 'Policing the Bars,' *Plexus* (September 1981), p. 2.
5. Elaine Henrichs, 'A Call to Resist,' *Big Mama Rag* (May 1982), p. 8. Note the absence of wimmin in her discussion of forming coalitions with national liberation struggles. While the intent to form coalitions is laudable, the effect may very well be the same as the US agriculture policy has been. Throughout Africa and other developing areas, the US has consistently supported males as the authorities in all spheres of the culture. By doing so, the US government has undermined the independence or significant contribution wimmin have had traditionally. In the same issue, the newspaper collective included an insert encouraging wimmin to participate in the conference referred to by Elaine.

Lesbian Separatist Statement from the closing session of the Jewish Feminist Conference, held in San Francisco, May, 1982.

The following was read by a group of very informally associated lesbian separatists at the Jewish Feminist Conference.

The Conference Organizers were 31 womyn: 30 lesbians and one bi-sexual. Among their opening statements, they said they wanted the conference to be a safe place for lesbians,[1] that some of the organizers felt the conference should have included (at least) the word 'lesbian' in its title, and gave some guidelines supporting lesbian visibility and defining the responsibility of heterosexual womyn present not to further lesbian oppression.

Many of the Jewish womyn who attended the conference and identified as lesbian separatists knew each other, or knew someone who knew someone who knew. . . . Although a lesbian separatist affinity group was scheduled to meet several times during the weekend, it met only once, and the meeting was apparently small and informal.

At the closing session, affinity groups that wanted to make statements had, theoretically, three minutes to address the conference, which, at that time, was a cafeteria full of approximately 200–300 Jewish womyn. Lesbian separatists had not written a statement prior to closing. But the first three closing statements went on at length. First, within a long and complex mother's statement, there was a reprimand about how boys should be allowed anywhere they wanted to be, there should have been no womyn or lesbian only spaces that excluded them. Next, a heterosexual woman reading, seriously, 10 rules for how lesbians should relate to straight women. Next a bi-sexual woman complaining about being oppressed by a strong lesbian presence. Someone got it together to start tapping shoulders, and suddenly there was a gathering of most of the separatists there, outside the dining room, clustered around the stairwell, trying to make our own statement. We were reminded to keep it to three minutes, and required to not 'answer' any of the previous statements directly.

In ten minutes in that hallway, a group of somewhere between 12 and 20 Jewish lesbian separatists with a fairly wide range of ages, abilities and class backgrounds, from several different parts of the states, agreed on the following nine points, at least enough to present them to the conference, within the guidelines we were given. Considering that this group contained womyn with coast-to-coast reps for being 'aggressive, pushy, emotional, hard to get along with & tough' (sometimes anti-semitism and anti-separatism go hand in glove), that we were able to do this with flexibility and efficiency seemed to be as much a statement as the statement itself.

Statement

1. We want the conference participants to recognize that the

93

impetus behind this conference came from our oppression as Jews *and* as lesbians, and that, as lesbians, we are always called on to include and speak to the needs of non-lesbians.

2. As lesbians we wouldn't be welcome at any other Jewish conference.[2]

3. We believe as a political principle that any oppressed group can separate themselves from their oppressors. And as lesbians, we claim that right.

4. This is one of the few places in the world where we can attempt to feel safe and we are proud to have made whatever safety we could for each other at this conference.

5. The lesbian and feminist communities say many of the same things about separatists as non-Jews say about Jews. We encourage the Jewish womyn here today to think about it; you might find a lot of similarities between lesbian separatism and zionism.

6. Jewish people have understood for centuries the need for separatism as Jews. The lack of separatist support at this conference is appalling.

7. Some of the separatists on the planning committee felt their positions were not respected as valid political positions, and experienced having a hard time being heard.

8. We support decent childcare, which we believe does not have to be at the expense of womyn-only space.

9. It is offensive to Jewish lesbian separatists to make any comparison between separatism and nazism or racism. Don't.

Notes

1. The organizers also made opening statements in strong support of working class, poor, differently abled, fat, Sephardic, young and old Jewish womyn, as well as Jewish mothers.

2. A xerox of a ruling by the Supreme Rabbinical Court, a small group of orthodox halachic Rabbis, officially declaring the lesbian contributors to *Nice Jewish Girls* 'dead' and 'non-Jews', was passed around in support of this point. Not many Jews, certainly very few lesbian Jews, take this group seriously (although some of us were relieved our grandmothers weren't alive to see it). Passing the flyer around was intended to emphasize the point that as Jews, lesbians need to look towards what we can make with each other, instead of looking for a way to fit in with mainstream Jewish cultures or religion.

Relating to Dyke Separatists
Hints for the Non-Separatist Lesbian

*Marty, with the help of
the dykes of S.E.P.S.**
1983

- Do not try and defend the 'humanity' of some men to a separatist. It's a waste of her time; she's probably already heard your argument hundreds of times and does not want to hear it again!
- Do not tell a separatist 'Yeah I hate men too except for my father/brother/son/cousin/ex-husband/faggot friend ... He's really an exception, he's really okay.' She doesn't want to hear about him or how you like him! Every male who has violated a female was loved and nurtured by some womon somewhere who thought of him as special.
- Do not protest in dismay or horror when we say pricks/puds/smegma/————— for whom are commonly referred to as men & boys. Maybe you think these terms are 'inhuman,' 'extreme,' 'horrendous,' 'unfair.' The crimes that men and boys have committed against womyn and girls are inhuman, horrendous and unforgivable. We name our enemy accordingly.
- Most womyn are survivors of men's rape and abuse. Most lesbians in one way or another have been the targets of male assault and sexual crimes. Don't assume that we are separatists because we have been unusually victimized by men.
  - Don't assume a separatist is a survivor of rape or incest.
  - Don't assume that she is not.
  - Don't assume that you are not.
- If a separatist *is* a rape or incest survivor don't assume her separatism comes out of her being 'controlled by her victimization,' that she 'can't deal with men because she's damaged,' and that if she were 'free of her victimization she could learn how to relate to and respect some men.'
- Especially for therapists & counselors: Do not conclude that a separatist should 'work through her anger at her father/brother/son/uncle/ex-husband/grandfather/stepfather (or *any*

* *Separatists Enraged Proud and Strong*, San Francisco, CA. Based on 'When you Meet a Lesbian: Hints for the Heterosexual Womon,' Taken from a poster by Day Moon Designs, Seattle, WA.

other males of *any* age at *any* time in her life) in order to let go of her rage and integrate men into her life.' This attitude is a very condescending power trip that says separatists can't know what's best for our growth and survival.

- Do not assume that it is a privilege for all separatists to be separatists, that we are all 'privileged lesbians' who can 'afford' to separate from men and run off some place free and safe from men.

- Do not assume that because we are separatists we have magical lives where we do not have to deal with men! Most separatists – whether living in rural, small town or urban areas – have to deal *daily*, *constantly* with men as our bosses, co-workers, landlords, social workers, doctors, jailers, neighbors, etc. They and their pricks are everywhere!

- Do you ever find yourself thinking, 'If she's a separatist, how come she's so friendly to the male landlord/repairman/boss, etc.?' Remember that we live in a world dominated by male power and authority. Because a separatist may exemplify what is seemingly 'common courtesy' towards males does *not* mean that we like or respect them. The pressures to like and 'honor' men in this culture are intense and all-pervasive. Some of us must employ culturally-accepted ways of relating in certain situations out of necessity for our *survival*. As is true with all oppressions, assimilation out of necessity only increases our invisibility.

- Separatists live with the added oppression of judgment, ostracism, and ridicule when we are out about hating men. It is usually much more acceptable for a non-separatist lesbian and definitely for strait womyn to express anger at men· because they can usually 'balance' that with also expressing like or respect for some men.

- Do not assume that all separatists are of light-skinned/WASP/Northern European ancestry, thin, ablebodied, middle/upper class and 'prime age' lesbians. There are dykes of color, fat dykes, Jewish, working class, disabled, physically challenged, very young and Old Gay dykes who are lesbian separatists. Many of us in fact struggle with added invisibility and not being taken seriously as separatists by other lesbians in our various communities as well as the larger lesbian community.

- If you are of light-skinned/Caucasian/Northern European ancestry do not assume that a Caucasian lesbian separatist is *more* racist than you are *because* she is a separatist. All 'white-skinned' womyn have grown up with the benefits and privileges derived from racism.

Likewise the charge that separatists are more classist, ableist, anti-semitic, etc. than other dykes and other people *because* we are separatists is a *lie*. As separatists we share the view that the oppressions that aim to destroy people who are of color, Jews, fat, physically challenged, mentally or emotionally disabled, old, etc. are abhorrent. We do *not*, however, have to like, trust, or want men in our lives in order to fight for a world free of these oppressions. We believe, in fact, that it is impossible for any total 'revolutionary' change to happen while womyn remain allied to men.

- Do not assume that an occasional womyn-only event should be plenty to satisfy separatists' needs. For one thing, most so-called 'womyn-only' events actually include boys. Being young, small, and dominated by adults' power does not make a boy female! An event, service, or space that is truly 'womyn-only' is rare, and events that are *lesbian*-only are almost totally nonexistent.

- Are you 'sick and tired' of hearing separatists' anger and grievances? Don't put your annoyance on us. Talk with other non-separatists, look at why you're threatened. Separatists are sick and tired of putting up day in and day out with other womyn – especially other lesbians – talking about and/or defending men and boys to us everywhere we go.

The Evolution of Lesbian Separatist Consciousness

Sidney Spinster
1982

Introduction

There is a tradition in Lesbian Separatist literature of writing personally from the heart, and identifying one's background and upbringing, because we each know that there is no such thing as objectivity. I have learned this, and many other things, from Lesbians who have identified themselves as Separatists much longer than I.

I am tall, thin, white, and relatively able-bodied. I grew up in a suburban nuclear upper-middle class gentile family with no religious identification until my mother and brother both got into a new age spirituality. My mother is a psychic healer. I am young and college-educated. I have been out for six and a half years, since I was seventeen.

I have been calling mySelf a Separatist for three years or so, largely I think because no one explained to me what it meant, really, before that. Of course all leaps of consciousness come from within, but I'm sure that this one would have come a lot quicker if someone had pointed out to me the glaring inconsistency between my firm advocacy of womon-only concerts, and my co-ed feminist consciousness, in a way that I could hear.

My first contact with self-identified Separatists was at a Separatist workshop I accidentally wandered into at the Lesbian Arts Celebration in The District of Columbia in the mid-seventies. The conversation, as I recall it, centered around man-hating. Being the young pacifist feminist Lesbian that I was, I nearly vomited. 'I'm a Lesbian because I love wimmin, not because I hate men' I said to a friend later. These words came back to haunt me again and again, from other Lesbians' mouths.

It was only after I read *Gyn/Ecology* so carefully, nourished by every word, that I could almost quote from memory any part of it, and then was told (to my disbelief) that Mary Daly was a Separatist, that it finally sank in.[2]

So there I was in college in Chicago, knowing lots of Lesbians but no Separatists except an acquaintance who was a well-known Separatist but lived on the other side of town. I had a thousand questions and I was very angry that I couldn't find answers to them ... when I knew that other Lesbians must have already figured out a lot of it. Where was the Separatist herstory and culture? I searched the New Alexandria Lesbian Library, many wimmin's bookstores, and later the Lesbian Herstory Archives looking for clues. I fantasized that one day I'd get a phone call from the Lesbian keepers of the secrets, who lived someplace I had not thought to look, and finally I would find my herstory and home.

Well, the phone call never came. But I picked up little pieces here and there, and Separatist friends here and there ... and eventually I felt that I had enough to share, so that no Lesbian should ever be as frustrated as I was at the beginning.

I wanted to record, crone-logically, the changes in Separatist consciousness over the years. Are there any patterns? Trends? Or, perhaps, are newer Separatists unrelated ideologically to early seventies Separatists? Where did all those Lesbians who once called themselves Separatist go? Have white Separatists been more, or less, anti-racist than other white Lesbians? Is the process of claiming the name Lesbian Separatist different for Lesbian

Separatists of Color, than for white wimmin? What are the additional forces which Lesbians of Color might have to face in choosing to become Lesbian Separatists?

To answer these questions I needed still more information. So I sent out a questionnaire to Lesbians who had called themselves Separatist previous to 1976. This sparked more conversations than questionnaire responses. A couple of Lesbians didn't believe in writing anything about Separatism for publication ... they believe that it is a secret oral tradition for initiates. Needless to say, they are angry with me. Others, some very close to me, would talk and talk to me about the changes in their consciousness but wouldn't let me write it down or let me tape them. They could not express why rationally, but in their hearts they felt they should not.

Early Origins

I am concerning myself only with modern Separatism here. There have always been Lesbians, and I believe, with or without the title, Lesbian Separatists. What I want to reveal right now is specifically the movement of Lesbians in the u.s. who have defined their consciousness/analysis/be-ing with the words Lesbian Separatism. This movement (if we can call it that) began around 1970.

> Separatism as a part of process was grounded in and evolved from the real experiences of active, committed lesbians in the grass roots projects which grew out of consciousness raising. Lesbian energy was the base for all the creative, direct action women serving projects in the early 70's. Independent women centers sprung up every place, abortion counseling, rape crisis, self-defense, self-help health were projects that required womyn only space. From this initial consciousness the ideas of separatism developed organically in many places at the same time.[3]

As a generalization that is true, but still there were early Separatists who never were a part of the wimmin's movement. Many Separatists come from radical backgrounds of some sort. The kind of radicalism varies from civil rights work to leftism to anarchism to radical feminism. From the small number of Dykes I've talked to from that period it seems as though working class lesbians and/or Lesbians of color were more likely to come to Separatism from a Lesbian background than from a wimmin's liberation C–R group, which tended to be white and middle class.

A few Lesbians claim to have invented their own Separatism very early on (pre-'71) but most heard of it through publications, friends, and Lesbian musicians like the Family of Womon band, Linda Shear, or Alix Dobkin.

The First Wave

Ah, working in the kitchens, here's what we found;
Scrubbing the floors, here's what we found;
Raising the children, here's what we found; and
Being with each other, this is what we found: that if we
Don't let *man*euvering keep us apart; if we
Don't let *man*ipulators keep us apart; if we
Don't let manpower keep us apart; or
Mankind keep us apart, we've won:
What I mean is: We ain't got it easy, but we've got it!

Alix Dobkin[4]

Spectre

We see separatism as working directly only with women. Any contact with males (especially male dominated groups) is indirect – primarily through the paper.... All our energy and time is spent with women and working on things that will further our liberation.[5]

This is the earliest statement that I've run across that is explicitly Separatist. It appeared in *Spectre*, a Lesbian newspaper in Ann Arbor, Michigan, which lasted about a year, from 1971 to 1972. Two wimmin published it, and most of what they printed were their own opinions on everything, and this means that today we have a good record of the evolution of these wimmin's consciousness at an early stage in their Separatism. They changed a lot, and each time they no longer agreed with something they said in an old issue they would update it in a new issue. There were also articles from other Lesbians all over the u.s.. From a herstorian's point of view, it is unfortunate that they did not believe in putting names on articles because, they would say, ideas are not private property.

They changed the subtitle of the newspaper three times from the 'paper of Revolutionary Lesbians,' to 'written by Revolutionary

Separatist white wimmin,' to 'by white Revolutionary Lesbians.'
They were trying to express their politics more fully and clearly
each time.

Oddly enough, they considered themselves to be communists.
Especially at first they stressed the idea that it was important that
the revolution be for all people, not just some, and they saw
themselves as connected with people struggling for liberation all
over the world. They knew that Separatism was a threat to male
power, but believed, too, that in some way it would be good for
them. At first they were sympathetic to radical men, Black
separatist men and transvestites and transsexuals especially. Later
they became more thoroughly man-hating.

They also changed their views about straight wimmin. At first
they didn't see much special about Lesbians except that we
shared our lives with each other and were committed to struggling
with wimmin-only. Then, mainly as a result of being in groups
with straight feminists, they became a bit more particular.

> So we want to ask our 'straight' sisters – why do you
> live the way you do? why do you continue to accept
> the priority of male values? why do you love only men?
> why do you really get so uptight when you come face
> to face with Lesbians?[6]
>
> I have had it. I am sick and tired of listening to
> women who spend most of the conversation defending
> MEN . . . talking about MEN . . .worrying about what
> happens to MEN and how it happens to MEN. I am
> sick and tired of listening to how we Separatists with
> our anger and male defined power 'objectify . . .' and
> don't treat half the human race as human beings . . .' of
> being told that we are making everything into sexual
> POLITICS *we* make sex so aggressive . . . that we deny
> humanity, . . . etc. Why the hell aren't they mad at men
> for objectifying women into property, meat, pussy –
> why aren't they mad at men for all the rapes – for all
> the roughness – why don't they notice that on every
> movie page there are ads talking about VIOLENCE:
> TERROR SEX: women don't make these movies.[7]

From the very beginning *Spectre* dealt with the variety of
experience which has surrounded various wimmin's lives. Classism,
racism, ageism, and the oppression of physically challenged wimmin
were not just issues to be dealt with by mentioning them in passing,
but a fundamental part of their analysis was fed by informed anti-
racism, anti-classism, anti-ageism, and anti-ablebodyism.

Racism in particular was of special concern to them. While white feminist groups were trying to get wimmin of color to join them so that they could claim they were not racist, these white wimmin thought that they had internalized racism, and that they should do their own consciousness-raising among themselves, not put wimmin of color into the position of having to educate them. They identified themselves as white to challenge the assumption that it's 'normal' to be white and only wimmin of color need to identify as 'other.'

The thing that really struck me about *Spectre* was that I don't think that these wimmin knew what kind of abuse they were getting themselves in for by identifying publicly as Separatists. How could they? They were among the first. They thought that they had discovered something new and exciting, and wanted to share it with everyone, even to the extent of losing over $700 of their own money on *Spectre* to get the word out. I think that they were shocked to find out that many wimmin hated them for it. Now-a-days most of us are familiar enough with our past to be aware of the possibility of fear-sparked hatred coming our way.

The Furies

Many more Lesbians are familiar with *The Furies* than with *Spectre*. For one thing many of their articles have been anthologized in several books from Diana Press. I find it interesting that Separatism is not directly mentioned in those anthologized articles, while it is in the original newspaper. The members of the Furies Collective had very different definitions of Separatism from each other. It looks to me like they glossed these differences over to present the appearance of a unified 'position.' The words that they all agreed on were 'Lesbian-Feminist' and 'womon-identified.' Several I believe saw Separatism as only one of several strategies, with a co-ed society as a goal. The *Spectre* wimmin, I think it is fair to say, saw Separatism as the only viable strategy for white wimmin to use to achieve liberation. By the time they stopped publishing they were uncertain whether men could ever be non-oppressive.

Charlotte Bunch wrote an article for *The Furies*, 'Perseverance Furthers: Separatism and Our Future,'[8] that caused quite an uproar for listing Separatism as just one of many separatist movements, and for suggesting that coalition work with men might be useful in the future.[9] Many Lesbians responded.

102

The divisions that exist between men and women and between women of different classes were the result of a conflict of interests. Just because we are now more conscious of our oppression does not mean that the power relationships have changed or that there is no longer a conflict of interests. From the article one could assume that it is now time for women to make alliances without a clear basis for allying and to consider alliances with men before separatism has even been made a strong political force is crazy.

Also, in discussing the limits of separatism, nowhere is its effectiveness as a serious tool to bring about change discussed but only its use as a way for different oppressed groups to get themselves together ...

Rosina Richter[10]

... Separatism is a necessary strategy if women wish to become a political force with a power base strong enough to challenge male power. Women must stop nurturing individual men and feeding the institution of heterosexuality. That energy must be given to other women in order that we stop identifying with a male identity and become that political force with a female identity....

... Surely it is not time to make alliances with men.... It is our hope that men will change. But we believe that they will only change at this point if we withdraw our support, our nurturance, our energies from them....[10]

Editorial by Lee Schwing and Deborah George

Charlotte Bunch responded that she agreed with Rosina Richter's definition of Separatism, and has always advocated it.

Temporary political alliances or coalitions with men around specific issues or goals are the only forms of working with them that we should even consider ... I think we do ourselves a disservice to assume that we are too weak to take advantage of coalitions when we judge them useful. A coalition made from a strong feminist base is not a repudiation of our Separatist autonomy. I ... reject the separatist purity that rigidly limits our political moves before a situation has developed or been analysed concretely....

She goes on to say:

> At what points do the separations and divisions that
> have become necessary among women help us build
> our strength and when do they leave us in an isolation
> and self-righteousness that is counterproductive? These
> are the really important questions about separatism –
> what has separatism become within the women's
> movement, and where is it taking us in the future?[11]

Putting aside the fact that many Separatists do not consider
feminism to be our movement, but rather that Separatism itself is
the movement, these are questions that Separatists should ask
ourselves regularly in our process of re-evaluation and growth.

Dykes and Gorgons

A year after *The Furies* was born, Lesbians were blessed with a
single issue of a newspaper named *Dykes and Gorgons* from the
East Bay area. One issue was enough to cause controversy from
coast to coast. Editorials condemning manhating sprang up in
numerous Lesbian and Feminist periodicals as a result.

> Just as sexism is the source of all our oppressions,
> maleness is the source of sexism. In order to rid the
> world of sexism we must first rid the world of men. But
> obviously we must also begin to deal with the racial
> and nationalistic and class divisions that men have
> created between us.[12]

What was new about *Dykes and Gorgons* – and what terrified
many wimmin – was that this document made it clear that a
Female-only world was what the collective that had produced it
had in mind. The Gutter Dyke Collective advocated eliminating
men. While the issue of killing men was not addressed, it was their
position that wimmin should not give birth to boys.

The Gutter Dykes also made one of the first public statements
that male-to-constructed-female transsexuals are not wimmin. At
this time 'Beth' Eliot, a transsexual singer, was performing at
womon-only events and Lesbian conferences. A few years later a
controversy emerged when Sandy Stone, another transsexual,
joined the collective that ran Olivia records, the most well-known
u.s. wimmin's music record company. In fact, Olivia was just
being born in Washington, D.C.

The Gutter Dykes believed in separation from straight wimmin ('men are the focal point of their lives'), and from certain Lesbians whose view varied greatly from their own.

> We would prefer to avoid a lot of fighting and start dealing with the 'fine' lines between us, as well as support each other in our arguments.

It is hard to describe the difference in tone between *Dykes and Gorgons* and the earlier publications. The Gutter Dykes seemed to know that they were going to offend many wimmin by directly stating what they knew to be true without softening it one bit for the sake of not turning off straight wimmin or non-Separatist Lesbians. This newspaper was not going to win many converts, at least immediately. It is best appreciated by Lesbians who already have some sort of Separatist consciousness.

Because they were not doing outreach they could focus on working out their analysis, as well as their understanding of the things which divide us. Discussions of racism by Third World Dykes, and classism by working class Dykes, were emphasized.[13]

Lesbian Separatism: An Amazon Analysis

By the summer of '73 Separatist groups were popping up all over. The Lesbian Separatist Group in Seattle, Washington (which later changed into The Gorgons) published a massive paper (nearly 100 pages) which became almost a handbook on Separatism for Lesbians all over the u.s. I say 'almost' because some Separatists by this time had created their own complex analyses that conflicted with that of the Seattle Separatists. However, this paper helped many Lesbians put a name to the feelings that had been growing within them, and to extend the details of their analysis beyond what they and their friends had come up with on their own.

> I first heard the term 'Separatist' when Liza Cowan and I got hold of *The Amazon Analysis* from Seattle. . . . We were blown away since we'd never read anything like it before.[14]
>
> *Alix Dobkin*

The Amazon Analysis was supposed to be published in book form in August of 1974, but never was. Instead, mimeographed copies were circulated around the u.s. from Lesbian to Lesbian. It was never promoted in any way, and yet it was treated as if it was a special Lesbian treasure. It became an underground Lezzie classic.

The Lesbian Separatist Group was comprised of four Dykes, all white, two Jewish, self-described as 'lower' to middle class. Three of them had some college education.

The paper is divided into six sections on Matriarchy, Patriarchy, Separatism, Lesbian Mothers, Problems of Our Movement (racism; classism; ageism; elitism; false divisions; destructive ideologies; human beingism; sexual minorities; reformism), Directions.

The section on Lesbian Mothers is interesting because it was an issue that had not been dealt with in the Separatist media up to that point. They believed it is the duty of the Lesbian community to provide childcare. They thought, however, that any Lesbian who chose to raise a male child was giving support to males like straight wimmin do. Furthermore, having female children was not a good idea, they thought, until Lesbians have some way to raise them outside of the patriarchal educational system, and until one would not have to have sex with a man to conceive. (These are simplifications of their positions.)

The part about racism is intriguing, especially because this group later changed their basic position about Separatism and wimmin of color.

These Lesbians stressed the necessity for white Lesbians to work with white Lesbians against racism. Originally, the paper went on to say that white Dykes should not use our Separatism to be 'divisive' among Third World people, when wimmin of color have chosen to work with men. They changed their mind about that later, and attached the update to the paper. All four of them had worked in the civil rights movement in the 60's and felt that the liberal guilt instilled in them during those years had pushed them into the position which they took at first. They concluded, basically, that it was racist not to see all wimmin as potential allies, not to credit Third World wimmin with the ability to see patriarchal society for what it is, and see also the fundamental division between wimmin and men.

The CLIT Papers
(Collective Lesbian International Terrors)

At the same time that all this was brewing on the west coast, Lesbians back on the east coast were getting down to business as well. The CLIT wimmin printed three long position papers in *off our backs* expressing their Separatist position on many many subjects. Perhaps *The CLIT Papers* was the publication that gave the largest number of Lesbians their conception of what Separatism is.[15] Few Lesbians agreed with everything they said, but many admired their sense of daring and humor. *The CLIT Papers* were clearly on the offense, launching attacks on (what they considered to be) patriarchal strongholds by revealing them for what they were.

The collective is completely anonymous in their papers. They do not identify their racial or class backgrounds, and I would like to see a thorough examination of these documents along race and class lines.

Their style is/was rambling, almost stream of consciousness, and yet when one looks closely one cannot help but believe that care was taken in the wording. I believe they were trying to break out of old prick styles of writing into a new Lesbian style, as the first step to a Lesbian language.

> We are exploding with ideas and an urgency to be understood. Therefore, we go off on alot of tangents that are just as important as *there are no main points*. Everything we say to each other is important. It may be difficult to read at first, but remember every sentence is a book.[16]

CLIT re-emerged in 1980 to bring us CLIT #4 in *oob* and *Green Mountain Dyke News*.

I believe there is a difference between early 70's and late 70's-early 80's Separatists, who I call first wave and second wave Separatists, respectively.

Most of the Lesbians I know who have named ourselves Separatist after '76 or so were greatly influenced by the writings of Separatist teachers like Mary Daly, Marilyn Frye, Julia Penelope, and Sarah Hoagland. This includes white Lesbians of all classes from poor to rich, and a couple of Black Lesbians. Unless we had access to an archives, or had first wave Separatist friends, it was only from these Lesbians' writings that we could find out about Separatism.

As I've said, some first wave Dykes did not believe in publishing, others did, but in a very underground manner. But *Gyn/Ecology* could be found in any bookstore, and *Sinister Wisdom* in any wimmin's bookstore.

Many first wave Separatists bitterly resented *Gyn/Ecology* for publishing with a prick publisher (church-affiliated no less), and for ripping off Separatist developed concepts and words while giving little credit in return. To many the radical feminism of *Gyn/Ecology* was a candy-coated version of Separatism, minus any race and class analysis. And if *Gyn/Ecology* is candy to them, then *Sinister Wisdom* is cream of wheat. This resentment explains a lot of the lack of communication between first and second wave Separatists. I think it would be valuable for first wave Separatists to look more closely at the newer work that is being done and see that it is not just a paler version of what came before, but has new things to offer.

I *know* it is valuable for second wave Dykes to learn from what has come before, and what Lesbians who lived through it have to say. Class analysis in particular was more astute in the first wave than in the second. Another thing those of us who are newer at this should learn is that many meticulous, plodding, scholarly pages often equal one sentence of direct revolutionary truth. *The CLIT Papers* often save time and refresh. After hours of arguing about the male children issue in terms of the relationship between access and power, or paring away the false selves (depending on whether I'm in a Frye or Daly mood that day), it is sometimes helpful and invigorating to simply say, in Liza Cowan fashion, 'I hate little boys.'

DYKE: A Quarterly

DYKE is a magazine for Dykes only: we are not interested in telling the straight world what we're doing. In fact we hope they never see the magazine. It is none of their business. If they see it we hope they will think that it's mindless gobbledygook. We are thinking in ways that are incomprehensible to them.

Penny House and Liza Cowan
DYKE #1 (Winter '75–'76)

In 1974 Penny House and I decided to publish a Lesbian separatist magazine, called DYKE A Quarterly. It was a magazine of Lesbian politics and analysis. It was outrageously separatist and equally stylish, much to the confusion of many readers, and the delight of many others. We sold to women only, allowed subs to women only, sold only in women's bookstores. We reprinted the CLIT papers and further developed separatist analysis. We published an issue in 1977 devoted to ethnic Lesbians with most articles featuring the development of Jewish Lesbian consciousness. The theme of the sixth and final issue featured articles on Lesbians and animals, including sex between women and animals. SCREW magazine reviewed us and called us 'sick.' We ran a long essay and interview about transsexuals, disputing the currently popular idea that men can become women. We published historical essays – JR Roberts wrote about Lesbian hoboes in the 1930's, we run a photo essay on Alice Austin, Lesbian photographer from the nineteenth century. We published in our final issue a forum on Lesbian Separatism. Our fourth issue was a poster accompanied by a tiny magazinelette. We had originally wanted to have varied formats, but our readers were too confused by the switch, so we gave up the idea.

After three years Penny and I decided to stop publishing. Our readership was not large enough to support the magazine, and we did not have the circulation to get enough ads to support us. We were pouring in lots of money not to mention time and energy and did not feel that we had enough financial or emotional support to continue. In my opinion it remains fresh and provocative to this day. I have yet to see a Lesbian magazine as beautiful and daring as we were. One reviewer said: 'DYKE magazine is more honest in print than most women are willing to be in the privacy of their own living rooms' and I believe that's true.

Liza Cowan, August '81[17]

DYKE, like every other Separatist publication, was attacked from its inception. It won over some with its slickness and humor, and lost some with its lack of an essentially anti-racist and anti-classist stand. Writings by Lesbians of Color and working class Lesbians were few and far between, even in the 'Ethnic Lesbians' issue.

One thing that was totally new about DYKE was its womon-only distribution policy. There had been tapes and documents that had been passed around exclusively inside the Lesbian community, but none that had been sold 'publicly,' in stores, that said 'for women only' on the cover. Today, since there have been several publications for Lesbians only it seems almost tame, but it was revolutionary in 1975.

I consider DYKE to be somewhere between first and second wave in its perspective.

The Second Wave

In the late 70's after DYKE went under, soon followed by *TRIBAD: A Lesbian Separatist Newsjournal*, which had been published at Fort Dyke at 49–51 Prince Street in New York City, there was no publication left for Separatists. Many Lesbians were disheartened and disillusioned with their groups, lovers, and Selves. It was at this point that a new sort of Separatist started to emerge.

Gyn/Ecology

Mary Daly is not a collective, not a group, she's not even a duo. It is no coincidence that just as the collectives had disbanded, and individual Dykes had become disillusioned with Separatism because of disagreements with other Separatists who define it differently, major work began to get done by autonomous Lesbians. *Gyn/Ecology* in particular portrays 'radical feminism' as a process of empowerment (an 'otherworld journey') for individual wimmin.

> It is a call to women who have never named themselves Wild before, and a challenge to those who have been in struggle for a long time and who have retreated for a while.[18]
>
> It is Crone-logical to conclude that internal separation or separatism, that is, paring away, burning away the false selves encasing the Self, is the core of all authentic separations and thus is normative for all personal/political decisions about acts/forms of separatism. It is axiomatic for Amazons that all external/internalized influences, such as myths, names, ideologies, social structures, which cut off the flow of the Self's original movement, should be pared away.
>
> Since each Self is unique, since each woman has her own history, and since there are deep differences in temperament and abilities, Hags should acknowledge this variety in all discussions of separatism. While it is true that all women have had many similar experiences under patriarchy, it is also true that there have been wide variations of the theme of possession and in struggles for dispossession. To simplify differences would be to settle for less than a Dreadful judgment of the multiple horrors of gynocide. It would also

impoverish our imaginations, limiting our vision of the Otherworld Journey's dimension. Finally, minimizing the variety in Amazon Journeyers' experiences, temperaments, and talents would blind us to the necessity for separating at times even from sisters, in order to allow ourselves the freedom and space for our own unique discoveries.[19]

This redefinition of Separatism, which exorcised all the remaining Leftist mass-movement mentality and replaced it with an anarchistic personalized (womonized?) network of wimmin in transition, for the first time clarified the difference between purity and Separatism . . . which I will discuss later.

The new definition allowed many Lesbians to understand, some for the first time, the patterns of resistance in all wimmin's lives, be it the resistance through visibility of butches and fems in the 50's and 60',[20] or the weapon of vulnerability as used by heterosexual wimmin.[21] For some Lesbians of Color the separation from white wimmin holds as much power as the separation from men.[22] To a Jewish womon who was forced to shave her head in a Nazi concentration camp, shearing her head is not likely to be as liberating an act as growing it long would be.[23]

Although Daly mentions the differences in the ways we become empowered and resist, and opens up the possibilities of their exploration more than most previous Separatist writers, she has been severely criticized for not taking her own challenge and exploring the race and class differences among wimmin instead of dwelling on the similarity of our position in patriarchy. I hope that these critics will allow this Dyke the room for growth and change that Daly herself has created among us.

The book was most appealing to college-educated Dykes, especially those who have positioned themselves on the boundaries of patriarchal academia. Marilyn Frye and Julia Penelope, for example, had been out as Separatists before *Gyn/Ecology*, but the appearance of Separatist documents by such wimmin has increased in frequency in the four years since then, as has the presentation of Separatist papers at wimmin's studies conferences.[24]

Living with Contradictions

Living with contradictions
Going against the grain
It's not easy

> Making my life work for me
> A good life, a sweet life
> A righteous life with women. . . .
> Life with women is not simple
> But it's quite fulfilling
> Through our conflicts, disagreements
> Strengthening the bonds between us.
>
> *Alix Dobkin*[25]

The boundary academic Separatists I have been referring to have made certain choices about which compromises are worth making for them and which are not. They have access to huge university libraries which contain lots of resources for understanding the way men think, and for unlocking the matriarchal wisdom which is sometimes discernible, although reversed, and contorted, and deformed, in the books of the boys. Faculty also wield a certain amount of power in the system which can be useful to give grades or degrees to Lesbians who need these things to achieve what they want to achieve. They are in a position to be visible to potential Dykes, and to teach wimmin the skills of articulateness and clear thinking they will need to survive.

Another way one might learn to live with contradictions is to get a job that, while it may involve working with males and/or getting low wages, gives one back something in the way of skill or material goods that is useful to Lesbians. For example, a Dyke I know talks about getting a job at a salvage company. She would make a deal with them that she would do certain work for them in exchange for being able to go in before the wrecking ball hits an old building, and take out whatever she wanted that was left. In this way she could gather materials for building her own house.[26]

Every Separatist must make choices about which separations hold the most power for us. We each must find the critical points of separation for ourselves. It is a process.

> I became a separatist gradually. It has been twelve years since I claimed the name of lesbian. Each year I come out a little more. I expect my coming out process will continue.
>
> Presently, I claim and affirm under tremendous pressure all of who I am — black lesbian separatist. To do so puts me in conflict with each of the groups from which I could reasonably expect support, nurturance and sustenance. It's a juggling act to maintain my sanity and to remember who my real enemy is.
>
> *Anna Lee*[27]

We may find that there are certain connections we would like to give up in this lifetime, but we can not at the moment. This conclusion often feels like failure to us. Lesbians have been so hard on ourselves and each other, we often expect too much too soon.

Many Lesbians who live in the country have told me they've discovered that it's worth it to be on good terms with their neighbors ... that not speaking to them brought unnecessary hardship to their lives.

On the other side of the coin, there is the excitement of discovering the most highly-charged points of separation. For some the vital thing is to live self-sufficiently on wimmin's land. For others developing non-patriarchal Lesbian-affirming ethics and language is the vital point. This, of course, affects where we choose to live, and how we choose to get money ... to the extent that we have choice in these things.

> Finally, when I went through my most uncompromising Separatist period (1975–76), I destroyed my entire embarrassing collection of gothic heterosexual romances and went through rather a difficult withdrawal.
>
> *Victoria Ramstetter*[28]

> ... the closer I got to a 'hard line separatist' (mainly '75–'77) the shorter my hair got.
>
> *Alix Dobkin*[29]

The second wave redefinition of Separatism casts a new light on statements such as these, as well as the more aggravating ones by anti-Separatists claiming Separatism is a fad or a phase some wimmin just seem to go through. It is not Separatism these Dykes are 'passing through' but the idea that it is possible and desirable to attain Lesbian purity on earth at this time.

In my mind this sort of purification is separate and distinct from Separatism *per se*.[30] While cutting off as many connections as one can with the straight world is a valuable thing to do, most Lesbians loosen up their standards when a state of purity ceases to be a healing experience. Unfortunately, since for so many first wave Separatists this purification is synonymous with Separatism itself, relaxing their standards means to them that they can no longer define themselves as Separatists.

> I stopped being a separatist ... because to continue meant I would have to do things that I did not want to do. ...

> I would have to stop being friends with a man who had been my friend for over seven years.
>
> I would have to feel guilty about being close to my sister, who was straight at the time.
>
> I would have to relate to everyone in the world on the basis of which they belonged in — straight; straight lesbian; says some good things so might be a potential separatist, etc. . . .
>
> I would have had to be willing to sit around and seriously discuss whether or not I would kill my father if it were necessary for the overthrow of the patriarchy.
>
> I was not willing to do any of these things.
>
> Joy Justice[31]

Now some of us may have done all these things (decided to kill our fathers, disown our sisters, etc. . .) and if one has one knows that these were not easy things to do. For those of us for whom these decisions worked, they worked because they were in their own best interests. 'Walloping off' some part of your life to fit some real or imagined party line never works.[32]

Many first wave Separatists I've connected with have said that while they were great dreamers in the early 70's and believe all the ideals they still hold to be good ones, they nearly destroyed themselves trying to live that dream perfectly in their real lives. They felt the revolution was on the verge of happening.

Where have all the old Separatists gone?

When I asked one first wave Dyke what Separatism meant to her she said, in effect, she could tell me *exactly* what she meant by it six years ago, but had no idea what it meant to her now. I believe this is because, once again, purification was so wrapped up in her definition of Separatism that when she became impure by her own standards her Separatism got all mushy and confusing.

I heard a former Separatist talk once about ceasing to be a 'hard-ass' and rediscovering 'human-kindness.' Instead of progressing into a Separatism she can live with, she had retreated into a hippie-rebel stance.

Unlike this woman, most Lesbians I know who no longer call themselves Separatist have not undergone a fundamental change in their analysis, but rather the word Separatist is inadequate to describe them. Sometimes this is because of their bad experiences with Separatists who define the word in vastly different ways. Others simply feel that separating is only a small part of the process that they are going through in their political lives. They want a name that reflects the richness of their philosophy; their love for Lesbians and commitment to our survival.

> Marilyn Frye and Carolyn Shafer prefer the term 'Lesbian Connectionist' and, to a great extent, I do, too. It seems more informative and descriptive since it's what thousands of us are doing when we make ourselves our first priority and insist upon regular woman-only space; when we consciously prefer and create it in our lives.
>
> *Alix Dobkin*[33]

Some first wave Separatists see nothing of value in second wave 'womonization.'

> We're not dangerous as individuals. We got scared of the political group and went back to being individuals in the economy.
>
> Mainstream culture prints liberal writings and calls it radical. The culture doesn't print radical writings (revolutionary political writings.)
>
> Careerism has ruined the movement. What is now visible as Movement is not radical. All the Dykes went home to get a lover and a job.
>
> *TRIBAD (Lesbian International Satellite Tribadic Energy Network)*[34]

Here are some first wave Separatists' comments on their evolution in the last decade:

> . . . discussions have made me more willing to examine my separatism for potential racism. I also see woman-baiting in some anti-separatist arguments: that the 'real world' is the world of men, that the women's community or culture is just an elite escapist fantasy.
>
> *Terry Wolverton*[35]

> I am a Separatist now and forever, and I am not a feminist. I came out as a lesbian and grew into a lezzie-separatist, and have never been involved in the feminist movement.
>
> My politics have not changed that much as I eventually would like to live in a lezzie-city or dyke town – or maybe we could have a state.

As a lesbian separatist – I separate and divide my energy into many lesbian forces. The spiritual – economic – and emotional growth of the lesbians within my circle of friends and the larger community – in which I am involved – Any leftover energy goes into my poetry.

I have spent the last ten years getting into the goddess – and sharing spiritual space with my lezzie sisters.

Vernita Gray[36]

Q: Have you made any refinements in your basic philosophy politics?
A: Yes – broader based politics – I believe in making progressive alliances from our position as a separate Lesbian movement.

Susan Cavin[37]

My old Separatist friends think I must be nuts. One or two of the women I used to hang out with think that my new community-mindedness, my enthusiasm for the straight business world and my involvement in the community-at-large is a regression. I disagree. I'm ready to join the mainstream on my own terms and I think they will have to be ready for me. So far their responses have been enthusiastic. And most of them know I'm queer and proud.

I still prefer to hang out with Lesbians. I still think there is a profound difference between men and women. I don't know why this is. I still support women only space, and enjoy it fully. Most people probably would not call me a separatist. I do, because I believe that separatism is an analysis, a way of figuring out the ways of the world. It doesn't mean to me that I can't be friendly or even be friends with men or participate in their world. I don't want them participating in a Lesbian world, and I guess that's key, a woman's world is of women only. I don't care if straight wimmin join. Just no males in that context. But it's not the only context in my life. I like variety and change. This happens among lesbians, among women in general and between women and men.

Liza Cowan[38]

Moving in our own time/space

When we identify our commitments and priorities to and with each other, we can become *acti*onary rather than *react*ionary. But as long as we rely on their rhetoric and unite within their systems (male left, feminism, socialism, etc.) we have no choice but to react to them. They are always doing something wrong. If we put ourselves in the position of not having to react to them, we will have the energies, knowledge, and time to take care of, and learn from each other as Dykes who have gathered with different perspectives.

Linda Shear[39]

Our Actionary Existence

I'm frustrated that my focus on consciousness has prevented me from discussing what we're actually doing in our lives now. I keep saying to myself: so what happens when we get the space we need, the womon-only space, the Lesbian-only space, the Separatist space? What have we done with it, what will we do with it? Do we look different, beyond the common ways we present ourselves as Lesbians (The Look, The Clothes, The Stance, that J.E.B., a Lesbian photographer, believes are unique to Lesbians), as Separatists? Do we love each other differently? Do we love the earth differently?

Country Lesbians and the *La Luz Journal* begin to record the lives of Lesbians building our world around each other. They are very tentative. In the case of *La Luz*, the space dissolved before it even got started.[40] I look to Lesbians on the land for the physical changes womon-space has brought about. There are many newsletters from various Lesbian 'lands' throughout the u.s. that record their changes. (I didn't put them in the bibliography because giving their locations would endanger them more than they need be.)

One northern farm I know of has carefully worked out many policies for the use of their land. Womon-and-Nature ethics. They have decided, for instance, to have one area which is animal space, off limits to wimmin. They have decided to burn brush off one area of the land to restore it to what they consider to be its 'natural' prairie state. It's good to hear of Lesbians who are carefully considering the decisions they make about their lives in nature, and coming up with politics that are new and womon-

117

identified instead of leaving old phallocentric theories of land-use unquestioned. Special Lesbian values are reflected in even our gardens, beyond just being organic. My friend Jennifer Weston has a round Wiccan herb garden which has many gyn-mystical qualities.

In the homes of Lesbians not in the country I find animals, herbs and sacred objects. The wimmin's books and records may be kept separate from the men's, and the lesbians' separate from the straight wimmin's. There is often a special place for our herbs, or for pictures of our favorite Lesbians. We sometimes have Goddess altars which we keep in order even if the rest of the house is a mess. Some of our homes are active homes that demand creativity. Typewriters, musical instruments, art supplies. Some are passive spaces with TV's, radios, stereos, dope, and instant food.

One eastern city had a Lesbian-only building for a year for businesses providing crafts and services for wimmin.

Linda Shear explores the possibilities of our emerging music; Elana Dykewomon believes a new Lesbian language with new letters is emerging from our Separatist space.[41]

Actionary Visions

Let's do what must be done – fight our oppression and create Lesbian freedom – let's stop doubting and turning away and frustrating our rage and our impulses toward making our own Lesbian space and territory. I want to hear concrete needs and goals and plans toward action.

Thrace[42]

The physical construct of economies, social systems, states on land mass gives these male ideologies more credibility. The male state has immediate sensory, social constructions of reality, while Lesbian Separatism does not. We suffer from lack of land, but this does not mean we have no lesbian society or are missing in action. Remember Marxist socialism had no land mass and was only an ideology until 1917. The socialist ideology has taken over half the world land mass within 63 years.

... Nothing will stay the same. Within fifty years, Lesbian Separatism will have land based societies around the world if we collectivize female property and resources into a unified network. This is the next logical step – international networking – for the Separatist/Feminist movement.

... Occupy the streets of patriarchy, disrupt patriarchy reality with assertions of our own liberated reality. Liberate the streets of women. Dykes must liberate reality!

CLIT Statement #4

You don't find positive visionary statements such as these from Separatists much these days. First wave Separatists guard their future visions closely now, having had them stepped on and laughed at for a decade. Maybe they have 'gone home to get a lover and a job,' but when asked what they are doing there they can often explain it in terms of gathering skills and resources for future use. For instance, many separatists are learning natural healing and survival skills to share with Lesbians. Many are making money to buy land, or start a press, or a town, or run a cassette company. I have faith that they will do these things and not get stuck in the straight world forever.

The idea of eventually taking over territory is a popular one. When parting with Separatists I am close to, so that they or I can search for a better place to live, we often express the belief to each other that we'll all live in the same place some day. How we will do that without putting us all in danger is unclear. Visionary works like *The Wanderground* are vitally important for Separatists to write,[43] so that we can figure these things out. One possibility is to take over a town gradually, until all the straight people move out for lack of jobs and companionship. Perhaps this is a way to go.

We must share our visions . . . and make them real.

> And that process of changin is important. It's the most important to us. There are some lesbians who are in a sense closer to us in terms of how they feel and all . . . but who we don't feel as close to at all as some lesbians who are committed to DOING something – to changin – to finding new ways – to figuring out what to do. And it's that commitment that's most important.
>
> *Spectre* #6 (1972)

Acknowledgments

The following Dykes helped me a great deal with putting my thoughts together for this paper, and getting my spelling right. They are not, however, in any way responsible, nor do they necessarily endorse the opinions implied or explicit in this paper. Likewise, I do not agree with everyone I quoted.

Joji Mednick, Elizabeth Fides, Vernita Gray, Susan Cavin, Nina Wouk, Robin Birdfeather, Tryna Hope, Alix Dobkin, Elana Dykewomon, Shuli, Liza Cowan, Anne Donnelly, Elaine Stocker, Bev, Mary Lee Sargent, Kathy Munzer, Jo Olszewski, Jennifer Weston, Iandras Moontree, Niomi, Luna Woden, Lois Addison, Marilyn Frye, J.E.B., Julia Penelope, and Sudie Rakusin.

My special thanks go to Sarah Lucia Hoagland, the Sep on the other side of town, for her friendship, encouragement, and copies of *Spectre* and the *Amazon Analysis*.

Notes

1. But then I was brave enough to be there, unlike many lesbians who stayed home on the pretext that they were protesting the exclusion of little boys from the event.
2. Although Mary Daly doesn't label herself a Separatist, many wimmin continue to identify her as such.
3. 'Chasing Balls for Big Bucks,' *Womynlovers* separatists' newsletter, 1, 1, p. 1.
4. 'Talking Lesbian,' on *Lavender Jane Loves Women* by Alix Dobkin, (Women's Wax Works, 1975; distributed by Ladyslipper Music, Inc., POB 3124, Durham, NC 27705).
5. 'How to Stop Choking to Death or: Separatism,' *Spectre* 2 (May–June 1971), p. 2.
6. 'Note to "Straight Sisters"! Time for a Turnabout,' *Spectre* 2 (May–June 1971), p. 6.
7. 'Battle Fatigue,' *Spectre* 4 (Sept.–Oct. 1971), p. 8.
8. *The Furies* 1, 7.
9. Charlotte Bunch spoke about writing for *Ms.* and *NOW Times* in an interview with Frances Doughty, 'Charlotte Bunch on Women's Publishing,' in *Sinister Wisdom* 13 (Spring 1980), pp. 71–77.
10. *The Furies* 2, 2.
11. Charlotte Bunch in *The Furies* 2, 3.
12. The Gutter Dyke Collective, 'Separatism,' *Dykes & Gorgons* (May–June, 1973), p. 17.
13. Bev, from the original Gutter Dykes, is still a separatist and has written for the *Lesbian Insider/Insighter/Inciter*.
14. Questionnaire response, 1981.
15. Thank you to Marilyn Frye for this point.
16. *C.L.I.T. Statement #2, Off Our Backs* 4, 8 (July 1974), p. 13.
17. Questionnaire response, 1981.
18. Mary Daly, *Gyn/Ecology*, (Boston: Beacon Press, 1978), p. xv.
19. Pp. 381–2. The use of the word *blind* to mean insensitive or stupid is unfortunate.

20. See Joan Nestle's article in *Heresies, The Sex Issue*. She is not a Separatist.

21. Sarah Lucia Hoagland, 'Vulnerability and Power,' *Sinister Wisdom* 19 (Winter 1982), pp. 13–23.

22. See Lorraine Bethel, 'What Chou Mean We White Girl?,' *Conditions* 5, and *The La Luz Journal* by Juana María Paz (Paz Press, 11. W. South St., Fayetteville, AR).

23. Thanks to Sarah Hoagland for pointing this out to me.

24. See Marilyn Frye, 'Some Notes on Separatism and Power,' now a pamphlet from Tea Rose Press, POB 591, Lansing, MI, 48823 and reprinted in an anthology of her articles, *The Politics of Reality: Essays in Feminist Theory*, (Trumansburg, New York: The Crossing Press, 1983), pp. 95–109.

25. 'Living with Contradictions,' from the *XX Alix* album, (Women's Wax Works, 1980; distributed by Ladyslipper Music, Inc.; see fn. 4 for address).

26. Thank you to Denslow Brown.

27. This name is a pseudonym for the Separatist who wrote 'One Black Separatist,' which originally appeared in *Innerviews*, 5, 3: POB 7516, Grand Rapids, MI.

28. Preface to her book, *The Marquise and the Novice: A Lesbian Gothic Novel*, (Tallahassee, FL: Naiad Press, 1981), p. vii.

29. Questionnaire response, 1981.

30. Sarah Hoagland helped me get this clear.

31. 'Visions,' *Sinister Wisdom* 4 (Fall 1977), 66–71.

32. Thanks to Shuli for this insight.

33. Program Notes, January, 1981.

34. 'Listen Statement #2, October, 1980,' *Green Mountain Dyke News* 1, 6 (November 1980), p. 6.

35. 'Including Ourselves in the Future: White Lesbian Anti-Racism,' with Tracy Moore, *Common Lives/Lesbian Lives* 1 (Fall 1981), 42–50.

36. Questionnaire response, 1981.

37. Questionnaire response, 1981.

38. Questionnaire response, 1981.

39. From the back cover of her *Lesbian Portrait* album, (Northampton, MA: Old Lady Blue Jeans, 1977).

40. 'LA LUZ DE LA LUCHA became Womyn of Color land in fall of 1977/78. By 1979 the land was empty. It is still in foreclosure.'

41. Elana Dykewomon has been a consistent strong voice for Separatism for a long time. Her work has a wide scope, and I recommend that Lesbians read it. Write to Diaspora Distribution, POB 19224, Oakland, CA 94619, for information.

42. 'Action Proposal for Lesbian Revolutionary Movement from a Lesbian Separatist's Position,' in *Fight Back!*, eds. Frédérique Delacoste and Felice Newman, (Minneapolis, MN: Cleis Press, 1981), pp. 301–5, and *The Lesbian Insider/Insighter/Inciter* 3 (April 1981), 12; 15.

43. In the original, uncut version of *Word Is Out*, Sally Gearhart said she would call herself a Separatist. In the TV version that part was cut. Whose change this was is unclear.

MAKING SEPARATIST CONNECTIONS:
RESISTING ASSIMILATION

Comparative Separatism

K. Hess, Jean Langford, and Kathy Ross
1980

The separatism of women is different from other separatisms in that it has no regional base. Therefore, the separation of women has little in common with Quebecois, Basque, or Puerto Rican separatisms, for example, which all aim at the nationalization of an already defined area. It is also different from racial separatism in the U.S. which is regionally defined to some degree. Native Americans have a clear claim on treaty lands. Chicano/a separatists feel ties with southwestern U.S. though Aztlan is often given more cultural than geographic significance. Black separatists have perhaps the most debated relationship to any one region (five southern states? Africa? existing urban communities?). Even so, Black separatism is in part a way of using, or trying to use, the ghetto as a power base. Women's separatism, on the other hand, is up against a status quo in which women are mostly integrated (the main exception being in the labor force). Racial exploitation historically required that people of color be separate from whites. The exploitation of women as women historically required that women live with men. Logically a regional base would give separatism a more nationalist bent. And practically that seems to be the case. Yet lesbian separatism also has its nationalist function.

Despite differences, there are some similarities between lesbian women's separatism and racial separatism, partly because the second wave of the feminist movement modeled itself in part after the movements of the sixties. Like many feminists, lesbian separatists would do well to stop imitating the methods and ideas of other movements and start analyzing them. We can recognize much of the rationale, and many of the dangers of lesbian separatism through a comparison with racial separatism. This comparison does not imply political support. We do support separate groups along lines of color or other oppressions within the feminist movement – for example, groups of older women or lesbians, ethnic women or lesbians, etcetera that are feminist. But as feminists we do not advocate any separatism that conflicts with the ultimate unity of women across lines of color, country, or other divisions. Nonetheless separatism is a means of organizing that has certain observable origins and patterns of development in any movement where it appears. Through a comparison of lesbian/women's separatism with racial separatism we can hope-

125

fully avoid errors that we haven't yet made. We can come to a better understanding of separatism's place in the feminist movement, its problems, its possible outcomes.

Origins of Separatism

Separatism is in part a response to the inadequacies of civil rights tactics. It tends to arise as an alternative to campaigning for equal treatment within the existing system. In the sixties, for example, Black liberationists got disillusioned with temporary stop-gaps against poverty, with the right to vote for racist candidates, and so on. Native American leaders got tired of getting no results through the 'proper channels' of protest with the Bureau of Indian Affairs and other white agencies. As for the women's movement, almost from the beginning there was radical and separatist opposition to the reformist and male–female integrationist National Organization for Women (though there should also have been opposition to the radical segregation in N.O.W. that made it an almost all-white group). Radical feminists learned from the example of racial separatists, being immediately unimpressed with sporadic openings in male job fields, token women executives, as well as impatient with the minor attentions paid to them within mixed radical groups. An old lesson was relearned: that oppressions like racism and sexism were not incidental social problems, but deliberate social policies of the group in power (white men). So, what was required was a revolution to overthrow that group. And the militant understanding that racism/sexism were supported by the real interests of a certain element of society went hand in hand with the separatist tactic of not working politically with that element. For racial separatists that element was whites. For feminist separatists it was men. (For while men of color do not benefit from white male rule in the countries where that *is* the rule, they do benefit from oppressing women of color.)

Militant separatism was not the only alternative to reformism, of course. Individual men of color and women of any color could and did join the integrated leftist revolutionary efforts. But the left has not taken much initiative in fighting racism or sexism. Much of the socialist left tends to treat race and/or sex as reform issues. This tendency ranges from dismissing women's liberation as a reform that can be accomplished within capitalism to believing that socialism will automatically end racism and/or sexism, to writing racism and/or sexism onto the post-revolutionary reform agenda, to considering racism and/or sexism attitudes to be ended through consciousness-raising. Whatever form it takes this tendency rules out the idea that racism and/or sexism are primary oppressions to be uprooted only by a revolution (economic and political as well as social) that specifically attacks *them*. So leftists oppressed by race and/or sex often have to spend a lot of time and energy trying to reform revolutionary organizations and ideologies that have racism and/or sexism at their base. Racial or feminist separatists have chosen instead to work out whole other ideologies and organizations directed at racism and/or sexism. . . .

A leftist perspective on separate movements contrasts with a separatist perspective. For leftists involved in separate movements the important question often becomes how can we best shape these movements to fit into the left. What feminist separatists are asking is: How can we become an autonomous movement? Separatists in general want separate movements not in order to gain leverage with the left or to train as vanguards for the left but in order to be truly independent of the left (and other politics). This does not preclude coalitions at a later time. Some women seem to think that the time for coalitions is here, and that feminist separatism is less necessary now that the left has made some concessions to women's liberation. But nothing the left grants us can ever take the place of a separate power base.

So separatism has been a response not only to the 'equality gradually' of reformist integrationism but to the 'freedom for you will follow' of leftist integrationism. Those who chose feminist separatism got sick of trying to convince men that women's liberation was in itself a revolutionary aim (in their spare time from pouring coffee, cranking the mimeo, and being fair sex game for any comrade). Those who chose racial separatism lost faith in the anti-racist militancy of groups who were busy using them as figureheads.

With the beginning of lesbian-feminism, female separatism rapidly led to lesbian separatism. Originally lesbian-feminism implied a form of feminism that specifically challenged hetero-sexuality as an institution. Nowadays lesbian-feminism is used simply to identify lesbians who are also feminists (and many times also socialists, or anti-imperialists, or anarchists, or political *in*activists). Lesbian-feminism has lost most of the specifically political meaning it briefly had. It does vaguely imply a common lifestyle, value system, media and sense of community or social network. Women's separatism, while it still exists (women-only groups), is largely lesbian in practice though it does signify a political difference with avowed lesbian separatism.

127

Cultural Identification

Another reason people quit the left is that it didn't offer the same opportunities to assert racial or sexual identity. If racial separatism, for example, had only been a matter of resisting white control, it would likely have been manifested in multi-ethnic organizations excluding white people. Instead it was manifested in separate organizations for each racial group. Separatism, for Chicanos/as and Native Americans, was partly a reaction to the threat of cultural extinction. For Black men it was partly a way of regaining their Black *man*hood. However, among racial separatists the emphasis on cultural identity has all too often only widened divisions between different oppressed races. It has also contributed to a reactionary stance toward women since the family and women's role in it are considered essential to transmitting culture. For lesbians, separatism was partly a way of releasing ourselves from an identification with men so strong that we sacrificed our interests to theirs. However, among lesbian separatists, the cultural emphasis has widened the divisions between lesbians and straight women much more than a simply principled political separation would have done. It has also served to widen the divisions between women of color and white women sometimes, since the search for women's culture has in many ways been an extension of the white hippie search for counter-culture. The search for women's culture has been carried on mostly by white women in ignorance of the cultures of most women in the world but in eagerness to lift a few things from the lifestyle and spirit of cultures of color.

Lesbian separatism is making some gestures toward understanding how all women (not merely young, white, thin, middle-class Christian women) are oppressed. But the impact of these gestures so far is small. Especially since lesbian separatists as well as feminists in general continue to deny feminism's *ability* to unite women. Some say, for example, that working-class women can't afford to separate from men; or that the family is essential to the freedom of women of color. Young white middle-class feminists who dominate separatism as well as other segments of the women's movement are too careful not to trespass on what they seem to consider oppressed-male territory: analyses of class, race, and age as they apply to women. Any feminist politics that persists in the myth that it is inherently relevant only to white young middle-class women will never succeed in making itself relevant to all women.

Nationalism

Most importantly, separatism, as we've said, refers to separate political organization and ideology. But for some it has also meant a separate nation. The nationalist facets of separatist movements analyze the oppression of their people as colonial or neo-colonial. Following from that their primary demand is for land, resources and an independent government and economy. So there was the Chicano suggestion that the southwestern states revert to Chicano control, or a hint that community control might eventually evolve into Chicano 'city-states.' There was the Native American proposal that tribal lands be made 'independent' enclaves, protectorates of the U.S. government. And there have been various Black blueprints for taking over sections of the U.S. or moving back to Africa and the adoption in spirit at the 1967 Black power conference of a resolution to initiate a national dialogue on partitioning the U.S. And recently there was the First International Lesbian Swim on Washington to demand a separate nation for women. (Actually the latter seems to have as much in common with the theatrical pie-throwing politics of the Yippies as it does with racial separatism.) Aside from the utopianism of these proposals (why, for example, should Native American tribes expect more than a neo-colonial status as nations enclosed by the U.S.?), there are many problems with the nationalist emphasis.

Nationalism is a means of survival and development as a people. But it is not a means of ending oppression or the abuse of a power. Nationalist revolutions usually choose economic structures designed to liberate the people from outside imperialism, not necessarily from class or any other oppression. Nationalists are fond of saying that a nationalist struggle is automatically a class struggle since national minorities and imperialized nations are mostly poor. But this sounds like rhetoric in view of the facts. A revolution which has an independent nation as its goal is much more likely to end there. In order to compete in the international economy nations predictably form their own strong centralized states and single out their own minorities to oppress. Only out of a real commitment to and identification with international revolution would come less oppressive policies internally and externally. Socialist revolutions have often succeeded largely because of their nationalist platforms (e.g. China). It's no coincidence therefore that these revolutions based in part on nationalism (especially as a way of combatting imperialism and the problems of underdevelopment) have not dealt well with oppressions within their borders. The nation-state is, after all, a large-scale model of the patriarchal family (the fatherland 'caring' for, policing, its loyal children and 'protecting' them from the world).

In the Native American movement a purely tactical separatism barely seems to exist, since separatism is almost always connected to the call for national sovereignty. In the Black movement nationalism and separatism came to be used interchangeably by some, or combined into one term (national-separatism) by others. We need to distinguish between separatism as a tactic (political separation) and separatism as a goal (separate nation). Lesbian separatists must confront the difference. We should be working not for a female state but for the end of sexism. We must fight for the freedom of all women everywhere.

Lifestyle Politics

Separatists in any movement stress the necessity of self-definition. To this end they try to control their own communities, culture and media as much as possible. For some it becomes their whole focus. Cultural revolution is essential, but it is not enough. Militancy requires a psychological shift from shame to self-confidence, from self-blame to anger. And revolutionary movements are definitely strengthened by a culture which directs people's lifestyles toward revolutionary ends. However, if and when the maintenance of a separate culture becomes its sole aim separatism becomes non-revolutionary. It tries to evolve toward freedom with cultural and psychological changes (changes internal to, confined to, the community or the individual).

This sub-cultural emphasis is in part a response to frustration at creating strategies to actually change the existing system. Leroi Jones, Black cultural nationalist, argued: 'We cannot fight a war, an actual physical war with the forces of evil just because we are angry. We can begin to build. We must build Black institutions in all the different aspects of culture.'[1] Certain militant stances of the sixties couldn't be maintained, for example attempted seizures of land (the seizure of Alcatraz by Indians of All Tribes and the brief seizure of Santa Catalina Island by the Brown Berets) and the 'urban guerilla' tactics. Some of those involved in those activities have turned from confrontations more to community work. This work consists of a lot of badly needed services offered by Chicanos/as, Blacks, Native Americans, Asian-Americans, Puerto Ricans to their communities: cultural centers, breakfast programs, free schools, health clinics, patrols to prevent police harassment. Feminists have followed this pattern also with clinics, rape patrols, child care cooperatives, et cetera. But too often the construction of a new lifestyle and institutions becomes an end in itself. So the strong community base which is a valuable part of separatism (and feminism in general) comes to be a substitute for a movement, instead of a support for it. And the services eventually usually become severed from any ideology. Instead of pushing forward more we stop at defensive positions of survival, self-improvement and shelter from the outside world.

Under these circumstances our little enclaves can exist only with the tolerance of the larger society. Separatism, racial or lesbian, is somewhat acceptable to liberals as long as it is not armed and militant. That is, as long as it remains a life-style alternative which provides badly needed services, thereby relieving the society-at-large of that responsibility. And separatism is not inherently militant. Without military strength or political organizations or clear ideology our little enclaves are totally defenseless. At any time the government can cut off funds and either release or simply lose control of citizen backlash. The government can allow the right-to-lifers and Nazis and Ku Klux Klan to become more and more powerful while it still plays liberal, withholding official sanction from the right-wing. At the same time it can casually cut down on welfare programs, civil rights, as soon as the cries of revolution die out. This is what the late seventies and conceivably even more the eighties are all about. . . .

Lesbian separatists need to think about what social-political-economic system would make freedom for women possible. We know capitalist democracy does not. Existing socialism hasn't yet and doesn't automatically. 'Pure' socialism is an unknown which existing socialist theory may not be adequate to create. It also doesn't make sense for separatists to keep aloof from the debate between socialism and anarchism. Much of the feminist movement is organized roughly along anarchist lines, whether or not it is conscious of it, using consensus, non-static leadership structures, and small groups. Many feminists, including separatists, go round and round in the anarchist-socialist argument without even recognizing it let alone making use of its history. Far from being just a leftist problem, anarchism versus socialism is intensely relevant to women. Do we have to design a future society or just a revolution? Can our culture be a useful tool? How useful? How much do our tactics have to reflect our goals in order for us to succeed? Can a 'dictatorship of the proletariat' evolve into a free society? Is hierarchy and/or the mystique of 'good leadership' our only hope? Or will it destroy the women's movement? If so, what are alternative types of leadership? Do we need a party? Or can we accomplish unity of purpose and action through a federation of small groups? We need dialogue on all these questions that takes the experience of other political movements into account. . . .

Note

1. Jones, Leroi, *Kawaida Studies.*

Lesbian Separatism:
A Historical and Comparative Perspective*

Bette S. Tallen
1983

The current debate over lesbian separatism within the feminist movement has focused on assertions that separatism is elitist, racist, and dangerous. These charges are levelled by straight feminists who seem to be afraid of being deserted in these reactionary times. They are also raised by some lesbians, including former separatists who have discovered the 'joys' of coalition politics. Particularly troubling are the attacks on separatism by lesbians of color, such as Barbara Smith, who view separatism as racist and elitist. As I shall argue later in this paper, such attacks can represent a distortion of the history and meaning of separatism.

It is the purpose of this paper to remind each other what the real meaning of separatism is. Marilyn Frye defined separatism as,

> . . . separation of various sorts or modes from men and from institutions, relationships, roles and activities which are male-defined, male-dominated and operating for the benefit of males and the maintenance of male privilege – this separation being initiated or maintained, at will, *by women.*[1]

Frye went on to remind us that all feminists practice some form of separatism in their politics, whether they work with battered women, or in women's studies programs or in any cause where they focus on their needs as women and organize with other

---

* I owe a tremendous debt to Billie Potts for her input, criticisms and insights. Thank you, Billie.

women.[2] By affirming this separatism what we are truly doing is engaging in a process of empowerment through the denial of access.[3] The oppressor traditionally controls access but when the oppressed group denies access that is a different matter. It is different because it is not imposed on us, but is rather an expression of individual self-worth by means of a declaration of autonomy. The key to separatism is the process of empowerment.

Separatism is not a fringe impulse but rather a deeply felt, articulate statement about the establishment of an independent, autonomous political movement. Lesbian separatism, like other separatist movements, is a response to systematic oppression and attempts by the dominant culture to annihilate and 'disappear' so-called deviant groups. It is the fundamental assertion of this paper that separatism is a reasonable and viable response to the attempt of patriarchy to either assimilate or annihilate or deny the very existence of dissident groups. We do not exist in their eyes except as the product of their projections, fantasies and nightmares, or as we are useful to them. Further, because of the power men have over women their perception takes on the nature of a survival threat.

I am reminded of a lesson I learned in college during an International Politics seminar. The professor, a Czechoslovakian national, who had fled in 1948, had previously been an official in the government. Immediately after World War II he had been placed in charge of the office dealing with the German minority. Hitler had invaded Czechoslovakia in 1936 under the pretext of protecting the German nationals who lived there. My professor was ordered, by the new Czech government, to expel any German nationals still living in Czechoslovakia after the war (they were afraid of Germany repeating its actions). My professor, in defending his actions, explained that nation states have three alternatives to cope with a significant minority (note: it did not even have to be a dissident minority): assimilation, expulsion or genocide. I can remember writing those three words down in my notes in a state of disbelief and shock. And yet, after some thought, I realize how accurate those comments are. The dominant system does not and actually cannot tolerate true active difference.

There is a further issue here, that of oppression. America has put tremendous pressure on immigrant groups to assimilate (I once had a student who called the 'melting pot' a blast furnace). Ethnic and cultural difference was not and is not tolerated until it emerges in a more sterile form. For oppressed groups this has meant the necessity to create survival networks.

> The separatism I was born into was Jewish Orthodoxy, twentieth-century american-Ashkenazic branch. . . . During the years I grew up in New York City this phrase ('separatism') meant something other than its current meaning. . . . It meant observance of the entire 'law' concerning food and *buying Jewish*. . . . It is only in Jewish circle dances that a Jew born to the passionate dancing environments of eastern-european transplanted separatism finds full and happy expression.[4]

Ethnic groups stayed together in the manner described above not only to maintain their cultural integrity but also to survive in the face of exploitation. To some, to assimilate (integrate) was possibly to achieve financial success but at the cost of cultural integrity. For most, separatism was not a choice but the only means available to insure the survival of one's family.

Black separatism is a particularly clear case in point. Black separatist movements, even though they include the largest movements in Black history, have often been ignored. Blacks in this country have in almost every generation created new and viable separatist movements. These movements, like lesbian separatism, were not only harassed by the white male patriarchy but were also subject to severe criticism by Black leaders. These movements were born out of the attempts of the white culture to systematically deny the lives of Blacks. By examining the history of the Garvey, Muslim and Black power movements we can see their strength and vitality.

Black Separatism

> I am invisible man. . . . I am invisible, understand simply because people refuse to see me. Like the bodiless heads you see sometimes in circus sideshows, it is as though I have been surrounded by mirrors of hard, distorting glass. When they approach me they see only my surroundings, themselves, or figments of their imagination – indeed everything and anything except me.[5]

With these words written in 1947 Ralph Ellison gave warning that yet another generation would newly discover the meaning of enforced invisibility. For many the response was the creation of yet another series of Black separatist and nationalist groups.[6]

Dr. Essien-Udom contends that Black separatism has a specific message and audience and arises out of a history of oppression.

> Nationalist leaders contend that the Negroes must become consciously aware of their identity as a group in America; they must realize their degradation and strive by individual and collective effort to redeem their communities and regain their human dignity. The Negro masses, unlike the middle and upper classes, are seeking a way out of a sociocultural environment, a spiritual and psychological impasse, fostered by the stubbornly lingering mores of slavery and complicated during the present century by the urbanization of American society.[7]

In this view separatism is a realistic and appropriate response to a history of slavery and oppression. Unlike integration this has a direct and primary appeal to poor urban Blacks. This can be seen quite clearly when we remember that the broadest based and largest Black movement this country has ever seen (and perhaps proportionally the largest radical movement in American history) has been a separatist one: the Universal Negro Improvement Association founded and led by Marcus Garvey.

The Universal Negro Improvement Association began in 1917, peaked in 1921 and had lost the great mass of its support by 1930. At its height Garvey claimed to have upwards of six million members; even his detractors numbered his followers in the hundreds of thousands.[8] Whatever the actual numbers there can be no doubt of his enormous impact and influence. The stated purpose of his organization was, 'To establish a Universal Confraternity among the race; to promote the spirit of race pride and love.'[9] The Garvey movement started a steamship company that at its height owned three ships. They also capitalized the Negro Factories Corporation that offered 200,000 shares of stock at $5 a share to be sold only to Blacks. The corporation developed many businesses, a laundry, a retail clothing store, a hat store and a publishing house. In addition, the corporation actively encouraged Blacks to open their own businesses and provided them technical assistance if needed. Garvey also formed the Black Cross Nurses as an alternative to the Red Cross.[10] Although most of Garvey's enterprises failed, many because of poor management, others because of outside interference, the intent is clear. These corporations were to be the core of, not only enhanced racial pride, but also the economic independence of Blacks in this country.

The timing of the Garvey movement was crucial to its success. There was a massive migration of Blacks to the Northern cities in the first two decades of this century. Many were lured there by industrialists and their agents who recruited very widely in the South. The Black press in the North, such as the Chicago *Defender*, also actively encouraged this migration. Many left in the hope of finding a new job, many with the need to escape Southern racism and the more active threat of lynching and other acts of violence, many to leave the deteriorating economic conditions in the South. Regardless of the motivation, these new Northern residents were quickly disillusioned with life in the North. Jobs became scarcer, especially after the end of World War I, conditions in the Northern ghettoes were abysmal, and there was a tremendous amount of increased racial violence by whites directed against Blacks in the North aided and abetted by the 'new' Klan. In September, 1917, some soldiers of the Twenty-Fourth Infantry regiment (an all-Black unit led by white officers) stationed in Houston got involved in a fight with local white residents. As a result thirteen soldiers were executed by the Federal government and forty-one received life-imprisonment.[11] The height of this violence was reached in the summer of 1919 (usually called the Red Summer – but just about all the blood spilled was from Blacks) when a series of race riots broke out all over the North (the most serious were in Chicago, where scores of Blacks were killed and injured).

These events, combined with the experience of many of the Black soldiers who had served in Europe (mainly in France) who were struck with the extreme difference between the treatment they received there and the treatment they received at home, led to the immense popularity of the Garvey movement. The contradictions between fighting a war that was supposed to make the world 'safe for democracy' and coming back to a country that systematically denied its Black citizens democratic rights were enormous. The Garvey movement, rather than representing an isolationist tendency, went right to the center of the problems facing Black Americans. Facing a system that was united in their opposition to the recognition of the lives and accomplishments of Blacks, a separatist movement that focused on the formation of racial pride through the achievement of economic independence and autonomy was quite attractive to most Blacks.

The responses to the Garvey movement from both whites and middle-class Blacks are significant in this regard. The white establishment, of course, opposed and harassed Garvey in an effort to discredit him and destroy his movement. The Federal attorney and an assistant district attorney in New York seemed to specialize in investigating Garvey, who, although he was only indicted twice and convicted once for mail-fraud, often complained about the amount of harassment. What little white support Garvey did receive came from certain parts of the Klan who supported his 'back to Africa' theme (which illustrates Frye's point about the difference between the segregation of white males and the separatism of oppressed peoples).[12] This support underscores the importance for oppressed groups to remain clear on the difference between separation and segregation – we must remain clear on the purpose and focus of our politics. Conservative and right-wing groups often attempt to undermine our politics by 'supporting' us on certain issues (e.g., the right-wing support of the anti-pornography movement).

Garvey had a number of Black critics as well, including A. Philip Randolph (the labor leader), W. E. B. DuBois, Chandler Owen (who along with Randolph, edited the *Messenger* magazine) and Robert S. Abbott (publisher of the Chicago *Defender*) and the field representative from the NAACP, William Pickens.[12] Eight prominent Blacks, including Owen and Abbott, sent an open letter to the Attorney General in 1923 demanding that Garvey's trial for mail fraud, which had been delayed, occur as soon as possible.[13] One student of Black separatism, C. Eric Lincoln, wrote about these Black leaders that,

> The emerging black bourgeoisie and the Negro intellectuals would have no part of him. Their attempt to mold the public image of Negroes as an intelligent sophisticated people was undermined by his constant harangues and the spectacle of thousands of his followers parading in flamboyant uniforms throughout the streets of New York City.[14]

I think, more to the point, rather than its being the color of Garvey's followers' uniforms that so angered the Black leaders, it was Garvey's message about separation, independence and autonomy as well as his vast popularity. Most of these Black leaders were primarily assimilationist and believers in integration. Their primary audience was not the poor Black in the ghetto but the emerging Black middle class. These Black leaders were embarrassed by Garvey's success, as well as his visibility.

But it was Garvey's emphasis on separatism, racial pride, independence, visibility and autonomy that won him such a wide following. Separatism, and in this case, separatist nationalism, was the most appropriate heart-felt response by Blacks to the oppression of white America.

Modern Black Separatism

Modern Black separatism, from the Muslims to Malcolm X's Organization of African Unity to Stokely Carmichael's Black power SNCC, has much in common with the Garvey movement. They, like Garvey, sought to unite Black people and reassert the values of racial pride, dignity, and, above all, independence from white society. At the center of all these movements is the expressed need for Blacks to redefine themselves, or as Carmichael and Hamilton put it, 'to recognize the need to assert their own definitions, to reclaim their history, their culture; to create their own sense of community and togetherness.'[15] These separatist leaders are all vehement in their rejection of both integration and assimilation: Malcolm X, perhaps the most significant modern Black Separatist leader, was particularly graphic in his rejection of integration and assimilation.

> It's just like when you've got some coffee that's too black, which means it's too strong. What do you do? You integrate it with cream, you make it weak. But if you pour too much cream in it, you won't even know you ever had coffee. It used to be hot, it becomes cool. It used to be strong, it becomes weak. It used to wake you up, now it puts you to sleep.[16]

And they are all clear in their advocacy of separatism. Malcolm X makes a vital distinction between separatism and segregation in his writing on separatism.

> The white man is more afraid of separation than he is of integration. Segregation means that he puts you away from him, but not far enough for you to be out of his jurisdiction; separation means you're gone. And the white man will integrate faster than he'll let you separate.[17]

This distinction between a segregation that is imposed by an oppressor and a separatism which is chosen by the oppressed is critical. Malcolm X articulates an important distinction between people of color excluding white people from their meetings and white people segregating people of color.

Even after Malcolm X left the Muslims, he stressed that the critical message for Blacks was to solidify their own community and racial identity. 'There can be no black-white unity until there is first some black unity.'[18]

Like the Garvey movement, all of these leaders and groups not only encountered significant white opposition and direct violence but opposition from Black integration leaders as well. Martin Luther King denounced the Muslims as 'one of the hate groups arising in our midst which would preach a doctrine of black supremacy, a new kind of bigotry as bad as the old one of white supremacy.'[19] Thurgood Marshall (now a U.S. Supreme Court Justice, then chief legal counsel for the NAACP) stated that the Muslims were 'run by a bunch of thugs organized from prisons and jails and financed, I am sure, by Nasser or some Arab group.'[20]

The white establishment reacted to these separatist movements quite strongly. The reactions ranged from police and F.B.I. surveillance to harassment, to the outright war waged on the Black Panthers. White establishment reactions to the integration leaders such as King were, interestingly enough, similar.

These criticisms and attacks notwithstanding, the Muslims alone attracted, at their peak, an active membership numbered in the hundreds of thousands. The Muslims also started a number of Black enterprises that are in most cases still quite successful.[21] They range from department stores, food stores to farms, barber shops, clothing stores and others. There are still Muslim-owned schools and universities.[22] Even one of Elijah Muhammad's critics, George S. Schuyler, New York Editor of the Pittsburgh *Courier*, wrote:

> Mr. Muhammad may be a rogue and a charlatan, but when anybody can get tens of thousands of Negroes to practice economic solidarity, respect their women, [sic] alter their atrocious diet, give up liquor, stop crime, juvenile delinquency and adultery, he is doing more for the Negro's welfare than any current Negro leader I know.[23]

As with the Garvey movement modern separatism also hits a responsive chord with poor urban Blacks. One young Black man said of the Muslims that they are 'telling the truth if they get killed for it,' while he saw other Black leaders as 'messing around with the Man ... when they know he ain't ever going to act right.'[24] (Lincoln described this as a typical reaction by a 'man in the street.') Blacks in the street seem to feel that the integration leaders are basically wasting their time, that white society will never open up sufficiently to allow them to enter.

Black separatist movements are by no means unique in this

139

country. American history, from its inception, consists of the stories of many separatist movements. The Puritans were quite clear in their need to separate from the dominant culture and religion and to establish their own territory and independence. Nineteenth-century America also contained many other separatist groups such as the Shakers and the Mormons. Malcolm X wrote, 'Separation is only a method that is used by other groups to obtain freedom, justice, equality or human dignity.'[25] Separatism is not confined to these shores; there are numerous examples all over the world (see for example some of the groups described in Norman Cohn's *The Pursuit of the Millenium* or the tribes mentioned in John Mbiti, *African Religions and Philosophies*). What most of these movements have in common though is: 1) existing in a situation with a dominant group that seeks to place its definition on the lives of oppressed people; 2) stressing cultural dignity; 3) being repressed by the dominant culture and enduring severe disapproval by many integrationist leaders; and 4) failing because of these pressures but nevertheless usually germinating another wave of separatism in the next generations. These groups continually re-occur because of their stress on independence and autonomy. However, it should be noted that those groups that are also nationalist often have a 'promised land' aspect to their ideas. Some of these groups, such as the Muslims, often also end up espousing a strict view of male supremacy.

Many immigrant groups in this country also formed separatist cultures. Billie Potts, in her perceptive article, 'Owning Jewish Separatism,' links her own lesbian separatism with Jewish immigrant separatism. I was raised in the same Jewish separatist culture. While my parents are not Orthodox, I can remember their teaching that the worst thing I could do would be to marry a non-Jew. Like Potts, I was instructed in the importance of cultural integrity and the dangers of assimilation. My father works in one of the few remnants left of that separatist culture – the funeral industry – where every Jew used to join a fraternal society or form a family circle and arrange their burials and purchase their cemetery plots years in advance. To this day, my father belongs to over seventy lodges and three synagogues. My parents exist entirely within a Jewish social network as well as a Jewish economic network. I was raised in the context of these survival networks.

Lesbian Separatism

Lesbian separatism must be seen in the context of other separatist movements. It too has grown out of a time of profound general societal crisis. It develops along with the feminist movement around a heightened awareness of our oppression as women and as lesbians. But separatism, while a part of the feminist movement, is in some ways different and larger. It takes the meaning of feminism seriously, so seriously that it pushes the meaning of feminism toward its ultimate implications. As Abbott and Love wrote: 'Feminists who have men in their lives . . . complain that the wonderful feelings of independence, self-possession and self-determination they have around women are shot down when they come home and are dominated by men in bed.'[26] As I noted earlier, Frye explains that all feminists are separatists to some degree, the degree to which they focus their energies on women and feminist concerns. The core of lesbian separatism becomes clear. Lesbianism is, at its center, a decision to direct one's primary energy towards other women. Further, a commitment to lesbianism necessitates a commitment to independence and autonomy. In a patriarchal society, a woman who lives without the support and protection of men must make a fundamental commitment to her own independence. There is something ironic about lesbians who say they are not separatist but actually live their lives as separatists.

Separatism is based on both a resistance to and a rejection of the dominant oppressive culture and the imperative for self-definition. Lesbian separatism, unlike some other separatist movements, is not about the establishment of an independent state; it is about the development of an autonomous self-identity and the creation of a strong solid lesbian community.

Straight feminists have historically had a very difficult time with lesbian separatists; they accuse us of being divisive. These charges are similar to those levelled by the Left whenever it examines any separatist movement. But their very protests, like the protests described in this paper, seem to derive from a fundamental belief that only working with men will solve the oppression of women.

More serious criticisms come from lesbians of color, some of whom view separatism as racist and elitist. Barbara Smith, for example, states that: 'white Lesbian separatism certainly played right into the hands of traditional racial segregationists.'[27] She appears to be implying that white lesbian separatists are more racist than other lesbians or feminists. However, even she backs away from that when she writes, 'I don't think that white lesbian separatists are more racist than any other white women in the women's movement.'[28]

Her argument is peculiar in several respects. First, she never explains exactly how white lesbian separatists play into the hands of male segregationists. If she is referring to the exclusion of men of color by separatist lesbians, then she is missing the critical point of all separatist movements: they are about empowerment and autonomy. They do not receive their strength from negative definitions or exclusion. Malcolm X, for example, did not deny the reality of the oppression of the white working class; rather he stressed the coming to power and identity that Black people must achieve before they could work with any whites.

I can understand, however, the pressures brought to bear by an oppressed group to support the men of that group. I've often been told about the importance of supporting Jewish men in their struggles. I have had difficulty with this because, while I do understand the nature of their oppression, I also see their extreme male supremacist stance. I don't feel that I can look to them for support in fighting sexism or racism. Excluding Jewish men from Jewish women's or lesbian groups is done, not to further exploit them, but rather to facilitate women coming to terms with our own oppression.

Smith also confuses separatism and segregation when she argues:

> This is the way that a separatist position, chosen on the basis of sexual identity, and racial separation, imposed as the result of institutionalized racial segregation, are made to seem similar and to spring from the same impulses, ignoring the history and politics of this country and the element of choice.[29]

Malcolm X, as quoted above, makes an important distinction between separatism and segregation, pointing out that segregation is imposed in order to maintain domination, while separatism is chosen to undermine that very domination. Separatist movements are based on choice and the seizing of power; they are not imposed by the dominant culture.

Finally, Smith seems to deny the existence of lesbian separatists who are women of color. Surely she isn't claiming that they are racist and segregationist. Smith is missing a vital part of her own history when she denies the value of separatism.

Charges that separatism is elitist are similarly wide of the mark. Separatist movements in our history have traditionally appealed to the poorest and the most oppressed; that is precisely the reason for their popularity. It is a clear distortion of history to call separatism elitist.

The primary point of this paper is to demonstrate that separatism is a frequent and viable response to a situation where a dominant powerful group seeks to define and control the existence of a dissident minority. Separatism is not a fringe impulse, nor is it an expression of privilege.

Lesbian separatism must be seen in the context of other separatist movements. As lesbians we live in a society that has either denied our existence or attempted to eliminate us altogether.

We also must learn from prior separatist movements that when other lesbians denigrate separatism they might well be doing it to protect some form of privilege. Just as middle-class Blacks opposed Garvey because they found him embarrassing, so do some lesbians who, because of skin color, class background, ethnic or religious background, or other manifestation of privilege, find separatist, blatant lesbians embarrassing.

Lesbian separatism, while understanding the way the white patriarchy oppresses some men, still believes that only women can fundamentally change our own lives.

> The separatism we lesbians need to create will have to be non-expansionist, more internal by nature. . . . By working toward lesbian separatist inner space and concretizations that do not further usurp this earth, lesbian separatism could evolve a theory and mode of living that acknowledges . . . everything is connected.[30]

Notes

1. Frye, Marilyn, 'Some Reflections on Separatism and Power,' p. 2, [reprinted in this anthology, eds.].
2. Ibid., p. 3.
3. Ibid., pp. 7–9.
4. Potts, Billie, 'Owning Jewish Separatism and Lesbian Separatism 1982,' pp. 3; 29. [Printed in this anthology, eds.]
5. Ellison, *Invisible Man*, p. 7.
6. In this paper I am equating Black nationalism (right to self-determination) with separatism (establishment of an autonomous self-identity). I contend, unlike Malcolm X (see *Malcolm X Speaks*, p. 19), that while all nationalism is separatist not all separatism is nationalist (i.e., not all separatists seek to establish a nation).
7. Essien-Udom, E. U., *Black Nationalism*, p. 17.
8. For a full discussion of Garvey and the UNIA see Edmund Cronon, *Black Moses: The Story of Marcus Garvey and the Universal Negro Improvement Association.*
9. Essien-Udom, *op. cit.*, p. 48.
10. Cronon, *op. cit.*, Ch. 3.
11. Ibid., p. 30.

12. Ibid., pp. 106–107.
13. Ibid., p. 111.
14. Lincoln, C. Eric, *The Black Muslims in America*, p. 64.
15. Carmichael, Stokely, and Hamilton, Charles V., *Black Power: The Politics of Liberation in America*, p. 37.
16. Malcolm X, *op. cit.*, p. 16.
17. Ibid., p. 42.
18. Ibid., p. 21.
19. Martin Luther King, quoted in Lincoln, *op. cit.*, p. 153.
20. Thurgood Marshall, quoted in Ibid., p. 148.
21. For more on the Muslims see Ibid.
22. Ibid., p. 93.
23. Ibid., p. 142.
24. Ibid., p. 163.
25. Malcolm X, *op. cit.*, p. 51.
26. Sidney Abbott and Barbara Love, 'Is Women's Liberation a Lesbian Plot?' In *Woman in Sexist Society*, edited by Vivian Gornick and Barbara Moran, p. 618.
27. Barbara Smith, Letter to *Sinister Wisdom*, in *Sinister Wisdom* 20, p. 102.
28. Barbara Smith and Beverley Smith, 'Across the Kitchen Table: A Sister-to-Sister Dialogue,' in *This Bridge Called My Back: Writings by Radical Women of Color*.
29. Smith, Letter, p. 102.
30. Potts, *op. cit.*, p. 30.

Bibliography

Abbott, Sidney and Love, Barbara. 'Is Women's Liberation a Lesbian Plot?' In *Woman in Sexist Society*, edited by Vivian Gornick and Barbara Moran. New York: Signet, 1962.

Carmichael, Stokely and Hamilton, Charles V. *Black Power: The Politics of Liberation in America*. New York: Vintage, 1967.

Cleaver, Eldridge. *Soul On Ice*. New York: Dell, 1968.

Cohn, Norman. *The Pursuit of the Millenium*. New York: Oxford, 1970.

Cronon, Edmund David. *Black Moses: The Story of Marcus Garvey and the Universal Negro Improvement Association*. Madison: University of Wisconsin, 1968.

Cruse, Harold. *Rebellion or Revolution*. New York: William Morrow, 1968.

Ellison, Ralph. *Invisible Man*. New York: Signet, 1947.

Essien-Udom, E. U. *Black Nationalism*. New York: Dell, 1963.

Frye, Marilyn. *The Politics of Reality: Essays in Feminist Theory*. Trumansburg, N.Y.: The Crossing Press, 1983.

————. *Some Reflections on Separatism and Power*. East Lansing, Michigan: Tea Rose, 1977.

Jacobs, Jane. *The Question of Separatism: Quebec and the Struggle over Sovereignty*. New York: Vintage, 1981.

Lincoln, C. Eric. *The Black Muslims in America*. Boston: Beacon, 1961.

Malcolm X, *Malcolm X Speaks*. New York: Grove, 1966.

Mbiti, John S. *African Religions and Philosophies*. Garden City, New York: Anchor, 1970.

Potts, Billie. 'Owning Jewish Separatism and Lesbian Separatism 9982,' *The Lesbian Insider/Insighter/Inciter*, 9 (December, 1982); 3, 29, 30.

Smith, Barbara. 'Letter to *Sinister Wisdom*,' *Sinister Wisdom* 20: 100–104.

———— and Smith, Beverley. 'Across the Kitchen Table: A Sister-to-Sister Dialogue,' In *This Bridge Called My Back: Writings by Radical Women of Color*, edited by Cherrié Moraga and Gloria Anzaldúa. Watertown, Mass.: Persephone, 1981.

Spinster, Sidney. 'The Evolution of Lesbian Separatist Consciousness,' *The Lesbian Insider/Insighter/Inciter*, 7 (April, 1982), 1, 16–23.

It Has To Do With Apples

Sarah Grace
1981

For lesbians, separatism is a volatile issue. There's so much talk, such heated debates. Friendships are broken and alliances are made strictly on the basis of one's feeling for or against.

With all the furor, you'd think it is a new issue. But it isn't.

My grandmother, Rivke, was a separatist of the first degree and lived her life adamant that she remain one. It wasn't exactly my brand of separatism. Hers dealt with gentile vs. Jew; mine has to do with men, but nonetheless. . . .

Rivke emigrated to the United States from Munkach, Hungary, in 1901, at the age of eighteen. Her family settled in Sharon, Pennsylvania, and it was there she met Mandel, fell in love and married him twelve days later. Her life, and his, was totally centered around and involved with Jews.

Rivke would have nothing to do with 'goyim,' her term for non-Jews. I can remember quite clearly her hatred and disdain for them.

She had reason, of course. I mean, talk about oppression! Her parents and grandparents were uprooted from their homeland, their friends, their businesses by non-Jews. Even in America, her American-born children were taunted and teased by gentile playmates.

Her disdain took various forms.

After an airplane crash, for instance, she would read the list of dead. If there were no Jewish names, she would dismiss the whole incident as trivial and no great loss. Jewish names on the list, on the other hand, evoked sorrow and often tears.

She lived her entire adult life consciously choosing to surround herself with Jews and avoid gentiles. She never had a 'cleaning lady' because she did not want *goyishe* hands touching the things she cherished. Gentiles were not allowed in her home.

Outside of the home, she was also discriminating and selective. She played cards with Jewish wimmin only, had Jewish doctors, did volunteer work in synagogues but not hospitals. She had no gentile friends – she didn't trust them. Even in business, she had contact only with Jews and chickens, as she worked with my grandfather in a kosher butchershop.

When I began dating we had conversations about the boys. It was obvious she just couldn't understand why a Jewish womon would have anything to do with a non-Jewish male.

'You're dating a boy named David, Mumele (her term of endearment for me),' she would ask, 'ah! Yidden (Jewish)?'

'No, gramma, he's not.'

'Feh! How can you stand to be with *Schutzum*?' (I'd rather not translate that word.)

She let me know in no uncertain terms that were I to marry a gentile boy, she would consider me dead and no longer speak my name.

Fortunately for me, gentile wimmin friends of mine weren't so awful. She understood that her ways were 'old-fashioned' and believed in the bonding of wimmin, and could make allowances for gentile girlfriends of mine. I'm certainly glad. It made things easier when I came out as a lesbian. At least I didn't have to contend with Rivke's programming on wimmin.

Her life was full, joyous – and separate. Separatism was Rivke's dream, Rivke's life. I am her granddaughter, and, as my mother, may she live and be well, often says, 'Apples don't fall from pear trees.'

For Rivke, being centered and peaceful depended on being in an environment that she chose, with people she trusted and could depend on for loving and support. She knew her enemies, and she consciously chose not to give any of her marvelous energies to them.

I feel at ease making the same sort of decisions. It's true that the focus of our separatism is different, but, after all, the underlying principles are the same. We all have the right to choose where to put our energy, and what sort of apples we will be.

'The Issue is Woman Identification'

Margaret Sloan-Hunter
1976

The interview with Margie Adam in Plexus (Feb. '76) surfaced feelings of anger and sadness in me, and caused me to reflect on my involvement in the Civil Rights Movement that led to my later involvement in the Feminist Movement.

As a black lesbian feminist, I am constantly amazed to see that our Feminist Movement cannot learn from Movements that have preceded it in recorded time. I find it distressing that years after this 'second wave' began, we are still debating and discussing the issue of men with all the energy we brought to that subject 10 years ago.

After Black Power and 'Black is Beautiful,' blacks for the most part stopped reacting to white people and racism, and most of our energy went into developing our psychic survival. Whites were moved out of Civil Rights organizations, and although some whites didn't understand this and were angry, most of the whites that had any sense were supportive and understanding.

A people that had been alienated from one another had a need to put energy into themselves and heal wounds that had been created by racism. It was not too necessary to have meetings and events labeled 'black only,' because whites simply knew they had better not come. Whites who were in close friendships or intimate relationships with blacks felt somewhat left out, but those who were sincere met with other whites and tried to deal with racism where it had begun: with them.

Inside those meetings we blacks did not have lengthy debates on whether whites should be admitted, nor did we agonize and make statements like: 'What about whites; they're human beings too?' Those blacks that were resistant had their consciousness raised on the spot or stayed home. But our female caste, which has been separated since just after that 'gynocratic' age that Elizabeth Gould Davis speaks of in her book *The First Sex*, is still feeling the need to include, and defer and apologize to men.

The issue is not closed or open concerts. The issue is woman identification. Lesbians have had a painful her-story in the Feminist Movement. And yet, we have always been there, whether it be on the board of N.O.W., or organizing radical feminist groups. For the most part, we have founded the presses, the bookstores, the credit unions, the women's centers. It is we who will carry on the culture in our poetry, prose and song. In spite of all the energy that has been generated by lesbians in the Feminist Movement, we are still at the place of 'excuse me.' If, as a Movement, we had really taken ourselves seriously, there would be no debate over open or closed concerts, meetings and dances. Men would simply know not to come because our Movement had been very clear, and proudly so, about our message.

Black separatism as a physical reality failed because most blacks didn't want the state of Rhode Island or a plot of land to till. The concept didn't fail, however. Black separatism failed because most blacks developed a black identification and made the revolutionary discovery that we didn't *need* white people. That was important because we thought we did and had depended on white people so much we couldn't imagine how we could exist without that support. Many of us blacks are now free to have equal relationships with whites, not because we *need* them, but because we want them.

If Lesbian separatism fails it will be because women are so together that we will just exude woman identification wherever we go. But since sexism is much older than racism, it seems that we must for now embrace separatism, at least psychically, for health and consciousness sake. This is a revolution, not a public relations campaign, we must keep reminding ourselves.

I am reminded of an incident in Chicago during the height of the Civil Rights Movement. A meeting had been announced to deal with Black Power, and it was understood by most that it was for blacks only. But a black woman showed up with her white man friend. A black woman felt extremely threatened by this and spoke up. Debates over 'what harm can one white do?' etc. went on for a few minutes. Then the woman stood up and shouted, somewhat frustrated: 'You don't understand. I am uncomfortable with his presence. I don't even know him, but I don't want him here.' At which point the black woman who had brought the white man turned to him and said, 'I'm sorry, you will have to leave; if one sister is uncomfortable, that is enough.' He left.

When those kinds of priorities are placed on us by ourselves and we put ourselves as women first above everyone else, then the racist and sexist society will know we mean business. After all, it is we who are changing the world.

Owning Jewish Separatism and Lesbian Separatism

Billie Luisi Potts
9982

The inside lesbian community struggles over separatism have been with us for more than a decade. These struggles have their ups and downs, in-times and out-times. In my view, the last few years have been particularly hard on lesbian separatism. It now seems 'out' for many reasons: 'inherent racism,' a 'naïve politic,' and most recently 'anti-Semitic.'[1] In addition to separatism being on the outs as a politically correct position, many lesbians who describe themselves as formerly separatist say it was an angry stage, or that they can't make a living working for/performing for women only. Others simply say that it doesn't have much to do with what they are currently choosing to do in their lives. Many activist lesbians now feel that working with politically sympathetic men is a necessity in the climate of rightwing resurgence that is america of the '80's. Coalition-building has become a strong trend.

Sidney Spinster's recent article on 'Separatism' for the *Insider/ Insighter/Inciter* [reprinted in this anthology, eds.] is, I believe, an important and clarifying attempt to come to grips with our separatist herstory and inner contradictions. My lover and I have been talking about doing a book about separatism. There are separatist anthologies in the works. I still define myself as a lesbian separatist. For me, the core of my lesbian separatism is womon-identification, making lesbians my priority, and not giving my energy and skills to men and their systems if there are any choices available. Separatism has always been for me an effective and workable response to oppression. Today's historical situation forces us to surrender some of our hard-earned monies (usually earned within the male structures), to the oil cartels, telephone and utility companies, food industries, landlords, banks and other mortgage institutions, to greater or lesser degrees, for there are so few choices in these realms. Even the decade-old dream of lesbian land self-sufficiency with its promise of release from single-parenting, high overheads, and food industry dependency is not a concretized reality. Land, having been grasped by men and turned into a commodity (along with food and healing), is resold back to us in a bewildering variety of entangling, patriarchally-evolved forms. Many of us work for 'the man' for basic survival wages, needing the dollars for ourselves and our children. None of this contradicts separatism for me, since it is the practical contradiction I have had to face all my life. Unlike many dykes who say they were born lesbians, I am a lesbian with a long heterosexual past, but a born separatist.

The separatism I was born into was Jewish Orthodoxy, twentieth-century american-Ashkenazic branch. For years I have been explaining and footnoting my experience to lesbians, Jewish and other. The major reason that I have found myself in this educatory situation is that I am forty-two years old and the specific separatist culture I grew up in has almost vanished from the american scene. This may seem a strange assertion to make, just as Jewish american lesbians are articulating our special identity and Orthodoxy itself is making a comeback on these shores. Neither the recent Orthodox revival nor the current Jewish identifying lesbian is particularly separatist, and certainly not separatist in the old way that characterized the first sixteen years of my life.

During the years I grew up in New York City, Jewish separatism was an organized, manifest, daily fact of life. Starting with the obvious, we ate Jewish food. In 1930–1950, New York City, this phrase meant something other than its current meaning. It didn't simply refer to keeping kosher[2] or eating Jewish style homecooking and bakery specialties. It meant observance of the entire 'Law' concerning food and *buying* Jewish. Meat, fish, dairy, and eggs came to New York City from Jewish producers who ringed the city in the nearby greenbelt region, the agricultural counties closest to the city. Even in predominantly non-Jewish neighborhoods (all of New York City was 'neighborhood' at the time), there usually existed a kosher butcher, an egg and dairy lady, an appetizer store where dairy and preserved specialties (pickled herring, pickles, smoked salmon, sturgeon, whitefish and carp, olives, dried fruits, nuts) were retailed, and a Jewish fish-market with 'live' tanks for carp. Often the tiniest of these stores were open only one or two days a week, their owners returning to their dairy and poultry farms for the rest of the farm-work week. Often, only the neighborhood egg lady came in to keep store, retailing the produce from her family farm and the products of a vaguely expansive network of brothers-in-law, cousins, 'lansmen.'[3] When families bought food from these particular retailers, we had the assurance of tradition, clan, and religious network that the eggs, dairy, meat and specialties were produced with rabbinical supervision, were in no way 'unclean.' Spiritual structures and economic self-sufficiency were conjoined in everyday life. The idea of going to a supermarket and purchasing a 'kosher-style' chicken from the 'kosher' section of the market, a chicken that had hobnobbed with 'unclean' chickens and foodstuffs, was unthinkable and had not yet come to pass. Two particular european traditions were carried on in these customs, that of bringing the produce of farms to town weekly, and the east-european village or kin-cooperative tradition (such as in the old Russian *mir*). A noteworthy Jewish element was the numerically high proportion of women conducting the retailing in town. European market ladies and euro-Jewish business women were visible in 'the old country.' Where I grew up there were no Italian or Irish women visibly keeping store in this way, but there were many Jewish women doing this sort of work.

What we wore was clothing made by hand by our mothers, aunts, grandmothers, great-aunts (sewn, knitted, crocheted), or at times bought 'out,' i.e. purchased in a store, at the neighborhood drygoods store. This establishment sold mill ends of fabric, yarns, sewing notions such as needles, thread, and loose zippers, some 'factory goods' (finished clothing), odds and ends of household necessities, and jobber's closeouts. Everyone participated in the hand-me-down network, and you saw the same blouses and skirts coming and going for years, in shul, in school, at family circle meetings, and hanging out the back windows of apartment houses, drying on clotheslines from Mondays through Thursdays. The lean years of the depression and World War II made it a moral obligation to save old clothes and recycle papers, rags, and string, all dutifully collected by handpushed (push-cart) labor-ragmen, peddlers, and pickers.

The fishmarkets opened only a few days a week, sold whatever was 'running,' had scales, and came in as local catch off Sheepshead Bay, Montauk, City Island, and the other New York shore points, in the days of clear waters. I didn't know what a lobster was, looked, or tasted like till I was sixteen, and always thought the gorgeous conch shells on display in the Italian fishmarkets were decorations. Only years later did I learn that edible sea animals had lived inside them. To this day, I carry insatiable cravings for these most mysterious forbidden foods: eels, squid, mussels, crab and lobster, even catfish; but my mind's eye sees the stern eye of the live carp as it swims claustro-phobically in the tanks of the Jewish fishmarket.

Money was borrowed from family, the 'union' bank (the Amalgamated Clothing Workers lending institution, downtown at Union Square), the breadwinner's pension fund if there was one, or not at all. Buying on credit or installments cost more and was for the 'goyim' (gentiles). If you absolutely had to borrow and had to pay interest, the interest had to go to the community (i.e., union banks, credit unions), or to another Jew. Asking interest on a loan within the family was, as my grandmother used to say, 'for the Morgans and the Rockefellers,' her equivalent of saying robber-baron goyim, to be tacitly understood as inappropriate to Jewish family ethics and solidarity.

As Orthodox Jewish children we went to our own Hebrew and Yiddish schools. Hardship, defined as health problems, distance and commuting, lack of money, frequently intervened in our lives. These hardships were recognized as the ordinary consequences of *diaspora* living. They were dealt with through a complex code of allowances, exceptions and compromises reached in accord with rabbinical consultation, study and understanding. If some of us wound up in public schools, with only after school traditional instruction, or in non-sectarian summer camps, it was tolerated. Of course, many of us were able to go to Jewish, always referred to as 'our own,' summer camps and resorts. At that point in time the camps and resorts were concentrated at the shore – the Rockaways, Brighton, Coney Island, or in *the* mountains, the Catskills. There were many more 'day-camps' than overnight camps, and family resorts, such as bungalow colonies, cottages, family hotels, were more common than children's camps. Summer living was a hodge-podge of collective shopping and communally-shared refrigerators and dining rooms, nuclearized bungalow living, large numbers of children staying with mothers, aunts, grandmothers over the summer weeks, while men and working mothers commuted to the summer places on oddly defined weekends (Friday morning through Sunday, Saturday night through Monday – to avoid travelling on the Sabbath). Class distinctions and assimilation levels were probably most pointed and painful, as revealed by your family's summer arrangements – or lack of them.

New York City Jews built hospitals that would provide kosher meals for patients, and ritual circumcision for males, and eventually accessible medical school education and training. We buried our own dead within twenty-four hours through Jewish cemetery plot subscription societies, lodges, and fraternities, at Mount Hebron, and later at Ararat.

We saved our pennies in glass jars and tin cans that had special penny slits in their tops. Every window sill, kitchen counter, cupboard, corner table, shelf, or china closet, had its penny can. We saved our pennies to plant trees and regreen the desert of Zion, for the orphans, for the aged, for the victims of cancer, to bring over the D.P.'s, for the B'nai Brith, for the Hadassah, for the yeshiva around the corner, for summers in the mountains. Secretly, some of us saved for guns, with the encouragement and explanations of persons nameless still after thirty-five years or dead, for the 'underground,' for the Resistance, for *it* to never happen again, for the defense of the Rosenbergs, for L. to be delivered out of the hands of the Stalinists to the hope of Israel. Dropping those pennies into their containers was more constant ritual than the prayers in shul behind the women's curtain. For years, the inner parts of me believed saving pennies would save the world. Some never clearly explained connection was deeply ingrained in me that money was power. Can you imagine how serious a little girl I grew to be?

Very little is written by american Jewish lesbians about the tension-antagonism generated by separatism/assimilation conflicts inside Orthodox households. When I was little, my larger family came together weekly to play cards on Sunday and have huge raised-voice arguments about whether Reform Judaism would end Jewish life, about the Bund,[4] about unions, about the possibility of pogroms and persecution in america, about Israel, about keeping the 'Law' or abandoning it.[5] These arguments went full speed ahead in Yiddish. Sooner or later, someone would shout in Yiddish, 'they should speak English or they'll set a bad example for the children.' It was a time when families raised non-English speaking children and then overnight reversed their language stand, their separatism, their maintenance of the 'Law.' Last week at my grandmother's unveiling, one of my aunts by marriage came up the path shushing her mother's flow of Yiddish, saying first in Yiddish and then in English, 'Now speak English, you're in America.' They have both been here for almost seventy years.

Assimilation was dreaded and sought after in the same breath and moment. There seemed to be an inside standard and an outside standard. It was a constant source of confusion. For years I thought it was because of internal Jewish confusion about where to take a stand. I now believe it stemmed from outside societal pressure, confusion, and hatred. From the inside, there was no question: if you didn't keep the 'Law' you were not a Jew. 'What were you then,' I would ask my grandmother. 'A free thinker and a whole person,' she would say. 'Can you stop being a Jew, just like that?' I'd say. 'No, you are still a Jew,' she'd answer. Life was one big contradiction. Whatever arguments went on internally, the face shown to the outside was that of a Jew. Having your nose redone was not only vain, it was a great betrayal. Sneaking a taste of lobster Cantonese was understandable. If you stopped keeping kosher or no longer sold your chametz away at Passover, change was tolerated. If you married a non-Jew you were ostracized, punished, excluded by the clan.

Even considering the contradictions, defensive arrogance, and narrowness separatism can produce, I still believe it fertile. Jewish Orthodox separatism as I knew it is now a ghost. It passed away, just as we euphemistically once said of our dead. It has left strange markers: bagel outlets in shopping malls, decaying Catskill hotels, 'egg creams' in California towns, one surviving Yiddish daily, acres of brothers and sisters resting in peace, their plots memorialized in polished granite, arched over by columnar stones carved in a dying language. The tiny, producing family farms were engulfed by rising agri-business, suburban development, industrial parks (???), the automobile's endless appetite for roads, pavement, and parking garages. The drygoods merchants founded retailing empires and built malls. The doctors, bankers, landlords, and lawyers multiplied. Generations of women organizers, machine operators, laundry workers, clerks, bookkeepers, and typists, writers, socialworkers, and healers were abused and disappeared into the stereotype of grasping, overprotective, self-enslaving, homebound, martyred mothers. My mother, grandmothers, aunts, and cousins, all 'went to business.' Who remembers where? The capital they generated financed their husbands and sons. Popular histories today tell us repeatedly that out of all proportion to our numbers in the general american population, Jews achieved upward mobility in the 'new world,' pushed open the doors of the Ivy League and the Seven Sisters' establishment, captured the post World War II literary scene, reinspired american activism and political resistance. In the process, we disavowed, dismantled, and disowned Jewish separatism. From that vanished separatism, my first, I learned that:

> Separatism defines and builds firm individual and group identity. It teaches how to survive as a minority culture within an oppressive dominant majority culture. Within it you learn early how to compromise on necessities, but also the limits of compromise; what are the absolutes to preserve. Separatism builds loyalty and community, focuses energy, and creates the only setting I have encountered for uninhibited joy and energy sharing. 'Mixing' with an oppressive surrounding society group drains energy and constantly limits rapport and sincere expression of feeling. It is only in Jewish circle dances that a Jew born to the passionate dancing environment of eastern-european transplanted separatism finds full and happy expression. And what of wimmin's circles?

Jewish separatism as I knew it is long gone. And here I am on the radical fringe, wondering whether lesbian separatism ever existed as a manifested reality, whether it too is in its death throes being assimilated by resurgent leftist-feminism and coalition-building, or whether it's actually just starting out. I'd like to suggest that we are still in the birthing of lesbian separatism. Self-defined, self-conscious, visible lesbian culture is not even in her adolescence. Our theory is in infancy. Unlike other separatists of the past, we are not bonded by centuries of common language, common experiences and rituals of birth, nurturance, healing, and death. The common circle dances we form are grafts. Our survival-support networks have so far been shallow or herstorically short, compared to native american people, Jews, or the dispersed tribes of Asia and Africa.

We have, I believe, too early and glibly assumed that our common lesbian oppression creates community and fundamental bonding, that all lesbians' first allegiance will be to lesbian solidarity. We have borrowed the rhetoric and distillations of other oppressed people's long and deep experience before we have become ourselves a people. We have grafted onto these borrowings our analyses and perceptions, naming this both our culture and struggle. But each of us has her own ethnic, religious-spiritual, personal-political identity formed prior to or alongside our lesbian identity. Our lesbian people is still a folk of divided loyalties. Some of us may want to be primarily identified as lesbian folk, others of us may not or cannot, in this time and place. Trying to recognize and understand all these divergences and divided loyalties is a tension in itself, over and above the tensions we deal with *eman*ating from the patriarchy. When we agree to disagree among ourselves, we run the risk of drifting apart as a lesbian people.

I believe that every lesbian is by definition a separatist to some degree. Once we commit our energies in a primary way to another womon and/or wimmin, we have made a statement of separation from the patriarchy. No matter what compromises we make out there in survival country, this separation runs deep. The extent of the definition and degree is a matter of pressure of circumstances, understanding, and choice; a dance we must all dance. The masculist societies from which we withdraw our energies know we are outsiders even if we do not 'know' it ourselves, even if we refuse to label ourselves, continue to work for the good of humanity, and remain deeply connected to our sons or fathers. My vision of lesbian separatist society is a gentle vision, one of organic growth and power, firm commitment to loving wimmin, non-violent conflict resolution, and refusal to support or participate in the current patriarchal greed for more, bigger, tougher, exploitation, abuse, and death. Perhaps for centuries our lesbian resistances and refusals to participate in patriarchal patterns will have differing paces, shapes, forms, and intensities. It seems impossible at this moment in time to easily resolve the multiple conflicts between societally inherited and given identity, and our self-defined, chosen paths toward whole-womon-being.

Over and above the patterns of patriarchy we are born into, separatism itself faces new factors. What calls itself american has hosted many forms of separatism in the past. Christian fundamentalists, from the self-proclaimed Separatists of seventeenth-century Plymouth Colony to the misogynist, authoritarian, worldly and 'successful' separatists of the Church of the Latter Day Saints, have peopled this land. At one time, the 'open' land of america called enticingly to generations of European enthusiasts and fanatics. Immigrants and homegrown religious visionaries preached separatism and attempted to form living communities that would manifest their visions. The land called to the hunted, the persecuted, and the denied of other places, to come and move onto the wilderness places. And the 'new' land in its turn obliterated, segregated, oppressed, and threatened its minorities, many of whom began to promote separatist utopian visions. There has been separatism along racial and ethnic lines, chosen for the purposes of self-preservation and self-definition among minority peoples in america, as well as separatism that grew out of abuse, exploitation, and ghettoization. It is a term that carries much inner explosivity and many different meanings accreted through history. I believe the separatism of the eighties has to deal with a differing situation, defined by the end of further frontiers on this finite earth.

The separatism we lesbians need to create will have to be non-expansionist, more internal by nature. We have been trying to separate along old separatist lines against a background of densely developed, patriarchally defined, owned and controlled structures. By working toward lesbian separatist inner space and concretizations that do not further usurp this earth, lesbian separatism could evolve a theory and mode of living that acknowledges the limited-resource time and place we live in, that pays its dues to the basic tenet of ecology: everything is connected. Acknowledging that we arise out of diversity and have prematurely assumed solidarity, we could turn our attention to creating ourselves as people through evolving rituals that mark and celebrate our births, coming-out times, healings, dyings. These evolutions will have to be full of sharings, recognitions, compromises. Years ago, friends of mine and I looked into the possibility of establishing a lesbian sacred ground for burials and ashes of our dead. What a welter of regulations, money, red-tape, prohibitions, and bureaucratic confusions spread in front of us! I wondered whether the Zornitcher Society[6] confronted the same barriers, and then remembered that Mount Hebron was 'in the country' way beyond the edges of the city as we know it today, when it was founded. Over seventy years of codes, protective statutes, and local ordinances have accumulated since the heyday of the Jewish separatist burial societies. Jewish lesbians today have to develop hybrid solutions and compromises about where our bodies will rest, or whether to be buried at all. I can no longer peacefully envision the remains of my earthly body resting between the polished granite markers of Mount Hebron and the thousands of brothers and sisters who would have sat shiva for me and counted me no-woman. What would preserve the threads to my ancient past if my ashes are scattered across the surface of wimmin's land? Putting off the consideration, or even dismissing such questions blocks the process of creating ourselves as a lesbian folk.

In these last few years, I have defined my lesbian separatism as a motherland of heart and mind. Out there in the geographical and physical world imprinted and impressed by man, I make my survival compromises. Inside the motherland, I reserve my psychic and spiritual, healing, and heart energies for myself and wimmin-bonded-wimmin. The first separatism I once knew eroded away, but lesbian separatism is still growing. Separatism as a strategy, as an empowering way of life, and analytical theory works[7]; its meaning, forms, and tactics change. There isn't any way to measure the influence of a particular separatism on the systems and structures it resists and separates from, for separatism changes both its supporters and adversaries.

I look back over the last decade at the pioneering efforts of lesbian separatists to create women-only space in print, in music, at events, and see that much of today's visible 'women's culture' arose from separatist vision and energy. We haven't needed new frontiers or wilderness land to create spaces in which we find our uninhibited expressions of lesbian insight and happiness. And through our example and energy, we have prodded heterosexual feminism and straight society into changes. Presses, events, rape crisis centers, women's centers, and the battered women's houses have been staffed and spearheaded by lesbian energy. We are in the habit of not saying this out loud or directly, for fear of losing support and funding, and jobs. Lesbian invisibility in sports, the academy, and the skill trades is a condition of survival, but we are there too, in great numbers. And many of us live as separatists in the areas of our lives that we *can* keep apart from male society, but tone down our lesbian being 'out there.' The rightwing, the Reaganites, and the anti-feminist backlash may attempt to roll back the changes, but there is no going back to the way it was. Process will come up with a synthesis that will incorporate the changes that have occurred, and we at the radical fringe will be pushing the struggle to the next border of changes. It is from the dark well of our separatist selves that we draw the resources to try the outrageous.

Notes

1.   Sara Bennett and Joan Biggs, *Top Ranking*, February 3rd Press, 1980, pp. 2–3; Combahee River Collective, 'A Black Feminist Statement,' in *Capitalist Patriarchy and the Case for Socialist Feminism*, ed. Zillah Eisenstein, Monthly Review Press, 1979, (the statement is dated 1977); Gloria Greenfield, 'Shedding' in *Nice Jewish Girls* (pp. 7–9), broadly equates lesbian separatism with 'the naïve notion that the demise of patriarchy will end all oppression,' and describes her movement away from lesbian separatism because of its failures to confront anti-Semitism (as well as the general feminist movement's failure to change its anti-Semitism). Coming from a minority culture, I have deeply recognized the question of sympathy-solidarity with men of my oppressed culture. I part company with wimmin who cannot politically recognize the pattern of passed-on further oppression that I grew up with as a daily fact of life. The treatment of women inside Jewish Orthodoxy was oppressive, abusive, hypocritical, and a source of severe pain to me when growing up.
2.   *kosher* – the term that covers the complexities of Orthodox Jewish dietary Law. Some of its basics called for separation of all meat and dairy dishes, foods, preparation utensils, utilization of meat slaughtered according to Law and supervised by a rabbi, abstention from pork, creatures without cloven hooves, and sea creatures that had no scales and fins. (See Leviticus, 11, 17 and 20.) The food aspects of the Law had the most immediate and observable influence on my life. Upon the death of my maternal grandfather, I went to live with my grandmother. She revealed herself to me as a 'free-thinker' and we theoretically jettisoned all aspects of strict observance, food and other (see below note 5). In actuality we went on purchasing only kosher meat and poultry, salting down red meat, cooking the same way, buying from the same suppliers, diligently avoiding everything we knew to be 'unclean.' We were never kosher enough for the rabbinical side of my grandmother's family. They came visiting with their own tea glasses and never ate any solid food at our house. The ferocity of one-upsmanship around keeping the dietary Law is hard to describe to wimmin who have not grown up with its prohibitions and severity. I have met several Jewish lesbians recently who say they keep kosher, and that it is easy because they are vegetarian and don't have to worry about meat/dairy problems.
3.   *Lansmen* – I have not found an English equivalent to this term, roughly translated as 'folk from the same country' (something akin to the Italian *paisan*), for it always carried a mystical kin-bonding element when used in my past.

4.   The Bund – specifically here the Jewish Socialist Labor Bund, Vilna, 1897. See Baum, Hyman, Michel, *The Jewish Woman in America* (New York: New American Library, 1975), p. 77.

5.   The 'Law' – here I am referring to the entire convenant, revealed statutes and the system of understandings, interpretations and accretions that grew up around it, forming the complex cultural-spiritual tradition.

6.   The burial society my grandparents belonged to, and through which my resting place is still assured via a complex series of subscription tradings and later emendations with other organizations. Even though these societies have eroded away to a large extent, it is not unusual to fly half way around the world to attend the funeral or unveiling of a loved family member and find yourself met, briefed and supported at the gravesite by a member of 'the society.'

7.   Marilyn Frye, *Some Reflections on Separatism and Power*, Tea Rose Press, 1977. This writer's definition of separatism as power through denial of access has been critical to my own re-evaluation of theoretical separatism. [Reprinted in this anthology, eds.]

Matriarchy: A Guide to the Future?

Carol (Murf) Moorefield
Kathleen Valentine
1983

Research into our past reveals that our present Separatist Movement was preceded by thousands of years of resistance by women who refused to accept oppression without question. Careful research has led us to trace the beginning of women's resistance to a time which male historians labels (quite appropriately) as 'pre-history.' Before his story began, we had Her Story, the story of the Matriarchy; that of strong women living separately from men; creating their own society, technology, religion; and building their own cities.

This herstory of independent living, creativity, and peaceful strength is important for Separatists to reclaim for several reasons. First, we need not repeat the mistakes that led us to a position of an oppressed group within the patriarchy. Second, our knowledge will enable us to move forward from a position of strength by building upon the skills and knowledge held by our Matriarchal Foremothers. Third, by examination of cultures different from our own, we can develop new ways of thinking which will help us to

159

overcome our Patriarchal upbringing.

In this article we articulate some of the theories we are developing while researching our Matriarchal past. Our theories are built upon research in libraries and museums, combined with the oral traditions of the Women's religion of Wicca which have been passed down from mother to daughter throughout the generations.

Contrary to the 'We've come a long way Baby' theory, which highlights times of women's worst oppression through the ages, a close examination of Herstory shows that the farther back in time we travel, the greater the role of the Goddess and of women.[1] The roles are interrelated, leading us to believe that she who controls spiritual power also controls temporal power. In some instances we find cultures where remnants of a former Matriarchy exist, in others we find Female Communities which were successfully maintained as separate political entities from one generation to the next. Female societies lived in peaceful coexistence with the Earth and surrounding Universe. In so doing, they created an environment in which women were able to develop, without impediment, a female world view. The view held by Matriarchal Women included seeing themselves as having an intimate connection with the Earth and all life. As the Goddess resides in all things, thus women saw themselves as sisters to the moon, sun, stars, rocks, plants, and animals. Life was seen as cyclic, with reincarnation as the ultimate circle. In conjunction with this universalist perspective, Matriarchists developed a technology, based on psychic skills, which replenished rather than depleted the Earth.

Our Foremothers knew the reality of man's inability to accept women as the creators and civilizers we are. That, combined with the male penchant for violence, caused them to build their societies in isolated or easily defensible areas.

One familiar example of a defensible city is Mesa Verde, located in southwestern Colorado, and built approximately 1066 A.D.. The inhabitants retained remnants of their Matriarchal heritage. This peaceful Indian tribe built their cities inside of caves located high in inaccessible cliffs. They themselves entered and left their dwellings by means of ladders which were withdrawn when threatened by invaders.

The archeological evidence (which is now part of a national park) indicates that the women controlled the agriculture, which was the mainstay of the community. Additionally, the religious societies were separated by sex. Each society had their own meeting place (an underground room called a 'kiva') over which a strict tabu existed against trespass by the other sex. The women held their secrets, including the secret of procreation and crop growth, and retained their power and magic by not revealing the source of their power to men. Consequently, it was recognized that women's first priorities and energies belonged to other women.

It is not known how this group of cities ended, although it is believed that the Cliff Dwellers moved on because of drought. Today's Pueblo Indians (including the Hopi) carry on some of the traditions of the Cliff Dwellers, including the building of apartment-style defensible cities, which are entered by the roof, and many of the religious traditions.

Çatal Hüyük, located in what is now Turkey, is another example of a defensible city. Like Mesa Verde, the women of Çatal Hüyük built their homes 'apartment-style' where they shared interlocking walls. The houses could only be entered through the roof, thus causing attackers to battle anew in each household in order to take over the entire city. When threatened, the inhabitants would withdraw their ladders, leaving invaders standing on the plain facing high walls. When Matriarchal Çatal Hüyük was finally breached, it was through the use of fire, which destroyed the city.

Çatal Hüyük lasted approximately one thousand years, from 6500 B.C. to 5600 B.C.. The archeological evidence shows the earliest inhabitants were women; and in later years, as Patriarchal invaders achieved entrance through violence, the women still outnumbered the males and retained much of the Matriarchal culture.

The relics left by the women of Çatal Hüyük show a peaceful, highly civilized society which worshipped a Goddess as Supreme Being. The archeologists excavated one square mile of the forty-square-mile mound which now marks the location of the city. As the walls were uncovered, intricate painting and wall sculptures were revealed which showed a concern with the Earth and with the animal counterparts who peopled the surrounding areas. The women had carried back the horns of giant cows (whose hornspread was twelve feet across) to decorate their shrines. Goddess figurines of great power shared shrines with the skulls of ancestoresses. A huge wall mural showed the eruption of the nearby volcano, and the sacred obsidian was used to create mirrors for ritual use. Paintings of animal transformation ceremonies, where women became leopards and vice versa, showed a reverence for all life. The burials in red ochre, depicting birth blood, showed a belief in reincarnation. Although the prevalence of shrines to the Goddess (forty in the one square mile excavated) show women who prized spirituality, that spirituality permeated their entire life. Tools and utensils (forks, knives, pottery, as well as weaving) were decorated with sacred symbols. The crops in the agricultural culture (the inhabitants were thought to be vegetarian) were dedicated to the Goddess, as was the weaving and pottery. Although the archeologists have not determined that these women had writing, they have determined that the women did have an intricate set of symbols, which was used extensively.[2]

This archeological dig, which is probably the most extensive evidence of a Matriarchal City, was halted shortly after it was begun, for 'political reasons.'[3] James Mellart, the British archeologist who led the excavation, was asked by the Turkish authorities to leave the country because of a supposed scandal he had been implicated in several years previously. The Çatal Hüyük site has since been left exposed to the elements, and the Matriarchal relics have been destroyed.

Defensible cities were only one method of insuring women-only settlements. Matriarchists often located cities in remote areas where it was unlikely that strangers would chance upon them. This gave rise to accounts scoffed at as 'traveler's tales.' However, the prevalence of tales on a world-wide basis of 'Isles of Women' leads us to realize that our separatist Foremothers (including Sappho) in fact found islands a friendly place to establish communities.

Island sanctuaries served a dual purpose: they provided both physical safety and access to spiritually powerful sites for religious shrines. These communities were often overlooked by Patriarchal raiders, and when attempts at invasion were made, the aggressors were easily picked off as they landed.

These Isles were often referred to as the 'Navels of the World' because of the presence of water on all sides. Living in close proximity to the sea enabled women to study the element water and to realize the relationship of the tides to their own body rhythms. Eventually women were able to merge their consciousness with water in order to control it, as the Empress Jingo of Japan controlled the tides to conquer Korea in approximately 300 B.C..

The accounts of the Romans, who travelled far in extending their empire, often mention the existence of sacred isles of priestesses in the Celtic realms of the North. Strabo wrote of one such isle near the mouth of the Loire River in France, inhabited by women of the Samnite tribe, where no man was allowed to set foot. Strabo related that 'Bacchic' rites were celebrated there; that is, the women participated in sacred sexual practices among themselves. On at least one other isle near Britain there were priestesses who also observed the mother-daughter rites of the death and rebirth of the grain, similar to Demeter-Kore rites in Greece, which included the sacred sexual practices. Mela, a Roman geographer, reported also that on the Isle of Sein near Brittany, nine sacred virgins lived alone, and were often consulted by the respectful mainland population as prophetesses and Keepers of the Sacred Lore.

Closer to home, islands of women were recorded in the Caribbean by early Spanish explorers. Columbus' journal told of Carib Indians who insisted that an Amazon society could be found on the island of Matenino or Mantenino, where women lived alone and engaged in 'male' occupations, including hunting and warfare. Males from nearby islands were allowed to visit solely for mating purposes at specified times; these men later took the boys born of these unions and the Amazons kept the girls. Columbus described this island as being near Hispaniola, and it is sometimes identified with Martinique. It is interesting to note that the labyris, that foremost matriarchal symbol of ancient Crete, was also found among the religious artifacts of some Caribbean societies.

The Spanish also discovered the sacred isle concept in Yucatan religion. In 1517 Hernandez de Cordoba named one such isle the 'Isla Mujeres' because of the large quantity of female idols at the island shrine to Ixchel, goddess of the moon, water, and childbirth. Cozumel, off the eastern Yucatan coast, also had an important shrine and pilgrimage center for Ixchel. By the time of the Spanish conquests, these were no longer solely for women, but the shrines to an important goddess-protector of women indicates a religious thinking similar to that of the Celts with their sacred isles of priestesses.

Myths about isles of women also occur throughout the Far East. The ARABIAN NIGHTS contains a story of a man who marries a strange woman who abruptly flies off to her island home of Wak-Wak where she commands an army of 25,000 strong and beautiful women. Traditional Arab lore placed this island near Borneo, and often versions of the tale mention that men were forbidden to land there.

Tales similar to that of Wak-Wak recur in other Oriental narratives and indicate the probability that they refer to historical, not mythological, places. European travelers record hearing of islands of women off the coasts of Japan, Korea, India, and East Africa near Zanzibar. Alternately, there are stories of women's isles situated in the Pacific Ocean. Jesuit missionaries heard of such islands from the Marianne Islanders; other such isles were described as existing off the Carolinas, Seychelles, Java and New Guinea.

Often included in the stories of female communities were accounts of the women's methods of procreation. Many of the old husband's tales were similar to Columbus' journal entry about Matenino where the males were allowed to visit at prescribed times for the purpose of procreation. However, other persistent myths occur which lead to speculation that ancient women may have had alternate means of conception. Two such myths concern the aforementioned Isle of Wak-Wak, and the Isle known as Gandei in New Guinea. On Wak-Wak the women were said to mate with the winds, while on Gandei they mated with the sacred tree. It is noteworthy that the New Guinea myth of the Gandei was passed down in secret by the men, thus hiding from the women knowledge about Amazons who controlled their own lives, unlike the women of the patriarchal tribe.

As mentioned earlier, Matriarchal women were highly spiritual, observing a 'pagan' religion which permeated all aspects of their lives. The science of the ancients has been labeled magic; perhaps because it was obvious that it worked, but why it worked was concealed from patriarchal observers.

It was essential for the womenfolk to observe and interact with nature in order to create the peaceful, sufficient, efficient communities necessary to maintain a separatist culture. Plants and animals were domesticated to provide a constant food source. Healing was accomplished through knowledge of the herbs in the nearby environment, as well as knowledge of how to direct life energies from one to another (the christians call this the laying on of hands). This same psychic energy may have been used to build the cities and shrines (as seen on Malta, Easter Island and the stone circles of the British Isles). Crafts, weaving, pottery, lapidary, tool-making and writing were invented; and rules of conduct were instituted.

In addition, on special occasions, such as Solstice or Equinox, sacred rites were performed which enabled the women as a group to grow in new ways and to better understand their relationship to Nature. Many of these rites involved a concept known today as theolepsy,[4] whereby women were taught to merge with the Infinite by dissolving the boundaries of the self through singing and dancing, drink and sacred drugs, and sex at prescribed times.[5]

These rituals were the means whereby women were initiated into the use of their psychic powers. As such, the rites themselves, as well as the knowledge imparted, were zealously guarded, and cannot be found in the writings of the patriarchy. There are, however, many references to rites in patriarchal cultures where only women were admitted. These rites were clearly remnants of an earlier Matriarchal heritage.

Women-only rites were common among the ancient Greeks, and were of great antiquity even in classical times, hearkening back to the days before the patriarchal takeover. The Demeter-Kore (mother-daughter) rites often contained rituals to release women's sexual power to make the grain grow. These rituals were conducted throughout the year as the crops reached different stages of growth, such as the Thesmophoria in the fall, the Skirophoria in early summer, and the famous annual Eleusinian Mysteries. No men were allowed into the most sacred parts of these rituals, and Greek writers more than hint about Lesbian sacred sexual practices at these observances.

Similar rituals were conducted in honor of the Greek Goddesses Artemis and Aphrodite as well as the enigmatic male god Dionysos, where originally males were barred from celebrating 'Bacchic' rites. In earliest times, only females of good reputation were allowed to climb the 8,000 foot Mount Parnassus and become maenads who performed orgiastic sacred dances on the heights, drinking wine and shouting 'evoi' as torches waved in the night.

Greece is not the only area where such rituals took place; only a few references can be made from the numerous known instances of female rites. For example, in Crete women danced in sacred groves before a Goddess who sometimes wore a crown of poppies. In Asia Minor, Cotys was worshipped by women with such enthusiasm that her rites became synonymous with 'immoral practices.' There were also hints of Lesbian practices in the American versions of voodoo ceremonies, as well as in many African and Australian ceremonies.

As feminist herstorians now recognize, at some point in antiquity a patriarchal takeover of the motherlands occurred, either through revolts of local men or armed incursions by nomadic patriarchal tribes. At some archeological digs the arrival of the Patriarchs can actually be documented, as in villages where the earliest remains show only female idols, then a burned layer occurs, followed by findings of predominately male idols in the remains.[6] The male takeover appears to have occurred all over the globe at different dates, as numerous Third World takeover myths demonstrate.

For example, on the Nullabor Plain in Australia, tribes today tell the fable of the women who hunted meat. This myth takes place in olden times, when a tribe of women lived together and hunted for food. It is observed that by living thus, the women broke patriarchal law, since they lived without men and followed male occupations. The women, probably holdouts from the patriarchal takeover, refused to change their ways, so that

Tchooroo, the Great Snake, turned them into termites.

In the Brazilian legend of Yurupari, it was related that women held power which was only broken by the action of a hero, Yurupari, who gathered the men and initiated them into a sun cult. It is interesting that the hero never touched a woman sexually. Additionally, at the tip of South America in Patagonia, it was told that in ancient times women ruled, and owned the sacred instruments and the hunting weapons. Tradition says the men finally revolted and massacred the female rulers.

The violence imposed upon Goddess worshippers is evident throughout the world where patriarchists instituted the ceremonies of 'sacrifice' to the Goddess. In order to destroy Matriarchal culture and place fear into the hearts of Goddess Followers, the invaders would select prominent women (often the priestesses, wise women, and virgins) to die a horrible public death for the Goddess. This is particularly evident in Aztec culture where priestesses were skinned alive and their skin donned by male priests in an attempt to steal the power of the priestess. [See 'An Invitation' by Sarah Lucia Hoagland in this anthology, eds.] Other artifacts show women with their breasts removed, their mouths gagged, raped, or their children murdered. This systemic violence was effective in destroying Matriarchal thought as many mothers refused to pass their knowledge and beliefs to their daughters in order to protect them.

As a direct result of the coming of the patriarchs, bands of women arose to defend the motherland, as the so-called 'myths' of Amazons illustrate. Greek classical writers never felt that Amazons were mythological but instead recorded the early Greco-Amazon Wars as actual historical events. It is clear from the sources that the Amazons were not Greek; in fact, the Greeks report Amazons in two distinct major geographical areas of the classical world – Asia and Africa.[7]

The African Amazons dwelt in Western Libya on the large Isle of Hespera on Lake Tritonis. At the time of the Greco-Amazon Wars, these Amazons were not a Separatist society, as they kept husbands who maintained the home while they were off serving in the army or performing other public duties. The Libyan Amazons worshipped the warrior Goddess Neith and the Gorgons were also associated with them in myth.[8] At some point the Libyan Amazons waged war against the patriarchs of Greece, and as the Amazons marched through Egypt, Isis joined the Libyan Queen Myrina as friend and ally.

The Libyans then moved through the Levant towards Asia Minor and the Greek Isles. Legend has it that on the Isle of Lesbos the city Mitylenê was named for the African Queen's sister, and the Africans also gave Samothrace its name, which means 'Sacred Isle.' These Amazons stayed on the Greek Isles for some time until the Greeks dislodged them in an all-out war. Queen Myrina was buried on the Plain of Troy after falling in battle, and the Amazons withdrew to Libya where even as late as Roman times the Matriarchal character of Libyan society was reported to linger still.

Asian Amazons were said to have founded the cities of Cyrene, Thebes, and the Artemis shrine at Ephesus. They were believed to have gotten as far as the gates of Athens in 1256 B.C. before being defeated. Athenians in classical times pointed to the tombs of women warriors along the invasion route, and they observed the annual tribute to the Amazons at the Theseus Festival.

The Greeks also say that somewhere in the East, on the banks of the Thermador in Asia Minor, or even farther on the banks of the Don in Thrace, lived a tribe of Amazons who carried crescent shields and a double-edged ax called the bipennis. These are the Amazons so favored in Greek art, wearing the Scythian cap and often depicted in the act of defeating a Greek warrior.

The Greco-Amazon Wars were considered actual historical events. The hero Theseus considered it a mark of bravery that he conquered Queen Antiope, and Achilles was elevated to hero status because he slew Penthesilea in the Trojan War. It is interesting to note that an actual historical queen, Tomyris, who killed the Persian king Cyrus, is presently being relegated to the role of mythological queen like Antiope and Penthesilea.

Amazingly enough, European travelers, as late as the eighteenth century, continued to report persistent tales of Amazon Tribes in the areas where the 'Greek' Amazons once roamed. Throughout the Caucasus areas and beyond were various reports of Amazons called 'Emmetsh' by Circassians, 'Aë Metzaine' by the Kalmuks, and 'Emmazuhn' by the mountain peoples of Tartary.

Classical India also had Amazon myths, the earliest known being a tale in the MAHA BHARATA, a saga glorifying the exploits of a branch of Aryan invaders in India, and dating back to an oral tradition of perhaps 1500 B.C.. In this story, Raja Aruna enters a land of women under the Rani Paraminta. The women are fighters who ride swift horses and wear pearls along with their weaponry. The Rani can shoot straighter than Aruna, but in the end she submits to the Aryan and marries him. Some commentators feel this story evolved from the Aryan invaders' encounters with native Dravidian women defending their land from the patriarchal onslaught, but in the end losing and being forced to intermingle with the conquerers.

Besides the accounts of Amazons defending the Matriarchy

during the patriarchal takeover, there are also travelers' descriptions of all-female guard units in Third World armies up to present times. These represent remnants of female independence lasting into the patriarchy as separate islands in a sea of masculinism. Male rulers kept these elite corps not because they preferred Butch women, but because the female units hearken back to a time when women ruled, and thus justify the male rule.

The most famous of these guard units was, of course, the Amazon Corps of Dahomey in West Africa. These Amazons, who lived separately from the male army, were respectfully called 'Mi-No' (our Mothers). They continued to fight to keep the little nation of Dahomey free as late as the 1890's. They were also clearly Lesbian, as reports of European travelers and the ever-present, ever horrified, missionaries clearly indicate.

Other African rulers, such as the king of Monomotapa in South East Africa, the king of the Behrs on the Upper Nile, and the Yoruban king in West Africa, also kept separate female guard units. In fact, as late as the 1960's, separate female units fought in the Malawi Independence War and were given an important border province to oversee after freedom was won.[9]

British colonial rulers also related that female elite corps existed in India as late as the nineteenth century, mostly in areas such as Hyderabad and the Deccan where Matriarchal traditions still lingered. Female troops were also observed in other Southeast Asian locales, such as Bangkok, Thailand, and Dutch Bantam.

These units continue to legitimize the male rulers' claim to the throne, and they also retain vestiges of their former prerogatives in the form of religious or political functions, such as casting votes in the king's election or in ruling separate provinces in an empire.

Although some of us, such as the aforementioned guard units, continue to hold a measure of power and/or prestige within the Patriarchy, only in the reestablishment of our own communities will we be free to develop to our fullest potential. Our Matriarchal studies have so far given us but a glance into the alternatives which are open to us. Continuation of these studies, combined with psychic development and exchange of ideas with our sisters, will enable us to develop 'Matriarchal Thinking,' whereby we move beyond the boundaries of our patriarchal training. Hopefully, the study of Herstory will enable us to move forward in the development of Woman-Identified theories, which will, in turn, help us to establish successful Separatist Communities.

Notes

1. For a full elaboration of this theme see Merlin Stone's *When God Was a Woman* (Dial Press, New York, 1976). This book is highly recommended reading for anyone who has not yet done so.
2. Mellart, James, *Çatal Hüyük*, McGraw Hill, New York, 1967.
3. Hamblin, Dora Jane, *Buried Cities and Ancient Treasures*, Simon and Schuster, New York, 1973.
4. For further discussion of the concept of theolepsy, see: Evans, Arthur, *Witchcraft and the Gay Counterculture*, Fag Rag Books, Boston, 1978; and Taylor, G. Rattray, *Sex in History*, Vanguard, New York, 1954. One should carefully note, when researching this topic, that when a writer refers to only women participating in rites involving sacred orgies, then this is clearly a reference to Lesbian rites. Similarly, if a reference is made to 'immoral practices,' the writer is referring to Lesbianism.
5. For further information on women-only festivals in the classical world, see: Harrison, Jane Ellen, *Epilegomena to the Study of Greek Religion*, University Books, New York, 1962; Kiefer, Otto, *Sexual Life in Ancient Rome*, Abbey Library, London, 1976; and Licht, Hans, *Sexual Life in Ancient Greece*, Abbey Library, London, 1971.
6. Many archeology books discuss burned layers without drawing any Matriarchal conclusions; for further information see: Childe, V. Gordon, *Dawn of European Civilization*, Vintage Books, New York, 1957; Redman, Charles C., *The Rise of Civilization: From Early Farmers to Urban Society in the Ancient Near East*, W. H. Freeman & Co., San Francisco, 1978; Trump, D. H., *Prehistory of the Mediterranean*, Yale University Press, New Haven, 1980; Wheeler, Sir Mortimer, *Early India and Pakistan*, Thames and Hudson, London, 1959.
7. Two books which give more detailed information on the classical Amazons while proffering outrageous explanations for the persistence of the 'myth' are: Kanter, Emmanuel, *The Amazons: A Marxian Study*, Charles H. Kerr & Co., Chicago, Illinois, 1926; and Sobel, Donald, *The Amazons of Greek Mythology*, A. S. Barnes & Co., Cranberry, New Jersey, 1972.
8. The Gorgons, who were lead by the famed Medusa (who may have been Myrina), were immortalized in Greek Mythology because of their prowess as warriors. The Greeks lost battle after battle to these women and consequently invented stories to justify their losses. Therefore they turned the Black women into terrifying monsters whose kinky hair grew snakes (a great Matriarchal power symbol). The very sight of a Gorgon turned *men* to stone, so the only defense was to run! The Gorgons were finally defeated by turning their own power against them (facing them with a mirror), as male warriors made no dent in their ranks through conventional warfare.
9. Taylor, Kathryn, *Generations of Denial: 75 Short Biographies of Women in History*, Times Change Press, New York, 1971.

BE-FRIENDING OUR SELVES:
THE PERSONAL IS POLITICAL

Gum Lin and Loy Yi Lung

Kathy Munzer
1982

I want to tell you a story about some wimmin who lived a very long time ago in the part of the world we now call China. The age in which they lived was called 'The Era of The Great Purity,' and it has been described as 'the epoch in which people knew their mothers, but not their fathers.' As the tale was told to me, there simply were no fathers.

Certain things were of great importance to these wimmim of long ago; one was their spirituality. They honored two Goddesses – one called Gum Lin and the other, who was her lover, Loy Yi Lung. The story is sung at the foot of Tai Ma Shan – Great Horse Mountain – of how Gum Lin, a village womyn, and Loy Yi Lung, the daughter of a dragon, saved the village from a long drought. As the land grew drier and drier, Gum Lin discovered a lake whose only access was through a gate. The key to the gate was in the dragon's lair which the dragon jealously guarded. She told Loy Yi Lung of her discovery, and together they cunningly devised a plan to get the key. Loy Yi Lung described how the dragon would crawl out of the lair to listen to her when she sang. So the two went to the dragon's lair and began singing. As the dragon emerged, Gum Lin slipped past and into the lair. While searching for the key, she came across precious jewels and golden coins. She could have taken them for her family and forgotten about the village, but she didn't. She found the key, and with Loy Yi Lung, went to open the water's gate. This is the tale that the wimmin sing as they stand upon the banks of Ye Tiyoh, Wild Swan River, at the foot of Tai Ma Shan.

What is not usually known about this story, however, is that the dragon was so enchanted by Gum Lin and Loy Yi Lung's singing that she offered them some of the jewels and gold to share with the rest of the village if Gum Lin and Loy Yi Lung would return to sing again. It is the story of these jewels that I want to tell.

The village wimmin appointed Priestesses to make altars and create rituals to honor the Goddess Lovers. Each Priestess was given a gemstone that once came from the dragon's cave, and thereafter she was called by the jewel's name. Each gem had its own mystical, protective and healing property and so the Priestess was given a title appropriate to her stone's power. Each wore her namesake gem set into a comb, earring, ring, pendant, or bracelet which blazed bright and gave her a magical, colored aura.

First there was Amber, and she was the Priestess of Healing. The lovely tint of amber is reminiscent of the Sun, and she embodied all the magic and healing powers attached to this star. Amber was forever mixing up herbs and plants into brews and potions for her sisters who fell ill. She would shine her amber ring into the cauldron and there would be much bubbling and smoke and a sweet, mysterious aroma would fill the air. No one stayed sick for very long with Amber around.

Next there was Bloodstone, and she was the Priestess of Defense. Bloodstone could cause severe tempests accompanied by thunder and lightening, and she could make herself invisible just by rubbing her bloodstone earring. This magical trait tended to make her mischievous, and no one quite knew when or where to expect her to show up.

Pearl was the Priestess of Writing, since this jewel of the sea has always been a symbol of wisdom, knowledge, and creativity. She fashioned her own bamboo pens and held classes for the other wimmin to teach them her craft. She always had a new poem or story to share, and the wimmin would say about her, 'She can make you laugh and she can make you cry all in the same breath.'

The Priestess of Music was called Jade since this stone has been known to symbolize knowledge, ingeniousness, and in its resonant quality, music itself. The air was always filled with beautiful sounds because Jade, of course, taught everyone her songs. She fashioned instruments and held daily classes so that all could learn her skill. Jade liked nothing better than performing and would wake everyone up in the morning with her singing and chanting and put everyone to sleep at night with her sweet gentle lullabies.

Another teacher-Priestess was the Priestess of Art – Agate. Because agate often has inclusions of minerals called dendrites, you can see in it fascinating pictures which resemble gardens, forests, or individual plants or trees. Agate would gaze into the stone pendant she wore around her neck and paint or draw the pictures the stone inspired. Her art combined the most beautiful colors and patterns, and everyone's hut was decorated with Agate's artwork.

Emerald was the Priestess of Ancient Wisdom since the emerald is known to bring back memory and promote mental prowess. She was not only a good storyteller of events gone by but she could also, by placing the emerald stone beneath her tongue, foretell the future. Emerald always had a group of wimmin around her wanting to learn more about the lore of their ancestors and asking questions of what was to come.

The last Priestess was Moonstone, the Priestess of Spirituality. Moonstone planned all mystical rituals during the full moon, when her gemstone was the most powerful. The moonstone has always been used in magical rites, and by gazing into the moonstone bracelet Moonstone wore on her wrist, the wimmin could see the moon's reflections and phases. Moonstone was clairvoyant and prophetic, and the full moon dances she planned for the wimmin had many effects. They brought good crops and harvests, aroused tender passions among lovers, and offered good fortune and happiness until the moon became full again.

All in all, these wimmin lived a harmonious life. They moved with the seasons and with the ways of Nature. All the Animals in the forest were their friends, and the Trees gave them shelter and, at times, good advice. They lived by a cool and soothing River and their village was surrounded by high majestic Mountains with rippling Hot Springs where the wimmin could relax and bathe together.

As Gum Lin had been a mortal womyn and Loy Yi Lung immortal, some of the village wimmin were mortal and others immortal; but you couldn't tell by looking at them which was which. Some of the wimmin had but one lover, some had more than one lover, and some wimmin preferred no lovers for periods of time. When entering into a relationship with another womyn, from what I'm told, each womyn had to promise three things – kindness, understanding, and friendship both during the relationship and after the relationship was over. As we all know, that sounds very simple, but sometimes loving someone makes you feel and react more intensely than you might want to. From what I've heard it wasn't exactly perfect even back then, but all the wimmin tried to be open and caring about each other because, after all, no one can really see into another womyn's mind and heart.

From what I understand, there was every kind of Animal imaginable living then, from pterodactyls and brontosauruses to cats and dogs. The Animals and the wimmin worked collectively and enjoyed each other's company, and there was a bond of friendship and loyalty among them. Some of the Trees were very old and wise and the wimmin learned much about deep friendship from them.

What spoiled things for these wimmin of long ago still spoils things for us today: stupid, vain, uncaring, unfeeling, hateful, greedy, bothersome men. The Animals and Trees heard from their sisters of far away that they were being hunted and killed and cut down and burned, and the Mountains were being desecrated. They warned the wimmin of coming disaster, for the men were moving closer and closer to the village.

The Priestesses called a council, and everyone attended. Amber and Emerald thought they would cast spells. Jade and Pearl offered to make weapons. Agate and Moonstone wanted to hold self-defense classes for everyone, and the Animals and Trees promised to help. But in the end they all waited for Bloodstone to speak, because she was, after all, the Priestess of Defense.

Everyone and everything was quiet and all turned toward Bloodstone. Her aura shown a darker green and red than anyone had ever seen. She had a faint smile on her lips and her eyes shown like glowing coals. 'Well my sisters,' she said, 'All of your ideas are worthy; however, if we stay and fight, though I know we will fight valiantly and win, some of the mortal wimmin among us will surely die. To me, not one sister's death will be worth the fight. As you all know, I can make myself invisible by rubbing my gemstone earring. I propose that all of us wimmin who have so much combined magical power conjure up the spirits of Gum Lin and Loy Yi Lung to help us all become invisible and remain invisible forever.'

And so it happened – the men came upon a barren stretch of land where there were no trees, no mountains, no water, no animals, and no wimmin. They did, however, report in their journals, found many years later, that they thought the place enchanted since at night, especially during the full moon, they could see colored lights looking very much like jewels shining suspended in the air. And they heard talking and singing and laughing as if a dance were being held.

Now the wise womyn who told me this tale swears by the Goddess that all lesbians, during the full moon, can see and hear or in some way sense these very same things ... that is, if we really want to.

Finally Out Of Drag

Gutter Dyke Collective
1973

Women are never given the real option of dropping out because they are the first building block of the male society: it is built on their backs. Whether it be economic or emotional, heterosexual women continue to support their men and continue to define their reality through their men's set of values, and continue to be used and abused by those very standards which set one woman against another. Those dykes who think they have dropped out of heterosexual society learn very quickly that 'coming out' on the streets can be a culture shock, a frightening experience of stepping back into the prick's sphere of influence. We find ourselves standing up to a system of morality that labels us queers because we would dare to put our arms around one another in public. A system in which the masculinists have purposefully channelled women into a standard set of sexist values by which we judge one another. We all are the products of rape. Most women continue to agree to that rape physically and psychologically, every day of their lives, and so hold a very low opinion of themselves because deep down inside they know they are being shit on.

By not relating to men on a personal level, the Lesbian or woman-identified-woman likes to think of herself as not giving energy to men because they are of no concern to her, since her *primary* relationships are with other Lesbians. However, by continuing to invite men into their homes, bars, dances; by seeing whom you sleep with as being a personal issue rather than the crux of our sensuality, the *politics* which all Lesbians have in common; by perpetuating the sexist patterns which we have all grown up in – calling one another bitch, chicky, and so on; by continuing to be an *invisible* minority and trying to convince ourselves that we should look like all other women because looking like a dyke would threaten women with a real alternative; by continuing to kow-tow to the same old male standards of beauty and feminine appeal – searching for a blonde blue-eyed lover or judging another Lesbian by the layers of skin that wrap around her body; – we too are being squashed by the male supremacist shitpile.

However, we can choose to struggle with one another in the comfort of our havens and to fight that prick world out there by stepping out from the folds of the invisible feminized masses. We are Lesbians because we love women. We are Dykes because we choose to create a new and open lifestyle to redefine our own images of ourselves. We are daring to challenge those old sexist stereotypes and, in doing so, we open ourselves up to the full brunt of the male supremacist society.

When I first heard the word Dyke it was in the early sixties. I was on a bus crossing town and a gang of tough looking, brassy women bounded onto the bus. The straight men began whispering 'diesel dykes' in their seats, 'cunt-lickers' and other 'cute' numbers like that. To the straight world, it is all black and white anyway. There are the butches and the femmes. All women are the femmes (otherwise they would be competing with the men) and those who try to break free of those stereotypes are called butches, or if they do fit into the grey matter inbetween, they're hippie chicks (meaning you can dress more freely but you are still attached to a man). It has taken many years of gay consciousness raising and struggle to take a derogatory word thrown at us for centuries and take it on in a positive sense. Because taking it on in a positive sense means we can redefine what it does indeed mean to be a dyke. We certainly can widen the definition. Dykes are springing up in every Lesbian community across the country and we sure do represent a varied cross-section of cultures merged into one dyke subculture. I am proud to be called a Dyke now. For me it conveys an image of a strong together Lesbian, one who can express her feminism in public. The time has come to stop blending in with the 'feminized' masses of women, to stop being that invisible minority. Lesbians have gone beyond the concept of 'woman' as so defined for us for eons by the male dominated societies.

They Tried to Make it Personal

Revolutionary Lesbians
1971

A little while ago, my best friend and I became aware of a problem. For a while she had been real uptight about being touched and she stopped responding in her usual easy and self-assured way that she used to when I would stroke or caress her body. So we asked ourselves questions ... what did my giving attention to her body mean? How had she been with other people? How had other people been with her in the past?

We began to see some stuff. For a long time she had always been very 'smooth' about reacting sexually. She'd given alot to the two people who she'd lived with during the 10 years before we did ... one man, and one woman. Both of them had taken alot ... and Sandy gave alot in terms of making them feel at ease ... comforting them. And that's what she did with her body too ... she tried to make them feel at ease and relaxed with her. She told me how the woman she'd lived with would go into fits of depression and self-hate whenever Sandy would tell her that Betty had hurt her ... which meant that Sandy had to comfort Betty, when Betty had hurt *her* . . . and Sandy's needs had to be shoved aside.

We recognized how much this was true of all women . . . that we're constantly comforting, putting aside our own feelings. How we sense, that as women . . . we're not valued by men . . . or by other women, so we make ourselves necessary by giving so much that the other person will be 'grateful' . . .

And then we tried to get at what it meant for Sandy to be loved for the first time, for me to respond to her openly and out of respect that's built on a lot of struggle. We asked what it meant for her to admit our love for each other by responding.

This time it became clear how hard it was for either of us to let the real depth of our love for each other in, . . . because in a society that rips everything away that we value . . . where we're betrayed over and over again when we have opened ourselves up to people and where we have been treated as a piece of meat by men . . . and by male-world women . . . it's real hard to admit to ourselves the love we felt for each other in fear that it would somehow be taken away. We felt ourselves constantly bracing our bodies for the possibility of one of us leaving the other . . . just so we could sort of shrug it off like it didn't mean that much to us anyway. . . .

And to let that love really sink in meant that we would really let ourselves in for FEELING what happened to us . . . and if we did bad things to each other it would HURT. We realized how we had both been testin things out . . . sort of feelin around . . . then numbing ourselves a little – just in case. . . .

But this time we both began to WANT to let all those feelins in. It was real clear that we really cared for each other and that we trusted each other . . . Sandy's body was just testin things out a little more . . . she was making a decision by lettin her body get cranky. Before it had been easy for her just to climb into bed, into an argument, into a 'relationship' and to 'comfort' the other person. She had trained her body to respond acceptably on cue. If she didn't respond right – well then all sorts of things might happen to her. She might have to face the fact that the other person didn't even care enough to notice that something was wrong . . . or she would be noticed and the other person would flee in the face of having to help her – so in order for Sandy to avoid all those terrifying possibilities (and they did terrify her for good reasons) she just got her body to 'behave.' She now talks about it as tho it had been a plane and inside the pilot who would take a nap and just put the controls on 'automatic pilot.'

I got really excited that her body was bein cranky and told her so. She just couldn't believe my reaction – she thought I was puttin her on and she began to cry . . . just from relief. I told her that sure it upset me a little . . . I wasn't used to her saying things like – 'stop – that tickles' or 'no – that doesn't feel nice,' but I was just really happy that she was lettin her body say things to me because I knew what a big thing that was. It meant that she was beginning to let me know her needs . . . her feelins – and she wasn't satisfied to just react to my needs. Our love helped us to love ourselves enough to begin to express our own needs and to ask the other person to take notice. That is real hard for women to do . . . cause that is something we never get to do . . . we are trained from the beginning to be an endless source of compassion and strength for everyone else.

A mother can't give into her cold . . . what the hell would happen to everyone? Look at all the women in 'service' positions . . . GIVE GIVE GIVE. . . . Men use women for this all the time . . . – even if a woman gets raped – she ends up consoling her boyfriend or husband – she reassures him and then hopes he won't hate her because she got raped . . . Women comfort men – they protect them from the world . . . from other men . . . to make it easier for the men. In the business world, the same thing happens . . . you put rows of women between the customer and the executive – if something goes wrong and the customer is furious – who do they yell at – who are they rude to . . . and that happens even when the customer knows what is going on because the people really responsible for things hide. . . . I know women who have been told in their secretary courses that their major purpose is to keep their bosses happy and to keep unwanted people away . . . they have been told that they are office 'wives.'

Everyday Sandy and I go thru this same process . . . asking ourselves what we are feelin – what memories we are having . . . what we think might have made us react the way we did . . . what our parents said about that . . . and we start asking things like who benefits from the way we were trained to act . . . what purpose does such training have, in the end? . . . how does this old value connect up to other things and how does all of this keep things running smoothly? And these questions, and many more are asked about the feelins we are havin or the experiences we are rememberin and tryin to work thru. We don't have our feelins and then at some later date examine them with a fine tooth comb.

What we know is that everything that goes on has a social reason . . . somebody is benefiting from all this shit coming down . . . and if you started talking about your most secret experiences or fantasies – you would soon find out that you ain't the only one . . . so a distinction has been drawn – and values placed on different parts . . . what men say or have been saying for ever is that what happens to you in your gut ... what you experience and others experience every day of their lives ... your whole life ... well that is called 'personal' and that don't mean shit ... because see that just happens to you and what are feelins anyway? Now 'political' well that's somethin else – according to them ... why that's real important ... and takes a lot of brain to follow ... and has to do with things like votin ... or if you are beyond reform politics ... well then it has to do with very HEAVY things ... like Dialectical Materialism and Economics and statistics. . .

BULLSHIT! There ain't no distinction between personal and political ... that distinction only exists for people who have a mighty big gap between what they say they think and what they do every day of their lives. . . .

Yes, they tried to pull it off – they tried to define politics as something abstract and away from you and from your lives. They can't afford for politics to be brought home ... to have us know that things that happen just aren't some sort of personal little events ... for if we begin to start makin connections – if we begin to understand what gets done in the family, in schools, at work, and if the rage that that knowin would release ever got started – why things would really start changin ... there's a lot of really angry women walking around ... and we aren't gonna believe those men (nor their male-world women agents) any longer ... we know that strong women, who are close to their feelins, and who don't have any particular investments in the way things are run, and who have real investments (like their lives) in things changin – who are filled with rage at what has been done and won't accept any excuses ... we know that women like that can tear this disgusting beast to pieces ... and well – that's what I call real political.

Fear

Vivienne Louise
1983

Upon commencement of writing a piece on lesbian separatism I was overwhelmed by numerous themes dancing soberly in my head. The all cleansing rage pulsing through the hearts of wimmin screaming for release from the prison of self-denial. Love of a richer and deeper kind than any professed in matrimonial terms of possession and conquest. Trust that reaches the gutsy planes of spiritual bonding through forthright honesty. The dissipation of patriarchal illusions breaking the shackles of a deadly contract. Decisions ushering in a new and yet very old age conversant with a natural meter and time. Ancient truths made known today through newly awakened vehicles of memory. The power to create and decreate given the constancy of faith, clarity and balance. And fear. That all pervasive entity rendering potential inanimate and driving forward energy into stagnant pools of conciliation and failure.

After due consideration I chose fear as the main theme recognizing its relevance to all issues of lesbian separatism because of its ability to immobilize by gradual weakening, leading to total enfeeblement.

Fear is False Evidence Appearing Real. It is the essence of fascism and the original pillar of patriarchy. Invalidation of internal assessment abilities and total reliance on external judgment is its goal. In other words, it is a controlling mechanism designed to destroy self belief and internal faith, replacing them with desired approval from outside sources. Debilitation results as self-love evaporates in an atmosphere of submissive behavior.

Lesbian separatism is a politic of empowerment. It touts the values of self love and acceptance promoting creativity of spirit and mind. It challenges demons of fear stripping those supporting realities of their intimidating wonder and exposing them as a plague of necrophilic addiction. Radical lesbianism is the reclamation of our most intimate power, the right to walk the planet free from the scourge of patriarchal terror.

As a seasoned activist I am not prepared to say that the disappearance of all men on the planet would also mean the disappearance of patriarchy. Unfortunately there are millions of wimmin who support and practice an ethic of top-bottom and who believe in the validity of fear. As long as trepidation is the song then dissolution will be the dance and helter-skelter the ball at which they're played.

As wimmin in this society we are taught to coddle and pamper our fears. We are encouraged to give in, yielding them full reign in our free will decisions and actions. Confrontation of any sort is not supported and acquiescence of a defenseless mode lauded. This promotes a message of weakness and an acquiescence of powerlessness. The acceptance of passivity leads to a failing sense of self belief and therefore a diminishing consciousness of personal power. It is at this stage that patriarchal values set in. Subscription to these mores is enforced by violence (mental, physical, emotional and spiritual) and promulgation of the lie that there is no relief from this violence. Thus a map with only one dead end road is presented when there are really many roads blocked by the sentry of fear.

Above I listed several issues relating to lesbian separatism: illusions, decisions, herstory, love, trust, rage and power. These areas and many not listed, are compromised daily because of deep pockets of fear.

We swallow illusions about the 'sanctity of ladyhood' like so many candy pills dispensed to troublesome patients. Exposing the destruction barely hidden behind a veil of pretense is disquieting for many of us. To finally see the hatred that men have for wimmin and to understand its relentless persistence is to look into the belly of the monster from within. It is alarming to know that this misogyny perseveres in the face of all placating actions on the part of wimmin.

The battered wife 'shuts up' but is still beaten. The dutiful secretary is punctual, accurate and conscientious. But never receives a raise, bonus or promotion. And in the face of so many contradictions many of us are still just too afraid to look and see.

Making the decision 'not to decide' is deadly. Its daily continuance can only lead to a state of ambiguity and confusion. Not setting values consistent with our own natures forces us to contort to an alien form. We gag on this force-fed slop but persevere in an adherence to its rules.

'Women's fashions' are dictated by men and wimmin in collusion with men. Together they produce clothes that obstruct the natural flow of a woman's body and often cause injury to that body. Rigid determination of 'acceptable sizes' makes it difficult for wimmin outside those boundaries to obtain reasonable clothing. This can lead to various forms of diet control which is often under pressured circumstances and therefore dis-eased. High heeled shoes are notorious for their deleterious effect upon a womon's pelvic region, but thousands of these monstrosities are sold daily.

Here is a clear situation of the power of wimmin to stop a brand of femicide. Simply not to buy these malevolent raiments and to insist, instead, on suitable clothing. But alas the fiend of fear raises its ugly head to cause a foreboding shadow, should wimmin really see the venom housed in those garbs.

Acceptance of a history where wimmin are placed in a position of insignificance cheats us of ancestral memories chiming matriarchal bliss. It denies the yearnings of our souls for ego satiation in the realm of past deeds. Our story, or herstory, has been quieted by destruction and misinterpretation. But I believe that each of us feels this omission and secretly longs for tales of wimmin triumphant.

I am sometimes encouraged in this belief by the gleam in a woman's eye after hearing a tale of heroine victory (that victory may be the independence of a prominent public figure or the exploits of an unconventional family member), or while quietly admiring a little known herstorical personality. The gleam may wax or wane but persists in its clandestine enjoyment.

Why then don't we demand a more full satisfaction? Because to open this box would be the beginning of the end. The end of the lies and consternations. It would bring the whole tangled mess to light and again many of us are afraid of what we might see. Afraid that the distortions are so twisted as to demonstrate nothing short of evil. The evil of hatred, fed and nourished by the actions of the hated.

Love between and among wimmin without supervision of men has always been strongly discouraged by the patriarchy. So much so that many wimmin live their entire lives without knowing the love of another woman, either as a friend, mother, sister or lover. Often any relationships that do exist (outside radical lesbian bondings) are timed for the convenience of some male influence. Even lifetime lesbians who have always known the lavender love of silver nights will closet that love to avoid scenes caused by male discomfort.

Again the demon of fear is controlling even our acknowledgement of something as naturally beautiful as love. Something as wonderfully invigorating as love. Something as exciting and fun as love. While meager rations of heterosexual dominance, exampled by rape and vivisection, are offered in its stead.

To have total trust is to have total honesty. To have total honesty is to have total clarity. And to have total clarity is to be able to see the total picture, detail for detail.

Many wimmin refuse to see the details. Refuse to acknowledge the total picture as evidence of a diabolical plan. Through the promulgation of illusions, indecision, suffocation of herstory and inhibition of love the boys have instituted a systematic identity designation plan. Wimmin are told what to believe, what to think and how to live. This diabolical scheme erodes the essence of personhood creating confusion in our own minds as to who we are. This leads to wimmin playing robot games in relationships seeking warmth from mechanical chill. Without the basis of self knowledge and understanding we are confused as to who 'self' really is. And without clarity on who 'self' is clarity on any other issues is basically out of reach.

Trust is a bonding based on honest lucidity stemming from

the courage to simply look and see. Fear of what we might see inhibits our ability to see at all. As long as we are insisting that apples are oranges we will never have fresh orange juice or homemade apple pie. The object will consistently evade our grasp as we insist upon a reality that simply isn't there.

Wimmin daily place faith and trust in the machinations of the patriarchy. Many give their love to men in an effort to affirm a trusting bond only to have it mocked through infidelity, double standards and mutilation. For men imagine no such equality with wimmin. They are committed to the brotherhood in continuance of the sham. Truth is always unwelcome in a con game, especially when the conee is eager to believe.

A high percentage of rapists in this country are men that the victim knew and trusted. These are men in which these wimmin have placed a large degree of personal belief and faith. They are their fathers, brothers, uncles, husbands, sons, boyfriends, etc. They are men who presently do or at one time did hold a high place in the woman's value system as decent, upstanding and trustworthy. Yet this faith is returned with brutality and desecration. These wimmin's bodies are split apart in the anxious ravings of maniacal conquest. Their very beings are destroyed and yet they persist in believing. Persist in believing that there are good men and there are bad men. Persist in swallowing the moldy tale that some men do respect wimmin and some don't. This persistence continues in the face of a judicial system that fails to prosecute rapists. It persists even though a woman's story is often questioned and she is submitted to a barrage of insensitive interrogation. It persists given the fact that verbally or non-verbally, a woman is usually blamed for the attack.

And even if the rapist is not someone that the particular womon knew, he usually is someone that some other womon knows, trusts and loves.

Surely this is a contradiction worth illumination. Surely anyone can see that men do hate wimmin and exhibit that hatred in a most pervasive way. Surely to place trust in a system, a someone, a being, that violates that trust in ways smacking of misogyny is to disrespect that trust. It is to give that essence a very low value.

Why is such a profound quality as trust continually debased with lies and deception? Because the demon of fear is keeping a close watch on all movements. It is halting any progression that promotes its banishment to the halls of hell. Blocking all movement out of its chains into a new and free reality. Resisting all advancement that demands its expulsion. Because it is in control and intends to remain so, but can only do that through our own complicity.

And then there's the rage. The rage that comes when all delusions are stripped away and naked verity is standing in its wake. The rage that arrives after exposure of the hypocrisies and threatens to overwhelm our major senses. The rage that shudders and shakes our foundation loosening old entrapment and molds.

This rage can allow us to see clearly but first we must experience it. First it must be worked through to its satisfactory conclusion. First its orgasmic heights of death then life must be embraced before its remedial powers can take effect. It is a cleansing rage washing away the confusion and ambiguity. It forces us to vomit all decayed matter in a volcanic eruption of fire and freedom.

Although this rage can bring relief from the ominous weight of self-deception, its intensity is immense. The force field projected from its core is pure lava spewing forth generations of agonized deception.

The force of this rage is enormous in its determination to be loosed. Once released it flees our systems in any way possible, leaving through windows and portals previously unexplored. All ways 'out' are sought and our beings experience a metamorphosis, not unlike the earth after an earthquake, tornado or tidal wave. There is an eradication of what was, making way for what is to be.

But the intensity of this cleansing can be personally all consuming. It can command attention constantly or at intermittent intervals. But it does demand sedulity and internal focus. Wimmin are taught to focus outward not inward and to look therein is to journey in a foreign land. It is to undertake an adventure on an unchartered course through a raging storm.

This rage is occasionally exhibited by wimmin in the justifiable homicide of men. They just get fed up, usually from some form of abuse, and release the rage from its caged jungle. Of course the patriarchy doesn't validate these actions and so they are considered insane or incompetent. But they are really the most sane and competent among us because they have battled the demon of fear and won. For at least one moment in their lives they experienced the cleansing rage and glimpsed its healing properties. They have heard the call from beckoning shores of self-possession and her song will always wax familiar in their minds.

After the purge comes the power. The conscious sense of relief from a bottled demon leads to a path of progressive contentment. It moves us into the vast expanse of our beings and bids us build a new reality. The wreckage of the past becomes the resources for the construction of the future. Knowledge of self, universal centeredness and social responsibility replace the assenting, cajoling servant. We now become empowered, determined spirit-forces marching to a new drummer and creating the dance as we move along.

The ability to create and de-create becomes manifest and the extinction of the patriarchy a matter of course. Through just our self-creation we will render this malevolence impotent and dead. It will die from lack of nourishment for we will be feeding ourselves; an act in direct contradiction to feeding it. We will watch it crumble but only from the corner of our eyes for our full vision will be on the manifestation of our own destinies.

This balance is peace supreme. It is what many claim to seek but are really afraid to have. It is the banishment of illusions, the decision to decide, the reclamation of herstory, the presence of true love and the formation of trusting bonds. It is all power supreme, eternal, ephemeral and beautiful. At this place we will see our true potential and be that potential.

But the road to this place is long and winding. It is strewn with debris and boulders blocking the way to an enlightened destiny. Its tangled vines cast shadows of admonition and punishment but it is the real road to life.

Fear is <u>F</u>alse <u>E</u>vidence <u>A</u>ppearing <u>R</u>eal. Through permeation of its structural essence with courage and determination we can see, feel and live on the shores of universal balance, social consciousness and personal acceptance.

Three Chinese Womyn

Lola Lai Jong
1981

Purpose

This paper is the beginning point to re-claim the life-loving ways of my foremothers: in the time of Ging Guen, my maternal grandmother, who was born and raised in the Kwangtun Province, CHINA, and spent most of her adult life in Shanghai, CHINA; in the time of Hung Puey, my mother, who was born and raised in Shanghai, CHINA, and is living in america; and in the time of Lai Jong, myself, who was born, raised and am living in america.

I will present the atrocity of footbinding with an analysis of the Sado-Ritual Syndrome that Mary Daly has named in *Gyn/Ecology*, and the purity rites and binds of marriage. I will name the individual acts of resistance which my foremothers and myself committed to sabotage the patriarchal system.

Footbinding Atrocity

The mutilation of footbinding was used in China by the patriarchy to create the difference between man and woman.[1] The Myth-Masters were able to assert their superiority and the inferiority of women by physically maiming women in this way. Footbinding guaranteed the immobility of women and bound them to the role of sexual object and breeder.[2]

History indicates that footbinding began sometime between the 9th and 11th centuries when Emperor Li Yu ordered a favorite dancer of the Imperial harem to achieve the 'pointed look.'[3]

> Li Yu had a favored palace concubine named Lovely Maiden who was a slender-waisted beauty and a gifted dancer. He had a six-foot high lotus constructed for her out of gold; it was decorated lavishly with pearls and had a carmine lotus carpet in the center. Lovely Maiden was ordered to bind her feet with white silk cloth to make the tips look like the points of a moon sickle. She then danced in the center of the lotus whirling about like a rising cloud.[4]

Thus, Emperor Li Yu tricked women into identifying beauty and dancing with bound feet.[5] The truth is there were less and less great dancers after footbinding started.[6]

'The Myth-Masters and other males who wielded economic and political power had decided that maimed female feet were essential for male approval and marriageability.'[7] Around the age of 7, a young girl's feet were processed for marriage.

> ... The bandage, about two inches wide and ten feet long, was wrapped in the following way. One end was placed on the inside of the instep, and from there it was carried over the small toes so as to force the toes in and towards the sole. The large toe was left unbound. The bandage was then wrapped around the heel so forcefully that heel and toes were drawn closer together. The process was then repeated from the

beginning until the entire bandage had been applied.
The foot of the young child was subjected to a coercive
and unremitting pressure, for the object was not merely
to confine the foot but to make the toes bend under
and into the sole and bring the heel and sole as close
together as physically possible.[8]

This mutilation took about 2 years to complete – the reapplication
of medicine, tightening the bandages as the '. . . flesh often became
putrescent during the binding and portions sloughed off from the
sole; sometimes one or more toes dropped off.'[9]

Then the Myth-Masters said, the bloody flesh-rotting stumps*
that once were feet would arouse the erotic passion in men, and
named them 'Lotus Hooks'; the lotus is the emblem of purity.[10]
The Myth-Masters dictated manuals on the concealment and
mystery of the proper care of the 'lotus hooks'; proper ways for
footbound women to sit and 'walk'; the art of the shoes; different
ways for men to sexually appreciate these mutilations, with advice
to them against removing the bindings so as to not destroy the
'beauty' – all this done to detract from the horror of the atrocity.

What the emperor sets, the nobility copies, and the lower classes
do their best to emulate.[11] (The lower a woman's class, the more
work she had to do, the larger her feet.[12]) By the 12th century,
women felt forced to carry out this atrocity on their daughters
because of the fear that men would find their daughters
unattractive and would not marry them. This served to fulfill two
more elements of the Sado-Ritual Syndrome: total erasure of male
responsibility in carrying out this mutilation, and women being
forced to become token torturers of their daughters.

The Myth-Masters referred to footbinding as a 'small perversion,' 'a curious erotic custom'; terms which minimized and
belittled the facts of this atrocity. This ritual mutilation quickly
gained normality and remained so for almost 10 centuries.[13]

The truth is that this maiming of women was deliberate. The

---

* 'Bound feet were crippled and excruciatingly painful. The woman was
actually "walking" on the outside of toes which had been bent under into
the sole of the foot. The heel and instep of the foot resembled the sole and
heel of a high-heeled boot. Hard callouses formed; toenails grew into the
skin; the feet were pus-filled and bloody; circulation was virtually
stopped. The footbound woman hobbled along, leaning on a cane,
against a wall, against a servant. To keep her balance she took very short
steps. She was actually falling with every step and catching herself with
the next . . .' (See Andrea Dworkin, *Woman Hating*, New York: E. P.
Dutton, 1974, p. 101.)

patriarchs needed a way to isolate women 'to ensure female chastity, fidelity and the legitimacy of children . . .'[14] to control our thoughts by controlling our exposure to the world . . . to control our movements . . . to control our education . . . to control our bodies . . . to control our lives.

Footbinding Resistance

Though the date is not precise, I have reason to believe that Ging Guen, my maternal grandmother, was born around 1900–1903. Her family was considered lower merchant class: the family business was a resale shop. When Ging Guen was between 9–12 years old, her feet were prepared for marriage through the male-defined ritual atrocity of footbinding.

Ging Guen was a resistor to the Will of the Male-Masters. She loosened the bandages as she sat behind the counter of the store every day. Several times, she took off the medicine bandages and hid them under the counter (later to be swept away by the servants, whose feet the Male-Masters allowed to grow naturally because they were needed to carry on the work). By these acts, Ging Guen was making a statement against the patriarchy: She would not tolerate the pain and deformity of the footbinding mutilation. Further, she was careful to imitate the walk of footbound women – the small tottering steps, the pained movement of the hip – and successfully hid her sabotage under the floor-length baggy pants and dresses that were worn by women in her time. Hung Puey, my mother, witnessed that Ging Guen was able to free all but the two smallest toes on both her feet.

I found other evidence of resistance to the Master's Plan of footbinding. The Myth-Masters' dominant formula of the thrice-obeying woman* was seriously challenged by the encouragement of women's literacy during the late Ming and early Ch'ing dynasties. The scholar-officials reacted to this challenge by directing didactic works at an audience of literate women to tell women how they should behave rather than accepting how they actually did. Most notable was Lü K'un, whose ambiguous attitudes toward women caused him to acknowledge that women were intelligent be-ings, while still reflecting the old beliefs of women's timidity, irresponsibility and limited moral capacities.[15]

* to '. . . fathers or elder brothers in youth, to husbands in marriage, and to sons after the husbands' death.' (See Joanna F. Handlin, 'Lü K'un's New Audience: The Influence of Women's Literacy on Sixteenth-Century Thought,' *Women in Chinese Society*, eds. Margery Wolf and Roxane Witke, (Stanford, CA: Stanford University Press, 1975), p. 13.)

This controversy was further stirred up in the late 18th century when the urban elite were influenced by Western attitudes and examples of Western women. Scholar-officials began to speak out against footbinding in the 1830's.

By 1897, a girls' school under the direction of Li Kuei, and an anti-footbinding society were established by a group of reformers who published Shih-wu-pai (The Chinese progress).[16] The 1898 Reform Movement advocated changes in the treatment of women among other Western-inspired reforms.

One vanguard thinker of this time was Ch'iu Chin. Though she combined feminist and revolutionary commitments, Ch'iu Chin held, as her main theme, the intense and total rejection of the traditional role of women.[17] According to one source, Ch'iu Chin helped form a natural-foot society after the Boxer Rebellion (1900–1901).[18]

> By 1911 at least 21 Chinese and nine missionary schools for girls had been established in Shanghai . . . As a result there were a sizeable number of girl students and women teachers who took part in demonstrations and other political activities and founded their own associations and their own press. . .[19]

But leftist women subordinated feminist goals to the broader one of social revolution,[20] which ultimately ended the 10 centuries of the footbinding atrocity. This is significant because footbinding did not end because it was recognized as a ritual mutilation of women, but it was stopped because women's productive labor was needed to successfully accomplish the Revolution.

Marriage Ritual

When Ging Guen was 13–14 years old, in anticipation of the onset of menses, her picture was passed to a matchmaker. The sale of the bride was negotiated between her family and that of the potential groom through the matchmaker. The groom's family agreed to pay an amount of money to her family for a pure bride. In a show of confidence of a pure product, Ging Guen's family used the money to purchase a sofa, comforters, pillows, china and bedspreads for the couple. The detail in which this ritual was practiced reflected the wealth and class of the families involved.

As if footbinding was not enough, the Male-Masters dictated a ritual packaging of the bride on the eve of the wedding. Women-servants, who specialized in preparing the bride for marriage, carried out the orders of the patriarchs. Ging Guen's body was bound with strips of cloth tied together in knots. The Myth-Masters said that this was necessary to prevent anyone from stealing her purity before the wedding. If any of the knots were loosened, the patriarchs would have beaten her. Within this binding was tucked a lucky-money envelope with a white handkerchief in it. (This handkerchief would later be used to gather proof of her virginity for the groom's family.) Then, Ging Guen and the servants went into the garden for the ritual of mourning the death of her childhood days, to prepare her for the role of a dutiful wife. It was also the last opportunity for her to play as a child with other children.

Three days after the wedding, Ging Guen's mother went to the house of the groom's family, where, by the judgment of the groom's family, she was rewarded several pigs to honor the proof of purity on the handkerchief. Ging Guen was ritually bathed and returned home with her mother where the pigs were roasted and the town was invited to join in the celebration of this significance.

In 1920, Ging Guen gave birth to Hung Puey in Canton. Later, the family moved to Shanghai, the center of many feminist activities, and Hung Puey grew up in a more liberated atmosphere. Her feet remained natural and her father, an educated man, advocated schooling for Hung Puey. However, the marriage ritual was still practiced by her family, and at 15 years of age, Hung Puey was sold for marriage in a manner quite similar to that of her mother.

Marriage Resistance

Hung Puey was subjected to many beatings because she liked to read instead of performing the duties of the obedient wife. According to the rule of the Myth-Masters, these beatings were carried out mostly by the mother-in-law. Hung Puey's husband also beat her because he said she was silly and her head was full of dreams.

Hung Puey was a resistor! She did not want to continue to tolerate this abuse, which continued to escalate for reasons I am not mentioning in this passage. After two years of this oppressive treatment, Hung Puey spoke with Ging Guen about committing suicide.

In the essay, 'Women and Suicide in China' by Margery Wolf,[21] we learn that suicide was considered an act that implicates others and was honored as a proper response to a variety of problems that offered no other solutions.[22] 'For a woman . . . (suicide) . . . is the most damning public accusation she can make of her mother-in-law, [and] her husband . . .'[23]

> To bring such disgrace to one's husband's family and so much trouble to one's natal family would not be likely to alleviate a survivor's original wretchedness. Male representatives from her natal family must, for their own face, indignantly demand explanations and guarantees of better treatment from her parents-in-law, no matter how 'inconvenient' bad relations with the in-laws might be. The girl must be taken home to recuperate (and probably to be berated for her hasty actions) and complicated negotiations must commence over her return, a journey her male relatives may be even more eager to arrange than her in-laws. By the time she returns, her husband's family has been humiliated by the negotiations, and by the gossip of curious neighbors; her mother-in-law has heard her treatment of her son's wife openly discussed by her women friends; and worse yet, the older woman may discover her son (who considers her responsible for managing his wife) looking at her askance. The family, as individuals and as a group, will resent this adverse publicity and the continuing attention the slightest row in the family brings. They are unlikely to feel very charitable toward the young woman who has caused them so much trouble.[24]

With Ging Guen's support, Hung Puey divorced herself from the abusive marriage and soon pursued an apprenticeship to become a dentist, vowing never to marry again. However, the attitudes of the Male-Masters pervaded and Ging Guen continued to advise Hung Puey to remarry. In 1947, Hung Puey honored her parents and married again, rising the morning after the wedding to pass the final exam and earn the certificate of dentist. In 1948, Hung Puey gave birth to my Sister, Sei Jong. Born in the USA and raised in Shanghai, Hung Puey's husband returned to the USA in 1948 to escape what he feared might be communist retaliation for his American citizenship. They joined him in January, 1949.

In 1949, Hung Puey gave birth to me. Even with the liberated attitudes toward American women in the 1960's and 1970's on the issue of marriage, my picture was requested by matchmakers when I was 15 years old. My mother held firm on her decision that I would choose whom I wanted to marry. In 1970, I married a man who was acceptable to my parents, and tolerable to me. To marry or not was not seen as an option at that time, and illustrates how pervasive the rule of the Myth-Masters was in my life. I had felt that who I had to be as dutiful daughter, wife, and mother, was not my perception of who I was. My focus was to honor my parents at the cost of denying my Lesbianism.

I am a resistor! In 1975, I learned more about the lives of Lesbians, and the music and literature of wimmin. I reflect now to the first time I heard Margie Adam's song, 'Best Friend (The Unicorn Song).' When she sang,

> ... And now that I am grown, my best friend lives
> inside of me
> The others smile at me and call me crazy
> But I am not upset, for long ago I found the key
> I've always known their seeing must be hazy ...
> Seeing is believing in the things you see
> Loving is believing in the ones you love*

I knew there were other wimmin who had felt the differences, and sighed in relief at the sanity of that statement. I began to focus on re-defining, in my own terms, what it meant for me to be a womon.

I noticed how often the topic of conversation was about men, and how quickly silence infected a conversation about wimmin. I often heard the Myth-Masters dismissing wimmin's perceptions as man-hating, silly, evil, naïve, insane. I felt the hopelessness from the physical maiming and mutilation committed against wimmin and I asked why the Male-Masters were so afraid of the power of wimmin that they had to hurt us like that. I found the truth: There is no reason. The Male-Masters destroyed our Goddesses and have mis-defined the images of our strength to that of Evil Eve and the Virgin Mary. The Myth-Masters have ordered cruel physical and mental atrocities to enforce their domination of wimmin.

In 1977, I broke out of the silencing that the patriarchy uses to enforce the rule of death-worship. I recognized that I had the power to stop internalizing the patriarchal misconception of womon as sexual object and breeder – to reject the divisions that they have imposed between myself and other wimmin. In working to break the division between myself and my mother, I learned that my foremothers and I were subjected to and celebrate our

* (See Margie Adam, 'Best Friend [The Unicorn Song].' *Margie Adam: Songwriter*, (Dixon CA: Pleiades Records, 1976).

resistance as acts of sabotage to the Will of the Masters. It was that resistance which has allowed me to affirm my lesbianism and my separatism.

With the support of other Lesbians who believe in the autonomy of wimmin, I focus my power to demand the right of wimmin to define ourselves, un-learn the lies and re-learn the truth of our life-loving ways.

Acknowledgments

I thank my mother, Hung Puey, for her patient support, for giving me information that had been silenced, and for trusting me to see the truth.

Notes

1. Andrea Dworkin, *Woman Hating* (New York: E. P. Dutton, 1974), p. 103.

2. *Ibid.*, p. 96.

3. *Ibid.*

4. Howard S. Levy, *Chinese Footbinding: The History of a Curious Erotic Custom* (New York: W. Rawls, 1966), p. 39.

5. Mary Daly, *Gyn/Ecology: The Metaethics of Radical Feminism* (Boston: Beacon Press, 1978), p. 149.

6. R. H. Van Gulik, *Sexual Life in Ancient China* (Leiden, Netherlands: E. J. Brill, 1961), p. 218.

7. Daly, p. 140.

8. Dworkin, pp. 98–99.

9. Levy, p. 26.

10. Maria Leach, ed., Jerome Fried, assoc. ed., *Funk and Wagnalls Standard Dictionary of Folklore, Mythology, and Legend* (New York: Funk and Wagnalls, 1972), pp. 645–47.

11. Dworkin, p. 103.

12. *Ibid.*

13. Daly, p. 141.

14. Dworkin, p. 103.

15. Margery Wolf and Roxane Witke, eds., *Women in Chinese Society* (Stanford, CA: Stanford University Press, 1975), p. 2. This is a collection of essays which came out of the 1973 Conference on Women in Chinese Society, held in San Francisco under the sponsorship of the Joint Committee on Contemporary China of the Social Science Research Council and the American Council of Learned Societies.

16. Mary Backus Rankin, 'The Emergence of Women at the End of the Ch'ing: The Case of Ch'iu Chin,' *Women in Chinese Society*, eds. Margery Wolf and Roxane Witke, (Stanford, CA: Stanford University Press, 1975), p. 54.

17. *Ibid.*, p. 57.
18. *Ibid.*, p. 48.
19. *Ibid.*, p. 54.
20. *Ibid.*, p. 40.
21. Margery Wolf, 'Women and Suicide in China,' *Women in Chinese Society*, eds. Margery Wolf and Roxane Witke, (Stanford, CA: Stanford University Press, 1975), p. 112.
22. *Ibid.*
23. *Ibid.*
24. *Ibid.*, p. 113.

Bibliography

Adam, Margie. *Margie Adam: Songwriter*. Dixon, CA: Pleiades Records, 1976.

Daly, Mary. *Gyn/Ecology: The Metaethics of Radical Feminism*. Boston: Beacon Press, 1978.

Dworkin, Andrea. *Woman Hating*. New York: E. P. Dutton, 1974.

Fitzgerald, C. P. *The Horizon History of China*. Norman Kotker (ed.). New York: American Heritage Publishing Co., Inc, 1969.

Leach, Maria (ed.), Fried, Jerome (assoc. ed.). *Funk and Wagnalls Standard Dictionary of Folklore, Mythology and Legend*. New York: Funk and Wagnalls, 1972.

Levy, Howard S. *Chinese Footbinding: The History of a Curious Erotic Custom*. New York: W. Rawls, 1966.

Schram, Stuart. *Mao-Tse-Tung*. New York: Simon and Schuster, 1966.

Van Gulik, R. H. *Sexual Life in Ancient China*. Leiden, Netherlands: E. J. Brill, 1961.

Wolf, Margery, and Witke, Roxane (eds.). *Women in Chinese Society*. Stanford, CA: Stanford University Press, 1975.

Craziness as a Source of Separatism[*]

Joyce Trebilcot
1983

I begin with a brief description of the events I label 'being crazy.' I am remembering primarily my life of the late 1950's and early 1960's, when I was in my late twenties.

[*] This essay is closely related to an earlier piece, 'Craziness and the Concept of Rape,' *WomanSpirit* 34 (Winter 1982).

The core experience was largely auditory. (Mary Daly [follow-
ing Nelle Morton's idea of 'hearing into being,' eds.] says 'In the
beginning is the hearing.') There were two stages. First, intrusion.
Men – male voices – would overhear my thoughts and want to get
in. The second stage was control. The invaders not only wanted to
get in, they wanted to take me over once they were in – there is
something they wanted to make me do. So they would scream
'Talk! Talk!' and I would be unable (as I thought then) to do what
they wanted, or (as I think now) I would refuse to do it. This then
is the core of the craziness – invasion and control, and the threat
of invasion and control.

I was drawn to participate, to allow the connection to happen,
but at the same time I would repeatedly block. I was drawn
because of the lightness and power of participation, and because
of my values – acquired primarily in Berkeley during the 'Beatnik'
time as a street person and student of dance and philosophy –
which made participating in 'ecstatic communion,' whether
through drugs or religion or art or sex or some other means, the
highest and consuming priority. Consciously, I accepted this
'experience ethic' (although I wouldn't then have put it in quite
the words I use here), but nevertheless (or perhaps even
'therefore'?), I would regularly block when it seemed that intense,
shared experience was in the offing.

As a result, I was in almost continuous emotional turmoil. I
cried a lot, and punished myself, and traveled, moving repeatedly
to new places in order to try again with new groups of people.
Trying to cross over, to move into and remain in a different
consciousness, seemed to me to be the most important, the only,
thing in my life. I kept trying to think about how to do it, to figure
out how to do it, but I never did. I ended up in prison (Rebibbia,
outside of Rome, 1962) where I was hardly able to communicate
at all (no one else spoke English and at first I spoke no Italian).
Throughout it all I was certainly separate.

This separating has its roots way back in my history. Long
before I was aware of hearing the voices of men trying to rape me,
I was subject to control by my mother and resisted it. To cite just
one example, my mother points out that I was rather late in
learning to talk, but that when I did talk, whole sentences, even
paragraphs, came out. What was happening, as she and I both
understand it now, is that my refusing to talk was a way of my
resisting her control of me. Mother wanted the baby to speak, but
the baby wouldn't do it. Later, I wouldn't say what men wanted
me to. And still later, as an academic, I have had 'writing blocks,'
refusing to write and publish philosophy papers in order to show
that I can survive, even as an academic, without doing what they

want me to do. I now understand all these refusals as resistances to rape, that is, to invasion and control by others.

My interpretation of these experiences has shifted over the years. At the most painful time, it seemed to me that what was going on was that I wanted to do what they wanted me to, I wanted to participate in what was going on, but I simply could not, I was unable, I did not know how. I had the sense that there was a trick to it, something I had to learn. I now understand this nonparticipation not as inability, but as refusal: it is not that I *could* not take part, but that I *would* not. And the reason I would not is that I wanted to protect myself from the assault, from the intrusion, from the loss of my own will. So I think now that while I at that time experienced myself as being unable to do something I wanted to do, I was in fact taking good care of myself. I resisted in order to continue as an individual – in order not to be submerged, subjected, merged.

The patriarchal term 'crazy' applies to all this, first, because I was certainly behaving in ways Western patriarchy takes to be typical of craziness – raving and crying. And when I talked about what was happening to me, my talk was 'crazy talk.' And I expect the conflict itself – between seeking and resisting psychic touching – counts as crazy, although there is not much discussion of that in patriarchy (but see Doris Lessing, *The Four-Gated City*). One who just merges and submerges is not crazy, and one who just refuses isn't either. The craziness is to keep putting yourself in the middle of the conflict, which is what I kept doing, in the hope of getting through it. (Later, of course, I learned to avoid the conflict, and for years now I've mostly stayed away from it.)

Now the part of all this which is a source of separatism is not the hearing of voices, or the being in conflict, or the running and crying; it is that deep-seated tendency to resist the rapist, to resist penetration. This resistance to control, which is essential to my kind of craziness but not exhaustive of it, is a preparation for lesbian separatism.

It is a preparation for the separatism part of lesbian separatism, that is, not for the lesbian part. Lesbian separatism consists not only in separation from men and from patriarchy but also in the creation of separatist spaces in concert with other lesbians. The craziness I have been discussing not only provides no preparation for this joining together, it makes one wary that the same conflict experienced on the occasion of psychic touching in patriarchy will (and it is true, it sometimes does) occur in lesbian space and so require a backing away even from separatists.

So making a commitment to separatism does not stop what they call craziness. The intrusive voices, the conflict, even the screaming and crying can all happen in separatist space as in patriarchy. There are some differences though. The most important is that lesbian separatists can be expected to be respectful, even supportive, of craziness – the kind I have described here and other kinds as well. Separatist culture can change the meanings not only of differences of race and class and physical ability and appearance; it also, surely, can change the meanings of differences in the ways we are spiritually (psychically, emotionally). I don't mean that the changes are already made. I do mean that there is hope here, as there is not in patriarchy – hope that the refusal to be controlled, which is at the heart of the craziness, may respectfully be given space.

My Poem

Rebecca Lillian
1981

This is a poem sneaked
off the library's IBM Correcting Selectric II
while no one else is in the office.

This is a poem to give myself
something, anything like my life to read
while I shelve 'progressive' books
that assume weddings, and Christmas.

This is a poem for me to read
while I write notices for books
overdue.

This poem is overdue.

This is a poem to read aloud
to finally hear the words JEWISH LESBIAN
even if spoken by me,
while everyone else is out to lunch.

This poem is my lunch.

This is a poem to steal copies of
off the library's Xerox machine
so I can give one to each sister who tells me

that separatism is too narrow
that I'm too negative just because
after
a day of shelving and processing and staring through
books that assume weddings, and Christmas
and after
eating my own damn poetry for lunch,
sometimes I want no more windows
only mirrors.

This is a poem for my mother
(who won't see it)
because she taught me
to believe that I am not Chosen,
but *choosing.*

This is a poem with my power
to separate myself,
and connect myself
from/with whom I choose
before anyone gets a chance
to do it for me.

Be-Friending: The Lust to Share Happiness

Mary Daly
1984

Separatism: 'a disposition toward secession or schism; especially: advocacy of withdrawal from a parent group (as a church).' *Webster's Third New International Dictionary of the English Language*

Separatism (Radical Feminist): 'a necessary disposition toward separation from the causes of fragmentation; especially: advocacy of withdrawal from all parasitic groups (as a church), for the purpose of gynophilic/biophilic communication.' *Webster's First New Intergalactic, Wickedary of the English Language*

Happiness implies biophilic communication. Such communication is ontological, implying deep interconnectedness with all be-ing. This interconnectedness can be expressed as follows:

> Everything that IS is connected with everything else that IS.

Crones will recall the 'first law of ecology,' as expressed by Barry Commoner, namely: 'Everything is connected to everything else.'[1] While this is a useful maxim as it stands, there is also something left unexpressed, namely the fact of disconnectedness, the breaking of the flow of natural interconnectedness, the manufacture of fractures of the Foreground Fraternity.

As a consequence of this fracturing there are, in fact, 'things' that are not biophilically connected. On the physical level, one need only think of plutonium, of agent orange, of the increasing quantity of hazardous wastes. On the psychic level, there are the plastic feelings, pseudo-virtues, and warped ideas discussed in the Pyrospheres. These products of the Predatory State ARE NOT, in the sense that they do not participate in the biophilic flow of be-ing. Of course they 'are there,' as barriers to our Realization of powers of be-ing. Only through such Realization can radical ontological communication be dis-covered. Analysis of this process requires cutting through the snarls that keep women in the State of Separation.

Separation and Reversal

One of the basic blocks to Be-Friending, that is, to radical ontological communication among women, is the embedded fear of separation. Terrified of the dreadful thing which in fact has already happened (although this event is unacknowledged), that is, of separation from their Selves, women in the Possessed state dread separation from their separaters/fracturers/batterers/flatterers. Therefore they are horrified by such words as the label 'separatist.'

Women confined in the phallic State of Separation, then, are characterized/crippled by inability to identify the agents of Self-blocking separation. They are victimized by the strategy of reversal. Just as the label 'man-hater' in Woman-Hating Society functions to stop thought, so also the negatively charged use of the label 'separatist' within the State of Separation hinders women from Be-Friending.

It is necessary to recognize that the life-blockers who have instituted the State of Lechery are radically separated from the natural harmony of the universe. Women who separate our Selves from the blockheads/blockhearts whose intent is to block our

Unfolding, our Happiness, do so out of radical commitment to communication. It is precisely the commitment and capacity for ontological communication that is feared by the blockocratic rulers, for this is what they lack.

Metapatriarchal women, who choose biophilic communication, understand that the foreground label 'separatist' will be used against us. The question is whether we choose to expend energy refuting this, or to 'save' energy by ignoring it, or to understand this word as a Labrys which we can sharpen and use.

The expenditure of gynergy in refutation is kept at a minimum by Shrewd Scolds. Wanton women understand that this is a waste, and even as Gorgons and Amazons we recognize that fixation on refuting is ultimately re-fusion with the sappers/drainers. The second alternative, ignoring the label, is functional only if one is truly ignorant. As worldly/Other-worldly Nag-Gnostics, however, we do *know* about the prevailing prattle-battle; we are not ignorant of this. To totally suppress this knowledge, to pretend it isn't there, is mind-mutilating.

The Metamorphic option, then, would seem to be the third, that is, to use the term *separatism* as our Labrys. On the one hand, it Names phallic separatism, which blocks and bars Life-Lust – the desire for ontological communication. On the other hand, it Names the choice of women to break from the artificial context of phallic separatism in order to affirm and live our radical connectedness in biophilic be-ing.

As a name for the movement of Metamorphosing women, therefore, *separatism* is what I would call a 'second order' word. For it does not emphasize the direction, or final cause, of our movement, which is ontological Metamorphosis itself, but rather an essential prerequisite of this movement under the conditions of patriarchy. Since, under these conditions, separation from those forces that cut us off from be-ing is necessary, it is not inaccurate for a radical feminist to call her Self a separatist. This name, however, unless used in a context of Lusty words, is inadequate. Since the whole point of feminist separation is biophilic communication/participation in Be-ing, it is bio-logical to conclude that these context-providing words will be Other words – words that signify such transcendent communication, for example, Spinster, Webster, Brewster, Fate, Muse.

For metapatterning women to wield the word *separatism* as a true Labrys, moreover, its positive meanings must be understood in conjunction with phallic separatism – the condition which makes metapatriarchal separation necessary. It is essential, therefore, to consider the meaning of phallic separatism.

Phallic Separatism

Recalling the description of cancer cells as characterized by a 'gross inability to communicate,' Websters may decide to consider the analogy with cancer as a tool for description of the phallocratic society. Crones have observed that there is a disorder at the very core of patriarchal consciousness, and that this consciousness both engenders and is engendered by phallo-centric myths, ideologies, and institutions in an endless necrophilic circle of separation and return. If there can be said to be a 'connecting thread' or commonality among all of these phenomena, that commonality is their disconnectedness from biophilic purpose.

The cancer analogy for contemporary society is widespread, of course. Few connect it with phallicism, however. Yet the somewhat accurate images in the contemporary imagination of how cancer 'works' expose a great deal. In the Prologue to Robin Cook's medical thriller, *Fever*, there is a vivid description of poisonous molecules of benzene attacking cells in the bone marrow of a twelve-year-old girl. As Cook describes the event:

> The [attacked] cell instantly divided and the resulting daughter cells had the same defect. No longer did they listen to the mysterious central control and mature into normal white blood cells. Instead they responded to an unfettered urge to reproduce their altered selves. Although they appeared to be relatively normal within the marrow, they were different from other young blood cells. The usual surface stickiness was absent, and they absorbed nutrients at an alarmingly selfish rate. They had become parasites within their own house.[2]

As a parable, this description can be Prudently applied as follows: Within the Virulent State of phallocracy women have been attacked and divided against our Selves. From the earliest times of the patriarchy countless mothers have been broken, and the resulting broken daughters have carried on the chain of fragmentation. No longer have the broken daughters been able to listen unhindered to the 'mysterious' telic centering principle within and become fully Self-actualizing women. Instead, they have been reduced to responding to the fettered/fathered urge to reproduce their altered – that is, patriarchally identified – selves in an endless circle of Self-destruction. Such forcibly altered women have appeared to be normal within the man-made milieu. In these altered women, the usual defenses are absent, and they have absorbed the 'nutrients' of misogynistic messages at an alarming rate. This patriarchal 'selfishness' is the result of starvation for real spiritual and intellectual nutrition.[3] Thus these members of the chain of broken mothers and daughters are unable to communicate unbroken messages of biophilia. Patriarchal women, then, have been reduced to the role of 'parasites' within their own 'house' – this planet, feeding into the mechanisms of reversal, distracting attention from the fact of patriarchal parasitism.

Yet the sources of wholeness are with women.[4] Consequently, many women, even under patriarchal rule, have managed to transmit mixed messages of biophilia and gynophilia to their daughters. The overcoming of phallic separatism, of the programmed separation of all living creatures from the telic centering principle of be-ing, will involve facing the horror of its workings and its effects.

One way of approaching the spiritual carcinogenesis that is patriarchy is to look at its own ideologies, as well as its myths, as the self-fulfilling prophecies which they are. One excellent example is the Aristotelian-Thomistic doctrine that women are 'misbegotten.' Relying upon Aristotle's biology in his work *De Generatione Animalium*, Aquinas, the 'Angelic Doctor,' wrote:

> As regards the individual nature, woman is defective and misbegotten, for the active force in the male seed tends to the production of a perfect likeness in the masculine sex; while the production of woman comes from defect in the active force or from some material indisposition, or even from some external influence; such as that of a south wind, which is moist, as the Philosopher [Aristotle] observes.[5]

On one level, many Hags have seen this as a laughable reversal, at which they can righteously roar. On another level, it functions also as self-fulfilling prophecy of the man-made woman. In the context of Amazonian analysis, 'misbegotten' as applied to women under patriarchy describes the deformity/conformity of women to male-made models or patterns. Thus women who, like patriarchal males, cannot listen to the telic centering principle within, are – on the foreground level – man-made, made-up, misbegotten. Women in this condition include not only the twice-born Athenas but also those immersed in passive stereotypic femininity.

Women in this Misbegotten State have been assigned to break/divide the daughters, to break in their daughters, to break down their defenses, to cut off their possibilities for Original communication. They are indeed unfettered in carrying out this male-ordered mission. It is important to scrutinize the remainder of the text cited above from Aquinas. He continues:

> On the other hand, as regards human nature in general, woman is not misbegotten, but is included in nature's intention as directed to the work of generation. Now the general intention of nature depends on God, Who is the universal Author of nature. Therefore, in producing nature, God formed not only the male but also the female.[6]

This text can be decoded as follows:

> As regards the man-made construct of 'human nature' in general, patriarchal women are not misbegotten, but are included in 'nature's' intention as necessary for the work of reproduction of the male-identified species. Now the general purpose of 'nature' depends upon patriarchal myth-makers, who are the universal Authors of 'nature'. Therefore, in producing 'nature,' these myth-makers formed not only the stereotypic male, but also the stereotypic female.

Simply stated, what this amounts to is the fact that patriarchally begotten, that is, misbegotten, women, serve patriarchal purposes, blocking the flow of Elemental be-ing. In order to comprehend the processes of Metamorphosing women's separation from this State of Separation – to actualize powers of Be-Friending – it is important to consider the effects of phallic separatism in women's lives.

The Effects of Phallic Separatism
In order to understand the effects of ontological dividedness, it may be helpful to employ a metaphor of wholeness. Returning to the idea of the holograph, Websters note that the basic meaning of this word is 'a document (as a letter, deed, or will) wholly in the handwriting of the person for whom it proceeds and whose act it purports to be.' The life of a wholly Present woman would manifest itself as wholly in her own 'handwriting.' That is, it would be clear that she has been the composer, creator of the Book of her Life. She would acknowledge many friends, Foresisters, contributors, but it would be evident that her words and deeds proceed always from her Self as center of focus and purpose. Gynographers would be able to detect her signature in all of her acts. Such a holographic, hologynic Hag would be an

inspiration, a signal of attainable Happiness.

In fact, Metamorphosing women sometimes experience such integrity. Yet the facts of dividedness are undeniable. Sirens, Sibyls, Soothsayers/Truthsayers must face this separation from our Selves. Feminists, seeking deep and faithful bonding with other women, have frequently been baffled and broken by repeated encounters with this brokenness. Many have experienced inexpressible grief and even despair.

To feminists, one of the most dis-spiriting experiences imaginable is to encounter in a woman an apparent inability to experience moral outrage at the atrocities perpetrated against her sex. This cannot be explained by ignorance of facts, when the facts are presented clearly and cogently. The puzzle is ineffably confounding: here is a woman, yet she seems unable to identify with the oppression of women – a condition which she must have experienced on many levels. She may, in fact, be sensitive to the abuses against almost any other group, while apparently feeling nothing about the common lot of women – in a word, gynocide.

To approach this problem it is helpful to Spiral back to the study of the passions in the Realm of Pyrospheres. Shrewds will have noticed in the Foreground to that Realm that in the traditional listing of the eleven passions, only one passion has no contrary, namely, anger. Unlike such passions as daring and fear, for example, which involve movements toward and from a 'difficult [to avoid] evil' that is not present, anger is a movement of attack upon an evil that is present. According to that analysis, since the 'difficult evil' is present, a movement of withdrawal is not possible.

There is a certain logic in this medieval analysis that should not be overlooked. Of course, Hags know that anger can be converted into such plastic passions as depression, hostility, anxiety. However, so can other passions be transformed into pseudo-emotions. The Nagging question remains: What exactly is different about anger? Is there really no contrary movement? Where does the anger go?

Shrewd women may obtain insight for approaching these questions by observing such phenomena as the current interest in the syndrome called 'multiple-personality disorder.' That this subject is particularly significant in relation to the topic of anger is suggested by the fact that according to one recent survey of some one hundred psychiatrists around the country the vast majority of cases of multiple-personality disorder that were 'seen' were women, and over 90 percent of the patients diagnosed and treated as 'multiples' had been severely abused sexually and/or in other physical ways for long periods during their childhood.[7]

Ellen Hale has pointed out that although multiple-personality has been sensationalized in such popular books as *The Three Faces of Eve* and *Sibyl*, it is currently receiving serious attention by some psychiatrists. Some of these professionals are now admitting that the disorder is far more common than previously acknowledged, partly because the condition has been misdiagnosed, often as the catch-all 'schizophrenia.' Hale cites Dr. Frances C. Howland of the Yale University School of Medicine, who has treated 'multiples' for years. Remarking that the possibilities in situations of danger are to fight back or run away, Dr. Howland stated: 'If you can't do either – as a child cannot – you can only do it symbolically. Dissociation is symbolic flight.'[8] The dissociation manifested in those diagnosed as multiple personalities is extreme. One psychiatrist claims to have identified 'startling differences in the brain waves of the alternate personalities of patients suffering from multiple-personality disorder.' Another study suggested that each personality may have its own memory. 'Multiples' may have abnormally wide vocal ranges and an extraordinary ability to alter speech patterns.[9]

Two of the cases cited by Hale will serve to illustrate the extremity of the abuse of women who become 'multiples.' Natasha (a pseudonym) was raped continually by her father from the time she was two until she turned sixteen. 'Until she was 12, the rapes took place with her mother's passive compliance and often with her active participation.' Natasha seems to have 127 personalities or personality fragments. Another woman, 'Sherry,' was tortured as a child by her father who played 'doctor' with her. His sexual torture of her was so vicious that she bled all over his white jacket. Among her father's other activites was throwing her pet cat into a incinerator.[10]

There is hardly a feminist (none, to my knowledge) who can read or even hear of such material with complete equanimity. One reason for this shared sense of horror may be an implicit recognition that a low-grade form of multiple-personality disorder is very common among women in patriarchal society. Indeed, I suggest that this is the normal/misbegotten condition of women locked into the phallic State of Separation. All women within sadosociety (even those with the most enlightened and well-meaning parents) have been physically abused and starved for healing, inspiring Self-images. Since mind (or soul) and body are not separate entities, such deprivation inevitably has physical effects.

To return to the questions posed above concerning anger, then, I suggest that Shrewds following this line of reasoning can find in the idea of a widespread low-grade multiple-personality disorder among women strong intimations of the answer to our question: What happens to the woman-identified, that is, Self-identified Rage of woman under patriarchy? Since women abused as children cannot fight back or run away, dissociation is a logical solution. I suggest that dissociation is the 'missing contrary' of the passion of anger. Anger can be seen as different from the other passions in this respect, namely, that when it is blocked, its movement or energy splinters into fragments within the psyche. Rage, then, can be seen as a convertible energy form. In the State of Separation this energy in women is frequently converted into the production of dissociated 'other selves.'

If this analysis is correct, then the key to escape from the State of Separation can be found by asking a precise question concerning patriarchally possessed women – women incapable of moral outrage on behalf of their own Selves and other women. The question, simply is: What is it that a patriarchal woman dissociates from? The response that seems most evident to a metapatriarchal thinker is that the dissociation is from her original identity as a woman – not as the sadosociety defines 'woman,' but as an Archaic, Elemental woman, which Jan Raymond has Named 'an original woman.'[11] This response leads to the subject of radical feminist separatism.

Radical Feminist Separatism

Weirds and Websters, wielding the word *separatism* as one of our many Labryses, can use this word to name our intent and actions that powerfully separate us from the Dissociated State, releasing the flow of Elemental energy. Thus understood, separatism is an essential aspect of gynophilic communication, for it separates a woman from the causes of fragmentation – the obstacles, internal and external – which separate her from the flow of integrity within her Self.

We can begin to understand the importance of such separation from the State of Separation by returning to the subject of Rage. We have seen that anger in the traditional sense is a movement of attack against the evil that is present. This raises the question of how the gynocidal evil of phallic separatism is 'present' to a woman.

In an earlier chapter [Chapter Three, 'Beyond Sado-Sublimation: Real Presence,' p. 147, eds.] I discussed the 'presence of absence' that characterizes phallicism. This kind of presence, when it invades a vulnerable woman, has as its target her very integrity of identity. Typically, when a little girl or a grown woman is sexually abused, she blames herself, feeling guilty and ashamed. Anger may not be her immediate reaction, because the internal 'fighting back' which is the passion of anger implies an ability to distinguish the Self and her motives from those of the attacker. The phallic presence of absence, however, translates itself within the attacked/victimized woman's psyche into an internalized presence of absence of the woman's Self. Feeling that she has been stained and defiled by the attack, the victim loses the capacity to Name the attacker and even to Name the event of violation as an attack. In such a case, she has internalized and identified with the evil.[12]

The evil, then, can be so present that it blends with a woman's own idea of herself. In order to attack this attack, she must disconnect her Self from the violator. If she is caught within the maze of patriarchal images of women as weak, despicable, seductive, dirty – images injected in early childhood into every woman within patriarchy – this may be precisely the move she is unable to make. Her incipient Elemental Rage, twisted in upon itself, splinters her soul.

The attack, of course, need not be physical. The perpetual bombardment of women's psyches with overt and subtle insults, often guised as courtesy, consideration, and respect, also inflicts the presence of absence within that immobilizes the impulse to anger. The dissociation that results will not be recognized as such within the State of Separation, which is also the State of Reversal. Rather, it will be accepted and fostered as normal and healthy.

The healing response to this condition is the providing of a *context* that affirms precisely that from which women under patriarchy have been dissociated, that is, identification as Wild, Original women. Feminist separatism, then, is a communal process, affirming the flow of connectedness within each woman – her Presence of Presence.

The history of women's struggles to provide and maintain diverse forms of 'women's space' has been a vivid testimony to the fact that men recognize this to be a crucial issue in the war to control women's minds. Many women, moreover, deceived by rhetoric concerning 'equality' and 'human rights,' have been willing to cede such hard-won space. Sometimes the attack upon women's space originates in socialist circles, whose propagandists manage to persuade white as well as minority women that since some men are oppressed, these men should have access to all feminist gatherings and events. These invasions are justified through ideologies that ignore the meaning and functioning of phallocracy/patriarchy as radical source of other forms of oppression.

Particularly instructive has been the virulent and often vicious undermining by university administrators of the efforts of feminists to reserve some Women's Studies classes for women only. Such classes can provide the occasion for true encounters with Metamemory, for perceiving and reasoning beyond the schemata of 'adult,' i.e., male-authored, memories. They can provide contexts for re-membering beyond civilization, for metapatterning. Therefore they must be undermined. The radical potential of freely thinking women is a threat to the very meaning of a patriarchal university. Indeed, such institutions are dedicated to the maintenance of the 'adult schemata' whose purpose is the destruction of Metamemory.* They are dedicated to the proposition that 'the programme of becoming happy ... cannot be fulfilled.'

It should come as no great shock to Crone-ologists to find that these institutions of 'higher learning,' which make every effort to impede the development of Women's Studies, also undermine Black Studies and 'honor' themselves by giving honorary degrees to fanatic proponents of the nuclear arms race. All of these practices are manifestation of the same program – the denial of the possibility of Happiness. Yet in this sordid setting there is still a struggle for the life of the mind. These institutions possess important re-sources for the stimulation of such life. Therefore, they remain an essential arena – a battleground, in fact – of the struggle for intellectual/e-motional autonomy that is feminist separation from the State of Separation.

It is important now to consider further the meaning of the context-weaving that can release the flow of Presence within and among women.

* The absurdity of the average history course is one illustration of this. There could hardly be a more dreary example of the emptiness of 'adult' memory's categories than History of Man 101. Here the milestones/millstones of male memory, which block out virtually all of the landscape, are weapons of assault and battery that grind down the student's potential for making any sense of the past or the present or the future.

Notes

1. Barry Commoner, *The Closing Circle* (New York: Alfred A. Knopf, Bantam Books, 1971, (1974), p. 29).
2. Robin Cook, *Fever* (New York: New American Library, Signet Books, 1982), p. 2.
3. These deep psychic levels of the oppression of women are cogently analyzed by Marilyn Frye in *The Politics of Reality: Essays in Feminist Theory* (Trumansburg, N.Y.: The Crossing Press, 1983).
4. Denise Connors has emphasized the need for recognizing and acting upon our knowledge of this fact, arguing forcefully that women have not

found wholeness (healing) at the hands of male physicians and should not expect this. ('The Social Construction of Women's Sickness,' paper delivered in the Feminist Lecture Series, Smith College, Northampton, Mass., February 17, 1983.)

5. Thomas Aquinas, *Summa theologiae* I, q. 92, a. 1, ad 1. I have written of this theory with mingled amusement and horror, in *The Church and the Second Sex* (New York: Harper and Row, Harper Colophon Books, 1975). The present concern is understanding it within the Sado-Syndrome of self-fulfilling prophesy.

6. Aquinas, *Summa theologiae* I, q. 92, a. 1, ad 1.

7. The survey, made by Dr Frank W. Putnam, Jr., a psychiatrist and physiologist at the National Institute of Mental Health in Bethesda, Md., was discussed by Ellen Hale, 'Inside the Divided Mind,' *The New York Times Magazine*, April 17, 1983, p. 102. Hale writes, concerning this high proportion of women (85 percent): 'This may reflect society's tendency to deal with a violent man – or his violent alternate – by throwing him in jail, while women more often are steered to the psychiatrist's office.'

8. Ibid.

9. Ibid., p. 100.

10. Ibid., pp. 101–2, 105–6.

11. Janice Raymond, 'A Genealogy of Female Friendship,' *Trivia: A Journal of Ideas*, 1 (Fall 1982), p. 7.

12. It is germane to this point to reflect upon the fact that some women, when asked whether they were raped, answered that they didn't know. See Andrea Medea and Kathleen Thompson, *Against Rape* (New York: Farrar, Strauss, Giroux, 1974), p. 26.

An Invitation

Sarah Lucia Hoagland
1983

I

(Part I was inspired by the showing of a slide in a slideshow on matriarchy by Carol Moorfield and Kathleen Valentine. The slide appeared at first to be of a drawing of a female Aztec warrior, for the figure had breasts. Upon closer examination, however, one could see it was the figure of a man inside a woman's skin, the skin of a priestess he had just slaughtered. You could see where her skin

*ended at his neck and at his wrists, at his wrists where her hands
dangled down, like idiot mittens.)*

He wore the bag of a priestess, her breasts shrunken and empty.
He emptied her then tried to fill himself. Clinging, controlling,
coring, he thought he would become her. He thought he gained
her power.

His hands reached out where hers had been, greedy, grabbing,
grotesque. Methodically he emptied her skin, believing he was
absorbing her power, then destroying what he could not have.
Like a boy.

He had resolved to introduce his own meaning to life.
Determinedly he destroyed Eve. ALL WITCHCRAFT COMES
FROM CARNAL LUST WHICH IN WOMEN IS INSATIABLE.
Delightedly he created evil. He believed he created purpose.
Purposefully, now, he struts.

Carnal lust. Witchcraft. Craft of the wicca, of the wild, of the
wooly. Fires burning, flames blazing, heat searing . . . Interruption.

Victorious he stood there, grinning. Look, Ma, no hands. Look
what I've done. Look at ME. His victory prevailed, the power of
terror, of disruption, of interruption, demanding attention. Attending, we rivet on him. For days. The predator-cum-protector.

He wore the bag of a priestess, he claimed to have her power.
Demanding our attention, he would have us believe he is her;
believe, indeed, she never existed. Startled, I look. Shocked, I
focus. Stunned, I stop.

Hypnotically he struts: back and forth, back and forth.
Horrified I stare in fascination. He can divert us. For days. He can
interrupt, terrorize, demand attention. But he has not killed the
spirit.

He has not killed the spirit, the spark of memory of who we
were. He cannot claim that power, the fires of the heath, the fires
of the hearth, the fire of the heart. Gold and warm, orange and
russet, stirring crackling, searing cauterizing.

He stole the bag of a priestess; but he can never kill the spirit.
Only we can.

I want to hold you and kiss you and taste you and move with
you and fill up with you and find the part of you within the part
of me that steps beyond the part they hurt.

II

Several male faculty are notorious on campus for their harassment
of female students.

She comes crying to my office.

The female faculty become outraged. Why do they become outraged? Why have they not been outraged? They live on the same campus as I. In a meeting they become outraged and after go home, outraged, to their husbands or their closets.

She comes to my office and names names, is willing to sign hers, wants to reclaim her dignity, wants to gain knowledge without harassment.

In a meeting they write a position paper telling the president all about IT, but not naming names. Outraged, the president encourages them to define IT and promises to issue a warning stating that IT is not permitted on this campus, will not be tolerated (by someone).

I say why talk to big daddy, why not develop guerilla training sessions for female students, help them organize so they can band together, take one class together, circulate an underground list of the harassers.

They look at me, say that's a good idea. They talk about the merits of wearing a wedding ring on campus. Then work for a year defining, trying to figure out how to separate harassment from male sexual advances, normal sexual intercourse. It can't be done, say I, any sexual advance from male faculty to female student is harassment. What can you expect from a lesbian, say they.

A year later the president issues his report. He says IT is a no-no. The faculty are delighted. The women have gotten big daddy to speak. The men now have new locker-room material.

She comes crying to my office. She is willing to name names, willing to start a process.

A woman, reputed to be in the closet, tells her he can and will sue for defamation of character. She warns, like a father warns his daughter.

To avoid threatening men, women comply with the masculine edict that eradicates female resistance, keep the protector as buffer from the predator, convince themselves that men should masculate. The women have chosen whom they will focus on, whom they will attend to. And it is not her or me.

I want to hold you and kiss you and taste you and move with you and fill up with you and find the part of you within the part of me that steps beyond the part they hurt.

She comes shaking to my office. She has been warned, don't use That-word. She has been told she might be labeled, that things can happen to her records. She was warned in good faith, like a daughter is warned. She was warned by a woman, assistant to a woman reputed to be in the closet.

213

The women are surprised, outraged. But soon they question what they can prove. They have only a student's word. The woman high up is offended, angry at the innuendos behind her back about her office. Why are you causing trouble, they ask me. They expect me to apologize to her. I go to her. I do not apologize but I acknowledge her, I ease the situation. And this is enough. I am surprised. But then I realize that semblance of smoothness, of things being alright, is all that is required; no disruptions.

My separate perception keeps me from losing bearings in my academy. I know what I want. And I know why I'm tolerated. I no longer understand women there who don't know such things. It is from there that I first saw the evolution of wimmin's liberation to ladies' auxilliary. That they live in fear is no longer an explanation.

She comes shaking to my office. But she makes her choice. She never fit in closets. Her focus is Lesbian. And she stands nearly alone.

I want to hold you and kiss you and taste you and move with you and fill up with you and find the part of you within the part of me that steps beyond the part they hurt.

III

She bursts through, she looks around. Arrogantly she moves her weight. From within her a force rumbles venturing out under heavy eyelids, telling of a passion still burning, whispering of a need still groping.

I said come walk with me, here in this space. It is special for me. For you. Sharply her eyes meet mine, her tension encircles me.

I said you can walk proud here.	She said my back hurts.
I said there can be bonding here.	She said I see nothing new.
I said you can take risks here.	She said I'm shut out.
I said you can find sisters here.	She said I'm alone.

I want to hold you and kiss you and taste you and move with you and fill up with you and find the part of me within the part of you that steps beyond the part they hurt.

I said we could create a place of belonging, a place of growing. A place where our Selves emerge through music, through videos, through books and magazines, through healing, the crafts, the energy, the stories, the lectures and readings, the rituals, the photographs, the gossip . . . through our focus. Here among the many and varied dreams of Lesbians.

The spark in her eye flickers. Sensuous rhythms reach out, electricity crackles.

She said I need you here.	I looked at her.
She said I have no power to speak here.	I said what are you doing now.
She said I'm being attacked.	I said I will not be always here.
She said then you betray me.	

I said let me walk here with you now. Take this mirror and find the fires. Gold and warm, orange and russet, stirring crackling, sparking burning.

I said this can be our center. We fight here and love and plot and weave and risk and hurt and get it wrong and laugh. Here, among Lesbians. We need not abide by all that develops. But it is to this space we can refer. Here we can focus. As Lesbians.

She said it isn't real.	I said no, this is not what I come from either.
She said I have been hurt.	I said yes, I know.
She said how do you go on.	I said this is what I choose.
She said I'm scared.	I said yes . . . so am I.

I want to touch you in the crease where arm meets shoulder, teasing you open, gently probing, rocking cradling, falling centering.

I center here, my Self settles here. I do not choose this in order to survive or from obligation to you. I do not find Self here; nor do I find community. Rather, I walk here, focus my attention here, grow here. And I find that in choosing this my source opens, my power develops, a reality emerges.

Because I find you here, walking too.

I want to fall laughing into your arms and hold you. I want to watch your eyes sparkle with delight at some exchange between us. I want to nibble and whisper and dream and suck and laugh and center and lick and talk and focus and nudge and argue and listen and bunt and joke and conspire and kiss and kiss and kiss and kiss and kiss . . . in the joy that we are Lesbian.

215

LIVING AS A SEPARATIST: THE POLITICAL IS PERSONAL

expatriate

zana
1981

once a month i reenter
the country i grew up in
like a true member of the underground
i slide quietly through
its edifices
collecting a few things
for my survival:
the oranges we cannot grow
candles and flashlight batteries
a bottle of ink.
as if time stopped
i find that country always
changed only in its fashions.
to its inhabitants it is the real
and i the escapist;
to me it is a neverneverland
oblivious to plutonium on highway 5
hidden feelings, and other
things that can explode.
when my countrywimin enter this place
we are stared at
our loose, worn clothing
our face hair
our skins dark
some from heritage
all from sun and soil.
and as for us, we stare
at relics of our past
garish painted faces
male bodies like misshapen trees
useless things upon things upon things
pushed at us to buy.
the people of this country
might sicken to see us kiss
or pour our urine on our fruit trees
but nonchalantly
they slap wrapped packages of dismembered animals

into their shopping carts
poison their own lands
with changeling chemicals.
i remember;
this is the country i grew up in
learning at my mother's side
how to make jell-o
and wondering
what was wrong
it must be me i thought
no one else is panicking
as they follow their programmed routes
well maybe they are, or
choose their struggles differently
i always was a foreigner
and daily i perfect my ways of separation
toward visiting this country
less than once a month

Separatist Symposium

Liza Cowan
1978

The Symposium included the response by Penny House, which follows this, and the response by the Gorgons which appears in the section Transformations of Consciousness: Examining Our Selves.

In September of 1977, Penny and I made up questions to send to self-defined Lesbian Separatist groups around the country. We had hoped the answers to these questions would help to clarify just who exactly Separatists are. In our cover letter we said: 'The nonSeparatists, and those who are quietly unsupportive, have hundreds of false and destructive fantasies about Separatism. Because we know that Separatism is not a monolithic ideology, but a collection of many different women's years of hard work and consciousness-raising, we have decided to send a question-naire to you.'
We sent this questionnaire to approximately ten groups and/or

individuals. One group wrote to tell us that they did not want to answer the questions because straight women and men might see the magazine. Another group, the Gorgons, sent us a collection of previously written essays which speak to many of the points we raised. We received no other responses.

I worked on my own answers to the questionnaire on and off for about three months. The questions we posed were difficult, and required a great deal of time and thought. We tried to ask the questions in such a way that would elicit responses not so much about the ideology of Separatism, but about who Separatists are. We have been feared, scorned and most of all misunderstood. We thought it was important for all Lesbians to understand that Separatists are not a bunch of hard-line weirdos, women with no feeling and no doubts. This is the impression given by anti-Separatists. We hope to show what a diverse group of Lesbians call themselves Separatists; to show that Separatism has no centralized laws, no rules and regulations.

In answering these questions I tried to be as open and honest about my life and my feelings as possible. I did this to help explain what Separatism means in my day to day life; how my beliefs and politics affect my dealings with my family, my community and my work.

How do you define Separatism?

I was brought up as an apostate (one who has abandoned her religious faith, vows, principles or party) Jew. I always knew that I was a Jew but I was barely conscious of what that meant. I know that many of the values and morals my parents handed down to me are Jewish, but I can only vaguely differentiate the Jewish from the Gentile, and at best it's a guess. Fortunately, there is a way for me to learn what it means to be a Jew: there are Jews I can speak to, there are books for me to read, there is a museum I can visit, there is even a country I can go to.

I was brought up as a heterosexual, patriarchal woman. I always knew that I was female but I never had a real grasp of what that meant. I know that much of what my mother handed down to me was feminine (of the female sex, womanly). I have been spending the past eight years learning to differentiate male from female. Unfortunately, there is no one I know of who knows truly what it means to be a woman. There are a few books written by women on this subject, but their speculations and discoveries are rarely more developed than my own. There is no women's country I can go to. There is not even a museum.

Lesbian Separatism is a vague title that explains only about 1/1000 of the way I think and behave. Last year Alix, Penny, Janet and I decided to quit calling ourselves Separatists because it was too imprecise; it seemed to mean too many different things to different women. Unfortunately, when word got around that we were no longer calling ourselves Separatists, many women began to think that we were no longer going to be so stubborn about having women-only spaces; it meant that maybe we no longer hated men, that we were going to be nicer and not so threatening to be with. It was quite terrifying to get the feeling from all over the country that we used to be monsters but that now we were going to be 'good'. When, on a concert tour, Alix announced from the stage that she was no longer calling herself a Separatist, some women actually clapped and cheered. It made us realize that it was our duty to continue to call ourselves Separatists because the word has become identified with issues and emotions that touch a raw nerve in the women's community — gender and sexual politics.

It seems that it is still too frightening for many lesbians to realize that they have the right to be exclusively with women, whether it is for a concert, a conference or a business, and that it is a right that must be fought for. I have travelled around the country meeting hundreds of Lesbians who live in a more Lesbian world than I do, Lesbians who live, work and socialize almost exclusively with other Lesbians, who will say to me that they are not Lesbian/Separatist. They 'personally' prefer to live with women, to work with women and to socialize with women, and yet they will not call themselves Separatists. They are not willing to commit themselves even to the idea of working to maintain the life they enjoy so much. There are Lesbians who will fight, lie, get sick or leave town rather than commit themselves to such a seemingly simple act as claiming a concert is to be for women only. Why is this so? The label 'Lesbian Separatist' has become the hot line to everyone's flushing-boy-babies-down-the toilet fantasy, and they run from it screaming. How did Separatism get such a terrible reputation?

When I say Lesbian Separatism I am talking about the analysis and observation that there is a profound difference between male and female, and the understanding that women have the need and the right to be together without males, and to define the world in our terms. Men 'rule' the world, but Mother Nature is a Lesbian. Men try to control Mother Nature and they try to control women. Lesbian Separatism is an analysis which shows women that it is possible to withdraw support from men, and a belief that withdrawal of women's support will dissolve the patriarchy.

Men, and most women, do everything in their power to make life uncomfortable for women who challenge the patriarchy. Most women do not really want to rock the boat; it is too frightening, and we are taught thoroughly to be passive. It is hard not to cooperate with the patriarchy; everything is involved. Every single piece of information, every action has to be understood and frequently challenged. Everything sent from the patriarchy tells us that this world was created by, for and about the male. All information from the patriarchy is colored by a male point of view. Challenging and dissolving the patriarchy means withdrawing support from male assumptions. Take, for example, the energy crisis. Men have decided, and informed the world via all their media, that there is a terrible shortage of energy, that it is a crisis. There is no shortage of energy. The sun can give us an abundance of never-ending energy, and there are probably at least twenty-five other simple, organic solutions to the 'energy problem.' Rather than explore these possibilities, most of which women would probably utilize in about fifteen seconds if we had the learning and access that men have, men prefer to fight each other for the money, power and domination that comes with scrambling for oil, threatening our health and lives with nuclear power plants, spilling wastes into the waters and throwing junk into outer space. It is clearly an S&M power game that they would prefer to play to the end of their days. By accepting the assumption that an energy shortage exists, we allow, even help, the 'crisis' to continue. That is just one example of how we support the patriarchy by giving power to their beliefs. We can begin to withdraw support with as simple an act as saying, 'I don't believe it; I refuse to give "power" or "energy" to this assumption. Without women's energy and power men will truly have an "energy crisis." '

Another assumption that must, I believe, be challenged, is the assumption of 'human being.' When I first became a feminist, I rejected the notion that there was any basic difference between men and women. I saw how the patriarchal analysis of the difference between women and men only served to keep women enslaved, and I believed that women and men had just been socialized differently. I still believe that we have all been socialized badly ... that the world could be a better place if men and women were socialized differently. But I also realize that it is men who have been in control of the socialization, no matter how often or how loudly men scream that it's 'all mom's fault.'

After I came out and started to spend more time and energy in exclusively female company, I began to realize just how different men and women really are. I realized, too, that seeing everybody as 'human' would help men stay in control and would keep women enslaved. It is in the interest of the patriarchy that women not realize that it is *men* and not 'human nature' that have created pollution, racism, the energy crisis, agribusiness, fast food, and every other symptom of the agony of life in the patriarchy. Men and women have known all along that there are enormous differences between the sexes, but I think that when it seemed clear from the first and second waves of the women's movement that women were going to make public this best known secret, and were actually going to do something about it, that men quickly realized that they had better hide behind the collective title of 'human,' thereby not having to take the blame for their crimes. Women, for many complex reasons, have, for the most part, accepted this and are frequently grateful for being recognized as 'human, too.'

Once I became conscious of the fact that men and women are so different, a realization that came from feelings, observation, analysis and support from other Lesbians who were making similar discoveries, it became clear that we know very little about what it actually means to be a woman. In order to explore the difference, to learn what it means to be a woman, and to exorcise that which is male from our own patriarchally trained brain patterns, it seems obvious that we have to remove ourselves from men. Hence, the title, Lesbian Separatist. The natural separation between male and female. The separation is as much emotional and intellectual detachment as physical withdrawal. In order to take control of my own life, I separate myself in varying degrees from men and their influence. I try to be constantly aware, on guard, alert to recognize, understand and challenge all patriarchal assumptions, attitudes and actions, whatever their source. This is a full-time job.

How do you act with the men you have to deal with in everyday affairs, such as supers, shopkeepers, servicemen, neighbors, men at your job? How do you feel about them?

Sometimes I surprise myself at how well I get along with so many of the men I have to deal with in my life. Everyone has to deal with men in this life, but I have had to spend more time and energy on men since I moved to the country four years ago than I had to in the city. I have heard from women who say that it is easy for me to be a Separatist because I live in the country. I guess they thought I could isolate myself on my own land and never have to deal with landlords or supers or men on the street. This common fantasy is wrong in two ways: first of all you can be a Separatist and still speak to men; second, being in the country does not mean moving away from men, since men live in the country, too. When I rented an apartment in the city all dealings with tradespeople were taken care of by the super, but now that I own my own house and land everyone has to deal directly with me. When our furnace starts choking and farting I know one or two things to do to relieve it, but usually I have to get on the phone and call the plumber. Our hundred-year-old house had wiring that was almost as old and we were afraid that all the extension cords and old wires would start a fire, so we had to call an electrician man to rewire the house. When the car breaks down we have to call the garage which is run by men. The gas for our stove is delivered by a man, the fuel for our furnace is delivered by a man, the UPS driver who comes to our house a few times a week for pick-ups is a man. When the roads are covered by a foot of snow and we haven't seen the plow all day, we have to call the highway department which is run by men. All these men have to be dealt with.

I have developed a standard way to act with men when I first meet them. I rarely smile, I am on my guard and make sure that they are aware that I will not put up with any nonsense. I have found that usually a man will behave much less offensively to me if I put him on the defensive first. Make him know that he will have to act right to get that smile; it doesn't come automatically just because he is a man. If you start right away smiling at them it makes them feel that they have the automatic right to treat you like a child or an idiot.

When I am having to throw a man out of a concert or some other women-only place, I take the opposite tactic. I stride right up smiling and give him a big 'hello' and a bigger smile. I say, 'Hi, I bet you didn't know that this concert was for women-only. You'll have to leave.' This takes them totally by surprise and it's very hard for them to fight or get angry when they are so off-guard and challenged by such an obviously friendly woman. I don't waste any time arguing, just take him by the elbow, smiling, and escort him to the door. So far, this has worked like a charm.

With my neighbors, townsmen and tradesmen, I have found it totally unnecessary and unpleasant to continue the no smile, 'watch out buster' attitude once I have gotten to know them. The same man delivers the fuel oil each time, the same man delivers the bottled gas, the same plumber comes, etc. Soon we learned that this one was born right down the road, that one went to school with one of our friends, another one's wife works in the post office and so on. We have developed a nice, courteous, friendly rapport. We have, after all, joined their community.

One of the reasons that I wanted to leave New York City was that I wanted to know my neighbors, to feel like I was part of a neighborhood. I tried and tried in the city but it was never satisfactory. Now I am happy to finally know most of my neighbors. I love to go to the supermarket or stores and know the shopkeepers and many of the customers. I love to wave to someone I know from the car, or stop on the road and chat about the weather or the hunters or whatever for a minute. At first we were not sure how people would take to us. Being Jewish Lesbians in a straight white Christian community could cause some problems. Much to our relief and delight, we found that as far as we can tell everyone has very nice feelings about us, and we discovered that we have very nice feelings for them too. They like us because we keep our house and yard looking clean and neat, and we are working to improve the land. We are polite, courteous, and respectful of them. We are 'good girls'. We don't live with men. We are not hippies. We help each other in times of trouble. We are nice people and they are nice people. We don't intrude in their lives and they don't intrude in ours. We have managed all this without betraying our principles and we are very happy about it. We love our neighborhood.

Some relationships are a little tricky. When my dog was a puppy I noticed one day that her gums were bleeding pretty badly so I took her to the vet. He was new in the neighborhood and we had only seen him a few times. My puppy had chewed some wood that had gotten stuck between her teeth and gums, and I was relieved that she was not sick. I told the vet that I had been worried that she was suffering from periodontal disease. He said, 'periodontal disease, that's a big word. Are you a dental hygienist?' I was so furious that I was dumbstruck. I went home in a rage and that night I had nightmares about him. We had to go back again, soon, and this time I had decided that I would not say a single unnecessary word to him. I glared at him; I was calm and very cool. It made him nervous. The next few times we went I gave him the same treatment, and he has behaved tolerably well ever since. Now, a few years later, I am a little less cold. He's sort of amusing to talk to for a minute or two, but every once in a while I have to remind myself not to get too jolly, because he's the type of man who likes to prove that he's smarter, funnier and more in control than anyone else, and the best way to control a situation like that is to be removed and cool, look at him like you might be thinking that he's an asshole, or that you just may not be paying attention to him at all.

At this time in my life I do not have to work with men, but I used to when I worked in radio. I always got along alright with them, although it was a drag to have to work for them and they fired me three times. I have found in all my relationships with men that the same rules hold true, don't smile unnecessarily (unless it's a tactic), be honest and direct. Be courteous and friendly if it's called for, but don't be afraid to let them know exactly what they are doing that is oppressive, disgusting or annoying. It's also best, and I try to remember this, though sometimes I forget, to remain calm and speak in low tones when you are annoyed with them. Let *them* get hysterical.

My number one rule for dealing with men is never to discuss Lesbians or Lesbian business with them. I have followed this rule 99-9/10 percent. It makes me sick when I betray this rule, but it teaches me to be even more careful and more on my guard next time. I only hope that all Lesbians are as careful as I am.

For the most part I loathe men. They bore me, they annoy me, they are dangerous and draining. I hate men, but every once in a while I like one anyway. By 'like' I don't mean it the way I would like a woman. It's an entirely different feeling, very superficial with no expectation of closeness. I have no desire ever to attempt to be close with a man, even if it were possible without great sacrifice on my part, which it's not. I figure that women are vastly more fascinating, deep, intelligent and creative than men, but we have been so damaged by men for so many centuries that many women are unpleasant and unreachable. Men are less creative, more destructive, less intelligent, harder, etc. but because they have for the most part been given every advantage and support available to all men, occasionally one or two can be jolly, amusing and interesting to talk to for a little while. I am always conscious of the maleness of every man, and all that implies, and yet I have a good time talking to them occasionally, and, yes, every once in a while, I meet one who I would trust in *some areas* as much as I would trust *some* Lesbians. Rather than to deny to myself that this is so, I prefer to accept that life is full of contradictions, and to know that through discussion, consciousness-raising and analysis, someday we will understand the meaning of it all.

How do you act with straight women you have to deal with in everyday affairs? How do you feel about them?

Most of the women I see in everyday affairs are shopkeepers, supermarket checkout women, the mail carrier and the clerks in the Post Office. I like them all very much and I am always happy to do business with them. I always try to be as friendly and sweet as I can be. I usually talk to them at least a little, but most of the time I am more eager to talk than they are.

Do you choose to have friendships with straight women?

This is one of the big dilemmas of my life. I would love to be friends with straight women but I have found it is extremely difficult, sometimes impossible. I love women and I have always liked straight women. I used to get crushes on them but every time I ended up crushed. The sad fact is that straight women are not willing to make the choice to care more for a woman than a man, and they have rarely returned my love and admiration in full. For the most part I have only been hurt, humiliated, rejected and made a fool of by the straight women that I have loved. From this experience I have learned not to have crushes on straight women, but I go right on admiring and liking them.

Many of the straight women in our neighborhood are strong, lively, independent, admirable and beautiful. The only Lesbians living anywhere near to us are twenty miles away and we are lucky if we get to see them every two months. Consequently, if I were not interested in having some kind of relationship with the local straight women I would end up speaking only to Alix and the animals. This would drive me crazy. I feel that it would be like cutting off my nose to spite my face. It is true that I have been hurt by straight women, but I am learning how to avoid this and it happens less and less.

It grieves me to realize that my straight friends care less about me than I do about them. When I became a feminist, I made a decision that women would always come first in my life. My friends here do not feel that way: they are not feminists, they have not made that choice. When I feel that they are caring less for me than I for them, I try not to take it personally; I just know that they have not made the commitment to women and that is that. What this requires on my part is that I not expect them to reciprocate my feelings. I have to force myself to care less for them than is natural or I will end up feeling ripped off.

It thrills me when a straight woman asks me about being a Lesbian. This has happened a few times in the four years that we have been here. Sometimes it is funny and infuriating at the same time, like when one woman said to me, 'Don't tell me, but what do Lesbians do?' Our neighbor women know that we are happy to tell them anything they want to know about Lesbianism. It is clear to us that they also hate men, though it is not clear to them, but they like to hear us speak about it, and we hope that our discussions give them support. We know many women who are curious about us and have become stronger because we are around.

One evening I was talking to a woman who I was just getting to know. We were talking about sewing, she is an excellent seamstress and I am just learning. I told her how hard it is for me to find clothes that I like and she asked me why, if I was . . . she couldn't finish her question so I finished it for her. Why, if I am a Lesbian and love women, do I want to dress like a man? Right, she said. I have heard this question a million times and I have a good answer and I enjoy talking about it. I told her about the history of Lesbians dressing like men. I told her that I feel freer from harassment in trousers, that I want people to know that I am a Lesbian, that men stole all the good clothes for themselves and that I refuse any longer to consider them 'men's' clothes. I told her that with a group of women I would feel comfortable to wear anything that strikes my fancy, but with men around I have to protect myself and also I have to let them know that I am not willing to be the object of their so-called affections. She was fascinated. She told me that she had never heard anything like that before; it really made her think.

When she asked me how I came out, I told her, and she said it made a lot of sense; she'd never heard it explained in such a way. She asked me what I did. I told her about DYKE and told her not to tell her husband what I had said about it; I explained that we didn't want men to know about the magazine. She didn't understand, but she said ok. I found out several months later that she was true to her promise and had not said a word to her husband about the magazine or about Alix's records.

I do not expect this woman to come out but I am happy to know that she knows a lot more than she did about what it means to love women, for a woman to trust women. I feel that I was able to give her some new insights, maybe to start her thinking about feminism. What did she give me, or is it just a one-sided relationship? Am I being ripped off by a straight woman? I think not. I enjoy speaking to her. I love making contact with women and I feel that during our conversation we were communicating, even though I was doing all the talking.

What is your relationship with your family?

I am the youngest of four children in a Jewish upper middle class family. I grew up worshipping my older brothers, adoring my sister, with mixed feelings about my parents. I was always passionately proud of my entire family. My mother and brothers were civil rights activists, and politics was the staple of all mealtime conversations. As I was growing up the family maintained fairly close ties. My brothers and I were quite eccentric, and that kept us close. We enjoyed a kind of zanyness that sometimes only we could understand. The first year that I lived alone and was lonely away from home I spent more time at my sister's house than at my own. My brothers and sister were there when I needed them. Our father had told us over and over *ad nauseam* that we should always be there for each other, that the family was the most important part of life, a Jewish sentiment to the core. I believed him.

When I was twenty, in 1970, I became a feminist and I began to take a closer look at my relationship with Polly, my mother. I wanted to know her as a 'sister' not just as a mother. I even interviewed her on my feminist radio show one night. She was very pleased with our new relationship, because I was beginning to try to understand who she was, not just mom, someone to whine and kvetch to, someone to demand attention from any time day or night. We started to have a good time together. Lou was a detached kind of father. Our conversations mainly took the form of him lecturing me. This was how he acted with all of us. Also, starting when I was fifteen he was usually very sick, and demanded a lot of attention and babying, although he was fairly subtle about it. He was proud of me doing radio and was compassionate each time I was fired, because he had been in broadcasting and was fired, too, also for political reasons. He was proud of my button business, and he loved the idea of my doing a magazine even though I would never let him see it. He loathed my being a lesbian.

When I came out I immediately told my mother. She was, at that point, ready to accept Lesbianism as a valid choice but only theoretically. I don't think she was surprised when I came out, but her reaction was powerful and long lasting. After a few months, when it was becoming clear that Alix and I were developing a relationship that was going to last, she began to panic. I wanted to tell Lou because I felt it was important that I talk about it on the air, and he always listened to my show and I didn't want him finding out that way. One day Alix and I were visiting at Polly and Lou's house, my brother and sister were there also. I broached the subject to them of coming out to Lou. Polly said it would kill him by aggravating his already weak heart. My sister thought it was unnecessary to tell him. My brother thought I should tell him since by not telling him I was having to lie all the time. I decided to tell him, but I waited for a few more weeks, at which time I told him without ever saying the words Lesbian, lover, couple or anything like that. But he knew what I meant.

During the same visit at Polly and Lou's, Alix and Polly and I were sitting around the kitchen table. Alix and I were holding hands. Polly told us not to hold hands, she didn't want to see us 'making love.' I pointed out to her that my brother and sister-in-law were always smooching and kissing and whispering sweet nothings in each other's ears and that she knew it made me sick to see them, but she had said nothing to them about it. In her mind it was different. At that point our relationship began to change. I began to feel like an alien in my own family.

The worst times were when Lou had his heart attacks. During his convalescences, Polly told me not to bring Alix with me to her house for visits: somehow seeing us together would trigger another heart attack and kill him. Many times I wished it would be that easy. It infuriated me that my parents would prefer to have fantasies that I was straight, and that by seeing me alone they could pretend that Alix didn't exist and therefore I was not a Lesbian. Polly wouldn't budge and naturally I was not allowed to ask Lou for his own opinion. For a little while the first time I went along with the program. Lou seemed on the verge of dying and I didn't want to cut myself off from my family at that point. My brother spoke to Polly on my behalf but it did no good. The crisis seemed to be past, Lou wasn't dead, and I decided that the only way to remedy the situation was to stop seeing and speaking to my parents. I did. It lasted for about a month till Polly was convinced that Lou was back to his usual semi-health, then she said that Alix would be welcome in her house. I decided to forgive her and we spoke about it a little. I was relieved to be able to see my parents again. The next year the same thing happened. I did not speak to Polly and Lou for several months, then Lou recovered and all was back to normal. My father never got that sick again so I don't know if my withdrawal treatment worked, or if Polly would have pulled the same trick had he gotten sick again.

During these years I rarely spoke to my sister. She lived far away, was busy with her work, school, husband and children. Her life seemed so different from mine. I occasionally saw one of my brothers, but it was not in my program to be speaking to any man more than I absolutely had to, and I was not interested to see my brothers.

Except for my mother and father I was totally out of touch with my family. This lasted from about 1973 to late 1976. I felt that my women friends were my sisters, Alix and Adrian were my family, and that was all I needed. I was a Lesbian Separatist and I began to deny the validity of my father's message of family importance. I had gotten in touch with incredible hatred for men and everyone who chose to be associated with them, and the thought of being close with my brothers and sister was incompatible with everything else in my life.

I saw my parents because they allowed us to stay with them on visits to the city, and because despite my alienation from men and straight women, I still loved them, especially Polly. My relationship with her was getting good, we were discussing real things: emotions, fears, spiritual investigations, and I felt very comfortable with her. She told me that when Lou died she would rather have an affair with a woman than a man. The men her age repelled her, they were egomaniacs, they had ugly bodies, etc. Her women-friends, she said, got more beautiful and interesting all the time. Later that day she called to tell me that she hadn't really meant what she had said, and that I shouldn't tell anyone. I knew that she had meant every word she had said, and told all my friends. One day we were sitting in her bedroom, I was going to be leaving soon to go back upstate. It had been five years since I first came out to her. We had been having a fabulous visit. She hugged me and told me that she knew that it would never work out, but she wished we could live together.

A week later my brother called me up to say that there had been a fire in their apartment and Polly and Lou were dead.

One of the many profound changes that this has brought about in all our lives is that my brothers and sister are now much closer. When they were all supportive of Alix taking an active and visible role in the funeral and other death-related public events, I knew we had it made. We discovered that we all had more in common than we suspected. We had all become involved in Judaism, each in our own ways, but each relevant to the others. My sister and I have rediscovered each other, we speak regularly, not just about our dead parents, but memories and analyses of our childhoods. Also, we share a passion in learning what it means to be a Jew. Now we have regular family meetings whenever we can all arrange to be in the same part of the country, and we stay in touch with each other.

This is a very satisfactory arrangement for me. When I was first a Separatist I thought that to be consistent with my politics, I had to abandon the notion of blood family. I learned years ago that the nuclear patriarchal family is bad for women, bad for society, bad for the world at large. Nevertheless, no matter what system we have for propagating the species we will always have relatives. Family, after all, is not man-made, it's woman-made. Having a family satisfies a great need in me, a need I suspect we all have. Separatist or not. Because I was born into a patriarchal world I make do with what I have. I can be friends with my siblings and cousins and uncles and aunts and still be a good Separatist. I don't bring my Lesbian business to my family and I don't bring my family business to Lesbians. Each satisfies a need, and they can remain quite independent of one another.

Is there any political work you do or would do with men?

In a crisis, for a short range project, I would work with men. Otherwise no. I want to change the world to a place where femaleness is the primary assumption. It is not possible for men to create this change.

Is there any political work you do, or would do, with straight women?

Yes. I am currently working with a local Planned Parenthood group to design and erect a pro-choice abortion billboard in a local town. A few months ago we were driving on a road not too far from our house and we saw a billboard showing a photo of a baby with the headline, '*Never to laugh ... never to taste sunshine ... fight abortion.*' It was at that moment that I realized that something had to be done, and that I had better help. Right To Life and anti-ERA forces are powerful and destructive and they must be stopped. A while ago Alix and I went to Albany to lobby to keep medicaid abortions; there were women from all over the state. It was the first time in years that I had done anything political with straight women and it was very interesting. I think it is vital to work with whichever women want to on such issues. If women lose the right to abortion we are back to square one.

Do you, or would you, do Lesbian work with non-Separatists?

My main Lesbian work is DYKE. Not everyone who works for DYKE is a Separatist, so the answer is yes. I would not, however, do Lesbian work with a group that was anti-Separatist. I have found that I prefer to do most of my work via the US mail, and basically I only work with my close friends, who are all Separatists. I am not a group joiner anymore, because all the groups I have ever been involved with ended with horrible fights, mainly over Separatist issues.

How is Separatism expressed in your Lesbian work?

My main Lesbian work is DYKE. DYKE is sold only to women and only at women's and gay stores. We do not sell subscriptions to men. We are aware that once in a while a man sees it, but after a certain point there is nothing that can be done about it.

As important as directing our circulation only to women is the fact that we write directly to Lesbians. DYKE is a magazine for Lesbians, and we have never had, nor will we ever have an article written by a straight woman, nor will we have one that is written for straight women although we do not mind if straight women read the magazine. In all the articles is the presumption that the reader is a Lesbian. We think that this is revolutionary. Women-only space is a fight I am willing to dedicate my life to.

Response by Penny House

Penny House
1978

The following is the text of a talk given at a Separatist workshop at the Eastern Regional Lesbian Conference in April, 1978, in New York City.

Over the years much of the misunderstanding of separatism that Lesbians have had is based on the perception that separatism is primarily an exclusionary vision rather than a positive focus on women. Along with this misperception goes the feeling that separatism and the separatist life must necessarily be grim, austere, isolated and emotionally narrow. It is true that among the broad range of Lesbians who have at one time or another defined themselves as separatists, that that tone, if not ideology, has often dominated. In the past couple of years, I've evolved an understanding of separatism in my own life in which the value of separatist analysis is not defined by what and who I have excluded from my life but rather on whom I primarily look to for satisfaction and whom I trust as comrades and supporters.

One tendency I've noticed in separatist literature as well as in other Lesbian writing is the notion that what makes a Lesbian politically trustworthy and correct can in some way be measured by the number of so-called privileges she has renounced. In fact, Lesbianism seems sometimes to be defined by some women as the giving up of privilege.

Creating a life for myself which is sustaining, satisfying and pleasurable is not contrary to separatism but is as much a reason for separatism as it is a right I feel all women should have.

The concept of pleasure as privilege and deprivation as duty has nothing to do with how I feel about devoting the best part of my energies and the most satisfying part of my time to women. Knowing or understanding that our conflict with patriarchy will be going on for longer than my life time makes me realize that the pace and expectations I set up in my life have to be ones I can live with and feel happy about for years to come.

So for practical and emotional reasons, separatism doesn't have to mean severing all ties with family and old friends and straight women, or having constant hostile confrontations with men you have to deal with on a day to day basis. Nor does it mean that I have to withdraw my interest or participation in the culture that surrounds me. But as a separatist I realize that it is through an association of women together that the implications of patriarchy and the damage we have sustained become clear, as well as the growth of our still primitive notion of what a world of women might be. Experiencing women's space and working with other women to create that physical, intellectual and emotional connection of women-only also provides me with the clearest analysis of the divisive and profoundly destructive patriarchal creations of racism, economic deprivation and class status.

The analysis that grows out of separatism of these truly evil male creations does not derive its power from guilt nor from feeling that I have to take on all the pain that any oppressed person feels. Rather my understanding of the damage done to me and to other women becomes clear to me in an intense and personal way through my focus and reverence for women, which is an expression of separatism.

Guilt is an exclusionary and remote-making feeling and to have *that* be the emotional basis of one's political life is destructive. Understanding my own historical legacy of oppression as a woman, as a Lesbian and as a Jew, and extrapolating what I feel about that in terms of the lives of the women I look to as allies, is

a far more productive and creative and sustaining foundation for
both political action and a sane life.

I Know I Take a Chance in Forming Words into Meaning: A Leap Over Wild Waters. Or, Talking Myself into Getting a Haircut

Susan
1982

1.

My grandmother died last week. She lived a long life. Was
productive in the ways middle-class early 1900's Jewish american
women were taught to be. She brought up three children and
helped raise four grandchildren. She painted, worked skilfully
with silver, knitted dozens of afghans – filling her children's
homes with her art – she kept daily journals of her and her
family's health and well-being.

I also got a phone call yesterday from a non-Jewish working-
class straight friend of some years ago. A woman who always
reminded me of a leopard with her spirited wild angers and
strengths. Janet told me a few days ago her son's father stuck a
gun in his mouth and pulled the trigger. I knew him years ago
when we all lived in New Hampshire. Besides his drinking and
unpredictable violence, he had a fascination with Hitler. This
deeply disturbed me. When Janet told me news of his death, I
wanted to tell her I was relieved he killed himself. One less prick
we have to kill. He did it himself. Saved us the work. One less
prick killing us. But I didn't tell Janet this because she was
mourning and I care for the Janet that is core stripped of that male
world around her.

Then I woke up this morning from a dream that involved Janet.
She was dropping me off at my house, this house where I live now
with three other Lesbians. We were parting and we both knew it
would be forever. In the dream I had her wristwatch on my wrist.
I knew the watch meant she would be taking me with her off into
her life, and would have to come to me to remember our time
together. We were separating, exactly as we really did years ago.
Her to her childhood world of male street survival, me to a
forming Lesbian culture. It was another step in my separating, this

ending, something I can see now only years after. I needed to begin to separate together with those who were separating in the same ways as I.

What I am writing about here is separating; different ways people separate and some of its meanings. Both my grandmother and Janet were not Lesbian womyn; but Lesbians do not have first claim to separations (nor are we the first culture to use Separatism or Nationalism as a means of survival). As a Jew my grandmother maintained strict separation from non-Jews. She related to goyim only in matters of necessity. Janet too separates. She does not act this out in her life; yet I am the person with whom she has shared the most deeply and completely in her thirty-one years of living. What Janet does is separates from men: separates from womyn: has separated from herself. It's all very complex, this issue of separating.

I am trying to understand. To figure out here with myself, my feelings and thoughts, this puzzle that has so many more pieces than I know how to easily work with. What I do know is about myself, and I start from here. From my grandmother(s), my Jewishness, my sensitivity to inter-personal dynamics, and my strong will to do more than survive, I have taken in an identity of Separatism. It is very much true that when I was sitting in that chair in kindergarten, not only was I a Jew and a Lesbian, but also a Separatist. I need to remember: as I held wax paper between our lips when mat feldman and I kissed in third grade, I was a Separatist. We separate in ways we can.

2.

I guess I could name this piece 'Ramblings on Being a Jewish Separatist Dyke Coming to Consciousness in the 80's,' and sigh at the struggle of what this means. I could ask: in terms of surviving in this world isn't it enough to have to deal with being a womon, a Jew, and a Lesbian that I need to add Separatism to my repertoire of reasons for oppression? But that question is not mine, it is their lies and fears taken in and meant to mask the truth of my life to me. I am a Lesbian-Separatist and it is not a choice. Not any more than being a Jew or a Lesbian were choices – they are identities and what I do is choose whether or not to listen to their voices.

3.

In the past week since her death I have had a constant and ever-present image of my grandmother which has followed me through my days and restless nights. I see her body laid out (under earth I helped shovel on top of her coffin as my family looked on not remembering this ritual of their so near pasts) – and I see her alive. I see her feeling feelings and taking breaths, her chest heaving with effort to grasp air.

4.
I just can't let my grandmother go. Not yet. I still have something to learn from her, something relevant to my life now. Today. Present. I know I need a deeper way of understanding a deeper way of knowing a politic less reductionist than often our Lesbian politic seems to be. There is direction for me in my grandmother's life. No matter what anyone says, no, I am not relieved that my grandmother has died; and I'll keep her alive just to spite that whisper I hear COMING FROM INSIDE ME saying: one family member dead, one less tie to the straight world. There has to be room for contradictions, for the realities of our lives, and I say this to myself as well as to anyone else. I cannot cut my hair just because this is the 'Dyke' thing to do. No matter how much we wish otherwise we do not exist only in the present time wholly in the here and now, and this can be an aid if we better learn how to use it. It is too late to go to my grandmother but it is not too late to learn from her life. I do believe we wear watches with different faces. Many of us wear faces that do not fit the mold. And why does it seem so many of us try to pour ourselves into it, from one container to the next, what good does it do to deny the many parts of our own and our sisters' selves and lives? Where do each of us need to go to do our re-membering? I think we each need the room to go there. To that place.

But at this time and in this country it is tricky and dangerous. Dangerous to merge into the present and let go of past, dangerous not to do this. A group of people, to take power in their otherness, need to claim it. We are Lesbians and as Lesbians we need to define and consensually embrace our own way. The assimilation of a culture serves to eventually erase that culture. The Diaspora (exile of Jews from our homeland) was intended to defeat the Jews by separating us. Rather than doing this, through the past several thousand years of exile the Jewish people have survived (even through the massive destruction of European Jewish life and culture by Hitler). It seems impossible for us to expect such to be true for our newly forming Lesbian culture. With the undermining forces many of us have felt so strongly in the past months becoming more a power and voice in our communities (the old 'Lesbianism is just a sexual choice' line, Lesbians putting more of their primary energies into men, Lesbians suddenly forgetting what it means to be a Lesbian culture, and so on) – I become very afraid. I do not want us to each have to start over again from isolation and fear. One of the reasons Jews survived and our cultures grew under the continual anti-Semitic oppressions and murder of our lives in Diaspora is because many Jews remained separate, individual lives and communities separate from whatever countries we lived within. This is a historical social reality for us as Lesbians to learn from. Will Lesbians get to a necessary place of strength and purpose before men decide to wipe us out with a more overt and violent form than they have used on us in the past dozen years? It is here where I understand and advocate the politic that calls for uniformity. Identifiability. Suspicion. Separation from the boys. We need to be very aware of their continued silent secretive ways of tearing us down. At least separation is a beginning for trusting we will survive, there is great power here we need to take. And there are many ways of separating, all do not need to be physical – go far past just the physical – though the physical is an important part of the whole. As a Jewish Lesbian I am ready to take on a strengthening Lesbian symbol, yet one that has been my legacy of Nazi dehumanization: the power in taking very short or shaved hair. (For years when I saw Lesbians with buzzed haircuts I was uncontrollably filled with fear. I have not forgotten yet I am ready to rid myself of this association that has followed me for many years.)

5.

I was talking to a non-Jewish friend the other night about myself as a Jew. As I spoke my fingers repeatedly ran through my hair, pulling it out to its fullest lengths, twisting its curls. I remembered the judgments and disdain its wildness and frizziness brought on me for so many years as a girl as I ironed and straightened and snipped away at its swirls. As I got older the textures of my hair changed and today when the weather is right my hair becomes again these swirls and waves. I am beginning in a new way to reclaim with awareness my Jewish identity and it is easy to understand why my hair symbolizes this identity to me and is now affirming. This identity is a place where I have gone and where I need to stay. I am afraid that by cutting my hair I'll make less visible this part of myself: I will be more visible Lesbian and less visible Jew. This struggle has been made more difficult for me because although my features are of Eastern European Ashkenazi Jew; often in my life I have been called Italian or Greek – anti-Semitism at this time and in this country has caused my Jewishness to be overlooked and denied. So, I grapple with identifiability and uniformity with more than one part of my identity.

6.

Some weeks ago before her death when my grandmother was sick I went with a non-Jewish friend to visit her. My friend waited outside the suburban Boston nursing home for hours while I was inside with my grandmother. That particular afternoon, after one year of not having seen my grandmother, the myth of senility kept me from thinking she could feel or acknowledge me. I left sad and frustrated.

I returned to Boston one week later knowing I must see my grandmother again and that weekend would be the last chance. During the time that passed between visits I remembered, gut level, that you can't tell a book by its cover: that I simply could not guess or judge my grandmother's emotional or psychosocial self. Although forgotten, I had known this once before. Albeit she stopped communicating with words and common gestures years before and took on the medical symptomology of 'senility,' that did not mean she was unaware of the people and environment around her. That afternoon I let go of assuming the unknown is not known because it is not consciously and culturally embraced. My grandmother was not a Lesbian but she was a Woman Jewish alive and feeling and we connected here. Our meeting that day although short in time was one I'll never forget. We communicated to each other acknowledging our connection and her dying between us.

> We spoke an ancient language
> far beyond words
> then in my dreams the following night
> there were vivid images of her
> my grandmother
> her body floating
> under water
> in a suspension
> of wait
> then striking visions of her
> my grandmother
> in a warm living womon's body
> as she stroked my arms
> held me
> alive
> breathing though I could not see
> her face
> my grandmother
> died
> the afternoon after
> the night of my dreams.

Sometimes it happens, this surpassing the ways of the wider world we live within.

7.
My grandmother died alone. Through experiencing her death I understand that for most of us, in our years of growing we are as alone as in our deaths. I would never have learned this without watching death, this process of life. We die alone as we live, essentially, alone. No one could have completely shared her dying with her; not the cessation of that last breath. Not in my grandmother's life. And there is a lesson here for me about being myself guided by an ethic that *I* come to; working through all the garbage to the life the root the core. My grandmother Hannah did this in the ways she could – I need to go further. As much as I can in my life I must not be manipulated by culture, subculture, individual, idea – unless it is by choice. It seems foolish to be afraid of aloneness, to deny it, for at one point we must confront it, no matter what we do in the years of our growing. This is so in the way of the wider world we live within; I hope for other ways, but do not trust that I or the earth shall live to experience them as more than fleeting moments.

8.
I am exhausted and furious at continually reading critical, hateful, and defensive letters, articles, and other such divisive writings in the Lesbian and feminist presses by non-Separatists about how Separatists act, think, and what our ethics and values are. It is simply not possible to define and categorize all Separatists together. Not only does this reduce the complexity of our lives, but it is oppression and it is painfully obvious – trying to speak for a group while not being a part of it. For reasons generated from that world of pricks like energy from nuclear power plants, the deepest truths in too many of our Lesbian beings are unable to be expressed, muffled, extinguished (for what appears to be shelter surrounds us and keeps us thinking we are safely warm and with light). At this point in time I believe there are too many Separatists closeted; many Separatists who do not name themselves; many who do not act out or make obvious their Separatism; many Lesbians bound by fear of the judgments that come from naming oneself a Separatist in the Lesbian communities.

My family waited for years to put my grandmother into a Jewish nursing home – this was the only fate my grandmother ever in her words spoke to us in her verbal voice, chose for herself

– but the wait was still years too long (many old Jewish people waiting); and so my Jewish grandmother lived her last years surrounded by non-Jews in a goyim nursing home. I hardly ever remember my grandmother at the Synagogue through my years of growing up, but does this matter? She was a Jewish Separatist yet very few people ever knew this.

9.

This is my rebirthing day today and one thing I have done for myself for this day was to get my hair cut. Cutting my hair has not made me feel any more or less Jewish, but the feelings and fears around this were deep and difficult and I am left with questions: why did I think I would lose my Jewishness when I lost my hair? Could it have been some remembrance of the stripping away of my identity in the past? Was I identified and killed because of my long wavy hair (ripped from my body in clumps of scalp and blood)? Or, in this life has my hair hid another identity? Allowing me to pass as straight and not have to carry the symbols of Lesbian openly on my body suffocating me a heavy coat in the heat of a summer day.

Today I have also put a Star of David around my neck.

10.

> The Star of David on my neck
> I wear
> having put it in place just two weeks ago
> in place
> of the Labrys
> that hung around my neck
> for some years.
> It has not been an even exchange
> not at all one oppression
> made visible
> for another
> made invisible.
> There is no comparison
> in my Lesbian experience
> to what I have felt
> the anti-Semitism
> I have felt with the Star of David hanging
> on my chest falling between my breasts.
>
> I realize a Labrys is a Lesbian in-group symbol
> (even at first glance
> like a cross it resembles

the ancient Egyptian Ankh
symbol of life
the same source
as the christian cross
later stolen
and turned into anything but
an object representing
life) –
it is safe
whereas a Jewish Star evokes rage and hate
in seconds
I have seen it take only
seconds to occur
suddenly this violent emotion there in my world.

I have just returned
home from a workshop for Jewish Lesbians and their
friends
a room full
of Jewish Lesbians
non-Jewish Lesbians
and Jewish women
to gaze upon.
I have just returned home from five hours of gazing
when I craved not gazing but grazing like a mare
in a rich field of grasses.

Many of us felt
Jewish Lesbians
that were there
in this year
in that room
felt alone
I feel felt
utterly alone with our struggles
with what we experienced there today
with our experience.
Even though we were surrounded by some others of
like mind
it takes more than one step to out of danger enter into
another time
(my grandmother Hannah did this in the ways she
could
I need to go further).

I wanted to scream to yell to cry out all the pain

but there were no feelings
at that moment
the moment
when I most wanted them
they deserted me
affected me like the turning away of a lover
when my body most spoke of desire.
There in that room back there
only moans and futile attempts
at holding on
to a non-Jewish, non-Separatist friend.

11.

I have answers
I have strength
I have a voice
and know the way
and it is not
with my grandmother
under the massachusetts earth
chest heaving to grasp life-breath
more dead than alive.

12.

My thoughts are rich of what I want my life to be; the struggle comes from trying to make this a reality. I know because of my birth sign of Cancer and my Jewish self, I want and must have family in my life; and the family I need is a group of Jewish Lesbian Separatists working against abuse and injustice with doing more than surviving, Lesbian Separation, at the base of our work.

In my thoughts we are out there blowing up churches and government buildings, kidnapping men whose capture will get us what we need, learning to kill. This is war we are in and I no longer deny it. I no longer deny our herstory as Lesbians or our history as Jews. I've moved very far from restrained polite thinking.

13.

For now women like Janet come with us. She has rebelliously lived the life of a straight woman and has never been given the free and open choice of loving with womyn, and I want so to give her that choice. But from what I have observed in my life heterosexuality is a reality for some and is too engrained to easily change; so I do

not have an answer for what to do with these women in a world
of just womyn – what of their happiness and becoming?

14.

My head spins when I think about the future
of this world
(for how many of us is this not also so?)
it seems never in our lives will the needed changes
come
(and how many times have we written this?)
but if not now
there may not be a place
for girls to play out
their lives
for grasses to grow.

I have few answers and many questions
and only know today that I want to believe
in that concept of karma
but helped along and in this life.
Boys that have violated
need to be violated
except one up on their particular crime against us
an act of rape of course
equals reason for death
but coming from my Jewish past
I hate violence and
fear tortured bloodshed,
so the killing must be done
with the least pain.

And how can we kill the Jewish boys
kill like the camps
six million men and women's
limbs, heads, bulldozed hills of dead people
showers of deceiving death
the ripped open bloodied bodies and crushed Jewish
faces
of the pogroms
and all through Jewish history?
I would rather
Jewish, men of color,
and others oppressed by white wealthy men
be considered differently
for their violence abusive death-loving living

somehow in this scheme —
but there can be no exclusions
men are men.

What has taken form
in this world on this earth can not
go on and men are
the clay forming the violent
horifying architecture.

15.

I write of killing men I hate
the violence and pain their habits reign
yet I do not know if I could ever do this
in any systematic fashion
I think of advocate
putting life out
like a match tossed into water
hissing
I do when I hear of torture and death
now with outrage
I'll never stop visualizing, imagining, remembering
piles of shoes hair of clothes the screams
the smell of burning bodies
enough blood has flown from men.
I don't know if it can be any more than wishing this
                                              hope
for a place where
women who hate thrust
mimic male violence
pawns of patriarchy, yes even
Lesbian pawns acting out patterns of
paternal pain
can begin to learn
how not to be life-
killing.
A starting over I am grasping for
a return for us
to the safety
of a loving mother's
lover's breast
all around us every day everywhere in every way.
I do not want to kill
but I ask for more than just an end to their acid rains.

And this is another voice in me here
speaking now
my heart aching for tenderness crying
for options without violence
I do not want the death touch
to be sanctioned wielded by womyn
my wishes are of men
dying out
those who have not committed direct violence
against womyn •
and leaving only womyn
and leaving only womyn born of womyn.

Yet I have heard this before, this idea
and now I am writing science fiction fantasy here.

16.

A lesson I take from my grandmother's life is in living, growth and survival, I must somehow live my life fuller than hers; she created but never shared her art with the world. This is perhaps why my medium is words rather than paints and yarns and metals, for me words move swift and easy. My grandmother was a Jewish 'outcast' whose emotional and primary social energies went solely into other Jews. Both my grandmother and Janet separated from the source of their pain and oppression; Janet waging a continual battle of self against self, and my grandmother, though living her life separate from non-Jews, never taking her actions to their logical conclusions: a radical perspective and politic, a place of empowerment.[1]

I have moved forward and have written many words that wanted to come forth from my fingers on this paper in the genres I have so far chosen, I have taken a leap over wild waters – now I am ready to cut more than my hair and leap over mountains, to fly. For my freedom, for expression of my being, it is time to create a space where I can hold up no barriers. A place where I can simply embrace and be embraced alone and with others. I do this at least here with my words.

Note

1. I got this concept of 'outcast status' and what it can mean in the realm of one's identity from a fascinating unpublished paper by Julia Penelope called 'The Lesbian Perspective: Pedagogy and the Structure of Human Knowledge,' 1976. The paper was delivered at the National

Council of Teachers of English Conference, held November, 1976. It is presently on file at The New Alexandria Lesbian Library in Northampton, Massachusetts.

An Interview with A Separatist, January 23, 1983

iandras moontree
1983

1. You call yourself a Separatist. What are your ideas about and definitions of Separatism?[1]

My deepest desire is to live in a world with other Lesbians, where murderous patriarchal oppression is unknown. i first got a glimpse of what it might be like to live in such a world when i attended the Michigan Wimmin's Music Festival. For once, i was somewhere where i could walk at night (and day) and not be afraid of attack or rape by a male. It felt wonderful to be in a space with all wimmin. i had freedom to peel away layers of protection. i had the opportunity to observe the various ways that wimmin relate to one another when males are not present, when we are in a predominantly Lesbian space. i'm not saying that there aren't any problems at the Festival or that everything is bliss and wonderful when only wimmin get together. i've been in many wimmin only contexts since that time, and believe me, i've seen problems. i think there are many changes that wimmin need to make before we are at a place where we are not oppressing one another with the 'prick within' us. The 'prick within' is the years/generations of brainwashing that we have absorbed in the patriarchal culture.

Two ideals are at the core of my beliefs about Separatism:

1) That males individually and as a class are a destructive, parasitic species that is/has been destroying the earth and dominating her wimmin ever since they have been on this planet. One needs only to read its recorded his-story, and to observe the male culture around us, to recognize its destructive force. Males have always dominated wimmin and groups they define as 'other.' Their goals are power and control. Males have not been solely socialized to behave in these ways, even though *their* culture perpetuates and supports *their* behavior. I do not believe that with the kind, unselfish help of wimmin they can be educated to change. i believe that males are a genetic mutation, who

biologically possess the traits that make them violent and death-oriented. In my opinion, coalition with males is short-sighted. It is another parasitic ploy to suck the life-giving energy from wimmin so that males can continue to live.

2) That in order to achieve the full and rightful place of wimmin, living in psychic and spiritual harmony on this planet, males must go. Coexistence with them is impossible. i don't think it's 'unrealistic' to think in these terms. We limit our possibilities and confirm their reality when we say: 'Well, males are here to stay, and we'll just have to learn to live with it.' The earth herself is rebelling against the crimes of mankind. Collectively, wimmin can, and should, help bring about patriarchy's downfall.

There are two things that wimmin can do to initiate these changes. First, we must withdraw our energy from individual males, male systems and institutions. In this way we stop validating and perpetuating their reality.

Second, we must begin to create an alternative to patriarchy – a wimmin's culture. We can begin to do this by creating womon-spaces. These are spaces where we can be safe to exorcise the 'prick within,' and to heal ourselves from the scars of patriarchal genocide; spaces where we unite outside the patriarchal culture and begin to develop ethical ways to relate with one another as different, unique individuals.

There are many things we must unlearn. Part of our ongoing ethics would be to break down divisive 'isms' and to use consensus, not assimilation, as part of our process. All wimmin need to recognize, as a species, our common struggle on a battered planet. We must recognize, too, the differences in our lives and avoid generalizations that tend to trivialize the experiences of another woman. Our priority should be to ourselves individually and to other wimmin.

Both withdrawal from patriarchy (making ourselves inaccessible to males) and creating womon-centered spaces and an ethical wimmin's culture are necessary to bring about major changes.

2. **How did you become a separatist? When did you first hear the word?**

I went through a multi-faceted process of change that took years. It began, probably, when i decided that i was a Lesbian. At that time, i decided consciously to give my emotional and sexual energy to other wimmin, and not to males. i didn't define it much beyond that at the time; but later i began to see other parts of myself that i wanted to share only with other Lesbians. Gradually, over the years, more and more changes took place that pointed me in the direction of Separatist politics.[2]

i think i first read the word 'separatism' in an old *Sinister Wisdom* article. Suddenly, i felt that i had discovered the words to describe how i felt. i felt not so crazy at all. Later i read different descriptions of separatism based on other people's oppression, and their strategies for using separatism to resist assimilation by a dominant group. I recognized connections between Lesbian Separatism and other forms of separatism and began to expand my concept of it.

3. What were your politics like before you became a Separatist? Looking back, do you see ways that you resisted patriarchy in your Lesbian life then, ways that you did not?

Before i became a separatist, politics, if you asked me, were democrat and republican; something the boys did with what they named government. i felt powerless to participate in any way that would create noticeable change. i had never heard anything about 'the women's movement.' i was raised in Wyoming and parts of the southwest. i graduated from high school in 1971. i came out when i was eighteen, after a brief marriage that lasted seven months. Even though some of my actions and thoughts were separatist, it was about nine years before i began to call myself a Separatist.

When i first came out, i decided that i was not going to live as a 'closeted' Lesbian. i felt that was too great a compromise to make. i chose to deal with the problems of being an 'out' Lesbian. During those years, i lost jobs, was kicked out of apartments, and my family disowned me because i would not deny my Lesbianism. At that time, i viewed being a Lesbian solely in terms of sexuality. i had no political ideas about my choice. i would tell people, 'No, i'm not one of those women's libbers,' or 'No, i don't hate men.' i didn't think there was an inequality between men and women. At least, i didn't see how it related to me specifically, or to wimmin in general. i did think that males had better choices than wimmin; but i didn't consciously recognize their choices as privilege.

i think i was born to be a Lesbian. It just took a few years to find the words to make it reality. From the time i was a little girl, i rebelled against frilly dresses, baby dolls and polite girl-like behavior.

During my childhood and preteen years, my fantasies were always of having an important relationship with another womon. i would fantasize meeting the womon of my dreams and spending the rest of my life vacationing with her. i always had crushes on girlfriends and teachers. But in my high school years, i began to date some boys. This was at the insistence of my mother, who was beginning to be less and less tolerant of this 'phase' i was going through. By the time i was sixteen, my mother's insistence became threats to have me committed if i did not finally get through this 'phase.' So, to assure her, and to keep myself out of an institution i dated boys and tried to act as though my 'phase' had passed. Deep inside, i knew it hadn't. i contemplated suicide. Instead, at the age of seventeen, i married. i hoped this would be the thing to cure me of the so-called 'sick' problem i had.

i really wanted to fit into the 'real' world. From everything i had been told about being a Lesbian, it didn't sound like a very good way to live. My information had come mostly from my mother, from movies like *The Children's Hour* and *The Fox*, and from books like *The Well of Loneliness* as well as psychology books on the subject of homosexuality. Mother always said that Lesbians never had lasting relationships; the movie messages were that Lesbians killed themselves; and the books said that Lesbians were lonely, mentally ill, immature and sick. It sure didn't sound like what i had in mind. None of this offered me the stimulation to form any insightful political tenets. i had no experience with other political movements, even the ones of the '60's from which i could draw analogies that related to Lesbian politics. i left Wyoming after i came out at the age of eighteen.

Between the time i came out, and the time i began to call myself a Separatist, which was about nine years, i lived in the midwest, still unaware of a women's movement or of Lesbian politics. i would define myself at the time as a bar-dyke. That is, i found other Lesbians to relate to in the local 'gay' bars. i still viewed my Lesbianism as a sexual preference. My lifestyle was similar to that of most heterosexuals. At least i tried to fit into their lifestyle, rather than to define a Lesbian politic or to identify myself with a Lesbian culture.

I think the single most significant way that i resisted patriarchy, both as an adult Lesbian and as a child, was that i survived. i am a survivor of incest, of attempted rapes, and of a battering, alcoholic mother. Many times i could have been dead; but instead i chose to keep fighting and to live. i resisted in many more ways: by choosing to become a Lesbian when i had no models to follow; by choosing to be 'out' and to live uncloseted, though i endured many oppressions for being out about my choices. i refused as a child to be programmed into a feminine role, and, as an adult, i decided against the feminine privileges awarded a womon when she marries.

i failed to resist patriarchy when i did not consciously question and challenge its rules and reasons. At one time, i didn't think as much about what was going on. i did not ponder how i was oppressed as a womon, as a Lesbian. For example, i have lost jobs because of sexual harassment, and never questioned the dynamics of the situation. i spent years believing that the incest committed against me was my fault. i have allowed myself to be harassed by males and ignored it because i thought, 'boys will be boys.' i have blamed wimmin for their own oppression because i thought they were making their own choices about what they got.

These were all things that undermined my survival. These were things that kept me separated from other wimmin and kept me from identifying with other wimmin in our common struggle.

4. Was moving out to land a political act for you when you did it?

Yes, but at the time, it wasn't a conscious political act. i moved from the city because i felt like i was dying internally, and that i was going to die, literally, if i continued to stay in the city. i was terribly unhappy for several years before i decided to leave. i had gone through months of depression and apathetic behavior. i tried to numb myself by abusing drugs and sleeping a lot. Nothing seemed to fill the voids i felt in my life.

One summer, i attended the Michigan Wimmin's Music Festival for the first time. After i came back, i felt angry, angry at how the world was around me. i lived in an area of town with a high percentage of rapes and attacks on wimmin. i was angry i had to be constantly aware of how close men were to me on the streets. i was angry that i had to put up with harassment; that i couldn't take my shirt off outside. i began to question the rules and authority of boys. i was depressed. i saw no sense to anything, no good purpose. i had one low-paying job after another, and i always struggled to make ends meet. i didn't feel any sense of community with other Lesbians. I had no political context in which to describe the things around me. I truly felt i might as well be dead.

After being fired from another job, i began to let myself fantasize about how i would like to live if i could choose without any limits. i thought about the childhood dreams i had of living in the country. i realized that my goal had always been to work for years, save some money and retire to the country, out of the rat-race on a few acres of land. i began to realize though, that on what i was capable of earning, i would never be able to save enough money to buy land. Besides, who said the world would be here in fifty years; that i could even buy land then; or that i would be physically able to homestead at that time? i began to wonder why i couldn't go ahead and live out my dreams *now*. Why should i wait? So, after losing my job, i began to plan for a move to the country.

My life began to revolve around this dream and the changes involved in making such a move. i began to read books on the subject of living on land, as well as books on the women's movement and wimmin's spirituality. i began to ask questions, and to examine things in a way i never had before. It was about this time that i became a vegetarian. And from the books i'd read, i began to tie together ideas about the politics of wimmin's spirituality and living on land with the politics of Separatism.

i spent the next six months writing to communities in the country in search of a place to go. i didn't know wimmin's land communities existed. That was yet another dream in the back of my mind. i worked on selling everything that i wouldn't need in the country and began to collect the things i would need to survive there. After six months, i found a small heterosexual community in southern Kentucky that was open to new people. i moved there with a few duffle bags, six hundred dollars, and some dreams about eventually living on Lesbian land. i was ready for some growthful changes. It was after i got to land that i began to recognize the move as political.

5. **Do you consider living on Lesbian land to be a Separatist act? In what way? Does living on land create change? How and in whom?**

Yes, i believe that living on Lesbian land can be a separatist act. It is the act of separating from the patriarchal culture, and it can be the act of creating something new. i think it takes some consciousness on the part of the Lesbian doing it. Not all Lesbians move to land as a separatist act. Some are there for various reasons, and live in a variety of ways. Some live in ways that 'ape' male culture. They have not exorcised their male values. But, i do think that living on land with other Lesbians can be a Separatist act when it is done from a conscious decision to deny access to men and create a healing environment for wimmin and the earth. But the Lesbians involved must be conscious and responsible about the process and the product that they are creating.

i don't see the move to land as escapist, or think that it is running out on your sisters who are left to fight the patriarchy in the cities. Living on land *is* fighting patriarchy and it takes a tremendous commitment to change, and a willingness to give up privilege. It is not simple or easy. Nor are Lesbians on land totally isolated from patriarchy. Males are still around, and Lesbians must find ways to deal with them. In fact, sometimes they are even more dependent on males if they live in an isolated rural area and have few wimmin to depend upon for survival support.

For example, when i lived in the country, one year i needed space to put in a garden. One of the heterosexual neighbors offered me space in one of their plowed fields. i didn't find it too compromising to accept the use of their land. They required nothing of me. Another of my neighbors was a quite obnoxious male. He had a nice spring that bordered his land and the land i lived on. The spring was the closest drinking water source i had. But because he required me to be nice to him, listen to him, and act a certain way toward him that i would not, he refused me use of his spring. i chose to get water a mile away rather than compromise in my dealing with him. In the country, as in the city, we still must make choices about which males we will deal with and what compromises we can make.

It might be true that some wimmin can buy a lovely estate on which to retreat from patriarchy. But after i visited several wimmin's land spaces around the country, it was clear that a lot of Lesbians on land are poor and struggling to live their ideals for change, with a commitment that comes from a sincere place in themselves.

6. Do you think Lesbians living in cities can be Separatist? How do you feel about living in the city? How do you manage to survive there?

I have heard Lesbians in the city say that they were Separatists once, but that they couldn't continue to live their ideals in the city. They felt compromised so much by working for and with males, and they could no longer continue to isolate themselves from the predominant culture around them.

i have to agree that compromises take a toll on our ideals and politics. That is why i think it is absolutely necessary to withdraw our energy and the access to our energy from the male culture. It is so easy to become assimilated by their culture while living in it, especially since our Lesbian culture has a long way to go. We are tied economically to the male system. This is true even of Lesbians living on land. But living in the city takes so much more time and energy. The average working class Lesbian must spend almost all of her time just maintaining housing, food, transportation and other essentials. There is little time and energy left for building a Lesbian community/culture. This is no accident. Patriarchy plans it that way.

i do think we can still be Separatists and live in the city. While we give a certain amount to the patriarchy through our energy on jobs and participation in their system, we can also create pockets of womon-only space, where we can renew ourselves, focus on our future visions and work out problems among ourselves. But, it's important not just to renew ourselves to go back out and get drained by the patriarchy. We need to have our sights set on the larger picture. Withdrawing our energy from patriarchy and creating new options must be a primary objective. Our priority needs to be on discovering ways to do that – ways to build a Lesbian culture.

While we're out in the patriarchy, we can have a tremendous impact if we act on opportunities. Sabotage is a technique that we can use strategically to undermine their system. We can organize ourselves and become a strong force against male institutions. i think we need to be working 'underground' among ourselves. Males and heterosexual women have more credibility and less to lose by making public statements against male institutions.

For this reason, heterosexual people should take more responsibility for challenging their society. They should be the ones doing protests against the draft, nuclear power plants and the pentagon. For example, I think it's great that churches are organizing against nuclear war and arms proliferation. i'm not saying that it is their issue and not ours. i agree that if the boys blow up the world, it's everyone's problem. But i do resent that it is Lesbians who are called upon to protest and help educate the masses. It's the vampire strategy all over again. Why should wimmin always be the ones to come in and clean up the messes that the boys create? Our priority in coalition needs to be with each other as Lesbians, as Separatists.

I continue to withdraw my energy from males and their systems. I work for wimmin as much as possible. i live on a low income and try not to consume many goods and services that keep me dependent upon the system. i barter for as much as i can, such as rent, dental care, etc. i take advantage of opportunities available in the city. For example, a tremendous amount of goods are thrown out for trash. i am always on the scout for materials from which to build a shelter when i return to the country. i buy used clothing, and give things i no longer wear to womon shelters. i belong to a food co-op, buy foods in bulk, and cook and eat at home. i steal from the patriarchy when i get the chance, and i sabotage their systems when i can.

7. What do you consider an ideal dyke future to be?

Ideally, it would be a world without males. But, more than that, we would no longer have the 'prick within' that we use to oppress ourselves and other wimmin. We would relate within an inter-dependent system of communities. And our relating would be based on ethical, spiritual ideals. Our psychic abilities would be used to a great extent. Our world would be void of destructive male technologies, and of objectification and dominance. There would be a great respect for the earth, a reverence for nature, a compatibility between wimmin and the earth. Of course, that's the *ideal.* i think we've got a long way to go. Perhaps it will take generations to unlearn some of the things that we've come to believe, as well as to re-learn how to live with one another in a peaceful, growthful way. i think it must begin in small groups, and between individual wimmin and then finally expand to encompass us all. Developing our ideal dyke future needs to be a process of living Lesbian Ethics;[3] of taking responsibility for ourselves as Lesbians and our actions.

8. You've hitch-hiked a lot while you've been a Separatist. How do you protect yourself from harm while doing so? When you were attacked, what did you do? What do you wish you had done?

i've hitch-hiked a lot because i do not own a car, and i refuse to be immobilized and isolated from other Lesbians. As for self-protection, i don't believe that there are any formulas, majik or otherwise, that can offer 100% assurance against an attack by a male. They are out there, and they do harm to wimmin. i am aware of this when i hitch.

   i do employ some common sense practices, though, to protect myself. i don't hitch at night. i don't (usually) ride with more than one male . . . never with more than two. i never get into the front seat between two males. i don't ride with males that are obviously on drugs or drinking. i also use several techniques to keep control of the situation. i avoid the topic of sex. i keep them talking (which usually isn't difficult) by asking them about their work or other topics that they are interested in. i maintain my space and keep them from coming into it. i do this by making myself look as large and as mean as possible (my cat taught me that one). i pop a clove of garlic into my mouth if they look like they want to get too close. i watch my body language. i don't give them adoring smiles, like het wimmin do. Instead i talk in a deepened, sure voice and keep a serious face. i take up as much room as i can with my body and aura. i stay clear on where i am going and always keep alert. i never let on that i'm scared, lost or tired, even when i am.

i also rely on a psychic sense. i work to draw myself the kinds of rides i would prefer to have. i concentrate and focus on what i want. i discharge tension and scared feelings. At the same time, i listen to the feelings i have, since perhaps i am picking up warnings. i don't believe that wimmin draw rapists to them. Nor do i believe that, when we are attacked, it is a karmic payback. But i do believe that we can develop and use our psychic abilities to help warn and protect us against danger. i believe too that we should be ready to defend ourselves physically. For those of us who can, we should keep in good shape and be schooled in a form of self-defense that teaches us to fight. The knowledge of how to use weapons is also important, and may become increasingly important in the future.

i have never carried a gun while hitch-hiking, mostly because of the hassle cops can give you if you're stopped on the interstate with it. I have carried a lock blade knife. But i wouldn't use it in most cases. i wouldn't pull it on a male and say 'Now you stop or else. . . .' i would use it in a situation where i could pull it, use it and get away. i don't believe that the possibility of having a weapon taken away from you is a rationale for not carrying one. i do think, though, that it's vital to know how to use it, when to use it, and to be prepared to use it.

i was attacked once while hitch-hiking. i was on my way back from the Michigan Wimmin's Music Festival. i was grabbed from behind by my breast by a truck driver. My immediate reaction was to pull away from him, and to just do something to make him let go of me. i turned and hit him a couple of times, but my blows did no harm. One thing i realized later was that i had forgotten the self-defense techniques that i had been taught. In a teaching situation, i would have been instructed to stomp on his foot with the heel of my boot, come up under his nose with my elbow, and then go for his eyes. But under the tension of attack, i forgot everything. i simply tried to get away. i think that fighting back is foreign to me. i'm not used to hitting anyone, even if they are attacking me.

Sometimes i wish i had beaten the male who attacked me. i wish i could have done something to make him afraid – afraid to ever attack another womon. If i had used a weapon, like a gun, and shot the trucker, i'd probably have been arrested and jailed. The

law frowns on man-hating killer dykes who kill males for
grabbing their breasts.

This is an issue that i continually struggle with. What do we do
about rapists and males who attack and batter us? To me,
passivity is not the answer. And the male law does not protect us,
or support us in our choice to protect ourselves.

**9. You take care of the Kentucky Collection of Lesbian Her-
Story. How does running an archives relate to your
Separatism?**

Before i left the city a few years ago, i purchased a number of
books on the topics of feminism, the women's movement and
wimmin's spirituality. I figured that since i was moving to the
country, i would finally have time to do some reading, especially
during the winter months. Within my first year on land, i began to
compile lists of wimmin's bookstores, land spaces and centers, in
an attempt to keep connected to other Lesbians around the
country. i didn't want to become isolated from the Lesbian
community.

i attended a Southeast Lesbian Network Conference in Tennessee.
There i met another Lesbian who was building an Archives. She
had a tremendous impact on me. i began to see the importance of
the work i had begun. For another two years, i collected books
and materials and continued compiling lists. The Collection nearly
outgrew my 12′ × 12′ cabin. Over the last year, since my move
back into the city, the Collection has grown tremendously.

Working on the Archives is related to my Separatism in that it is
a project that keeps me centered. It gives me a focus for
networking with Lesbians. It is what i do to help create a Lesbian
Culture.

i believe that one of the main ways that males have maintained
a powerful control over wimmin is limiting the information we
have on any given topic. They virtually control written records.
This is a powerful propaganda tool for them. They feed us the
information they want us to have. From it, we form the construct
of our reality. Information about our past, a time before wimmin
were colonized by males, has been destroyed. The bible was
inserted as the record of beginnings. It is the foundation for their
propaganda. All along the way, wimmin have been systematically
wiped from recorded his-story, and our stories replaced by lies.

A few months ago, i saw a slide show about wimmin in
literature. It was blatantly devoid of information about Lesbians
of color and working class Lesbians. Even when we can find some

recent records about Lesbians, they usually represent upper middle class Lesbians who were privileged enough to get their work published. It is difficult to find information about the lives of 'common' Lesbians.[4]

Right now, and in the past fifteen years, there has been a wealth of publications/periodicals being published by Lesbians. There are many wimmin's presses that are publishing books that would, for one reason or another, never be published by the mainstream heterosexist presses. Lesbians are doing a tremendous amount of work politically in their own communities, and our lives are filled with a rich herstory of stories and experiences. i believe that it is extremely important that we begin to collect writings about our lives, writings that document our resistance and tell of the *common* Lesbian, both of color and white, and of the other diverse groups in our community. We are aware of the repressiveness of the times in which we live. But i believe that we have not yet seen the extreme of repression, and i see that it's coming. Our documents are the records that keep us from being silenced again. We must be the ones to tell our stories to the Lesbians who come after us.

Notes

1. Sidney Spinster provided the interview questions. A special thanks to her for the encouragement and support she gave to me to include something in this anthology.
2. Thanks to Jenna Weston, Sidney Spinster, Laura Haller and Sarah Hoagland for discussions, feedback and writings that have contributed to my formulation of ideas about Separatist politics.
3. The term Lesbian Ethics comes from Sarah Hoagland.
4. The term 'common Lesbian' comes from the publication *Common Lives, Lesbian Lives*.

Out of the Bedroom

Jorika Anna
1982

Total silence. I imagined her with her mouth fallen open, or maybe just twisted a bit. Scream out, shock the silence – be an apologist for extremism. No, no, I won't say anything. Did she hang up? Be forceful, emphasize. I *can't* say anything. Be rude, be . . ., be . . .; I just want to hang up.

I had just informed my friend of my decision to become a separatist. After I hung up I settled back, queasy in the stomach but immensely relieved. And I thought: I will return to them, word for word, their silences.

My sudden, though not unpredictable, decision to be a separatist ended my justifications to people who had/could not make the same decision. Satisfying the need to be honest by telling and explaining, I never begged for approval. So for the next couple of weeks friendships disintegrated as I told each one that I no longer needed or even wanted their opinions. Most of the helpless liberals responded with: 'Well, I think it is good that you're doing what is true to your own self.' Obviously they thought just as highly of Nazis, if they were true to themselves. Without my friends' awareness of it, the gap between us expanded.

The process of disentanglement, though ultimately liberating, grew to be very exhausting. Face to face with old problems, resolving them, hearing the ring of finality. I cannot say it didn't hurt. It did. Since few of my friends before were lesbians, much less separatists, the resolution of my heterosexual friendships meant the end of all heretofore existing life. A ring of finality came without a definite practical sense of where I was going; the ring of futurity so far sounding only in the abstract. I knew I wanted to put my energies toward lesbians – well, where the hell were they! The fault was mine: I had put my energies toward the wrong people in the past and now faced picking up the scattered pieces and re-directing them. So while 'loner' was not the label I had picked for my regeneration, it has, at least temporarily, become part of the definition for my separatism. It will be several years before I develop relationships with lesbians which will have some semblance of stability, before I have a truly positive sense of myself as separatist, as dyke, and particularly as lunatic.

I chose to become a separatist consciously and deliberately. One day I was not, the next day I was. I knew of separatism but could not see myself within the label: I saw separatists as wimmin who lived on all wimmin's farms and *never* saw men or the likes of them, particularly since they weren't forced to work with them. This did not seem an evil to me – it was actually very enticing. Once I settled on such a farm, *then* I could call myself separatist, but not until then. Meanwhile I (deliberately) lost contact with many male friends and continued to make only female friends. I was asked to be the token separatist on a feminist panel at my college; I refused out of anger at their stupidity for thinking that *any* separatist would want to speak to them. Personally, though, I didn't catch the hint. A more complex definition of separatism finally dawned on me when I met several separatists in, of all places, my hometown. Listening to them talk, I found their goals and ideas not so different from mine. We differed mainly in places where they were definitive/definite and I was ambiguous; I vacillated on several points for lack of courage or support since I was usually alone in my opinions among my friends. With them, though, I found support. I took a deep breath and became more definite; I admitted to myself that I thought this about one thing, and that about another.

And so I collected pieces, as if from a large jigsaw puzzle scattered long ago. I still do, holding them in my hand until I figure out what to do or where they go. Nobody ever told me the rules of this game – I make them up as I go along. Still fragmented, yes, yet quickly learning my patterns and abilities in making separatism livable rather than abstract.

Resolutions. There are still so many. Have I resolved my separatism with my college education? No, every day I consider dropping out. I live with the contradiction of wanting to learn but only having access to a patriarchal institution. I am not rich (though not exceedingly poor) and this is a contradiction in our society. Until we take the money away from the boys and create something they can't take from us, we (will) live with contradictions. In some areas we have no choices, or rather the choices always have unpleasant consequences. I define my life and work as separatist because I am committed to resolving these contradictions, not because I have already done so.

Still, I traveled a good distance in the last year. Basic conflicts about lesbianism disappeared upon the eve of my separatist decision; separatism completes the process of my lesbianism. It makes it whole, not limited to simply my sexuality or anything else. Thus 'coming out' as a separatist was much more difficult than the first 'coming out.' The first was a sexual definition and I thought, in my naïveté, that *my* acceptance of my sexuality was the biggest hurdle to leap. Thus for a while I still 'existed' in their heterosexual/male society, until I figured out that they neither would nor could truly accept me. As long as I stayed in their society, defined my lesbianism only in terms of my sexuality (a level they could handle), I defined myself in their terms. I believed them, at least in part, when they said: 'Well, that doesn't really change *our* relationship' or '*That* doesn't need to be brought up here.' I was lesbian when I was in my bedroom, according to my straight friends. Out of the closet and into the bedroom.

261

But no more. I do not believe them; I no longer listen.
And I have come out of the bedroom. To stay.

Risk

Sarah Valentine
1982

A call goes out to lesbians. A group is forming to work on issues
of survival for social change. Women's group that asks for lesbian
womoon. The group wants the spectrum of womoon, lesbians are
not represented. Lesbians come excited ... apprehensive. Each
lesbian coming with private concerns, goals and fears. Gathering
together in a lesbian caucus our shared goals are spoken. Survival
issues represent our lives. Old scars are exposed to one another.
Can we work with straight women? Is the time right? We want to
work with straight women. The distance between lesbians and
straight women groups has grown large in each lesbian's life. We
are anxious about working with them. We are proud lesbians.
Proud of ourselves, our struggles and our sisters. Lesbians seeking
a sisterhood. Wondering, hoping to believe that it exists. Can we
respect straight women's choice to be with men? No lesbian feels
comfortable with the question. No lesbian feels she can fully give
support to such a choice. If a woman does her work. If she
understands what men do to women, how dangerous men are,
how can they stay with men? It is essential in dealing with survival
to understand that men are killing women. To name men as our
enemy. Lesbians need the hope that the gap between lesbian and
straight can be bridged. Sisterhood can be achieved. Yet we refuse
to be defensive with women. If the question arises we will go
around it, rather than fight.

We walk into the straight women's group strong. We have
responded to a call to work with women. Energy high and flowing
we meet the group with equal numbers 10/10. The agenda holds
promise. Work will be done concerning lesbianism. A dialogue,
speak out, of our lives. Lesbians strong in coming to the group.
We come with a desire to bond. We will speak openly and
honestly about our fears and dangers of working with straight
women. Lesbians sitting tensely in a malformed circle. Each
lesbian, individually, speaking her innermost truth. Groping for
words, a lesbian's hand, voicing the rage of a wild anger.

'I don't understand why you're staying with men! One out of two batter. 60% of womoon-children are victims of incest by men living in their homes. Uncles, fathers, brothers, kin, "trusted men" that *you* invited into your home. Men are dangerous and kill womoon.'

'You use our spaces and energy as vacation grounds, take our energy and feed the enemy.'

'Diluting our life politics, making liars of ourselves, in the hope that you may be reached and begin to hear.'

'I don't see the womoon in you.'

'You divide us, claim to speak about us in sisterhood, misconstrue our words and vision.'

'We carry the battle. We are the front lines. We will be killed for the struggle that frees you. We will be fed to the enemy by you in an effort to shield yourselves.'

Each lesbian voice rising to define her rage. Seeking dangers within herself. Struggling to understand and cut it loose. Pulling out words that reflect our very being, touch our core. Each lesbian shaking in her anger reaching for another lesbian's hand to pull her out of the void. We found each other's hand, connected over tables around obstacles. In this way we were able to speak.

Across the room straight women retreat within. Their eyes are blank. Walled against the meanings of the sounds. Their ears are shut to the struggles and strength of lesbian lives. They speak back, reflect what it is that they have heard. What they understand to be the lesbian's pain. Lesbians will begin to perceive the work that needs to be done. Work that will enable us to work together, to bond.

'I heard we are allies.'
To whose fight a voice inside me replies.

'I heard that you feel lesbians are carrying the load.'
What are you bringing to the war sister?

'I heard your anger. I heard your pain.'
But can you feel it? Is it as painful for you? Does it rip you open wide and dripping? And I begin to spin outwards.

Anger, Pain. I get stuck in the rushes of feeling within.

The upheavals, the searing, the woman-hating within. I push feelings aside, deal with it later. Place work in my suitcase to take home after the meeting. I need to listen to the straight women. Try to find a place of bonding, of understanding. Desperation? Another to place in my suitcase.

> 'I also heard why are we with men?' Spit out. The load
> I feel lightens. Is the womoon breaking through? The
> womoon recedes as I perceive the 'we'.

The lesbians loosen their tightly bonding hands. Hands that have tried to fill the empty space. We break to the next room. We need to find our lesbian strength. We are in shock at the straight women's words, the lying. The straight women break laughing and talking among themselves. We are angry that our truth has been met with avoidance and lies. Lesbian falls upon lesbian. Because we are blood sisters we understand. Misdirected anger and frustration. Yet understanding does not soften the blows. 'Why did you not speak?' 'Why are you numb?' The knowledge that each lesbian has her own skills and shutdown points is lost. 'Did I speak too long? Was I too angry?' We break apart, spinning into our separate lonely voids. The space is not safe for lesbians. The straight women tell us that we must leave so that the building can be locked up. There is no time for the lesbians to reconnect. We stand huddled outside. Trembling in our rage, unable to cross the void, to reach each other and ourselves, we wander off into the night. Seeking private homes, safe havens to fall apart alone in search of our private lesbianism.

Straight women I am angry. I feel women-hating within. The work we brought for you to do has turned to my need for work. You sat bunched together shutting out lesbian truth, womoon truth. Straight women I am raging. Once again my sisters are divided. In trying to reach out to you we cut ourselves. Straight women, I see no womoon, in you. I am coming to realize that the enemy has many forms. He even takes the shape of a woman.

Album Liner Notes from *A Lesbian Portrait*

Linda Shear
1977
Edited by Sid Spinster

My concerts . . . (in 1975) were for wimmin-only, and most of my audience *was* Lesbians. I learned, however, that to passively 'allow' my concerts to be *mostly* Lesbians was just not good enough. When I began to aggressively perform for Lesbians ONLY I experienced just how true that was. The power and energy in the room were huge and uniquely beautiful. I began doing Lesbian only concerts early in 1976. We continued the distribution (of the album) to wimmin-only. Now, Tryna and I can no longer distribute the album to straight women. All of the music, lyrics, and composite intentions are for Lesbians.

I believe in my own power, and I believe intensely that you as Lesbians and as Lesbian audiences have a tremendous amount of power. We must now define our needs for Lesbian music; we must carefully inspect and judge what is now being documented as *our* music and sentiment. There is energy being created in front of us that is defining our futures. We must recognize our power as Lesbians and be certain to create our Lesbian definitions in front of ourselves. We must take our power seriously and be determined to be discriminating about what is being called 'our' culture. *Wimmin's* music is for all Wimmin. *Our* needs are not the needs of all wimmin. *Our* needs are the needs of Lesbians.

I wrote a song called Family of Womyn in 1972 [printed in this anthology, eds.]. It was the second song I had ever written. It was inspired by the naïve but good intentioned sentiment of myself as a Lesbian Feminist, by the Lesbian Feminist movement of the time, and by the first Lesbian Band in the country, 'Family of Womyn'. I was one of the four musicians, and the band had been named by the drummer, Ella. Joan Capra was the violinist. After a lot of growth and self-reclamation, I learned and experienced that Feminism was an institutionalized, closed system which required us Lesbians to dilute our energies and form coalitions with straight Feminists who carried our strengths, knowledge and energies away from us. They took us to our enemy. As Lesbianism became the obvious growth-producing, nurturing, and centered analysis, I stopped performing the song Family of Womyn. I no longer wanted to be identified with the feminist movement. The song had originated in feelings and definitions that had become subversive to my goals, and the goals of other Lesbian Separatists who were then emerging. We were most definitely not all sisters. In 1975, during a rehearsal, I began to re-experience the song. I had a new perspective. I changed some of the words, the tense, the tempo, and the intention of the lyric and music. I realized that I could embrace a Lesbian future for us Lesbians by recognizing our potential in the present, and by validating what we could have in the future. I had the right, power, and knowledge to change my past work by combining my present reality with all of my hopes for us in the future. When I sing about the Family of Womyn, I am now singing about the family of the highest common denominator, the Family of Lesbians.

As the class of Lesbian, many of us have experienced the pain of having been scapegoated. We are scapegoated not only by our naturally defined enemies, but by each other. I believe that the scapegoating we do to each other comes from our frustrated energies. A large part of our frustrated energies with each other is caused by the ugly lessons of the male left, the patriarchal systems, and by our own self-hate. The lesson is: do not validate each other for what we each, as individuals, do best, or for what we can learn to do best. Strive instead for commonality. Do not strive to excel at your own skills. You might threaten another womyn who is just learning about her own abilities and powers. A system which negates the value of excellence will cause us frustration because we are by our very definition of self (Lesbian) always striving for a *quality* of skill. It is our lack of systems for validation that causes us to feel threatened by each other's strengths. We become frustrated; the frustration causes pain; the pain becomes anger which is remanded to the ugliness of scapegoating. We now need to center our energies and create those systems which validate and encourage each other as individual Lesbians. We have a lot to learn from each other, and we have a lot to teach.

I am a Lesbian Separatist. I have heard and read about how boring and irrelevant Lesbian Separatism is. I have read statements of Lesbians who say they *used* to be Separatists. I guess they got tired. I look forward to the time when we all recognize our commonality as Lesbians; when the concept and analysis of Lesbian Separatism is *so well utilized* that we all take off from there to claim our future; a time when there is no more need to discuss the *basics* of the analysis. I wrote this song with the hope that we will all recognize where our source of power comes from. We have learned that we cannot hold the patriarchy exclusively responsible for the ways we oppress each other in race, class, age, ethnicity, body type, etc. As the class of Lesbian we can begin to effect changes in ourselves and in our systems that can result in larger distances between ourselves as tribes united and the obvious vested interests of patriarchal systems. When we identify our commitments and priorities to and with each other, we can become *acti*onary rather than *react*ionary. But as long as we rely on their rhetoric and unite within their systems (male left, feminism, socialism, etc.) we have no choice *but* to react *to* them.

They are always doing something wrong! If we put ourselves in the position of not *having* to react to them, we will have the energies, knowledge, and time to take care of and learn from each other as Dykes who have gathered with different perspectives.

I heard about a Jeanne Dixon prediction that a space-ship occupied by wimmin-only was going to land on this planet. I have often fantasized that we Dykes got dropped off here by mistake, and that our source-mothers would come back and collect us. After hearing Dixon's prediction, I concluded that they were on their way. I wanted to fill them in on what had happened here, and encourage them to hurry up! If they contact you first, please send me a telegram.

Family of Woman

Linda Shear
1972

Looking through a future window
Breathing in the coolness
Of the young moon
All the colors of a shifting
A once dark sky

Women passing through the world
Sharing tears and struggle
With the strength of miles behind
We are bringing in the dawn

Family of woman we've begun
Family of Woman we will become
Family of Woman we are tearing down the walls
Family of Woman we are more than slaves and dolls
Women sing of mountain moving days, the day is now
Armies made of lovers should not fail
Woman order is changing and the future time is sung
Sisters I can feel you
I can touch you
I can need you

I can kiss you
I can love you
Dawning of a new beginning
Ancient anger goes on living
Through the souls of women who have touched
And find time to grow

Sister lovers building fury
Throwing out the lies and stories
Making room for touching in a new way
We are bringing in the dawn

Family of woman we've begun
Family of Woman we will become
Family of Woman we are tearing down the walls
Family of Woman we are more than slaves and dolls
Women sing of mountain moving days, the day is now
Armies made of lovers will not fail
Woman order is changing and the future time is sung
Sisters I can feel you
I can touch you
I can need you
I can kiss you
I can love you

Battle Fatigue . . .

Revolutionary Lesbians
1971

I just feel all blocked up . . . and I don't see how we'll ever get the paper written and put together or that it will be any good at all. I am just feeling so tired and low . . . and then raging fury explodes inside my head for a moment and I tighten my whole body. It feels like what battle fatigue should feel like . . . that's what it must be . . . struggle fatigue.

Before – whenever we sat down to do the paper (even last time when we were hard pressed) I felt full of energy. Now I just feel sort of constipated . . . with depression, frustration, anger – anger hell! . . . raging fury. It has been a hard year in general – but now things are beginning to get through to me and the strong pressures of the past few months have taken their toll.

First it was Elinor gettin into nursin school and us having this discussion about whether we should come-out at nursing school and fight the shit that we knew would be coming down . . . liberal friends warned us about stepping out of line – and how if she made the slightest peep, she would be kicked right out. But then we figured – shit! – we can't hide and not fight . . . we can't ask others to put themselves out on the line if for great reasons that we can make up about surviving and all that – we don't do it. So she stood up and started fighting. I went the day she started. Jesus, was I proud. Elinor has guts . . . next to her I am a first class chicken-shit. Oh I talk better than she does . . . say things more 'coherently' and stuff – but she has the real guts in the collective . . . if she can't always say it – she can *do* a hell of a lot. And there she was in a roomful of 250 nursing students with a hysterical giggling academic nurse as an instructor in a 'human' (read: white, male, middle-upper class, heterosexual) development class. The tension in the class was awful. Our pulses broke 100 and mine made it to 120 (told you I was the chickenshit). But she started asking questions about the material, challenging the way the class was structured – the values that were being handed down as tho they were scientific facts (all dutifully copied down by the class, of course) . . . she was fantastic. But you know what she got for it . . .? The hatred (through gritted teeth with sometimes smilin faces . . . lock-jaw smile hatred) of 250 'coeds' (and believe me I use that word with all the contempt that it carries . . . women who say in a voice full of sighs . . . 'I'm not oppressed . . . I am liberated . . . oh . . . and don't they look so nice in their white doctor's jackets . . .'?). Those 250 women (let me be more specific . . .) those 250 white women think she is a 'queer' and run out of the bathroom when she walks in and they ignore her when she asks them questions when she is studying for those horrible anatomy exams. Now and then one of them will be nice and talk to her . . . which means a fight because she is 'so mean to those nice doctors.' That's how it went for 2 months of her trying to do things – gettin no support from any of the white women there – coming home frustrated and angry – on the brink of tears or already crying because of all the shit. And it would happen day after day and it drained me until I was afraid that I wouldn't have the energy to comfort her on a really bad day. Then we faced things and knew we couldn't fight like that everyday . . . not because we wanted to protect a cushy job . . . but because it was really wearin us down.

Somethin is happening to me right now . . . I got started talkin about what had happened to Elinor and I really got into it – but as soon as I tried to get down to how I feel . . . try to get in touch with what is happening to me – well then I freeze. I cross out stupid abstract paragraphs . . . I stop and stare at the paper for minutes on end . . . I guess I know why. I am scared to death. Anger has always meant helplessness to me . . . gettin angry in a situation always meant blowin it . . . and I am so full of anger right now at so many things . . . I would rather punish myself with a depression and take it out on Elinor by being a cranky than face what is beginning to bubble up inside of me. Oh I wrote about rage in the last issue – but that weren't nothin to what is goin on inside of me . . . because of what a strain it has been lately . . . because of what is happening to us separatist women all over the country. (See there I go off again . . . away. . . . I am scared to death to get down to talking about what the hell has been happening . . . and that's because I am still shuffling to the goddamn people who are ripping all of us off . . . to the people who TAKE TAKE TAKE and *never* give a goddam thing . . . I am scared because a lot of those people probably read this paper and I still tense up or flinch whenever something is said by me or Elinor to make them uptight.

It happened again . . . I began to zoom in on those feelings and whamo . . . gibberish. . . .

But I know something important is happenin . . . because as I read this over to Elinor right now I started to cry when I got to the part about me.

I have had it. I am sick and tired of listening to women who spend most of the conversation defending MEN . . . talking about MEN . . . worrying about what happens to MEN . . . why it happens to MEN and how it happens to MEN. I am sick and tired of listening to tales of happy marriages or about the exceptional men (and of hearing myself say – well then they should be working with other men to change themselves). I am tired of listening to how we separatists with our anger at male-created and male-defined power 'objectify and don't treat half the population as human being . . .' – of being told that by our making everythin into sexual POLITICS *we* make sex so aggressive . . . that we deny humanity . . . etc. Why the hell aren't they mad at men for objectifying women into property, meat, pussy – why aren't they mad at men for all the rapes – for roughness – for not caring if they have much real satisfaction in their lives . . . why don't they notice that on every movie page of every paper there are ads talking about 'VIOLENCE! TERROR! SEX!'. Women didn't make those movies. . . .

Right about now someone will usually say 'well change is hard and you have to make it as easy for someone as possible and it really is hard for women to admit things about men because of their investments . . .' BULLSHIT! Change is hard . . . it shouldn't be made impossible but I also just don't understand why all the caring about the hardness of change goes into women who have a lot of male, class, and racial privilege . . . why does so little of it go towards the women that have to make changes without any or very few privileges to make it easy? Why do we care so little for the really ripped-off in this place?

I don't know what kinds of decisions and changes you people think we have made – but you seem to think that the changes we ask of women tied to the male-world are too great. Listen! revolutionary separatist women have made some very painful changes without much support. Some have among other things faced the reality of marriages and gotten divorces . . . some have separated from their male-children (I can hear the intake of breath and see the appalled faces) . . . some have lost their economic security by no longer holding onto their careers that they worked for all their lives . . . others have told their parents about their lives and had to face the consequences of that action. A lot of women have stopped taking all the shit with a smile and started to fight back – and they catch more shit – but somehow it seems better not to go happily along in the kinds of things that happen in this place. And those are only a few of the changes that revolutionary separatist women have gone through . . . and believe me . . . believe us . . . none of those decisions were easy. Nobody is asking you to do something that hasn't been done before . . . hasn't been faced before – and by one of us.

There is a big difference between discomfort and oppression. All too many women in this society have known that for their whole lives. But to a lot of women who are into 'women's lib' this will have to be learned through changin – changin investments and privileged positions.

My anger isn't just because we get 'bugged' a lot – not just because women who have no desire to change themselves, their positions, and this society want to come and have a few hours 'chat' about our rather strong positions – and therefore waste our time and energy. My anger is because it becomes only another 'interesting' (if rather tense) discussion and they never do a damn thing. And it is a pain in the ass to always be stuck with the responsibility of making the conversation honest – by not just nodding and keeping things comfortable for everyone. It isn't just a pain – it is a fantastic drain on energy – and I resent putting that energy into merely 'interesting' discussions.

My anger – my resentment – my feelings that I am the wrong one because I allow myself to get caught in those asinine discussions comes from the gut experience and knowledge that as long as women direct their energies toward men – towards male goals and values – nothin will change. And each day that things don't change – more women die – more women are raped – more women have their whole lives and sense of dignity stripped from them ... more young people are murdered and beaten by their parents – more black women face their double oppression ... but then I forgot ... WE are the ones who are accused of bein 'insensitive' to the dignity of human beings.

Tell me – why is it so much more humane to be 'sensitive' to what makes someone 'uncomfortable' than it is to be angry and resentful at what happens in this society because of that comfort. WHY? And why is there such a fantastic value placed on 'talking'? I have a feeling it is because then it won't dawn on anyone to ask 'what have you done lately?'

All this stuff has become more and more important because we are not the only women in the country who get into these conversations with male-world women and gay men and.... And because we have had to give our attention – it is demanded after all – for they only want to spend an hour or so talking about these issues with us (but then there are so many of them and so few of us – so an hour for them is an hour for them – for us it is one more hour spent talking to one more woman who hasn't got the slightest intention of doin a goddamn thing – why does it never occur to them to sit down and talk to each other?). We have spent more time with other separatist women and when we start talking about what has been happening in our lives we start talkin about our feelings of frustration with our conversations with male-world women – and we nod as someone else starts talkin about how pissed she is at the gay men for asking for so much time and energy – or someone else tells of a meeting with women's liberation and GLF and how the male-world women came and fawned all over the gay males – but avoided the lesbians as tho they were lepers ... we find out that we have all been interrogated about 'monogamy' – when male-world women don't even have the slightest idea about what the hell kinds of relationships we have in the first place ... and they sure are right there to talk about awful 'butch/femme role-playing' when it never occurs to them to ask themselves about their own role-playing – it never seems to dawn on them that before there was any open support for women lovin women – there was only one model for loving women ... and that was men lovin women. One of the effects of all of this is that we seldom have time to get down to talking about the things that really matter to us ... how we feel about each other ... what anxieties we have about being with each other ... what we have been working thru ... what we want to strive for now. ...

But we are learning – learning what gives us strength and energy and what drains it. Separatism first meant takin the splits from males – then splittin from the male-world of values, attitudes, etc. and it means a lot about building the world with women. But we don't have infinite energy and an infinite amount of time.

I think male-world women should just go and ask their males for comfort, support, understanding, etc. . . they should ask for strength from males and not from women (of course they might just have to face some very nasty truths if they did that – and the women's movement guarantees that that won't happen at this point) because when they get support, comfort, and strength from women all that seems to happen is that it makes them stronger for their men . . . it means that they have more understanding and energy to give to men – and by giving it to men they not only do not give it to other women – they get it from women and give it to men. Well – they'll just have to get along without our energy in that little exchange.

As revolutionary separatist white women we give our time and energy to women in struggle – to women who are not passin that energy onto men – to women who are facing what their positions of race and class privilege do to other women and are committed to changin those positions.

On Separatism –
And the Perils of Having a Man Around the House

Anita Cornwell
1982

When I joined the Women's Movement a decade ago, it seemed to me that, generally speaking, the Lesbians were more at ease with themselves than were most of the straight women. Worse yet, to my surprise – and horror – I soon discovered that at least some of those straight women who were 'Making The Revolution' were letting men lay the same trip on them that most of our more 'unenlightened' Sisters were doing.

Then ever so slowly, I reluctantly but inevitably came to the conclusion that 'This Revolution ain't gonna work this time around either.' Naturally, I kept that opinion to myself because I disliked the idea of dumping cold water on such a beautiful parade. Besides, who would have believed me?

Now, however, I believe it can be said. To put it bluntly, in spite of much rhetoric to the contrary, the Women's Movement is stymied because men are determined to retain their male privileges which permit them to exploit all women whenever they so desire, while most straight women are just as determined to hold onto men as long as they possibly can, even if it eventually leads to their destruction.

Way back in the 19th century, Elizabeth Cady Stanton, one of the more prominent Feminists, wrote, 'The true woman is as yet a dream of the future.' I believe she meant that women were so crippled by repression and brainwashing and had been for so long that only in some future era would the world be able to see what a real woman was like. Unfortunately, although we now stand at the brink of the 21st century, we are no closer today to seeing what the *true* woman is than they were in Stanton's day.

That is because in spite of our having made several tiny steps forward, most women are still emotionally tied to their oppressors, and even when they are old and gray and have long since been discarded by men, they still cling to that mancenteredness that hangs over all straight women like an ancient curse.

And, yes, I don't see how being obsessed with men can be called anything but a curse. Inevitably, all women who associate with men on an intimate basis will sooner or later become only so much fodder in a meat grinder. To some extent, *all* women in all patriarchal societies are subjected to this meat-grinder process, but those few women (mostly Lesbians) who are fortunate enough not to become suckered into close intimate contact with men are seldom wrecked in quite the same way most heterosexual women are.

Of course, I am aware what many of these women are apt to say when such matters are brought to their attention. They come up with that old 'think of the species' cop-out. And it is a cop-out. If the species cannot survive unless half of it remains enslaved, *then it doesn't have the right to survive*!

Besides, if men continue to run the world, the species is doomed anyway, because if men don't destroy the world by their unbelievable greed, which causes them to ravage and pollute wherever they go, then their lust for power is going to ultimately lead to a nuclear war which is much closer to a reality than most of us care to contemplate.

Now, I suppose the burning question of the hour is 'Will Separatism help this deplorable situation?' The answer is probably yes, no, and maybe so, which is not to be facetious, not in the least.

One of the most disconcerting things that I have found in dealing with some young white women is that they seem to harbor such impractical ideas at times. Perhaps that is true of some young Black women also, but given the racist nature of this society, even today no Black woman can go around with her head stuck in the clouds very long, if she wishes to survive.

No one likes to talk theory any more than I do, but I believe it is imperative not to mix theory with reality no matter how good the theory may be. Worse still, it seems that so many of these young women believe their theory is the *only* theory, and she who does not wish to follow same is 'politically incorrect,' and is therefore not to be trusted.

Also there often seems to be a tendency to get hung up on impracticalities that have little or no bearing on our actual situation. For example, I heard of one woman who complained that in a group discussion it came about that women would be expected to shoot their male relatives 'Come the Revolution.' And those who would not agree with that concept were looked upon with suspicion.

Now aside from the fact that most of those women probably did not own a gun and probably could not hit a paper bag ten paces away even if they had one, just what in the name of heaven would make anyone think that a few women could ever win a shooting war with men who not only control all of the armed forces and police departments, etcetera, but also control all of the gun factories and the illegal gun traffic as well?

In fact, when you come right down to it, one could say the same thing about women that many of us have always said in response to those Black Militants who demanded a separate country – women already are separate in this country, and in all other countries that I have ever heard of.

First of all, I believe it is important that we realize we will probably never get a uniform set of circumstances to fit all groups of women. In other words, we must recognize that different women and groups of women are coming from different backgrounds and have different problems and/or needs to deal with.

But that does not meant those women cannot make some contribution to the Revolution. And I truly believe that the only kind of warfare we can successfully wage is a guerrilla-type warfare, not with guns or bombs, but with ideas and strategies. It has always seemed to me painfully clear that the main obstacle standing in our way of waging a successful revolution is the seemingly innate reluctance of most straight women to change their behavior patterns toward men.

At the same time, these otherwise intelligent women seem utterly incapable of learning from experience. In other words, they have observed from infancy the sexist behavior of their fathers toward their mothers. Finally, they grow up and marry and then act 'surprised' when their husbands treat them in the same contemptible fashion. Not only that, but many of these women will marry one dude after the other, always with the same results. And always they are 'surprised' that they have been so ill-treated. Perhaps one of the reasons for this is that most children are still being brought up today as children were brought up during the 50's – the 1850's that is – with a strong father running the show, and a submissive mother running her ass off serving father and the children, *especially the male children.*

I have often felt that at least one of the reasons so many Black women of the over-forty generation (and beyond) are so independent is that many of us grew up in households where the father, for any number of reasons, had long since departed. Although most of these mothers had men friends and male relatives, their daughters were not subjected to a daily dose of having to watch their mothers being dominated by men.

In addition, most of these mothers knew that if their daughters were to survive, they had to bring them up to be independent, self-supporting women. Frankly, I was extremely shocked when I first entered the Movement and heard so many white women say they had been brought up with the idea that some man would take care of them.

One of the commandments that my mother continually drummed into my head was, 'Always make your own money.' As a variation on that theme, I was told, '*Never* take money from a man.' And to complete the holy trinity, she warned, '*Never let any man beat on you!*' My mother preached that doctrine to me from my pre-school years until the time I entered college, and by that time it had become an innate part of my nature. And I submit to you that if all mothers had done likewise with their daughters, the world would not be as it is today because men would not have the stranglehold on it that they now have.

If you want to get a true picture of the horrible indignities that so many straight women have to endure, you don't need to read Feminist literature. Just get a batch of Dear Abby columns and retch. In one of the last columns that I read about two months ago, a mother wrote in to say that her 13-year-old son had taken to beating her up the way his father used to do!

Obviously, we face an almost impossible task. I don't believe we will ever see any appreciable change in the status of women unless we can first see that all children – especially all female children – are brought up in an egalitarian environment. Secondly, we must somehow establish a truly Feminist mass media to counteract the unrelenting brainwashing that the male media now subject all women and men to. And thirdly, we must somehow get women to stop worshipping male gods and supporting male-dominated religions.

Of course, there are many other areas that need attending to, but if we can get going on those three, at least half the battle will be off to a running start. And yes, I believe a lot of this can be done by those who want to separate from men and/or man-centered women.

We need to enlist any and every strategy we can think of. And if that includes settling into the wilderness and having nothing to do with those who disdain going off into the wilderness, then so be it. But let us not forget that when the nuclear bombs start flying, there will be no hiding place. Not even in our little hut in the wilderness that we have declared 'off limits' to our oppressors.

Gut Feelings

Gutter Dyke Collective
1973

Most of us are aware, somewhat of how Third World lesbians/ women are subject to racial oppression. Race is not an issue that can easily be dealt with or eliminated. There is a deep-rooted stereotyped racism in each of us that usually never surfaces or only when one is actually pushed up against a wall. I feel that race is a matter of grave importance that should not ever be overlooked or slighted. Third World women are often the victims of very painful experiences that come from white peoples' insensitivity and unawareness – feelings that will always be a part of us.

My own racial background is still a rather confusing aspect of my identity. My mother and grandmother were born and raised in Puerto Rico. My mother's father came from Spain. My father's family all originate in Italy. As a child a very clear distinction was made (by my mother) between white and black Puerto Ricans.

Naturally, my sister and I were told that we were white. Since we are all light-skinned, I never questioned her.

From a very early age I learned it wasn't cool to say that I was Puerto Rican. In my catholic school and all over new york being Puerto Rican was tantamont to being Black. Anyone with a Spanish surname or accent was constantly hassled. However, it was okay to be a dark-skinned Italian or Irish or Polish, or even Greek. The neighborhood was very ethnic. There was a tremendous push in school to identify with one's nationality. I suddenly realized that I would have to cover up my mother's 'nationality', if I wanted friends, by saying she was Spanish. I also developed a great pride in being one half Italian and felt very lucky in having an Italian surname. My secret didn't last too long. It was a small community and my mother was compelled to go to the school a lot for various reasons. The girls that now knew who I was never let me forget and made it a point of making nasty comments about Puerto Ricans in my presence. However, I was in no position to defend anyone. My mother had drilled into me that there were good and bad Puerto Ricans and that everyone else was naturally bad. Fortunately, I was able to see through some of it.

My main problem was not having any culture to identify with. I wasn't taught Spanish or familiar with anything relevant to the culture. There was much resentment towards me by most Puerto Rican females because I *could* 'pass' so easily. An immediate barrier would also be created since I didn't know the language (that being one of their bonds and an effective way of cutting up honks in front of their faces).

After leaving grammar school and going to high school, I didn't have any more problems concerning my background. All I had to do was lie, since my mother was not expected to attend high school parent-teacher meetings. My home was also not the place where I could bring friends – for fear of them meeting my mother and then avoiding me. I didn't perfectly understand, either, what I was hiding, because I believed that being Puerto Rican was just another nationality and shouldn't warrant so much discrimination. But I was also aware of the pain my mother felt when people didn't understand her (verbally) and then would make snide remarks at her. Seeing all the shit that was thrown at Puerto Ricans all over the city, I knew I didn't want any of it.

No one had ever confronted me for not dealing with my background until I moved into a women's collective a few years ago. We were all trying to struggle with the ways we oppressed each other so I thought I could be honest for the first time in my life. Some of the women wouldn't believe that I didn't know the difference between Puerto Ricans and white people. It suddenly became obvious that Puerto Ricans were part of the Third World. (I had actually begun questioning things when the Young Lords (a Puerto Rican liberation group) said it in new york.) Now fully conscious of my new identity, I didn't know how to relate to it. Being a woman and a feminist I didn't want to belong to an organization that sought to equalize Third World men's power with the white man while leaving the women down in the dumps.

The dilemma I face is one which most Third World feminists face also – that of not having an organization where we could belong, to discuss ways of dealing with the racism that surrounds us through a female perspective. There have been various Third World women's and lesbians' groups. But although they are not male-dominated, they are usually male oriented in that they visualize a united front of Third World peoples (male and female) fighting the oppressor (white society). It would be good if lesbian/feminists could get together around our Third World identity.

So, here I am, still without a real identity living in a dyke collective and relating mostly to white women. My sympathies and fears (fears of being crushed and annihilated because of racism) lie with Third World women; usually overcome by guilt, I can't work and struggle with them. Because of the inherent racism in the community, I'm not upfront with most dykes – although very defensive when I catch a racist comment. My idea would be to have a super utopia amongst dykes, but that isn't realistic at this time. Therefore, we are compelled to say who, what, and why we are because we do oppress each other. And the only way to eliminate oppressions is by forcing lesbians to face it and struggle around it.

One More Contradiction

Naomi Dykestein
1983

Although I define myself as a Lesbian separatist, and have for over four years, it is often frustrating for me to read articles or letters in womyn's publications by other dykes defining themselves as separatists. More often than not it ends up being something written by some privileged white, middle-class, able-bodied, thin woman whose analysis of oppression is that 'sexism' is its primary (if not sole) form, and that all other issues – such as racism and classism – are either false 'divisions,' or else will magically disappear at some point (probably after all womyn move to the country à la *Wanderground*), when we all blend together into one homogenized Lesbian culture/lifestyle. It is not surprising to realize that the most visible dykes defining as separatists are those with the most privilege and the most access to being published. What makes me cringe in a mixture of anger and embarrassment is that these womyn somehow come to represent 'separatism' and separatists in general – denying my existence, and the existence of any other separatist who might be working class, poor, Jewish, and/or womyn of color, as well as fat and/or disabled. For most of the womyn I know, race and class are not just 'issues' to 'work on'; they're the ongoing realities of our lives – sometimes both as oppressed and oppressor. For me, it means dealing with the anti-semitism which is a constant in my life, as well as the light-skinned privilege I've always had, and the ways I continue to act out of that. It means living with the effects of classism, but also recognizing the real privilege/power I have over poor/lower class womyn. It means being fat, but also able-bodied. Nothing cancels anything else out – I have to leave room and take responsibility for them all.

So, for me it makes sense to have separatism seem like just one more contradiction in my life. I don't feel my survival allows me the luxury of thinking I can sever ties with my people. It's important for me to realize that my survival as a Jew is as much in question as my survival as a Lesbian – sometimes even at the hands of my Lesbian 'sisters.' Therefore, I often become nervous when I hear white/gentile dykes criticizing a Jewish womon, or man, or the Jewish state or Jewish culture/'patriarchy,' or whatever. It's not that I need for anything Jewish to be immune from criticism, or don't believe those criticisms can be necessary or true. It's just that I can't always trust the motives behind them, or that the womon doing it has recognized her own potential anti-semitism in criticizing something she probably couldn't hope to understand.

While it's true that, as a separatist, I believe that men's power structures and needs are at the root of all oppressions, I also see a real danger in blaming our own racism/classism on men, and not recognizing the choices we make, and the benefits we receive. I think maybe the main weakness of separatism is the potential to see ourselves only in the ways we can be oppressed – just as powerless victims – while avoiding taking responsibility for the power we do have, especially over each other; the ways we can and do oppress each other.

At the same time, however, I struggle with these realities with the understanding that if I expect change/growth/commitment anywhere, it is from dykes and not men; that there has not been a single recorded society on earth where men don't rape womyn; that there has never been a successful male revolution where womyn have not continued to be defined by and in relation to men's needs. I recognize that no man is made pure by virtue of his oppression (it has been painful to accept that about Jewish men); that the most oppressed man alive still has access to womyn he can fuck over; that just because a man is 'decent' to one womon (and it's always his choice) is no guarantee he's not raping/beating/killing some other womon. I've come to believe that men are unable to deal with power on any level; that their inclination is to dominate, whether it is womyn, the earth, or other men – they assume an inherent right to stick it in whenever and wherever they can.

I resent automatic assumptions about who separatists are and what's behind any of the decisions and choices we make. It's true: separatists are loud, angry, pushy, uncompromising, man-hating, and obnoxious – we do not shut up and we are not 'polite' womyn. But those 'criticisms' sound uncomfortably familiar – they're the same complaints made about Jews in general and Jewish womyn in particular. No coincidence, I think, considering the large percentage of Lesbian separatists who are Jews – which is something else I've come to realize is no coincidence. We come from a heritage of separatism – it's been one of the main ways my people have survived, and is an essential part of our culture(s). I grew up in an observant, ethnic Ashkenazic home, where one of the worst crimes a Jew could commit was assimilation. I learned young the importance of struggling constantly against cultural/physical genocide; of naming the enemy; of maintaining an entirely separate way of life (sometimes at great cost); of refusing to be defined and absorbed by that enemy. My bobbe always used to warn me: 'Scratch the surface of a goy, and you'll find an anti-semite.' – and that's been a valuable lesson that has proved itself over and over again. In this context, Lesbian separatism becomes not only a logical outgrowth – in my life it feels almost like an inevitable one.

I think it's time that each lesbian separatist's voice becomes recognized for just that – one dyke's voice, not necessarily representing anyone other than herself. And I think it's time to accept the importance of making room for and listening to womyn whose voices are not heard often enough; to not be threatened by our differences, but strengthened by them.

Some Thoughts on Separatism

Sarah Grace
1982

– i am at the michigan festival, summer, 1980, sitting in a small circle of wimmin and talking about mothering. the workshop is billed as one for lesbian separatist mothers. i am feeling grounded and centered as i never feel 'out there.' with the naïvity of pollyanna, i think it is going to be wonderful to be with other separatist mothers. it should be very fine – after all, we share many of the same problems.

but it isn't.

being a separatist with sons is relatively easy for me to maintain, since i am privileged by their living with their father, to whom i gave custody. but one of the others isn't so fortunate. she defines herself as a separatist and is struggling with the issue of living with a son. we never discuss how she might creatively solve her problem, because one of the members of our group, in the elitist position of having one daughter, bitterly berates both of us. she declares that we are not separatists since we have alliances with pricks. she verbally attacks us for not being separatist enough. the discussion never gets beyond that.

this mother, asking for help in coming to some sort of life decision, might indeed arrive at a decision that she isn't a separatist. but i wish we could have come up with something a little more creative than the suggestion that she put ground glass into his peanut butter and jelly sandwich. she leaves the group feeling worse, feeling more confused, than when she began. i leave devastated.

– i run into an acquaintance, a straight woman, who has asked me to take part in a jewish sabbath service. wimmin will have the major roles. i am excited about participating. she also asks my lover to play 'hatikvah' on her recorder and they are arranging to meet at our house to go over the music.

'can i bring my husband?' she asks.

we tell her we'd rather she didn't, without going into any lengthy explanation that our home is womon-only space. at midnight, our phone rings and it is she, telling me that if her husband, her best friend, is not welcome at our home, she won't come either, and to forget about doing the music.

we neither play the music nor go to the service.

– a member of my lesbian support group has brought a problem to us. she has recently gone to an alix dobkin concert and ever since then has been shaken and angered by the hatred of men openly expressed there and with the resounding support and cheers for alix's comments. so she brings this anger to our group. two of the members are myself and my lover. both of us are separatists who maintain womon-only space in our home and have only very rare exceptions to that. those exceptions pertain to the landlord and a few of my sons who are allowed only into the room that she and i use for an office.

for two hours we listen to our friend direct a tirade at all separatists. every time i try to interject my own feelings, i am angrily shouted down. i get more and more withdrawn as each minute passes. after the group disbands it takes me nearly an hour to work out, with many painful tears, that i don't have to sit and listen respectfully to my position being attacked, to hear how 'fucked' separatism is because, if all wimmin felt as we do, who would take care of the boys of the world, who will see to it that they are raised 'different'?

the common thread is separatism, seen as the ultimate threat to the patriarchy. we stand as obstinate symbols of denial for all that society holds precious and dear, the antithesis to humanism. we don't need men, we don't solicit or want their support, their wars, their prick philosophies. and we are not afraid to say so.

as separatists we strongly identify as womon-loving-wimmin. many of us believe that even the most compassionate, the most sensitive among us cannot raise sons who are 'different' in a male-dominated culture. and we are under attack for being separatists. sometimes, as in the first incident, from among our own separatist sisters.

yet i believe that lesbians need to at least have compassion for each other. arriving at a self-definition of being a separatist isn't easy. it means that each of us has given deep thought to what we are saying about ourselves, has dedicated our energies and our strength and our minds toward wimmin only, with minimal contact, and certainly minimal energy, going to men.

very few of us are so fortunate that we are totally independent of men. we need to survive financially, and that often means gritting our teeth, putting on protective armor and going to work with the boys. some of us take alimony from our ex-pricks. we *aren't* totally separated yet, and it will be years before we can be.

i am not a humanist. i am glad that i have to deal with my

sons on a very limited basis. i hold my separatist space precious and, while i may occasionally tell conservative straight folks that my separatism merely means that i don't give energy to men, i know inside i hold very dear my fury at pricks and that i believe it to be fully justified. day-dreaming about being on a hit-squad is a favorite pastime.

there is strength in diversity. with our differences in culture, experience, beliefs and philosophies we create a wondrous textured weaving. and with that, we bring a divergency of dearly held values and beliefs, which we cherish and will defend loudly. but there is a need for compassion, an urgency that we allow other wimmin their own beliefs and at least try to understand them and give them room to exist.

i would hope that, as lesbians, we could begin to put energy into building paths toward each other's houses, not fences between them.

x-tra insight

flyin thunda cloud, rdoc.
1982

i often have found myself (especially recently), defending my separatist stance, az i am a dyke of coloua & i do reside in the south. i used to identify myself az a black dyke, now since i've been delving into my & many otha sistahs of coloua, i identify az jamaican west indian & cherokee (native amerikan). i really want to address an emotionally charged subject, from the view that i see/hear/feel from.

the issue of my separatism came up again wif a womin of coloua who did not personally feel that she need to link with her native amerikaness. she tole me she felt very hurt because i made the statement that yes i am a dyke of coloua, but i cannot go home runnin to mommy or daddy if the shit wears completely thin and none of my dyke friends want anything to do wif me. being of coloua and separatist iz a heavy duty thing especially if you live in the south. because az this dyke tole me, it's expected of you to work on issues that affect the general (if you want to identify wholly az afro-amerikan, which i don't) issues, such az housing for blacks/jobs/the economy, etc. . . .

it seems to me that so many of my sistahs of coloua (in particular black, amerikan born) forget the lies the black man tole in order to get us to believe that *we* (my black sistahs older than me) were submitting/compromising *no* part of us, by allowing our cunts to be pierced by dark penises, filling us full of poison & *many* unwanted babies, during the so-called black revolutionary (or so many thot) time, late 60's early/middle 70's.

i get very irritated when i hear dykes of coloua trash on separatism az a whyte girl's trip, cause it's not. even now, the black and otha males of coloua (but in particular black males) are assuming what they think iz their male prerogative/right by coercing black wimmin 2 have sex wif them unda the pretense of contributing to a very strong black nation. it seems that since black womyn (well for the most part, then again?) found out what the shit these fucks have been up to, the fucks have chase whyte pussy, jewish pussy, have raped/killed whyte wimmin, because of their rage at the 'un-womanly' black womyn, that will not 'up' for a black man, like she 'should,' which i see az bullshit. i'm only 25, want to live to be much older, but like the commercial, the wine remembers, well i remember their lies/broken promises, the countless black sistah lives lost in vain 4 a revolution that never truly happened. what did come out of this waz a much more increased state of awareness *identity*, everyone wanted to find it. i don't know very much about womyn's rights, i know about the womyn's movement of that time period only from what i read, cuz i waz very young, but i waz very insightive. it felt like a huge plot had gone down, & womyn (later dykes emerging) were getting the wool pulled down over the eyes – hurt/bitterness/rage & *not* hatred, prompts me at this point to be a dyke separatist. i follow my *own* rules of conduct az to how i choose to display my separatism. i have a kind of anarchy, i follow the realities of the world in which i *have* to exist (for financial/racial-ethnic pride, reasons this means i meet black pricks on a day to day basis). & whyle i am *not* about hatred, i see putting lots of energy az a *waste* of my/or my sistah's valuable time energies. all we need do iz withdraw from dealing with men & begin lovin *ourselves*/join with dyke womynkind, celebrating who we are, instead of speaking of *separate* 3rd world matriarchies. why iz it so hard for some womyn to see/feel/hear/taste with *all* of our 'listed' senses, & the x-tra insight that comes naturally with our being open to our womynlyness? i up for no one. i put out for no one; the only way that i will put out iz if a womyn wants to put out equally with me, if she will let me make love to her, az i let her make love to me; if we have coloua powa in bed, 'gyneferous!'

az a writta, who iz black/red/brown, and very proud of it, i must deal with the issues of survival which my lova and i feel very acutely az parents and 4 this moment, az dykes (particularly dykes of Coloua). things are ruff indeed, and sometimes reganomics haz us fightin one anotha, which izn't cool at all. we are both separatists, which really suited me fine, az i'd hate to have to slug it out with any womin about faggots, or male chyldryn (frankly i don't dislike male chyldryn until their moms make their having penises such a great big fuckan issue). i have a lesbian mom co-mom/friend of kid support network, and i have hooked up with dykes with male kids. i make it known that UMOJA iz a support network for any dyke with any chyld. but i do not have male kids. i had once said that i wouldn't mind havin male kids, but now since i have this very separatist political head, i'm not quite sure i could deal with seeing a waving penis, changin a stinking diaper. i also am a rape/incest survivor, and it haz taken me four years 2 deal with the anga/frustration i felt about all of that, and whether or not i'm angry with anything prick because of it. so i don't know.

it sort of hurts, but we're used to being alone weekends. we may move soon, to a place where there will be dykes to talk wif, be friends wif, who won't ask shitty questions, but will be supporting of our separatist stances, and support iz very important when you have a very separatist head. there's so much more i can say, but *not* at this writing. i just wanted to add another voice to the din of voices defending dyke/separatism az personal political choice. why don't we just give all praises due to the dyke imagination/vision, & go about things the way that feels comfortable? & quit creating separatisms where there are none.

Why Be Separatist?
Exploring Women-Only Energy

Alix Dobkin
1982

In many minds I have become a symbol of 'Lesbian Separatism,' whatever that phrase may represent to whomever might be using it at whichever point in some process she might be going through at that particular time in her life.

Nevertheless, there seems to be an unspoken, undefined myth of 'the Lesbian Separatist' who never, ever chooses to interact with men and who expects all women to do likewise. For me, Lesbian Separatism has always meant a consciousness, an analysis, and a commitment to the well-being and best interests of women in general and Lesbians in particular.

Marilyn Frye and Carolyn Shafer prefer the term, 'Lesbian Connectionist' and, to a great extent, I do too. It seems more informative and descriptive since it is what thousands of us are doing when we make ourselves our first priority and insist upon regular women-only space – when we consciously prefer and create it in our lives.

'Closed' is a word which has been used to describe an all-female community gathering. Once again women are being measured in relationship to men, who are not members of our community and whose appearance in it would probably offend most of the women there. I would love my father to see me in concert, but I have no right to expect every other woman to understand what a nice man he is. When I see a man at a woman's event a portion of my feelings closes down. Conversely, when I know that I am in the exclusive company of women I feel safe enough to 'open up.' Using the negative, self-defeating, 'closed' to characterize women's space is true only from a man's perspective. For a woman it is a lie.

And we have just barely begun to scratch the surface of what it means to be only with women. Those of us who have been consciously seeking out this precious time know how different it truly is and how little we actually know about it. We are eager to learn more and are frustrated by the way of life which constantly denies our sensibilities and overwhelms us with obstacles. Being with women is so wholesome, healing and liberating, and yet so often devalued, so often thwarted or laced with guilt by those who do not or will not understand the essential necessity of women-only space and time for women's well-being, and who, perversely, measure it according to the absence of men.

Building lesbian self-sufficiency

I have abiding faith in Lesbian survival and well-being. We are courageous outsiders. We have less emotional investment in men and their institutions.

It has been said that as a general rule men act in order to 'make things better' while women act to 'keep things from getting worse.' Well, in spite of our actions to date, the eighties are getting worse for women in those areas of life directly controlled by men: economic survival, racial and cultural repression and public health. Astrology predicts and Ronald Reagan promises that conditions shall worsen. Both point to 'self-sufficiency' as the key to survival. I agree. These times appear more scary than those past because there are so many more disasters waiting to happen.

Being self-sufficient as Lesbians has to do with taking our lives seriously and with a perspective on what our real needs are as opposed to the needs men manufacture for us. If we act in accordance with our own best interests, which to me means making the best use of all our resources, it seems obvious that racist, classist, anti-semitic and related attitudes and behaviors are not workable. This is an integral part of my separatism. Such work in our interests is the process and substance of our lives. Everything I do, and everything you do, with women is a part of this process if there is a consciousness about it. Sounds grand, doesn't it? Well, it is. And it is revolutionary. Evolving means skill building and we do it over the kitchen table, in our bedrooms, at parties, meetings, support groups and with those sharing special connections. I like to consider concerts, workshops and potlucks to be part of this process. For years I have been writing, talking and singing about how much women like me love and need women-only space. The particular sort of energy present at a concert of and for women only is not like any other. There is a unique rapport which women find only with each other. It's a bond you can't deny. And a thrill!

Notes on the notes

The above are excerpts from 2 sets of program notes which I have written and distributed at concerts over the past few years.

For the reasons outlined in some of the 'Notes' I find myself identifying less and less with the specific term, 'separatist,' although I have neither abandoned my passion for Lesbian sensibility and women-only time and space, nor my disgust for male violence, nor my rejection of the women and life-hating values of the male culture which perpetuates it.

The high quality of Lesbian consciousness impresses me more and more as does its usefulness in my everyday life. My unique position as a 'professional Lesbian' allows me to appreciate this perspective more than most but in no way invalidates it for others. A Lesbian who is alert to her identity and therefore to her own self interest is served well. Despite discouraging experiences with Lesbians, despite feelings of betrayal, disappointment and anger as a result of interactions with Lesbians, despite the discovery of Lesbian faults, flaws and foibles I am more and more impressed with the courageousness implicit in a woman's choice of a Lesbian identity especially in the face of revived anti-Lesbian sentiment. Some of this sentiment reveals itself within our own ranks, often under the guise of 'anti-separatism.' It has become so fashionable in some circles to discredit separatism within the past few years that I have resisted disassociating myself with the label even though I have felt less comfortable with it. Reluctant as I am to hold on to an outworn identity, I detest allying myself with the trendy compulsion to repudiate my separatist past.

The 'anti-separatist' cop-out

There's been much discussion of 'outreach' and a 'broadening of perspectives' from Lesbians lately. It's an excellent strategy, but does not impress me as a goal in itself. It seems to me that when some of these women embrace 'outreach' they are also forgetting who they are and what they know. The term itself comes close to being code for a denial of Lesbian identity and Lesbian community. Expanding beyond old definitions and guidelines is natural and healthy and is surely what a good many of us are now doing with our lives in one way or another, but I have some trouble with the language and its implications. Maybe it's because some Lesbians, especially 'former separatists,' have used these words in simplistic ways to indicate a weakness, a lack in ourselves which we must now fill with a male presence.

It depresses me to learn of a Lesbian who turns to men and the culture I generally reject. The immaturity of this assumption (that Lesbians are inadequate) becomes clear if we ask, what did you expect? It's as if these women are comparing our fledgling institutions with the mammoth and elaborate institutions of male society. Yes, of course we put each other through hard times, but it seems short-sighted to abandon a terrifically long-term vision after only a few years' effort. I can no more go 'back' to the emotional investment and dependence which was part of my definition as a heterosexual woman than I can kiss my elbow.

I prefer to learn about Lesbians going 'out' and not 'back' into the world of men. I still call it 'the fake world,' and I still participate in it. This has always been the case for me and for every other separatist and non-separatist I know. There are other reasons to go outside the women's community. I, myself, would like to be a role model for straight women. I would like to help make it easier for women to come out. I want to promote joy and pride for women in general and Lesbians in particular inside and outside of the Lesbian-feminist community. There are other values and causes which are important to me, and other identities, including that of 'human being,' but it is my Lesbian core identity which gives great, long-lasting meaning and currency to my life.

Those who discount Lesbian-hating, who dismiss Lesbian specialness and contribute to Lesbian invisibility, when I know that they know better, hurt and insult me. To me these are casualties of the heavy artillery trained at Lesbians ever since the dawn of man. What I refer to as 'the Lesbian community' has been the target of direct negativity ever since the early seventies when we first realized that we had such a thing as a community. Lately though, the over-all, general atmosphere is particularly successful in promoting anti-Lesbian and anti-separatist bias. The current intrusive environment encourages repudiation and compromise of Lesbian values. Being a Lesbian or a separatist is now, according to some, 'old fashioned,' 'out-of-date,' 'irrelevant' or just plain 'politically incorrect.' Such negative labeling strikes me as a rejection of our own history, a superficial capitulation to male assumptions and male authority. In other words, it seems like the same old shit to me, but with up-to-date packaging.

In spite of this small wave of forgetfulness there are many Lesbians who are still working, thinking, communicating and interacting consciously with Lesbians for conscious Lesbian purposes. We have been adding new dimensions to our basic analysis by incorporating a consciousness of the importance of anti-racism, work against anti-Semitism, considerations of ableism, fat issues and other relevant topics. We need not abandon separatism in order to include issues of concern as long as they affect Lesbians. 'Separatism' has become more of an assumption than a definition. It remains an important part of my identity. It is a foundation of original woman-identified theory, and the self-righteous critics of separatism are left with a dead horse – their own paranoia – to beat. The rest of us have moved on and taken the principles of our separatism with us.

To Rose

Vernita Gray
1983

You were seven in seventy
and I was
                beginning my separatist journey

past the role-playing in the few bars
that admitted a black lesbian if she
had 47 ids and a birth certificate.

Seeking the depth of communal sharing
with lesbians
i shifted my attention and energy
to us/
　　/we lesbians.

looking and seeking
to share a lifetime of love

creating/ourselves
a structure.

We lesbians make a lot of noise in bed
and out of bed.

There are always choices
and the commitment to passion

searching for the flow of beauty
uninterrupted –
　　　　　　　　the depth of loving

We lesbians make a lot of noise
in bed, and out of bed

but mostly we get up
and go our own ways
take paths
that sometimes separate up the road.

being the same
is not
always enough

I journey past the sounds of ugly racist
comments from so called sisters.

i took/take steps away from those
sounds, but still I can hear
the polite tones saying and silencing.
How dare you act out anger. I'm from a
good Irish family and we don't act that way
Saying – how dare you act black, womyn – and if
you can't act white then don't act. don't say. silence
it is no longer anger
but irritation as i explain once again
I'm not Allison
I move on my journey from these sounds and
racist tones.

to pause and boogie with black sisters

and to heal
while continuing to journey.

to create and seek
new space
separatist space

searching for the witches
and healers
who can touch

the touch of the fairy princess
    the wonder of the witches
As i journeyed and you read
    children's books

we both knew the fairy princess could

We believing in our power
you, thinking it make believe,
and I believing we have and
will continue to reclaim that
power of touch.

When the wicked witch turns the man into a frog

In the seventies I journeyed into separatism
loving lesbians
creating within myself a strength of stability
while working on
                    working out
                    moving into a collective
                    working on a collective newspaper
                    going to family of woman concerts
                    learning how to spell collective
                    and consciousness
                    sometimes taking space
                    choosing between birkenstocks
                    and boots
                    having a pot-luck
                    going to a rap group
                    liking alix dobkin
                    getting on the stage at the 1st
                    michigan music festival and asking
                    the collective to call it what
                    it is — a lesbian music festival

It was the Bicentennial year by then
you were a teen
probably wanting to leave home and
have your own space
and i wanting to buy some space
place – where only dykes would have the keys
and control the locks.

                     only dykes had the keys
    in that space we would
build an altar
to the goddess because we
have found her

our souls magnify the goddess
our hearts rejoice in her beauty
for we are graced with power to
choose to create ourselves

Seeking lesbian/spirits
              spirituality
             sharing
        in creating our power.

      power
          power

Now, I hear it called power and praised
        by lesbians who are into
        the diversion of
        whipping and tie-dying into violent fantasy

I hear on this journey past
spirit
        to sex

I hear it called power
over womyn over the other

I love loving – gertrude said

I love loving too, gertrude

And at my altar I pray we
redefine power and come out of
the bedroom – throwing off those
tied up fantasies – keying up and into
loose into loving each
seeking power over our lives
not emulating our oppressor.

in the bedroom
   A
   journey past these diversions
to work

        work/work on our racism
     work on our consciousness
             work with ourselves
     key into that violence and let it go.

My great great grandmother had no choice about
                                       violence
        slave she could not sleep without worrying
night after night
she had no keys
     There were no keys for my curly haired
     Semitic sisters in concentration camps only the
     long nights.

I have journeyed to the depths of
my ancestors' pain of real powerlessness
and come now to rejoice in the choice
the beauty of my lesbian life
separating with lesbians
              who have rings filled with keys

We lock up and go off to dance
under the moon at night

You are no longer seven, now we journey
                    together

Sharing our loving lesbian energy.
searching and journeying together.
and separate.
     free
     seen
     loved.

LESBIANS AS MOTHERS: STUBBORN QUESTIONS

The Ancient Matriarchy of Atlantis

Juana María Paz
1981

Act I Scene I

(The scene is a goddess temple in the ancient queendom of Atlantis. Anatolia, the first queen, is addressing a priestess of the temple Diana.)

Anatolia: The phallus problem, again. I can't imagine what you expect me to do about it. I don't understand it. Perhaps the elderwomyn can explain it to us. Exactly what do the priestesses want?

Priestess: Those of us who are priestesses of the Goddess temple are very sincere in our dedication, my queen.

Anatolia: Your dedication is renowned throughout Atlantis, my priestess, and I honor it. What is it that you wish me to facilitate?

Priestess: If you would, my queen, the priestesses and myself are quite appalled at this practice of the mutants to remove their outer genitals and place them bloody and warm on the temple of Diana. Several priestesses vow to leave the temple if this outrage continues. We understand that you have sent sages to speak to the mutants before. We thought that, perhaps, if you as queen and facilitator of all things would take an interest in the poor creatures that our land had pledged to be kind to. . . .

Anatolia: Please don't quote me. It gives me a headache. Are you really suggesting that I bring the dreadful creatures here?

Priestess: It was quite eloquent and moving, my queen, when you spoke before the counsel as a young seer of protecting and revering the mutants as every other living thing on our land. I was a young warrior at the time. I remember it well.

Anatolia: My former eloquence is always being remembered on these occasions. I honor you, my priestess, and I will use all my powers of facilitation with every womyn on the land to see what can be done about the mutants. Why do you suppose they come to the temple at all? Why don't they go off and fish or something? I thought they liked that.

Priestess: It seems, my queen, that the mutants possess a cruelty towards life that is unknown on our land. The teachers

297

thought it best to bring them back where they could be taught respect and kindness.

Anatolia: We were never taught respect and kindness. They were always just a part of our spirits. I'm afraid these mutants will be our undoing if we do not heed their ways.

Priestess: The priestesses have spoken, my queen. We must get about our work. We are planting new gardens outside the temple, you know, vines with the kind of fruit you like so much.

Anatolia: Of course, the priestesses are wise, as always. You must work with the givers of life and not be continually confronted with these monuments of death in the temple. I'll think of something. Someone will be willing to deal with the mutants. Perhaps the elders will tell us. I will call for Cilia, the wise one, and see what she has to say. I will send word to the temple when I have found a possible solution.

Priestess: May the ancient goddess be with you, my queen.

Anatolia: And you, my priestess.

(The priestess exists. The queen goes through another door and calls to a womyn in the next room.)

Anatolia: Agea, the mutants are soiling the temple with their phalluses again. The priestesses call upon me for a solution. Have you any counsel?

Agea: None, my queen, only to drown the last one of them before they prove our undoing. They bring no good fortune to our land. We have spoken of it before. My counsel has not changed.

Anatolia: It is true, Agea, that you are a great wise womyn, but Atlantis has made a vow to revere and respect all living things. What would you have me do?

Agea: Call upon the womyn to admit that we made a mistake. Many unexplained accidents have come among us since the mutants came of age. Our warriors would be glad to take them off to sea and leave them there.

Anatolia: I fear their mothers, our sisters, would never allow it. What do we do now?

Agea: Perhaps the science womyn can tell us, my queen, how this happened. We used to be all of one body; the old days, I remember them well. The first mutants were just being born when I was a young student. Cilia and I were in the same class. We had many profound discussions on the care and responsibility of womyn to our mutant children.

Anatolia: Dreadful creatures that they are. Would that we had drowned the first of them. They've brought us nothing but evil spirits.

Agea: It is true, my queen, and the responsibility to find the solution or the womyn with the solution falls to you as facilitator. Perhaps Cilia has some counsel. I can bring her to you if you would like to stay and think awhile. I have nothing further to say about the mutants. I am weaving more cloth for the Priestesses' robes and they will be wanting them before many days. I do not choose to waste time on the mutants. Shall I take a walk and visit Cilia's lessonrooms?

Anatola: You are a great friend and seer, Agea. Yes, please, see if Cilia will come to me.

Agea: May the spirit of the ancient goddess be with you, Anatolia.

Anatolia: And you, Agea.

(Agea leaves and Anatolia turns to the window to meditate. Shortly after, Cilia enters, in a flurry.)

Cilia: Anatolia, you had need of me . . .

Anatolia: And in such a state, my mother, and have you emerged this moment from your bath?

Cilia: In fact, I have. I was bathing while Agea came to speak to me. It is a very hot day, my queen, even for Atlantis. She said you were disturbed, that it was about the half-womyn again, so I came immediately.

Anatolia: And have you brought me something, my love? I like it when you bring me things.

Cilia: I believe I have some rose petals from the bath here in my pocket if you would wish . . . oh, here, a little wet, I'm afraid. I did come in a great hurry, knowing you were probably upset.

Anatolia: It is no matter. Perhaps next time you will bring me a rosebud. Agea spoke to you of the matter at hand?

Cilia: Indeed, my queen. I do not know of a solution if we cannot live with them. As you so eloquently said, many years ago, they are living breathing creatures to be revered and respected like all others. . . .

Anatolia: Cilia, my friend, friend of my mother, teacher of my grandmother, please do not speak to me of these memories. I have heard nothing else all day. It is your counsel I need, not mine. Why do they come to the temple? Why do they not go off into the forest to live?

Cilia: They are destructive of the land and their mothers will allow only so much discipline against them. Also, it seems some of our womyn have chosen to make love to the mutants. I believe that's what keeps them hanging around.

Anatolia: Make love, as you and I? How could they possibly? What would they do? The mutant has no reproductive organs.

Cilia: That remains to be seen. It seems some of our womyn have discovered that by placing the half-womyn's outer genitals in the birth canal a tickling sensation is brought about.

Anatolia: A half-womyn's outer genitals in the birth canal! It is incredible. A good thing my honored mother, your friend, is at sea with the lost mariners and not here to see what outrages befall our land. Surely I can do something, Cilia. I am the queen.

Cilia: It is true, you are the queen, Anatolia, but it is respect and communication that you have at your disposal, not authority.

Anatolia: That is very amusing, Cilia. Where did you arrive at that description?

Cilia: It is from your oratory at the counsel many years ago when Atlantis chose a method of coordination and facilitation in the land. Shall I quote you?

Anatolia: Please don't. And stop reminding me that this queen business and sparing the mutants was my idea. What should we do?

Cilia: It could be suggested that the mutants be taken to another land to live. But as some are very young I doubt their mothers would allow it. And the word of a mother for her child is always sacred.

Anatolia: It seems, my lover, that the half-womyn strangle us with our own morality. Let us speak no more of it for now. Tell me why you are taking a bath in rose petals – some brave warrior in your class, perhaps? You may scarcely have thought of it but I've always hoped I held a sacred place in your heart. At times like these you are the one I look to for wisdom and encouragement. None of the other womyn wish to deal with the halves of themselves and who can blame them? They are dedicated to the forces of life. I am very tired, Cilia. How many years since my mother has been gone?

Cilia: Over twenty, my child. I have tried in my ways to make a home for the daughters of warriors who do not return. I have the school, you know, and any time you are tired of this work. . . .

Anatolia: I know, my friend, but I feel it is not time for me to leave here. In a year perhaps, or two, but as the elders said at the counsel of Atlantis many years ago, Anatolia, the orator, who asks for a queendom and one seer to facilitate works in the land, Anatolia, the orator, must commit herself to her truth and if we choose the way she has counseled then she and no other must be queen. I am very tired, Cilia. We will think of this further.

Cilia: You wish to be alone to meditate on this matter?

Anatolia: I was just going to ask if you have plans for the evening.

Cilia: If I may answer in my own way?

Anatolia: Of course.

Cilia: There are many plans to be carried out in Atlantis but none that I revere more than being in your presence. Shall I come at dusk?

Anatolia: Please. And you will bring me a rose, not in pieces this time, the whole thing?

Cilia: Not in pieces, my friend, the whole thing. May the goddess be with you this day, Anatolia.

Anatolia: And you, Cilia.

(Cilia leaves.)

Act II

(It is later the same evening. Anatolia brightens the lamp at her bedtable and turns to speak to Cilia.)

Anatolia: I wonder how it seems to you to make love to me as my mother before me and my grandmother before her, perhaps? Am I any different? Am I like my mother, Cilia? Would your friend have been proud of her daughter?

Cilia: My friend would have loved you as I do, Anatolia, more, perhaps, if that is possible. I, too, think of you as a daughter, as well as a lover. You are many things to me and I see that you are much distressed by the mutant curse. Curse that it is upon our land to have halves of ourselves born to our womyn. Thanks be to Diana for bringing me three hearty daughters, all warriors on the sea.

Anatolia: Ah, yes, my daughters, too, feel the calling of the mariners to the sea. My eldest daughter vows to bring forth my mother from the sea. I fear I will lose all my daughters to the sea. It is a generation of mariners we have raised. In truth the warriors tire me sometimes with their tales. Look there, it is a dragon's tooth or some such object, a monument of death I call it, yet I must keep it on my altar or the young warrior who brought it to me will be much offended.

Cilia: The same warrior sought counsel from me. She is very intrigued with you and desires to make love to you. She fears you find her foolish.

Anatolia: I am the central meeting place. They tell me before they come and go on their journeys so one womyn, at least, in Atlantis, will always know where everyone is. I am sometimes the first to see their treasures. Why do they bring me bones? Why don't they bring food and new methods of planting, knowledge of better water systems and living environments? Why don't they stay home and do house-work? All the cleaning of the temple here falls to me, you know. As with the mutants, womyn direct their energies elsewhere.

Cilia: The warriors are young my queen. They long for adventure. They seek the impossible to test their powers.

Anatolia: The impossible is already here. What are we going to do about these wretched mutants? I've used all my powers of facilitation to contact every womyn on the land. Even the psychics in the mountains who descend once a year refuse me. They are very indignant. They do not wish to be disturbed in their rituals ever again. I fear that I have offended them. They say we should destroy the mutants or learn to live with them. They will not. They were very strong when they spoke years ago of preferring the peace of the mountain to living with halves of themselves. The answer is always the same, Cilia. The solution, I fear, is beyond me.

Cilia: What do you usually do?

Anatolia: Someone usually comes to me with a task they need performed or want to share with someone else. Since I am in touch with every womyn on the land I usually know who to send her to. If I don't, I send letters or messengers to whoever I think is most likely to be interested or know who else might be. Like when Thilia wanted to build a new temple we found a womyn on the south side to do the building plans but some of the stones required for the roof were too big to lift, slide or dig out. So we sent messengers out and found a womyn by the sea who was perfecting a way of making stones move by playing certain notes on a flute. It saved a lot of work and those same womyn are working together on the new theater. You may have noticed them outside surveying the dimensions.

I have called upon our scientists again about the mutants.

Cilia: I fear you are alienating those womyn. They say you, above all in Atlantis, blame them for the curse of the mutants.

Anatolia: I do not blame them, my friend, I simply want them to do something. What can I do? I am not a scientist, a mixer of potions, a maker of medicines. I simply facilitate between womyn who have the same wants.

Cilia: You have been a good queen to us, Anatolia.

Anatolia: And you a good teacher, Cilia. Will I be wise like you when I grow older?

Cilia: I am no wiser than other womyn, my friend. I simply listen more closely, perhaps, than they.

Anatolia: Meaning that I don't listen? I listen to the science womyn. They say they can explain the phenomenon but have not the power to stop it. The Tribunal of Atlantis must meet again they say and propose a solution, then they will look for a scientific way to bring it about. Something to do with radiation and the sun stroke of the last generation. Do you understand it, Cilia?

Cilia: Indeed, I teach the phenomenon in my classes.

Anatolia: I'm not interested. I only want it stopped. I don't suppose we could do something with the sun?

Cilia: I'm afraid our knowledge of the stars has not reached these depths, my friend.

Anatolia: Just a thought. I'm getting desperate for a solution. I hear there has been another phallus sacrifice in the temple this day. The halve's mother came to see me when she finished tending his wounds. It was quite dreadful. She had his blood on her robes.

Cilia: Still, it is not womyn's blood spilled.

Anatolia: Yes, that is true, but it is a terrible thing. The halve's mother was quite upset, doesn't know what to do with such a creature as an offspring.

Cilia: Who did you send her to?

Anatolia: I suggested anyone and everyone. No one in Atlantis knows what to do with the mutants. She will not hear of the creature being destroyed or set out to sea. She is afraid of what will become of the creatures without her. We have truly nursed these mutants with our life's blood.

Cilia: So what is your solution?

Anatolia: I can see none. The tribunal must meet again. I fear this issue is the most divisive of all. Even when we debated the planning of whole cities, the routes of long journeys, the education of daughters and warriors, we had not this chasm between us. Womyn is pitted against womyn. The mutants' mothers despair at their actions but will not allow them to be restrained. The others hold themselves above the mutants and will not even speak of the creatures. I heard tell today of a womyn who refused to eat at the marketplace because a group of young mutants were crowding together telling jokes about the womyn and throwing fruit at each other.

Cilia: May the Goddess save us. The creatures are vile.

Anatolia: Cilia, it is nearly dawn. I may have to face the High Priestess today with no solution. This has never happened before. Will you stay with me now and help me think this through? Perhaps there is something, an idea or possibility, that we have not thought of.

Cilia: My friend, I have watched you grow and blossom from a babe in arms. I was at your mother's side when you were born and I hurried back to be at your side when your mother failed to return from that journey so many years ago. You were just a girl then and I wondered what direction your thoughts would take you in. For a while I thought perhaps you would become our best orator or join the priestesses in their rituals instead of this lonely path you have chosen. Yes, love, I will stay with you now and help and think and walk with you to the Tribunal when the time comes — with or without a solution to present to the womyn. Come now and sit by me. Let's remember the good times, the days when your mother walked among us. Remember that story she used to tell about the womyn who ate the moon? Perhaps the solution is not accessible to us now. Perhaps only the future holds the answers we seek. And perhaps if we sit here together as two friends and bring the sum of our womyn's knowledge to the problem a solution will reveal itself. In any case, your mother was my oldest friend. As her daughter and my friend also you hold a special place in my heart beside her. Whatever happens at the Tribunal today I am with you. The womyn will understand if we need their help in finding a solution and our lives and culture will survive no matter what happens today.

Lesbian Mothers

Alice, Gordon, Debbie, & Mary
1973

We have all chosen not to be mothers because of our realization of the oppression our own mothers faced. All mothers are oppressed by being forced to do constant childcare with no real power over the factors affecting the child's growth or her life. Mothers are placed on a pedestal and adored, at least in the abstract, but they are not respected. They are expected to be the embodiment of wisdom, love, peace, etc. and at the same time relegated to what society considers some of the most menial work. They are given much of the responsibility for making sure that their children properly internalize society's rules and yet are given no say in the formulation of those rules. Mothers, according to the psychiatric profession, always love their children too much or too little and are either too powerful or too submissive.

Mothers spend most of their time taking care of (by working either inside or outside of the home) or worrying about their children. Child care for them is a responsibility which they *can't* slough off. Most of the time this activity prevents them from being involved in a complete way either in society or in the movement.

Not only are lesbian mothers oppressed in the ways that all mothers are oppressed, but since lesbian mothers often are not associated with men, they suffer additional economic oppression, as well as the constant fear that their children will be taken away.

We have already expressed our belief that it is a waste of time and energy, for at least white lesbians, to raise male children. But we feel equally strongly that the choice should be hers, not the government's or the father's. We believe that the right of lesbian mothers to keep their children is a right which all lesbians should support.

Further, we think, given the lack of adequate facilities in the larger society, that it is in the interests of the lesbian community as a whole to provide for adequate childcare so that lesbian mothers will be free to participate fully in the movement. But we can't see, as we've said before, lesbians wasting energy on male children, and we believe, therefore, that the lesbian who keeps a male child has placed herself in a contradiction analogous to that of the straight woman. Although her participation in the movement is valued, we can not see that any lesbian has the responsibility to waste her energy on childcare for that child.

We have noted with increasing dismay the number of 'lesbians' in Seattle who have decided to sleep with a man in order to have a child. All the reasons we've heard for having a child seem messed up. Basically, they seem to boil down to two. The first is that for security and continual love, a child is even better than monogamy. The second is that they feel that they, and maybe only they, can raise a child in a non-sexist manner so that the child will become a non-sexist 'person.' We feel that the first reason is too great a demand to place on any child. We feel that the second reason ignores the individuality of the child and the fact that society has as great a part in the socialization of a child as do the parents.

There are plenty of children in this society who need to be cared for, and we don't see that having your personal egg cell involved in the formation of the child should be all that important. (We would like to second the Gutter Dykes' proposal, in *Dykes and Gorgons* #1, that the best way to deal with the question of men in future societies is for women NOW to refuse to have any more children with men. We believe that technology is almost to the point of extra-uterine birth, cloning, and the ability to produce a baby through the union of two egg cells.)

As our movement grows we hope we will be able to really get into communal raising of girl children. They are our future. They, as all women, can be a source of energy and valuable ideas for all of us, and a lesbian community seems to us to be a good environment to grow up in.

Right now, however, we see childcare as an enormous drain of energy on our still embryonic movement and, although we feel the responsibility and desire to do childcare with and for the female children of lesbians, we see no need to add more children at this time, especially since the only way to get one is to sleep with the oppressor.

We realize that the lesbian mother of any child has often had to struggle much harder than a straight woman, to make a life for herself and her child and thus often has a larger emotional investment in her relationship with that child than the straight mother has with her child. We don't think that lesbian mothers should be forced by community pressure to immediately part with male children if they are not comfortable with this political decision. Lesbians should be supportive of those lesbian mothers as they work out this difficult contradiction.

As white lesbians, however, we recognize, as we've stated before, that the genocide being practiced against third world people might prompt a different choice to these questions on the part of third world lesbians. We want to respect those choices.

This article should be read in conjunction with 'Separatism,' page 31.

Addition to the 1st Printing of *Lesbian Separatism: An Amazon Analysis*

Alice, Gordon, Debbie, & Mary
1974

The four of us are rethinking and rewriting *LS: AAA*. Diana Press will publish the new book in August.* There are several changes that we are making and we look forward to your criticisms. One of our errors is so grave, however, that we do not feel we can wait until August to acknowledge it. We believe that we have already done a great deal of damage to third world lesbians by our non-supportive attitude due to our position on third world women in the paper.

In the paper you are about to read we say that because many third world people face genocide in a white dominated society, lesbian separatism may not apply to third world women. We said that we felt third world women did not have to give up their male children. We also said that, as white lesbian separatists, we shouldn't use our politics to be divisive to third world movements. We now feel this is wrong.

Males created their own cultures, strikingly similar everywhere in the world. From these cultures came wars of conquest. Racism and classism were instituted to justify the purposes of war. Sexism was the basis of the overthrow of the matriarchies by men in all cultures. Men of all cultures subjected women to violence, and at various times continue to do so. Racism and classism have often been only excuses for more advanced patriarchies to overthrow cultures which retained more matriarchal customs. The basic purposes of patriarchal cultures still are to perpetuate themselves and consequently to keep women separated from each other so we won't rise up against men.

We think patriarchal culture is dangerous and disgusting. We therefore intend to overthrow it for our own physical survival and our happiness. We therefore do not condone any behavior of any woman which serves to support men. We do not want any men to retain the power they have or to gain more power. Any support of men will inevitably be converted by men to strength, used to further subordinate women. Our happiness lies in our ability to support women and to convert that strength into the rebuilding of matriarchal culture and the undermining of patriarchy. We are appalled to find that we four have been unconscious collaborators with the enemy in our position on third world women.

We analyzed why we took that position. Our original feelings

* This manuscript was supposed to have been published by Diana Press in August, 1974.

on the subject were close to our current position. But the more we talked about racism and about lesbian separatism and third world women, the more confused we got. Because we had been involved in civil rights and the left, we had a lot of experience with anti-racism. We habitually accepted this as a positive force in our lives and didn't actually realize that all of this education had been just as patriarchal as the pro-racist educations we had had previously. We particularly became confused by the two teachings: white people should never interfere in third world affairs, and the genocide of third world cultures and peoples is of more urgency and importance than anything else.

We now publically reject such education designed to enable men to gain more power and to divide women from each other, such education based on dividing people along artificial lines, patriarchally imposed, instead of along the basic and original division of sex. This male teaching tells third world women that their first obligation is to stick with the males of their race and that their liberation as women is not as important as helping men get more patriarchal power. Women are told to think that the genocide of particular male cultures is more important than the fact that all matriarchal cultures have been dealt a death blow and that all women are facing gynocide. Consequently, third world women and white women have been separated from each other more than ever. For years we have been politically forbidden to support each other's struggles for survival as women, they because it would be supporting the supposed enemy, white women, and us because we were not allowed to interfere in the third world community because we were the oppressor. Yet all four of us who wrote this paper have had experiences where privately, during those male movement years, third world women and ourselves acknowledged our natural close feelings and trust. Racism and genocide are very real. We feel that it is important that we develop a feminist way to oppose them, rather than re-warming the new left's methods which were bound to fail because they weren't anti-patriarchal. We do not believe white women are the real enemy to third world women. We do not feel women who still relate to men are the real enemy to lesbians. Almost all of us act sometimes as enemies to others but potentially we can all be allies. Men are not potentially our allies because it is their culture we have to destroy, and this makes all the difference.

We realize that while we are only potential allies that there are a lot of problems. As lesbians, we do not work with straight women. Some third world lesbians, in addition, may not be willing to work with white lesbians. And so on. This is because there are real privileges involved which give some of us more power than others. Such power gives us a stake in the male system which may lessen our desire to fight. Until straight women stop relating to men and become lesbian and until those who have inherited privilege because of race or class can learn to non-oppressively handle these privileges (which we cannot just get rid of as long as this male culture stands), we cannot expect to have a united lesbian movement. Because we are not united does not mean we cannot act to destroy the basic cause of oppressive divisions, patriarchy, and to alleviate the effects of privileges within our movements. Thus many of us shall eventually be able to unite, and build a powerful feminist society.

We still believe that white lesbians should not impose white culture on third world lesbians. However, we believe that we have accurately analyzed this society. We believe that third world women are as capable as we are of perceiving the patriarchal nature of the society and acting accordingly.

Where the Boys Aren't!!

Nancy Breeze
1982

Last Christmas, when my college-aged daughter arrived with her boyfriend for a visit, I considered calling the local women's resort to inquire about their December policy on male children. But we ended up going to Cumberland Island, instead.

The male child issue swirls relentlessly through our community endeavors, often dividing us and our energies. Having raised three of this species myself, (and hearing the wife of one say that she only wanted daughters, not sons), I feel I can be considered somewhat of an expert. Because times were different back then, my children, unfortunately, were raised very conventionally. So, I am related to three young men who possess most of the traditional beliefs. Their father's attitudes, the general cultural practices, and my own learned powerlessness, taught them about women's 'proper place.' Of course, each one thinks he is very different from the sexist father or usual males. Their anti-war activities, and dropping-out of college, encourage them to define themselves as non-traditional, and they assume that also means non-sexist. However, the Hare Krishna one believes women have a 'special

309

place,' the married father-of-two jokes that his wife can have some of his beer but no money of her own, and the 20-year-old regrets that I no longer wield a cookie sheet.

When I first got involved in the women's movement, I was surprised to hear the mother of a two-year-old boy say he had already picked up so many of the cultural maleness norms that she just didn't want to spend her time and energy trying to combat that. I didn't know what she was talking about. Whether or not he was a boy, her schedule, of working as an apprentice carpenter and organizing women in construction, would have left her little time for single parenting. So she let her former husband raise the child in another city. At that time I thought her decision was based on the practicalities of time and energy. Since then, however, I have become more aware of the cultural impact on small children, and I can see that it is an overwhelming job to try and raise any child without pre-determined sex roles. Yet, as the mother of one boy put it, we have more patience with a girl who wants to 'be a lady,' or join Brownies, than with a boy who is boisterous.

I think we could argue forever about what these women who already HAVE male children should do. And some say, 'How can we change society if we leave the boys to their fathers?' This usually comes to a head at women's conferences. Otherwise, it is relatively easy to make personal decisions about our own situations, not complaining about other women who make different choices. There is enough work for all of us; each one doesn't have to do the same thing. But, when we get together for a weekend, or a week, to work and play together, what do we do with the children, male or otherwise? A recent matriarchy conference was, ironically, labelled 'anti-mother' by some, because boys were banned. No doubt the organizers hoped to avoid a volatile issue which they feared would overshadow what, to them, was the purpose of the conference.

Instead of screaming at one another that we 'shouldn't abandon the babies,' or, alternately, that 'we are continuing our oppression,' we need to join together to come up with solutions. The quantity of children, whatever their sex, being produced, under the societal heterosexuality and motherhood norms, can always keep us busy and distracted. It's tempting to consider a way to turn off the flow, but, since motherhood is perhaps the greatest consciousness-raiser around, we must assume that the lesbian-feminist community will have to deal with what seems an inexhaustible supply of children. One solution: the Michigan Music Festival organized a program for boys, run by selected men at a separate site, while the mothers and sisters were at the festival. This seems a practical answer. Although some mothers were worried that the boys would feel excluded, others believed that this kind of experience would neutralize some of the 'superiority' notions that boys inevitably pick up from the larger society.

It seems to be a matter of priorities. We are continually being forced to make painful choices about what to do with the limited amount of time and energy remaining after we have earned enough money to pay the rent and buy the groceries. A traditional way of deciding would be to defer our present needs for the future needs of others, especially our children. Today's mothers, however, are less likely to be coerced by the dependent nature of small children into confining their activities to child-oriented ones from the moment of birth until time for kindergarten. Therefore, I have been surprised to find mothers of boys waging such vehement attacks on women-only spaces. They seem to feel threatened by the possibility of going where their sons would not be welcome, even when the boys are not with them. This contradiction suggests that women's expanding self-definition can often bump guiltily into the internalized age-old limits, and that the motherhood identity can be pervasive. This does not indicate that such limited identity is 'natural,' or unchangeable, but that we may still need to struggle against the bombardment of traditional messages, which are designed to keep us in our place.

Although I don't advocate ignoring the next generation, I believe it is a mistake to focus all our attention on changing the little boys, (and girls), while leaving the 'big boys' free to continue their planet-destroying practices. It is possible that the next generation of women, not having been subjected to a lifetime of being taught that everyone else is more important, will not feel as conflicted as many of us do about putting ourselves first. Recently, I was explaining to a seven-year-old friend that I liked my granddaughter's teacher because she encourages her to like herself. My friend looked at me in astonishment. 'You'd have to be crazy not to like yourself!' she said. The dawning positive self-image of these little girls can expand, uncurbed, when boys are absent from their environment.

Women have always valued women-only spaces, although this has rarely been acknowledged. When we have basked in the suburban morning coffee, the ladies' sewing circle, or the weekly beauty parlor visit, we have told ourselves that we are just 'passing the time' until our husbands or boyfriends come home. However, now that women are buying land and constructing women-only resorts, we are challenged to validate the age-old truths that we prefer space unpolluted by male energy. It seems obvious that there's no way we can be kept 'down in patriarchy' once we've experienced the reality of WOMANSPACE!

The Tired Old[1] Question of Male Children[2]

Anna Lee
1983

As we try to do so many things differently than have been done before, we sometimes lock ourselves into old patterns. One of those old patterns is to concern ourselves with male children. Wimmin have always been responsible for children, especially when their behavior turns out to be socially unacceptable. This is the old pattern. Now, within the lesbian community we still see ourselves as responsible in that way. If we want to change society and if, as things have gone up to now, male children grow up to be men, then it seems that one of our 'chores' is to be responsible for male children by seeing that they become non-sexist. And since male children raised within the lesbian community seem to be about as sexist as their counterparts in the straight, non-feminist world, we wonder what we have done wrong.

We have done nothing wrong. To believe we are responsible for the sexist behavior of male children, to see ourselves as responsible for the failure of male children to adopt non-sexist values, is to labor erroneously under certain assumptions. In the first place, this belief involves the assumption that our generation of political activists is the first to realize that male behavior is generally unacceptable. In addition such a position carries with it the belief that our mothers and grandmothers felt it was OK for their sons to brutalize wimmin. Thirdly, insofar as we believe that our mothers and grandmothers were aware of the unacceptability of male behavior, the belief that we are responsible for male child behavior involves the belief that our mothers and grandmothers were totally incompetent in this area whereas we, somehow, are utterly different in our rearing abilities. These are assumptions that we must face directly.

In addition, the belief that wimmin are responsible for changing male behavior seems to involve the belief that if only mothers would teach their male children to be less aggressive and to respect wimmin, everything would change. This is simply not true.

Within the black community, sons were taught passivity in order to enable them to survive in a world committed to lynching black males. An aggressive black male simply would not survive. So, if teaching male children non-aggression and respect for wimmin is viewed as a means of changing our sexist society, well we already have such cases and it hasn't made any difference in how those males treat wimmin. In fact, a black male reveres his mother as a strong womon and claims he would do anything for her. At the same time, he is out on the street pimping, leaving 'his' babies for 'his' womon to care for, and abusing wimmin. I believe such efforts would yield similar results in white males, but I will leave that topic to those who care about it.

As wimmin we have been strong. We've taken care of business. We have been available for our children – whenever they have wanted us. And what have we gained? It is arrogant and sexist for us to believe that our mothers before us erred, that now we can correct their mistakes and raise male children differently so that male behavior we object to so much won't happen anymore. It is also arrogant and sexist to believe that wimmin as always are the ones responsible for whether male children grow up to be acceptable in a society that gives wimmin no power.

The above assumptions are present as discussions occur about the need for wimmin-only space. Marilyn Frye has discussed separatism in relation to who has access to us and who doesn't. Historically, males have had access to us. If we include them in wimmin space, how is that different than what has gone on before? The argument that boys need to see strong wimmin interacting with each other and caring for each other carries the arrogant assumption that today's adult males did not see that as boys. Certainly they saw it in the black community.

The belief that we are responsible for the behavior of male children avoids the reality that wimmin do not hold power in the boys' world. By inviting them into our spaces we perpetuate the historical, sexist pattern of assuming wimmin are responsible for something they have no power over (the attitudes which male children absorb from a society that discredits and undermines wimmin of all ages). Further, we assume that non-sexism and sensitivity will be perceived by male children as a reasonable trade-off for power. For it is power that any boy is offered upon reaching manhood. Some get more than others but all get to join the old boys' club and in case you didn't notice that is what runs this world. What we as wimmin can offer little boys is not power. If you were a little boy which would you choose – power or sensitivity? Be honest.

A final consequence of the belief that wimmin are responsible for male children is an incredible focusing of attention (once again) on males while taking females for granted (once again) and assuming they can and should take care of themselves. Girls grow up with the same options we have. When we invite male children into our spaces we devalue our daughters. We discount our daughters by considering boys' power only in relation to ourselves. That is, many wimmin convince themselves that since boys are smaller than they are, boys are harmless and have no power. Even this consideration is a false belief that implies adult males will respect adult female institutional authority in the same way they respect adult male institutional authority, and will never or rarely side with a male child (or male student) against an adult female.

Aside from this false implication, the belief that boys are harmless ignores entirely the reality of wimmin-children and so devalues them. Have we forgotten how little boys would terrorize us at school and at recess? Have we so easily forgotten what little boys do to little girls? Have we forgotten that this terrorizing took place under the noses of strong, adult wimmin? In a time when we are trying to understand the experiences and reality of wimmin different from ourselves it is ludicrous that we ignore those whose experiences we once had.

In womon-only space how safe will wimmin children feel when they see those who terrorize them welcomed by their mothers? Secondly, in a womon-only space such as the Michigan Womyn's Music Festival, if boys see girls and the mothers of girls walking around without clothes on, what will they say the next week in school to their classmates — that they saw really strong wimmin interacting in a caring way? Finally, in womon-only space where we do have some say as to what goes on and are not in the immediate shadow of male authority, little boys still terrorize womon-children. Ask the womon-children.

What is it we have decided to offer our daughters? Are we not saying that their safety and comfort are not our concern? And in doing so are we not implying that the needs of wimmin are still not important or as important as the needs of men, beginning that devaluation with the needs of wimmin children?

Wimmin-only space is limited. It is limited by location and duration of time. It is to be cherished. It is wrested from the powers that be. It is a place for us to heal ourselves, nurture ourselves, grow and change, and relax with each other, a place which would enable us to go out into the boys' world and survive with our sense of self somewhat more intact. Should we not transmit the message to male children that they cannot expect access to wimmin whenever they want? Should we not be concerned about giving support to young females who face the same options we do? Should we not cease to accept total responsibility for what happens in a world when we don't have the power to control what happens in it? Wimmin-only space is important. Without it the gains we have made would not have been possible. If we hadn't been in a safe environment, the talking and growing would not have happened. I do believe that wimmin who argue for inclusion of males of any age ignore at what cost we have built our communities – fragile though they are. Our communities are still fragile, and, in light of this reality, who are we going to focus on and value?!

Notes

1.   I use the word 'old' in the sense of persistent.

2.   I want to thank Julia for her helpfulness in pointing out places in my paper that needed to be clearer and Sarah, thank you for taking the time to do such extensive re-writing of some of the passages. I of course take full responsibility for the opinion expressed.

For Women Who Call Themselves Lesbians –Are You Thinking of Getting Pregnant?

Bev Jo
1984
Supported by Linda Strega (California, U.S.A.)
and Rose Ruston (Wellington, New Zealand)

Well, your decision affects all of us and there are some things we'd like to say about it.

BECOMING A MOTHER DOES *NOT* MEAN . . .

1.   . . . . that you are really normal at last.
2.   . . . . that you are now finally a *real* woman.
3.   . . . . that you are a loving, unselfish individual.
4.   . . . . that you are politically courageous.
5.   . . . . that you are now more oppressed than Lesbian non-mothers.
6.   . . . . that you will own your children.

7. . . . . that if you have a daughter she will become a Lesbian.
8. . . . . that if you have a son he will be the exceptional non-sexist male.
9. . . . . that you are not bringing another rapist into the world.
10. . . . . that you are creating Lesbians of the future.
11. . . . . that you will be able to re-live your life through your children.
12. . . . . that you have a right to expect or demand that other Lesbians take care of you and your children.
13. . . . . that you have a right to inflict another male on our Lesbian communities.
14. . . . . that you have the right to inflict another male on our world.

BUT BECOMING A MOTHER *DOES* MEAN

1. . . . . that you will be treated with more respect and privilege in the world.
2. . . . . that you will be treated with more respect and privilege among Lesbians.
3. . . . . that this increased privilege will be at the expense of Lesbian non-mothers.
4. . . . . that your privilege will be more if you have a son.
5. . . . . that you are fulfilling a male-defined role of femininity and Motherhood.
6. . . . . that you are doing what you have been programmed to do since you were born. (Now you'll have a real doll to play with.)
7. . . . . that you are participating in a reactionary choice to join the het baby boom that is part of the U.S. right-wing backlash.
8. . . . . that you are sentencing yourself to at least an 18 year commitment.
9. . . . . that you will have less time and energy to take care of yourself and other Lesbians.
10. . . . . that you will always have a primary commitment to your children that will take precedence over close Lesbian friends and lovers.
11. . . . . that you are contributing to more hardship in all of our lives because your babies will be our future competition for housing, jobs, resources and possibly food and water.
12. . . . . that you will replay some of the same destructive roles you played with your family.
13. . . . . that you will be more caught up than ever in the

circular trap of dependent and caretaker (which is already a trap for those of us who are alcoholic or drug dependent or grew up taking care of a parent who was).

14. . . . . that it's likely your children will later hate you because they did not grow up with all the privileges of a normal, nuclear family.

15. . . . . that they are likely to hate you just because of the power you have over them as a Mother, whether you wanted that power or not.

16. . . . . that you will be vulnerable to being institutionalized by them when they grow up and you grow old.

17. . . . . that you are most likely creating more heterosexuals.

18. . . . . that *no matter what you do*, if you have a boy, he will terrorize and attack girls and later, adult women, and statistically will very likely be a rapist.

19. . . . . that if you have a son and daughter your son will probably molest and rape your daughter.

20. . . . . that it will not be a rare event if *you* are raped, beaten or killed by your son when he gets old enough.

21. . . . . that you will be playing with sperm, which is a heterosexual act (and offensive to most Lesbians).

22. . . . . that the process of being pregnant and giving birth is also a heterosexual act.

23. . . . . that you are risking getting V.D. or AIDS and passing them on to other Lesbians.

24. . . . . that you are weakening and permanently altering your body, and shortening your life span, making it more possible to bleed to death, have toxemia or a stroke, become paralysed or even get cancer. (The dangers of pregnancy and childbirth are a well-kept secret.) Motherhood can be lethal.

We Have to Ask the Question: What is Happening?

Baba Copper
1981

Birth defects are the single greatest health problem of the young. (March of Dimes)

Cultural Death/Rebirth – An Evolutionary Process

The question 'What is happening' is meant as an evolutionary question. In the past, the popular concept of evolution was limited by the model of biologically inevitable change achieved imperceptibly over eons of time. More recent theory acknowledges the possibility of very rapid modification and includes culturally determined biological adaptation. Human passivity toward evolution can no longer be justified. Each of us becomes a representative of the species, empowered by our particularized participation in the whole, to identify and interpret the evolutionary potential of our culture.

I ask the question as a lesbian separatist and as a representative of my species. Since patriarchy has been the world-wide cultural norm for several millenia, I consider it evolutionarily significant that my identity category even exists. Our presence among the forces of female resistance is just as much a measure of patriarchal disintegration as are the statistical trends of genetic illness and deformation, pollution, resource depletion, accelerated violence or mechanization run amok. It would seem that male-dominated culture is running out of time in this frame, on this graph, within this pulse. Cultural transformation is neither easy nor quick enough, threatening the evolutionary process itself with the greed of its death convulsions.

What form did we think that the decline of patriarchy would take? If we tell ourselves often enough that it isn't as bad as we know that it is, then we will not have to think about the complicity which our survival demands. Everyone clings to her toehold of safety. We wait. As our personal statistics give us glimpses of the never-named epidemics which surround us – the little children living out their short lives under oxygen tents, the friends sickened by the toxicity of their work, the jagged sexualized violence of the angry men, the seven o'clock news of hunger or torture or armed suppression, the babies deformed within their mothers' wombs, the leaky reactors – we wait. What exactly are we waiting *for*? Revolution, in the age of scarce resources? Strikes, marches, non-violent protest, civil disobedience – in the age of managed media and political police? Terrorism, in the age of nuclear détente, political assassination, hostage peoples, counter-insurgent massacres, refugees? Sabotage, in the age of spills, lethal contamination, delicate supply systems? Each of us is vulnerable, dependent upon the system to maintain itself, to provide distribution of food, emergency services, and sanitation, information, jobs. As the world contracts, all compete to avoid being one of those who slide off the edge.

I would despair, but I see at the same time the flourishing cultural exploration of lesbians – wimmin consciously defining our lives outside of patriarchal limitations. This tension between the worlds which I bridge has a deeper meaning, I believe, than simply personal experience. Our presence in these times is for me evidence of a cooperative adaptation to the changes which the future demands. Evolution is not simply the survival of the most aggressive – the patriarchal named 'fittest.' For humans, it must be a genetic/social adaptation *within* the nest patriarchy has fouled. Future survival of the species will depend upon radical changes of values, reproduction, and tools into models which do not reflect male domination/competition. Where else can this work be done?

Evolutionary Consciousness – Future Visions as Political Guides

[Women] must start being tender and compassionate with themselves and with other women. Women must begin to 'save' themselves and their daughters . . . . [An] effect [of this] would be the creation of a secure and revolutionary source of emotional and domestic nurturance for women, without which the courage for survival might falter and which, at this point in history, only biological females seem to know how or are willing to provide.
(Phyllis Chesler, *Women and Madness*, p. 301)

As the larger culture crumbles, lesbians are moving out into the nothingness of cultural invention. The rending of male 'civilization' is creating outlaw wimmin. Any wimmin who resist compulsory heterosexuality or involuntary motherhood or economic slavery are by patriarchal definition outlaw wimmin – renegades. Often separatists. Our resistance demands cohesion, not only for defense, but in order to invent new ways of being. Since possibilities for a female-named future for any of us as individuals are remote, we are learning to adapt as best we can to survival within chaos. Chaos is full of opportunities, as well as casualties.

If lesbians as a category are to avoid being among the casualties of patriarchal disintegration, then it is necessary that we develop between us mutuality and solidarity *over time*, from one generation to the next. This demands clear namings of our long-range goals. We must become strong seers who envision a world in which all females have absolute control not only over their reproductive life but also the milieu which informs the next generation of mothers. It is the shared vision of the future we *want* which will create it, as it becomes our expectation. It is irrelevant that we do not know how to achieve the circumstances we envision. There is absolutely no way 'from here to there' without first naming to each other where it is we want to go.

When I think about a post-patriarchal future, my vision is one of a world without war, rape or all the variations on human slavery history has always known, including wage slaves. I envision a consciousness shared world-wide that would allow wimmin to reject for the whole culture knowledge or inventiveness which denied the overriding value of inter-dependence between peoples and their environment. What I am talking about is a restoration of an undisturbed genetic/social evolutionary process within our global matrix. Limitation of human births to the demands of ecological balance, as the females of some other species do instinctually, is unimaginable within the social expectations of obligatory heterosexuality. Female sexual autonomy would assure species reproductive responsibility. The biological and psychological roots of a female-named technology would, I believe, maintain clean air and waters, fertile soils, wild places and space for all the species. It is to this vision that I bring my experience of land-based separatism and its meaning for me.

Land-Based Separatism, A Personal Account

The connection between food production and women is an ancient one, symbolizing the extension of female responsibility for the feeding of her young beyond the breast. Worldwide, women are being separated from the land and food production by machines and their male owners. At the same time in this country there are many lesbians who are struggling to purchase and work land. The life they live is neither easy nor secure. Although there always have been single rural women, the social phenomenon of large numbers of country dykes is probably new. Most are couples on private land, but in my county there are six lesbian-owned communities. Although many country dykes participate in a wide variety of political activities, most of them are at the same time saying through their life style: 'I want to live gently with the other creatures of my climate; I need to be more responsible for the food I eat; I want to return my wastes to the soils which support me; I am learning to use the energy of the sun, wind and water which flow around me; I want to coalesce with others like me in a celebration of loving the planet, the moon and the sun who pull upon my body.' These values were shared by those of us on land who identified as separatists.

Above the refrigerator in the kitchen of the community in which I lived hung a hand-printed creed, taken for granted by the wimmin who shared the land. It reflected convictions peculiar to the separatist consciousness from which it sprang:

> Until there is no place on the Planet Mother where access to, or use of, a womon's body or labor can be taken by force, or legally acquired, or exchanged under duress for basic livelihood, then we will seek separation from those who advocate or practice these abominations against wimmin. We will refuse all males our essential energy, or nurture, or life through our bodies.

Living on land which was owned and worked by separatists changed our perspectives in ways which I believe are not possible otherwise. To explain this, let me trace our process in establishing ourselves as separatists. When our collective first discussed the issue, we were very innocent. We were lesbians, weren't we? We certainly didn't want men around. But what about repair men, delivery men, meter readers? Male neighbors could be deterred by a new gate at the top of the hill. We would read our own meter. Although we acknowledged that there was some maintenance we could not do, and some loads we could not haul up the mountain in our pickup, we solemnly pledged to stretch our skills, to find wimmin experts, to never call for male help without exhausting all other possibilities. Fathers, sons, brothers, ex-husbands or gay men friends were not welcome on the land. No man was to enter our quiet valley without consultation among us and adequate forewarning.

A year and a half later, many things had changed, but male-free space still was of high value to us. Mostly, we worked and played naked in the sun – weather being the primary justification for the clothes we wore. Visiting wimmin often found the emotional impact of our freedom unnerving. Confronted by the depth of their fears – fear of country darkness, fear of the voyeur, fear of male violence – many found that they must consciously struggle with irrational responses to the absence of threat. We heard a lot from them about the shedding of the armor of their city conditioning, as it took place. Also, some of our own attitudes shifted gradually. We became acutely territorial, so that the presence of hunters in the valley on the edges of our land infuriated us. The isolation of the land, as well as encounters with rattlers, modified our attitudes toward weapons. Our separatism was less rigid toward male workers from whom we need to learn, and at the same time, became more passionately ideological.

As the demands upon us grew, the 'male child of a lesbian mother' problem emerged, bringing with it a new level to our exploration of the meaning of separatism, and divisions among us. 'A rule is a rule' said one. 'Flexibility is the essence of accountability' said another. 'We can not be all things to all wimmin' said another. 'There are other places she can go with her son.' 'I'll leave myself rather than cope with some nasty little boy!' A clear absence of consensus. We scheduled Separatism for our weekly consciousness-raising meeting. We returned to the subject over and over, raising new doubts, asking new questions, but maintaining our no-male stand. (We always had been open to heterosexual women although we were insecure about what was carried back to their men about us.)

We were the only separatist land in our area. Lesbian backlash was severe. Some local wimmin would not visit our land; others exchanged fierce disapproval of our 'nazi' politics. Many potential supporters or members of our community never paused to explore the rest of our politics or our personalities, once they heard that we were separatists. We seldom knew their definitions of separatism, so vigorous was their rejection. Strong anti-separatism seemed to spring from homophobic sources, even in lesbians. As always, the assumption that our stand was molded from a negative base left us vulnerable. We tried to affirm our choice to be with wimmin as a way to coalesce our energies, in a search for the unknown. Some heard us.

Separatism as the Development of Pro-Daughter Consciousness

When the shaman wears the mask of a deer, she is filled with a knowledge the deer has. Entering the body of the deer gives her a way to discover the knowledge of her own body.
(Susan Griffin, *Pornography and Silence*, p. 72)

Instead of defining separatist spaces as excluding males, it is possible to see them as pro-daughter spaces where single wimmin and mothers can be innovative in their relationships to the daughters and each other. Female-only space is a symbolic extension of the lesbian resistance to nurturance of males. All women, including lesbians, are imprinted with the patriarchal imperative of ascribed power through the role of mother/of/the/son. Layers of mythic brainwashing contain religious admonition (the Virgin Mary), psychological guilt-gripping (*Portnoy's Complaint*) as well as lots of real life rewards. Women as life givers and life sustainers tend to fall into false doctrines of love. Our fallacy has been to trust that our sons will not enslave our daughters.

There is a lack of feminist analysis of the mother/of/the/son trap, and at the same time most lesbians feel painful ambivalence about the female socialization which they experienced as daughters of patriarchal mothers. Self-hatred has been the primary lesson, as mothers sacrificed their daughters to the demands of the cultural sadism of patriarchy, shaping them for victimhood, sexual service, and economic dependence. Mothers also teach their daughters how to mother. The continuum of this largely unconscious process is, I believe, a key to cultural evolution. There are primal possibilities latent in female-to-female teaching in the service of anti-patriarchal values and expectations. Separatist redefinitions of motherhood are past due.

I was the only mother on our land. Not only was I the only womon who had borne a child, but I am the 62-year-old lesbian mother of a 23-year-old lesbian daughter, who also lived on the land. It has been eleven years since I escaped the obligations and goals of patriarchal motherhood. She and I have been inventing mother/adult daughter relations as we go.

On the land I found new teachers of motherhood, new insights of its potential. The deer grazed just outside the fence which surrounded the orchards, gardens and houses. Mothering for the doe means teaching which herbs and bushes are safe to graze, where the sweet water can be found even as the summer parches the earth, how to stop motion so that the dappled light obscures instead of reveals, which humans are dangerous, how to watch for the ajar gate to harvest the tender garden, how to avoid the rattler, how to outrun the dog, when to group with others and when to go alone. I recognized that my seeing was distorted by my humanness, but this I sensed by watching: the mother never favors the young buck, for it is the doe who must learn survival, to adapt to change, to cooperate within the group. She is the one who must have the full power of her own initiative and the will to make choices, not only for herself, but in her time, for her young.

The deer I watched survived by adaptation to the circumstances of a rapidly deteriorating environment. In a hundred years their primary predators have shifted from four-legged to two-legged creatures. The deer and I avoided the same tormentors. When a forest fire set by men to flush their prey swept through our valley, it burnt many of our basic survival needs – the water tanks, fences, orchard, barn. For the deer, the loss was even greater. Gone was the cover which hid them from the hunters. The ground was bare of green. Until the rains renewed their forage, they ate the crisp singed leaves of the oaks. They are strong survivors. We have much to learn from them.

Lesbian Mothers

The mother and the lesbian are two polarized images on which male subjectivity has projected some of its deepest fears and hatred of women. The lesbian mother is a contradiction; she is not supposed to exist. Perhaps among other reasons, because her existence suggests that no woman, even one who has married and borne children, necessarily belongs to a man or men.

(Adrienne Rich, Foreword to *The Lesbian: A Celebration of Difference* by Bernice Goodman, p. 2)

I feel that the assumption is justified that all females of all species have many more 'instinctual' impulses than can be identified by observation. An example of this is the ability of the female of many species to reduce her average reproductive rate when her eco-range is overburdened. Species reproductive responsibility is an instinctual response *of the female alone* to environmental pressures. Human females also function at a 'doing without knowing why' level, later legitimizing our actions by left-brain rationalizations. Most of us know that, just as humans are endangering all other species, so we are ourselves an endangered species. Lesbian culture is a species survival tactic, the only exploration globally of consciously non-patriarchal values and mores. Separatism is the cutting edge of that social mutation. As we unconsciously gauge the magnitude of the damage to our habitat, we instinctively plot a reproductive and nurturing adaptation.

Lesbian mothers teach their daughters new lessons by example. Gone is the cultural impotence and involuntary servitude of the patriarchal mother or grandmother. The lesbian is the mother-who-can-not-be, by heterosexist definition. Stripped of legal motherright, she usually carries the multiple responsibilities of earning *and* home care. The lesbian mother shows her daughter the full dimensions of the workmaker, the one who copes, the decision-maker, the one who names. She sees herself, not as lacking the presence of a father for the child, but fully sufficient without him. Sufficiently mothered daughters are learning to be the creators of their own circumstances. Sufficiently mothered daughters are being taught to avoid the divisions of age, race, and class which arise to diminish the bonding of wimmin. Above all else, lesbian mothers are sexually autonomous wimmin who act upon the human potential of differentiation between eroticism and reproduction. Their control over their own sexuality and at the same time the product of their bodies, is their primary gift to all the daughters who can hear it. It can be taught; it must be.

The Lesbian Daughter/Mother as an Evolutionary Model

. . . the first love object for all children is the mother. Our deepest, most primary connections are to her. If this is the case, then the male child is primarily in a heterosexual position and the female child is in a homosexual position.
(Bernice Goodman, The Lesbian: A Celebration of Difference, p. 15)

We need to 'study' ourselves more systematically, since we represent the only subculture which is consciously attempting real detachment from the normalcy of male-supremacy. Lesbian separatist mothers especially are like fish out of the water trying to explore the possibilities of amphibianism. The metaphor which comes to my mind is a remarkable TV documentary I saw about the tree-frog of Eniwetok, the coral atoll in the Pacific where scientifically empowered men exploded an experimental hydrogen bomb. In the twenty years from the fatal zero on the countdown, a species of fish had evolved from the waters of the lagoon to the sparse trees of the atoll, where they survived by catching insects nocturnally. As the bulbous eye of the tree-frog winked at me from the screen, my identity merged with hers for one nauseous moment. In only twenty generations the mother fish had pushed her daughters out of the water, toward the step they must risk death to learn: breathing. The daughter/mothers taught each other from one generation to the next. Very rapid change is disorienting for mothers. For countless generations we mothers have resisted the gaseous experimentations of our daughters, teaching them to remain in the water. Finally, and perhaps too late, we recognize that it is time to acknowledge the potential of tree life. (The tree-frog is an ex-fish, just as I am an ex-heterosexual.)

Another metaphor which I believe is relevant is that of the crowded rat experiment. As reported through the androcentric bias of male researchers, 'social breakdown' took place as the result of crowding the rats. The dominant male rats established territories where they had sufficient space and 'kept' preferred females. Other males engaged in homosexuality. Many females became 'poor mothers' who trampled their nests instead of nursing their young. To my evolutionary eye, the rats were showing signs of trying to adapt to the circumstances to which the researchers had subjected them. The females were reducing their burden of reproduction by the means available to them. Not rearing young is just as natural an act as rearing them. However, for the researchers, homosexuality and female-controlled infanticide are such deep patriarchal taboos that it was impossible to report them without condemnation. Cultural adaptations to overpopulation, diminished resources and genetic pollution when initiated by females will inevitably be named 'social breakdown' by men.

There are no future facts. The future can always be seen in the trends of the present; successful prophesy relies on being able to pick the significant trends from the insignificant. The trends which I perceive likely to be projected into the future are:
- more wimmin are coming out every day
- perhaps as many as six-and-a-half million US women who self-identify as lesbians are remaining in their marriages only because of their fear of losing their children through legal action (source: Lesbian Mother's National Defense Fund)
- single motherhood is statistically the fastest growing familial structure in the US
- more lesbians and single women are choosing to reproduce using a donor
- a recurrent subject of research and speculation among lesbians is techniques to avoid the conception or birth of male children
- more lesbians are acknowledging their unwillingness to mother sons, and acting upon those feelings

The separatist vs. anti-separatist debate over the nurturing of sons is a painful reality most of us have experienced in raw forms. Often it divides white wimmin from wimmin of color or strong ethnic roots, economically secure wimmin from poor wimmin, and non-mothers from mothers within the lesbian community. Lesbian mothers committed to a male child are understandably defensive about the debate which swirls around them. Like aware mothers of every preceding generation, they believe that they can do better – that their son will be an anti-sexist adult. There are good indications that in some cases real changes are being made, despite the imprinting of the cultural sadism which predominantly socializes the male.

Lesbian feminist futurists (like Sally Gearheart) are admonishing both women and men that planetary life depends upon the female's ability to contain male power through severe limitation of the proportion of males in the total population. Although Gearheart optimistically envisions that males could voluntarily take responsibility for their own proportional decrease, there are others who take a more active stance toward this goal. Some lesbians exchange information about the potential of parthenogenesis in articles, newsletters, workshops and ongoing groups. Other wimmin are using amniocentesis to determine whether or not to carry their pregnancy full term. However, the number of wimmin involved in the new determination not to bear or nurture males is very small, insignificant in comparison to the large number of women worldwide who still practice female infanticide.

Separatism as One Process in the Politicization of Lesbianism

By analyzing and comparing the significance and meaning of different kinds of separatism, lesbians are reaching for an important tool in our own culture-naming process. We are touching ourselves with the power of feedback, thus altering the potential of our actions (feedback being the partial reversion of the *effects* of a process on its source). As the numbers of land-based separatists grow, more wimmin will be able to provide the environment for group mothering of the daughters, freer from pollutions of the bonding process. Our belief in the innate ability of wimmin to generate knowledge and ethics which derive directly from *our* experience, *our* biology, *our* psychology allows us to breach the limitation placed by patriarchal sympathizers upon political life in the present. We thus test-through-being new parameters of female autonomy.

Bibliography

Chesler, Phyllis. *Women and Madness*. New York: Doubleday & Company, Inc. 1972.

Goodman, Bernice. *The Lesbian: A Celebration of Difference*. Brooklyn, N.Y.: Out & Out Books, 1977.

Griffin, Susan. *Pornography and Silence: Cultural Revenge Against Nature*. New York: Harper & Row, 1981.

DRAWING LINES: MANHATING

in the dream

Jan Hardy
1981

they brought her/handcuffed and bruised
to a bare wooden room/i watched
through a window covered with grey dust or soot/
they stripped her
hammered her with questions
somehow i could hear/i knew what they wanted
though i had never seen this woman before/
when she would not answer
they forced her to a table/held her down/
a ring of men's faces grey in the glimmer
of a naked bulb hanging over her head/
again they demanded/a hand like a club, lifted
blocked the light/the seconds before
more terrible than the blow

they called her by my name
and she did not deny it

i couldn't stop shaking/crying/knowing that her life
was buying my own
and i saw through her blackened eyes
the fist drawn back/striking/again and again
saw through the blackness of her closed eyes
the naked yellow light/the ring of men's faces/
felt the crack of my skull/my arms and my legs
held down/broken
i stood watching
safe/for the moment/in my body

they called her by my name
and she took it for her own

she lay on the table/
they beat her into consciousness
finding their mistake they called her name and still
held her down/to finish their work/
spread her legs while one man
wearing white took a scalpel
cut careful incisions/

like small bloody rays from the angry sun
of her vagina/
the doctor's voice/authority/kindness/
said the operation would widen her/
make what was going to happen/a little easier

he was the first to rape her
and every man ripped her further apart
i fell to the ground outside
covered my eyes with my fists/choking/huddled
in a pile of bricks and ashes/
for the first time i saw
the soldiers in the street
they brought me to the room
handcuffed but unhurt/
they had taken her away/
i stood by the table/her blood/dried
and clumps of hair matted to the wood/
then i knew they had wanted me
not on that table/but standing outside/
they wanted me to see
a woman tortured and killed
for loving a woman/for wearing her name
like a prison number/
they wanted me to witness/a woman killed
for being a woman
they wanted me/and others like me/not dead/not yet
but alive and afraid
and silent/it is for that woman
i write this poem

Remembering: A Time I Will Be My Own Beginning

Jeffner Allen
1982

Lesbian separatism is, for me, the ongoing action of every lesbian feminist who will be her own beginning. I will be my own beginning: I remember myself, my body, my world as a source.

Integral to remembering is man-hating: A difficult stance because it requires a fidelity to what is real in ourselves.[1] Through philosophical reflection that constitutes a vital aspect of my own rememberment, I will show how man-hating is an element of lesbian separatism.

Touching, feeling, imagining, fighting, thinking, caressing, I remember myself. I remember the possibilities in my future, the actualities of my past, the openness of my present. I remember the members of my body, the actions that form my body as lived. In remembering, I am.

Remembering shapes my existence within a temporal horizon. The horizon of temporality is not neutral. Whenever the profiles of my memory, like the horizons of time, are erected by men, I cannot remember myself. At such moments, male domination not infrequently forces me to remember myself as essentially and 'by nature' the Other who 'is' only in relation to men. I, dismembered, disappear into nonexistence.

Yet, quite clearly, I am here. In everyday life I undergo and envision an experience of stopping the time and memories of patriarchy and of unfolding a temporality in which I am myself.

According to Greek mythic history, in late Mycenean times the oracle at Delphi engaged in a remembering of herself. As a priestess of the earth goddess, Ge, she descended into Earth's caverns and returned with prophetic wisdom. Whenever the oracle spoke of a community's past, future, or present, she remembered back into, ahead of, and within herself as a source.[2]

The Delphic oracle remembered herself as an originary source of time-consciousness and historical being until Apollo killed her. The Delphic oracle, embodied as a female dragon, was slain by Apollo. Apollo appropriated and occupied the oracle's prophetic tripod. Zeus stopped Earth from sending dream oracles to warn humans of the oracle's impending danger. Chronos, with the passing of time, turned the dragon into a male so it would be a more 'worthy' opponent for Apollo to combat.

I remember, only with great difficulty, the oracle who was an originary source of time and history. When I look back at the so-called 'origins' of Western civilization, I see only the Pythia who is *not* herself. The Delphic oracle is said to remember only because Apollo possesses her: 'At Delphi . . . Apollo relied on "enthusiasm" in its original and literal sense. The Pythia became *entheos, plena, deo*: the god entered into her and used her vocal cords as if they were his own.'[3] Apollo becomes he who shapes the horizons of time and history. He commands wars and peace, decrees laws, legislates art and music. The oracle, robbed of her own memories and bodily members, becomes the vehicle of Apollo's utterances. She is made to sit on Apollo's ritual tripod and, finally, is replaced by a male priest called 'the prophet.'

Today it is neither possible nor, perhaps, even desirable to return to the originary remembering of the Delphic oracle of Greek mythic history. What is significant is the oracle's meaning, and loss of meaning, for me as I remember myself.

From the Delphic oracle to modern times, men's expulsion of Mnemosyne, she who remembers, has attempted to make impossible the free, open and spontaneous, remembering of ourselves. Whenever our history has passed through the events of ancient European culture, we have been forced into dismemberment. Yet, even though the oracle has been expelled not once, but over and over again, something of her remains.

I pass through memory after memory, looking for the body of experiences which I and my friends have lived together. Amidst an unending series of images possessed by men, a moment quite different in kind appears. Surrounded by its possibility, I may, perhaps, exclaim, 'I hate men!' After all, as Adrienne Rich writes,

> Am I to go saying
> for myself, for her
>
> *This is my body*
> take and destroy it?[4]

In the anger and irony of this statement, man-hating emerges as having been just below the surface all along.

A cautionary voice of the gate-keeper's memory may promptly echo the command of patriarchy: One ought not hate men. Joanna Russ states in 'The New Misandry':

> It's nothing new for the oppressed to be solemnly told their entry to Heaven depends on not hating their oppressor.... (1) You do something nasty to me. (2) I hate you. (3) You find it uncomfortable to be hated. (4) You think how nice it would be if I didn't hate you. (5) You decide I ought not to hate you because hate is bad. (6) Good people don't hate. (7) Because I hate I am a bad person. (8) It is not what you did to me that makes me hate you, it is my own bad nature. *I – not you – am the cause of my hating you.*[5]

I may echo the voices of men, 'Be assertive, not aggressive. Don't confront: don't hate men.' Perhaps I need 'positive thinking,' a 'personality change.' Am I OK? Am I 'hung up'? Smile! Smile! It's not 'normal.' Don't hate men. Hate myself — that's fitting for women. Fit in. Selective amnesia begins again.

But, NO. Man-hating is not a matter of taste. It depends not upon my personal whim. Man-hating is my response to men's violence against women. According to FBI statistics alone, every three minutes a woman is raped and every eighteen seconds a woman is beaten – by a man.[6] The ultimate mark of man's possession of women may well be the ethic of suppression by which he forbids women to hate him.

A faint voice of the gate-keeper's memory may propose, with the greatest of diplomacy, 'I hate not men but what it is men do in this culture.'[7] Yet, to hate the 'sin' but love the 'sinner' continues a patriarchal and Christian morality that posits a pure human nature, or essence, behind men's actions. According to Thomas Aquinas, hatred is always preceded by and arises from love. Hatred is a disorder of the will and the root of sin. One cannot hate God in his essence, for God's essence is Goodness. Nor can one hate the True or the Good in their essence. Likewise, one cannot hate one's neighbor, for hatred would be opposed to the love that we have 'naturally' for him.[8] I, the diplomat, deny all essential characteristics that men have assigned to women and claim that we are our actions. With regard to men, however, I am caught in dangerous patriarchal essentialism. I insist that men are essentially good, regardless of their actions.

If I say, 'I hate not men but what they do,' I remain divided against myself, dismembered. I hate myself and not my oppressor. In contrast, when I say, 'I hate men,' I use language well. I say what I experience: *I* hate men.

My hatred of myself appears in a new perspective. Hatred of wo-man is hatred of that aspect of me bound to man, of myself as the twin essence, or 'wife' of man.

Man-hating may be considered an antagonistic division between object (woman) and subject (man). Woman, the supposedly passive object who can be only in relation to men, rebels against and ruptures with men, the transcendent subject and Creator. In this context, man-hating is not the 'battle of the sexes,' it is not an incessant cycle of men vs. women, women vs. men. Nor is man-hating a stereotypic 'heroic hatred,' a battle between heroic wills. Heroic hatred is insatiable. Upon vanquishing its enemy, heroic hatred goes off to seek another. Heroic hatred depends, and thrives, on a situation in which there must always be an enemy. Man-hating, in contrast, threatens at its core the patriarchal world of strife and fragmentation. Man-hating places in question all heroic ability, namely, all antagonistic activity that exists solely for its own sake.

Man-hating posits an end to those very conditions which set it in motion. Man-hating is without the ineffectiveness of resentment. Anger no longer suffices, for in anger I act against an individual who has power over me, rising to his level to get even. My anger, instead, turns to, and is grounded in, hatred. Hatred begins with the assumption that there is an equality between object (woman) and subject (man) and ends in the breakdown of all patriarchal definitions of women.

In man-hating, I explicitly identify and break with the reproductive memory that leads to my dismemberment. I no longer claim to be wo-man, the counterpart of man, she who is possessed by men. I posit my own freedom. I place myself with all who will be women no longer: lesbians.

Man-hating brings me memories of strength by which I begin to gather myself in productive remembering. Here, man-hating appears as grief at an injustice, as a deep bereavement and caring.[9]

Whenever man-hating is thought solely in a patriarchal context of woman vs. man, it fails to appear as an adequate paradigm for radical change. In a patriarchal and Cartesian sense, once one begins with a dualism, man-woman, one is stuck with it. I cannot bring it about that men have never existed. That men have existed, is, in fact, an 'irremediable dimension' of my life.[10] One may even protest that man-hating intensifies my painful experience of men, as the violators of women. Adrienne Rich writes,

> Fantasies of murder: not enough:
> to kill is to cut off from pain
> but the killer goes on hurting.[11]

My experience that 'the killer goes on hurting' has, however, a freeing explanation. Guided by etymology, the echo of my deep though often hidden experience, I find that 'to hate' [from old English *hete*, akin to Old High German *haz*, hate and Greek *kēdos*, care] is to experience an absence of justice, a violation of one's rights, a state of being injured, oppressed. Hatred is grievance at an injustice. Hatred includes the pain and sorrow, fear and anger, originating from an injury. Hatred is a deep and poignant distress caused by bereavement. Just as anger is grounded in hatred, hatred is lodged in grief. Hatred emerges in grief for the dead, funeral rites, mourning. My hatred arises from a loss, but not the loss of my 'other half,' as patriarchal dualists engaged in preserving forever the twin essences man and woman, or masculine and feminine, often say. My hatred of men is, rather, my experience of the loss of myself and others as autonomous subjects. My man-hating is grief for myself and other women at the loss of our bodies and memories, time and history.

At the same time, to hate is also to care: for a deceased friend, for a living friend, intimate and beloved, for a group of persons or communities. The opposite of hate is 'not caring' [*akēdia*], apathy, sloth. My intense and active love for what is most intimate, most dear, may be accompanied by man-hating. If 'the killer goes on hurting,' it is because men continue to bereave women of ourselves as free autonomous subjects *and* because I continue to care for myself and those intimates who are close to me as individuals who are whole and free.

Springing forth from caverns deep in the earth, Mnemosyne designates a central aspect of lesbian feminist self-constitution. The persistence of my dismemberment is but an indication of the fragments and limbs of women which appear in the field of patriarchy. Yet, by care, which is found at the center of my hatred of men, the fragments are remembered into a time in which women are with women, a time, even, when wo-man as a class can disappear. The caverns of Mnemosyne speak anew only when there is 'heard, as it were, the echo / of an echo in a shell,' when unaccustomed memories and a new attunement to remembering lead 'through spiral upon spiral of the shell / of memory that yet connects us.'[12]

Notes

1. Pamela Kearon, 'Man Hating,' in *Radical Feminism*, edited by Koedt, Levine, Rapone (New York: Quadrangle, 1973), pp. 79–80. See also, for discussions of man-hating, Elly Bulkin, 'An Interview with Adrienne Rich,' in *Conditions* Two (1977), pp. 53–66; Connie Salamore Velmadaughter, 'Man-hating,' in *Majority Report* II, 6 (October, 1972), pp. 13, 14; Monique Wittig, *Les Guérillères*, trans. David le Vay (New York: Avon, 1971), p. 76.

2. H. W. Parke, *A History of the Delphic Oracle* (Oxford: Blackwell, 1939), pp. 4, 17; H. W. Parke, *Greek Oracles* (London: Hutchinson, 1967), pp. 14, 35, 36.

3. E. R. Dodds, *The Greeks and the Irrational* (Berkeley: University of California Press, 1966), pp. 70, 71, 73; Julian Jaynes, *The Origin of Consciousness in the Bicameral Mind* (Boston: Houghton Mifflin, 1976), p. 322.

4. Adrienne Rich, 'Natural Resources,' *The Dream of a Common Language* (Norton: New York, 1978), p. 65.

5. Joanna Russ, 'The New Misandry,' *Amazon Expedition*, eds. Birkby, Harris, Johnson, Newton, O'Wyatt (California: Times Change Press, 1973), p. 27.

6. Elizabeth Pagedale, 'Women-Hating Film Elicits Strong Protest,' *The Reader* (Chicago, March 13, 1980), p. 10. See also Ntozake Shange, 'with no immediate cause,' *nappy edges* (New York: St. Martin's Press, 1972), pp. 114–117.

7.   Robin Morgan, *Monster* (New York: Vintage, 1972), p. 83.
8.   Thomas Aquinas, *Summa Theologica*, trans. Fathers of the English Dominican Province (New York: Benziger Brothers, 1947), pp. 714–717, 1341–1344.
9.   Ernest Klein, *A Comprehensive Etymological Dictionary of the English Language* (Amsterdam: Elsevier, 1966), pp. 13, 530, 707; Liddell and Scott, *Greek-English Lexicon* (Oxford: Clarendon, 1925), p. 946; *Oxford English Dictionary* (New York: Oxford University Press, 1972), p. 1263; Eric Partridge, *Origins: A Short Etymological Dictionary of Modern English*, 4th ed. (London: Routledge & Kegan Paul, 1966), p. 2, 280; *Webster's New Collegiate* (Massachusetts: Merriam Co., 1973), p. 525.
10.   Jean-Paul Sartre, *Being and Nothingness*, trans. Hazel E. Barnes (New York: Citadel Press, 1966), p. 388.
11.   Adrienne Rich, 'The Phenomenology of Anger,' *Poems: Selected and New, 1950–1974* (New York: Norton, 1966), p. 200.
12.   H. D., 'The Flowering of the Rod,' *Trilogy* (New York: New Directions Books, 1973), p. 156.

This is the Year to Stamp Out the 'Y' Chromosome

Gutter Dyke Collective
1973

As a further definition of our feelings, ideas and lifestyle, we call ourselves *man-hating* dykes, which is not the negative, time-consuming declaration that it seems. To simply ignore men in this world is impossible. We are constantly bombarded with their pollution and destruction. It surrounds us – from the air we breathe and food we eat, to the scarcity of jobs, to the subtle rape of our minds by their media and society, to the very real rape we meet in the streets, at work, and even in our homes. The privilege of ignoring men is not concretely feasible for most women.

Considering the majority of us were brought up to believe males to be superior and desirable, regardless of the other truths our inner sensibilities told us, it is important that we recognize them now for the real enemy and danger that they are. Although our anger has been suppressed, it is a good and healthy reaction to the way we are treated in this world. Our oppression is *real*. If we react the way we have been conditioned, we sublimate our rage and turn it into fear or suicide. Or else we throw it off onto each other and tear our friends apart. In-fighting and divisiveness have always been the primary weak points of the women's movement. We ridicule each other for our defense mechanisms and survival techniques and do the man's job for him. Our differences are real, whether they are race, class, age or lifestyle, but the oppressions we place on one another originate from men.

We can relate across our barriers if we take care not to deliberately use our man-made differences to hurt each other. We may first have to start with small affinity cells and struggle with each other in order to distribute power equally and not hold our privileges over one another, but we can do it without unleashing the major part of our anger. We can do it with understanding. But that anger we feel is still there. If we are 'live' lesbians and are even half-awake, we have righteous anger and the way to deal with it healthily is to direct it at those who are destroying us and the planet – men. Again, we want to make it clear that this doesn't mean we spend our time with hate rising from us like steam, but rather that, by the very decision to consciously direct our rage at the deserving ones and not inwardly, we are freeing ourselves to relate with warmth and sensitivity to our own selves and to each other. By our defining the enemy as all males, we are freeing ourselves from forming any kind of energy draining and oppressive relationships with them, and do not give them even an impersonal friendliness in our daily confrontations with them. (And any necessary interaction with them *is* a confrontation and power struggle. They are used to tapping our time and feelings when they choose, whether it is starting a conversation on line at the store or expecting a smile on the street. When you resist responding with the appropriate gesture of humiliation and subordination, they meet you with hostility and even threats of violence.)

Some of us never experienced heterosexuality and so escaped personal pressure from men. Through awakening to our feminism and oppression, we awakened to our anger and hatred of men. Others of us experienced the rape on a more humiliating personal level and our loathing grew out of our heterosexual experiences. But for all of us it is necessary to define ourselves as women, a natural life force and an entirely separate category from men, the predominate death-force on the earth.

The Workshop

Sylvia Foley
1981

Eddie called for attention listen everybody it's time we got started can we get started please he waited for people to stop talking this is a workshop on separatism and togetherness in the gay community gay and lesbian community someone said from the back gay and lesbian right Eddie said now please let's remember that we're here to learn from each other okay he sat down and looked at me do you want to go first I shook my head no last okay then Max why don't you start

my mother was a steadying influence in my life Max said she was a strong woman much stronger than my father he grinned at the circle of faces believe me I know it sounds strange but I still prefer the company of women most of the time everyone laughed he crossed his legs and looked down at his hands I think we gays have to stick together especially with Reagan running the country and if we split off into factions he looked pointedly at me we are going to get nowhere that's all I have to say for now

people clapped Ralph your turn Eddie said well I agree with what was just said Ralph said we have to work with each other toward our common goals listen I am still close with my ex-wife she lives out in California now but I call her on business all the time it's been my experience that women are a hell of a lot smarter than us men he laughed but seriously I have a couple of lesbian friends I see no reason not to work together he sat back in his chair to show he was finished all the faces turned toward me

well I'm the separatist here I said I smiled and leaned against the back of the folding chair I felt a little like the bull's eye on a target there were very few women there maybe five I decided to play it cool if possible first let me say that I think there are times when gays and lesbians can work together however I don't think we have common goals in the long run what do you mean a man in a green shirt said his voice rising wait a minute Eddie said let her finish we'll have time for discussion after the man sank back in his chair and pressed his lips together okay where I'm coming from is a lesbian-feminist head I said sexism is the bottom line here look gay men are still men you have privilege because you are men you have the money the power and lesbians don't that's where I'm coming from

I stopped and took a deep breath I knew already there was no way to say what I had to say but as long as I'm here I thought I'll do it look I just don't think we're fighting for the same things I think the gay movement oppresses lesbians as women gay men have no stake in changing things why should they after all but we have a stake for me it means revolution not reform I could feel myself losing them they were looking at me with blank closed faces the women weren't tying in as far as I could tell I tried again I'm just trying to tell you separatism is survival to me that's all

thank you Eddie said people clapped again now we'll have questions anybody here have a question they'd like to ask our panelists yes go ahead back there

I like girls a man wearing grey socks said and I agree we need to stick together I don't see what all this separation is about none of us have civil rights women I said we are women not girls how would you like to be called boy I was getting angry I couldn't help it oh it wouldn't bother me girls women what's the difference I really don't see what the big deal is that's exactly what I'm talking about I said you don't see you're a man and that gives you cock privilege the man's face started getting red

Eddie interrupted quickly let's not get out of hand here please does anyone want to respond to that last statement a hand went up Judith's hand she's right Judith said it does matter we are not girls the trouble is that lesbians have problems men don't have abortion rape lesbian motherhood women can't even get the jobs men get so there's no money it all boils down to male privilege I relaxed a little and smiled to myself it was just like Judith not to say cock out loud anyway Judith said I myself am not a separatist but I think we need them they spearhead the movement we need their radicalism she sat back and no one said anything for a minute anyone else Eddie said

I think if we isolate ourselves into factions we'll all get killed a man said I think it's crazy anyone else Eddie said a woman leaned into the circle she had short hair and she looked tough well I don't mind being called a girl maybe it's because I'm older I take it as a compliment and besides the word lesbian has a horrible sound it makes me think of perversion she shrugged I'm just a gay girl that's what I am the men were smiling and nodding their heads I felt sick to my stomach everyone had something to say everyone began talking there happen to be both men and women in this world it's ridiculous to act as if one half the human race doesn't exist we're all people as far as I'm concerned a man's voice said this right on another man seconded

I didn't say anything right away they were all talking they sounded threatened to me out loud I said Eddie I want to explain something go ahead Eddie nodded he looked nervous

I didn't want this to turn into a shouting match I said Max

leaned forward well you should say what you feel I know I said I can see I'm not getting through I just don't think we're fighting for the same things I am tired of putting energy into men even gay men because whether you want to see it or not all men are socialized to be misogynistic I sat back and waited for my head to get blasted for that one

what do you mean misogynistic we're telling you we want to work with women the man in grey socks said he said women like a dirty word because of that girls business earlier what do you mean not the same fight we need the same reforms we're all gay here

I said no we don't well okay I'll concede we need some of the same things changed maybe but reform isn't really what I'm fighting for you don't understand

his face was a rumple of anger okay he said then tell me so I can understand why don't you

no fighting Eddie said we are here to learn not to argue points now calm down and try to listen to the other person's point of view Eddie looked very anxious I told myself to be cool

I took a deep breath and started again what I've been trying to tell you is that lesbians have been shafted by both the women's movement and the gay movement some of us are damn tired we were out in the streets marching for ERA and better divorce laws we were out demonstrating in front of the Ramrod the night those two fags got shot but we get very little support when it comes to lesbian issues I'm a separatist because I'm tired of being used and forgotten I'm in this for me now lesbians I stopped there and looked around the room people were shaking their heads and whispering among themselves I was very tired but I felt proud I didn't care anymore I said what I came to say

I think you're crazy someone said from the back if the black men and the black women had separated off from each other during the sixties where would they be today jesus christ maybe I'm too old a woman said I just remember the McCarthy era too well I guess this separatism stuff sounds like suicide to me Eddie looked at his watch listen it's almost eleven we have to wrap this up does anyone have any last comment to make I think we've all learned a lot here tonight

Max's hand went up yes go ahead Max Eddie said I just want to say that I feel sorry for you Max said you seem like an intelligent person and I'm an intelligent person I am willing to learn from you but I can't if you refuse to cooperate that's all I have to say

well then thank you all for coming Eddie said I would like to thank our panelists for being here there's coffee and Harry made some cookies you are welcome to stay and socialize a bit he sat down everyone clapped the circle broke up people headed for the coffee urn Eddie rubbed his eyes then he leaned over and tapped my knee to get my attention I was sitting there thinking about how to leave quickly listen he said I hope it wasn't too upsetting for you

no not at all I said I knew I'd be the token separatist here tonight I'm sorry more women didn't come though we usually get more of them Eddie said I guess the topic scared off a lot of them you made some good points he grinned at me you know if I were a woman I'd probably be a separatist myself

there you go I said listen I'm pretty tired I gotta get going sure he said thanks again I picked up my knapsack and my jacket and headed for the door there were little knots of people standing around talking one or two of them spoke to me I kept moving I didn't feel like talking anymore when I got to the door Max was sitting in front of it with his legs stretched out he pulled them in when he saw me coming hey you're okay he said I know you don't really hate men maybe we can sit down and rap some more sometime he was smiling so all his teeth showed I looked at him I let the door bang shut behind me

Popular Separatist-Baiting Quotes And Some Separatist Responses

Marty with help from the dykes of S.E.P.S. 1983*

'By hating and ostracizing men you're doing to men what they've done to us.'	There's no such thing as 'reverse discrimination.' This concept is based on the idea that an oppressed group has equal power to their oppressors.
'You're shutting out half the world's population.'	Patriarchal culture tries to

* SEPARATISTS ENRAGED PROUD AND STRONG, San Francisco, CA. Based on 'When You Meet a Lesbian: Hints for the Heterosexual Womon'. Taken from a poster by Day Moon Designs, Seattle, WA.

343

brainwash us that a bottom-line of woman's role is to take care of men. We're taught that we *owe* them our energy. We do not!

Besides: There are a billion & 1/2 womyn in the world of which millions are lesbians. There's not the time or possibility as it is to relate to and deal with the needs of all these lesbians — why even consider wasting time on pricks!

'How can you hate that little boy — He's *just* a baby.'

Contrary to popular fairytale notions of sexless, adorable children:
— Children learn bigotries at a very young age.
— Little pricks *do* grow up.
— Boys oppress girls.
— Boys can & do oppress, rape and abuse womyn of all ages.

'He's not a man, he's a faggot.'

Faggots *are men* and are just as oppressive as straight men.

'He's not a man, she's a transsexual, and she identifies as a lesbian.'

Cutting off their balls and taking female hormones does not make men into womyn!! The presence of a prick &/or XY chromosomes disqualifies one from being a woman. A womon is much more than the mere absence of these. And
A PRICK CANNOT BE A LESBIAN!

'It's easy for you to hate & reject men, you're a separatist. *I* have a difficult, complex relationship with my father/

There's apparently a myth that separatists have simple and uncomplicated emotional struggles around men.

brother/son, etc.; it's a hard struggle for me.'

'I used to be a separatist. It was an important phase, but now I've grown out of that phase; I've matured beyond separatism.'

Many of us used to be separatists and we still are! Separatism is *not* a phase for us – it's a personal and political vision that's integral to our lives.

'We need to leave behind one-sided, narrow-minded, simplistic, detrimental, irresponsible ... politics; we need to join together to fight all oppression.'

Sounds good. The more dykes who leave behind working within male-infested, prick-defined politics, the more chances we have for truly comprehensive and powerful change.

Separatists vary widely in our personal pasts and present experiences. We share the common bond of choosing Lesbians first and naturally repudiating our oppressors who have hated, abused and murdered us in every culture in patriarchal history. Working to separate from men is a VALID, HEALTHY, SELF-AFFIRMING NEED & CHOICE!!

Coming Out Queer and Brown

Naomi Littlebear Morena
1981

Clara: Now why is it i hear so many people ask me, 'Why are there not very many Latina Lesbians involved in the feminist movement?' Well one thing for sure, if i was in the barrio right now i'd be scared to 'come out.' Not too many cultures i know of approve of their kids goin' queer, especially Catholic ones, altho' i seem to have met a big percentage of uppity presbyterian dykes.

In the barrio you have straight brothers and sisters quoting that now famous line about the women's movement being a white woman's trip filled to the armpits with bulldaggers and castrating bitches and of course no self-respecting, 100% Mexican will have jackshit to do with that unless you don't mind being called a vendida, sellout; and if shaming you into the closet doesn't work, thank the Virgin Mary for good old-fashioned guilt. 'The Raza will simply perish,' if you're not there to have 1/2 dozen babies and who wants that on their conscience? The only way out is to walk hand in hand with your man and together battle the white devils of oppression.

Let's face it, if you've got the bucks together, it's easier to leave town, unless you're lucky enough to live in a big city; i wasn't. i ended up here by accident; i thought Oregon was somewhere near New Mexico. What did i find when i stumbled into the women's community? A gauntlet of white women on one side and straight leftists (ex-boyfriends) on the other.

'Welcome Sister of Color (east L.A. i corrected). So you want to be a lesbian? Well never mind about that, that's a bedroom issue. First brown sister let us tell you that we're right here to support you and your brown brothers in your fight against right racist imperialism. By the way do you speak Spanish.' Look I said, i wanna do C.R. and come out brown and proud, you know get down and get angry about the truth about brown macho in the barrio loco, and i want a bumper sticker and a mother nature is a lesbian button. Well forget that shit. Here's your script sister and here's how it reads: 'Woman of Color becomes Mascot at Meetings, Woman of Color meets Karl Marx, Woman of Color becomes politically correct, Woman of Color decides who to boycott and call racist in the community, Woman of Color brought to you live from Dammasch State Hospital, Daughter of Woman of Color Part II' and don't it seem that the only other women of color you meet are all either marxist, communist or middle class.

There is encouragement to 'play up' the oppressed minority image; you'll get a lot more mileage in the community, not to mention respect and maybe fear. And when i didn't make friends with Maria Gomez, the only other Chicana in town because she was so straight and uptight about her boyfriend getting bad vibes when he walked into a Lesbian Rap Group at the women's bookstore, they called me an isolationist. It's bad enough that they think we're all distant relatives without assuming *all* women of color think alike and should get along. To my sisters i say, either you have a short memory or no memory left at all. And to the white sisters i say my colorful and oppressed brothers would just as soon run over me in their cool chevrolets if they knew i was a dyke.

Don't tell me that i don't understand these 'poor angry young men, starved for personal power'; take a look at what the white man has done with all that personal power. Do you dare think people of other races lack ambition? Behind every angry young man, regardless of his color, is a repressed angry woman with no power at all. Oh it's fine to dump on the white man; everyone dumps on the white man, even white men. It's almost a fad. White lesbians can down rap their oppressors and denounce their class background, but for a brown woman to denounce her brother/oppressor, it's a political crime.

Clara: i am pissed at this double standard, it ain't too far in my memory that those guys were lowriding down the passing lane of my life, following me down the streets, leaning over to shout 'Hey esa, chake it but don't brake it,' a half a block later filled with slurps and whistles 'Ay mamacita, i got something that could split a woman in half.' Oh yeah sucker, if i had a propane torch i'd fry your huevos rancheros.

But you know i never said it too loud and i still can't or someone would say i was racist or you must be hanging out too much with those man-haters who wanna kill little boys and dios mio how did i get involved in all this name-calling, get me to the confessional. i think i'm gonna go back to being catholic.

It's a hell of a lot easier to call someone racist than for a chicana to call her 'brother' a sexist jerk. Bureaucratic bullshit, but it works; it keeps us all safe and out of the way in a double deadbolt closet.

i agree, me and my 'brother' both been screwed by the system, but when he starts screwin' me he is the system and when white liberals start telling me to 'take it but don't shake it' they're the system too.

TRANSFORMATIONS OF CONSCIOUSNESS: EXAMINING OUR SELVES

The Awakening

Lee Lynch
1982

Sun splashed against the porch screen as summer breezes lifted the leaves and branches of the wide old tree outside. Momma sat sleepily on the large, thickly cushioned rocker. Every afternoon her two daughters sat to either side of her; Lillian sat stiffly on the edge of her straight-backed chair and darted forward at each sound in the street, while Nan rose more slowly to witness and judge Lillian's observations.

'There she goes now,' Lillian exclaimed, her index finger a stiff extension of the thin hard line of her body. 'I told you so. Can't spend a day without him. She's like a drug addict. Has to see him up at the corner every day or she thinks he won't come to see her at night. A lot she'd be missing if he didn't,' she finished sarcastically.

Nan raised her limp, heavy form off the flowered cushion of her rocking chair, looked at the figure hurrying through the schoolyard across the street, and sat again, exhaling, like an inflated pillow whose plug has been pulled. She shook her head and chuckled. 'Can't get enough of him, can she, Momma?'

Momma, her short white hair neat under its matching net said, 'Tsk, tsk,' and smiled with pleasure.

'Momma always appreciates a good joke, don't you, Momma?' Nan asked approvingly.

'But this is no joking matter,' Lillian protested and snapped her cigarette case open. 'Not at all, not at all,' she repeated, tapping a cigarette against the arm of her chair. She picked a green splinter out of the filter and jabbed the cigarette between her lips before she continued. 'The neighbors are all up at arms! Madge Dougherty with her poor sick mother is beside herself with what goes on there weekends. She doesn't want her two girls to get the wrong ideas, you know. That's an impressionable age, the early teens, I well remember.'

Nan and Momma both looked as one away from the retreating figure in the schoolyard and looked defensively toward Lillian. 'Nothing *we* did, I hope,' Nan giggled.

'Certainly not,' Lillian snapped past the cigarette that jumped on her lower lip while she talked. 'Shut up, Alexander,' she called suddenly to a blue canary who had begun to sing in his cage in the corner of the porch. She adjusted the gauzy pink scarf which surrounded her pin curls.

'None of those goings on in our family,' Momma asserted.

Nan shifted her weight more comfortably and pulled her dress down over her knees. 'If it was just one I'd understand better. But it seems like a new one every year.'

'Doesn't it, though?'

'And she had a perfectly good husband.'

'Drove him away, they say.'

'Needs a lot of men.'

'Do you think so?' Nan asked thoughtfully, finishing with her dress and picking up a *Reader's Digest* to fan herself. 'Do you think that it's her body that needs them? Or just her mind?'

Alexander sang again briefly and Lillian glared at him. 'It's all in her head, of course,' she replied, stabbing the ashtray with her blackened cigarette butt. 'No one needs that much you know what,' she ended in a hiss.

'I guess she thinks she's no good unless a man wants her. Otherwise why would she need them all?'

'Nanette, what makes that worthless bird my boys never clean sing? There's something in her. She was brought up just as good as us. Her poor mother would be mortified.'

'Devil made her do it,' Momma chortled slyly, rubbing the few stiff white hairs on her chin.

Lillian darted forward. 'Let me pluck those for you, Momma,' she demanded, examining them close up.

Momma waved her away with her fleshy pink hand. 'Don't be bothering me, you,' she admonished. 'God put them there for a reason.'

'Maybe god has a reason for her to carry on like that,' Nan suggested.

'Who? Momma?' Lillian wanted to know. 'Who?'

'That little trifle we're talking about. Maybe we need women like that to keep the men amused so the rest of us can have some peace.' Nan let her head drop to the back of her chair. Her hair was colored blonde and was thin. Wisps of it escaped the pink curlers around which it was rolled. 'Always touching and poking. They can't think of anything else, it seems.'

'Except betting away the money,' Lillian added.

'The horses,' Momma said, rocking and nodding. 'The horses and the drink.'

'Speaking of the drink, there goes poor old Frank.'

'Poor old Frank,' Momma echoed.

Lillian craned her neck to see Frank stumble down the street. 'Disgusting,' she said as she stared at the disheveled figure. 'To think you were his girl once.'

'That was before I even met Ned, Lily. I never did intend to marry that old drunk.'

'There but for the grace of god go I,' Momma nodded to herself. The daughters nodded vigorously in agreement while the bird began a new chorus. Lillian turned to chide him until her eye was caught by the man's cautious approach to a tree in a secluded corner of the schoolyard. 'Oh, no,' she whispered in horror.

'What?' Nan asked, pulling herself forward to the screen excitedly. 'He's not, is he Lily?' Lily glanced threateningly at Nan, shushing her and pointing her chin at Momma who was absorbed in straightening the doilies under her forearms and repinning them. Nan and Lillian sat back slightly in their chairs, but kept their eyes on the man.

'What is it?' Momma asked, sensing something.

'Nothing you want to see, Momma,' Lillian answered evasively. 'There, it's over, you can look now.' She lowered her voice. 'He relieved himself over in the schoolyard.'

'Do you believe it?' Nan asked and suddenly began to laugh nervously. 'Momma could have seen! If school was in session the little girls . . . !'

'Never mind the girls, they'll have to put up with that kind of thing all too soon when they're married. But what an example to the boys! *My* boys.'

'They'll be like that soon enough anyway,' Nan observed.

'Not my boys. If I ever catch them doing a thing like that, I'll skin them alive. My boys will not be rummies like old Frank or lose their paychecks as soon as they get them. You'll see.'

'Glad I only have the little girl. I don't have to beat any of that piggishness out of her.'

'Well, mine won't grow up piggy. You can mark my words.'

'All alike they are,' Momma said, shaking her head. 'They're all alike, every last one of them.' Nan smiled and lifted her chin while Lillian sat stiffly furious and looked down the street. 'I'm raising my two boys to make their wives happy. They'll be different. I don't care about what anybody says,' she complained with tears in her voice.

'Look, look!' Nan cried, proudly spotting something before Lillian did. 'It's the honeymooners,' she giggled, 'fighting again.' A man and a woman walked together down the street, glaring ahead of themselves, not touching.

'They had a fight already, it looks like,' Lillian whispered loudly, distracted from her mother's criticism and ready to return to her post. 'Why she puts up with him, I'll never know.'

'They say it's for the kids.'

'All six of them,' Lillian sneered.

'Once with him should have been enough, I'd think,' Nan looked slyly at Lillian over Momma's head.

'She can't possibly get any pleasure from it,' Lillian concluded. 'It's hard enough with a man who doesn't hit you.'

They craned forward again to hear as the couple passed under the porch. 'The language!' Lillian breathed, outraged. 'To his own wife!'

'Words *I've* never heard before,' Nan winked at Lillian who did not spare her a glance.

'Shh,' Lillian admonished. 'They're fighting about him going to work. He's telling *her* to go to work if she needs more money,' she whispered.

Nan clucked. 'The nerve. Why, that's all men are good for is bringing home the bacon.'

'And their troubles.'

'Not a drop of good in any of them,' Momma added, leaning heavily on the arms of her chair as she struggled to her feet. Her stockings were rolled around her thick ankles and spilled over her low black shoes. Her dark flowered housedress had bunched behind her around her girdle and the silky material eluded her stiff fingers as she tried to grab and pull it into place.

'Here, Momma,' Lillian offered as she rose and jackknifed behind her mother to help her.

'Here,' said Nan simultaneously flailing for a hold on the dress from her chair.

'Why you still wear these girdles I don't know. You're old enough to relax.'

Momma winked. 'Maybe the boyfriend will come by today.'

'Boyfriend my foot,' Lillian ridiculed her.

'What would you do with a boyfriend, Momma?' Nan wanted to know.

Lillian stood in the doorway calling after her. 'Where are you going? Use my bathroom down here. Don't walk up all those stairs to your place.' She went back on the porch muttering to Nan, 'Embarrassed, I suppose, to use anybody's but her own.'

'Do you blame her? After all those years living with Poppa? She finally has a little privacy. A bathroom all her own. A bed all her own. An apartment all her own except when you can't stand it down here and go up to her. You must spend half of your life up there.'

Lillian relaxed and sat down after she heard her mother finish climbing the stairs. 'Thank god I have it. My little refuge. When he,' she lowered her voice, looking around the porch, 'when *he* starts drinking you don't know *what* he'll do. He doesn't bother the boys. They've started protecting *me*, young as they are. But there's nowhere else I can go. Last night, Nan, he smashed my fresh baked pie on the floor. Ruined it. Then when I cleaned it up he wanted to you know what.'

'I don't understand them, I just don't.'

'Don't tell Momma.'

'No, no, I never do. I don't want her hearing about my fool of a man either. I'm sick of the horses. He found my refrigerator money yesterday. The money I've been saving for a new one? I think Sheila deserves something better than mushy ice cream, poor little girl.'

'To the betting parlor?'

Nan laughed. 'Where else? Right down to old man Reilly's cigar store. But I couldn't say anything, you know. He won.'

'Did he now?'

'He's buying the refrigerator *and* school clothes for Sheila. Taking her shopping himself,' Nan boasted.

'Trying to win her favor after all the meanness.'

'He doesn't fool her, though.'

'Good for her.'

'She says she doesn't want any new clothes,' she whispered. 'No plaid skirts like all the little girls are wearing, no little patent leather shoes. I must admit, I don't understand the child, Lily. All she wants is another pair of those flannel lined jeans like we got her last year out in the country when we visited *his* folks.'

'Do you suppose it's a stage?'

'I don't remember any stages like that when I was eight. Do you?'

'No. Momma always dressed us in the prettiest little white starched dresses no matter how little there was, didn't you Momma?' Nan asked as her mother stepped onto the porch. She leaned over to smooth the afghan on Momma's chair.

'He did his best, poor soul,' Momma said as she sighed into her seat. 'Did his very best.' Her eyes twinkled. 'Wonder what his worst could've been,' she chuckled.

The daughters laughed loudly. 'Momma, you're a scream,' Nan heaved, recovering from her laughter.

'He was your father, though. You must respect him. Respect the dead.'

Lillian straightened indignantly. 'After how he treated you?'

'He couldn't help it. He had a tough time of it.'

'He didn't have to take it out on you, though, Momma.'

'Who else did he have?'

Nan shook her head. 'No one, I suppose. Poor Poppa. He should have been rich. Being poor drove him to drink.'

'Like it drives some men to gamble,' Lily looked significantly at Nan.

'Or to hit their wives.'

'It all comes of trying to raise a family and keep a home together.'

'Forgive and forget,' Momma advised.

'Still,' Lily mused, 'sometimes I wonder if we'd be better off without them.'

'Don't be ridiculous,' Nan scorned her. 'Of course not. How could you raise two boys alone? How could I take care of Sheila properly?'

Lillian stubbed out another cigarette. 'And our lovely flats.'

'My nice new refrigerator,' Nan beamed.

'Grin and bear it,' they agreed in unison when Momma started to say it again.

'Would you like some lemonade?' Lillian asked.

'Sounds delicious,' Nan said. 'If it's not too much trouble. And I can bring out those lovely fresh cupcakes Sheila picked out on the way over.'

'Won't take me but a jif. No, Nan, now sit and rest your old bones, I'll bring it out.'

'You'll need help carrying it,' Nan insisted, righting herself on her short wide legs. 'No more argument. I'm helping.'

As the sisters left the porch, Lillian quickly and purposefully, puffy Nan following slowly, Sheila at last let herself open her eyes. From the porch cot where they had instructed her to nap while they visited she gazed at her Grandmomma's back. She never could sleep through their talk, though they always thought she did. She wondered what Grandpoppa had done to Grandmomma. Was it just the same old stuff her father and uncle did to her mother and aunt? She hoped it wasn't worse. Quietly, she sat and looked up at Alexander the canary. He blinked at her. She winked at him. 'Why do they live with men?' she whispered to Alexander. He blinked again and flapped his blue wings. '*I* ain't going to, bird. You can bet your sweet tailfeathers on it,' Sheila pledged.

Momma turned her slow bulk toward Sheila. 'Awake, rascal?' she asked.

'Um-hum,' Sheila answered, pretending to rub sleep from her eyes and stretching noisily.

'Cupcakes coming. And lemonade,' Momma offered warmly, opening her arms. Sheila blundered over to Momma, still feigning sleepiness. She walked between Grandmomma's open legs and let herself be enfolded by her fleshy arms against her soft breast. Sheila sighed and had no intention of leaving Grandmomma's arms. Ever.

C.L.I.T. Statement No. 2

C.L.I.T. Collective
1974

Introduction

The C.L.I.T. Collection is written by C.L.I.T.s. We intentionally prefer not to write under our own names for these reasons: we are trying to put into practice some of our sentiments about breaking the star-system described in C.L.I.T. Statement No. 1. We don't want to make a name for ourselves as thinkers or whatever you think we are. We are making it safe for ourselves not to be bought off by *Bitch* or *Viva* magazines who want a feminist to write an article for them to make their sexist stuff appear feminist. They aren't going to ask Oedipussy Tuddé to write for them, are they? We don't want to be known for getting out information that every lesbian is entitled to know. We do not believe that ideas should be bought and sold in capitalist competition style. That is a man-made thing; just like the buying and selling of land and air waves (for radio and tv stations). Pretty soon they are going to start selling land on the moon to men; the moon just like the earth is woman – it's utter blasphemy to womankind. But men are used to buying and selling women; they started it all. The idea of ownership of women, land, air, earth, thoughts, feelings is all the same – male. Male wrongheadedness that goes against everything that is woman, as is the intent. We are trying to unwind from Western patriarchy's hype about keeping your ideas to yourself or else someone will steal them. Thinking of ideas as commodities in the market place is a split with nature, woman, ourselves. 'How can anyone steal an *idea*?' is what the woman asks the Man who doesn't know what the hell she is talking about. We don't want men to know what we are talking about in the first place; and second, ideas, thoughts, feelings are to be shared. It is male to keep an idea to yourself. They are meant to be floating from one woman to the next without money signs, a male concept, attached.

The pseudonym also has a freeing effect. We can write whatever we want in any style without the fear of someone telling us we are *bad* writers. So we have more room to experiment with writing. It takes alot of weight off most of our shoulders who are nervous about writing.

A crucial note about our writing: we think most things written – textbooks, books, magazines, newspapers, etc., are written in the *language* of men because men, not women, are their audience. And men are stupid. So is their language – they hardly ever know how to say anything directly to each other (legal language, business language, presidential and politician language, academic language, New York Times language, Watergate language, etc.). In fact, their entire language is based on secrecy – how to look like you're saying something without saying *anything*. Therefore, most writers who are men anyway and naturally think (if you want to call it that) in a stupid vague language, and have no idea about what creativity is, usually only put one or two ideas out in an entire book and spend the rest of their booktime giving examples of what they mean to say. They just rephrase the original vague idea over and over so that their stupid male readers can follow the gist of the book.

Our audience is lesbians. Who are real smart women. Therefore, we think we can write with many ideas that don't need to be explained in tedious male fashion because women intuitively know what you mean. Women have an infinite capacity to feel another's meaning and intent. I've seen women understand anything, even men. So we are literally packing our articles with hundreds of thoughts and feelings that in the male community would deserve a book written about each idea. We appeal to your woman instincts in reading us – just to understand what we are saying. After that point, you can decide for yourself. But listen to us as a woman first. We are exploding with ideas and with an urgency to be understood. Therefore, we go off on alot of tangents that are just as important as *there are no main points*. Everything we say to each other is important. It may be difficult to read at first, but remember every sentence is a book.

Right now the Media State is involved in the most important war game plan of the century – they are defining what a lesbian is to the people of America as if lesbian was a new word. This is a typical mind-fuck media move to co-opt the thrust of what lesbians actually mean – women of resistance, women who cannot be controlled by the man. Everyone involved in this mind-fuck – the Media State, the mother/housewives (their most significant target population to explain what a lesbian is) and the lesbian who is being explained away – are all playing their appropriate parts in this game.

The Media State which is again disguising itself as the

condescending liberal, civil-rights oriented, humanitarian teacher of the rabble masses is sending out the message to Nixon's children that lesbians are something almost like people and you should accept them at work but don't let your daughter marry one. The Media Mindfuck is their false plea for acceptance of the lesbian from the people when it is the Media State that has always been the oppressor of lesbians; now they are pretending to be a defender of the faith when they are actually controlling and defining our new image. Never let your oppressor define you – that's what has hurt us all along. They are defining lesbians from their point of view, not from ours.

The role the straight woman mother/housewife is playing in this mind-fuck is that she never heard of the word lesbian. 'Gosh, honey, I never even thought women could do that together' she says to her suspecting husband. She is letting the man tell her what a lesbian is; playing dumb, an old stance, to dissociate herself from the lesbian to let her man and The Man know that she never thought about loving women and resisting men. 'Oh, really, how cute – but I don't feel that way.'

The lesbian's role in the game is that she is excited and hopeful at the crumbs the Media State and its supporters are throwing at her. Oppressed people always act this way – it comes from starvation. The lesbian is starved from having had her existence ignored or ridiculed for so long and thus regarded by her oppressor and herself (accepting the oppressor's definition of herself) as illegitimate, criminal and deviant that she is surprised (which is the Media State's intent – take them by surprise) and excited that her existence is now being recognized and discussed in the homes of American 'normals' that she'll take anything. It's like signing a contract that you never expected to come through, and then reading the small print when it's too late. (Movie scout signing someone who thought she was ugly and could never be in the movies precisely because the movies for the last 50 years made her feel ugly by only showing cultural WASP straight 'beauty' and making other women ugly ducklings, undesirables, etc. Then one day they sign her up to be the latest avant-garde ugly duckling. Ugly duckling is ugly duckling is ugly duckling.)

'Never give a sucker an even break' has always been the Media message. Intended result: within a year or two at best, the lesbian will be locked into her new media image and accepted in the oppressor's definition of herself (which is not herself). When we, she wakes up and sees the small print and screams 'this isn't me, this is just as oppressive as the way they used to treat me' (ignore, ridicule) – it will be too late on the Media clock. No one will listen, not even David Susskind. They'll say 'we dealt with the lesbian issue – no one wants to hear about it anymore.'

Now onto the bloody specifics of how the Media State is eating lesbians for lunch and guess who's coming to dinner? We begin with death around the CAMPfire where they roast lesbians as marshmallows for laughs.

Camp

Daddy is a piece of shit who demands respect. He sets the stage, the original stage set (the scene of the crime) is the family living room. Heterosexual life is therefore based on artifice. Every player has her/his part and dialogue. Class determines who speaks how (archie bunker or laurence olivier). Watching soap operas or grand operas is watching other people's living rooms. We watch the Hamlet family drama or 'As the Stomach Turns.' As a survival tactic, the child who was clever and resilient enough to withstand role-playing damage, who distanced herself/himself enough to see the farce of heterosexual family life (usually either a tomboy girl or a sissy boy) laughed (faggot) or grieved (dyke) themselves into deviance. The two sexes have different ways of dealing with this oppression: males can afford to keep on laughing at momma, having no heart, no ability to emphathize with momma who is the real victim of family life, because he is at heart a *hole* and has nothing to offer himself or anyone else. Therefore artificiality and desecration of woman does not offend him. He wants daddy's position of privilege and power over women. His concept of women has now become to dress momma like a drag queen, which turns them on. Straight son wants momma, fag son wants daddy. The fag reenacts the scene of the crime to high drag caricature. If he prefers the masochist femme he wants daddy to want him as a sex object and dresses in momma drag. If he prefers the sadist butch, he competes with daddy to beat up on and/or fuck momma drag (queen).

The female, being a natural *whole*, and empathizing with the mother victim, yet does not wish to return to the scene of the crime to re-enact the tragedy as mother-victim herself (being daughter victim is enough in one life). She cannot tolerate the artificiality that faggots call camp, that she knows is pain. So the adult tomboy runs from the family to life, love, emotion with other women. Adult sissies in big cities carry purses, walk poodles, dress straight women and themselves in Macy's windows in three million feathers, laugh together, fuck each other and call it camp. The straight male equivalent of camp is existentialism, the ashcan school of writing, pop art, death-absurdity, the shit school of writing (norman mailer), theater of the absurd, etc.

Originally, camp was used by faggot-sons as comic relief and distance from the weird family scene. Enter the Media. The media, acting as son of detestable daddy, and seeing the threats posed by the existence of oppressed groups turned radical-political, follows faggot-son's tactic of caricaturing the threat: black men in army fatigues mincing down the street in platform shoes, Joe Namath wearing women's pantyhose on national tv, Rockefeller's agent Andy Warhol (who Valerie Solanas was smart to shoot) popstar portraying 'Women in Revolt' as drag queens. The Media, with its liberal-educate-the-masses front, in the name of sexual liberation, is stabbing dykes in the back by trying to lump dykes into the campy freak show context of the new decadence, the avant-garde nostalgia for Berlin in the 30's, the radical chic, hip, trendy, with-it, 'in' garbage bag of: transvestites, glitter rock, Mick Jagger and David Bowie (the androgynes-misogynes), Bette Midler, Tracy Young and Susan Sontag (fag hags), the bisex-boom ('Bloomie's bi's' – a Saturday afternoon cruise at Bloomingdales), Soho parties where straight art molls (mauls) dress up for a night as 'lesbians.' The above trash is MALE PATRIARCHAL SUPPORTIVE junk that is being blended with the term 'feminism' to make it look like the Women's Liberation Movement leads to that kind of 'sexual liberation' as we just described. Which has nothing to do with the Women's Movement or sexual liberation – in fact, the stuff that the Media State supports and labels is counter-revolutionary to the Lesbian Feminist Movement. They are trying to smear our name. Guilt by association.

Legitimate Theater

The Media caricature of lesbians extends beyond camp into legitimate theater: the human drama of queer women struggling to be recognized as normal people, slobs like everybody else. We're not like anybody else in this rotten patriarchy – we're not male and we're not straight women. The Media hype which the faggots push too to get their full MALE privilege is that 'just because you do something different in bed doesn't make you any different from straight people in the work world.' That's true for faggots because they are males living in a male society. But it's bullshit for dykes. Loving women makes your whole life, your consciousness, how you see and experience this male world differently from the average patriarchal supporter. But dig how the Media tries to make us look like *them*, straight! The David Susskind Show, topic – Gay Liberation – showing faggots and lesbians together (which is a smear for lesbians) in straight roles of doctor, nurse, psychologist, lawyer, advertiser, priest, middle-class consumer, talker, dreamer, shitter, etc. The queer as see-I-can-act-straight-too blob. The New York Post articles, on homosexuality in females, selected three 'couples' as examples, all of whom were prototypes of the middle class heterosexual consumer unit ('if you make yourself invisible enough you can ignore everyone and everyone ignores you'); the more gregarious couple describes how they were invited out to dinner with two straight hetero couples who were also married. 'They talked about the P.T.A., and the Garden Club, and the American Legion, just as though we were any other couple. We used to get invited every year to the American Legion Dance. Of course, we never went.'

Bi-sexuality

Bi-sexuality has now been declared 'in' in New York (the Media Capital of the world) by all the N.Y. Media which means the Media State has declared bisexuality ok for the provinces although it will take a couple of years to filter down the sewer. Bisexuality has also been presented as one of the points scored by the lesbian contingent of the Women's Liberation Movement in their effort to advance the sex life of the human race. Lies. Dykes don't know any humans. They know men and they know women. Straight women are not what dykes call women and therefore do not lust after them as straight women like to think. Straight women think, talk, act, cross their legs, dress, and come-on like male transvestite femme drag queens. They are something which stepped out of an S & M male fantasy world (which we wish would step back in and leave us alone) which has no reality in the woman world, the dyke world. We don't know any dykes who are confused enough or hard up enough to go to a straight woman's bed – so we wonder who these 'radical dykes' are that New York Magazine and other rags have reported are strong-arming via feminist guilt-tripping poor straight women into bed. Lies.

The only creatures who push bi-sexuality are straight women, men (especially latent faggots), and the Media State. For different reasons, of course. Straight women want a little excitement in their lives (especially their sex lives) because men are dull both in and out of bed. They rip off a lesbian in bed because a lesbian can make them feel something between their legs that they didn't know was there; once discovered, she takes this knowledge back to a man's bed and can now have better sex with men either because she has regained feelings between her legs or because she tells him how to do it. Reconnaissance Mission completed. She also calls up New York Magazine and gives them a feature article on what it's like to sleep with a 'radical dyke.'

The now 'in' bi-sexual woman is still functioning under her oppressor's definition of herself, of woman whose existence is measured only in terms of her *sexual* worth. Everybody knows women together are more sensual than any other sexual combination. The Hare Krishna's counterpart to the Bible states that women are 9 times lustier than men. The witches were burned for being lustier than men and making sexual pacts with the devil – for millennia men have twisted this sexual truth to make women appear all pussy and no brain.

The truth of the matter, which all patriarchies since their conception have tried to suppress, is that women are not only superior sexually to men, but also intellectually and emotionally and every other way except for physical strength. So the bi-sexual woman who thinks she is so smart and hip-in to go rip off a lesbian in bed so that she too can have a superior sex life to man and yet keep her male privilege by association with men – is stupid. She missed the full import of what a lesbian is – not just a piece of sexual dynamite but a woman who has broken through the patriarchal confusion of centuries to realize that a brilliant and beautiful (fully equipped emotionally and intellectually) species called women have been imprisoned and made to associate with a totally inferior species which attempts to justify this imprisonment by making the prisoners think they are stupid and inferior (the reversed truth) and need to be locked up and taken care of by monsters. The straight woman who calls herself 'bi' maintains her imprisonment by keeping her male privilege, but is having a better time in prison now thanks to the Media State. Just like they let the slaves dance to release tension and have a good time while keeping them slaves, they now let the women sleep with each other for the same reasons. Bi-sexuality maintains the patriarchy. Lesbianism understood is a revolt against the patriarchy.

The only ones who understand this are dykes, the Media and the smart pricks who talk their women into being bi-sexual. Men have always been turned on by two women making love so they vicariously get off on the 'lesbian affairs' of their straight women. They make the woman tell them about it in great detail while they make love so they can both come. The liberal chauvinist wins the reputation of being 'in,' a 'liberated man,' while controlling the entire sexual situation. 'He's not a chauvinist pig like other men – he *lets* me sleep with women.'

Ah, but the Media State's advertising campaign to legitimize bi-sexuality as a Women's Movement 'feminist political stance' is even more grotesque. The patriarchy has all available P.R. units out pushing the human being theory hard, and we mean hard. They want women to think men and women are becoming more alike, that through WLM we have learned to take the best of both worlds and come out with this wonderful androgynous bi-sexual human being. They are trying to keep the confusion around sex lines intact, the sexual confusion of women the patriarchy runs on like fuel. Let's take a closer look at the lies. First, it is impossible for women and men to become more and more alike because all men are terminally male which means jealous hole/woman killer. There is nothing good women can get from men. The only thing a woman can get from a man is money, also known as prisoner's coupons. Men have everything to gain from this blurring of the sexes lie – it allows them to disguise their true identity as woman killer and at the same time rip off women in a cooler way. Take emotions. She projects her emotions on to him (although he has none) and makes them both believe he has some. But it all comes from her.

Everybody knows from the first minute the WLM hit that feminism meant lesbianism. The patriarchy to preserve itself had to blur the meaning of lesbianism into bi-sexuality which means no political insight into who the sexes are, what the patriarchy is about and only seeing the difference between men and women as sexual (that women are better in bed) which is common male knowledge. Bi-sexuality is a Media plot which keeps women in economic, emotional, intellectual and consciousness bondage to men while sexually the girls are allowed to play.

Language

The farther back you go in patriarchal time, the more complex the language (Sanskrit, Greek, Latin). The later it gets in patriarchal time decline, the less meaning in the language. (The Greeks had three words for love; we have one.) Patriarchs praise the English language because one word has so many different meanings – you never know what anyone means – the male intent, because they don't mean anything. The earlier languages had more words, each with a different meaning; the speaker then could say exactly what she meant and be understood with ease. The reason for this is that the farther back you go in patriarchal time the closer you are to pre-mal(e)-historical matriarchal language. Men, unlike women, are not and never have been gifted in communicating. The only thing males know how to do with language well is mind-fuck, to take female language and blur its meaning by misuse. Also remember males are incredibly dumb on their own. Take for example what a cock culture does to *three* parts (this is a very deep analysis) – head (what they call intellect), heart (what they call emotions), and either cock or cunt (what they call sexuality). Can you imagine how many different words women in pre-patriarchal time had for what males call in a single blurt, emotions? For intellect? In cock culture we measure intellect with an I.Q. test. The matriarchs probably roll over in their graves with laughter at today's male stupidity.

Males call science, their great weapon over nature, the ability to *name* the unknown, to be able to describe it *physically* (outward appearance) when you see it again, then to compare this physical description with other things that you are familiar with, then to make endless artificial tables *categorizing* the new thing with the old things. Does that sound brilliant to you? Nature (woman) resists man's name-calling. They can name clouds, but can they make it rain? (The U.S. military spent 21 million dollars in the 1960's trying to seed the clouds over the Ho Chi Minh trail to make it muddy – it didn't work.) Can they stop rain, an earthquake, a storm, a flood, a tornado? But they can name them. Does it sound like you really have knowledge of a woman to say, 'oh yes, that's a Linda,' then to describe what she looks like, then to compare her to Jane's and Mary's, then to categorize her (what men call full understanding in science), i.e., to trap the name Linda on paper between the name Jane and Mary and draw lines between them? Real deep. That's how men think. They name everything, but they don't know anything about the disease or the health of anything. Nature resists man's name-calling. But men, unlike nature (woman), become what their name is. And to the extent women have lived with men (disease) for centuries and taken on his disease, women too can be named and accept the name calling; this is the woman who is as far away from her nature as man is from mother nature, the straight woman.

The Media State we live in which evolved late in patriarchal time is hysterically male (its logical endpoint) in its use of language. The later it is in patriarchal time, the more male; hence, the more meaningless and stupid everything in the culture, especially language, becomes. The Media State is the most anti-woman, anti-nature, i.e., MALE, thing devised by man – it's control of communication *en masse*. Men try to *control* everything they don't understand, which is just about everything. And if there's one thing men really don't understand, it's language. (Girls are good in English, boys are not, and if a boy is the school correctly concludes he's *effeminate*.) Men build elaborate artificial frameworks of disguise and control to cover their natural stupidity in language. Enter the Media State.

The Media State amplifies the characteristic male ineptness with language. Men, like their generalized counterpart, the Media State, never say what they mean or mean what they say. They have two styles of mind-fuck: 1) there is the man who talks all the time and says nothing, like the radio; but men have mindfucked women by making that projection of themselves onto women into the stereotype of the 'woman who talks all the time and says nothing'; and 2) there is the strong, silent type who is well-documented in Media script (Gary Cooper to Robert Redford) who move around with hardly a word and when a woman pushes them up against the wall to say something emotional for god's sake, they look down and say, 'I can't put what I feel for you into words' – the mindfuck is that the empty-headed male gets the woman to project what she thinks is deep feeling to match hers onto him when he really doesn't have any feeling. So the Media matches the man. The Media bombards us with meaningless phrases over and over on radio and tv to the point when language means nothing. American school children studying in the heart of the Media Empire can do schoolwork and 4 other things while watching tv and/or listening to the radio – simply because the media is not saying anything. TV media men even say that the reason they can put a thoughtful show on tv every now and then is that the impact of one thought-provoking show is deadened by the barrage of shit and stupidity that they hit viewers with the rest of the week. Over and over language misused and overused.

Women communicate intensely in a complicated way without speaking. Men cannot and this scares the shit out of them. And when women talk, they wouldn't think of speaking without mixing emotions with words, unless they're imitating men (the professional woman) or doing straight seduction numbers which is the way you operate with men – it's the only thing that turns them on – artifice. Men freak when women speak emotionally simply because women are on a higher existence level that men could not reach even with a ladder. So men trash speaking with emotional intensity and make their non-talent into a social virtue – the ability to speak ridiculous mindfucking stale languages (legal, business, doctor) that are like them – they attempt to sound important but mean nothing. They try to make women feel stupid for not understanding these languages that are essentially meaningless. (Watergate legal talk.)

Since men have been taking women's language apart for millennia and rendering it utterly meaningless slop, it comes as no surprise that the Media State has gunned down feminist language by misuse, overuse, diffusion and defusion. The Media State has taken the language of the Women's Movement and distorted it so terribly that women in the movement even misuse it. We have one group going off with one understanding of feminism, another group going off with another – DIFFUSION – and the two shall never meet. By calling men and straight women 'feminist' and picking conservative reactionary male-identified women to be 'feminist' stars and parading them in the media, they have totally *defused* the word, feminism, to the point where every male transvestite in America thinks it's a 'feminist.' The Media State has defused the language of the WLM where everything means nothing. If every woman in America is a 'feminist,' as you are led to believe by the Media, why then are we still living in a patriarchy?

ALL THE ABOVE PLOTS ARE WORKING

Separation: Room of One's Own

Mary Daly
1978

Writing of male bonding, J. Glenn Gray asserts: 'While comradeship wants to break down the walls of self, friendship seeks to expand these walls and keep them intact.' Sisterhood has nothing to do with breaking down 'the walls of self,' but with burning/melting/vaporizing the constricting walls imposed upon the Self. Moreover, female friendship is not concerned with 'expanding walls and keeping them intact,' but with expanding energy, power, vision, psychic and physical space. Sisterhood and female friendship burn down the walls of male-defined categories and definition. However, hagocratic separatism/separation is not essentially about walls at all. Rather, it is expanding room of our own, moving outside the realm of the War State, War Stare.

Having thus separated female bonding from male definitions, Crones can approach the questions of separation and separatism in new ways. The dictionary reports that we should understand the term *separate* to be derived from the Latin *se*, meaning apart, and *parare*, meaning to get ready, set. Without bothering to dispute the correctness of this etymology, it is still possible to look at the word another way, to see in it the Latin word *se*, meaning

367

self, and to see also that the Latin *parare* is the root of the verb *to pare*. When Spinsters speak of separatism, the deep questions that are being asked concern the problem of paring away from the Self all that is alienating and confining. Crone-logically prior to all discussion of political separatism from or within groups is the basic task of paring away the layers of false selves from the Self. In analyzing this basic Gyn/Ecological problem, we should struggle to detect whatever obstacles we can find, both internal and external, to this dis-covering of the Self.

It is Crone-logical to conclude that internal separation or separatism, that is, paring away, burning away the false selves encasing the Self, is the core of all authentic separations and thus is normative for all personal/political decisions about acts/forms of separatism. It is axiomatic for Amazons that all external/internalized influences, such as myths, names, ideologies, social structures, which cut off the flow of the Self's original movement should be pared away.

Since each Self is unique, since each woman has her own history, and since there are deep differences in temperament and abilities, Hags should acknowledge this variety in all discussions of separatism.[1] While it is true that all women have had many similar experiences under patriarchy, it is also true that there have been wide variations on the theme of possession and in struggles for dispossession. To simplify differences would be to settle for a less than Dreadful judgment of the multiple horrors of gynocide. It would also impoverish our imaginations, limiting our vision of the Otherworld Journey's dimensions. Finally, minimizing the variety of Amazon Journeyers' experiences, temperaments, and talents would blind us to the necessity for separating at times even from sisters, in order to allow our Selves the freedom and space for our own unique discoveries. Acknowledging the deep differences among friends/sisters is one of the most difficult stages of the Journey and it is essential for those who are Sparking in free and independent friendship rather than merely melting into mass mergers. Recognizing the chasms of differences among sister Voyagers is coming to understand the terrifying terrain through which we must travel together and apart. At the same time, the spaces between us are encouraging signs of our immeasurable unique potentialities, which need free room of their own to grow in, to Spark in, to Blaze in. The greatness of our differences signals the immensity/intensity of the Fire that will flame from our combined creative Fury.

Whereas discussions of relations between men and women eulogize the so-called complementarity of opposites, an Amazonian analysis of female friendship/love dis-covers the fact that the basis of woman-identified relationships is neither biological differences nor socially constructed opposite roles. As Jan Raymond has observed, rather than accepting a standardized 'difference' (femininity), Lesbians/Spinsters find in our authentic likeness to each other the opportunity to exhibit and develop genuine differences. Rather than relying upon stereotypic role relationships, Amazon friends/lovers/sisters cast our Selves into a creative variety of developing relationships with each other. Since there are no models, no roles, no institutionalized relationships to fall back upon, we move together and apart in ever-varying patterns of relating. As each friend moves more deeply into her own Background she becomes both her earlier and her present Self. At times this re-membered integrity makes her appear Strange to her friends, and since the latter are also re-membering, the encounters of these older/younger Selves can be multiply Strange. This Dreadful Strangeness is part of the terrain of the Other-world Journey. It is essential to the Amazon adventure.

Women who have the courage to travel can see the absence of standardized roles as an asset, for such roles inhibit our struggle for truthfulness and fidelity. Heterosexist society does not reward Lesbians for friendship and fidelity to each other. Therefore, the way is clear for honest Amazon bonding. Since we know that our friendships will not in the final analysis yield social approval, we are free to seek Self-approval. We are free to follow our passion for Self-centering. As de Beauvoir correctly points out, men and women are always playing a part before one another. In contrast to this, Lesbians need not pretend. As she observes: 'They [these liaisons] are not sanctioned by an institution or by the mores, nor are they regulated by conventions; hence they are marked by especial sincerity.'

Such sincerity involves risks. Since woman-identified relationships are unrestrained by mystification over biological and role-defined differences, there is often great intensity and turbulence in be-ing together. It has been observed that sisterhood involves stages when one seems to be stepping off a cliff, and that, mysteriously, the ground rises under the Journeyer's feet. That ground is the Self's own confrontation with her reality, her truth — a confrontation made possible and unavoidable by her unprotected situation. Having defied the patriarchal protection racket, she finds her Dreadless Self.

Paradoxically, then, it is the likeness of women that makes room for our otherness, our wildness, our strangeness. The creation of separate female-identified psychic, mythic, semantic, physical spaces is necessary for likeness and wild otherness to grow. Each individual Amazon must have such room of her own, and she must be free to communicate the light and warmth generated in the privacy of her own room to the hearts/hearths of other Hags, and to receive their luminous energy.

Isolation of female-identified women from each other – a basic tactic of patriarchy – does not quench the individual woman's Spark, but contains it in a dampening environment. Each such woman, locked into the damp dungeon assigned to her by the misogynistic State, must struggle to maintain her own sense of reality against the prevailing lies. When she makes contact with even one other Sparking Self, the combination is conflagration. Each woman sees her own knowledge of reality confirmed in her sister. The possessors' spell is broken. Their prisons are reduced to ashes as these Sparking Selves energize and re-energize each other, giving each other the incendiary incentive.

Crones kindle the Fury of our own kind against the godfathers who burned our foremothers. The uprising of Cinderellas from the cinders/ashes of our mothers is the righteous Renaissance. In our rising together, Hags affirm the true identity of our foremothers who were burned as witches during the alleged 'renaissance.' We affirm the reality hidden by the 'wicked stepmother' image – the reality of the women of Wicce, whose fire still burns in every Haggard heart. This uprising of Amazon Fire, our life-loving, be-ing, is the hellfire deserved and dreaded by the Grand Inquisitors. If its purpose were merely to consume them it would be less effective. In fact, it is simply the expression/expansion of gynergy for its own sake, and this transcendence of Fury itself in the Renaissance of Fire. In its light, the patriarchal male is forced to see his history of holocausts, to re-view the multitudes of women sacrificed as burnt offerings to his gods. This is his unbearable 'beatific vision,' his Last End.

As the Sparking communication occurs, Hags do not haggle over 'equality,' for we know there is no equality among unique Selves. Noting that one definition of the term equal is 'capable of meeting the requirements of a situation or a task,' Jan Raymond observes that what each asks of the other is that she be equal to the task at hand. Crones expect and en-courage each other to become sister pyrotechnists, building the fire that is fueled by Fury, the fire that warms and lights the place where we can each have a loom of our own, where we can spin and weave the tapestries of Crone-centered creation.

Note

1. I want to separate my position here from an attitude of 'tolerance' for

differences among women. A common definition of *tolerance*, given in Merriam-Webster, is 'a permissive or liberal attitude toward beliefs or practices differing from or conflicting with one's own.' This attitude of 'different strokes for different folks,' while appearing to support originality, is in fact often repressive. The tyranny of tolerance is often the source of silencing/erasure of strong-minded Hags – who are labeled 'intolerant,' 'extreme,' and 'narrow.' However, if we look at Merriam-Webster's first definition of *tolerance*, we find an interesting clue for an analysis of genuinely gynocentric respect for difference. *Tolerance* (which is derived from the Latin *tolerare*, meaning endure, put up with) is defined as 'capacity to endure pain or hardship: ENDURANCE, FORTITUDE, STAMINA.' The variety which Crones respect in each other has as its basic precondition and common thread the endurance/fortitude/stamina needed for persevering on the Journey.

The Agent Within

oedipussy tudeé
(of the C.L.I.T. Collective)
1974

Part 1

I am a queer who has been trained in the male art of sociology. For the last four years I have been teaching students that a stable male society does not have to spend alot of money on social control. I mean, they don't have to hire one cop for every one member of that society because of the socialization process. This is common sociological knowledge. When applied to women, and it is never talked about in patriarchal universities, it is deadly.

By socialization, male sociology means the process of learning to become human. By socialization, I mean the process of learning to become MALE, that is learning the appropriate Male values, attitudes, and rules of behaviour that function to maintain the patriarchy. (Aside to the reader: If you are a biological male and learn to become male, I will call this socialization; but if you are a woman and learn to become male (identified), I will call this MALe-FUNCKTALIZATION or for short, MAL-Function of the Ovarian Intellect.)

When MAL-Function of the Ovarian Intellect occurs, what we actually have is a male conscience inside a biological woman. This is very bad for the woman and very good for the patriarchy. It

371

creates an existential tension between the woman body, her natural woman feelings, thoughts and the contemptuous, whipping, S & M, hostile, jealous, punishing male conscience. The woman is constantly working against herself for the Man inside her and she thinks she is a virgin. It should be obvious by now that once men are socialized and woman are MALe-FUNCKTALIZED the patriarchy does not need to hire cops on a one-to-one basis for citizens of the state. Because through the mechanism of the conscience which has been manhandled by P-men (patriarchy men) and P-women (family, teachers, nuns, the primary socializers), that is, once our conscience has been fucked in the name of the patriarchy, we have a cop inside ourselves walking the beat of our hearts every minute of our lives.

If you are a man with a cop inside, there is no tension; there is something primordial in the nature of men to be cops. They created the concept and every male society has them. It is one of their key moral and intellectual heavy concepts – Cops and Robbers, Good and Bad (and *Ugly*). Men are very *deep* thinkers. Men are also very cheap. They find that MALe-FUNCKTALIZATION, the internalization of the male ethic inside the female, is a much cheaper way to deal with the age-old patriarchal problem of social control of women than hiring massive police forces.

They get all the mileage out of women that they can in the process of literally fucking the woman out of them. Who do they (the Patriarchy) get to do 90% of the heavy socialization/MALe-FUNCKTALIZATION for the MALE state? From the cheapest labor source in society, of course – WOMEN! Housewives and mothers who you don't have to pay anything; nuns and teachers (who are mostly female). Who but women could do such an effective, credible job of convincing infant women that they should listen to daddy? Not only do women do the job well, but they do the job with love. Now after the State has gotten all the mileage out of mothers and wives it can – it doesn't even have to bear the expense of getting rid of the women who turn wise in old age after being discarded by men. Because there is a self-destruct mechanism built into the roles of wife and mother in patriarchies. The job itself kills off these women after they have raised their children.

Being a dyke, I think of social control alot. Especially the grass roots kind that comes out of the average citizen's eyes – the disgust, disapproval in the eyes of socialized P-men and MALe-FUNCTALIZED P-women when they catch sight of the wonder and beauty of a lesbian sliding down the street. P-men and P-women have this remarkable gift of knowing how to spit with their eyes at lesbians. Do any of you lesbians ever wake up in the morning and feel not wanted? That's because you aren't.

A lesbian is a woman who during MALe-FUNCKTALIZATION did not lose all of her Ovarian Intellect; that is, her body rejected the maleness imposed upon her by the patriarchy, leaving her enough of the female principle to love the female in her and other women. Further, by separation from the P-men and P-women, she has been able to exorcise some of the MALe-FUNCKTALIZATION attitudes toward herself and move on to a higher stage of life called SUCKTALIZATION where she is learning with other women the joy of being a woman without a man inside her. SUCKTALIZATION is very good for the woman and very bad for the patriarchy. She is out of line; she is a woman of resistance; she is fighting against the cop inside her. What will the patriarchy do to control her now?

Part 2

Easy: from a societal level, the patriarchy tries to co-opt, neutralize and make a new economic market off the movement (as we discuss in C.L.I.T. Statement No. 2) to scatter and scramble brains and energies. From the individual level, they set dyke traps to trip up the lesbian who thought she was free because she purged the male cop conscience inside her until she is unexpectedly ambushed by the cooler, smarter agent the patriarchy sent to do her in. That agent is the straight woman who has been living inside her for years, the 'woman' the patriarchy trained her to be, the patriarchal patsy who will cook for her killers and dig her own grave out of politeness. The most dangerous enemy of the dyke is the straight women she spent years being modeled into, an unpaid agent for the P-men created in their perverted image (man's walking, fucking rib) solely to trap and choke the baby dyke in herself and in any other woman she finds resistant to man. The patriarchy not only works to sabotage the movement of women as a group but also strikes hard at the individual level by continually socializing us to be agents against ourselves. It's the double fuck that men can't resist – cram a cock up your ass and down your mouth at the same time.

The most dangerous dyke trap the patriarchy has set for us is located inside every woman who grew up in the patriarchy. When in dyke danger, we always revert back to being straight. Which by definition means fucking the dyke in us and in other women; anytime we are not acting like a dyke, we are acting like a straight woman. And that concerns the patriarchy.

An agent is a provocateur, someone who takes aggressive action to create incidents over artificial man-made issues or to inflame real, sore problem areas among women which cause resentment, irritation, and anger aimed at splitting the members of the movement against each other and, in the end, themselves. I think there are many agents in the WLM, but most are not getting paid for their service job for the patriarchy.

To figure out how and where agents are doing damage to the movement we must look at the so-called 'political' divisions and splits that divide and conquer dykes. What we must find out is which of these divisions are ours that stem from real woman issues and which ones are theirs – man-made that have been put in our heads by paid agents and the inadvertent agents within each of us, the straight woman working with free rein out of ignorance and false consciousness about her real position inside the patriarchy. The splits seem to fall into these camps:

1. third world black vs. white dykes
2. third world spanish vs. white dykes
3. middle class vs. working class dykes
4. lesbian separatists vs. lesbians who do not want to separate from straight feminists
5. age differences among dykes including movement seniors and freshman dykes

The question is: which of these are ours and which are man-made splits in the dyke community? We urge everyone to rethink these divisions in terms of this question. C.L.I.T. will in the next batch of articles discuss each of these splits at length. We begin our answer with class.

We think that the armored class divisions among women, especially in the dyke community, are man-made and appeal to the straight patriarchal woman in all of us. Middle class dykes are mindfucking working class dykes pretending not to understand what it is they are doing that could irritate their working class sisters. Straight women mindfuck. Any woman who wants to can empathize with another woman's situation and listen to the things that hurt her and not do them anymore. But the middle class dyke does not want to admit that she and all the people she grew up with have oppressed other women all their lives without even knowing it. She thinks it's impossible for her to have done so. Although the same dyke can clearly see how straight women fuck other women over in return for male approval or security when in the case of rape she sides against the raped woman with the man saying she asked for it instead of identifying with the raped woman. That middle class dyke who thinks she understands straight so well fails to understand that any time she acts out of her class position or attitude she too is acting straight.

Working class dykes can smell a class number faster than most feminists can sniff out a sexist remark by a man. Middle class dykes have not reached that level of sensitivity about classism which means they are acting as straight woman agents against dykes. The working class dykes, who have the most female sensitivity about class insults done to women, have been pushed to the point of not wanting to be around any women who are not working class because the middle class dykes, who have almost no class consciousness, have been playing straight lady mindfuck games of 'I don't know what you mean' even when they're caught in the act of a classist remark or act. Who *but* the man and the straight woman who needs approval and security from the man benefits from women feeling so alienated from other women? If middle class dykes cannot get it together enough to raise their consciousness to a point where they can at least recognize a classist remark or attitude when they hear one, then they don't deserve to call themselves dykes and should go back to the straight world which digs on that kind of hurting women.

The beginning step for dykes to crash the class system in the movement is for middle class dykes to reach the high pitched sensitivity that working class dykes instinctually have about the pain, injury and insult the class system causes women. Only when all dykes are sensitive to each other's class pain and can talk about class without hurting each other, can we move on to dissolving the man-made divisions of class among women.

Even though all class insults are aimed at your mother's sex life – that's a diversion. Women don't mean anything in the class system by themselves. A woman's status or position in social space, her class in every patriarchy in the Western world is determined by either her father's or husband's position in the power turf struggle among men. Yes, women belong to races and classes and take the abuse of their man's low position or the privilege of his high position, but what it's really about is whose husband or father is on top or bottom or confused in the middle of the power game. What do you think the term illegitimacy is all about? It's not for lack of a mother that a child is called illegitimate. Although mama gets most of the insults for a family's class positioning, it's daddy (the size of his green prick) that determines how you comb your hair, whether you shop at Korvette's or Sak's, which neighborhood you live in, who your friends are, which high school you go to, whether you go to college and if you do, which one, your accent, how well you speak the English language, how many words you know, the clothes you wear, who your heroes are, etc.

One agent we are not aware of that is doing alot of class damage inside the movement is daddy's little girl. Much movement attention has been focused on the roles of straight woman as wife, mother, sex object, girlfriend – all adult woman relations with men that undercut solidarity among women. The childhood relationship of daughter-father has rarely been discussed. Discussions of women as daughters usually focus on the mother-daughter relationship. But the daughter-father relationship has done more damage by preventing strong relations among women possibly than any other straight relationship. Whose little girl you are, who your daddy is, determines your class position and privilege or lack of it. Dykes have mistakenly assumed that they gave up their straight class privilege by virtue of being a lesbian, that is, by forfeiting men in terms of husband status and privilege. What no dyke has given up is her daughter privilege or the defenses and pain that came from lack of it. Until we kill off the false sense of security or insecurity we derived from our father's position in the patriarchy, we are still holding on to our class attitudes and privilege. To hold on to the view of the world you got from daddy's position in the meat market when it hurts other women and makes you mistrust or fear women who have a more or less powerful daddy than yours is allegiance to daddy instead of women. It is the work of the straight woman inside you, your agent. Kill it before it kills you and the movement.

Another indication that the class problems in the dyke community are patriarchally induced by paid agents and the agent within is that the upper class mysteriously is not being discussed. Who's doing the fighting? Working class and middle class are again battling each other to the death. The upper class has always outsmarted both the lower classes into thinking that no upper class existed that was benefiting from all their turmoil and class warfare. That's precisely why the class system has remained intact. The upper class pretends for us they don't exist and we believe them. They pay the middle class to do the dirty work of running all their institutions; hence, the middle class only sees people like themselves managing the institutional world and falsely assumes it is their world since they feel so comfortable in it. Working class people only run up against the middle class rulers of institutions who tell them they cannot see the dean, that the doctor won't accept a check from them, that they wouldn't have a case in court, etc. and are constantly getting fucked over in the institutional world – so they falsely assume that it is the middle class's world too.

Some thoughts Norma Pontes wrote in a paper on Massification will help explain.

Massification means the process of dividing an oppressed population(s) into separate groups that view other oppressed groups as enemies rather than the men at the top who planned the group prejudices and fabricated the tastes and confusions of the oppressed groups to eternally keep them down. Examples: the divisions sociologists refer to as race, class, ethnic, religious, educational, occupational, etc. The Media State is primarily in charge of this operation of massificating people although other institutions of the ruling class's State like church, family and school play into it, especially the social science scholars who refine and elaborate discussion of these divisions. It is the mass media that does the heavy duty work of making oppressed people identify and address themselves as members of a mass, rather than as individuals. Norma talks about how little *thinking* people who are massificated do, especially women. It is part of the process of massificating women, giving women their image to themselves and to other societal groups, that women are not in the habit of thinking. Norma says that, instead of thinking, mostly we hold opinions, which she defined as 'internalizations of positions,' that we learn from a massified group that we belong to or from the media addressing us as a member of a massificated group. The main thing about massification is that no one is an individual in the pure sense; we are members of different groups and sub-groups which are falsely divided along confusions that the ruling class and its strong arm, the Media State, wants to maintain so that their power will not be threatened by an attack of consciousness.

What is most interesting about massification is that the individual thinks that his or her tastes are their own, original, personal; I call these people, which is most of us, massividuals. After we fall into a certain income group, for instance, we begin to take on the fabricated media tastes that the media says we have to begin with. The Media State manufactures Puerto Rican taste, Jewish intellectual taste, California taste, lower middle class taste, radical camp, radical chic and Bronx taste, Newark taste, Miami taste, bourgie taste, and nouveau bourgie taste, etc. And then the massividual walks into a room and says 'I'm from California' – 'oh, really, how could you tell?'

The most tragic joke of all is for women to take on these tastes or massificated attributes anyway. And worse to defend them to the death as if it were a personal defense of themselves when in fact it is more a defense of the media's right to massificate us. To be more accurate, to defend middle class or working class tastes or attributes is essentially a defense of the upper class, the real patriarchs who designed the class system and through the media maintain it. They are the fathers of middle class and working class tastes, values, and attitudes; the upper class is the only class that benefits from our having middle and working class mass-personalities and ways of life. It is no accident that the upper class is omitted from class discussions in the women's movement except for an abstract reference to them occasionally. If you listened to movement discussions of class seriously, you would walk away thinking that there are only two classes in the class system. The reason for this incomplete grasp of the class system is also due to massification – most of us have never seen the upper class way of life or hardly one member of the ruling class; we have no sense of what they look like, how they dress, how to detect one largely because the media purposefully never mentions them as a class group to protect their invisibility, their power. But the media spends vast amounts of time delineating middle from working class (Archie Bunker as opposed to Marcus Welby). The upper class world is small (1% of the U.S. population, if that much) and is like an invisible other dimension functioning above all that most of us never see or know about but that controls our entire lives, even the way we perceive the class system. Everybody's father or husband or brother (the men in your family, the men you used to date, go to school with, etc.) who are not in the ruling class are dildoes. Most of us have never seen the real pricks of America, the ruling class men.

Another mindfuck that has been done on both the lower classes (middle and working) is the misuse/overuse media mispeak translation of Marxian class analysis and his term, bourgeois. Marx used the term bourgeoisie to mean nobility, land owners, owners of production and not middle class as we mean it in America today. But when most leftists today use bourgeois, they mean middle class. It's curious how the ruling class and their media have even worked Marxian class analysis to the point that we think the middle class is the enemy of the people instead of the ruling class.

So not only do we need to deeply explore the daughter straight woman in us that is hanging on to the class attitudes, confusions, prejudices and pain we got from daddy, but also we must understand the invisible upper class that we omitted from movement discussions of the class system. We can never destroy the class system and especially sabotage the plans the controlling class has for women and the WLM unless we start battling the real prick, the ruling class, and stop falling into their gameplan of fighting each other.

Our essential argument is that class is a man-made monster that offers nothing women moving on to an all woman world can take with them without damaging themselves and other women. The entire class system functions to cripple women and keep them defending the man inside them. Nothing we have learned from being working class or middle class encourages the woman in us to come out and be with other women. Our class positions have given us misconceptions about the woman inside us and the women around us; it makes us mistrust or fear other women. And we will keep having reasons to mistrust and fear as long as we have an agent within.

Problems of Our Movement

Alice, Gordon, Debbie, & Mary
1973

Other sections of this manuscript are reprinted in this anthology.
(Eds.)

Although the present lesbian movement is less than five years old (and any kind of lesbian movement in the U.S. is less than 20 years old), we have developed many internal problems which threaten its future. Some of these are carryovers of attitudes and oppressions of the larger society. From this society and from other movements we've also brought in oppressive styles of work. In this section we'll discuss the following problems:[1]

1. Racism
2. Classism
3. Ageism
4. Elitism
5. False Divisions – 'political' vs. 'cultural' lesbians; 'Old' vs. 'New' lesbians.

Straight women and male left groups have also introduced some destructive ideologies to the lesbian movement. In Seattle, the three major ones we've had to deal with are:

1. Human-being-ism

2. Sexual minorities
3. Reformism

Racism

White lesbians have not dealt with our racism to any greater extent than the rest of the white population. If we had any beliefs to the contrary, these beliefs were burst at the 1973 West Coast Lesbian Conference in Los Angeles. At this conference, which attracted some of the most politically conscious lesbians from all over the nation, racism was most apparent: It took five tries before a workshop on racism among white participants could be convened; few third world women had the privilege of being able to leave work to come, or felt comfortable enough among white lesbians to come; a non-antagonistic statement by third world lesbians presented the second night was not taken very seriously by most white lesbians; a report by the workshop on racism was booed; one speaker was allowed, if not encouraged by most lesbians, to engage in racist behavior and speech; and a proposal to play a tape made by a third world lesbian explaining her feelings about the speaker's overt racist behavior towards her was also booed.

Many white lesbians are in awe of the strength of third world lesbians who have to suffer incredible daily oppression because of race, sex, and lesbianism and are, by virtue of the combination of these factors, excluded not only from the dominant culture, but from just about every sub-culture as well. White lesbians have opted to ignore the necessity to make an attempt at reducing this oppression by not working among white lesbians to reduce racism in our own community. We have no excuses for this treachery on our part and realize that racism and patriarchy are so inextricably linked that an attempt to fight one without fighting the other is stupid. We must immediately begin serious work on annihilating our own racism and the racism of other white lesbians, as well as the racism of the society.

Many white lesbians have been falsely believing that there was not so much racism among ourselves, not conscious that the reason our community has not been attacked often by third world lesbians for its racism is that for many, if not most, third world lesbians our community is the only place they can be. To attack white lesbians and risk isolation is a privilege third world lesbians often feel they can not afford, though they are constantly oppressed by our behavior. For us to profess to love other lesbians in any more than a sexual way and not put our efforts into reducing the pressures of racism on third world lesbians is hypocrisy.

Part of our fight against our own racism is for us to become actively involved in opposing the genocide and oppression being committed daily against third world people. Our way of fighting must be consistent with our lesbian separatist ideology. We believe that we should actively oppose the oppression of *all* third world people, and defend their right to define their own movement, while we don't necessarily support their politics. Naturally, we feel closest to third world lesbians and to third world women, but if those women choose to work with third world men we can not allow their position to in any way diminish our support for the struggle against racism. Further, if these women choose to unite with third world men because of the tremendous oppression they face, we should not use our lesbian separatist politics to become divisive.

There has been a lot of tokenism and paternalism shown towards third world lesbians who have chosen to work in the lesbian movement. Writings in the lesbian publications in the past two years have frequently focused on classism and sexism but rarely on racism. In Seattle, the fact that the 'movement' has been dominated by one or two social cliques has excluded all but a very few third world lesbians from involvement in the movement (as well as excluding all lesbians not around the university community).

Part of our work against racism will be in coalitions with third world people and probably with straight white women and even white men. This does not mean that we intend to work in any sexually mixed community. We believe that our work in those coalitions will be to articulate and build support in the lesbian community. Nor will we stand for sexism or heterosexism in these coalitions.

Classism

Lesbians who formed the current lesbian movement were, for the most part, from cross-classed[2] or middle-class families. Because of the type of movement they initiated and perpetuated, poor or working class lesbians have felt excluded. This movement defined rigid sex roles as lower class (which is not true), instituted middle-class youth-culture chauvinism in many forms, held long meetings at inconvenient times and without providing child care, ignored gut responses in exclusive favor of abstract theorizing, listened condescendingly to women who were not as aggressive or articulate in a university-approved fashion, reacted with giddy excitement to women who got jobs as janitors, bus drivers, or cab drivers because these women had supposedly broken into male fields when working class women have held these jobs for years and don't consider them much fun, exalted women in any professional field no matter how oppressive the field to working-class women[3] (for example, social workers, psychologists, teachers) and used specialized and unnecessary words to convey simple thoughts.

Women from the poorer working class and some cross-classed families and women currently in the poorer working class either had to feign feelings in order to appear 'in' the movement or left the movement entirely. Many of these lesbians are now justifiably reacting with anger. Some middle-class women are beginning to work on changing their classist behavior.

Most of the writings of lesbian publications on classism are very personal, which is good. But some of them also lead to confusion when they begin to advocate all kinds of personal solutions to this very political problem.

Many middle-class women are reacting to complaints about their behavior with guilt. Reacting to guilt instead of understanding that the destruction of classism is necessary to their own survival in this society as well as the more immediate survival of working class women is not only a waste of energy, but it is unlikely to produce any real solutions. People reacting to guilt can not think clearly, act clearly, or evaluate their actions clearly.

Failure on the part of all of us in analyzing classism has also made it difficult to either make demands on middle-class women or to react to the demands that have been made. Many demands and reactions don't make sense. Some lesbians from working-class backgrounds have asked women from middle-class backgrounds to resume or begin jobs as social workers, teachers and the like, which they assume middle class women can get through their privilege, while at the same time condemning these jobs. Such jobs directly oppress working class women who are the unfortunate 'recipients' of these 'services.' Other demands have included that middle-class women take these jobs and support individual working-class women from their salaries, or that these salaries be used to create movement jobs with high salaries to be filled by working-class lesbians. All of these proposals ignore what happens to a person's behavior and ideas when they assume a middle-class mode of living with its attendant expectations and privileges. Middle-class women respond to these sorts of demands by salving their consciences by trying to 'help' an individual woman while they oppress tens of women in the same position as part of their jobs, and drive themselves crazy in the process.

These demands by working-class women are partly in response to the insulting 'downward mobility' and 'slum-adventuring' practiced by some women of the youth culture. Not only do middle-class women glorify poverty but they ridicule women from the working-class who maintain some security because they can not fall back on parents, college degrees, or contacts during periods of illness, arrest or other misfortune. Being on welfare or food-stamps is an affirmation of supposed inferiority or failure to a person from the poorer working-class while the person from a middle-class background on welfare can gloat that they're ripping off the system (which is often a misconception).

Classism has been particularly oppressive to lesbians as a group. It seems that nearly all lesbian fiction up to very recently portrayed lesbians as being rich and perhaps even Parisian. One member of our group, when she was in high school and sleeping with women, did not think of herself as a lesbian since she thought all lesbians lived in Paris.

In some large cities there is almost a caste system among lesbians. Lesbians with surplus money attend relatively expensive restaurants and cocktail lounges with high cover charges and expensive clothes standards. Those lesbians who work at less professional jobs or who make less money go to different bars. Though there are relatively few lesbians altogether, mixing of classes may not take place.

In most cities, lesbians share one or two bars with lesbians of all classes, since they don't make enough money as a whole to support many bars. They may be so insensitive to each other as to misinterpret sexual cuing or to expect different courting or sexual behavior from a lesbian of another class. This is oppressive to lesbians of all classes.

White families especially are sometimes cross-classed. They often move from one sector of the working-class to another, from a position of more privilege. They can also move from the petty-bourgeoisie to the working-class, and back again. Lesbians may thus experience and reap the rewards of more or less privilege at various times in their lives. The effects of all the levels we go through stay with us (subjective) while our actual present class (objective) may change and affect our attitudes. Thus, the poorer working-class is often spoken for by lesbians who are objectively middle-class but from working-class backgrounds, or by lesbians who are objectively poorer working-class but who are still very middle-class subjectively.

Obviously, even extreme personal changes in middle-class women will only halt some of the oppression of poorer working-class lesbians. Some things can be done to remedy the classism of the lesbian movement. Strikes can be supported. Responsibility for children can be shared. Institutions such as food coops and women's clinics can make special efforts to make their services more available and convenient to poorer working-class women. Lesbian institutions that develop must make sure that on the first, most basic levels, participation of poorer working-class women is assured. Those lesbians who have privilege that is not oppressive to others should share it. Ultimately, however, classism with all of its real-life oppression will not end until the patriarchy is overthrown and matriarchy reinstated.

Ageism

One of the means devised by patriarchal society to keep what was once a more clear and powerful enemy, women, separated from each other is ageism. Ageism pits daughter against mother, or any older woman against any younger woman. In addition, patriarchal ageism pits every woman against herself for virtually no woman feels she is the right age. She is, in succession, deprived of her legal and social rights, then deprived of her right to choose and live her own life, and finally deprived of any useful function in society. She is supposedly too young and naïve, and, as she ages, finds that no one will listen to her experience. Women within any age group are further separated by being forced to compete with other women in that group.

In addition, patriarchal society, with its drive for profit, eliminates those segments of the population from participation in society who are not yet needed for production and who are detrimental to the process of training new employees who have many 'serviceable' years of life ahead. Both the young and the old who are in these categories are, in this advanced stage of patriarchy, barred from contact with society and each other. This separation between old and young serves to destroy any sense of historical continuity in all of the individuals who live under such a system. Ageism thus limits each of us to our isolated experience, and to the history which those who rule us choose to put forth.

Ageism presumes that all people grow physically, mentally, emotionally, and experientially at the same rate regardless of the fact that each of us comes from a different environment, background and genetic code. This means that each of us who does not fit into the preconceived notion of development must suffer. That virtually no one fits into that notion is ignored by patriarchy in its quest for order.

Ageism destroys part of every person who is not in a position of power. It hurts more privileged women less than it hurts women from the lower classes.

Ageism affects lesbians in some ways to a greater extent than it affects heterosexual and bisexual women because it denies their right to sex and to go to bars to meet other lesbians (when they are under age). But in some ways lesbians are less affected by ageism since we do not look to men and male standards for our feelings about ourselves. Standards set by ourselves for ourselves are less restrictive and more natural. Heterosexual and bisexual women are forced to disassociate from themselves in some way because they can never meet the standards the men have set for them and they have internalized.

Ageism in the lesbian movement is an oppressive reflection of ageism in society. It is used on women perceived as older and on women perceived as younger, so that five years spent in the movement will assure anyone of the opportunity to experience it on at least one side, if not to practice it as well.

The lesbian movement is encouraged in its ageism by some of the institutions of the larger society. The liquor laws are one outstanding example. There's nothing quite like the feelings of camaraderie a lesbian gets when everyone at a meeting or a demonstration adjourns to the lesbian bar, except her, because she's under age, or the warm glow of sisterhood when someone says: 'You're 17? Why I could get in trouble just talking to you.' Or there's the feeling that your ideas are being listened to when you hear, 'I felt that way too, when I was your age.'

On the other end, there's that sexist, male-left proverb, 'Don't trust anyone over thirty,' or the oft-expressed feeling that 'old-world dykes are fucked-up.'

'Older' lesbians (from about 23 on) don't listen to 'kids.' Younger lesbians don't listen to 'her, she's as old as my mother.' Or, conversely, younger lesbians feel intimidated by the experience of older lesbians, or desire to imitate the oppressive role behavior adopted by some of the older lesbians in response to the situations the older lesbians came out in. Older lesbians are often envious of the situations younger lesbians are coming out in. Sometimes they try to evaluate their own experience in the light of ideas and ways of behaving that weren't even dreamed of while they were doing all the 'fucked-up' things in their past.

Of course, everyone feels bad or alienated, and the movement is deprived of all sorts of valuable experience, ideas, talents, and dreams.

We have no magic answers for ageism. Although all of us in the study group have tried to be sensitive to each other on the question, we still find ourselves doing ageist things to each other. When we do, we try to talk about it, understand it, and prevent its recurrence.

Elitism

Elitism is a very common problem in women's and lesbian groups, as it was in the male left. Essentially, it consists of the control of information and communication, if not actual decision-making, by a small group of self-chosen individuals. Often elites are based on previous class privilege, especially on contacts made in college. Sometimes it's a matter of a small group of women knowing each other from previous movement activities and becoming incapable of really integrating new people into the organization. Needless to say, elites tend to be white, male (in mixed groups), straight, or upper-class.

Elitism can be exacerbated by having some individuals paid and working on movement activities full-time while others work at straight jobs and do movement work in their 'spare time.' Those who are around the movement activities more learn more, make more of the quick decisions, develop close ties with others who are around, talk to more people, etc. They often appear to be so much more up on things that 'part-timers' (often putting most of their non-sleeping, non-working hours into the movement) feel that they don't have the expertise to question what the full-time movement woman says. (Of course, since 99% of movement work is unpaid, it's mainly the upper class, or in rare cases the middle-class woman who can become a full-time 'heavy.') The full-timers begin to resent the women who aren't 'doing as much' and often start guilt-tripping the others into ceding more power to them.

Elitism is often confused with leadership. But one of the problems of the elites is that they *don't* take the responsibilities of good leadership – they don't share information or aid communication (they act like vacuum cleaners, gathering up all of it in sight and getting it inside of them). They don't help provide women with all the information they need to make decisions, but rather, they make the decisions for them, and they make it extremely hard to use the experience and expertise of all of the women in the movement.

We are aware that paying women for their movement work has been urged as a way to help remedy the classism of the movement by enabling some lower-class women to work full-time in the movement. But we think that in general this will just exacerbate the problems of elitism and create a division between the newly privileged lower-class woman and the rest of the lower-class women. In other words, this form of tokenism leads to elitism. Perhaps collectives and the rotation of jobs are at least part of the solution both to the survival problems of lower-class women and to elitism.

Small closed groups, whether for study, action, or rapping, or a combination of these functions, are often criticized for being elitist, especially if they are, as a group, staffing or maintaining a movement center. On the other hand, many lesbians feel a need to work closely with and make a commitment to a reasonably small number of sisters who are making a reciprocal commitment. We think such groups should keep in mind the problems of elitism, of becoming isolated, and of taking some of the responsibility for integrating newly-involved lesbians into the lesbian movement.

Further, there's a problem because a structureless group often gives the appearance of being very democratic and anti-elitist, whereas, actually, there is a small group who is making decisions through the control of information, etc. These apparently democratic groups (like SDS) are often especially oppressive to less privileged members because the ultra-democratic facade precludes recognition of these problems by simply denying their existence.

One other form of elitism is big city chauvinism. This is the attitude that, if it isn't happening in Berkeley, or New York, it's not happening anywhere. Contacts and information flow to and from these big cities, while others get feelings of inferiority or at least the feeling of being completely out of touch with what's going on.

Of course, a discussion of elitism wouldn't be complete without discussing the whole question of super-stars. In the lesbian movement, this has been particularly disgusting because 'our' two main superstars are an avowed 'bisexual' – Kate Millett – and a woman who continues to live with a man – Robin Morgan – both of whom refuse to recognize (and have publicly and forthrightly refused to recognize) that who you sleep with DOES have political meaning.

Certainly, we don't create superstars, the media does, in an attempt to distort and destroy our movement. They purposely pick on the most privileged, most individualistic and least (to them) politically threatening of us, so that the real voice of our movement will not be heard. Let us make it clear right now that the lesbian movement has been and will continue to be built by all the lesbian collectives, groups and individuals who have been working, often unrecognized, in the areas in which they live – talking with, working with, acting with other lesbians. We see superstars as parasites who are making a living and a career by representing themselves as the spokeswomen for all of these lesbians.

When a woman writes an important book or does something else that gains outside recognition, she has the option of keeping to the collectivist theories of our movement or of allowing herself to be catapulted into superstardom. She has that option. Some lesbians choose collectivity and the movement, and some choose stardom and its attendant isolation. We find it hard, therefore, to consider superstars as victims, since they chose the path they now walk. We would also like to point out that there are many women in the movement who are writing good things, making good speeches, doing good art, etc., and that it takes a certain amount of privilege to get the leisure to spend three years writing a book. There should be some way for the movement to give more of its members a chance to develop rather than it being left to a person's individual privilege.

But what worries us more than the superstars themselves are the lesbians (and there are many) who engage in the adulation of these superstars. A superstar can blither out some unsubstantiated inanity which will be printed, read, quoted and taken as gospel.

Lately, superstars have been heard to complain that we are oppressing them by our criticism and trying to squelch their creativity. We would like to point out that we all like to think of ourselves as creative and we are not into squelching individual creativity. But we believe that creativity should be used to help our movement and thus our personal survival, not to use our movement to build an individual's fame and fortune on our backs.

We see the Women's Press Collective in Berkeley as a positive form of creativity in the movement. But superstars do our movement great harm because they misrepresent what the movement stands for by making it appear that the lesbian movement is about being the follower of a star. Thus, they destroy any self-respecting lesbian's desire to get involved in the movement.

In our section on directions we will talk about more satisfying structures for the lesbian movement.

False Divisions: 'Political' and 'Cultural' Lesbians

The division between 'political' and 'cultural' lesbians became one of the unarticulated issues at the West Coast Lesbian Conference. We don't want to dwell on this issue here, but we see the division as a false dichotomy. Our lesbian culture is VERY political in that to be a truly lesbian culture it must shake the very roots of male supremacy. Our culture – our shared music, art, poetry, fiction, crafts, theater, etc. – brings us together and articulates our lesbian vision. It also speaks the pain of our experience under patriarchy. We agree with the statement by the Family of Woman [Band] that lesbian separatist music is very political.

But we also see work in the sector that is more traditionally viewed as political to be important. We must learn how to fight, to discuss issues with each other, and how to work together to get the power we need to build and defend our lesbian nation. Although we are not into reformism (see section on reformism) we believe that we must find ways to collectively fight our daily oppression under patriarchal capitalism. Otherwise, the men who rule us will not only take the small space our movement has created for our culture, but the outside oppression will move back into our heads and ourselves and squelch our creativity and love for each other.

We do not view politics as uncreative hack work. We believe that political actions are also works of art that can bring us together and let us feel our collective power.

At the West Coast Lesbian Conference artists were used by the conference organizers to blur our political differences and stop political discussions. Artists were also forced to compete as 'entertainers' for mass audiences. This was oppressive to all the lesbians involved.

There is no such thing as apolitical art, or apolitical entertainment. Years of experience with the mass culture should have been enough lesson to us all that culture either supports or opposes the dominant male-supremacist system.

False Divisions: 'Old' and 'New' Lesbians

Problems have arisen between lesbians who have come out recently and those who came out some time ago. The problem seems to be two-fold. Many lesbians who have come out recently are young, while those who have been out are older (of course). Age differences and therefore differences in outlook and experience are nothing new (see section on ageism). But many older lesbians have always been suspicious of new lesbians, largely because of the number of straight women who 'experiment' with 'lesbian experiences.' (See section on separatism.)[4]

An additional problem has come about because of the number of women who have come out through the Women's Movement, a recent phenomenon. Many of the latter came out under what appears to the older lesbians to be relatively 'easy' conditions within a very supportive environment. Because of this, older lesbians mistrust them because it was so easy for them and because they did not suffer as much as they had – and experienced the terrible pain and loneliness that most lesbians have experienced at some time in their life. (This is in no way implying that coming out today is easy.)

Also, some of the older lesbians feel jealous because it *had* been so hard for them. This jealousy is particularly hard to deal with since many of these same lesbians have been working and fighting to make the way easier for those who will follow later. They don't want coming out to be a terrible trauma, and yet they (wrongfully) resent it when it isn't. These attitudes must be struggled with. No lesbian wishes the pain and damage on any other lesbian; yet we value the experience and understanding that it has brought.

On the other hand, older lesbians feel oppressed because of some of the attitudes the new lesbians have towards them. They feel that the new lesbians lack an understanding of the value of *their* experience, and why they are the way they are (now). Because many older lesbians used to be primarily concerned with survival, or because they didn't see alternatives, they may have adopted oppressive ways of relating to each other, such as heavy stereotyped roles.

This is not to say that younger and/or newer lesbians (even those who came out through the women's movement) do not do oppressive sex roles. All lesbians should work towards an understanding of why oppressive sex roles develop.

In addition, many younger lesbians look down upon older lesbians because the older lesbians didn't make a conscious political choice to be lesbians. We feel that new lesbians must acquaint themselves with these and other aspects of older lesbians' lives and culture. They must educate themselves before they criticize.

We feel that these differences, while sometimes oppressive, can be overcome, and therefore must be struggled with. We do not need to jeopardize our potential unity with each other because of divisions which boil down to the various ways the Man divided and conquered us.

Destructive Ideologies: 'Human being-ism'

One of the major political attitudes among Seattle lesbians (as in the women's movement here in general) is what we've labeled 'human being-ism.' This political line runs basically that 'we're all human beings. There are good human beings and bad human beings, sexist human beings and human beings who are struggling with their sexism, racist human beings and human beings who are struggling with their racism, etc.'

Some lesbians extend this ideology even further: 'Since we're all human beings then of course we don't want to sleep with a sexist human being, but it doesn't matter whether the human being one does sleep with is a male or a female, so long as she or he is struggling with their sexism.'

We can understand part of where the willingness to accept this ideology is coming from on the part of many lesbians. The early gay and women's movements were mainly reformist movements (see section on reformism), involved in gaining basic recognition of their 'humanity' (i.e. their right to exist on some sort of equal level with, as it was then seen, 'straight white men') from the ruling male elite. Furthermore, as the women's movement began to give at least token recognition to lesbians, lesbians began to hope that for once we wouldn't have to feel estranged from the majority of women. Somehow, it didn't seem like that great a compromise to accept what they did in bed, if they would accept what we did in bed.

Unfortunately for all our hopes and good vibes, patriarchy has created (or is reflective of) some very real divisions that can't be smoothed over with the term *human being*. Men get privileges *off* of sexism and women are oppressed by sexism. Men are in power in patriarchy. Women are kept powerless by those men. We are not prepared to take a position on whether men are a separate biological species or not. At this time that question is somewhat irrelevant. Their male culture has created for them a daily life experience that is so different from that of women, and so diametrically opposed to that of women, that they behave as if they're from another planet.

Furthermore, we think the 'human being' ideology is dangerous for the lesbian movement because it prevents us from seeing our enemy as anything more than an amorphous set of bad attitudes that we all share. Thus it becomes impossible for us to define an enemy or to determine who are our allies or potential allies.

No man, no matter how he 'struggles with his sexism' even approaches in his daily life the constant oppression women feel from men. Often men even use the excuse of struggling with their sexism to demand more energy from women.

As we've stated over and over again in this paper, it does matter whether you share love, energy and physical intimacy with other women or whether you surrender your love, energy and body to a man who is oppressing you and other women. We see sex with men as an act of capitulation and of sucking up (often literally) to the oppressor, and we see making love with women as a way of sharing our strengths and building women's community.

We are not surprised that, given their objective life-styles, straight women have developed and subscribe to human being-ism, because only that kind of a theory can rationalize what they do. But we think it's a fatal mistake for lesbians to buy that ideology.

Destructive Ideologies: 'Sexual Minorities'

Within the straight women's movement lesbians are still thought of as one of the 'sexual minorities.' Even many lesbians tolerate being lumped together with such people as gay men, fetishists, transvestites, transsexuals, bisexuals, sado-masochists, necro-philiacs, scatologists, pederasts, those who practice bestiality and others.

All 'deviations' (except homosexuality) are extensions of the sexual objectification/power/dominance way that men in this society relate to everything. Pederasty, sadism and bestiality are acts of wanton cruelty and are extremely exploitive of helpless people and animals. We in no way identify ourselves with people who commit these acts and in no way condone them. In the case of other 'deviations' we see patriarchal society as being hypo-critical and oppressive in its condemnation of these people when they are only acting out extensions of patriarchal sexuality. We do not see gay men who do not engage in these violent practices as being 'deviants.'

Seeing lesbians as a 'sexual minority' ignores and obscures the fact that who or what a person relates to sexually is a matter of political significance. Seeing lesbians as a 'sexual minority' ignores all but the sexual aspect of lesbianism. The emotional, political, and all other aspects are overlooked. The phrase 'sexual minority' evokes the concept of deviance, and emphasizes that deviance, thereby recognizing heterosexuality as the standard and giving bisexuality more legitimacy than lesbianism.

Another popular view of lesbianism is that of the 'alternative lifestyle.' This view is equally oppressive because it, too, sees heterosexuality as the standard.

We can not let straight society, or 'straight' feminists, define us. We reject this way of thinking of ourselves and we are building our own concepts and standards.

Destructive Ideologies: Reformism

Some lesbians have gotten involved in the basically male 'sexual law reform' movement or the basically straight 'equal rights for women' movement. They have gotten involved out of their need to fight our oppression as lesbians, and have been involved in many courageous struggles. Many of us have, at one time or another, been in these struggles, or in similar struggles in the civil rights or anti-war things:

1. Lesbians' basic oppression is NOT due to laws, though some laws oppress us, but it is due to the fact that patriarchal society is completely the opposite of lesbianism. Patriarchal society views women as men's tools and as existing for their pleasure. Lesbianism is the practice of women existing for themselves and each other.

2. There is no way any given reform, or any number of reforms in combination, will ever change the basic nature of this society. Reforms are simply changes in the way the same small group of white men will rule, but they don't change or challenge the fact that they do rule.

3. Reforms are often turned against us because we can't control them. For example, reformed abortion laws have been used to force abortions on women on welfare. (This is not to imply that the abortion reform movement did not actively oppose or protest forced sterilization or abortion.)

4. Because of the reasons listed above (that lesbians are oppressed by the very nature of this patriarchal society) lesbians end up fighting for reforms that are often not very directly related to our lives.

5. Many of the women who fight for any given set of reforms are dishonest with the people who they are trying to 'organize' since they know all of the above things but don't acknowledge that to those people. Thus they create cynicism among all but the already cynical 'political heavies' towards any kind of political action.

We DON'T believe in ignoring our day-to-day oppression while we build for some abstract revolution. (In the section on directions and projects we will deal with some concrete proposals for action.) We believe that it's very important to fight cases of discrimination against lesbians in the areas of jobs, housing, sex-laws, child custody, etc. But we believe that only a lesbian movement with the clearly articulated vision of building a matriarchal society can avoid fighting the losing battle of going from one fight for reform or defensive action to the next without ever getting closer to building our vision.

Every action we take, every leaflet we write, every demonstration we build, must reflect our perspective on WHY this injustice has occurred and how we see it as ultimately being remedied. Further, they must be aimed at building a sense of power and unity among lesbians.

Notes

1. We are not at this time discussing the important problems of sex roles, sexual objectification, monogamy, and non-monogamy in small groups, sizeism, etc., because of lack of space.
2. 'Cross-classed' refers to women who have experienced living in several different classes throughout their lives. 'Cross-classed' has also been recognized by the term 'hybrid' in the *Furies*.
3. 'Poorer working class' refers to the 'lower class' in sociological terms and to the less privileged portion of the working class in Marxist terms. We don't believe Marx adequately defined the term 'lumpenproletariat,' so we therefore include the permanently unemployed in the working class.
4. Reprinted here in the section, Separatist Basics. (Eds.)

Response by the Gorgons

Gorgons
1978

We are Lesbian Separatists because we love women and want women to be happy. Women have an awful life in patriarchy. We want to change that. We are building a Lesbian Separatist political movement which actively opposes patriarchy. We are learning how to relate non-oppressively to each other. We are teaching ourselves skills and knowledge that help us in our fight against patriarchy and that will help us build a Lesbian society where women can be happy.

During the patriarchal revolution, which lasted thousands of years, men forced themselves and their society, patriarchy, on women through rape, witch burnings, destruction of women's knowledge, and many other kinds of attacks on women. Though many women had fought against the men, the men eventually won because some women had cooperated with them and possibly because women had not developed war technology. In the establishment of their patriarchy, men set up many systems of oppression: race, class, age, looks, fat oppression, and more. These oppressions and their interrelationships operate for the benefit of men, divide women from each other, and keep women in allegiance with men.

Patriarchy accords power to every man. He can rape. He can have better access to jobs than can women of his race, class, age, etc. He can sexually objectify women. He can have a wife. These are a few of his rights as a man in patriarchy.

Straight women collaborate with patriarchy by putting time and energy into men. This individual support helps men maintain their male power, and a straight woman's commitment to men keeps her from effectively fighting for women. There are other relationships in which women and Lesbians support men. This does NOT include the contact with men we are forced into all the time in order to live.

As long as patriarchy exists, women will not have the power to act for the benefit of women because patriarchy does not accord women power, only privileges. Men often directly offer some of their privileges to women in friendships, marriages, and families – it can be money, jobs, houses, security, etc.

This is different from men who, although they vary in the amount of race and other privilege they get, always retain their maleness, which is the basic power in the patriarchy. Men are also the ones who retain the power that comes from oppressions like class or race, even though they might share their privilege with some women. It is this difference that makes it possible for women to deal with differences in race or class or looks or fat and makes it impossible for women and men to ever work together by 'dealing with male privilege.'

Lesbians and other women can also get privilege in patriarchy through race, class, age and other oppressions. Any time a Lesbian or other woman accepts a privilege she can get because of oppression, she is dividing herself from those Lesbians and other women who don't have access to those privileges and therefore is helping patriarchy. For example, white women don't have the power in patriarchy to enforce white supremacy. That is up to white men who make the laws, establish the social system, etc. White women get lots of privileges off of white supremacy but cannot control what or how much privilege they will get. The men do. Every man not only gets privilege off patriarchy, but he also has the power to enforce it, or make changes in it, or distribute what privilege he has control over. The difference between men and women involves not only privilege but power. Although there are sometimes incredible differences between women in terms of privilege, no woman has it within her power IN PATRIARCHY to change the class, race, age, fat or other oppression system. It does mean that these differences can be worked out whereas the power difference with men can not.

Lesbian Separatists are working hard to get women to stop collaboration with men. Lesbian Separatists are fighting patriarchy's oppression among ourselves, in the Lesbian community and in patriarchy. And we won't quit fighting until we have a non-oppressive Lesbian society.

Although many Separatists believe that men are biologically disposed to destructive behavior, we do not base our analysis on men's behavior, both historically and now. We can not discount the effects of culture and history. We know who created patriarchy, its culture and history, who benefits from it and who perpetuates it. And that is men.

This is reality. 'Humanist' theories, ideals, of some sort of non-sexist men, are disproved by the *reality* of the men we all have experiences with – as fathers, brothers, rapists, sons, 'comrades,' and friends.

Some Lesbians believe we should work with 'revolutionary men.' Many of us have been in the left and worked with these men. We've witnessed their open ridicule or quiet 'tolerance' of the women's movement and their hatred of Lesbians. Just recently the Revolutionary Committee split off from the Weather Underground accusing the Weather Underground of planning to infiltrate and destroy the women's liberation movement for the last seven years. We've been to demonstration after demonstration, and group after group, where support for black liberation or the Vietnamese struggle meant support for men and an increase in their power over women. We've even worked under conditions of 'women's leadership' only to find that pricks at crucial moments simply ignore that leadership and assert their prick power.

Men took over the trade unions women started in the early part of the 1900's. The 'socialist' revolution' in Cuba meant imprisonment for Lesbians, some of whom had worked for years for the 'Cuban revolution.' With some variation the same situation exists in every socialist country. Sure, women and Lesbians have fought and died in all these struggles, but in the end, it turned out to be one group of men getting power from another group of men. Just because a man promises women a fair deal doesn't mean it will happen.

A collaborator is a woman or man who works for the other side in some struggle, therefore betraying their kind. For example, President Thieu of South Vietnam who worked against the Vietnamese struggle. Collaborators have no power in their own right. If a collaborator is given power, it is not power to act for their own kind, but against their own kind.

For example, Dixy Lee Ray, the Governor of Washington State, is a Lesbian. Yet, she can't rule for the benefit of Lesbians, she can only rule for the benefit of men. If she were to start ruling for the benefit of Lesbians she would be removed because she has no power of her own to hold her position. She is a 'figurehead' put up by men. Ray does not rule as a Lesbian, but in spite of it. Bella Abzug was a figurehead woman who started to ally with women. She's not in congress anymore, her defeat aided by liberal, radical and 'feminist' men.

At different times in its history, patriarchy has chosen to rule through women. Yet male privilege and power remained intact and the women have been tokens, lasting just as long as they pleased the men.

This is different from the definite male powers and privileges mentioned earlier. Many Lesbians believe that most men are just collaborating with the few men who rule. But men have lots of good reasons to fight for patriarchy, male power and privilege, and they do. They aren't just collaborators fighting someone else's war, and they know it.

Women and Lesbians get power and strength from separation from men. But some refuse to take the consequence of separation – the loss of privilege that men give women. This reminds us of the straight women who use the women's movement to gain power in their individual relations with men, or on their job, and yet deny being 'women libbers.' It is using Lesbian Separatists, and other Lesbians who want to build an independent movement, without making a commitment to us. Further, if men were a group Lesbians should be working with, then Lesbians would find an increase in power by working with men, not a decrease. Just because men are 47% of the population doesn't mean that we can't win against them. When men overthrew women they were even less than 47% of the population. Modern history is full of small countries being beaten by big countries. Men dominate women now although they are only 47%, and depend on women for reproduction, as well.

We are part of, and want to build a Lesbian Separatist movement. Therefore, we don't work *individually* with non-Separatist Lesbians. We have done many things with non-Separatist Lesbians and believe in working with them in a principled and organized way. We relate to all women as potential allies and make our ideas available to them. We are in support of an independent women's movement, and we believe that the only way it will be truly independent is when it is Lesbian Separatist.

We don't believe in working with men because we don't work with our enemy.

Lesbians and Lesbian Separatists come from a variety of class backgrounds, are of different races and ages, and suffer size, fat and looks oppression. We are oppressed by the assumption that Lesbians are white, thin, Christian, class privileged, and somehow non-age oppressed. As Lesbians we can and must fight all oppressions, and we don't need to work with men to do it. And anyone who thinks we do invalidates the political choice many Lesbians make to fight against our oppression through the Lesbian movement.

About socialist theory – that is, theory based on the assumption that the economic structure is what is at the root of all oppressions: it is wrong for socialist Lesbians to identify themselves as Lesbian feminists, since feminism is the belief that there is a struggle between men and women which is the basis of the oppressive patriarchy men created, and in this struggle feminists take the side of women. If Lesbians believe in socialism, then they should identify themselves as socialists, not feminists, otherwise they are confusing the issue.

We believe Lesbians find it repulsive to work with men not just because men are sexist and difficult to work with but because the revolution men would create will not change the patriarchal nature of the society any more than previous male 'revolutions' have done. As long as patriarchy is around hierarchies and oppressions will survive and this makes working with men not just discouraging and oppressive but also self defeating.

In Defense of Lesbian Separatism: A Response to the Combahee River Collective Statement on Lesbian Separatism

Doreen Worden
Isabel Andrews
1981

You say:

> ... Although we are feminists and lesbians, we feel solidarity with progressive Black men and do not

advocate the fractionalization that white women who are separatists demand. . . . (In *This Bridge Called My Back*, eds. Moraga and Anzaldúa (Persephone Press, 1981), p. 213.)

. . . We are Socialists. . . . We are not convinced, however, that a socialist revolution that is not also a feminist and antiracist revolution will guarantee our liberation. . . . (*Ibid.*, p. 213)

. . . we reject the stance of lesbian separatism because it is not a viable political analysis or strategy for us. It leaves out far too much and far too many people, particularly Black men, women, and children. . . . We must also question whether lesbian separatism is an adequate and progressive political analysis and strategy, even for those who practice it, since it so completely denies any but the sexual sources of women's oppression, negating the facts of class and race . . . (*Ibid.*, p. 214)

Joint Response:
We are lesbian lovers and companions who define ourselves politically as lesbian-separatist sympathizers.[1] We are white, ages 47 and 50, and 'came out' at the ages of 41 and 45. We have chosen to live in semi-retreat, devoting our energies to economic necessities, clearing out our heads, enjoying, and strengthening those areas of our communities which are supportive to wimmin, especially to lesbians and other poor wimmin. We focus much energy on recovering our relation to the rest of the natural world, and recovering some of our spiritual-material heritage as wimmin, including our heritage as healers. In economic terms, we are poor and always will be. We are combining our response to your statement.

Doreen:
I don't want anything to become 'the way to think' and 'the answer' – that's a totalitarian approach. I think that's a masculine way of thinking. There always have been separatists e.g. Amazons, gypsies, religious communes, etc. There always will be separatists – lesbians and other varieties of outlawed beings. When a society gets very totalitarian, separatists become more visible to each other, because everyone else becomes more 'the same.' The North American society we now live in is a non-community. Everybody is fragmented. What the separatists try to do is to get a bunch of fragments together.

Lesbian separatists didn't invent prejudice based on gender and sexual orientation. That's what we're doing battle against. Your accusation is like a white man accusing native leaders who want self-determination of being racist, when what they are trying to do is survive as a people.

I think we (wimmin) have a tendency to put down any ideas wimmin have about social structure. We have to check first with a man or a male analysis to see if it checks out. But almost anything is worth trying when living under a totalitarian patriarchal system.

What is the *real* horror thing about separatism? Is it *really* the exclusion of men? Is it *really* the exclusion of boy children?

I think the real horror thing is that we won't go along with the majority. *Lesbian separatism implies diversity in the social order.* Marxists can't tolerate such a concept.

Isabel:

We are not advocating fractionalization!!! We are trying to heal ourselves of the worst effects of this fractionalization!!!!!!!!!!!!!!!!!!!

How can you assume that we 'negate the facts of class and race' simply by drawing together to pool our resources and heal ourselves of the worst effects of batterings?????????????????????

You have defined yourselves as lesbians and feminists.

How dare you reject the way that a whole section of other lesbians are attempting to combat their own oppression?????????????????????????????????????

I have nothing but respect for your stated goals of combining the battle against heterosexism with the battle against racism, sexism and classism. But what are you doing in practice? In another statement you omit heterosexism from your list of things which must be eradicated before we can be free ('we are not convinced . . . that a socialist revolution that is not also a feminist and anti-racist revolution will guarantee our liberation. . . .'). And in your other statements quoted, you are scapegoating white lesbian separatists.

Why could you not just say 'we reject the stance of lesbian separatism because it is not a viable political analysis or strategy for us.' That is a position consistent with identity politics. But you then take a second stance, contradictory to the first. It is this *other stance* which says, 'We must also question whether lesbian separatism is an adequate and progressive political analysis and strategy, even for those who practice it . . .' It appears that this contradiction is due to your attempt to combine identity politics with marxism.

There are many varieties of lesbian. They partly, but only partly, depend on age, race and class. They also partly depend on ideology, which cuts across the lines of age, race and class.

All lesbians are, by definition, separatists, because we have moved away from a dependence on relations with men. We can accept that we are separate or deny it, but it is always there; the brotherhood makes sure it is always there. Yet none of us is consistently separatist. Even if we spend 100% of our time with other lesbians, or in solitude, the patriarchy is still there with us through the conditioning it has implanted in us.

I believe it is a given that we must respect each other's niche, our way of surviving, providing we do not actively harm others. At the same time we may know it is not our niche. One thing that all lesbians have in common is that we run out our lives trying to find a niche, a cell, a family, a community, where we can be ourselves. In the periods when we are lucky enough to find one or create one, we protect it with all our power.

A FAMILY: for the Combahee River collective it is a socialist, feminist, anti-racist, anti-heterosexist cell. For many white lesbians it is a lesbian-separatist cell. For myself and my lover it is a retreat to the bush country where we form our own cell or family.

We all share the need that you are expressing of trying to make sense of the future, of trying to project an analysis that offers hope. I reject a separation of matter and spirit. You reject the significance of our biological programming; I attempt to better understand it and I assure you that concern has nothing to do with bigoted supremacy, but has lots to do with the question of human survival.

Your collective sees a form of socialism that is feminist and anti-racist as the only way forward. I see the only way forward as one where wimmin of all races, cultures, ages, sexual preferences and class backgrounds recover our ancient and original role as the spiritual-material leaders and civilizers in human communities.

Speaking of the white wimmin that I know and see in my neck of the woods, I don't think we'll ever accomplish that unless we more consciously separate from men to rebuild our resources.

That may not be necessary for native lesbians or black lesbians or other lesbians of color. I understand that some are not forced to the same absolute necessity of separating from men of your cultures, since they are usually not in the powerful ranks of the brotherhood. I sympathize with the position of poor men, including poor white men, who are used by the boys at the top. But as a lesbian, I must consciously choose to use my limited energy to support those who are most likely to return some support to me. That's what I see politics as being all about.

Who are white lesbians? Why are we such a threat to you

when we separate from men?

In patriarchal terms, we are the least powerful group of whites in each and every class level, in each and every age bracket, among wimmin as a whole and among gays.

Here are a few facts of life for lesbians in canada. 1) In the current political battle over entrenchment of human rights in the canadian constitution, it looks like some scraps will be thrown to Native people and to wimmin as a whole. But the efforts to have lesbians and gays included never got to first base. This is because, in canada generally, homophobia is even more pervasive than racism or sexism and so homosexuals are the scapegoat for everyone else.

(2) On the issue of homophobia, the record of the white left is barbaric. The middle of the road left (ndp) has only recently given us significant support in response to the nazi-like raids of meeting places for gay men in Toronto. The big communist parties still say we are a sickness under capitalism. Only a few others give us support – some feminists – socialists, Wages for Housework, some gay men, some trotskyists, a few independents and some of the christian left. The 'official' women's movement is often silent around heterosexism because of their goals of upward mobility and their dependence on government grants, although I think that they are now beginning to think of us as embarrassing but necessary front-line troops.

The articulation of lesbian separatism in canada has hardly begun, but of course all white lesbians are separatists in our bones – we have to be – how else can we escape from the closet? But in canada there are comparatively few lesbians who are out of the closet in public, so we badly need each other for our sanity. Hence the fear of political clarification among us because it inevitably leads to further fragmentation of a very shattered group of women. Yet this clarification is being forced on us by a privileged few among us who shit on separatists because we make our outlaw status more obvious, and by others who do not understand that they are 'dumping.'

Wherever I see lesbians, I see the self-destructiveness that comes with being an oppressed group, but among lesbians who call ourselves separatists, I also see group attempts to halt that destructiveness. People break off into cells primarily to heal themselves and to try to achieve some kind of internal harmony. Separatists seem to know they must de-program themselves and try to make contact with *the rest of* the natural world. *This is the hope I see in separatism. It is in what all the separatist cells learn and re-learn about self-healing. Self-healing can only happen by renewing some relevant contact with the rest of the natural world.*

402

When that happens, we will have created a very powerful counterforce to human self-destructiveness.

Note

1. Since this article was written (in Dec./81), Isabel has changed her political self-definition to separatist.

Trying Hard to Forfeit All I've Known

killa-man
(of the C.L.I.T. Collective)
1974

There are probably many forms of social control aimed at lesbians that many of you know about that we don't. I urge you to write about them if you've experienced or are aware of these controls, these dyke traps. One of the primary intents of social control is to keep you *confused* about your oppression, so confused that you keep what you know to yourself. It is time we told each other *all we know*, the beginning step of reconstructing the ancient woman wisdom that patriarchies have spent centuries trying to smash.

Delineating sophisticated forms of social control of women, especially lesbians, is precisely what the movement has to do now before we are blurred out of existence without even knowing why the movement suddenly disappeared. Consciousness is everything. Getting women to see that they are not getting the same *physical* (body, money, property) privileges as other groups is not difficult compared to getting them to see the *mental* violence done to them every day by patriarchal reality. No one is safe from it. Especially dykes because they represent the most threatening type of woman inside a patriarchy, the highest woman consciousness that must at all costs be obliterated if the patriarchy is to be maintained. Dykes are out on a frontier, and we will not survive intact, in the way that we hope for, unless we know where the mine fields are. Dyke consciousness is hand-to-hand combat with patriarchal reality. Everyday.

I think many lesbians are walking around with a false consciousness about their place in patriarchal reality right now. The patriarchy has spent a lot of media time trying to make us feel that we are out of danger because we have 'freed' ourselves from emotional dependence on the man. They have focused our attention on straight women showing us in technicolor how much better off we are than the women who are still emotionally struggling every day with a man, whether he be husband or boyfriend. That's a diversion and a lie. If all patriarchal reality's oppression of women was just a matter of getting emotional strength and independence from men, women would have been free a long time ago. Because *everybody* knows that women are emotionally stronger than men. The battle of the sexes, which all those cute books on love, sex, and now 'feminism' as misconstrued by straight would have you believe, is not one-to-one man/woman emotional warfare. The Media State is sending out an old pack of lies rewrapped and packaged as 'feminist' cigarettes which lesbians are buying. The message is: it's the men that you've *known intimately* like your father, ex-husband, or ex-boyfriend that hurt you; so if you're a lesbian you leave them and go to women, or if you're straight, you try to teach the men you know how to treat you more equally. So lesbians feel a 'fake free' because they don't fuck men, and especially when the Media shows them straight women pulling teeth with their men. Straight women have helped the Media State give lesbians this false consciousness that they are no longer in the patriarchy's hands by hanging around lesbians and telling us not to leave them before we bring them up to our level. Straight women do the same number on lesbians men are doing to them now.

The Media State and its supporters know that a woman can empathize with *anything, anything* fucked up and below her like men. Isn't that what the 'good woman' in patriarchal history and movie scripts is about? And men can't identify with anything but themselves. The Media State knows the difference between women and men more than we do. So they get women to aid and abet the enemy, they make her feel sorry for the poor man – what will he do without his woman? They use art and media stories to get straight women to feel sorry enough for men so that they'll stay with them. The same number straight women do on lesbians. When in both cases women should be objectifying men as enemies, and lesbians should objectify straight women as patriarchal conspirators and stay the fuck away. But the Media men know that women have a hard time objectifying anything but themselves as sex objects and play on women's feelings for all they're worth.

.I have sat through lesbian meetings where lesbians still spend heart time talking about how to make a woman's world without hurting men, stepping on their toes or feelings. As if they had some. Oh, they have toes, but the only feeling men have I've witnessed is self-pity. They have a lot of instincts like territoriality, protect your turf or woman, whatever they think they own – but I don't call ball ingredients like testosterone, feelings or emotions. So isn't it curious that you can't even get most lesbians to say they are man-haters? Instead they say: 'Oh, I don't really hate men now that I'm a lesbian, I never have to be around any. They just don't affect my life anymore.' That is what I call the lesbian false consciousness. When don't we have to be around men? Don't we ever walk the streets, buy groceries, deal with some patriarchal bureaucracy, ride subways, trains, or drive cars, see police, repairmen, don't men live in our buildings in the cities or live around you in the country? If you work, aren't there any men around supervising you? If you're in school, don't you have any men teachers or have to sit with men in class? If you go to a hospital, aren't there any men doctors or patients around? The lesbian answer is: 'Oh, *those*; well, I never pay any attention to them.' Take a good look the next time you're in what they call public which means man's world; look at those men you *don't know* and dig on how much attention your body and mind pay to trying to avoid paying any attention to pigs, who are paying a lot of attention to you making sounds to scare you, stepping in your way or not moving so you have to walk around them and yield to their right of way. And why is it that women are afraid to walk the streets late at night? Is it because of the men they've *known intimately*? No, it's the *unknown* prick waiting out there in the darkness, patrolling the streets looking for easy prey, woman. Even the most down and out bum in New York has a whole repertoire of intimidation numbers to pull on women. No matter how far down you go in the prick hierarchy, every prick knows how to corner a woman, make her feel unsafe. And they all do it everyday, even your good daddies and your shy brothers who never told you what they do to the women they don't know.

'But we are not man-haters. No sir, we don't hate what is killing us off every day.' That's what you're saying when you're not man-hating, I think. I also think it's no accident that women are afraid to come out as man-haters in patriarchies. The Media and pricks know that women have picked up a real heavy masochistic streak from having to live with men ever since the matriarchies fell to men. So we are used to sticking up for and standing by the monster and taking out our rage on other women. James Joyce said: 'History is a nightmare from which I am trying to awaken.' I don't think lesbians have awakened yet, have come to full waking woman consciousness yet.

Consciousness is the primary weapon and defense women have

over men. And dykes have more of it than straight women because symptomatically they intuitively stay away from men and the death vibes. To me, politics and consciousness are everything and the same thing. Your political ally is someone who sees patriarchal reality from the same vantage point or level of consciousness as you do. Man-made divisions among women along class and race lines have obscured the consciousness dimension of life which is a much truer, clearer (once you forfeit all you've known as woman in a man's world) gauge of who your allies are.

The kinds of consciousness I can see so far in the world that cut across race and class lines are: the business consciousness, the religious consciousness, the S & M consciousness, the consciousness of violence, of nationalism, of patriotism, of 'keep things as they are – don't make any waves,' the avant-garde consciousness, and the male revolutionary consciousness. They are all terribly political. Think on each one yourself in the detail that I am going to discuss the football consciousness. Football fanatics found in the male species are political allies because their collective consciousness is on the same level; they view the world pretty much the same way; they perceive patriarchal reality from the same point of view.

You know who I'm talking about, the men who watch or listen to football on tv or the radio all the time and are ready to kill their wives if they make them miss 2 minutes of a game on the weekend; they know all the players since 1910; their fantasies are about being the football hero and they think of the world and relations with people and in business in football imagery (like Nixon). Life to them is among men, tough, homosexual juvenile glory. Life to them is competition, winning and losing with grace, pledging allegiance to the flag and praying hypocritically about 'winning's not everything, Lord, it's how you play the game, but Lord give me the strength to go out there and give those bastards hell, give them all I've got. Make me stronger and faster than mine enemies, help me kick the shit out of the weaker and slower and help me know when to punt, thank you, lord, grrrrr.'

Real women to them *are* cheerleaders, majorettes, flag girls, homecoming queens, but you only have sex with the ugly girls in the peanut gallery or the ones who'll do it in the back seat after the game, but you don't take them to the dance, either. Youthful bodies are everything – you're out of the game when your body loses its beauty and youth unless you're a man and can become a wise coach about football. But they don't have middle-aged majorettes, do they, boy? Doesn't this football fanatic consciousness sound like mainline 'life' in patriarchal America? Listen, team, it's no accident that our President always uses football imagery.

Football fanatics are political allies. They are men who come from all class and race sectors which is not to say that your position in the game is not determined by your class and race. There aren't many black quarterbacks are there? But just the same, all the boys with this mentality know how to rise to the top of the goal-posts whatever their starting position was (class, race determined).

Oddly enough football consciousness does not cut across sex lines. Women are not addicted to this mentality; it is not their level of politics. Women mostly *pretend* not to understand what seems to them intuitively to be brutal and senseless.

We are all socialized to be reactionaries. That's what keeps the collective consciousness of patriarchal society so low. We are all afraid of new ideas; we trust the lowest common denominator of consciousness, everyday reality of patriarchy, more than we trust ourselves. We are ready to fight every she who says something to contradict patriarchal reality the first time we hear it as if each one of us were a self-appointed defender of patriarchal reality. It reminds me of a cop who was giving me a hard time about being late for car registration one day. He acted as if by being one day late I was attacking *him* instead of the state law. I couldn't get over it that he saw himself as the state, as the law. It was as if I had insulted him personally. Women do the same thing – defend patriarchal reality as if it were our own, when it clearly is not. There's hardly anything in patriarchal law, patriarchal institutions, patriarchal economy, whether it be capitalist or communist (a false division anyway – it is either state capitalism or individual capitalism with an elite group of men at the top).

Every dyke is under as much pressure and criticism and attack from the media and the everyday world of reality as President Nixon has been in the past year from the press (for different reasons, of course). The only thing is that Nixon's attempt at mental murder is obvious and they put his name in the paper. They don't put dyke in the paper and they don't use your name, but the attack is just as heavy.

There is no such thing as men of conscience – the language which is the first social institution has been utterly ruined and confused by these weird combinations of putting the term male, or men, which connote killer, with words like respectable, honorable, etc.; anything connoting something pleasant or right or good, to be admired, etc. The term male means killer of woman before language became so confused on purpose by men. Every time you see the word male, men, etc., replace it with killer of woman and see how the phrase reads.

It is as if we had been drugged for centuries, had shock treatment, which is what living in close proximity to males is anyway if you are woman which means you have an acute sensitivity. Men teach that it is bad to be overly sensitive – connoting an extreme. In fact, they don't want women to feel right or trust their sensitivity because it will lead women to never go near the death rays that emanate from males.

Waking up is painful; woman coming to trust her sensitivity and perceptions is painful, because the male world is painful to be experienced with female sensitivity.

Lesbian-Feminist-Separatism: Radical New Beginnings*

Anne E. Schulherr Waters
1982

I. Moving Toward Honesty: Exploring Some Possibilities

Introduction

Whem I am alone I do not have to worry about thinking compromise politiks so as not to offend anyone. I am accountable only to myself, and I think radically without censure. I do not fear being with myself. Alone, there is no one around to socially sanction my thoughts, ideas, movements, ways of being. Alone, I am free to imagine a lesbian existence without compromise – or at least try to imagine such situations. For me, this imagining is a step toward creating lesbian space. And this freedom of being, non-compromised, is the kind of lesbian reality I want to move toward creating among lesbians. I believe such a space is possible only to a limited degree in dialogue between lesbians and nonlesbians. I believe such a space is possible either alone or with other lesbians. The next few pages are thoughts I have about some of my experiences. In these ponderings I imagine a world free of 'heterosexual presence,' a world where 'heterosexual' has been rendered senseless in the sense that heterosexual presence and value assumptions are absent. I call this section 'crystallizing,' because I focus on frequently non-re-cognized aspects of inter-action.

Experience

I am at the wimmin's bookstore. I trip and tumble, falling gently into a lesbian's warm arms. She, catching me, smiles. 'Easy,' she says, helping me to gain my own balance, my own control. There is nothing awkward in this movement. The action is easy, smooth, not rushed. There is a regained sense of my own balance with the support of a dyke. Gynergy is easy flowing. Empowerment is present in the mutual, shared experience of validating lesbian presence.

Pondering

My interacting with lesbians is sometimes very different from anything I encounter with nonlesbians. Many lesbians are not conscious of bumping into each other *in the same way* nonlesbians, or especially lesbian and nonlesbian, are. Around the counter corner, around the edge of a chair, through the doorway, past the hallway ... we touch, and sometimes in the touching, empower. We have brief moments of support, encouragement, of glee, fear, excitement. Such exchanges are clear and vivid exchanges of communication. Our gynergy is often translucent. We know what we feel, and, that we feel. We are aware of touch. In fact, we like and enjoy touch. Touch is verbal, audial, visual, physical.

Experience

I am at a convention. A lesbian is blocking the hallway. I gently place my arm around her, nudging by. Lesbians gather through the doorway. They touch and move about the room. I am afraid to enter. Then, I turn around, squirreling my way past lesbian bodies to enter. I am met with a lesbian smile. I perceive lesbians in the room. There is a calming. I am validated by lesbian presence. Partly, I let down my lesbian guard – I am in supportive, empowering space.

Pondering

There are no hidden messages that I feel – nothing undercover – we enjoy the touching, the seeing, the feeling of lesbian presence. I like open empty spaces and also rooms full of lesbians. We are not always afraid of our own charges, as we may be in nonlesbian oriented space. We melt among ourselves. Creating lesbian space and presence is creating space for trust and honesty among lesbians. *To create lesbian space is not to create an alternative to patriarchy, it is to create new space, new values, new be-ing(s)*. In shedding ambiguity of what we are creating, we can shed the potential for deception, distrust, and betrayal. Lesbian space is the presence of lesbian-identified values.

Experience

Reading:
We were warm and satisfied. Sitting three to a seat, we

are all touching, our parkas rubbing noisily together. Outside the car, it is cold, and snow lies piled on either side of the highway; inside, we are bundled together, touching and laughing. . . . The material of our parkas rubs together deliciously, scrunching and crunching. Something happens here, I think to myself; this is important.[1]

Pondering

I know 'this' lesbian's experience *in a similar way* that I know my own. She knows my experience in a way nonlesbians cannot know it. It is known by the experience. The experience re-cognizes the reality and names/claims/owns that reality. Inter-acting crystallizes lesbian knowledge, lesbian presence. Every lesbian experience is both unique and the same. We find ourselves, and through the self-knowledge, the social validation of lesbian presence, dis-cover each other. Hmmmm . . . every lesbian writer knows the experience of experiencing and the experience of writing the experience of lesbian experience. This is qualitatively different, I believe, from nonlesbian experience.

Experience

In the hugging is lesbian presence. Our strong bodies reassuringly accepting as we come together. It feels good . . . duration is irrelevant. Our clothes press together and the softness of the flesh, rubbing, pressing, meeting the gaze, the touch. Lesbian bodies touching, verbally, audially, visually, physically.

Pondering

In the touching, there is no trace or thought of fear. I feel our beauty, openness, valuation. Rejection is now inconceivable. I meet lesbian existence and acknowledge the validity of lesbian existence, lesbian presence. It is a moment of dis-cover-ing. The experience cannot be not acknowledged. It is *that* strong, *that* present, *that* moving. We move toward a language of our own creation with which we communicate – to a new validation of be-ing-in-the-world, a new valuing.

Re-Ponder-ing

Lesbians frequently communicate bodily when we bump into and brush against each other touching, empowering. These are not only physical events. These events are common among us; I believe they carry a special significance of respecting, knowing, and appreciating our bodies as not separate from our lives, from our presence of lesbian values. Lesbian communication occurs through eye contact, in touching, by knowing each other in our ideas, our bodies, our experiences, our reality. It is the lesbian in us that knows.

Experience
Listening: 'But I want to love wimmin. Logically, it makes sense. Rationally I want to. Morally I feel I ought to. But I simply am not attracted to wimmin. I don't have those feelings. Besides, *it's* all too difficult. You are asking me to give up a lot.'

Pondering
As of yet I know of no appropriate response to this claim. Whenever I hear it, I feel rejected, like being told I belong to a class of unattractables. The same wimmin who make this claim also argue that they love individual men, not men generally as a class (they have all found the 10%!). So the information I process is that they are unattracted to the class of wimmin, and are attracted to specific men. If these heterosexual women were attracted to a lesbian, would they continue to claim they were not attracted to the class of wimmin? that the lesbian they were attracted to was a 'special' case? What is it to not be attracted to a class? To be attracted to a class?

Actually, what I want to know is, if nonlesbians really are not having the close intimate intense feelings lesbians are having for each other, why not? Is there a psychological or physical resistance to the thought of being attracted to lesbians? to one like oneself? to oneself? To what extent is patriarchal misogyny relevant to this situation of lesbian turn-off. I believe the presence of patriarchal value conditioning is profoundly relevant to this issue. And it does not go without lesbian notice that heterosexual privilege and safety is granted when wimmin negate/deny the presence of these feelings for wimmin. Heterosexual privilege is taken away/given up when wimmin acknowledge lesbian desire. Male personal/political purposes are being served by the denial of wimmin-loving-wimmin. Is this really a place to dissolve our discussions between lesbian and nonlesbian feminists? It is precisely at this point that I would like to hear more dialogue between lesbian and nonlesbian feminists. If feminists really do care for wimmin, why is it we never encounter such comments as, *'Oh, if I really could love a lesbian, what beauty I would find!'*

Nonlesbian response to lesbian presence needs to be examined by feminists, though it may be personally, physically, emotionally, and psychologically difficult for many heterosexual women to do. But the burden of examining the misogyny of heterosexism should not continue to fall on the lesbian shoulder, especially if feminists are committed to struggling to improve *all* wimmin's lives. Perhaps, analogously, we can say that it is not easy for any womyn to analyze a battering situation. But it will be healthier for the womyn being battered.

411

An-Other Side

In contrast to these experiences I have named, it is important that we re-cognize also the struggles against racism, classism, and other oppressions within the lesbian community. Many of us are frequently pained, even among lesbian-feminists, by the ignorance and assumptions of oppressive behavior that wreak confusion in our hearts and intolerance in our be-ings. Consider the complexity of Audre Lorde's Black-lesbian-feminist dream experience.

> To the white woman I dreamed standing behind me in an airport, silently watching while her child deliberately bumps into me over and over again. When I turn around to tell this woman that if she doesn't restrain her kid I'm going to punch her in the mouth, I see that she's been punched in the mouth already. Both she and her child are battered, with bruised faces and blackened eyes. I turn, and walk away from them in sadness and fury.[2]

To further illustrate this complexity, we do not know whether the womyn was a lesbian. We do not know whether the child is a female child or a male child. If a lesbian womyn or a female child, in what other ways could the misogny of physical abuse also have been laid upon these victims? And what of the silence between these two wimmin?

In comparing loving with painful experiences, it is important to continually re-cognize the complexity of lesbian pain, where it comes from, and how it is sustained in the white-male-supremacist conditions that act to internalize oppressive values and behavior in our minds, in our community, in our lives. It is especially important, however, to know that we do have the strength and will to create kinds of spaces amongst ourselves, as lesbians, that can move toward value analyses and casting our loving of wimmin into every act, word, and thought. We can learn to mediate our experiences with wimmin by seeing the truth of each other's and our own lives, not the false reality patriarchies have conditioned us to see. We can learn to see, hear, feel, and touch with our lesbian-feminist intuitions, hearts, and bodies as well as our minds. And, as we move toward creating loving spaces, we must pay close meditative attention to our feelings, and inspect them with loving lesbian caring. We must listen keenly when we hear about, for example, a poor young lesbian, who may turn up at free rap groups intermittently, will never be seen at the expensive concerts, and one day appears at the lesbian bar, battered by her

412

lesbian 'lover.' We must listen and pay close lesbian attention to the conditions of our lesbian lives when we hear these stories.

Accountability of Nonlesbians

In an earlier essay discussing the politiks and power relationships in Women Studies classes I wrote: 'If we are to nurture our women's culture, we must validate all women's voices that are not oppressive to us.' This includes validating and giving credence to those voices that are not oppressive to us as lesbians. I went on to say that 'we must silence all those voices that are oppressive to us.' This means we must stop the lie-telling. We must, by using our wimmin's ears of experience, listen to potentially oppressive voices of our sisters, and act on, rather than be victimized by, these voices. We must also re-cognize why it is not always feasible to compromise our discussions with nonlesbians, allowing them to pretend that our lesbian relationships are similar to their personal relationships, or even that all lesbian relationships are the same. That their reality and our reality is different is quite clear, and these differences are important, and need to be re-cognized as important. It is also quite clear that lesbian relationships are as diverse as our multi-cultural individual lesbian lives.

If we fail to acknowledge these differences of experience of lesbians among both lesbian and nonlesbian, there will be deep deception among feminists. With deception honest dialogue ceases, and dishonesty leads to betrayal, unfair advantage, and oppression of the powerless. Lesbian relationships, especially perhaps those involving racial difference, cultural difference, class difference, physically and emotionally challenged lesbians, differently abled, need to be explored more fully; for the truth of our *individual* lesbian lives is at the heart of our lesbian community, lesbian culture. And, we sometimes need to step over into a safe space where we can speak the reality of our lesbian lives. These spaces need to be supported, encouraged, and respected by nonlesbians.

Most lesbians I know act differently in heterosexual lesbophobic spaces than they do in lesbian-only spaces. There is an aura of heterosexual protection on the part of lesbians in mixed spaces — go easy, says the lesbian to herself — do not let lesbophobia become rampant — be polite and don't frighten your sisters. There is no clear reason that I can determine that this responsibility for heterosexual women's protection must fall on the shoulders of lesbians already oppressed in heterosexist space. The blatant politeness of lesbians toward nonlesbians frequently eats up lesbian gynergy, gynergy that could be more constructive.

The general message internalized is that lesbians need to protect the nonlesbians; do not get over-emotional translates do not get emotional translates be reasonable translates compromise translates silence translates leave all your lesbian stuff outside. Lesbians are forced to interact in this way from their minds, not their hearts or bodies. I am sometimes made physically sick by the silence enforced on lesbian presence; I am frequently tired of experiencing the nonlesbian-protection-racket forced upon lesbians. Hardly ever do we read about heterosexual women challenging heterosexism. Perhaps nonlesbians are unaware of this environment – like the fish unaware of swimming in water. I believe that with few exceptions only lesbians grasp lesbian oppression in heterosexually dominated space. A glance, a nod, an understanding – a touch, a word, a communication – a dialogue between two lesbians validating the prevalent reality *can have* revolutionary potential we need to tap. But, supporting silence is not breaking the silence. Acknowledging shared reality must become active. Both lesbians and nonlesbians need to articulate our experiences of silence. We need to push our dialogue through these gaps carrying with us a consciousness of lesbian-feminist values.

Lesbian silence, especially, is frequently experienced in Women Studies classes, at conferences, at meetings, in beds. I know the lesbian world of silence and the lesbian communication of this silence. I live lesbian silence, and I cannot name the nonlesbian experience of experiencing lesbian silence. The silence persists for many reasons: inability to articulate lesbian experience; inability to believe the reality of what is being said; inability to translate to a language that nonlesbians would readily understand; inability to move beyond the conceptual breakthrough that has just been experienced; inability to gently articulate lesbian objections, especially when faced with frustration and anger when there isn't a strong lesbian presence; inability to believe whatever is said will be taken seriously.[3] To move beyond these inabilities will require developing new ways of communicating; will require lesbians and nonlesbians taking lesbian experience seriously – more seriously than we ever have in the past.

Lesbian silence sometimes occurs when lesbians compromise lesbian-feminist politiks so that nonlesbian wimmin will accept us. An example of such compromise with nonlesbians can be seen in a relatively recent slide show put together by a group of Boston feminists entitled 'Straight Talk About Lesbians.' The title names the perspective. This film is supposed to be about lesbians, yet the message that showers across the screen is clearly a straight justification of lesbianism. 'Look,' the screen subtly suggests, 'we shouldn't be feared, because we are similar to you.' Nothing could be more false in my own experiences with lesbians – especially lesbian-feminists. Nonlesbian wimmin may have a lot to fear from lesbians. We may change their entire lives, their entire way of be-ing. Every womyn who encounters deep, intense, and meaningful relationships with lesbians has a lot to fear – she may become one! Yet also, in naming herself lesbian, she may have much to be joyous about as well.

Second, lesbian experiencing is not like nonlesbian experiencing. If lesbians' experience was like heterosexual women's experience, it would be true that nonlesbians would have nothing to interest them in being lesbian themselves. It is a heterosexist lie to indicate that lesbians are like heterosexuals; and it is more: it is preposterous! My experience with lesbians, especially lesbian-feminists, is not like my experience with nonlesbians at all, including nonlesbian-feminists. There is a myriad of changing interpersonal relations among lesbians. Ironically, nonlesbian wimmin continue to define lesbians as 'women who are looking for a new lifestyle.' This is ridiculous. Lesbians have quite sophisticated lifestyles – lesbian-feminists especially are out to create more than lifestyles! We are creating new modes of communicating, new ways of be-ing. Such creations sometimes necessitate separate lesbian-only space. This lesbian space may not be a sufficient condition for exploring our deepest values and desires toward creating lesbian culture, but it is a necessary condition for stepping away from the predominance of hetero-sexist values, perspectives, and might. Nonlesbian accountability to lesbians means sharing in the process of unmasking male-supremacist lies about lesbian lives. It means encouraging truth telling about lesbian lives and supporting and encouraging those conditions necessary for creating lesbian-feminist values. And, it also means participating by questioning heterosexist values in the form of presuppositions and assumptions that nonlesbians bring to the world – accountability demands truth-telling for all wimmin.

Accountability of Lesbians

When the pamphlet by Adrienne Rich, 'Women and Honor: Some Notes on Honesty Among Women,' began circulating in lesbian hands, lesbians took a fresh interest in discussing honesty among dykes. During many discussions the word 'silence' became a code word for the inarticulation of oppressive experiences within lesbian communities. Though I have personally been in some sense preoccupied with breaking silences among lesbians, to seek openness among lesbians, I have also experienced the power of lesbian silence as a tool of communication in oppressive situations. The breaking and creating of silence is manifested in our actions, in a body language which has been described not as being vulnerable, but as being sensitive. Our silences can point us to areas of concern. There is touching in the meeting of a glance. How frequently we say, 'It is/is not in her eyes.' I hear with lesbian-feminist critical eyes my lesbian and feminist sister's voices – I hear sometimes in silence, in witness. I know frequently whether a womyn is a lesbian-feminist by her critiques of patriarchy. I know by the reality of the analysis, by the truth (or denials), by the background values that inform the perspective she brings to her life and work. We know, many of us, who we are though we may not have met. We know in a way that we know each other's voices. We know in a way that nonlesbians could not possibly know – in a way nonlesbians could not feel about these voices.

I learn from the articulation of lesbian experience from a lesbian perspective in a way that nonlesbians do not. I am proud of lesbian-feminist analysis, especially, in a way that I do not believe nonlesbian-feminists can share. There is a common struggle for articulation that I re-cognize in reading lesbian-feminist words. Our already existing lesbian-feminist consciousness exemplifies our work as it passes through the mailboxes, and is experienced at various wimmin's events. It has been my experience that lesbian-feminist strength of analysis means digging deeper, thinking harder and longer, reading with special interest and intensity papers our nonlesbian sisters are not reading. I frequently know lesbians by their conversation, their knowledge of lesbian culture, lesbian space, research of questions nonlesbians have left untouched, and especially by the background values they bring to their work.

Lesbian-feminists read lesbian analyses and critiques of Black-Feminism, Jewish-Feminism, Liberal-Feminism, Chicana-Feminism, Hispanic-Feminism, Anarcha-Feminism, Native-American Feminism, Third-World-Feminism – we read all of these analyses *with lesbian sensitivity*, recognizing the multicultural diversity among ourselves. All of these readings have fed into developing Lesbian-Feminism and lesbian-feminists, globally. Lesbian understanding of wimmin's experience has been necessary to having knowledge of how patriarchal systems systematically destroy the conditions conducive to wimmin-loving-wimmin. Lesbians have a special stake in understanding how these systems operate to keep all wimmin subordinated to male supremacy.

Lesbian-feminists must encompass diverse feminist analyses to know ourselves and our politiks as lesbians, as feminists. Of course, nonlesbians may also read some of these materials, but not *in the same way* or *for the same reasons* lesbians do. Why no one has made this clear before is confusing to me. To ignore this aspect of lesbian bonding among feminists is to ignore the lesbian of lesbian-feminists; it is to allow heterosexism to operate among feminists.

To ignore the lesbian of lesbian-feminists is to perceive only what is advantageous for the perceiver. To ignore lesbian presence is to be complicit in naming lesbian absence where there is lesbian presence. Lesbians and nonlesbians alike need to re-cognize our already existing myriad of wimmin connections with each other, but not at the expense of lesbian presence. Lesbian presence is fundamental to the destruction of male-supremacy, and the emergence of wimmin-loving-wimmin values. Lesbian-feminist presence is fundamental to feminism. Lesbians as well as nonlesbians need to re-member our lesbian-feminist community — to re-member lesbian-feminist values, and begin to take our lesbian lives seriously in the struggle to move toward a lesbian-feminist ethic. Lesbian accountability can begin with lesbians taking ourselves seriously, globally.

Exploring Tensions of Me and You

The problem of separation from the opposite sex is much more simple and translucent to our understanding than is separation among wimmin. Though for heterosexist women, neither separation seems to be clearly understood. As lesbians, especially, we know wimmin are cut off from relating to the colonizers of a male-supremacist culture on any equal basis, by virtue of their being wimmin. That one sex is valued over another in all cultures is a block to equal relations among the sexes. Some heterosexual women believe this sex inequality can be quantitatively balanced by inequalities in other areas, for example, income. I do not hold this view. Oppressions are not so simple as things we can put on a scale and balance. The moral issue of oppression is harm done, unnecessary pain. To try to balance one oppression over another is precisely to participate in the game the white-male-supremacists desire us to participate in — it is to betray the complexity and sensitivity of our lives, to view ourselves as superficial.

Feminists who attempt to balance inequalities of oppression in their relationships are not perceiving the complexity of specific victimizations of wimmin. Against those who would insist that to be a woman is a cultural concept, and that wimmin's oppression of sexism stems from the conditions and context of male culture, I feel compelled to insist that it is more. The difference in biology between the sexes is a significant difference. Feminists who have backed away from this re-cognition have been inclined to hold that individual relationships can transcend the cultural differences; that they can have equal relationships with men, interracial relationships, interclass relationships that are equal because of this ability to transcend indoctrinated cultural attitudes. Feminists who hold that the biological difference between wimmin and men is significant will be drawn to lesbianism. If the biological bases of male-domination play a significant role in the oppression of wimmin, heterosexual-feminists are going to have to deal with this. And simple rejection of the lesbian-feminist biological analyses will not do. These analyses, for lesbians especially, need to be taken seriously, as seriously as we take the lives of all wimmin. It is true that male attitudes and behavior toward wimmin are profoundly immoral – I know of no word sufficient to express the moral outrage of the culture men have created. But more, wimmin as wimmin, as different biological be-ings, be-ings whose biology has played an important role in their victimization, need to courageously consider what the nature of these biological differences means for all wimmin. How are biological differences important, not only in male cultural control, but in our most intimate relations – our physically intimate relations?

But what are the reasons lesbian-feminists might want to separate from nonlesbian-feminists? What seems to be a minor reason is because nonlesbians will most always take the opportunity to control separatist wimmin's spaces by talk about men. This effort to dominate lesbian space, especially with talk that presupposes a truce with men is necessary, necessarily hinders the potential for lesbian presence, lesbian values. When the presuppositions and assumptions are changed, the potential for seeing changes. When my head is not always turned around having to respond to how to control, placate, and tend to men, my head jumps in the opposite direction, and I see things that I had not seen before. My being-in-the-world is different; I perceive things I had not perceived previously.

Among wimmin there is a constant struggle pulling us in two directions. We want to be who we are – touching, sensitive, lesbian-loving-lesbians. And yet, in mixed lesbian/nonlesbian spaces we are constantly reminded by body language (at least) that nonlesbians are 'man-loving-women' . . . a phrase that translates into 'we do not love wimmin in the *same way* that you do' (what way?) that translates into 'we do not love lesbians like you do' (how?) that translates into 'we love the class of wimmin, not individual wimmin!' Earlier in this paper I discussed conflicts of some wimmin who claim not to be attracted to any womyn. I think I want to say that wimmin not attracted to any womyn may not be attracted to the class of wimmin, and surely not the class of lesbians. This needs to be spelled out more clearly, but that needs to be done by those who are claiming to be attracted to classes. It presents a conceptual barrier among lesbian-feminists and nonlesbian-feminists in our dialogue. Because I am a participant in the dialogue complicit to supporting and maintaining this barrier, and am harmed by this barrier, I will offer óne lesbian-feminist perspective on the problem.

How do I, as a lesbian, explain nonlesbian-feminist claims about loving the class of wimmin, of being committed to wimmin as a class, but not to any individual womyn? I must admit, their claims confuse me! I *am* attracted to individual lesbians, individual wimmin. I'm not even sure I want to entertain the notion of being committed to a class rather than individual members of that class. This tension is evident, in almost every discussion of lesbianism I have ever held with a heterosexual feminist. This tension is experienced and known differently by lesbian-feminists than by heterosexual-feminists; it is also *resolved differently*. However much male logic can create *classes* of people to be attracted to, I find in my own lesbian experience, I am only attracted to *individuals*. And I *value* individuals, not classes. And I love with my heart, through my body and mind.[4] I love with my entire lesbian-be-ing-in-the-world.

Sometimes, the loving of classes, not individuals, means 'we love lesbian-feminists' minds, not lesbian bodies.' Other times, of course, it simply means we need your support, your gynergy, when the expression of caring is merely a form of coercing wimmin's lesbian gynergy for interests already specified by a particular group. White-middle-class-heterosexual-feminists have a herstory depicting occasions of this interaction. This attitude of mind acceptance, gynergy acceptance, and body rejection, is antagonistic to a lesbian-feminist sensibility and politic. 'We do need positive images of our bodies, all our bodies, every facet of them, every pose we assume as we change and grow. . . . If we really do believe that being a Lesbian comprises every aspect of our beings, then it cannot be true that any single facet of our lives is more central than another.'[5] And if, as feminists, we believe our hearts and minds should not function separately, we will need to mend this false dichotomy of human interaction endemic to male logic and experience.

When heterosexual-feminists love women colonizers as individuals and claim to love lesbians generally as a class, they are not loving wimmin individually – they do not love even one single individual particular womyn. Further, they frequently claim to be incapable of doing so. Is this important? Heterosexual-feminists, it seems to me, love the idea, not the body; they love the ideology, not the being, not the experience of wimmin-loving. (How reflective is this of male inability to love wimmin?) Nowhere has this distinction between ideology and experience been more clearly or sharply drawn than in a recent article by Jackie Zita.

> The truth I am trying to find begins with the lies between us. Have You Never Felt that Pull toward a woman? Have you never wanted to touch another woman and receive the same from her? What stopped you? By what authority have you turned away from women? What tugging have you smothered deep inside? Honesty between women demands that we talk about this . . . All of your choices are predicated on a commitment *not* to *do the same for women*. What you fail to see is the betrayal of women carried out in your life.[6]

Jackie's dialogue is a familiar one for many lesbian-feminists and nonlesbian-feminists. The dialogue exists between both lesbians and nonlesbians; it also occurs among lesbians. It is a dialogue of acceptance, or more properly, non-acceptance. It is a dialogue of mis-communication – a dialogue about non-touching, about fear of knowing, of making a commitment. A nonlesbian friend of mine has recently spoken of this fear.

> Many women are afraid of loving lesbians because they fear they will like it, and they are not willing to suffer the social stigma attached to being a lesbian in any society.[7]

The wimmin who make these decisions are some of the same wimmin who claim to be struggling to alleviate the oppression of all wimmin, but fail to see the beauty of womyn-loving, focusing only on the oppression of lesbianism. How easily these nonlesbian-feminists forget that the personal is political – and, the political is personal. Every time we forget or turn away, all wimmin are betrayed, and honesty among wimmin is smothered.

Though many heterosexual-feminists have understood Jackie's dialogue to be a challenge to justify their heterosexuality, we can read the dialogue as an expression of honesty. There is a distance between the lesbian and nonlesbian. They are living in very separate realities – the nonlesbian is much more entrenched in the authority of patriarchal reality, in both the language she uses and her values we see this difference. The nonlesbian is, the lesbian is not, colonized. Nothing of value would change if the lesbian and nonlesbian slept together – nothing would change unless they arrived, each one, at a total stepping away from, separation from, patriarchal heterosexist values. Stepping outside of male supremacist values is a necessary step to engage in womyn-loving. It requires a re-analysis of heterosexist values, including, if we reject the mind/body dualism, an understanding of *touching* as a special, unique, and commonplace mode of potential interaction. When the inter-acting of touching no longer requires an analysis, when we are free to know our bodies as well as each other's minds, only then will nonlesbians begin separating from heterosexist values, begin the de-colonization process.[8] This de-colonizing of wimmin requires thinking, acting, and being within a different set of values, and commitment to those values when hard times come: It requires a deep love of wimmin, capable of intense individual relationships with lesbians.

In raising the issue of accountability, I want to put my lesbian finger on something else that is very important in understanding lesbian-feminist and nonlesbian-feminist interaction: the heterosexual 'no-saying' to lesbians. This is destructively separatist. To more clearly understand feminist-separatism, we need to understand this dynamic of heterosexual women as elitists – as heterosexists denying lesbian bonds. This aspect of heterosexual-feminists as elitist needs to be accounted for at least as much as lesbian-feminist-separatism. We need to ask who is denying access to what and why. Who has power and privilege (however superficial) in a heterosexist culture? Who is getting access to what and why? And, who are the agents complicit in maintaining current distributions of power and privilege, and whose values uphold this distribution by what technique? Finally, who is nurturing, and how, those who are benefiting from and maintaining the oppressive power dynamics of wimmin's lives? In lesbian-feminist and heterosexual-feminist interaction, could it possibly be that heterosexual elitism is not being seen? Or does it go unnamed, and if so, why? Are heterosexual-feminists maintaining any kind of power over lesbian-feminists by denial of heterosexual elitism, by invisibility of lesbian-feminist values?

Hanging onto this same thread, we need to ask what lesbian-feminists are gaining, if only superficially, in supporting the politics of heterosexism. I believe the gains are concrete – it includes participating in heterosexual privilege. We need to examine why some dykes are stepping on the necks of other dykes, in academe especially. Where is the support for lesbian scholarship that existed at least to some degree in Women Studies several years back? Lesbians are getting pushed back into the

421

closets, and it is not always heterosexuals who are doing the pushing, though it is a manifestation of heterosexism. I would like to see more feminists, whether lesbian or not, ask themselves to what extent they are supporting lesbian-feminism? lesbian analysis? To what extent are lesbians losing lesbian-feminist perspective, being forced into (coerced, sometimes politely) interacting with the colonizers. Fear of doing lesbian-feminist analysis is real – we are talking bread and butter issues – *and we need to get these cards out on a lesbian-feminist table* in dialogue with both lesbians and nonlesbians.

Exploring the possibilities of honesty, of eliminating the potential for betrayal, requires getting clear about contradictions of lesbian silence. We need to be clear about who is striving to create lesbian presence, the emergence of lesbian values, and who is blocking this effort. The former are lesbian-feminists. The latter may be lesbians or nonlesbians – I don't think I would call them feminist. Sometimes, when I am experiencing lesbian silence, or am in a room where another dyke is experiencing it, I think we could really learn a lot by asking 'Will the real feminist let herself be known, and let us know how we will know her?' I think we can know who each other is by the values we share passionately through our everyday lives and interactions. The puzzles of feminism may be abstract, the actions of our values, however, are concrete, identifiable, nameable, and revealing.

II. Creating Separations and Withdrawing

Creating Separations

It is my experience that lesbian-feminist space is sometimes made within heterosexual-feminist space, just as wimmin-only space is made within patriarchy. However, when lesbian-feminist space exists within a dominant heterosexual-feminist space, the values dominating the space are sometimes heterosexist values. This is the difference between lesbian-feminist space within dominant heterosexual-feminist space, and lesbian-feminist space *qua* lesbian-feminist space. In lesbian-feminist space, lesbian-feminist values dominate and inform our interactions.

Removing myself from mixed lesbian-feminist/heterosexual-feminist space is a freeing of myself from heterosexual lesbophobic oppression. It is allowing me to be. Experiencing lesbian-feminist oriented space occurs alone or among lesbian-feminists. This kind of space validates lesbian experience, lesbian lives. The value shift from heterosexual-feminist to lesbian-feminist space means tabooing the taboo of touching, sharing, the experience of knowing, creating lesbian culture and lesbian values. I don't mean to imply here that in lesbian-feminist space wimmin are not sometimes uncomfortable touching each other – but I do want to emphasize that touching, whether verbal, audial, visual, physical, or otherwise, is perhaps valued differently in lesbian-feminist space.

To validate being me, that lesbian womyn who awakes every morning with the knowledge of my lesbian existence, requires a very different kind of space than does validating heterosexuality. This validation requires a space where I can be free to express myself, to create lesbian self-knowledge. Lesbian-feminist-separatism means moving toward honesty, openness, knowledge, communication, and empowerment of each other via shared knowledge of lesbian presence creating lesbian culture.

Lesbian-feminists cannot always stop psychological rape. But we can and must sometimes remove ourselves from likely situations where others have power over us. It is obvious to me why lesbians, when given the choice, prefer non-oppressive space. This often means space where lesbians try to get free from heterosexual value assumptions, which have been internalized, which form the core of nonlesbian experience. Heterosexuality, as an institution, informs all nonlesbian interaction (and some lesbian interaction that has and has not yet been examined). It is essential that nonlesbians understand how deep heterosexist values of misogyny are and how they affect behaviour and attitudes toward wimmin. It is essential to lesbian survival that we view heterosexuality as an institution of the patriarchy. The necessity to share a world free from heterosexual might, in our own spaces, is at the heart of the lesbian-feminist emerging culture. Whether or not that culture emerges remains to be seen. Partly it will depend upon lesbian strength and ingenuity to create new values, new desirable modes of being-in-the-world. Lesbian-feminist space must have the capability to transform our behavior patterns and attitudes that exemplify our values. It must also enable us to comfortably name our experience, and validate the self-knowledge and values we strive to create and live in our lives.

Whereas heterosexual-feminists fill spaces patriarchal values carve out, lesbians are seeking radical change of a quite different nature. A complete *values upheaval* and *epistemic questioning* is intrinsic to lesbian existence and presence.

There is no difference in viewing the *fact* that wimmin love wimmin in this world, whether from a nonlesbian or a lesbian perspective, with the exception that lesbians awake to this self-knowledge, and what it means for the living of our lives every day. What it means for the living of our lives is a continual acting upon

423

our *value* of loving wimmin. And this *is* an important difference. Lesbian existence informs all lesbian activities. There is a difference placed on the value of lesbian presence for lesbians and nonlesbians. Some lesbian-feminists want nonlesbians to say lesbian presence is OK – i.e., you can live in our world too (and give us your gynergy). This is toleration assimilation politiks, and it is important that lesbians and nonlesbians re-cognize it as such if we are ever going to be honest about what kind of space we are moving in with each other. Other lesbian-feminists are not concerned with nonlesbian sanction. We know we are not simply OK, but that we are wonderful luscious loving lesbians. The question is not a lesbian question for us – but rather, the question is what to do about heterosexual-feminists who question the need for lesbian-only space. When we encounter these experiences, we need to ask who wants to control and dominate space, how do they want to do it, and what is it they want to prevent from happening.

In a recent anthology discussing separatism the charge is made that lesbian-separatists specifically have no race or class analyses. This is simply false. A brief survey through the literature shows that struggling with racism and classism differences has been central to many lesbian-feminists in their search to understand and know wimmin. In fact, lesbian-feminist politiks is the only politik I know of that has (during the 2nd wave of feminism [1968–present, eds.]) consistently struggled to encompass analyses of racism, classism, ageism, physicalism, and many other 'isms' among ourselves (though sometimes lesbians ignore heterosexism for the sake of compromise politiks with nonlesbians). My own awareness of racism and classism evolved through years of meeting with lesbians at the bar – my lovers/sisters who were Native American, Chicana, Hispanic, Asian, Black, and Anglo informed my sensitivities to lesbian lives. Our diverse politiks frequently are expressed on the dance floor, in discussions waiting for the bathroom, on the barstools, and bumping with each other while sharing the juke-box. Our awareness, recognition, and acceptance of our diversities has been central to communicating with each other as lesbians, and continuing lesbian culture.

Presence of both body and mind helps carve lesbian existence and space. My lesbian experiences are sometimes experiences shared by and articulated by lesbian writers. I don't think that lesbian presence is really understood very well by nonlesbians. I do know that lesbians empower me to know myself in a way nonlesbians, feminists or not, do not, and perhaps, cannot. I believe nurturing lesbian knowledge requires lesbian space to grow and learn unhindered by heterosexuals and heterosexist values.

I do not want to suggest that lesbian space is not sometimes painful. I know how we hurt deeply and intensely when it is difficult to make sense of our interactions. But the space for new kinds of relationships, for epistemic lesbian self-dis-cover-ing, can exist among lesbians creating new ways of be-ing.

Separating and Pulling Back

Many lesbians and nonlesbians, and feminists of both groups, think I am too sensitive about the value I place on lesbian interacting, on lesbian self-knowledge, on lesbian touching. My lesbian sensitivity/sensibility, however, has taken root over the years becoming a part of me that is not separate from my self – not separate from my political analysis. Rather, lesbianism is central to my analysis of wimmin's oppression. My sensitivities of lesbian interaction are woven into my identity and into my re-actions with all wimmin. In claiming a lesbian-feminist presence, I pull back from heterosexist imposed interpretations of reality, I re-cognize: my being a lesbian is a direct result of powerfully valuable experiences with other individual lesbians, *not* with nonlesbians. And, these experiences and lesbians are important to me. I have the potential to sleep with, dance with, touch in many ways, love, and share a knowing with lesbians of diverse multicultural backgrounds and with diverse knowledge of lesbian identity. I do not have this potential with nonlesbians. I can not know my lesbian self through nonlesbians, but only in contra-distinction to them.

It is essential to my continuing self-knowledge that I re-cognize that my own abilities to care and love wimmin, lesbians, were nurtured in me by lesbians; they are a direct result of learning to value lesbians with an individual, personal, deep, intense, particular that I do not observe in nonlesbian interaction. Only with lesbians can I sometimes feel good about falling in love for an hour, a day, a week, a month, years. And, though our modes of lesbian interacting may vary and change, there is a special lesbian loving with the lesbians with whom I share lesbian presence.

Though sometimes we may ask ourselves, as Cherríe Moraga names the question 'How to get over this one?',[9] we know our lesbian loving creates a lesbian way of be-ing in the world that helps each other and ourselves get over, strengthening our love in the getting over, to 'radical new beginnings.'

I believe it is a mistake to conflate lesbian-feminist and heterosexual-feminist interaction and goals. It is a mistake of great significance to lesbian identity, to lesbian presence. Lesbian space is not nonlesbian space. This ought to be clear to anyone who has a sense of the English language. They mean different things. I have sometimes experienced a sensitivity, an exploratory openness of a differing kind that occurs in lesbian-feminist-only space. This may be only a difference of degree, I'm not sure. But the interaction, the epistemic knowing of lesbian space, is different in kind from that of heterosexual lesbophobic space. This much I am sure about in my own life.

Lesbian ways of being, of experiencing lesbian presence, of knowing lesbian existence, have, for me, been validated only by lesbians. Further, my experience in lesbian-only space has helped me to articulate my values. I have come to know that loving and valuing individual lesbians is an *act of sabotage* in a misogynist world – an act not participated in by nonlesbians. Yet it is more. It is also the discovery/creating/epistemic validation process of lesbian culture that draws me to lesbian space. Without lesbian space, there is no lesbian-feminist existence, only the presence of an absence. When I touch lesbian-feminists, I know what values I am validating. I do not get this sense of validation from nonlesbians. Only lesbians are pleased and accept rushes exchanged between us, the 'thisness' of our experience, the 'nowness' of our presence. Our excitement about ideas is not restricted to our minds. We allow ourselves, each other, together and alone, to think/feel through our bodies and our hearts, as well as our minds. Nonlesbians are frequently frightened of exploring these lesbian experiences and embarrassed by them. We, however, as wimmin-loving-wimmin, are guided by our own intuitions in discovering the complexity of lesbian loving, anger, and beings. Lesbians only can validate loving wimmin individually, with our minds, bodies, and hearts ... informed by the gynergy we share through that special bond which is a bond of distinctly lesbian identified presence. The possibility of creating these bonds requires lesbian space:

> ... taking ourselves seriously is determining who has access to us, and that involves some basic form of separatism.[10]

Notes

* This piece is part of a longer essay. I borrow the concept of 'Radical New Beginnings' from Jackie Zita, a gentle friend who works toward creating new forms of life.
1. Julia Penelope Stanley, 'And Now For The Hard Questions,' *Sinister*

Wisdom #15, Fall, 1980, pp. 99–100.

2. Audre Lorde, *Zami: A New Spelling of My Name*, Persephone Press, Inc., (Watertown, Mass) 1982; p. 5. Now distributed by Kitchen Table: Women of Color Press, Inc. (N.Y., N.Y.).

3. I want to mention here that these reasons seem to me to be similar reasons we experience silence among wimmin related to many different systems of oppression we experience as wimmin and members of other oppressed groups simultaneously. We become frozen in our interactions, blocking the possibility of love, of life, between us.

4. This fact was brought home to me by a warm friend whose lesbian presence is felt in St Louis, Chris Guerrero.

5. Julia Penelope Stanley, op. cit., p. 103

6. Jackie Zita, 'Female Bonding and Sexual Politics,' *Sinister Wisdom* #14, pp. 12–13.

7. Azizah al-Hibri very gently pointed this out to me during a very difficult conversation we were having trying to get clear about why heterosexual women 'want' to 'be' heterosexual. St Louis, Missouri, 1981.

8. The work of Joyce Trebilcot and Claudia Card is very important in moving toward this direction. Lesbians are developing new ways of being, and part of this task, I believe, does require lesbian-only space. See especially Joyce's article in *Womanspirit*.

9. Cherríe Moraga.

10. Sarah Lucia Hoagland, 'Lesbian Ethics,' *The Lesbian Insider/Insighter/Inciter*, 1982.

FRENCH SPEAKING LESBIAN CONSCIOUSNESS: RADICAL LESBIANISM

The Straight Mind[1]

Monique Wittig
1980

In recent years in Paris, language as a phenomenon has dominated modern theoretical systems and the social sciences, and has entered the political discussions of the lesbian and women's liberation movements. This is because it relates to an important political field where what is at play is power, or more than that, a network of powers, since there is multiplicity of languages which constantly act upon the social reality. The importance of language as such as a political stake has only recently been perceived.[2] But the gigantic development of linguistics, the multiplication of schools of linguistics, the advent of the sciences of communication, and the technicality of the metalanguages that these sciences utilize, represent the symptoms of the importance of that political stake. The science of language has invaded other sciences, such as anthropology through Lévi-Strauss, psychoanalysis through Lacan, and all the disciplines which have developed from the basis of structuralism.

The early semiology of Roland Barthes nearly escaped from linguistic domination to become a political analysis of the different systems of signs, to establish a relationship between this or that system of signs – for example, the myths of the petit bourgeois class – and the class struggle within capitalism that this system tends to conceal. We were almost saved, for political semiology is a weapon (a method) that we need to analyze what is called ideology. But the miracle did not last. Rather than introducing into semiology concepts which are foreign to it – in this case Marxist concepts – Barthes quickly stated that semiology was only a branch of linguistics and that language was its only object.

Thus, the entire world is only a great register where the most diverse languages come, to have themselves recorded, such as the language of the Unconscious,[3] the language of fashion, the language of the exchange of women where human beings are literally the signs which are used to communicate. These languages, or rather these discourses, fit into one another, interpenetrate one another, support one another, reinforce one another, auto-engender, and engender one another. Linguistics engenders semiology and structural linguistics, structural linguistics engenders structuralism which engenders the Structural Unconscious. The ensemble of these discourses produces a confusing static for the oppressed, which makes them lose sight of the material cause of their oppression and plunges them into a kind of ahistoric vacuum.

For they produce a scientific reading of the social reality in which human beings are given as invariants, untouched by history and unworked by class conflicts, with a psyche identical for each one of them because genetically programmed. This psyche, equally untouched by history and unworked by class conflicts, provides the specialists, from the beginning of the twentieth century, with a whole arsenal of invariants: the symbolic language which very advantageously functions with very few elements, since like digits (0–9) the symbols 'unconsciously' produced by the psyche are not very numerous. Therefore, these symbols are very easy to impose, through therapy and theorization, upon the collective and individual unconscious. We are taught that the unconscious, with perfectly good taste, structures itself upon metaphors, for example, the name-of-the-father, the Oedipus complex, castration, the murder-or-death-of-the-father, the exchange of women, etc. If the unconscious, however, is easy to control, it is not just by anybody. Similar to mystical revelations, the apparition of symbols in the psyche demands multiple interpretations. Only specialists can accomplish the deciphering of the unconscious. Only they, the psychoanalysts, are allowed (authorized?) to organize and interpret psychic manifestations which will show the symbol in its full meaning. And while the symbolic language is extremely poor and essentially lacunary, the languages or metalanguages which interpret it are developing, each one of them, with a richness, a display, that only logical exegeses have equalled.

Who gave the psychoanalysts their knowledge? For example, for Lacan, what he calls the 'psychoanalytic discourse,' or the 'analytical experience,' both 'teach' him what he already knows. And each one teaches him what the other one taught him. But who will deny that Lacan scientifically acknowledged, through the 'analytical experience' (somehow an experiment) the structures of the Unconscious? Who will be irresponsible enough to disregard the discourses of the psychoanalyzed people lying on their couches? In my opinion, there is no doubt that Lacan found in the unconscious the structures he said he found there, since he had previously put them there. People who did not fall into the power of the psychoanalytical institution may experience an immeasurable feeling of sadness in front of the degree of oppression (of manipulation) that the psychoanalyzed discourses show. In the analytical experience there is an oppressed person, the psycho-analyzed, whose need for communication is exploited and who (in the same way as the witches could, under torture, only repeat the language that the inquisitors wanted to hear) has no other choice, (if s/he does not want to destroy the implicit contract which allows her/him to communicate and which s/he needs), than to attempt to say what s/he is supposed to say. They say that this can last for a lifetime – cruel contract which constrains a human being to display her/his misery to an oppressor who is directly responsible for it, who exploits her/her economically, politically, ideologically and whose interpretation reduces this misery to a few figures of speech.

But can the need to communicate that this contract implies only be satisfied in the psychoanalytical situation, in being cured or 'experimented' with? If we believe recent testimonies[4] by lesbians, feminists, and gay men, this is not the case. All their testimonies emphasize the political significance of the impossibility that lesbians, feminists, and gay men face in the attempt to communicate in heterosexual society, other than with a psychoanalyst. When the general state of things is understood (one is not sick or to be cured, one has an enemy) the result is for the oppressed person to break the psychoanalytical contract. This is what appears in the testimonies along with the teaching that the psychoanalytical contract was not a contract of consent but a forced one.

The discourses which particularly oppress all of us, lesbians, women, and homosexual men, are those discourses which take for granted that what founds society, any society, is heterosexuality.[5] These discourses speak about us and claim to say the truth in an apolitical field, as if anything of that which signifies could escape the political in this moment of history, and as if, in what concerns us, politically insignificant signs could exist. These discourses of heterosexuality oppress us in the sense that they prevent us from speaking unless we speak in their terms. Everything which puts them into question is at once disregarded as elementary. Our refusal of the totalizing interpretation of psychoanalysis makes the theoreticians say that we neglect the symbolic dimension. These discourses deny us every possibility of creating our own categories. But their most ferocious action is the unrelenting tyranny that they exert upon our physical and mental selves.

When we use the overgeneralizing term 'ideology' to designate all the discourses of the dominating group, we relegate these discourses to the domain of Irreal Ideas, we forget the material (physical) violence that they directly do to the oppressed people, a violence produced by the abstract and 'scientific' discourses as well as by the discourses of the mass media. I would like to insist on the material oppression of individuals by discourses, and I would like to underline its immediate effects through the example of pornography.

Pornographic images, films, magazine photos, publicity posters on the walls of the cities, constitute a discourse, and this discourse covers our world with its signs, and this discourse has a meaning: it signifies that women are dominated. Semioticians can interpret the system of this discourse, describe its disposition. What they read in that discourse are signs whose function is not to signify and which have no *raison d'être* except to be elements of a certain system or disposition. But for us this discourse is not divorced from the real as it is for semioticians. Not only does it maintain very close relations with the social reality which is our oppression (economically and politically), but also it is in itself real since it is one of the aspects of oppression, since it exerts a precise power over us. The pornographic discourse is part of the strategies of violence which are exercised upon us: it humiliates, it degrades, it is a crime against our 'humanity.' As a harassing tactic it has another function, that of a warning. It orders us to stay in line and it keeps those who would tend to forget who they are in step; it calls upon fear. These same experts in semiotics, referred to earlier, reproach us for confusing, when we demonstrate against pornography, the discourses with the reality. They do not see that this discourse *is* reality for us, one of the facets of the reality of our oppression. They believe that we are mistaken in our level of analysis.

I have chosen pornography as an example, because its discourse is the most symptomatic and the most demonstrative of the violence which is done to us through discourses, as well as in the society at large. There is nothing abstract about the power that sciences and theories have, to act materially and actually upon our bodies and our minds, even if the discourse that produces it is abstract. It is one of the forms of domination, its very expression, as Marx said. I would say, rather, one of its exercises. All of the oppressed know this power and have had to deal with it. It is the one which says: you do not have the right to speech because your discourse is not scientific and not theoretical, you are on the wrong level of analysis, you are confusing discourse and reality, your discourse is naïve, you misunderstand this or that science.

If the discourse of modern theoretical systems and social science exerts a power upon us, it is because it works with concepts which closely touch us. In spite of the historic advent of the lesbian, feminist, and gay liberation movements, whose proceedings have already upset the philosophical and political categories of the discourses of the social sciences, their categories (thus brutally put into question) are nevertheless utilized without examination by contemporary science. They function like primitive concepts in a conglomerate of all kinds of disciplines, theories, and current ideas that I will call the straight mind. (See *The Savage Mind* by Claude Lévi-Strauss.) They concern 'woman,' 'man,' 'sex,' 'difference,' and all of the series of concepts which bear this mark, including such concepts as 'history,' 'culture,' and the 'real.' And although it has been accepted in recent years that there is no such thing as nature, that everything is culture, there remains within that culture a core of nature which resists examination, a relationship excluded from the social in the analysis – a relationship whose characteristic is ineluctability in culture, as well as in nature, and which is the heterosexual relationship. I will call it the obligatory social relationship between 'man' and 'woman.' (Here I refer to Ti-Grace Atkinson and her analysis of sexual intercourse as an institution.[6]) With its ineluctability as knowledge, as an obvious principle, as a given prior to any science, the straight mind develops a totalizing interpretation of history, social reality, culture, language, and all the subjective phenomena at the same time. I can only underline the oppressive character that the straight mind is clothed in in its tendency to immediately universalize its production of concepts into general laws which claim to hold true for all societies, all epochs, all individuals. Thus one speaks of *the* exchange of women, difference between the sexes, *the* symbolic order, *the* Unconscious, desire, *jouissance*, culture, history, giving an absolute meaning to these concepts when they are categories founded upon heterosexuality or thought which produces the difference between the sexes as a political and philosophical dogma.

The consequence of this tendency toward universality is that the straight mind cannot conceive of a culture, a society where heterosexuality would not order not only all human relationships but also its very production of concepts and all the processes which escape consciousness, as well. Additionally, these unconscious processes are historically more and more imperative in what they teach us about ourselves through the instrumentality of specialists. The rhetoric which expresses them (and whose seduction I do not underestimate) envelops itself in myths, resorts to enigma, proceeds by accumulating metaphors, and its function is to poeticize the obligatory character of the 'you-will-be-straight-or-you-will-not-be.'

In this thought, to reject the obligation of coitus and the institutions that this obligation has produced as necessary for the constitution of a society, is simply an impossibility, since to do

435

this would mean to reject the possibility of the constitution of the other and to reject the 'symbolic order,' to make the constitution of meaning impossible, without which no one can maintain an internal coherence. Thus lesbianism, homosexuality, and the societies that we form cannot be thought of or spoken of, even though they have always existed. Thus, the straight mind continues to affirm that incest, and not homosexuality, represents its major interdiction. Thus, when thought by the straight mind, homosexuality is nothing but heterosexuality.

Yes, straight society is based on the necessity of the different/other at every level. It cannot work economically, symbolically, linguistically, or politically without this concept. This necessity of the different/other is an ontological one for the whole conglomerate of sciences and disciplines that I call the straight mind. But what is the different/other if not the dominated? For heterosexual society is the society which not only oppresses lesbians and gay men, it oppresses many who are in the position of the dominated. To constitute a difference and to control it is an 'act of power, since it is essentially a normative act. Everybody tries to show the other as different. But not everybody succeeds in doing so. One has to be socially dominant to succeed in it.'[7] For example, the concept of difference between the sexes ontologically constitutes women into different/others. Men are not different, whites are not different, nor are the masters. But the blacks, as well as the slaves, are. This ontological characteristic of the difference between the sexes affects all the concepts which are part of the same conglomerate. But for us there is no such thing as being-woman or being-man. 'Man' and 'woman' are political concepts of opposition, and the copula which dialectically unites them is, at the same time, the one which abolishes them.[8] It is the class struggle between women and men which will abolish men and women.[9] The concept of difference has nothing ontological about it. It is only the way that the masters interpret a historical situation of domination. The function of difference is to mask at every level the conflicts of interest, including ideological ones. In other words, for us, this means there cannot any longer be women and men, and that as classes and as categories of thought or language they have to disappear, politically, economically, ideologically. If we, as lesbians and gay men, continue to speak of ourselves and to conceive of ourselves as women and as men, we are instrumental in maintaining heterosexuality, I am sure that an economic and political transformation will not dedramatize these categories of language. Can we redeem *slave*? Can we redeem *nigger*, *negress*? How is *woman* different? Will we continue to write *white*, *master*, *man*? The transformation of economic relationships will not suffice. We must produce a political transformation of the key concepts, that is of the concepts which are strategic for us. For there is another order of materiality, that of language, and language is worked upon from within by these strategic concepts. It is at the same time tightly connected to the political field where everything that concerns language, science and thought refers to the person as subjectivity and to her/his relationship to society.[10] And we cannot leave this within the power of the straight mind or the thought of domination.

If among all the productions of the straight mind I especially challenge structuralism and the Structural Unconscious, it is because: at the moment in history when the domination of social groups can no longer appear as a logical necessity to the dominated, because they revolt, because they question the differences, Lévi-Strauss, Lacan and their epigones call upon necessities which escape the control of consciousness and therefore the responsibility of individuals.

They call upon unconscious processes, for example, which require the exchange of women as a necessary condition for every society. According to them that is what the unconscious tells us with authority, and the symbolic order without which there is no meaning, no language, no society, depends on it. But what does women being exchanged mean if not that they are dominated? No wonder then that there is only one unconscious, and that it is heterosexual. It is an unconscious which looks too consciously after the interests of the masters[11] in whom it lives for them to be dispossessed of their concepts so easily. Besides, domination is denied; there is no slavery of women, there is difference. To which I will answer with this statement made by a Rumanian peasant at a public meeting in 1848: 'Why do the gentlemen say it was not slavery, for we know it to have been slavery, this sorrow that we have sorrowed.' Yes, we know it, and this science of oppression cannot be taken away from us.

It is from this science that we must track down the 'what goes-without-saying' heterosexual, and (I paraphrase the early Roland Barthes) we must not bear 'seeing Nature and History confused at every turn.'[12] We must make it brutally apparent that structuralism, psychoanalysis, and particularly Lacan have rigidly turned their concepts into myths — Difference, Desire, the Name-of-the-father, etc. They have even 'over-mythified' the myths, an operation that was necessary for them in order to systematically heterosexualize that personal dimension which suddenly emerged through the dominated individuals into the historical field, particularly through women, who started their struggle almost two centuries ago. And it has been done systematically, in a

437

concert of interdisciplinarity, never more harmonious than since the heterosexual myths started to circulate with ease from one formal system to another, like sure values that can be invested, in anthropology as well as in psychoanalysis and in all the social sciences.

This ensemble of heterosexual myths is a system of signs which uses figures of speech, and thus it can be politically studied from within the science of our oppression; 'for-we-know-it-to-have-been-slavery' is the dynamic which introduces the diachronism of history into the fixed discourse of eternal essences. This undertaking should somehow be a political semiology, although with 'this sorrow that we have sorrowed' we work also at the level of language/manifesto, of language/action, that which transforms, that which makes history.

In the meantime in the systems that seemed so eternal and universal that laws could be extracted from them, laws that could be stuffed into computers, and in any case for the moment stuffed into the unconscious machinery, in these systems, thanks to our action and our language, shifts are happening. Such a model, as for example, the exchange of women, reengulfs history in so violent and brutal a way that the whole system, which was believed to be formal, topples over into another dimension of knowledge. This dimension belongs to us, since somehow we have been designated, and since, as Lévi-Strauss said, we talk, let us say that we break off the heterosexual contract.

So, this is what lesbians say everywhere in this country and in some others, if not with theories at least through their social practice, whose repercussions upon straight culture and society are still unenvisionable. An anthropologist might say that we have to wait for fifty years. Yes, if one wants to universalize the functioning of these societies and make their invariants appear. Meanwhile the straight concepts are undermined. What is woman? Panic, general alarm for an active defense. Frankly, it is a problem that the lesbians do not have because of a change of perspective, and it would be incorrect to say that lesbians associate, make love, live with women, for 'woman' has meaning only in heterosexual systems of thought and heterosexual economic systems. Lesbians are not women.

Notes

1. This text was first read in New York at the Modern Language Association Convention in 1978 and dedicated to the American lesbians.
2. However, the classical Greeks knew that there was no political power

without mastery of the art of rhetoric, especially in a democracy.

3.   Throughout this paper when Lacan's use of the term 'the unconscious' is referred to it is capitalized, following his style.

4.   For example see Karla Jay, Allen Young, eds., *Out of the Closets* (New York: Links Books, 1972).

5.   Heterosexuality: a word which first appears in the French language in 1911.

6.   Ti-Grace Atkinson, *Amazon Odyssey* (New York: Links Books, 1974), pp. 13–23.

7.   Claude Faugeron and Philippe Robert, *La Justice et son public et les représentations sociales du système pénal* (Paris: Masson, 1978).

8.   See for her definition of 'social sex' Nichole-Claude Mathieu, 'Notes pour une définition sociologique des categories de sexe,' *Epistemologie Sociologique* II (1971); translated in Nicole-Claude Mathieu, *Ignored by Some, Denied by Others: The Social Sex Category in Sociology* (pamphlet), Explorations in Feminism 2 (London: Women's Research and Resources Centre Publications, 1977), pp. 16–37.

9.   In the same way as for every other class struggle where the categories of opposition are 'reconciled' by the struggle whose goal is to make them disappear.

10.   See Christine Delphy, 'Pour un Féminisme Matérialiste,' l'Arc 61, *Simone de Beauvoir et la lutte des femmes*, which appears in *Feminist Issues*.

11.   Are the millions of dollars a year made by the psychoanalysts symbolic?

12.   Roland Barthes, *Mythologies* (New York: Hill and Wang, 1972), p. 11.

One is Not Born a Woman

Monique Wittig
1981

A materialist feminist[1] approach to women's oppression destroys the idea that women are a 'natural group': 'a racial group of a special kind, a group perceived *as natural*, a group of men considered as materially specific in their bodies.'[2] What the analysis accomplishes on the level of ideas, practice makes actual at the level of facts: by its very existence, lesbian society destroys the artificial (social) fact constituting women as a 'natural group.' A lesbian society[3] pragmatically reveals that the division from men of which women have been the object is a political one and shows how we have been ideologically rebuilt into a 'natural group.' In the case of women, ideology goes far since our bodies as well as our minds are the product of this manipulation. We have been compelled in our bodies and in our minds to correspond, feature by feature, with the *idea* of nature that has been established for us. Distorted to such an extent that our deformed body is what they call 'natural,' what is supposed to exist as such before oppression. Distorted to such an extent that in the end oppression seems to be a consequence of this 'nature' within ourselves (a nature which is only an *idea*). What a materialist analysis does by reasoning, a lesbian society accomplishes practically: not only is there no natural group 'women' (we lesbians are living proof of it), but as individuals as well we question 'woman,' which for us, as for Simone de Beavoir thirty years ago, is only a myth. She said: 'One is not born, but becomes a woman. No biological, psychological, or economic fate determines the figure that the human female presents in society: it is civilization as a whole that produces this creature, intermediate between male and eunuch, which is described as feminine.'[4]

However, most of the feminists and lesbian-feminists in America and elsewhere still believe that the basis of women's oppression *is biological as well as* historical. Some of them even claim to find their sources in Simone de Beauvoir.[5] The belief in mother right and in a 'prehistory' when women created civilization (because of a biological predisposition) while the coarse and brutal men hunted (because of a biological predisposition), is symmetrical with the biologizing interpretation of history produced up to now by the class of men. It is still the same method of finding in women and men a biological explanation of their division, outside of social facts. For me this could never constitute a lesbian approach to women's oppression, since it assumes that the basis of society or the beginning of society lies in heterosexuality. Matriarchy is no less heterosexual than patriarchy: it is only the sex of the oppressor that changes. Furthermore, not only is this conception still imprisoned in the categories of sex (woman and man), but it holds onto the idea that the capacity to give birth (biology) is what defines a woman. Although practical facts and ways of living contradict this theory in lesbian society, there are lesbians who affirm that 'women and men are different species or races (the words are used interchangeably): men are biologically inferior to women; male violence is a biological inevitability . . .'[6] By doing this, by admitting that there is a 'natural' division between women and men, we naturalize history, we assume that men and women have always existed and will always exist. Not only do we naturalize history, but also consequently we naturalize the social phenomena which express our oppression, making change impossible. For example, instead of seeing birth as a forced production, we see it as a 'natural,' 'biological' process, forgetting that in our societies births are planned (demography), forgetting that we ourselves are programmed to produce children, while this is the only social activity 'short of war'[7] that presents such a great danger of death. Thus, as long as we will be 'unable to abandon by will or impulse a lifelong and centuries-old commitment to childbearing as *the* female creative act,'[8] gaining control of the production of children will mean much more than the mere control of the material means of this production: women will have to abstract themselves from the definition 'woman' which is imposed upon them.

A materialist feminist approach shows that what we take for the cause or origin of oppression is in fact only the *mark*[9] imposed by the oppressor: the 'myth of woman,'[10] plus its material effects and manifestations in the appropriated consciousness and bodies of women. Thus, this mark does not preexist oppression: Colette Guillaumin has shown that before the socioeconomic reality of black slavery, the concept of race did not exist, at least not in its modern meaning, since it was applied to the lineage of families. However, now, race, exactly like sex, is taken as an 'immediate given,' a 'sensible given,' 'physical features,' belonging to a natural order. But what we believe to be a physical and direct perception is only a sophisticated and mythic construction, an 'imaginary formation,'[11] which reinterprets physical features (in themselves as neutral as any others but marked by the social system) through the network of relationships in which they are perceived. (They are seen *black*, therefore they *are* black; they are seen as *women*, therefore, they *are* women. But before being *seen* that way, they first had to be *made* that way.) A lesbian consciousness should always remember and acknowledge how 'unnatural,' compelling, totally oppressive, and destructive being 'woman' was for us in the old days before the women's liberation movement. It was a political constraint and those who resisted it were accused of not being 'real' women. But then we were proud of it, since in the accusation there was already something like a shadow of victory: the avowal by the oppressor that 'woman' is not something that goes without saying, since to be one, one has to be a 'real' one. We were at the same time accused of wanting to be men. Today this double accusation has been taken up again with enthusiasm in the context of the women's liberation movement by some feminists and also, alas, by some lesbians whose political goal seems somehow to be becoming more and more 'feminine.' To refuse to be a woman, however, does not mean that one has to become a man. Besides, if we take as an example the perfect 'butch,' the classic example which provokes the most horror, whom Proust would have called a woman/man, how is her alienation different from that of someone who wants to become a woman? Tweedledum and Tweedledee. At least for a woman, wanting to become a man proves that she escapes her initial programming. But even if she would like to, with all her strength, she cannot become a man. For becoming a man would demand from a woman not only the external appearance of a man but his consciousness as well, that is, the consciousness of one who disposes by right of at least two 'natural' slaves during his life span. This is impossible and one feature of lesbian oppression consists precisely of making women out of reach for us, since women belong to men. Thus a lesbian *has to* be something else, a not-woman, a not-man, a product of society, not a product of nature, for there is no nature in society.

The refusal to become (or to remain) heterosexual always meant to refuse to become a man or a woman, consciously or not. For a lesbian this goes further than the refusal of the *role* 'woman.' It is the refusal of the economic, ideological, and political power of a man. This, we lesbians, and nonlesbians as well, knew before the beginning of the lesbian and feminist movement. However, as Andrea Dworkin emphasizes, many lesbians recently 'have increasingly tried to transform the very ideology that has enslaved us into a dynamic, religious, psychologically compelling celebration of female biological potential.'[12] Thus, some avenues of the feminist and lesbian movement lead us back to the myth of woman which was created by men especially for us, and with it we sink back into a natural group. Thirty years ago we stood up to fight for a sexless society.[13] Now we find ourselves entrapped in the familiar deadlock of 'woman is wonderful.' Thirty years ago Simone de Beauvoir underlined particularly the false consciousness which consists of selecting among the features of the myth (that women are different from men) those which look good and using them as a definition for women. What the concept of 'woman is wonderful' accomplishes is that it retains for defining women the best features (best according to whom?) which oppression has granted us, and it does not radically question the categories 'man' and 'woman,' which are political categories and not natural givens. It puts us in a position of fighting within the class 'women' not as the other classes do, for the disappearance of our class, but for the defense of 'woman' and its reenforcement. It leads us to develop with complacency 'new' theories about our specificity: thus, we call our passivity 'nonviolence,' when the main and emergent point for us is to fight our passivity (our fear, rather, a justified one). The ambiguity of the term 'feminist' sums up the whole situation. What does 'feminist' mean? Feminist is formed with the word 'femme,' 'woman,' and means: someone who fights for women. For many of us it means someone who fights for women as a class and for the disappearance of this class. For many others it means someone who fights for woman and her defense – for the myth, then, and its reenforcement. But why was the word 'feminist' chosen if it retains the least ambiguity? We chose to call ourselves 'feminists' ten years ago, not in order to support or reenforce the myth of woman nor to identify ourselves with the oppressor's definition of us, but rather to affirm that our movement had a history and to emphasize the political link with the old feminist movement.

It is then this movement that we can put in question for the meaning that it gave to feminism. It so happens that feminism in the last century could never resolve its contradictions on the subject of nature/culture, woman/society. Women started to fight for themselves as a group and rightly considered that they shared common features of oppression. But for them these features were natural and biological rather than social. They went so far as to adopt the Darwinist theory of evolution. They did not believe like Darwin, however, 'that women were less evolved than men, but they did believe that male and female natures had diverged in the course of evolutionary development and that society at large reflected this polarization.'[14] 'The failure of early feminism was that it only attacked the Darwinist charge of female inferiority, while accepting the foundations of this charge – namely, the view of woman as "unique." '[15] And finally it was women scholars – and not feminists – who scientifically destroyed this theory. But the early feminists had failed to regard history as a dynamic process which develops from conflicts of interests. Furthermore, they still believed as men do that the cause (origin) of their oppression lay within themselves. And therefore the feminists of this first front after some astonishing victories found themselves at an impasse out of a lack of reasons for fighting. They upheld the illogical principle of 'equality of difference,' an idea now being born again. They fell back into the trap which threatens us once again: the myth of woman.

Thus it is our historical task, and only ours, to define what we call oppression in materialist terms, to make it evident that women are a class, which is to say that the category 'woman' as well as the category 'man' are political and economic categories not eternal ones. Our fight aims to suppress men as a class, not through a genocidal, but a political struggle. Once the class 'men' disappears, 'women' as a class will disappear as well, for there are no slaves without masters. Our first task, it seems, is to always thoroughly dissociate 'women' (the class within which we fight) and 'woman,' the myth. For 'woman' does not exist for us: it is only an imaginary formation, while 'women' is the product of a social relationship. We felt this strongly when everywhere we refused to be called a *'woman's* liberation movement.' Furthermore, we have to destroy the myth inside and outside ourselves. 'Woman' is not each one of us, but the political and ideological formation which negates 'women' (the product of a relation of exploitation). 'Woman' is there to confuse us, to hide the reality 'women.' In order to be aware of being a class and to become a class we have to first kill the myth of 'woman' including its most seductive aspects (I think about Virginia Woolf when she said the first task of a woman writer is to kill 'the angel in the house'). But to become a class we do not have to suppress our individual selves, and since no individual can be reduced to her/his oppression we are also confronted with the historical necessity of constituting ourselves as the individual subjects of our history as well. I believe this is the reason why all these attempts at 'new' definitions of woman are blossoming now. What is at stake (and of course not only for women) is an individual definition as well as a class definition. For once one has acknowledged oppression, one needs to know and experience the fact that one can constitute oneself as a subject (as opposed to an object of oppression), that one can become *someone* in spite of oppression, that one has one's own identity. There is no possible fight for someone deprived of an identity, no internal motivation for fighting, since although I can fight only with others, first I fight for myself.

The question of the individual subject is historically a difficult one for everybody. Marxism, the last avatar of materialism, the science which has politically formed us, does not want to hear anything about a 'subject.' Marxism has rejected the transcendental subject, the subject as constitutive of knowledge, the 'pure' consciousness. All that thinks per se, before all experience, has ended up in the garbage can of history, because it claimed to exist outside matter, prior to matter, and needed God, spirit, or soul to exist in such a way. This is what is called 'idealism.' As for individuals, they are only the product of social relations, therefore their consciousness can only be 'alienated.' (Marx, in *The German Ideology*, says precisely that individuals of the dominating class are also alienated although they are the direct producers of the ideas that alienate the classes oppressed by them. But since they draw visible advantages from their own alienation they can bear it, without too much suffering.) There exists such a thing as class consciousness, but a consciousness which does not refer to a particular subject, except as participating in general conditions of exploitation at the same time as the other subjects of their class, all sharing the same consciousness. As for the practical class problems – outside of the class problems as traditionally defined – that one could encounter (for example, sexual problems), they were considered as 'bourgeois' problems that would disappear with the final victory of the class struggle. 'Individualistic,' 'subjectivist,' 'petit bourgeois,' these are the labels given to any person who had shown problems which could not be reduced to the 'class struggle' itself.

Thus Marxism has refused the attribute of being a subject to the members of oppressed classes. In doing this, Marxism, because of the ideological and political power this 'revolutionary science' immediately exercised upon the workers' movement and all other political groups, has prevented all categories of oppressed people from constituting themselves historically as subjects (subjects of this struggle, for example). This means that the 'masses' did not fight for themselves but for *the* party or its organizations. And when an economic transformation took place (end of private property, constitution of the socialist state), no revolutionary change took place within the new society, because the people themselves did not change.

For women, Marxism had two results. It prevented them from being aware that they are a class and therefore from constituting themselves as a class for a very long time, by leaving the relation 'women/men' outside of the social order, by turning it into a natural relation, doubtlessly for Marxists the only one along with the relation of mothers to children to be seen in this way, and by hiding the class conflict between men and women behind a natural division of labor (*The German Ideology*). This concerns the theoretical (ideological) level. On the practical level, Lenin, *the* party, all the communist parties up to now, including all the most radical political groups, have always reacted to any attempt on the part of women to reflect and form groups based on their own class problem with an accusation of divisiveness. By uniting, we women are dividing the strength of the people. This means that for the Marxists women *belong* either to the bourgeois class, or to the proletariat class, in other words, to the men of these classes. In addition, Marxist theory does not allow women any more than other classes of oppressed people to constitute themselves as historical subjects, because Marxism does not take into account the fact that a class also consists of individuals one by one. Class consciousness is not enough. We must try to understand philosophically (politically) these concepts of 'subject' and 'class consciousness' and how they work in relation to our history. When we discover that women are the objects of oppression and appropriation, at the very moment that we become able to perceive this, we become subjects in the sense of cognitive subjects, through an operation of abstraction. Consciousness of oppression is not only a reaction to (fight against) oppression. It is also the whole conceptual reevaluation of the social world, its whole reorganization with new concepts, from the point of view of oppression. It is what I would call the science of oppression created by the oppressed. This operation of understanding reality has to be undertaken by every one of us: call it a subjective, cognitive practice. The movement back and forth between the levels of reality (the conceptual reality and the material reality of oppression, which are both social realities) is accomplished through language.

It is we who historically must undertake the task of defining the individual subject in materialist terms. This certainly seems to be an impossibility since materialism and subjectivity have always been mutually exclusive. Nevertheless, and rather than despairing or never understanding, we must recognize the *need* to reach subjectivity in the abandonment by many of us to the myth 'woman' (the myth of women being only a snare that holds us up). This real necessity for everyone to exist as an individual, as well as a member of a class, is perhaps the first condition for the accomplishment of a revolution, without which there can be no real fight or transformation. But the opposite is also true; without class and class consciousness there are no real subjects, only alienated individuals. For women to answer the question of the individual subject in materialist terms is first to show, as the lesbians and feminists did, that supposedly 'subjective,' 'individual,' 'private' problems are in fact social problems, class problems; that sexuality is not for women an individual and subjective expression, but a social institution of violence. But once we have shown that all so-called personal problems are in fact class problems, we will still be left with the question of the subject of each singular woman – not the myth, but each one of us. At this point, let us say that a new personal and subjective definition for all humankind can only be found beyond the categories of sex (woman and man) and that the advent of individual subjects demands first destroying the categories of sex, ending the use of them, and rejecting all sciences which still use these categories as their fundamentals (practically all social sciences).

To destroy 'woman,' does not mean that we aim, short of physical destruction, to destroy lesbianism simultaneously with the categories of sex, because lesbianism provides for the moment the only social form in which we can live freely. Lesbian is the only concept I know of which is beyond the categories of sex (woman and man), because the designated subject (lesbian) is *not* a woman, either economically, or politically, or ideologically. For what makes a woman is a specific social relation to a man, a relation that we have previously called servitude,[16] a relation which implies personal and physical obligation as well as economic obligation ('forced residence,'[17] domestic corvée, conjugal duties, unlimited production of children, etc.) a relation which lesbians escape by refusing to become or to stay heterosexual. We are escapees from our class in the same way as the American runaway slaves were when escaping slavery and becoming free. For us this is an absolute necessity; our survival demands that we contribute all our strength to the destruction of the class of women within which men appropriate women. This can be accomplished only by the destruction of heterosexuality as a social system which is based on the oppression of women by men and which produces the doctrine of the difference between the sexes to justify this oppression.

Notes

1.   Christine Delphy, 'For a Feminist Materialism,' in *Feminist Issues* I, 2 (Winter, 1981).
2.   Colette Guillaumin, 'Race et nature: Système des marques, idée de groupe naturel et rapport sociaux,' *Pluriel* 11 (1977).
3.   I use the word society with an extended anthropological meaning, since strictly speaking it does not refer to societies in the sense that lesbian societies do not exist completely autonomously from heterosexual social systems. Nevertheless, they are more than simply communities.
4.   Simone de Beauvoir, *The Second Sex* (New York: Bantam, 1952), p. 249.
5.   Redstockings, *Feminist Revolution* (New York: Random House, 1978), p. 18.
6.   Andrea Dworkin, 'Biological superiority, the world's most dangerous and deadly idea,' *Heresies* 6:46.
7.   Ti-Grace Atkinson, *Amazon Odyssey* (New York: Links Books, 1974), p. 15.
8.   Andrea Dworkin, op. cit., p. 55.
9.   Colette Guillaumin, op. cit.
10.   Simone de Beauvoir, op. cit.
11.   Colette Guillaumin, op. cit.
12.   Andrea Dworkin, op. cit.
13.   Ti-Grace Atkinson, op. cit., p. 6: 'If feminism has any logic at all, it must be working for a sexless society.'
14.   Rosalind Rosenberg, 'In Search of Woman's Nature,' *Feminist Studies* 3, 1/2 (1975): 144.
15.   Ibid., p. 146.

16. In an article published by *L'Idiot International* (mai 1970) whose original title was 'Pour un mouvement de libération des femmes.'
17. Christiane Rochefort, *Les Stances à Sophie* (Paris: Grasset, 1963).

Separatism and Radicalism:
An analysis of the differences and similarities

Ariane Brunet and Louise Turcotte
Québec, 1982

(Translated by Lee Heppner)

In this article we will attempt to establish a connection between two tendencies in lesbian political thought, both of which are concerned with revealing the profoundly political dimension of lesbianism. This 'political dimension' helps us gain control of our own lives so that we may better understand our role in a social revolution in which we must be actively engaged.

We must stress that the two political tendencies belong to two different cultures: lesbian separatism comes from the U.S.; whereas, for the purpose of this article, radical lesbianism is particular to the French-speaking lesbians of Québec. It is no exaggeration to say that of the two cultures, the Québec culture is relatively unknown. The existence of six million French Canadians[1] within this vast English-speaking continent is, unfortunately, rarely recognized by our lesbian sisters in America.

It is not my intention in this introduction to discuss the history of Québec, its struggle against oppression, its nationalist fight for independence, the Québec 'separatist' movement, the feminist or lesbian movements.[2] I will simply mention that during the summer of 1983 the 'Amazones d'hier, Lesbiennes d'aujourd'hui' collective (of which the authors of this article are members, together with Genette Bergeron and Danielle Charest) toured the U.S. with a video whose title is the same as the name of our collective and which deals with French Canadian lesbians in Montreal.

During the tour, we realized how unaware Americans are of our very existence. We also realized that although our concerns seem at first glance to be the same, we found we approached similar concerns in different ways. The different priorities we give to our common concerns clearly reflect the scope of our cultural diversity. It is vital that we become aware of this diversity and that we enter a new era of communication, taking our differences into consideration, rather than letting the dominant North American culture dictate the political path of the lesbian movement. Only on these conditions will it be possible to build up an international lesbian movement. It is only by being open to each other, with all our ethnic, racial and national diversity, that we can ever be, to use a popular phrase in Quebec, 'visible to each other.'

French-speaking lesbians in Quebec, who experience 'isolation and oppression as a minority within the vast English-speaking population of North America,'[3] need contact with Canadian and American lesbians as well as those living in other French-language countries. Many of us make an annual pilgrimage to Michigan; being in a community of 8,000 lesbians does wonders for the morale. What we have to do now is take this experience even further and increase our contacts.

Ariane Brunet

This article was first written after a lesbian conference held in October 2, 1982. In a workshop on radical lesbianism, participants discussed the differences and similarities between lesbian separatism and radical lesbianism.[4] Because this article was originally written for Quebec lesbians who wanted to deepen their understanding of what lesbian separatism is, we have revised it for purposes of publication outside Quebec, keeping only the actual comparison of the two political tendencies. Nevertheless, many of our readers will be familiar with the extracts quoted here from separatist writings; we have included them because we are writing from a radical lesbian viewpoint.

We believe it is important to stress at the outset that the notion of 'lesbian separatism' originated with American lesbians and that the word 'separatist' has a completely different connotation for Quebecers.[5] Moreover, it is difficult to give an exact definition of 'lesbian separatism' because there exists a great variety of separatists, each with her own understanding of the word.

We first consulted those who had *written* on the subject. For us, one of the problems regarding the great divergence of opinion on lesbian separatism is the absence of a historical continuum for analysis. Looking through the various separatist texts written since the early 70s, one has the impression that each was written with no regard for the historical context of the existing literature.

Nevertheless, two distinct positions can be discerned.

First Position
1a) Lesbian separatists who define themselves as feminists and advocate separation from men in their political thinking as well as

in their daily lives. This position was put forth in *Amazon Analysis* (1973).

> Lesbian Separatism is inherently linked with feminism, the ideology and practice that considers woman prime. . . . Lesbian separatism is feminism carried to its logical conclusion . . . no other ideology speaks to all our needs, no other ideology will or can destroy patriarchy and male supremacy and build an egalitarian matriarchal society.
>
> (p. 43)

A similar position was taken by *Tribad* (a now-defunct publication of New York separatists).

This line of thought is based on the historical existence of an ideal society of women: the matriarchy. But it fails to take into account that at the time the matriarchy emerged (that is, when woman's capacity for reproduction began to be glorified through fertility rites), the institution of heterosexuality also took form. Matriarchy and patriarchy go hand-in-hand . . . from the power of the Mother to the power of the Father. But what about the power of lesbians? Unfortunately, the history of the Amazons is usually considered to be just an aspect of the matriarchy.[6]

Proposing a return to the matriarchy as a solution does not confront the institution of heterosexuality as such.

1b) The authors of *The Furies (1972–1974)* and *Feminism First: A Lesbian Separatist Analysis (1980)* also identify themselves as feminist lesbian separatists. *The Furies*, however, linked male supremacy (a term also used by *Amazon Analysis* and *Tribad*) directly to heterosexism. *The Furies*: The important point in the 1970 manifesto

> *Woman-Identified Woman* and in any lesbian feminist political thought is the fact that in a male supremacist society, heterosexuality is a political institution: it is then evident that lesbianism, like heterosexuality, is as much a political force as a personal lifestyle. (Charlotte Bunch, 'Learning from Lesbian Separatism,' *Ms.*, November 1976)[7]

We believe these two political forces are antagonistic by nature, since the one, heterosexuality, can ensure its political power only through the destruction of the other, lesbianism. The first is the political institution of the dominating class and the second, the power of revolt.

On this point the 'feminist' analysis leads to confusion. It is only lesbian radicals and separatists who have pinpointed hetero-sexuality as the fundamental institution of male power. Feminists have denounced patriarchal institutions such as the family, schools, work, religions, and the media as proponents of sexism. Lesbian radicals and separatists have restored to this word the major element that was missing: HETERO/SEXISM. Feminism deals with only half the reality: trying to maintain the Man/Woman (hetero) relationship while struggling with its most oppressive form (sexism). In fact, heterosexuality is the cause of sexism.

1c) The Feminism First group define themselves as 'tactical lesbian separatists'; that is, they advocate the use of lesbian separatism as a means of giving priority to feminism and adopting a feminist perspective of all oppressions:

> The term lesbian separatism has been used to express many different politics. To us it means, most impor-tantly, not a way of promoting exclusively *lesbian concerns*, or a way of *protecting* lesbians from heterosexism in political groups, but a possibility of prioritising feminism. We want to distinguish clearly between *women's interests* and *men's interests* so that we can act in *women's interests*. The institution of heterosexuality blocks this process by encouraging women to see our interests as identified with men's instead of opposed to them. (our italics)[8]
>
> (p. 59)

Again there is a tendency to equate feminism with lesbianism, with no mention whatsoever of the manner in which lesbianism has been treated by the feminist movement. To use 'feminism' in place of the word 'lesbianism' is to imply that they are synonymous! To do this omits recognition of the way lesbians have been ignored historically by feminists. 'Not promoting exclusively lesbian concerns' or 'not protecting lesbians from heterosexism in political groups' amounts to not having a lesbian perspective – hence the name of the group, Feminism First. It seems to us an easy matter to 'prioritise feminism' when speaking about women's *interests/rights* and lesbian *concerns* ... But in that case, how can such a line of thought be described as 'lesbian separatism'?

Of all the groups mentioned above, only The Furies have

ascribed a political significance to lesbianism, and they are also the only group to set themselves apart from the straight feminist movement. (See Ginny Berson's article 'The Furies' in *Lesbianism and the Women's Movement*, Diana Press, 1975, p. 18.) (Even today, can anyone claim the existence of a lesbian feminist *movement* identified as such and having a *lesbian* feminist politic? Is it not more accurate to say that there are simply many lesbians in the straight feminist movement?)

Second Position
2a) The second position, which gives no exact definition of lesbian separatism, is expressed in the form of clearly-identified publications such as *By and For Lesbians*. It is therefore more of a political affirmation than a political analysis as such. Through these publications, various kinds of analyses are put forth, all of which are focused on lesbianism. Other publications of this nature are *Lesbian Connection*, *Lesbian Insider/Insighter/Inciter* August 1980 to February 1985, and December 1985 to May 1986, and *Common Lives/Lesbian Lives*, to name only the better-known ones.
2b) Because there is no universal political position among lesbian separatists, many lesbians have expressed their separatist convictions in music, poetry, or theoretical writings. For some, the audience to whom their music or poetry is addressed is as fundamental an issue as the content itself. Linda Shear, for example, gave her concerts for lesbians only; her intent was to include us clearly in her music and to encourage us to identify as lesbians. Elana Dykewomon first wrote her poetry 'for women only' and then 'for lesbians only.' Alix Dobkin, too, gives concerts exclusively for women.

A number of academics have used their theoretical work to develop a lesbian separatist politic: for example, Sarah Hoagland, Marilyn Frye, and Julia Penelope. Their separatism has developed out of academic research that denounces the heterosexist use of language at all scientific and socio-cultural levels. They dissect the hetero-patriarchal system, rediscover our lesbian history, and build up a lesbian perspective, each according to her field of interest.
2c) We feel it is important to mention that all the texts cited in this article were written by white lesbian separatists. Some non-separatists associate separatism with racism (cf. 'Notes for a Magazine,' Adrienne Rich, *Sinister Wisdom* #18). Actually, it is not a question of separatist politics being racist but rather of some white lesbian separatists having racist behavior, as do some white lesbian feminists, radicals, etc.

A number of articles denouncing racism have appeared in separatist reviews. Some black lesbians define themselves as separatists, and they too have all the possible variations in political thinking.

Through these two positions we can see the diversity of separatists and separatist philosophies.

Radicalism

Based on the examples given earlier, it seems to us that separatism does not constitute an analysis in itself, since the overriding principle conveyed by the separatist literature of the 70s and 80s has been feminism.

One of the crucial differences between radicalism and separatism clearly revolves around the acceptance of feminist analysis and, consequently, the use of the word 'woman' (or rather the American spellings 'womyn,' 'wimmin,' 'womon,' and the recently recognized 'womyn-identified womyn').

To use this word is, once more, to dissimulate the reality of lesbians. 'Woman,' even in its orthographic variants, is not interchangeable with the word 'lesbian.' It takes its significance from the hetero-patriarchal system, inseparable from the Man/Woman relationship, and is therefore, in the words of Micheline Grimard-Leduc, 'annexed to male reality.'[9] The term designates not only a biological concept but also the socio-cultural concept of second-class citizen. Changing the spelling is not enough to change the social reality. 'Woman' is part of a consensus, a hetero-patriarchal perception; it has no connotation of breaking-away or autonomy. Only the word 'lesbian' conveys a sense of separation, independence, going beyond the borderline.

From whom are we hiding our reality when we speak of a '*womyn's* culture' and a 'Michigan *wimmin's* musical festival'? When the authors were stopped at the Michigan border in 1979, the American border guards asked us whether we knew that 90% of the women at the festival were lesbians. Who are we fooling besides ourselves? We are playing into society's hand and perpetuating the idea that lesbianism is only a different kind of sexuality. We lesbians create the culture, the music, the separatist environment, so why the equivocation? To maintain our unbearable situation as cheap labor in the 'women's' movement? We are strangers to the very culture we have just created.

None of the separatist analyses we have studied are based on the one consideration that is vital to any awareness of our reality: namely, that we are *lesbians* and not women. Society makes us invisible by calling us 'lesbian women,' that is, 'women' with an abnormal or perverted sexuality. Feminists see us as 'women' whose sexual preference is to be considered among all the other demands of feminism – a way of co-opting us into the fight to improve the subjugated condition of women in the hetero-system. *It is therefore imperative to any radical analysis that we define ourselves as lesbians.*

Radical lesbianism confronts the very basis of society: *heterosexuality*. And to be a lesbian, whether politically aware or not, is to be outside the concept of 'woman.'[10]

Feminism has never confronted heterosexuality as a political institution that enables the male class to oppress and exploit the female class. This institution defines woman as sexually accessible to male power, as a reproducer of men and the nourisher of their power. Heterosexuality is the institution that creates, maintains, and supports men's power. Without woman's subjugation to heterosexuality, man could not survive on his own, or so he thinks. Women's service to men – voluntary or forced, paid or unpaid – is what generates men's power and enables them to continue living on women's energy. And heterosexuality has its ramifications at all levels of society; it is the source of all other oppressions.

Heterosexuality is the pivot on which men have based the norm and created the origin and the measure by which all relationships are structured. The concept of difference is inherent in heterosexuality. That concept, as explained by Monique Wittig in 'La Pensée Straight,' makes us view the 'other' as different. The sexuality of the other (*hetero-*), of the other who differs, who is different *from* me, determines my own sexuality, reality. But to view one as 'different' one has to consider one's own difference as the norm because one has the power and the control. The concept of difference – heterosexuality – is a system of value judgment that sees one as superior and the other as inferior: dominant and dominated. Nothing in biology indicates that our biological differences can affect our social behavior. The sexuality of the other (*hetero-*) is that which sets me apart as different. Men, through heterosexuality, have devised their own concept and thereby constructed a system that generates all oppressions.

Now, lesbian feminists accept heterosexuality as the norm; it is the 'compulsory' nature of heterosexuality[11] which implies that a 'choice' between lesbianism and heterosexuality is possible. But, instead of beginning with the proposition that heterosexuals exist, we must begin with a more obvious proposition: Lesbians exist. We have always existed; we have always loved ourselves and rejected the so-called heterosexual imperative. But, in the writers' view, the writing of Adrienne Rich reverses this proposition, implying that compulsory heterosexuality and lesbian existence are somehow parallel. According to this thinking, if we have been able to become Lesbians in a heterosystem, then our very existence can be used to validate their assertion that heterosexuality is *their* choice. If resistance to heterosexuality is possible, then hetero-feminists can justify their belief that they, too, have made a 'choice.' Whereas in the past Lesbians were 'bad' because we didn't 'choose' hetero-sexuality, now we are 'good' because our lives are used to validate their 'choice.' This line of thought is evident in an editorial in a Quebec feminist magazine, *La Vie en Rose*. In this editorial, the magazine collective wrote that Adrienne Rich's article on com-pulsory heterosexuality had greatly influenced their reflection. What comes out of that 'reflection' is: '. . . But the existence of lesbianism gives all women the possibility of living heterosexuality with more freedom and less obligations and, ultimately, the possibility of choice.'[12] Our goal as Lesbians surely cannot be that we want to choose heterosexuality. For us, that cannot be what we mean by 'freedom.' And so we are used by feminists; our lives, the fact of our existence which they think should be impossible, are co-opted to feed the heterosystem. Our 'choice' thus guarantees the validity of theirs! Once one has recognized the 'compulsory nature' of heterosexuality she's rid of the obligation to follow the norm. She can now willingly follow, thus moving in a new direction, entering a new understand-ing of heterosexuality – consensual heterosexuality.

By this circuitous route, from compulsive heterosexuality we move on to a 'consensual' heterosexuality and we can view hetero-sexuality and lesbianism as sexual choices, leaving the political significance of those 'choices' to a non-threatening 'future' collective awareness.

The concept of compulsory/consensual heterosexualities is one and the same, undeniably linked to phallocracy. There cannot be any choice of one, or the other, and even less 'parallel/choice' between heterosexuality and lesbianism: domination and auto-nomy. How can one choose between the political institution of the dominators and the power of revolt of the dominated class? How can one compare the enforced accessibility of women with the sexual autonomy of lesbians?

Sexuality is power. The sexual subjugation of women leads to their economic, social, and political domination. Lesbians, who have no sexual relations with men therefore have an economic, political, and social perspective that goes beyond the M/F sexual categories.[13] To be a lesbian is to refuse to be a woman. That is not to say that lesbians are not viewed by the society at large as women and therefore oppressed as such, besides being repressed as lesbians.

455

Some lesbians cling to feminism because they say that lesbians are the ones who really apply feminist principles to our lives: 'Feminism is the theory, lesbianism is the practice.'[14] But how can we practice a theory that seeks to accommodate heterosexuality? Feminist movements, both the first and second waves, have always ignored lesbianism. And when they weren't denying our existence, they were guilt-tripping us for creating divisions among women and frightening them. Are we to suppose that rape, the heterosexual act par excellence, and woman-battering are not frightening? Who is really creating divisions: Man/Woman (hetero-) relations, or love of women? Feminism is neither our politics nor our history; it has never included 'non-political' and non-feminist lesbians. Hence the importance for radical lesbians to refer to feminism as HETEROFEMINISM.

Although our analysis differs from the separatist writings discussed earlier, a radical analysis nevertheless goes hand-in-hand with separatist practice. For us, separatist practice means breaking off from heterofeminism and the gay movement and living a life that revolves essentially around the increased visibility of lesbians as a political force capable of fighting all forms of hetero-oppression.

The similarity between radical and separatist lesbians is our lifestyle and our sense of lesbian ethics; and radicals have an even more evident political link with those separatists whose political affirmation is 'FOR, BY AND ABOUT LESBIANS' or 'FOR LESBIANS ONLY.' They start from the basis of their reality as lesbians, and although they fail to make the connection that lesbians are not women, in practice they work together as lesbians. It is important that any analysis of our oppressions be linked to an analysis of the cause of these oppressions: the hetero-system. Only we, as lesbians, can establish this link without compromise.

It should be impossible to analyse any type of oppression without making the connection that lesbianism signifies the eventual destruction of the hetero-patriarchal system.

Notes

1. During the 60s, the term 'Quebecers' gradually came to be used instead of 'French Canadians' to refer to the French-speaking inhabitants of Quebec – even though, to be exact, it designates the entire population of Quebec, 20% of which is not French-speaking. The term was adopted by Quebec separatists in order to stress their difference from the rest of Canada.
2. Since the 60s, Quebecers have associated the term 'separatist' with the fight for national independence and separation from Canada. The words 'lesbianism' and 'separatism' are therefore rarely associated in Quebec, since confusion would be inevitable. The question of lesbianism

and nationalism (i.e. separatism) in Quebec is the subject of an article which I am now writing and which I hope to publish in English. (Ariane Brunet)

3. Taken from Anne Michaud's article on the experience of Quebec lesbians at the 1982 Michigan festival, published in the review *Amazones d'hier, Lesbiennes d'aujourd'hui*, vol. I, no. 2–3, December 1982.

4. The first version of this article was published in *Amazones d'hier, Lesbiennes d'aujourd'hui*, vol. I, no. 2–3, December 1982.

5. See Note 2.

6. In the video '*Amazones d'hier, Lesbiennes d'aujourd'hui*,' Ariane Brunet puts forth the idea that there were two periods in Amazon history: pre-matriarchal and post-matriarchal. She also makes a definite connection between the Amazons and lesbians.

7. This extract was translated into French in 1977, and then the original English could not be retraced; so the paragraph cited here is actually an English translation of the French translation of the original version.

8. *Feminismo Primero/Feminism First*, Tsunami Press, P.O. Box 22913, Seattle, WA 98122. $3.00.

9. Taken from a book written and published by Micheline Grimard-Leduc: *L'Île des Amantes*, available from Micheline Grimard-Leduc, P.O. Box 461, Station N, Montreal, Quebec H2X 3N3. $8.00 (CAN).

10. This concept was first developed and explained by Monique Wittig in her article 'On ne nait pas femme,' in the review *Questions Feministes* #8 (May 1980). You can get those articles translated in English in a magazine called *Feminist Issues* from San Francisco.

11. This idea was discussed by Adrienne Rich in 'Compulsory Heterosexuality and Lesbian Existence,' in the review *Signs: Journal of Women in Culture and Society* 5, 4 (Summer 1980).

12. Translated by Ariane Brunet from the 'Editorial' of *La Vie en Rose* (June, July, August 1982).

13. Monique Wittig 'La Pensée Straight,' in *Questions Feministes* 7 (February 1980). Available in English in *Feminist Issues*.

14. A herstory of this phrase can be found in *A Feminist Dictionary*, ed. Cheris Kramarae and Paula A. Treichler (Boston: Pandora Press, 1985), pp. 160 and 229. [Eds]

Splits in French Feminism/Lesbianism

Marthe Rosenfeld
U.S.A., 1986

To English-speaking audiences feminism in France often evokes images of ivory tower intellectuals debating with one another

457

about conflicting and abstruse theories. While a large body of theoretical writing on different aspects of female oppression has appeared in francophone books, journals and leaflets, the Mouvement de Libération des Femmes, known as the MLF is as activist as women's liberation movements in other parts of the world. Indeed one of the characteristics of the 'new' feminism which emerged in the wake of the student-worker rebellion of May 1968 was the participants' attempt to maintain a closer relationship between their personal experiences and their political involvement.[1] For example, a number of feminists in the early 70's demonstrated their solidarity with women on strike at a hat factory in Troyes and they discovered in the process the numerous oppressions of their working-class sisters.[2] Similarly a group of unmarried mothers, often denigrated within the MLF, showed their support for the female strikers at the cloth mills of le Plessis Robinson and Issy les Moulineaux.[3] Another characteristic of the women's liberation movement in France in the early 1970's was the variety of groups such as the Petites Marguerites which later became the Féministes Révolutionnaires, the Trotskyite Cercle Elisabeth Dmitriev, the group of the University of Paris at Vincennes where the first 'women only' discussions took place, neighborhood groups in Paris, Marseilles, Lyons. This proliferation of groups revealed a desire on the part of the women to find ways of taking action in opposition to the rigid discipline of traditional party politics; they insisted on keeping the women's liberation movement open to everyone and to different ideas, without structures, without a leader, without a name.[4]

In August 1970 a handful of people went to the Arc de Triomphe to try to break the wall of silence which surrounded the oppressive conditions of women by placing a wreath on the tomb of the unknown wife of the soldier. But the police quickly arrested and later released the demonstrators. When the media reported this event using the term *Mouvement de Libération des Femmes* by analogy with the American women's liberation movement, it had given a name unwittingly to the feminist movement in France.[5] The importance of such a movement appeared in light of the terrible dilemma which teen-age girls and women with unwanted pregnancies were facing at that time. To expose the horror of the repressive laws driving those in need of an abortion to resort to dangerous practices and remedies, women of the MLF collected signatures in 1971 from figures of the stage, the screen, the intellectual world as well as from unknown people willing to defy the government by stating that they had had an illegal abortion. The militants among the signatories demanded that abortion become available free of charge. The Manifesto of the 343 as this appeal came to be known, like the demonstration at the Arc de Triomphe, received wide publicity in the press and thus helped to bring the MLF closer to women in different parts of the country. But the initial willingness of various groups to work collectively towards common goals soon gave way to dissensions and disagreements.

Two principal currents began to coalesce around this time: the Féministes Révolutionnaires represented by such early radical feminists as Christine Delphy and Monique Wittig and Psychanalyse et Politique headed by psychoanalyst Antoinette Fouque. While the former identified with the struggles of the suffragettes, believing as they did in the value of militant action to fight for women as a class,[6] the latter preferred to discuss such issues as female sexuality, women's relationship to writing and to the unconscious, the development of a 'feminine' identity.[7] Unlike the Féministes Révolutionnaires who reject the socially constructed image of woman, Psychanalyse et Politique basically accepts society's definition of the genders, influencing their followers to extricate all 'masculine' traits from themselves.[8] The conflict which pitted the Féministes Révolutionnaires against Psychanalyse et Politique reflected profound ideological differences between these two groups.

One of the characteristics of the women's liberation movement in France has been the diversity of its tendencies as well as the multiplicity of its groups. While the majority of the women in the movement appreciated the freedom of expression which this wide choice afforded, Psychanalyse et Politique accused the others, particularly the Féministes Révolutionnaires, of subordinating the ideals of the MLF to personal ambitions. Believing that they constituted the only real challenge to the patriarchy, Psychanalyse et Politique did not hesitate to monopolize and eventually cancel the feminist meetings held at the Beaux Arts school in Paris.[9]

In 1973 Psychanalyse et Politique founded a publishing house under the name of des femmes (women/of women/some women). Those who had used this generic term to sign their own texts or leaflets viewed this development with misgivings, for they were now compelled to find another signature. Others however looked favorably on the fact that women were beginning to take responsibility for bringing out the results of their creative efforts.[10] The following year Psych et Po opened the first of their des femmes bookstores in Paris. Only in 1976 when three of their authors (Monique Piton, Erin Pizzey and Mireille Deconynck, ex-

Barbara) testified in public of the difficulties they encountered in their relations with that group and when the editors of des femmes turned the tables on the plaintiffs by suing them for slander did a large number of women in the movement break off with Psych et Po and its various companies.[11] October 6, 1979, three years after this incident, when 50,000 women marched in Paris for legalized abortion, Psychanalyse et Politique, which had joined that project late in the game, seized control of the head of the demonstration not in its own name but in the name of the Mouvement de Libération des Femmes. Facing the cameras and the journalists they tried to give the outside world the impression that their own questionable slogans represented the views of the entire procession.[12]

For a long time a tyrannical sect had asserted its authority abroad as the only true representative of the women's liberation movement in France. But it went even further when it transformed itself that very year into a legal association consistent with the law of 1901. The initial MLF had now become the exclusive property of Psych et Po.[13] This crude appropriation of the title of a highly diverse movement posed a grave danger for its future growth and development. By seizing feminist names and symbols for itself Psych et Po tried not only to gain control over the rest of the movement but to undermine it as well.[14] Thus the group's monthly publication *Des Femmes en Mouvement* which drew a completely reactionary picture of feminism as one of the main pillars of Western bourgeois societies, continued to erode the vitality of the French women's liberation movement. Although feminists tried periodically to combat the power politics and distortions of Psych et Po, their fear of revealing to a hostile world the spectacle of internecine quarrels and conflicts prevented them from bringing the matter to a wider public.[15]

Less divisive than the enmities which separated Psychanalyse et Politique from the rest of the women's liberation movement is the recurring split between Marxists and radical feminists. On the one hand MLF groups such as the Femmes en lutte and the Cercle Dmitriev not only advocated the overthrow of the capitalist system, they also believed that the struggle for a classless society would lead to the liberation of women.[16] On the other hand radical feminists such as Christine Delphy and Monique Wittig, though in sympathy with the workers, rejected the notion of class struggle as a theoretical basis for the development of an autonomous women's movement.

In an article entitled *L'ennemi principal* Christine Delphy shows that the link between work and remuneration is not the same for women as it is for men. Because of the division of labor based on gender, wives in patriarchal societies are expected to raise the children and to do the housekeeping in exchange for their support but without any monetary compensation. When working outside of the house, they continue to be held responsible for domestic services and thus face a double work load. The male wage earner on the other hand sells his work for a fixed salary and with a clearly spelled out time frame.[17] Since classes according to Marx are defined by the worker's relationship to capital, his theory could not account for women's exploitation within the family. Hence Delphy's belief that we as an oppressed people should make alliances only with those revolutionary groups committed to destroying the patriarchy.[18] Monique Wittig similarly opposes the Marxist theory of class struggle, for she believes that we as a subjugated group under patriarchy constitute a distinct class, indeed that we are the real proletarians.[19]

In view of the priority which radical feminists give to female issues and of the strict discipline of leftist political organizations, French women would find it difficult to maintain the class struggle approach. The problem of working in mixed groups would be compounded by the burden of dual loyalties. Many women in the class struggle current would find it necessary therefore to move away from the MLF or to leave the organized Left.[20]

But the toughest conflict of all proved to be the feminist/lesbian rift – a rift which shook the French women's liberation movement to the core. This split, which would develop into a major battle in the 1980's, began to appear in the movement from its inception. Thus the lesbians who had been working since the early 1970's on the most visible aspects of women's oppression: rape, enforced pregnancy, domestic labor, the relationships between women and men, found themselves excluded by heterosexual women in the MLF as soon as they tried to bring up the question of lesbian invisibility.[21] To fight against this censorship the lesbians created a new group in 1971, the Gouines Rouges (the Red Dykes). But their voices were quickly submerged by the large number of gay men who tended to monopolize the discussions at the General Assemblies of feminists and gays.[22]

As an early militant who had witnessed the erasure of lesbianism within the movement again and again, Monique Wittig tried in 1975 to organize a lesbian Front. Seeking above all to challenge the institution of heterosexuality with its oppressive roles and norms, this group would break with the MLF as well as with the feminism of homosexuals and heterosexuals. However, fears that this separatist position would lead to an enormous backlash turned many women against that project.[23] The quarrel between lesbianism and heterosexuality as political strategies was not new therefore when *Questions féministes* reopened the debate in 1980, but it assumed a particularly harsh and public stance. As both sides expressed their points of view in that journal, a brief history of the magazine should help to untangle the different strands of the argument.

In 1977 five radical feminists: Colette Capitan Peter, Christine Delphy, Emmanuèle de Lesseps, Nicole-Claude Mathieu and Monique Plaza founded the collective and the journal which went by the name of *Questions féministes*. Like Simone de Beauvoir, who had agreed to be the senior editor of that magazine, the members of the collective as well as the other contributors argued that the laws, the customs, the institutions of the dominant culture have built the myth of woman as a creature belonging to a weaker group and that this myth, which passes as a 'natural' phenomenon, has been used by the ruling class to keep us powerless.[24] In a lead article of *Questions féministes* on the appropriation of women, a text which was to serve as a guide for the radical lesbians, Colette Guillaumin coined the word 'sexage' after the word 'esclavage,' a term which brings out the similarity throughout history between the appropriation of slaves by the dominant class and the appropriation of women by the class of men.[25]

Differences of opinion began to surface between the radical and moderate factions of the collective around 1979. But the seventh issue of *Questions féministes* brought the debate between lesbianism and heterosexuality into the open thanks to the publication of two major articles. One of these by Monique Wittig entitled *La pensée straight* shows that the existence of a heterosexual discourse, which tends to universalize the straight point of view, is oppressive not only to lesbians and gay men but to all women, indeed to all those who are 'in the position of the dominated.' The other, an essay by Emmanuèle de Lesseps called *Hétérosexualité et féminisme* analyzes the compatibility of heterosexual desire with feminism and concludes that one can be both feminist and heterosexual though not without contradiction.[26] While the former article does not mention the heterosexual feminists, the latter views lesbianism as a tendency already determined in childhood and thus denies the element of choice as well as the political dimension of sexuality.

Passionate debates on this number of the magazine in which lesbians began to articulate their vision of the world spilled over into the French women's liberation movement. From March to June 1980 various factions of the MLF organized meetings, debates and demonstrations to discuss such questions as the conflict between heterosexuality and feminism, strategies to combat rape and violence, the desirability or non-desirability of participating as feminists in the other struggles of our time. But the radical lesbians of Jussieu criticized the stifling of political lesbianism within the movement as well as the secrecy surrounding past quarrels.[27] In the heat of the debate which pitted feminists against lesbians, insults flew back and forth. Indeed the absence of any communication or dialogue between the two sides reinforced the myths and the rumors which circulated against the lesbians.[28]

The same issues which separated the lesbians from the feminists in the movement also brought about a split in the collective of *Questions féministes*. In June 1980 the radical lesbians of Jussieu organized a meeting in a hall where other lesbians had displayed posters that criticized heterofeminism for its complicity with the patriarchal system. The initiators of the conference wanted to present their own position papers for discussion. But the heterosexual feminists preferred to discuss the less explicit posters. From this meeting came forth the caricature 'hétéro-collabo . . .' a term which gave the lesbians in the movement a bad name and the resentment which had accumulated against them now exploded. On the one hand a homosexual and a heterosexual feminist decided to oust the most visible lesbian in the collective unless she repudiated her position; on the other hand two lesbians and another woman made common cause with the challenged member, thus expressing their choice for radical lesbianism. As neither side could lay claim to a homogeneous membership, the rift was not due to the defence of 'sexual interests,' it grew out of a basic ideological conflict. Nevertheless the group agreed by common consent to produce another issue of *Questions féministes*, a last number which would serve as an open forum for the expression of every point of view. But in spite of the lesbian group's repeated affirmation of the importance of such a debate for the movement as well as for the readers of *Questions féministes*, the other side reneged on its commitment.[29]

In October 1980, *Questions féministes* as well as its collective, which had been legally registered according to the 1901 law governing newspapers and periodicals, dissolved over the conflict between lesbianism, heterosexuality and feminism. Having shared the ideological position of the first editorial and contributed to the magazine's unique point of view, all the members had signed a written agreement October 24 pledging never to publish another review that would bear the title *Questions féministes*.[30] Four months after this event the lesbians learned, through an interview which Simone de Beauvoir had given to *La Revue d'En Face*, that the other party of the ex-collective was publishing *Nouvelles questions féministes*: the same title, the same graphic appearance, the same budget, but with the adjunct 'new' in front of it.[31] To expose this breach of faith, the lesbian group, after numerous efforts towards a private resolution of the conflict, including a visit to Simone de Beauvoir and to Editions Tierce, the first publisher of the magazine, had no choice but to take the matter to court.[32] The trial, contrary to the rumors that the other side of the collective circulated, focused exclusively on such publishing issues as titles, copyright laws, format and the material means of production of a journal.

A tragic irony of the splits in the French women's liberation movement is the fact that some of the people who condemned the imposture of the group Psychanalyse et Politique, its falseness, its distortion of events, its unjust appropriation of a name, are the very same ones as those who silenced the lesbians and who destroyed *Questions féministes*. In the '70's Psychanalyse et Politique, with its obsessive desire to become the sole representative of the women's liberation movement in France, used the acronym MLF in the hope of controlling, manipulating and ultimately discrediting the feminist struggle.[33] In the early '80's a minority faction of the radical feminist magazine *Questions féministes* took over the journal, eliminated five lesbians from its collective and proceeded to launch another review, using the same title, but with the well-known advertising device of the word 'new' in front of it. To justify this annexation of a name as well as the purge of five lesbians, Delphy labeled the ousted group as 'lesbian separatists.'[34]

A major consequence of the death of *Questions féministes* is the loss of a place in which radical lesbians can publicly express their vision of the world and their theories. The pretence that *Nouvelles questions féministes* continues the work of the original magazine is a concomitant result of this drama. For the similarity of that title must not conceal the fact that the lesbian voices were excluded from the collective and that the radical lesbian analyses which had given *Questions féministes* its unique character died with that magazine. Moreover, the erroneous opinion, first expounded by Delphy, that the radical lesbians are responsible for the divisions within the movement is being reiterated in a more recent account of the events. Thus even Claire Duchen, who presents both sides of the question, implies in her book, *Feminism in France from May '68 to Mitterand*, that lesbianism, by claiming to be a subversive practice, creates a hierarchy of political correctness which also divides women.[35] This argument ignores the fundamental inequality between lesbians and heterosexual feminists in a world which recognizes only heterosexuality and which condemns us to silence. It is not the lesbians who divided the movement or who brought *Questions féministes* to its untimely end; once more it is the power of the class of men which has divided us.

Marked by struggle, argumentation and dissension, the splits in French Feminism/lesbianism are exemplary in many ways of the tensions and conflicts which have divided women's liberation movements in other countries as well. One of the lessons which emerges from this tumultuous history is that without the courage to challenge those forces that oppress us both from within and from outside, without a passion for justice and a thirst for the truth, our movement as a revolutionary force for social change will disintegrate.

Notes

1.   The term 'new' feminism is used to distinguish the MLF from earlier feminisms, currents which hark back to the time of the French Revolution.
2.   Cathy Bernheim, 'C'est la vérité . . . mais c'est pas une raison pour le dire,' in *Chroniques d'une imposture*, ed., Association du Mouvement pour les luttes féministes, (Paris: Primavera, 1981), p. 7.
3.   Feminist leaflet dated February 2, 1972 in the 1972 file of documents on the *Mouvement de Libération des Femmes*, Bibliothèque Marguerite Durand, Paris.
4.   Cathy Bernheim, *Chroniques*, p. 5.
5.   Anne Tristan and Annie de Pisan, *Histoires du M.L.F.*, préf. Simone de Beauvoir (Paris: Calmann-Lévy, 1977), p. 55.
6.   Monique Wittig et al., 'Pour un mouvement de libération des femmes' (original title), *L'Idiot International* (May 1970).
7.   'Interview with Antoinette Fouque', remarks gathered by Catherine Clément, *Le Matin*, 16 July, 1980, p. 13.
8.   Anita Rinda, 'Le MLF en récollection', newspaper clipping in the folder of documents on *Psychanalyse et Politique*, Bibliothèque Marguerite Durand.
9.   Cathy Bernheim, *Chroniques*, p. 13.
10.   *Ibid.*, pp. 14–15.
11.   MLF group calling itself *Notre mouvement nous appartient*, 'Vous avez dit "commercial"?' in *Chroniques*, p. 8.
12.   *Ibid.*, pp. 8–9.
13.   *Ibid.*, p. 10.
14.   Marie-Jo Dhavernas, 'Des divans profonds comme des tombeaux', *Chroniques*, pp. 1–10.
15.   Simone de Beauvoir, préface in *Chroniques*; see also Christine Delphy, 'Libération des femmes an dix,' *Questions féministes*, 7 (February 1980), pp. 3–13.

16. Feminist leaflet distributed in Brussels to the International tribunal of crimes against women (March 1976), in the folder of that date on the MLF, Bibliothèque M. Durand.

17. Christine Delphy, 'L'ennemi principal', in *Partisans, Libération des femmes: année zéro*, Nos. 54–55 (July-October 1970), pp. 122–171; trans. 'The Main Enemy,' *Feminist Issues*, 1, No. 1 (Summer 1980), pp. 23–40.

18. *Ibid.*, p. 172.

19. Wittig, 'Pour un mouvement de libération des femmes', *L'Idiot International*.

20. Claire Duchen, *Feminism in France from May '68 to Mitterand* (London: Routledge and Kegan Paul, 1986), pp. 27–30.

21. 'Monique Wittig et les lesbiennes barbues', interview with Wittig by the magazine *Actuel* in *Mainmise*, Montréal (May 1974), pp. 63–64.

22. *Ibid.*

23. For a parable of the negative attitudes in the movement which prevailed in the French capital, see Monique Wittig, 'Paris-La-Politique', *Vlasta*, No. 4 (May 1985), pp. 11–41.

24. 'Variations sur des thèmes communs', editorial article, *Questions féministes*, 1 (November 1977), pp. 3–19; trans. 'Variations on Some Common Themes', *Feminist Issues*, 1, No. 1 (Summer 1980), pp. 3–21.

25. Colette Guillaumin, 'Pratique du pouvoir et idée de Nature (1) L'appropriation des femmes', *Questions féministes*, 2 (February 1978), pp. 8–9, 21–23; trans., 'The Practice of Power and Belief in Nature Part I: The Appropriation of Women', *Feminist Issues*, 1 No. 2 (Winter 1981), pp. 3–28.

26. Monique Wittig, 'La pensée straight', *Questions féministes*, 7 (February 1980), p. 50 and Emmanuèle de Lesseps, 'Hétérosexualité et féminisme', *Questions féministes*, 7 (February 1980), pp. 55–69. Wittig's article was translated under the title: 'The Straight Mind', *Feminist Issues*, 1, No. 1 (Summer 1980), pp. 103–111.

27. Des lesbiennes féministes radicales de l'ex-collectif Q.F., 'Lettre au Mouvement Féministe, Paris 1ᵉʳ mars, 1981', *Amazones d'hier Lesbiennes d'aujourd'hui*, 1 No. 1, Montréal (June 1982), p. 38.

28. *Ibid.*, p. 34.

29. *Ibid.*, p. 36.

30. *Ibid.*, p. 37.

31. 'Sur quelques problèmes du féminisme: entretien avec Simone de Beauvoir', interview carried out by Geneviève Brisac, Marie-Jo Dhavernas, Irène Théry. *La Revue d'en face*, Nos. 9–10 (first trimester 1981), p. 14.

32. Letter by the radical lesbian feminists of the ex-collective Q.F. to Adrienne Rich et al., *Amazones d'hier Lesbiennes d'aujourd'hui*, 1, No. 1, Montréal (June 1982), pp. 40–41.

33. Liliane Kandel, 'Une presse "anti-féministe" aujourd'hui "Des Femmes en Mouvements" ', *Questions féministes*, 7 (February 1980), pp. 37–44.

34. 'Interview with Christine Delphy: French Feminist', carried out by L. Cottingham in *off our backs*, 14 No. 3 (March 1984), pp. 10–11.

35. Duchen, *Feminism in France*, pp. 22–25.

Motherhood

Claudie Lesselier
France, 1981

(Translated by Anna Livia)

There is a pro-motherhood trend developing in the States, for example, particularly among lesbian separatists. Here in Europe the same opinions are being expressed, as is born out by the discussions we had at the conference in June 1980, and the first issues of the Genevan lesbian journal, CLIT 007. One article in CLIT discusses the different methods women are experimenting with to conceive a child without masculine intervention. It seems that many lesbians are waiting impatiently for the right method: 'Tomorrow, according to the latest rumour, a woman will be able to have a child all by herself. Two women will be able to have one together. It'll be fantastic, a lesbian dream come true.' (The woman who typed the journal seems to have escaped the collective delirium). No analysis of the social significance of motherhood, of why lesbians want children. The only problem discussed is the risk that all this research will come to nought because 'men are too worried about the power they have over us via their paternity to allow it to be taken from them.'

My immediate reaction was surprise as I've never, even as a little girl, remotely wanted a child. I could not imagine being responsible for someone else. I have never been able to identify as a 'mother'; had I been tempted, my experience of family oppression, and my analysis of it, would quickly have dissuaded me! Someone might say that since I don't have any children, and don't want any at any price, I have no right to talk about motherhood. That would be to treat it as a private affair, not a social, political question. If, however, it is absolutely necessary to trot out personal experience, I am the daughter of a 'mother' (of a father, too) and it wasn't all bad either!

So I joined an FLR[1] group which was working on motherhood, a group which did not function terribly well. Motherhood is one of those issues which everyone agrees it is impossible to discuss with even a minimum of objectivity, distance[2] from one's own

467

experience and contradictions and those of other women. This paper, therefore represents no one's opinions but my own.

I think it is vital to understand HOW MOTHERHOOD IN OUR SOCIETY IS A CONSTRAINT, AN OPPRESSION, AND, AT THE SAME TIME, VALIDATED. THAT DEMANDING 'THE FUNCTION OF A MOTHER' IS IN DIRECT CONTRADICTION TO OUR STRUGGLE. That said, I would like to make it clear that I would never criticise a lesbian for having had children; I do not have to face the problems she now faces. What I am criticising, and find contradictory to radical lesbianism, is that a lesbian should demand the SOCIAL STATUS OF A MOTHER, should raise her 'function as a mother', or someone else's, in discussion. How can a woman who has broken away from society want to bear children for that society?

The subjection of women to a reproductive function, in whose name they are forbidden some roles, forced into others, kept out of some areas and confined to others, is an essential element in the systematic exploitation and oppression of women by men. In short, it is a function which justifies the social division and hierarchy of the sexes, a device to lock women inside 'woman's nature'. Compulsory motherhood may vary in strength depending on the society and the period, but it is always there.[3]

It is accompanied, however, by an IDEOLOGICAL APPARATUS OF POSSIBLY UNRIVALLED PROPORTIONS

- guilt: women are considered (and consider themselves), incomplete, unfulfilled if they are not and never have been 'mothers';
- validation of the reproductive function in the 'motherhood ideal';
- exaltation and exaggeration of 'motherly love';
- compulsory motherhood is internalised as 'desire for a child'.

It is interesting to summarise, briefly, how this ideological apparatus has been constructed in the West. The ideology of motherly love, 'obligatory love' as Elisabeth Badinter calls it,[4] developed toward the end of the eighteenth, beginning of the nineteenth century alongside the confinement of women to the home (and the confinement of children to the home, and the development of institutions designed to support or replace the family). At the same time a whole network of controls over the work of 'mothers' was built up (medical, philanthropic, legal and psychological). We might also consider the more recent evolution in attitudes toward, and legislation about, unmarried mothers which Odile Dhavernas outlines (in 'Droit des Femmes, Pouvoir des Hommes' ['Women's Right, Men's Power'], Editions du Seuil).

There has been a development in the family structure towards a 'mother-child' unit, which is much more stable than that of a male-female couple, the father being either absent or variable.

The conclusion I draw is, essentially, this: A MOTHER IS NOT SIMPLY A WOMAN WHO HAS CHILDREN ... SHE IS A WOMAN DEFINED BY HER CHILDREN, A WOMAN ENCLOSED IN HER FUNCTION, A FUNCTION IN WHICH SHE IS BOTH OPPRESSED AND VALUED.[5] According to Freud, the child is the woman's 'penis substitute'. It would be difficult to find a more forthright admission that the reproductive function both reproduces and shores up the phallocratic system whereby women are worthless while mothers are valued; or, to make the contradictions clearer, for a woman who is aware of what is at stake to embrace this function willingly.

In my opinion it is essential not only that radical lesbians fight against this role which has been foisted on women, but also analyse how 'the desire for a child' is a purely social phenomenon, denounce, and refuse to be part of overvaluing the maternal role. I think it is wishful-thinking to imagine you can be a 'different kind of mother' in this society, bring your children up 'differently' so they escape social norms, so your son does not grow up a male chauvinist, nor your daughter repeat the patterns of oppression. Wishful-thinking also to imagine you can avoid the fundamentally dependent nature of the mother-child relationship, with all its consequences including the rebellion of the dependent. Wishful-thinking to imagine you can produce children without re-producing society. It seems to me that a lesbian in particular who wants to become a 'lesbian mother' is in fact only asking to be recognised as a 'normal woman', TAKING ON, DEMANDING, THE STATUS OF OPPRESSION, AN OPPRESSION GIVEN SOCIAL VALUE BECAUSE OF ITS FUNCTION. The desire to be recognised as a 'good mother' despite, (or because of?) one's lesbianism is evident in CUARH and FAHM[6] demands around divorce.

This leads me to the mother-daughter relationship, from the daughter's point of view ... a very complicated relationship which a lot of women (myself included) have found particularly painful.[7] The mother's role in the family is to transmit to her daughter, in the name of the father, patriarchal values, obligations and prohibitions. Because of the mother's function, if the daughter rebels, her rebellion and hatred are directed at her mother. Her father, less involved in day to day repression, can play the good guy, his reputation unscathed. Oppression comes basically from men as a class, thus from the father of whom the mother is only an instrument ... but I will not accept that she is a purely passive instrument. She is, only too often, responsible for her part in the process of reproducing oppression.

The only solution to this conflict is to destroy the mother-daughter relationship and replace it with a woman to woman relationship involving equality and the possibility of exploring contradictions with an objectivity and political consciousness unknown in any 'mother-daughter dialogue'. Feasible? Very rarely.

Psychiatry or, more precisely, child therapy is relentless in its attack on the 'devouring', 'suffocating', even 'castrating' mother, cause of all the child's problems, thus avoiding any examination of the alienating and oppressive mechanisms at work in the family.[8] Monique Plaza elaborates: 'I suspect that the vast apparatus of hatred against mothers is one of the most prodigious and effective bastions of misogyny'[9]. Certainly, but it is important to distinguish clearly between the hatred of men and the hatred daughters may feel toward their mothers.

Where does men's hatred come from? Or rather, why does their hatred of women take that particular form, which seems to contradict the high value placed on mothers? Could they be jealous of the capacity to have children? Might they even desire to seize this power from women and make it their own?[10] We know that in ancient times men were ignorant of their role in reproduction. According to some anthropologists (Cf Evelyn Reed 'Anthropologie et Feminisme' ['Anthropology and Feminism'], Denoel) the discovery of paternity was one of the causes of the enslavement of women in monogamous marriage and in society generally. Numerous myths, and male fantasies, would appear to reveal a fundamental fear in men of women and women's sexuality; perhaps their fascination with 'the creation of life', an act which is so mysterious to them, transforms into hatred[11] ...

Following these questions, which hardly begin to scratch the surface, I would like to end by stressing the need for a radical lesbian examination of the structure of the family, the oppression of children and adult-child relationships.

The oppression of children, of 'minors', has its roots in the family and extends to the whole ensemble of their social status. Lack of freedom, lack of choice over all the important aspects of their lives, absence of legal rights, denial of their sexuality, material dependence ...[12] What is the relationship between the oppression of women and the oppression of children? Can adult-child relationships, or rather women-girl relationships, be other than power relations? Could a children's (girls') struggle have links with our own? If so, how can we encourage it? Etc...

Few women have spoken about paedophilia, though it is highly probable that some lesbians have experienced it. Gay men contend that the paedophilic relationship is the antithesis of the suffocating, possessive maternal relationship, of confinement in the family. They assert that they do not exert power over the child but, on the contrary, allow him to express his desire and exercise his autonomy. (Cf the works of Tony Duvert . . .)

Adult-child relations in institutions outside the family are almost all the province of women, in the context of the 'feminine professions'. These professions were the first, moreover, to be open to women (apart from clerical and manual work) and are often claimed by women themselves as their 'natural vocation'. Can a lesbian involved in these professions have a different kind of relationship with the children, or does the institutional framework wipe out any initiative she may take?

As women THEY WANT US PERPETUALLY TIED TO CHILDHOOD IN ONE WAY OR ANOTHER: as a mother, an elder sister, nursery teacher, children's song writer . . . 'WOMEN AND CHILDREN FIRST'. Both weak, dependent beings . . . CAN WE SUBVERT THIS LINK IN ANY WAY? OR SHOULD OUR PRIORITY BE TO DESTROY IT, REFUSE TO REPRODUCE IT IN ANY FORM, EXPOSE THE VALIDATION OF OPPRESSION, BEFORE BUILDING, ON ENTIRELY DIFFERENT BASES, RELATIONSHIPS BETWEEN INDIVIDUALS?

Notes

1. Front Lesbien Radical (Radical Lesbian Front).
2. I believe that for any collective discussion, any work on our lives and contradictions to take place, and get anywhere, distance and objectivity (wherever possible) are basic requirements.
3. When the Eighteenth Century economists were considering the importance of the population factor, reproduction was the first so-called 'private' event to be given social and political status. In this way motherhood was brought, legitimately, under the sway of power politics. Cf, for example, the repressive measures which were brought in after the First World War in France against the neo-malthusians and those, more radical, who called for a 'womb strike' (Ronsin, *La grève des ventres*, [The Womb Strike], Aubier). Cf fascism and nazism, cf Mediterranean and African societies etc . . . as concerns violence and forced motherhood.
4. E. Badinter, *L'amour en plus* [may be translated as either 'Love into the bargain' or 'Love extra', translator's note] Denoel; numerous historical works on the evolution of the family; Donzelot *La police des familles* [Policing the family], Minuit; *Disciplines à domicile* [Discipline at home], *Recherches* No. 28.
5. Feminists have widely denounced the slavery of motherhood, the

burden of unpaid labour and alienation which bringing up children entails etc... (Cf *Maternité esclave* [Motherhood enslaved], written collectively, 10/18). They seldom denounce the other aspects ... (They must, however, be aware of them as so many of them have children.)

6. Femmes Accusées d'Homosexualité et Maternité [Women Accused of Homosexuality and Motherhood]. A group in Lyons which is fighting for divorced lesbians to get custody of their children.

7. There are numerous works on this subject, and on motherhood in general: Luce Irigaray *L'une ne bouge pas sans l'autre*, [One does not move without the other] Minuit; Monique Plaza, 'La même mère [The same mother] *QF* [*Questions Feministes*] No. 7; Adrienne Rich *Naître d'une femme* [Of Woman Born] Denoel [Virago]; Christine Ollivier *Les enfants de Jocaste* [Jocasta's children], Denoel; Nancy Friday *Ma mère mon miroir* [My mother my mirror] Laffont etc...

Bellotti (*Du coté des petites filles* [Little Girls]) and C. Ollivier (above) show that mothers do not generally treat their daughters with the same tenderness, nor the same sexualised gestures as they do their sons ... Does this not create the lesbian prohibition, the prohibition of love between women?

8. Except the anti-psychiatry movement which denounces the family as the cause of mental illness. Cf D. Cooper *Mort de la famille*, [Death of the Family], R. D. Laing *La Santé, la maladie mentale et la famille* [Health, Mental Illness and the Family]. Though they certainly don't write from the perspective of male-female class struggle and I have many reservations about their theories.

9. 'La même mère', *Questions Feministes* No. 7.

10. Hammer and Aller's hypothesis in 'La science de la reproduction', *QF* No. 5.

11. See W. Lederer *La peur des femmes* [Fear of Women] and Carloni and Nobili *La mauvaise mère*, [The Bad Mother], Payot.

12. See Christiane Rochefort *Les enfants d'abord*, [Children First], Grasset.

Feminism and Radical Lesbianism

Claudie, Graziella, Irene, Martine, Françoise
1981

(Translated by Anna Livia)

This article comes from the work and discussions of five lesbians in the Front.[1] It is not a definitive statement. It is simply the formulation of questions, lines of reflection, and the beginnings of an analysis. It will, of course, be developed during and after the conference.[2]

We have kept the same method of presentation as we used in our work, that is a written framework showing the genesis of our discussions, and a point by point critique of this framework.

A. Our Critique of Feminism

1. Repressive, guilt-tripping practices toward lesbians. Profiting from their energy and their work while forcing them to deny their lesbianism. Accusing lesbians who want to be visible of 'being divisive'. Discrimination, scorn or indifference toward 'apolitical' gay women.

Critique

Repression of Lesbianism should not be put first in a critique of Feminism. Only in some groups has it taken on an all-inclusive form (negation of the very existence of lesbians; paying attention only to purely heterosexual problems). It has only been politically promoted against political lesbians (not against lesbian feminists) i.e. those who sought to establish an all-encompassing political movement based on Lesbianism. In radical feminist groups, for example, lesbian feminists active in the MLF [French Women's Liberation Movement], working on questions of 'identity' politics, have been completely accepted.

'Divisiveness' – an accusation levelled particularly at political lesbians as soon as they expressed the remotest desire for an autonomous movement, or made any analysis criticising the heterosystem to any extent. The complaint that 'lesbians cause divisions between women' seems to us to come, essentially, via the theory of spontaneous stages. This is a theory that each woman must climb a certain number of rungs in the ladder before she reaches the platform of Feminism and Homosexuality. It is suggested that women have only a partial knowledge of oppression, which they must digest before passing on to the next rung. It is our duty, of course, to feed them each crumb of wisdom, putting all our energy into the task, but only giving them one little mouthful at a time.

But this technique: a) is always accompanied by the terrible fear of 'isolation' as though a woman becoming conscious of oppression would take fright and gallop away. At the end of the day, 'consciousness', knowledge, remains an object of terror, something negative which can only hinder the struggle. b) always entails constructing a monolithic mass movement for the majority of women, merely gathered together as women, without clear political objectives. The final characteristic of this technique is to call all those who are not in favour of an immense heterosexual hotchpotch, its consciousness raised by slow degrees, terrorists. Saying what you think of the heterosystem i.e. of oppression, becomes an act of terrorism.[3]

2. No calling into question of heterosexuality as the *politics* of men as a class. At best, heterosexuality is challenged as the 'norm' in the name of sexual freedom, which amounts to placing Lesbianism and Heterosexuality on the same level, reducing the problem to a question of sexuality. Heterosexuality is even justified as a 'battle ground' for the struggle against men (and lesbians are nothing but cowardly deserters . . .) see *QF* [*Questions Feministes* – Feminist Questions] No. 7, E. de Lesseps 'Heterosexualite et Feminisme' [Heterosexuality and Feminism]. *La Revue d'en Face* [the Review Opposite] No. 9/10 special collaboration.

Critique
Develop the idea that heterosexuality = the politics of men as a class. The heterosystem in general, and heterosexuality in particular, make possible the material conditions necessary to them, and the ideology which they embody; these systems maintain the exploitation and oppression of women as a class by men as a class. The heterosystem is the very cornerstone of society; not challenging it, not endeavouring to destroy it, makes any so-called struggle for Women's Liberation hypocritical and pointless.

It seems to us of fundamental importance to repeat that heterosociality and heterosexuality are the essence (the very substance) of heteropatriarchal, or phallocratic power. Indeed, it is not possible, even as a strategy, to posit the existence of a patriarchy outside its own infrastructure, and subsequently a heterosociality and heterosexuality as an a-political invention. This has always been Feminist reasoning: to cut the concept of 'patriarchy' off from its essence, which permits them, in the final analysis, to 'fight' something immanent, disembodied, ephemeral, a kind of god (the symbolist campaign of psykepo is a direct expression of this Feminist theory). This idealism is evident in every Feminist analysis; power never has any basis, any roots, so there is no strategy to fight it. Everything becomes a series of abstractions, without connection, the class of men merely a collection of individuals.

3. Refusal to envisage a strategic separation from men: Feminist campaigns end, in fact, in an improvement, a recuperation of male/female relations (look at the problems of campaigns around abortion, contraception, employment, battered women, rape . . .)

Critique
The idea of strategic separation from men needs to be developed (an obvious consequence of challenging the heterosystem), shown as a refusal to collaborate with the oppressor class. Whereas feminism, even radical feminism, leads to a false struggle in which it denounces men as the enemy class, but conducts campaigns which aim only to reform and regulate life within the same system of exploitation and oppression.

4. Refusal to encourage all activists to develop their political theories (in other words, promoting a deliberate vagueness reinforcing the power of an elite and supporting the ideology that: 'Scientific method is a male value, lived experience and tangible reality is women's province . . .'). Thus no real attack on *naturalism*: in fact, *the feminist (facade of) anti-naturalism (ill-) conceals an anti-lesbian naturalism* (see S. de Beauvoir, *The Second Sex*, chapter on 'The Lesbian'). Moreover, anti-lesbianism can only be the expression of a naturalist concept.

Critique
The refusal to promote political development amongst all feminist activists is seen essentially in the affirmation (repeated above all by Delphy, cf *Nouvelles Questions Feministes* [New Feminist Questions] No. 1) of the 'diversity of the movement', as many MLFs as there are groups, etc. . . in effect implying the (naturalist) idea that any and every group of women is fighting oppression (whatever we do as women is Feminist, subversive etc. . .) One of these anarchosyndical pearls of wisdom being the Marais 1000,[4] a tendency which proved to be the quintessence of this cult of spontaneity. Each woman is a Feminist tendency in herself, no theory is possible. The movement is all-important, the objective counts for nothing. Hence the perpetual whirl of spinning-tops, a systematic questioning of every proposition, every analysis. It becomes a deliberate inability to draw any lessons from the past. But this doesn't fool us. It indicates the presence of a hidden leadership behind the scenes, a leadership which is the more

dangerous for not being structurally recognised. One of the consequences of this deliberate vagueness has been that all lesbian groups with similar positions have been accused of sectarianism and stalinism . . .

The idea that naturalism is anti-lesbian needs to be developed. Anti-political lesbianism: the refusal to see radical lesbianism as a political position, an attack on the phallocratic system. The assertion that lesbianism is merely a question of sexual preference can only be justified theoretically by a naturalist concept of desire (lesbians desire women not men). If 'desire' is not political, it can only be a question of nature (instinct, or to give it its more modern, psychoanalytic form: drive).

But, if desire, including men's desire, is not political, then heterosexuality must be seen as natural. It's very interesting to examine this position. We already knew that for Feminists heterosexuality is, basically, natural (even though they have made superficial declarations to the contrary) but this shows that for them, too, we continue to be seen as *against nature*.

It is obvious to us, on the other hand, that lesbianism is anti-naturalist, not only because it is political, but also because, consciously or not, it is antagonistic to feminisation. That some lesbians still consider themselves against nature is another problem.

5. Ambiguity of the term 'feminism'. The predominant meaning of this term is 'fighting for women', whereas we want to destroy Men and Women as social categories. The term Radical Lesbianism makes separation from men very clear (see Monique Wittig *QF* no. 8).

Note: Some Radical Lesbians have made the following objection:
- why can't we retain the term Feminism and give it our own meaning?
- Isn't the term '*heterofeminism*' more accurate in understanding our criticisms?

Critique
The term 'Feminist'
- generally speaking being a feminist means fighting for women
- there's a short step from here to 'Feminism equals woman', thus to be anti-feminist can only mean being anti-woman. (We need to think about the naturalist origin of this position).
1. Feminism is the theory of men and women who claim to fight

for the liberation of women without attacking the heterosystem. Feminism is a totalitarian theory which claims to be alone in its fight against the oppression of women.

2. Some Radical Lesbians remain attached, for historical (and other) reasons to the term Feminism, asserting that Feminism is indeed the struggle for women's liberation, that the logic of this struggle is political lesbianism and that any Feminist who is not also a Radical Lesbian, is not a real Feminist. This concept is dangerous insofar as:

— it causes general confusion which, given the state of our resources, we will be unable to dispel quickly. (Any more than the subtle confusion fostered by psykepo[5] between Feminism and the MLF was dispelled in most people's minds)

— moreover, declaring feminists, our political adversaries, to be non-Feminist and thus, to a certain extent, eliminating the problem posed by the existence of a relatively powerful movement, is to underestimate the adversaries in question and to deprive ourselves of the means of fighting them.

3. The term Feminism refers to women, which is scarcely appropriate for us since we are struggling to destroy sex classes and, particularly, because our struggle starts from the only social, political position capable of validating it, the separation from men clearly expressed in the very term which describes us: Radical Lesbianism.

4. The preceding analyses make it clear that while the idea of heterofeminist 'recuperation' may have been a stage in our critique at the beginning of our analyses, it can now only appear redundant.

It is interesting to reflect whether there is a feminist orthodoxy, as there is a marxist or christian orthodoxy. In effect, according to those lesbians, we are, logically, witnessing the domination of a revisionist tendency within the feminist movement. We might also consider whether this Radical Feminist tendency, comparable with Radical Lesbianism, exists anywhere other than in the mind.

B. Lesbians outside Feminism

1. It's important to analyse the potential of the Front Homosexuel d'Action Revolutionnaire [6] [Revolutionary Front for Homosexual Action or FHAR] from its inception: firstly because it was founded by lesbians, secondly because it appeared at the same time as the MLF. We need to explain why this homosexual movement, mixed politics notwithstanding, was unable to develop as an autonomous (independent of the MLF and of Feminism)

Lesbian political movement. Why were some of the lesbians who provided its impetus quickly led into a double activism (lesbian and feminist) in order to silence what had been the essence of their struggle, i.e. Lesbianism? The failure of the FHAR to develop into a lesbian movement forced some lesbians into the MLF, reinforcing it and devoting all their energy to a struggle which was not their own (even if, at that time, they did not have the same analysis of Feminism as we have now). However, many lesbians had joined the MLF before becoming feminists, hoping to meet gay women. Others who never set foot in it, not feeling involved in the struggle joined the Radical Lesbian Front by a non-feminist route (possibly via gay groups, etc. . .)

2. We also need to analyse the role that the Groups des Lesbiennes de Paris[7] [Paris Lesbian Group] (see Masques No. 1[8]) may have played. This group's impetus was provided by non-feminist lesbians (who rejected feminism as a recuperation of heterosexuality) although a large number of lesbian feminists passed through it.

C. Lesbians within Feminism

On the other hand, there have been quite a few lesbian groups (Gouines Rouges[9] [Red Dykes], Lesbian Feminist Groups, etc. . .)

1. These groups did not see lesbianism as the basis of their politics, but accepted the division
    - *lesbianism* as lived experience, emotion, sexuality, culture
    - *feminism* as the political dimension

2. They were thus unable to get beyond discussions about 'personal experience' (more often than not, in fact, there were a series of personal accounts without any real analysis) to form a collective political practice. They all ended up disbanding.

3. Why were there these limits and setbacks?
    Possible explanations:
    - the weight of the *feminist norm*: lesbians being victims of the idea that the only theory-ideology-politics in women's interests is Feminism.
    - lesbians may have supported this theory because of a highly internalised guilt complex where Feminism seemed to be a respectable security for Homosexuality.

Critique

It's important to recognise that some lesbian groups did not base themselves purely on 'personal experience'.

Examples: the group which formed after the publication of Masques No 1 was organised specifically around a critique of this issue of the journal and the line it took i.e. a denial of sex classes and, therefore, a denial of the exploitation and oppression of women as a class by men as a class. The group took an entirely opposite stand insofar as it wanted on the one hand to support Radical Feminism and, on the other, to criticise all the lesbian analyses of the women who produced the journal.

Another group sought to reinforce Radical Feminism with the weight of political Lesbianism. This group refused to understand that they were still arguing on the enemy's terms, perpetuating the illusion that they were appropriating and transforming Radical Feminism.

We think it is also important to remember
- the theoretical inability (see feminist analyses) to understand or develop a specifically lesbian politics starting from our social practice and specific position in society.
- misunderstanding, and thus mythification of the struggles of the past.
- the pseudo benefits we might derive from political activism with straight women.

In a movement where lesbianism seemed (to some women) to be the logic of Feminism, we were cast in the role of seducer, precisely because we were seen as the most 'coherent' and 'logical'. (It is interesting to note, once again, that heterosexual 'conversion' to lesbianism seems to occur exclusively in bed. This process continues in (both) MLF(s), thanks to the wonderful ladder theory. What a sense of power!)

D. Ten years of MLF history

It is not due to chance that no feminist has been able to produce a remotely convincing analysis of this history (see C. Delphy 'Liberation des Femmes an 10' [Women's Liberation, the 10th year] *QF* No. 7; G. Fraisse 'La Solitude volontaire, pour une politique des femmes' [Voluntary isolation, toward a women's politics] *Revolte Logique* [Logical Revolt], special issue: the Laurels of May; *Temps des Femmes* [Women's Times] July '81. In fact, only a radical lesbian perspective can shed light on this period. Not that we claim to have made that analysis, that evaluation. They still need to be made.

Questions

1. Reevaluating the 'radical feminism' (of the seventies).
What are we to make of its role at the beginning of the MLF during the wave of revolt, denunciation, breaks with traditional politics and the new awareness of numerous aspects of the exploitation and oppression of women?

What are we to make of its role in relation to lesbianism? Didn't it contribute to the denial of lesbianism (even though most Feministes Revolutionnaires were lesbians)?

What is quite clear:

The deadends of its theory

Its inability to define a strategy

Its refusal to tackle heterosexuality head on (take another look at C. Delphy's 'L'Ennemi Principal' [The Main Enemy] in *Partisans Liberation des Femmes annee zero* [Supporters of Women's Liberation, year zero]).

Critique

Although it is important to analyse the Revolutionary Feminist tendency within the MLF, it seems to us equally important not to confuse the personal behaviour of individuals with an objective analysis. No analysis of the Feministe Revolutionnaire tendency can be made without reference to FHAR.

2. Psykepo: archetype of the socialist Feminist tendency which, despite appearances, has remained a coherent group for 10 years, drawing its justification from naturalist theory.

3. Several years of hegemony, of 'class struggle feminism' (in the traditional sense) or 'socialist feminism' aiming only to bring women's struggles into line with male organisations on the far left (i.e. a proletariat-bourgeoisie concept of politics).

4. A somewhat hazy period distinguished by a number of initiatives (violent action, 'reclaim the night', feminism as a 'comprehensive political force', 'horizontal coordination' . . .)

Were these attempts to break out of . . . or to water down feminism?

It does not seem that it could, at heart, have been a question of either, but, rather, of the desire to reinforce a (more radical) current which already existed in the MLF (see above). It could not, in any sense, have been a question of breaking away since each action remained inside the framework of feminism and was based upon it. No lesbian perspective emerged during these actions, not to speak of a lesbian, or lesbianist, analysis. Theories of violence cannot be equated with theories of Lesbianism. Not all violence is lesbian, even if Lesbianism is 'violent'.

5. The situation today
   - alliance between a brand of Feminisme Revolutionnaire (having lost much of its 70s radicalism) and a brand of Socialist Feminism (forced to accept its own autonomy, given the almost total disappearance of the Far Left).
   - serious crisis ... revealing the dead end Feminism has come to, but denied by feminists who attribute the difficulties to outside causes: deradicalisation, psykepo, the media ... (see the editorial of *NQF* No. 2)
   - How will they get out of this dead end? several hypotheses: increasing institutionalisation?
   development of a Marxist socialist feminism (see 'Marxisme et Feminisme' discussion organised by 'elles voient rouge' [they see red])[10]
   - What if they don't get out?

Critique

We believe it is incorrect to pose the question 'what if they don't get out?' It would, in effect, deny the nature of feminism. Feminism cannot reach a dead end, it is in itself a dead end to the liberation of women. If we believe that Feminism, or Feminisms, are theoretical incarnations of the phallocratic system (or the heteropatriarchal or sexist system, see current discussions in the lesbian movement) we cannot logically believe they could develop into the liberation struggle and then fall into a cul de sac. We should, rather, analyse what makes it intrinsically a dead end, a theory of how to recuperate oppression. (We should not deny even the minimal advantages it can bring to heterosexual women within the structure of oppression.) The crisis of the MLF points out more clearly what Feminism is; but, as a product of the dominant ideology, (although at present principally organised by women) it adapts to material reality and takes different forms. If tomorrow the principal tendency were socialist (or marxist) Feminism, this would simply display its ability to adapt, rather than any qualitative change. The MLFs, like anything else, could easily take on a different appearance.

Since Feminism, despite what it has tried to make us believe (see the editorial in *QF* No. 1), has never been a scientific theory capable of analysing objective reality as a whole, of making strategic responses and fighting to transform this reality, it is time to speak clearly of our fight against it. It is not because its practice proceeds logically from its first premises that we reject, abandon and fight it. On the contrary, it is because it is one of the finest con-tricks in history. What is this scientific theory which 'forgets' its heterosocial bases in its analysis of reality? (All we are doing here is following C. Delphy's own accurate reasoning in 'Pour un Feminisme Materialiste' [Towards a Materialist Feminism] which appeared in *L'Arc* on S. de Beauvoir and women's struggle. Her reasoning runs as follows: it is pointless to dwell upon premises which are thus revealed as vacuous in each individual discipline; we know that the basic premises of sociology, for example, entail the denial of the oppression of women and consequently,

- are unable to take it into account; are unable to find at the end of the journey what they set out denying
- can *only* conceal it and thus contribute to perpetuating it.)

What are we to make of this 'anti-naturalist' discourse which includes the theory of complementarity via heterosexuality (man + woman = child) in its basic premises, justifying oppression and exploitation? What are we to make of this theory which under pretext of not cutting itself off from, or being understood by women [DES FEMMES], conceals from them the cage in which they live, even though they must gild the bars of the cage with texts, demonstrations and demagogy. What effect can the straight guerilla tactics of pills and abortions have on exploitation? The only possible strategy of the (various) Feminisms is reform according to the will of men. (Sexist slavery has a rosy future before it.)

It is also important to analyse the significance to the MLF of

- the creation of the FLR [Front Lesbien Radical – Radical Lesbian Front]
- the departure of many lesbians, particularly the most radical, from the MLF
- the contradictions created by discussions on lesbianism.

Having talked so much about it, it was impossible that many women should remain indifferent. (Cf *La Revue d'en Face* which felt obliged to make an apology for heterosexuality; 'Elles voient rouge' who want to 'take account of the lesbian dimension'; the creation of MIEL[11] etc. . . .)

E. Radical Lesbianism

1. Its appearance nearly two years ago is not a matter of chance. Causes:

- *the crisis of Feminism* removed one of the obstacles, gave us more space, made it urgent to create an alternative . . . (but we also contributed a fair bit to putting it into crisis!)
- the convergence of several kinds of challenges to Feminism (although they did not consider themselves challenges to Feminism, but of dominant ideologies and practices).

Critique

'The crisis of Feminism gave us more space'? Is that really a reason? Had Feminism been flourishing (in reformism and Heterosociality, naturally) would the beginning of a Lesbian political consciousness have been impossible? We did not become radical Lesbians through defiance (any more than we become Lesbians through defiance!) It is more likely that the institutionalisation of Feminism, as well as a certain maturity (after the joy of 'being women together'), combined with the development of feminist theories which were inconsistent and led only to a dead end, and theories of feminist heterosexuality (tending towards mixed politics), paved the way for the emergence of Radical Lesbianism.

There is no crisis of Feminism, unless we reduce Feminism to a single tendency in the MLF. It would certainly be wrong to deny that radical feminism is in crisis, but it does not represent either Feminism or the MLF.

If this tendency is at a crisis point, it is because we have, in an essential way, collided with it head on. Radical Lesbianism developed from a critique of this tendency, among other reasons. It was by then impossible to stop its development. The next logical step was the creation of an autonomous lesbian movement (independent of Feminism).

As we examine the historical development of a political tendency it is important to look principally at its own internal contradictions, not at pre-existing contradictions (Feminism, Lesbianism inside the MLF). Otherwise we would only be able to see lesbianism in relation to Feminism, and the FLR in relation to the MLF.

The role played by the convergence of different kinds of challenge has been seen above. We know very well, moreover, that the vast majority of these 'challengers' remained in the MLF.

2. What should we do in relation to Feminism?
   - autonomy (minimum requirement)
   - we think it is essential, at the present time, to separate from Feminism, allowing our own ideas to progress. (But the problem is to unite around the question we posed at the

483

beginning: should we give the word Feminism a new meaning, or not?)
- we also need to reflect on the history of the MLF:
  what are the deadends?
  any gains expected? or is there nothing positive?
  what impact has it had on women, society, men as a class?
- and a political dilemma:
  what replies should we make to the questions numerous women have on this issue?
  what arms does an analysis of the past give us in our struggle?

Critique
- what attitude should we adopt toward the lesbian currents within Feminism? (Obviously we need to examine the means we employ to reach lesbians as a whole.)
- It is important to 'collectivise' our knowledge, documents, historical texts, personal accounts, etc. . . . as the basis for collective work.

Notes

1. Front Lesbien Radical (FLR) [Radical Lesbian Front].
2. Conference held in November 1981 to which this text was a contribution among others.
3. I.e. is considered a deliberate obstruction of a movement for the 'rights' of women.
4. Its real name was 'Les Mille et une tendances'.
5. Psychanalyse et Politique, a tendency based on a naturalist perspective which tried to achieve the hegemony of the MLF by appropriating the name (Mouvement de la Liberation des Femmes) as its own trademark.
6. A gay group active from 1971–1973.
7. Active from 1978–1980.
8. Mixed gay journal published from 1979–1984.
9. The first lesbian group in the MLF (1971–1973).
10. Journal of a tendency of feminists who were at the time members of the PCF (French Communist Party).
11. Mouvement d'information et d'expression des Lesbiennes, Lesbian-feminist group, started in 1980.

How gay to be 'different'!

Isabel Dargent
Belgium, 1981

(*Translated by Anna Livia*)

Excuse me, did you say 'gay and lesbian'? Two 'new differences' in one basket? Is it a new political party? a new fashion? a new perfume? Does it come from the left or the right? In the name of DIFFERENCE (read your history books!) there has been, up to the present day:

— millions of years of the *subordination of women* by men, apart from Lilith, the Amazons, lesbian guerillas and resistance fighters, in other words: us.
— *rape*, the ultimate expression of this domination.
— *racism*, integral to patriarchy, capitalism and fascism.
— *homophobia*, toxic product of heteropatriarchal society.

Nowadays they do their utmost to silence the voices of the oppressed, in this context lesbians and all women, using the euphoric (because apolitical and idealist) discourse of difference. This discourse has been masterfully *orchestrated from the new right to the new left* (Partito Radicale), Pro Vita and the straight feminists, the unions and gay integrationists (GLH, CCL etc.) . . . Consequently, while there was some hope of social subversion yesterday, today, the eve of the elections, resembles a funeral dirge, thanks to you. 'Campaigning for the *legitimation of homosexuality* entails *an expansion of the norm, reinforcing* rather than threatening it in any way,'[1] we quite agree.

There has, in fact, never been any future in the ballot box, or in 'differences' . . . They lead only to oppression.

As lesbians we draw support from this observation for our 'radical' theories and practice because:

— under the innocuous appearance of sexual orientation, the concepts of heterosexuality and homosexuality camouflage two antagonistic political tactics. The first, heterosexuality, entails the appropriation of women as a class by men as a class. The second (homosexuality) has the potential for resisting that appropriation.

Consequently the position of lesbians within this oppression is quite the reverse of that of *gay men who benefit, despite everything, from the social advantages of belonging to the class of* men; *it is impossible for us to share the same battle-ground since our objective interests are antagonistic.*

So what do the Belgian Homosexual Associations think they're doing calling for a 'Festival of Homosexuality', for the rights and sexual freedom of 'gay men and lesbians'? As radical lesbians we will not beg for our rights, nor plead with anyone for our 'freedom'.

In the everyday details of our revolt, in the international solidarity of our struggles, we create and live out **Lesbian Resistance.**

[*leaflet handed out on a mixed gay demonstration in support of Eliane Morissens on 24th October 1981 in Mons*]

Note

1.   Since a radical perspective (i.e. without political shortsightedness) is a lasting treasure, we strongly and warmly recommend the article: *Attention a la Marche!* [Beware of the march!] by our sisters in Paris, Les Lesbianères, to whom we owe much of our self-taught resistance!

Leaflet handed out at an abortion demonstration in Brussels, 3rd October 1981

(Translated by Anna Livia)

When heterofeminism[1] still seemed like feminism we lesbians worked alongside heterosexual women, demanding not only total depenalisation of abortion, but even maternity rights (c.f. the Homo-L leaflet 'Women at an Abortion Day – Why?')

This has been going on for nearly ten years and we reckon we've done enough! It's still the same old people who profit from the ambiguous liberation of 'WOMAN': your (new) men . . . Now more than ever, as heterosexual campaigns reach a dead-end (abortion in the private sphere, equal pay in the public sphere) and their ineffectiveness (compromised and recuperated by mixed politics) . . . they pave the way for men to take back what they lost.

This situation has led us, as lesbian feminists in a number of different countries, to adopt radical new analyses and strategies of resistance and open hostility toward the class of men.

Which is why, although we are demanding total depenalisation today, we believe this campaign is insufficient (reformist) because abortion (and the repressive measures which go with it) are a logical consequence of patriarchal heterosexuality, itself a form of repression and constraint for all women (whether they are aware of this or not).

In a society where men's relations with women are still based purely on power and perpetual violence, women carry the whole limitless burden of so-called 'liberated', 'natural' sexuality and 'shared' parenthood. . . .

'Liberated Sexuality'? . . .

What about rape (marital rape, for one) and harassment in straight couples (bisexual couples, polysexual, traditional or progressive couples), in the family, the street, at work . . .?

To prove our point for us, a heterosexual group has organised a 'referendum on rape'. In their campaign for 'demystification' at all costs, they can find no better explanation than to put it all down to myth. They add that 'like all myths, we believe it expresses less reality than desire, a desire expressed so far only by men.'

So the origin of rape, like the origin of racism and fascism, is in myth! A case of 'advanced socio-liberal-phallocracy'. Well you can't stop progress, or collaborationist opportunism.

'Natural Sexuality'? . . .

Entirely regulated by medical intervention, on the one hand, (the pill, tubal ligature) or artificial intervention on the other (coils, diaphragms to start the list).

'Shared Parenthood'? . . .

Shared with the 'new' fathers, one imagines, only it's still the mother who breastfeeds!

. . . And that's why you men are quite happy to join the women on this demonstration, because they're the ones who risk having an abortion, while you can continue to fuck (as you so 'respectfully' put it) in peace.

NO TO REPRESSIVE ABORTION MEASURES
NO TO THE OPPRESSION OF HETEROPOWER!

Radical Lesbian Feminists

Who are we?

Lesbian feminists who share the following radical analyses: all women are oppressed, both as a group and individually, by men as a group; this oppression is the first human oppression and thus the basis of all others (e.g. capitalism); the clash of interests between men as a group and women as a group, and hetero-sociality (a system constructed by heterosexual logic, hetero-sexuality and heteropower) are the foundations of this oppression.

Our aims:

The formation of a (consciousness of) a class of women which will lead to maximum separation from, and minimum collaboration with, men as a group; a movement (network) of hostile resistance to men as a group.

Note

1. Reformist political position whose aim is the amelioration of patriarchal heterosexuality.

WARNING!
Heterosexuality may damage your health!

Vanille-Fraise (Vanilla-Strawberry)
group of political lesbians
Switzerland, 1981

(*Translated by Christine Lac*)

Heterosexuality is normal, is natural ... so they say: chronic vaginitis, cystitis, infections of the womb and the Fallopian tubes, sterilities, worsening of cancers, greater tendency to develop varicose veins, sensation of heaviness in the legs, phlebitis, lung embolisms, hemiplegia, disorders of vision, hearing problems, headaches, flatulence, weight gain, stretch marks ...

These are some complications due to the use of 'truly safe' contraceptives devised by male researchers to have their partners available to them thirty days out of thirty.

On the other hand there are the complications due to unwanted pregnancy: abortion and its after effects, (risks of infection or haemorrhage . . .) anxiety, vomiting, premature birth, post partum depression, etc. There are also complications due to multiple pregnancies: anemia, demineralization, enuresis, prolapse . . . and also to be mentioned, there is vaginitis, frigidity, and the psychologically draining menopause.

All these illnesses are more or less the consequences of heterosexuality; all are used to have us believe that we, women, are more fragile, more frequently sick. The practice of heterosexuality, almost compulsory, well served the medicalization of the woman's body by male doctors and physicians.

The period between 20 and 40 years of age is the prime of life when we should be least sick. However it is during that very period of time that women see their medical expenses increase. And most of those expenses are due to heterosexuality.

You never gave a thought to that?   and yet . . .

[*This flyer was distributed during a union-organized demonstration of parties of the left, a demonstration to protest against the cost of health care, that took place in Geneva, Switzerland on November 9, 1981. It was subsequently reprinted in Clit 007.*]

The Mind-Drifting Islands

Micheline Grimard-Leduc
Québec, 1982

Introduction

This paper is part of a book, 'L'île des amantes' ('Lesbian Lovers') Island'), half-essay, half-poetry, I originally wrote in French about the island as a basic symbol in lesbian culture.[1] The main argument runs as follows: the Amazons existed; their tribes were a basic primitive form of female social pattern; and if there are so many legends of female-only islands, it is because the Amazon tribes often lived on islands. When these Amazon societies were destroyed by male supremacist societies, lesbians became the heiresses of an ever-menaced culture that had to move from islands of stone and sand to psycho-spiritual shelters, or 'mind-drifting islands.'

489

I am aware that my perspective has its own limitations, for example a North American white middle-class education, which in my generation (1950–1960) translated into Québec Catholic classical studies.[2] As with any research that is deeply motivated, I know that mine is not over and I do hope that it will contribute to a further knowledge of our multi-faceted culture.

The mind-drifting islands

In her book, 'Sappho',[3] Edith Mora writes that Sappho participated in the political feuds between Lesbos noble families, who were horse-breeding landowners, and the merchants and shipowners, as a result of the latter group's increasing power. Her 'pamphlets' against the new 'democracy' caused her to be exiled twice in her lifetime. I do not really care about the oligarchic quarrels that triggered these exiles; my main interest lies firstly in the geography of these exiles.

The most historically acknowledged exile is the second one, the one in Syracuse (Sicily); it is worthwhile noting that we are dealing with banishment to an island. But her first exile, less well-known, was to be sentenced to a few kilometers from Mytilini, in a small village named Pyrrha. This exile at first seemed strange to my electronic age mind used to transatlantic flights; what was the fuss, how could one feel exiled when banished from one's city to what might be called a suburb? Exiled to one's own island . . .

I could play with the word itself, 'ex-isle,' 'cast out of one's isle,' but my main purpose is to examine the concept of exile, a conception that reaches far beyond the sole geographical aspect, as shown by Sappho's ostracism in Pyrrha.

For me, the idea of exile includes two elements:

1) the banishment is *imposed upon* and not decided by the person herself;
2) a *rooting out* of the social self, a wandering situation where one no longer shares a collective system of values.

Patriarchal history has resorted to exile to solve unwanted political or legal situations by casting out used-up emperors, criminals, too 'progressive' elements, and sometimes even entire communities (Acadian population).[4] Each of these were sent far away from their native country, often to inhospitable islands. And this uprooting inevitably had a profound impact. For Sappho in Pyrrha, exile meant precisely this uprooting; she lost contact with her own collectivity, she was no longer in the social flow of mutual acknowledgement, she no longer partook in collective values. In her time, a few kilometers sufficed.

As lesbians, our collective and individual story has been one of estrangement since the breaking up of the Amazon tribes by male supremacy. Collectively, we have been deprived of our Amazon structures; even considering them as nomadic, they nevertheless constituted a social canvas into which individuals could weave their collective identity, the kind of collective identity that is necessary for strong ego sanity.

This 'de-possession' of one's social self fits well into Marx and Hegel's definition of alienation; one is alienated, because one is deprived of oneself by outside forces; one no longer possesses oneself and becomes the plaything of conquerors and events.

The uprooting of lesbians is an historical fact that breeds its sequels well into our contemporary individual lives. We no longer tap from our roots and this shows in our behavior and attitudes, to the greatest satisfaction of male supremacists. Furthermore, we have forgotten where our oppression has come from; we have forgotten that the cause is exterior to ourselves.

We are left out, and we are left with this paralysing fear, this ontological uneasiness, this dread of being. The kind of oppression that induces choking instead of anger and revolt; oppression that splits the personality. Indeed, without any collective identity, forced into cultural wandering, and without being able to determine the external causes for this exile, what choices are there for a lesbian to maintain minimal sanity?

A first solution is to blot out the feeling of estrangement and assign it to one's overly sensitive imagination, to think that the whole thing will straighten out by itself, as long as one conforms to the norms and adopts this 'strange land.' Women also adopt these 'alien' values and go so far as to estrange themselves with the stranger. As spouses, women do receive a few more social and economic benefits, even if 'well-adapted' lesbians get around well. But since lesbians have not crossed the ultimate threshold of submission to male ownership in their private lives, their situation remains precarious. Indeed, since a lesbian does not intimately belong to a man, she is a 'graft' that will be rejected by the male system at any sign of crisis. 'What is not mine, is against me . . .'

Bitter deception lurks behind the 'melting' stance. We shall never be able to melt into a male-dominated society because of its heterosexist political mechanisms, where there is no such choice as heterosexuality for women.

There is the self-destructive solution that runs the gamut from drugs, alcohol, smoking, up to suicide, not to mention conventional psychotherapy and various psychosomatic illnesses as a result of the uneasiness of being 'different,' a 'difference' that is epitomized by the notion of a 'third sex.'[5] How far will this schizophrenic scenario take us? This set-up is remarkably appropriate for ghettos, couples in hiding, closet cases, and all the alienated souls that think of themselves as being alone of their kind in the world.

Presumably, I am forgetting other solutions. But there is one other I think of: a solution that often coexists with others and which has its own little schizoid tinge, that is, to seek shelter in a fictitious inner world. To build, by imagining, an island inhabited by lesbian lovers and to hold onto it mentally. I am presently creating a fantasy where I can forego the distress that arises from my 'strange' condition. Am I trading my first estrangement for another one into fantasyland?

Freudian goblins are sarcastically laughing all around ... Yes indeed, I am fleeing. Running away is symptomatic of any situation where one is deprived of one's self as a social being. I build my own land of refuge. And I have come to think that every lesbian, through the ages and throughout continents, has built, be it for no more than a short moment, some sort of a shelter. And I am also convinced that this refuge took the shape of an island. The flight to the island is a symptom of uneasiness, a sane reaction against the restlessness caused by a destructive social environment.

I ask, is our inner island but a reaction? Living as 'outcasts' on this vast island, planet Earth, are we but reaching an island of imprisonment?

If we try and shed our passive attitude toward this exile, I think we can get around it, turn this prison-island upside-down into autonomy, into at least psychosocial autarky. This means a first subversive step to overthrow the established 'order.' One of the devices that holds this order functions like this: each of us being deprived of collective points of reference by which to 'plug' into a sense of reality, we tend to develop negative mental attitudes, which in turn impede our building up of a collective reality!

This is the kind of vicious circle we must break through. It is important indeed for male society that we be crazies, cute or harsh crazies, never mind, and thus each of us reassures herself by secretly thinking about others who are 'even crazier.' The system relies on our schizophrenic 'abilities' in order to insure an isolation that it does not even have to enforce since it comes from ourselves; the detachment from our own selves and from others. Of course, as long as my dream-island is known only by myself, I actually live on a prison-island, in sheer isolation. In Italian, 'isola' means island ...

But as soon as ! *share* my dream with another lesbian, I start breaking through the alien circle. This single act of communication materializes the dream. By this exchange we build reality. Communication and schizophrenia are antitheses; I am no schizophrenic if I am actually able to communicate.

Psychiatric diagnoses are meaningless when crazies, 'lost minds,' start sharing their dreams and, most of all, start to mold them into reality. Who is going then to send us off in exile to an island we call our own island? Who will impose banishment on us when we are already elsewhere?

If our exchanges enable us to rebuild a social fabric, collective values, an economy? (wow! what a dreamer!), who would still talk of uprooting? Perhaps one of the causes of confusion around lesbian separatism (as I view it) is a misconception of the 'island' as a ghetto in contrast to the island as autonomy. The ghetto-island stays in the closet, providing short-term security; the autonomy-island means the building up of a community, with a collective visibility.[6] It means a *positive* choice, a long-term bet on a *different* society. There is a qualitative leap between these two conceptions of our 'island.'

I admit that to choose autonomy and visibility is no piece of cake; fear and insecurity do not vanish instantly, but they are transformed. Fear that arises from oppression, paralysing fear, is replaced by the more realistic fear of repression. Even with the inevitable phantasms which pervade any kind of fear – most of all the fears we have plenty of time to contemplate – fear of repression is based on concrete data, exterior facts that can eventually be verified and sometimes overcome. One is then concerned about the consequences of one's own actions in the course of affirming oneself. Quite different from the fear of being!

Fear of repression does not make for easy living, even when we try to establish a network of communication, and sometimes because we try to do so. Each of us is not necessarily ready to take chances and risk visibility as much as her sister; communication between us acts both as a stimulus as well as a frustration or a deterrent. 'Why is she still in the closet? Why is she bullying me so soon into visibility? Should I involve my lover in my deeds? I am not allowing her to be vocal . . .' Couples, groups, friendships are sometimes torn apart by this shadowy fear that is not so easy to pinpoint. But there is still a longing.

We wish our island could materialize in a flash, somewhere; and we would rush there to organize our own society. But the unleased demography of male societies would soon find us, be it by plane, boat, or what-have-you; for in the face of these societies, there is no possibility for the existence of independent females, for a lesbian society. Female autonomy cannot and must not be. So, we create small islands, we are small islands. Each time a lesbian reveals herself to another lesbian, she is this island to land on. From countryside to city, from city to city, from continent to continent, across generations, and couples, and groups, overcoming the fear, each time we become visible to one another, we create the island. We are an archipelago that drifts through time and geography and allows us mutual recognition and the support of a social fabric.

That is the whole meaning of lesbian works, magazines, videos, movies, research, all these shaping our collectivity into reality. A collectivity that has bones and flesh in each of us thinking of herself as partaking in an actual lesbian community.

I realize that in addition to our individual 'in-case-of' investments in male society there still are racial and social clashes between us; conflicts that seriously slow down the building of our community. Ours is not always 'a rose garden.'

I even happen to think of our island as a swamp when I am fed up and pessimistic. But I still prefer it to the islands that bloom on tv commercials, with male voice-over. Our island is inhabited by real females, by lesbians. Instead of the voice-over, I would rather imagine Ioanna's voice through her letter: 'I am now sitting on our small garden, at Glyfada; it is awfully hot, but I have just watered the flowers, everything is wet, and I am feeling good. I am happy to know that you are doing fine, that you are content with your milieu. That is something. Perhaps, near the end of our lives, many of us will gather on an island. At least, let us dream of it.'[7]

In a corner of their living room, Betty and Ioanna have built a small-scale lesbian village. The little houses are waiting. I can picture them. There are red ones . . .

'Lesbians are not women' ('Les lesbiennes ne sont pas des femmes'). In these words Monique Wittig summed up her paper on the straight way of thinking, 'La Pensée straight,' a work that contributed to bringing out into the open the ideological conflict that had been latent amongst the editorial staff of the French feminist magazine, 'Questions Féministes.'[8-9] Conflicts on this question about the meaning of both words 'lesbian' and 'woman' have been sprouting in almost every feminist and/or lesbian circle with more or less hostility.

In the preceding pages, I have tried to avoid the use of the word 'woman,' except in those cases where I wanted to describe a social entity altered by his-story. Among the various possible verbal acrobatics, I chose the word 'female' for its biological semantics: a biological entity derived from some chromosomic organization, characterized by genes XX, displaying some hormonal and morphological configuration, blah, blah, blah. Far from being adequate, this term still makes me feel clumsy; for I am once more trying to word – hence to think of – our own entities with an alien language, the male language. I agree the 'male/female' division is typical of the straight way of thinking, but it is more readily restricted to biology than is the highly social dichotomy 'man/woman.'

Actually, even if this truth might conflict with a few literary theories, words do not float in a sea of immunity, one cannot play with them lightheartedly. Words are dependent, dangerously dependent. Their existence, their frequency of use and, most of all, their meaning depend on a consensus. Words must be 'approved' by a collectivity in order to be commonly used and even then, their use is limited to a meaning that also had to be approved! In social regimes where inequality is the rule, it is the dominating group who gives the approbation or not. Such is the case of male supremacist societies where men decide on the meaning of words, syntax, etc. Language then becomes a most powerful means of domination because it is both pervasive and discreet.

Monique Wittig has aptly shown that the conception of 'woman,' which apparently refers to a natural entity, actually is a camouflage for negative, downgrading socio-cultural semantics.[8] The actual downgrading mechanism is now no longer possible to decipher – and so less likely to confront – since it is attributed to 'nature.' If the word 'woman' has received phallocratic consent, if its use is current, it is because it is politically useful for male society. Through a biological smoke screen, 'woman' refers to a social entity, moreover an ancillary, downgraded entity.

Numerous feminist writers – Simone de Beauvoir leading the way[10] – have brought to light the inferior position of women in a patriarchy. As it is, feminist analysis seems to have focused only on that observation. Marilyn Frye[11] who went further in her analysis by including a discussion on the lesbian situation in patriarchal society, compares women's position in society to that of stagehands and cheerleaders for the masculine 'drama.' The staging of the play would be impossible without them, but they are pushed into the 'background.' If they want to play some 'role' in the foreground (a possibility that Marilyn Frye does not seem to consider), I think they must meticulously conform to the image of the 'real-woman' as epitomized by male transvestites. In the masculine staging of femininity fantasy, Guildas[12] are more likely to appear as 'real women' than all the stagehands who try to resemble them with loads of make-up, etc.[13]

The only 'visibility' allowed to women is one of a reality

completely *annexed* to man's. An independent, autonomous female reality is perfectly unthinkable to the master's logic. Such a reality cannot, hence, must not emerge, for it is the 'king' ('rex') and only he who assigns the 'realm,' reality.[11]

If I do conceive myself as an autonomous entity, if I am not privately dependent on a man, if I have stopped focusing on the male show and I now focus on what it has always tried to hide, how shall I call myself? 'Woman,' this word that sets me back to dependency, to inferior being? When I call myself a 'woman,' the word describes the inferior situation this society imposes upon me and which draws its daily burden; but *it also perpetuates the erasure of my autonomous self.* The word 'woman' pushes my intimate life back to nothingness; it blots out a way of living that generates my whole vision of the world, a way of living that is eroticism with/for my sister, eroticism that fuels my will to live. Then, how shall I call myself?

I call myself a *lesbian.* My reality is indeed invisible for male society. In the face of men, a Lesbian is a 'monster' regarding both nature and logic; this monster is 'anti-nature,' 'anti-logic.' We are not in the 'realm,' we are not in the masculine reality. As if to reassure themselves – and hold down women in their 'right' place – men pornography the 'monster,' that is, they reduce 'it' to utilitarian fantasies such as David Hamilton's teens or Nazi 'kapos.' There is not the smallest hint of lesbian reality in pornography; it wants to prove that lesbians are but fantasy robots programmed by and for men. (This masculine obsession is still a paradox: if lesbians do not exist . . . .)

Many lesbians refuse the 'label': do they assume for themselves the male fantasy, or are they 'crushed' by it? Is it because the word 'woman' allows one to 'pass' and feel less vulnerable? I agree that in a straight environment it seems less complicated to use the 'woman' password than to try to demonstrate one's lesbian reality. But when we are together, expressing our intimate selves to one another, assuming our reality among ourselves, what is the point in refusing to call oneself a lesbian?

At the time being, I have not found any other word that is both understood in many languages and that holds up so well the meaning of our autonomy, of our radical rupture from this man's world. Since our intimate life roots itself elsewhere than in male 'reality,' we, and only we, can give ourselves a reality visible to us, because of the words we choose. In this way, we send signs to each other, we *de-sign* reality, positive signals which in turn transform our way of thinking. This simple word 'lesbian' brings forth the vision of the island; in spite of the mirages, this word draws the contours of our collectivity to reveal the shape of our island.

At the other end of the island semantic spectrum, there is the esoteric island. Delving into esoterism is not my main hobby nor preoccupation, but I was interested in observing cultural evolution through esoteric symbols. Esoterism and its most valued symbols are not static; they have changed during the ages, thus reflecting important cultural trends if not actual cultures. According to J. C. Pichon,[14] chronology of myths is the following:

- 20,000 to 15,000 years ago: era of the Mother-Goddess, associated with earth, with stone;
- 13,000 to 12,000 years ago: the hyperborean virgin, associated with the boat, with harvests. In this period it is presumed that the glaciations that were to come had already been predicted (hyperborean: beyond the cold);
- 11,600 to 9,500: period of the Sun when physical beauty and strength are exalted;
- 9,500 to 7,300: the Circle, in which serpent, egg, water and lunar cycle are associated. It is the era of the 'Wise,' that is the prophetesses; truth/science is a way of living rather than a faith.

  Lilith seems to represent the converging symbols of water and stone; water springing from stone, and stone emerging from water.
- 7,300 to 6,200: Gemini, the 'twins,' where similarity, 'homogeneity' becomes incarnate in 'fraternity' (here comes the order of the brothers); the Wise are obliged to step aside for the entry of the 'Magi,' those who praise images, prefering appearances in lieu of truth.

What follows is his-story . . .

This chronology is quite inspiring. One could work hard before exhausting all its implications. But let us look at a few of these.

It is already remarkable that: 1) there was an era of the Virgin; 2) this period corresponds to the advent of agriculture; 3) it happened before a glaciation. That is, in favorable climatic conditions, there was a Virgin-centered culture. It is most likely for Amazon culture to have been flourishing at that time.[15]

Moreover, there is a surprising detail for our modern conceptions: harvests are not opposite to the boat! What could it mean? These populations were not limited to the fields, whilst others would have sailed the seas. This contradicts the usual barriers that anthropological studies put between sedentary, agricultural populations, unskilled at sea, and sailor populations, always on the move for fishing or trading. In the era of the Virgin, they sailed and developed agriculture.

Amazon tribes could have been these populations, even if they were not as sedentary as present anthropological criteria would dictate for the notion of agricultural society. At least, Amazons were contemporary to and respected by these populations.

The solar myth has been largely engulfed by patriarchal society; it is almost its symbol, but there is no proof that it has always been the case. Nevertheless, I will skip it to examine the lunar cycle.

All the meanings of 'wisdom' testify of an era that had great in-depth, profound thought. And then, there is this Lilith myth, today's quintessential symbol of evil, that was an eminent symbol in the Circle era, a symbol of autonomy, where the two nourishing elements, water and earth, are fused, giving existence one to another. Lilith is the outstanding autarky, the island emerging from the waters (it resembles Aphrodite's birth, 'born of the foaming sea'), water springing amidst the island; the self-contained island, an abhorred symbol in male esoterics.

I surmise that witches' 'circles' are a direct heritage from this period.

Lilith is evil by male standards, because she is self-sufficient. She is the she-serpent that ruins the artificial fruits 'marketed' by the magi following. They who want to force everything into uniformity and replace true science and search of truth with show and appearance. She who is self-sufficient is the egg, the nestling-serpent, the self-generating circle.

The Wise of the Past and of today 'spin a spiral,' as would say Mary Daly.[16] Perhaps this spinning comes from our continual moving, at least in our minds. We have been spinning a spiral, a circle that generates itself by its displacement in time and space.

Since the time Amazon tribes were chased into oblivion, we survived on continuing to draw this time-space revolving spiral. The width of the spiral being narrowed each time male aggression intensified and destroyed many of us; but still moving further in the time dimension, for in this dimension figures are not important, as long as the movement keeps going.

Coming out to land on one's island

In the 'Coming Out Stories,'[17] Sarah L. Hoagland compares 'coming out' with 'coming home.' It has been such a long exile away from our island that when we get in touch with our lesbian identity, it is the same as reaching a longed-for country.

This is at least the strong impression I got from my first night of love with a woman. If I write 'night of love' it is not meant in terms of technique, but because of my perception of the event. Actually, that night almost ended in a rebuff. In spite of this, I felt thoroughly at peace with myself in the morning: I knew that I had come to my coherent self, mind, heart, body, all of them blending into one emotion. I felt I had reached the land I had been traveling towards, delayed by so many detours. At last, I was coming home! I even remember the physical feeling of landing on an island. There would be a lot to discover in this island, but there I was! The wandering had come to an end.

At first there was the discovery of the inner, individual island, where senses are slowly untied and then followed the discovery of a community by learning visibility; a long process that spans a lifetime.

For many of us this discovery demands real traveling, because social pressure is too high in the environment we were raised in. As if to introduce at least a few kilometers between us and our family, in order to make the discovery possible. Is not family the main transmitter of the so-called 'heterosexual' patriarchal values? There are lesbians who have all their lives been traveling across oceans, others through libraries, without ever reaching their island. By what astonishing loop of the spiral do we succeed?

As an answer, I will recall legendary Morrigan.[18] Morrigan, the wild mare, celtic morn, she, the strength-giver, is dawning on our island.

Notes

1. Micheline Grimard-Leduc, *L'île des amantes*, (Montreal, 1982). Available from Micheline Grimard-Leduc, P.O. Box 461, Station N, Montreal, Quebec H2X 3N3. I am greatly indebted to Ariane Brunet for the friendly but thorough critical discussions she shared with me in the course of this work. Diana helped me with the translation from French to English.
2. At that time, classical studies were offered at the 'collèges classiques,' a private system of education extending from secondary to college level.
3. Edith Mora, *Sappho*, Paris: Flammarion, 1966.
4. The Acadian population inhabited, in the 18th century, areas of today's Canadian Maritimes. In 1755, families were split apart by the British military authorities and were chased away on small craft. Those who landed somewhere ended up on the Boston coast, in North Carolina, even in Louisiana, others in the Magdalen Islands and elsewhere in the Gulf of St. Lawrence.
5. Radclyffe Hall, *The Well of Loneliness*, London: Jonathan Cape,

1928. The idea of a 'third sex' reminds me of a lobotomy without scalpel.

6.   J. Steakly makes an interesting distinction between 'ghetto' and 'community' in an interview for *Gay Community News* 9, 48 (June 26, 1982).

7.   Letter from Ioanna Kouklakis, July, 1981. Glyfada is an Athenian suburb.

8.   Monique Wittig, 'La Pensée straight,' *Questions féministes* 7 (February 1980), ed. Tierce, Paris.

9.   The magazine '*Amazones d'hier/Lesbiennes d'aujourd'hui*,' Montreal, ran a series of papers on this debate in its June, 1982 issue (vol. I, no. 1).

10.   Simone de Beauvoir, *Le deuxième sexe*, vols. 1 and 2, (Paris: Gallimard, 1949).

11.   Marilyn Frye, 'To Be and Be Seen: Metaphysical Misogyny,' in *Sinister Wisdom* 17 (Summer 1981), 57–70.

12.   Guilda is a male transvestite in Québec show business.

13.   Transvestism and transsexuality is a complex matter in which I doubt that male and female motivations are symmetrical. And I think that as far as male 'drama' is concerned, male transvestites *perform* the femininity fantasy, while male transsexuals *embody* it. God-like surgery allows for the existence of a world of men and *women, without any female!*

14.   J. C. Pichon, *Histoire des mythes*, (Paris: Payot, 1971).

15.   I suspect female-only tribes to be echoed (unintentionally of course) in classic Hellenic words such as 'ethnos' and 'genos.' 'Ethnos' explicitly refers to specific people or a race, and 'genos' to gender, species. Xenophon writes textually: 'female "ethnos," male "ethnos",' and Plato: 'female gender, male gender.' These words bear more radical meanings than the term 'sex' and the 'human gender' melting pot.

16.   Mary Daly, *Gyn/Ecology: The Metaethics of Radical Feminism*, (Boston: Beacon Press, 1978).

17.   Julia Penelope Stanley, Susan J. Wolfe, eds., *The Coming Out Stories*, (Watertown, Mass.: Persephone Press, 1980). [Now out of print, eds.]

18.   Merlin Stone, *Ancient Mirrors of Womanhood*, vol. I, New York: New Sybilline Books, 1979. Morrigan: 'mor-gen,' that means both 'morning' and 'strength-generating.'

AFTER-WORDS:
ONE FLAMING LETTER

Separatist

Caryatis Cardea
1984

what i am thinking
will never be forgiven

men
are destroying
the world

should they discover my heresy
    and they do
    a little more each day
it would not be condoned

i say to my sisters
men
are destroying the world

and my sisters say
it is not men
who have done this
they are not alone to blame

it is caste and class
it is nation
it is religion and race
and i say
who has done these things
not a one is organic
    rising like lava
each has been planned carefully
and executed

executed i say
maimed raped murdered
poisoned drugged
buried alive
raped

and my sisters say
gender is nothing
it is culture and the role of mothers
the exploitation of labor

it is not men

and i say to my sisters
i know what i believe
    that every crime
    has a perpetrator
    and every criminal
    has a victim
and i do not speak of laws
written down by men
but of ethics so cosmic
they are of the very stuff which holds
the world
in balance

and they
and we
    the womyn
are violated
every moment

of every day

year after year

for centuries

and i say to my sisters
men are destroying
the world

and my sisters say
coalition androgyny
unity
we all must work together
because
men
some men
may be destructive
but they can be healed
they are only the later form
of little boys
poorly trained

in a culture
whose root and purpose
we will not name

and i say to my sisters

caste yes and class and religion
heterosexism and hatred yes
of queers and jews and dark skinned people
fear of nature
animals slaughtered and held captive

magic banned

and the love
of womyn by womyn
abhorred
and outlawed

war and the weapons of war
prison and the tools of torture
these things i will not forgive
languages obliterated with their cultures
        and sometimes their people
radiation and chemical dumps
land laid waste
minds laid waste
the hunger of millions
        a prerequisite of society
the domination of children
        a necessity of power

the slavery of womyn
        a deep and primal desire

confinement intimidation genocide
starvation rape torture incest terror
pain poison terror rape

rape

and we scream in the night
and we agonize in the day
who has done these things

and i say to my sisters
men are destroying the world
and my sisters say
no
there are institutions
beliefs and prejudices
we must struggle to erase
we can stop their institutions
but we need not confront
the ones who built them

and want them
and profit from them
and love them
and rebuild them
and rebuild them
and rebuild them on our bodies

but no
my sisters say
it is not
men
not men
not
men

and i say
to my sisters
but it is

The Mystery of Lesbians

Julia Penelope
1984

I want to thank my good Separatist friends who questioned and challenged me to clarity and encouraged me to say what I wanted to say: Alix Dobkin, Sarah Lucia Hoagland, Emily Levine, Jennifer Lynne, Kate Moran, Jeanette Silveira (a fine editor), Linda Strega, Bobby Lacy, Anne Leighton and Sarah Valentine. My gratitude doesn't imply that these Lesbians agree with my descriptions or interpretations of events; what appears here is my story alone, and its presentation, which owes so much to their criticisms, remains my responsibility alone.

Retrospective

Sometimes, it seems as though it's almost **too** easy for us to forget who we are. I had, until one night in August, 1983, when I remembered. I was standing in a bar in Montréal called The Bilitis. I didn't like the name, because Bilitis was the name a French pornographer, Pierre Loüys, gave to the fictional daughter of Sappho he created for his own purposes. But the name also reminded me of the Daughters of Bilitis, the first Lesbian organization in the U.S., founded in 1957 by Del Martin and Phyllis Lyon in San Francisco, a continent away from where I stood in 1983. It reminded me of being a Lesbian in another time. I remembered my excitement at 19 when I found out there was a magazine, *The Ladder*, published by the Daughters of Bilitis and available on newsstands in large cities. I remembered how long I've been a Lesbian, the several ways I've named myself, and how long I've fought to defend and maintain the integrity of my life and the feelings that make my life what it is. I remembered publishing my first articles in *One* magazine in 1962 and *The Ladder* in 1963. In that bar in a strange city, knowing only the two Lesbians who'd brought me there, I was home. There, I touched once more my own origins in the Lesbian and gay bars of Miami and Miami Beach in the 1950's and '60's. My first community. My first sense of belonging somewhere.

In Montréal, I remembered who I am. I liked the bar. It was full of Lesbians, all kinds of Lesbians. I couldn't move without touching or being touched, and the air was humid with the moist smell of Lesbians, thick and sexual, busy with the sounds of Lesbians being Lesbians, shouted, exclaimed, whispered, angry, defiant, aloud. I was among my kind, my people. Overcome with joy, and myself, I danced. (Actually, the dance floor was so small and crowded that I could only stand in one place and weave and wiggle and snap my fingers to what I managed to hear of the music, but I was dancing in every cell of my body. It was all I could do.) I was dancing with Ariane Brunet of the Amazones d'Hier, Lesbiennes d'Aujourd'hui Collective, while Louise Turcotte, also a member of the Lesbians-only Collective, stood by our table because there wasn't any place to sit down. In the company of these fine Lesbians, I danced for the joy of being a Lesbian among Lesbians, for having the strength of my will, for hours.

I was wonderstruck. Why? I've been in Lesbian bars ever since the night I snuck, terrified and illegally, into Googie's on 17th Avenue in Miami in 1956, because I had to be with my own kind so desperately. Since that first frightened excursion, I've been in the dyke/lesbian/gay bars of New York, New Orleans, Atlanta, Danbury, Conn., Houston, Tampa, San Antonio, Austin, Santa Fe, Albuquerque, St. Louis, Kansas City, Omaha, Chicago, Minneapolis, Madison, Wisc., Boston, Los Angeles, Seattle, Denver, Washington D.C., San Francisco, Wichita, and Mexico City (where we had to sneak into the bar because the Lesbians who'd offered to take me there were afraid of being seen going into the place)[1] as well as those in Miami and Miami Beach. I've felt a lot of emotions besides terror and joy in these places: disgust, despair, loneliness, desperation, self-pity, thrilled, lustful, sinful, evil, daring, sophisticated, naïve, worldly, hopeful, degraded and degrading, exploited and exploiting, put down, assaulted, ignored, ugly, beautiful, wanted, unwanted, lost, you name it. (I felt and named what I was feeling according to how I understood my experiences at the time.) I knew, from one end to the other, the range of what being a Lesbian means, from intense joy to extreme pain.

There could have been no surprises for me at the Bilitis in Montréal in 1983; I could have been in any one of many dyke bars on the North American continent. The names and locations of our bars may change like the weather in Nebraska, and the decor may range from J. C. Penney's Frontier Rustic to Neo-Plastic Interstate Motel Contemporary, but the atmosphere of Lesbian space remains remarkably predictable and, therefore, comfortable.[2] Therein lies the essential mystery hinted at in my title. I was a Lesbian among Lesbians, even though some of the customers in the Bilitis might never claim that label for themselves, and would've been insulted if I had called them 'dykes.' So what if some of those wimmin[3] preferred the safety of calling themselves 'bisexual' or 'gay,' thereby accepting the dubious protection of identifying as members of a male group? In that place, each of us was proclaiming, in her own way, that she was refusing the heterosexual imperative and taking the risk of acting on her feelings and convictions. Some of us had declared our Lesbianism over and over, out of desperation and a will to survive; some had become Lesbians, changed their minds, wavered, and returned. Others were probably still in the process of coming to understand that they were Lesbians, not yet entirely aware of what their identity might come to mean to them, might cost them. Some were there for 'kicks,' others were there because they were lonely. But we were there, in all our phases, the 'for real' and the phony, together.

Remember the excitement of discovering that a friend, co-worker, old high school acquaintance, or sister is a Lesbian? Remember the sense of *confirmation* that discovery brought both of you, and how that established a connection between you? Do any of us get that excited when we find out that another woman is heterosexual? Is it POSSIBLE to even talk about 'discovering' that a friend is 'heterosexual'? Is it a unique event when heterosexual women finally find each other and connect? Do they tell their friends 'the story' about the meeting for weeks after?

In that bar in Montréal, I remembered who I am and why I do the things I do. I remembered the time when I believed that I was 'the only one.' I remembered fears and pain, but, most of all, I remembered the integrity of my self-knowledge, how the threads of my experiences are woven into the patterns I call my Self, and I reclaimed for myself my commitment to change what it means to be a Lesbian in this world. It is so easy to forget what we've refused, what we've survived, and to take each other for granted. I had forgotten, or chosen not to remember, until that August night in Montréal put me in touch with my joy *and* my pain all at once, and called to consciousness my abandoned dream of a Lesbian community.

So profound had my estrangement become that I had forgotten who I am. I am a Lesbian, yes. I can be independent, strong, defiant, stubborn, arrogant; I can survive, alone, but only in a very narrow sense of the word. The quality of my survival requires – is defined in terms of – the existence of a community of Lesbians. Even though it isn't my purpose here to describe explicitly what I mean by my use of 'community,' I need other Lesbians to affirm me, support me, challenge me, encourage me, argue with me, tell me I'm full of shit, and tell me I'm wonderful; I need to know as well that there are safe places for me in this world, places where I can be stupid, wise, silly, profound, trite, or original, make mistakes, undo my mistakes, make bad jokes and a few good ones, without constant fear of being cast out. I discovered in Montréal that I no longer believe there is such a place for me. Whatever potential for safety with other Lesbians I'd once envisioned now seemed impossible and far-fetched.

In a strange city, in the unique aura of safety provided by anonymity in a crowded bar, I realized I'd ceased to believe in the Lesbian community I'd thought I was helping to build. Instead, I'd become an outcast from outcasts with no place to go. Having touched that pain, withdrawn from it, and touched it yet again, I knew I had to find out why I'd let go of my vision. More hopefully, I needed to discover, if possible, a way back to it, or, failing that, to fashion new frameworks for ordering and interpreting my life.

The Mystery of Lesbians

I'll repeat here, briefly, some things I've said before (in other articles) because certain aspects of my experience are integral to what I want to say here. I cannot omit them, because, like everyone else, my interpretations and descriptions and responses to events and situations are framed by my past experiences. That is, although what I say here is based on my experiences and perceptions of events and I cannot, for that reason, expect every Lesbian to agree with my interpretations, I believe that other Lesbians will understand what I'm talking about and be able to substitute similar experiences of their own that had the same effect on them. I've always been a Lesbian. I've never thought of myself as anything *but* a Lesbian, even though, at earlier stages in my life, I called myself 'homosexual,' 'queer,' and 'gay.' I accepted from the people around me the words I used to describe who I was. At 9, 12, and 15, I didn't know or care that the words I used to name myself were insulting or damaging to my self-concept; I took the labels offered to me for my identity in much the same way that I chose cereals at the supermarket – without consciousness. It didn't bother me in 1954 that 'homosexual' and 'gay' referred primarily to males; I took those labels as I found them, without meditating on their sense or the possible cost to my sensibilities. What I knew, with certainty, was that I loved other wimmin and wanted to spend my life loving them.

Never having entertained the idea that I might be a heterosexual (even though everyone around me kept insisting that I was if only I'd admit it), my Lesbianism was never a choice in the way that many speak of it now. My Lesbian identity has never been merely a 'preference' for me; it's not an identity I casually selected from a Baskin-Robbins sexuality counter. Heterosexuality wasn't an 'option' for me. Heterosexuality was forced on me from all sides and at every moment of my life until I managed to escape the adults who were so set on coercing me into a mold that suited them, not me. Heterosexuality wasn't a 'choice,' it was an attempted imposition, a way of being I found repulsive and demeaning.

I was attracted to, sexually excited by, and comfortable only in the company of women. I found men stupid and arrogant (a combination of traits I don't like in anyone), egotistical, presumptuous, and mean. I didn't like men when I was growing up, and I've found no reason in the intervening years to change my opinion of them. (The very few exceptions I've met simply aren't quantitatively significant enough to warrant revising my generalization.) I don't regard myself as somehow 'more' of a Lesbian than others who did go through a heterosexual phase in their lives. Each of us has come by her own path to embrace what being a Lesbian means, and our experiential differences can be, should be, a primary source of our strength. I want you to understand that my Lesbianism is who I am, and it's always been that way for me. I could not have been other than I am and continued to live. If there was an 'alternative lifestyle' for me, it was death, not heterosexuality. I would have killed myself, and did try, before I would have tried to live as a heterosexual.

There is something else you must know in order to understand my perspective and its origins in my experience: I've never been able to 'pass' for heterosexual. Not that I haven't tried. I understand the desire, the temptation, the need to at least LOOK like everyone else. I understand the benefits to be gained by 'passing' for something one isn't. I've missed the privileges of heterosexuality, including the rewards for successful mimicry, and felt that lack painfully. I wanted the goodies, and have many times wished fervently to be able to 'pass' for a heterosexual. Living on the outside of the heterosexual system made me acutely aware of the validation and support that wasn't, and wouldn't be, forthcoming. But I've always looked like what I am, a dyke.[4] When I've tried to look like a heterosexual, I was a failure, and I always felt ridiculous and laughable and, therefore, humiliated. My choice, in my circumstances, was to brazen it out.

It would be easy for some to say, 'Oh, you're just as bad about stereotyping Lesbians as society is,' but that statement ignores the fact that I've lived my life AS society's stereotype. As a result, I didn't have many girlfriends while I was growing up; mothers made it clear that their daughters weren't allowed to associate with the neighborhood queer. My isolation began when I was a child, but it was only the beginning. As I became aware of my difference and discovered that I wasn't the 'only one,' I learned simultaneously that lesbians who could pass, thereby escaping more overt methods of social punishment, didn't want to be associated with me, either. I was too 'obvious' when 'discretion' was the code word for 'passing.' Only outrageous faggots and bardykes weren't afraid to be my friends, because they, too, had nothing to lose by being seen with me. From our isolation and defiance we created families and 'homes' within which we were assured that we were loved for ourselves. In the bars, we lived in constant danger from both the nastiness and violence of het tourists and the vice raids that accompanied every political election. Not one of us was safe anywhere else. On good days, we were called names, jeered at, mocked, and ridiculed; on bad days, we were assaulted, raped, beaten up, and killed.

Isolation is nothing new in my life; I've spent my life being lonely, and trying to 'fit in' some place in order to end my isolation. (This isolation, which isn't self-chosen, shouldn't be confused with 'being alone,' which is chosen.) You need to understand these things about me to comprehend my intense hopefulness in 1971 when I heard that the contemporary Women's Liberation Movement (WLM), at that year's NOW convention, had announced that Lesbianism was to be recognized as a valid and acceptable lifestyle for women. It's hard to admit that I felt relief, hope, even gratitude, as groveling as that seems to me today. But I was tired. Isolation is an exhausting, painful way to live that makes simple survival seem a hopeless aspiration, and the radical politics of the then-lusty WLM appeared to be a chance to end my involuntary isolation, a way to find a community within which I would be accepted as a valuable, contributing member. If radical feminism[5] could change the quality of my life as a Lesbian, I was more than willing, in exchange, to work to improve the lives of other women, all women. If these women were going to fight to make my being a Lesbian easier, I was equally committed to the seriousness of their issues.

I believed, when I first became active in the WLM in 1972, that radical feminist analysis offered me a coherent way of interpreting and understanding my experiences as a Lesbian. Indeed, early feminist radicalism did give me a consistent and coherent basis for making sense of my experiences and acting to change both the way I perceived myself and related to other wimmin. So thorough-going and logical were the insights and explanations I learned from that feminism that I found myself gradually withdrawing from gay male organizations (GLM) and friends in order to remove myself from the omnipresence of their concerns and behaviors and, thereby, to focus my energies on wimmin's and Lesbian issues in a more concentrated, less fragmented way. The more I identified with radical feminism and, as a consequence, understood my experience as female, the less able I was to see my destiny as linked to that of GLM.

First to go was my support for drag shows, which I'd once enjoyed; now the misogyny repelled me. Then, I began to realize how much of the gay lifestyle I knew so well simply wasn't mine. I didn't hang out in bathrooms seeking quick, anonymous sex; I didn't go to Interstate rest areas for a 'night out.' 'Cruising' for sexual partners in public places, with the exception of bars, had never been a part of my life. (And any dyke will tell you that even 'cruising' among us is significantly different from the way that gay men cruise.) More tellingly for my own analysis, pederasty, sadism and masochism, water sports, and a variety of 'kinky' sex behaviors were, and remain, nonexistent in my life as a Lesbian. (That other females who prefer such sexual activities also call themselves 'gay' and identify their interests with those of GLM supports my early conciusion.)[6] Although I numbered among my close friends several gay men, and although I'd come to my feminism through my involvement in GLM, the latter simply didn't address the problems and issues of my life as a Lesbian or

as a womon. I ceased to call myself 'gay' because I finally
understood that the 'gay life' I'd thought I was living since the age
of 15 wasn't *my* life at all, and the 'gay slang' I'd been using for
15 years was primarily a vocabulary for talking about male
sexuality, not mine. In 1972, I finally used the word *Lesbian* to
name myself. The first time was scary, but I managed to get the
word out. I wasn't 'gay' from that time forward, although I did
participate in 'gay' events and collaborate politically with gay men
when I thought we shared compatible goals.

Now, it might seem that some of the preceding realizations
should have been obvious to me long before 1972, but that's how
it was for me. Yes, there'd been times when I felt uncomfortable
among gay men, and times when gay male friends humiliated or
angered me, or both. But I was an outcast, and, as an outcast, I'd
sought companionship in the only place I'd been able to find it.
Imagine, then, my excitement and euphoria when I discovered
strong, energetic, out dykes active in WLM. At first, like many
Lesbians, I divided my energies between WLM and GLM, but,
ultimately, I made a choice. Caught between the sexism of gay
men and the heterosexism and Lesbophobia of heterosexual
feminists, I chose to commit myself to that movement whose ideas
and analysis had first excited me and then given me a foundation
for changing myself in ways that felt good, feminism.

Of course, **AS A LESBIAN** I have many issues in common with
heterosexual and celibate women: rape, battering, incest, sex-role
stereotyping, and sex discrimination, to name only a few. But I
want to emphasize here that, for me, I needed validation and
support for my Lesbianism, *positive* responses that I couldn't get
anywhere else in this society. Not unpredictably, involvement in
the WLM was a trade-off for me. In exchange for having *MY*
issues and concerns dealt with seriously, I was willing to listen
attentively and offer reactions when heterosexual wimmin talked
about their struggles for equality in relationships with men, even
though I had no similar experience of my own and I couldn't
understand why they were so determined to make heterosexuality
'work' for them. But they were, and I accepted their issues with
the seriousness I expected in return. It was that early promise of
acceptance that won my allegiance to radical feminist ideology in
1972.

And, indeed, I *did* find heterosexual feminists who were
seriously committed to Lesbian issues and problems during the
early years of my involvement with the WLM. Some of those
wimmin are still around, but, as the years have passed, I've found
myself more and more seeking the company of wimmin who call
themselves Lesbian-Feminists or Separatists. Why? Because the

trade-off I'd believed would occur failed to become a political reality; I did not find a serious commitment to Lesbian issues in groups controlled by heterosexual feminists, and I felt continually patronized and degraded in my attempts at dialogue with them. Remember when *Ms.* (May 1980, p. 20) reprinted (from *New Women's Times*) a message placed in an 1879 time capsule by a Lesbian, but *DELETED* her statement that she loved other wimmin? Instead of listening to me and other Lesbians when we tried to explain why visibility and acknowledgement were so important to us, heterosexual wimmin tried to convince us that all women were 'the same' regardless of their 'sexual preference,' reducing Lesbianism to a carbon copy of their lives with men. Not only is it simply false to suppose that the life of a Lesbian is identical to that of a heterosexual woman, but that reductionism enables heterosexual feminists to ignore both the constant and tangible *rewards* they derive by living as heterosexuals and the brutal reality of socially condoned persecution of Lesbians. As a result, I came to feel less and less comfortable among the heterosexual wimmin who called themselves 'feminists' but urged me to 'keep a low profile' because my obvious Lesbianism would discredit or harm the WLM or who asked, when I protested being made invisible as a Lesbian, 'Well, what do *YOU* people want?' (No kidding. I'm not making this up. I was asked just that question by a 'feminist' in 1977.)

By 1980, again exhausted, this time by trying to persuade heterosexual feminists to take seriously the realities of Lesbian oppression, the economic and social benefits they received because of their relationships with men, and the stark contrast created by sexuality, I stopped participating in 'feminist' groups with heterosexual wimmin. I withdrew unhappily from a movement that was determined to make the Lesbians within its ranks invisible in order to 'reach out to **ALL** women,' when the phrase 'all women' clearly excluded Lesbians as members and potential beneficiaries of political action. A movement that was committed to creating the façade of a coerced 'unity' that ignored Lesbians and was anxious to avoid 'frightening away potential converts' who, assumed to be heterosexual to a woman, 'would be scared off by "radical extremists".' A movement that was timidly requesting male validation of its retrenched politics, instead of demanding the social reconstruction necessary to make the U.S. a safe place to be a female. At the same time, I want to point out that I wouldn't need to focus attention on the second wave of feminism if it weren't also true that, without it, I wouldn't be talking about the existence or non-existence of a 'Lesbian community' or a 'Lesbian Movement,' and we wouldn't have a journal called *Lesbian Ethics*. It was the WLM, with its weaknesses and strengths, its contradictions and insights, and its tensions and breakthroughs that called forth in many of us the vision of Lesbians living and working together. I don't think it's coincidental that so many Radical Feminists were also Lesbians. We had nothing to 'lose' from telling our truths.

The radical feminism that had demanded an immediate end to the centuries of patriarchal subjugation of women was eroded until all that was sought was a paper reform, the ERA, which would acknowledge (nothing more, mind you) that women are 'human beings, too.' How that acknowledgement of 'equality' with men would establish our right to live without male interference and control has yet to be explained.

It wasn't only heterosexual feminists who abandoned the dream of a 'feminist revolution'; Lesbians, too, accepted without much protest an appeasement program which had, as its explicit goal, the task of making something called 'feminism' less threatening to men and their women. Feminists loudly proclaimed that the 'women's liberation movement' would 'liberate' men as well as women, thereby transforming Feminism into a banal 'humanism.' Remember the *Plexus* (March, 1979) interview in which Charlotte Bunch equated 'the birth of new ideas, the continual moving into new territory' with 'humanism'?

> We need to expand our base of support and to expand the number of women who see themselves as having a stake in humanism. . . . Radical feminism has been the place where new ideas came into being, ideas which later spread to the other, more organized parts of the Women's Movement and then began to be taken up by society. . . . We need growth and enrichment which comes from interaction with people who aren't like us. . . .

What is now being called 'feminism' is indistinguishable from the 'human growth potential' movement, and women who call themselves 'feminists' speak psychobabble fluently, a dialect that enables them to avoid talking about real pains and real issues. Of course, Charlotte Bunch, who'd been a member of The Furies Collective, isn't solely responsible for the devolution of WLM into neo-humanism; she was telling her 1979 audience what they wanted to hear. She helped them to rationalize the redefinition of feminism in the U.S.

What happened on our way to the 'feminist revolution?' The threat of angry male reprisals (a real fear, by the way) intimidated wimmin into redefining our principles. The focus of our politics became, not what we could do to improve the lives of women, but how we could live more comfortably with men. Cohabitation with **men** was substituted for a thorough-going social revolution.

What happened to our vision of a 'Lesbian community'? No one talks about such things anymore unless it's in a derisive, sarcastic, or apologetic tone. Why do I have trouble believing that our present disarray, apathy, and internal conflict is 'just another phase' on our way to something 'better'? Was it, as some would say, merely a PERSONAL dream, a private, non-collective desperation that deluded me into imagining that Lesbians might create spaces where we would be valued and taken seriously? Yet, I know that there were other Lesbians who shared that dream; we talked about it so often. I know that there are Lesbians who still hold that vision, who still talk about it, who silently cherish it in a time when its mention has become an embarrassment. Where are we? Without caucusing, without convention, we've withdrawn into our private and isolated lives. Faced with the heterosexual betrayal of a movement from which we'd hoped for so much, we silently shelved our dreams of freedom and accepted the lesser goal of individual survival, a sort of spiritual 'scraping by' that's as bleak as it is exhausting.

In Montréal, when I touched once more the mystery of being a Lesbian, the miracle of Lesbian survival against all odds and in spite of the tremendous social pressures to deny our feelings, I also recognized the loss of my own hope, a loss whose recognition demanded grieving.

Having relinquished my dreams, I grieve. But I also keep trying to understand what happened and what didn't happen. I keep hearing all those 'feminist' voices urging me to reembrace invisibility, cajoling me to patience ('It's not *your* time yet'), demanding my acquiescence to the substitution of humanism for feminism. Those voices – placating, angry, insulting, declaring the politics of appeasement as the new face of 'feminism' – convince me that I, and I believe WE (radical feminists, Separatists) have been sold out; worse, we've collaborated in selling ourselves out, betrayed by our own willingness to believe in the voices of wimmin, our own hopes for a better future.

Surprised, I realize that I'm angry at being caught off-guard. Angered, I admit that I'm hurting because I failed to protect myself. Hurt, I'm surprised once more because I believed I wouldn't need the defenses against men and other women acquired during a lifetime in a lesbophobic society; worse, I believed, and acted in accordance with that belief, that my own best interest lay with the 'best' interests of other wimmin as they conceive them. *But that naïve belief assumes that other wimmin believe that their 'best interests' lie with all other wimmin; further, belief isn't enough – they must also consistently choose to act in terms of that belief.* Talking about one's commitment to wimmin's issues simply isn't *enough*; each of us must be willing to live that commitment on a daily basis, and that commitment must determine our choices and how we make them. But I know how few wimmin believe that their own lives will be significantly improved by acting in concert with other wimmin, how few dare to entrust their aspirations to the success or failure of women's political action. Of those who say that their self-interests lie with feminist politics, not many will opt for the possibility of failure with other wimmin when backed up against the wall.

What the evidence points to, and reinforces over and over again, is the fact that wimmin as well as women persist in seeing their 'best interests' as inextricably bound up with those of men. Wimmin/women will, time after time, ignore betrayals and hypocrisies they wouldn't think of tolerating in each other in order to link their own destinies and aspirations to those identified by men.

Why would wimmin, especially Lesbians, ignore their own experiences with men (rape, battering, incest) in order to attempt to coerce me into associating with men? How did it happen that, having committed myself to wimmin's issues, I'm informed that my commitment is dubious if I'm not working to 'liberate' men as well? Why is refusing to give my energies to men, all men, racist or classist? Why would wimmin/Lesbians demand that I work with men in order to prove that I'm 'trustworthy'? What on earth could have persuaded so many Lesbians that the men with whom they share one or more oppressions are more reliable and more likely to protect them than I am? Such assertions 'make sense' only if one assumes that what will benefit men will also and certainly benefit women, and I have yet to hear of ANY male group that plans to make ANY WOMON'S life any better. There are NO MALE GROUPS that make feminist issues priorities. How would working with men of any kind promote my well-being?

That programs and actions prioritized by men might be diversions or even hoaxes is easily ignored by wimmin/women who simply cannot imagine their lives as distinct and, yes, SEPARATE from those of men. Realizing how difficult, perhaps impossible, it is for women/wimmin to imagine themselves as having unique and identifiable interests APART FROM those of men, I must abandon a commitment that has informed and given meaning to my life. Then the hurt and anger return. A part of me prefers to believe that wimmin *are* capable of PUTTING OURSELVES FIRST, and another part of me resents my decision to put aside illusions in favor of a reality I cannot deny or ignore.

I Must've Dozed Off

I think there are many reasons why feminism and its current practitioners now repel me, and I see no way that the gulf between contemporary feminism and Separatism can be bridged. Separatism is a politics of insight as well as vision; it names the horror that is heteropatriarchy and imagines a safer world for Lesbians. At the core of my Separatism is my commitment to loving myself and other Lesbians to the best of my ability. In order to do that, however, I've also had to commit myself to actively UNLEARN-ING the self-hatred I was taught from the time I was a child, and that self-hatred takes many forms, not all of them immediately apparent. Being a Separatist is also an energetic, dynamic politics that requires constant alertness and evaluation. NOTHING in my life or in specific situations can be taken for granted; every decision, every impulse, every idea must be weighed, questioned, poked at. I must continue to reconstruct myself, emotionally as well as intellectually, or I risk stagnation and hypocrisy. Worse, I risk self-betrayal. If I fail to believe, each day, that I can be other than I am, if I cease to believe that I'm capable of redefining myself, then my commitment is without substance.

In contrast, the WLM has lost its early enthusiasm and the force of conviction has been drained from its rhetoric, which now echoes the bland, sluggish liberalism of the Democratic Party in the U.S. Certainly, one might have expected that the WLM would lose some of its early energy and enthusiasm with the passage of time, but that occurrence alone won't explain the simultaneous exhaustion of the mental resources of the movement's thinkers or the continued disintegration of its logic and coherence. Of course, one can point to notable exceptions, like *Pure Lust* by Mary Daly (Beacon, 1984) or *Right-Wing Women* by Andrea Dworkin (Putnams, 1983), but they've survived in spite of the WLM, not because of it, their analysis and perceptions undimmed by dreams of 'a slice of the pie.' Or, one could object to my observation by asserting that 'times have changed and WLM has changed with the times,' but that won't account for the continued decline of feminist businesses, the disappearance of wimmin-only spaces, the utter lack of interest in issues that don't include men as part of the agenda. In short, the once enthusiastic support for the spaces available only to wimmin and Lesbians and the politics that made

OUR issues the central focus of our lives have dissolved, only sporadically revived by one group or another. (And even at such events there is an almost tangible aura of nostalgia.)

Is it possible that the world has changed so drastically in 15 years or that men have altered their attitudes and behaviors so radically that the analysis of radical feminism simply no longer applies, is no longer viable or meaningful in wimmin's lives? Did the 'feminist revolution' come and go one night while I slept and I missed it? I doubt it. I cannot accept any of these possibilities as adequate explanations for the demise of radical feminism.

The erosion of radical feminism in the U.S. has been gradual, and time may prove that it was inevitable as well. Individual experiences may differ from mine, but each of us can, I think, supply examples of her own that illustrate equally well the processes of internal destruction. I'll describe my perception of what has happened as starkly as I can: During 1977, International Women's Year, the organizations and 'leaders' of the U.S. WLM saw an opportunity to build a large political constituency, a movement of NUMBERS of women. The urge to count bodies, the belief that numbers is a more significant index of political strength than political consistency, required that feminism be made more palatable to women in general, but especially to the conventional, particularly housewives and others to whom the Eagle Forum had more appeal. Note that, when feminist recruitment strategies were being formulated, it was never suggested that LESBIANS should be the focus of active recruitment. No. The concern has always been 'attracting' heterosexual women into WLM. (In a sense, recruiting heterosexual women into the movement has served to recruit Lesbians, because so many wimmin shed the façade of heterosexuality once they're given permission to love themselves and other wimmin. Hence the felt 'need' to continually find and bring in *more* heterosexuals as their numbers dwindle.)

Once the QUANTITY of bodies took precedence over the QUALITY of one's commitment, feminists wholly adopted the male definition of 'politics,' thereby committing the U.S. WLM to issues formulated within the context of heteropatriarchal political games. 'Feminist politics' became identified with issues sanctioned by the male political framework, and, by focussing on the passage of the ERA to the exclusion of all other issues, feminists tied the fate of the WLM to the whim of male politicians and their female cohorts. Once bound to the limitations imposed by hetero-patriarchal definitions of the 'political,' feminism, as a politics independent of male concerns, could only evaporate.

Steadily, in bits and pieces, radicalism, and its proponents, have been silenced within the WLM as the media personalities (most visibly) set about to redefine and, thereby, dilute the very ideology on which the movement itself was founded and through which it has grown. The emphasis on female autonomy and independence from men is simply discounted; Lesbianism is trivialized and heterosexuality reaffirmed as equivalent 'preferences,' or Lesbianism is made invisible as one among many 'alternate lifestyles'; being a feminist no longer means that one is pro-abortion. In short, any woman can call herself a 'feminist' if she wants to without having to change any of the assumptions she's grown up with and without seriously altering the structure of her life. (I realize that in many contexts, it's quite 'daring' and 'brave' to label oneself a 'feminist,' as nondescript and unthreatening as that word has become, but that fact indicates HOW MUCH we've lost.)

Feminists, in what is one of the grandest follies and delusions of our times (with the exception, perhaps, of heterosexuality itself), have undertaken to make feminist ideology 'respectable,' and set about the rather easy task of disavowing the radical analysis that has been the backbone of the WLM. Many non- and anti-feminists have been, of course, more than willing to help in this process, and the erasure of radical feminism as a presence, however marginal, in U.S. society has been accomplished with a minimum of noise. And, yes, radical feminists allowed this gutting of WLM to occur, but, in our defense, I must also point out that we have neither the numbers to outvote the reformers in floor battles nor the national media visibility that would enable us to present our protests to larger numbers of wimmin. Against the strength of their numbers, we have only the strength of our convictions. Against the range of their media appeal, we have only our irregular periodicals and (necessarily) limited and confidential mailing lists. Against the funds available to liberal feminists, we have only what monies we can raise from our own pockets.

The results have been predictable. Some of us, at first, protested, but we were collectively and individually silenced. Feminism has become, very quickly, the new humanism of the twentieth century, indistinguishable in its political program from garden-variety liberalism. It is a movement that purposely and consciously betrayed its ideology, abandoned its principles, forgot its aims. Anyone can join; misogynists like Alan Alda and John Irving are celebrated as 'feminists,' and support, however tainted, is gleefully sought and accepted, from Mobil Oil, Virginia Slims, and the Playboy Foundation. Those of us impolite enough to challenge such 'progressive' actions find ourselves isolated as 'extremists.' The values first articulated and accepted by early feminists are set aside as 'idealistic,' 'unrealistic,' or, insidiously, 'anti-feminist.' We have, indeed, sold out and been sold out. The values first articulated and acted upon by early feminists have been put aside; most importantly discarded were those aspects of feminist analysis which put wimmin and our issues first, the analysis which validates our experiences of oppression, enjoins us to act on our own behalf, an ideology which can teach us to value ourselves and other wimmin, first.

But along the way, 'oppression' has been abstracted from its immediate social expression so that the agents of wimmin's oppression, men, can be pitied as the 'victims' of their own power and dominance. The radical assertion that 'The personal is the political' is twisted into the notion that anything and everything a woman does must be supported and validated regardless of its sources or ramifications. (This distortion has been criticized by other radical feminists, in particular by contributors to *Feminist Revolution* [Redstockings, 1975], but they attribute its proliferation, erroneously I believe, to 'cultural feminists' [as opposed to 'socialist feminists']. They consider 'dyke separatists' a sub-class of the 'politically-misguided' cultural feminists.) To challenge a woman about her choices and decisions is said to be 'unsisterly,' and we are enjoined to accept without question the doctrine that no woman can be wrong. This distortion of 'the personal is political' makes it impossible to challenge heteropatriarchal institutions like the family, marriage, and the heterosexual framework such institutions protect and perpetuate. If individual men aren't the oppressors of women, then heterosexual women can blithely continue their lives without having to think about WHY being heterosexual is so 'preferable.'

Once oppression is removed from its locus in common female experiences of violence at the hands of specific and identifiable males, the only logical agent for oppressing women is that vague entity 'society.' If 'society' is responsible for oppressing women, one can say, quite logically, that it also oppresses men. Somewhere in that 'logical' sequence, the fact that men benefit from oppressing women in personal and economic ways disappears. By converting 'the personal is the political' into the assertion that every woman's experience and perceptions are equally valid, women who claim they aren't 'oppressed' by men, or who refuse to see the necessity for creating new social structures, have become the voice of WLM.

Well, of course, everything now looks much easier than it did before. Radical change is no longer necessary because our society is pretty much OK as it is; there are simply a few 'misunderstandings' between women and men that need to be cleared up and all will be well, superficial stuff like who'll take out the garbage or run for President. Consciousness raising groups, those early groups where we'd not only articulated and identified our common experiences of oppression under the dominance of men but conceived of independence from them as well, have ceased to exist. Wimmin have abandoned the idea that each of us is responsible for the necessary work of examining every assumption we've grown up with, dismantling the social imperatives in our minds that bind us to male domination, and reprogramming our self-conceptions for autonomy and independence. The experience of any woman, however unexamined, unquestioned, and utterly conventional, isn't open to question, and we hear, more and more frequently, that we can't 'judge' each other. As though feminism is ideologically empty, without its own values and principles.

'See Jane Blow It'

Freudianism, marxism, judaism, xtianity, all these and any other conceptual frameworks of the heteropatriarchy, are in direct ideological conflict with the Feminism I learned in the early '70s. Rather than subject the framework of values within which they were raised (e.g.; xtianity, judaism, socialism, capitalism) or educated (e.g., jungian or freudian psychology) to critical examination, latter-day feminists have attempted to infuse such ideological structures with 'feminist values.' Instead of letting go of heteropatriarchal ways of describing the world, people, and events, they have tried to revise such conceptual frameworks so they could feel more comfortable within them. In order to avoid the complicated task of changing their own ways of thinking and behaving, reform feminists set out instead to introduce a few minor revisions in the heteropatriarchal agenda, leaving themselves and social institutions largely unquestioned and unchanged. If we think of ideological frameworks as though each was a house, with a foundation, an internal structure, and several different rooms, so that marxism is a house, freudianism is a house, xtianity is a house, etc., what is now called 'feminism' is nothing more than one, tiny room in each masculist ideology. Feminism has no house of its own. Feminists have torn it down, because they didn't have any confidence in the way it was built. Was our construction so shoddy that we were afraid to try and live in it? Instead of having a 'home' of our own, we now have cramped rooms rented to us by xtians, freudians, marxists, socialists, etc. (Is this why so many Lesbian spaces like our coffeehouses, are in the rented basements of xtian churches?)

'Women's athletics' is a good example of how reform feminists have moved into a little room in a heteropatriarchal framework instead of building their own house. (Note that it's not called 'feminist athletics.') In universities, the money has usually been provided by the (still) all-male football team (and not without considerable resistance). Given the social stereotype that women must be feminine, the associated assumption that athletic women are, somehow, 'less than women,' i.e., Lesbians, and the fact that any financial support for female athletes would have to be sought from men, wimmin committed to female athletics simply continued the pro-feminine, anti-Lesbian propaganda that has characterized women's sports in the U.S. for as long as I can remember.[7] Now, however, with the prospect of financial rewards in the foreseeable future, the anti-Lesbian campaign has become more vicious. The existence of Lesbians in athletics continues to be vigorously denied or, when the evidence is unarguable, dismissed as quantitatively insignificant; Lesbians are coerced, threatened, and intimidated into staying in their closets, denying themselves and their lovers, and adopting those behaviors and modes of dress that will enable them to pass for heterosexual.

Because so many female athletes are Lesbians, the consequences were predictable. Consider, for example, the now-dead women's pro-basketball league. In order to sell the athletes as sex objects to their male fans (no one cared what their Lesbian fans thought), the athletes were *forbidden* to go to women's bars. The immediate cost of becoming a professional athlete for every woman was the curtailment of her personal life, limitations imposed on her freedom of movement. One player, for example, who'd been seen going into a women's bar, was immediately traded to another team. Ironically, her male fans, for whom she was a sex symbol, were so outraged by the trade that the owners of the team had to back down and reinstate her. Lesbians in athletics are *a fact*. There's no way to make 'compromises' like this one (compromise is a polite word, this was a *sell-out*) and expect anything but personal destruction of the women so man-handled. A Lesbian who chooses her identity first and refuses to deny it cannot be an athlete. Wimmin who should've known better accepted without question the heteropatriarchal framework of athletics.

The basic premises of athletics in the U.S. remain what they've always been, essentially competitive and identifiably militaristic in their structures: winners/losers, offense/defense, domination/submission. These are essential, institutionalized dichotomies in our society, and we cannot ignore the fact that they justify violence as a way of life, 'explain' the systematic destruction of women's minds and lives, and promote war as a 'necessary evil' in the world. These dichotomies aren't 'harmless' or inevitable ways of conceptualizing ourselves and others. As a result, we act out of and perpetuate a violent dualism when we refuse to challenge women who accept them.[8] **WHOSE INTERESTS ARE WE SERVING?**

Don't get me wrong. I'm as thrilled as any other womon when I watch women's athletics and see women striving for a goal, succeeding, and being rewarded for their perseverance. I watched avidly as female athletes won medal after medal in the 1984 Olympics. But we cannot ignore the COST of such accomplishments, the PRICE that every single one of us must pay for such individual achievements, and we cannot stop asking if such gains are WORTH the utter betrayal of feminist values. We cannot, for example, pretend not to notice the USES to which such women are put as evidenced in the decidedly patriotic, imperialistic, militaristic descriptions typical of ABC's coverage of the 1984 Olympics. While the sportscasters were, on the one hand, patronizing in their treatment of the female athletes, they were, on the other hand, utterly glib when they talked about how the U.S. women 'dominated' the basketball court or compared the coach of the U.S. women's volleyball team to General Patton![9] Some women have made some gains in the world of athletics, but they must, in exchange, allow men to make whatever use of them will immediately benefit heteropatriarchal society and perpetuate its underlying assumptions.

Most importantly, for me, I cannot pretend that any of these compromises have made it any easier to be a Lesbian. If anything, it's become more difficult as a result, rather than less. I'm unwilling to concede that much has been accomplished if the quality of a Lesbian's life is improved materialistically at the expense of its psychological quality. It's harrowing and demeaning to live with the constant fear of discovery; the more one believes she has to lose economically, the more terrified she becomes. A few women have made perceptible gains for themselves, but what about the invisible, the unknown, the uncounted Lesbians? Are we so inept, so unresourceful, that we must be grateful for so little? Are we so desperate that we'll abandon **all** our principles in order to accept **any** crumb tossed to us by the patriarchy?

Emily Levine[10] has suggested an analogy from carpentry that illuminates how the process of compromise has functioned to erode radical values in WLM. In carpentry, when one has several boards that she has to cut down to the same size, each succeeding board must be measured, not by matching it with the board just cut, but with the *FIRST* board cut. By measuring the length of each board against the first one, the carpenter insures that every board ends up the same length. If she makes the mistake of measuring each successive board against the one cut just before it, she'll discover, when she finishes, that none of the boards are the same length. As the number of boards cut between the first one and the last one increases, so, too, does the extent of the error in measurement.

Similarly the individual compromises we've made in WLM haven't seemed 'dangerous' or 'unreasonable' taken one by one. Cumulatively, however, they've gradually added up until WLM no longer *has* a political viewpoint distinguishable from humanism. Weighing compromises against the one we made only the day before has made each particular concession seem negligible. Measuring the politics of the contemporary WLM against the radicalism of early second-wave Feminism, though, reveals how far short we've fallen of fulfilling those goals. Each compromise has moved us imperceptibly away from radicalism on our own behalf, until the gap between what we said we wanted and what we have (or are likely to achieve) has destroyed the framework we set out to build.

> As our right-wing enemies have gained in strength and
> arrogance, women have become more and more afraid
> . . .
>
> *Dworkin*

In an effort to enlarge the 'appeal' of WLM and 'attract' more women into its burned-out ranks, every issue that might 'turn off' a prospective 'feminist' was euphemized into extinction or abandoned altogether. Our failure to examine critically the *means* of realizing the radical goals of early feminism led, inevitably, to the eradication of the goals themselves. What is unspeakable too easily becomes the unthinkable.

I'm tired of 'movement women' who play only to men and worry about what 'they' think. I'm tired of women denying my existence because I'm a 'political liability.' I'm tired of being ignored and trivialized because I'm a Lesbian; I'm tired of being hushed up, quieted, and made invisible so other folks can get on with 'their business.' There is no struggle for human dignity (call it 'rights' if you will) that is 'trivial.' There is no instance of the abuse and exploitation of the powerless by the powerful that is justifiable. I am not attempting to ignore or dismiss other people's existence by claiming the significance of my own; I am, once more, trying to make a space for my existence, my dignity, my importance.

I'm objecting to the way other issues have been used to diffuse and disperse feminist energies, to turn the WLM into Mother-hoodism, to make us responsible for *solving* problems in the world that we didn't create, to force us into nurturing men, again. and cleaning up after them, again, when they've made yet another mess. The radiation leaking from nuclear sites, is, after all, piss on the toilet seat on a grand and lethal scale. Men either don't care enough about anything to clean up after themselves or, used to their own power and the habit of wielding it, they've become accustomed to having someone else, usually women, clean up their messes for them. Like the guilt-ridden wife blamed for her husband's 'ring around the collar,' politically-conscious wimmin choose to ignore or dismiss male causation, because acknowledging it would then require developing an adequate means of neutralizing it. If men washed their necks, ring-around-the-collar wouldn't exist; there would be no 'problem' to solve. If men didn't like war, and the toys of war, the thrill of killing, and the promise of death, the world wouldn't be like it is. War, like dirty necks, is a by-product of male manufacture.

Yes, Let's Talk about Men

The 'split' in the WLM has never been defined or examined, because it's not a subject we can talk about without a lot of anger and pain. Attempts to describe the 'split' usually deteriorate into name-calling, scape-goating, and then withdrawal by those participating. The issue of *Maenad* (Winter, 1982) that tries to figure out the 'split,' called 'The Lesbian/Heterosexual Split,' wavers somewhere between sincere, but simplistic efforts to mend the breach and ferocious anti-Separatism. To label our division as a 'Lesbian/heterosexual split' is erroneous, because many Lesbians refuse to choose wimmin and will not give up their masculist values, and some heterosexual feminists show, time and time again, that their commitment to feminist values is reliable and consistent. It would be more accurate to characterize the 'split' as one between Separatists and Radical Feminists on the one hand and Assimilationists on the other, with Coalitionists waffling around uneasily somewhere in-between.

Separatists, for example, maintain that the only way to free ourselves from male domination is for all females to withdraw from men, to withhold from them our energy, our nurturing, our care-taking of them; only in this way, we believe, we can erode the foundation of male power and control over us. Male power is based on female complicity in our own powerlessness; to say 'no' to male demands on our bodies, our minds, our energies, is to take power for ourselves. The Assimilationists, in contrast, maintain that the only way to liberate ourselves is to 'struggle' with men, educate them about their sexism, nurture them through the painful changes necessary to a thorough-going social revolution.

That is the essential ground of the split that divides the WLM: **What do we do with men?** To say that they're 'half the population' and can't be ignored begs the question. All of us know they exist. Separatists and Radical Feminists assert that men use women's labor and energies as the basis of their domination. If we are to free ourselves, we must first deny them access to the nurturing on which they depend. Liberal and Reform Feminists, in contrast, claim that we'll liberate ourselves by working with men and convincing them to change. Both Assimilation and Coalition, in order to sound like plausible political goals (or strategies) presuppose Separatism, but the success of Coalition *requires* Separatism as the power base for political trade-offs, whereas Assimilation entails the necessary denial of Separatism in the formulation of its program.

Lesbians who choose to work with heterosexual wimmin misconstrue the issue of giving energy to men, and reduce it to sex, as though that were the significant distinction. Carole Anne Douglas, defending her 'token good heterosexual feminist' quotes Ti-Grace Atkinson to the effect that '. . . it is more important what you're willing to die for than who you sleep with' (*Maenad*, p. 60). And I agree. The 'real' issues that we refuse to talk about have to do with our values, the frameworks we use to make our choices and order our priorities. Unfortunately, we frequently choose *what* we're willing to die for on the basis of *who* we sleep with, and that's the 'grain of truth' that makes the reduction to 'sexual preference' sound plausible. The fact remains that, *generally* speaking, it is more likely that I'll be able to rely on a Lesbian than a heterosexual feminist.

That generalization is based on my experience and observations. Because heterosexual feminists choose men as their sexual partners, their allegiance to other feminists and, especially, to Lesbians is divided and ambivalent, at best, or nonexistent, at worst. Because they maintain intimate emotional relationships with men, they see their 'best interests' as more likely to be served by Assimilationist politics; that way, they don't have to confront the nature of their investment in men and they can enjoy whatever benefits come their way as a result of their male connections.

Lesbians, though, have made a choice; at some point in our lives, we crossed a line. We put behind us the heterosexual privileges offered to us and acted on our feelings for other wimmin. That single decision is the basis of my Lesbian politics. We said 'no' to the social pressures and rewards that demanded our self-denial. In spite of the fact that many Lesbians remain 'in the closet' and get whatever they can by pretending to be heterosexual, in spite of the fact that many Lesbians cling to whatever privilege dribbles down to them from working with gay men, I continue to look for my surest support, caring, and understanding among Lesbians. Even when they don't share my Separatist politics, they do share many of the same problems of survival that I experience daily.

In contrast, although the aspects of my experience that I'm likely to share with a heterosexual feminist may seem somehow 'broader' or more general, the range of commonality between us is little more than a narrow strip that must constantly be renegotiated if mutual benefits are to come from our political association. It might seem, for example, that 'equal pay for equal work' would be a common issue on which we might profitably work together, and, to a limited extent, that's true. But the reality is that many Lesbians need jobs before 'equal pay' becomes an issue to them, especially 'out,' 'open' Lesbians. (I've put the words *out* and *open* in quotation marks to emphasize the lack of connection between a Lesbian and a heterosexual feminist in even the most obvious aspect of our lives, economic well-being.) Most blatant Lesbians, whether for physical or political reasons, or some combination of the two, as in my case, cannot find jobs, and the ones available to us are factory work and other low-paying occupations. Our Lesbianism keeps us at the bottom economically. Many professional jobs are closed to us by law, in some states, or by tacit maneuvers, and the latter is the prevalent method because, quite simply, Lesbians don't have legal rights in the U.S. Since we don't have any 'rights' to be violated, our economic lives are both peripheral and extremely fragile. One might or might not get a job, or a raise, or a promotion because she's female; we don't get jobs because we're Lesbians, but we certainly lose them for that reason and that reason *alone*. Even Lesbians who choose to remain 'in the closet' live in an illusory security, because disclosure almost always means ruin for the Lesbian whose identity is discovered by employers.

From the time we're born, quite literally, we are told we're heterosexual; our parents take for granted that the primary objects of our emotional and sexual responses will be men. From nursery school on, our teachers, some of them Lesbians themselves, determine what we'll learn and how we learn it by assuming, first, that every female in a class is heterosexual. Sexual harassment by male teachers (and employers) assumes that every female is heterosexual and, hence, their legitimate prey. If such treatment is insulting, degrading, and humiliating for the heterosexual, it's doubly so for the Lesbian.

The media depend upon the heterosexual majority for their credibility and viability. If we destroyed every book, movie, sitcom and piece of music, from opera to new wave, that assumes the heterosexuality of its audience, there'd be no 'entertainment.' The real theme of *Yentl* was the triumph of heterosexuality; the intense emotional relationship that developed between the two women (but only because Yentl was cross-dressing) had to give way to heterosexual conformity. (Ask yourself, for example, why couldn't the two women abandon the charade that brought them together and forget the man altogether? The movie could have developed in that direction, but didn't!) Advertisements, on television, radio, billboards, and in newspapers and magazines, **sell**, along with cars, toothpaste, and diet colas, **heterosexuality**. The Diet Pepsi and Levis ads now showing on TV are good examples.

From the mundane to the tragic, heterosexuality is the subject. How can something touted as 'natural' need so much PR? Lesbianism is, as Sally Gearhart said years ago, A MIRACLE!! And a **MYSTERY**. HOW, without guidance, encouragement, accurate information, images and words to nurture us, do we manage, finally, TO CONCEIVE OURSELVES?? HOW, in spite of derision, incarceration, violence, and poverty, do we find the courage TO CREATE OURSELVES?? I don't know, and wish I did. Like cockroaches, we live in the woodwork of society, in its tiny cracks and crevices, finding our way to each other. Like cockroaches and dandelions, all attempts to eradicate us have failed; if anything, overt efforts to thwart us strengthen our resolve and make us more stubborn.

Separatists, and some radical feminists, have told the truth that other women don't want to hear: **WE'RE AT WAR**. Men are the enemy, and heterosexuality makes wimmin collaborators in their own betrayal. I'm not using a 'metaphor' here; I'm speaking literally. Yes, there is a 'battle of the sexes.' What is so painful and terrifying about acknowledging that fact is that we **didn't declare this war**. We didn't *choose* to be at war. It may be a war we're going to lose, every day of our lives. It may be a war we can't win. In every aspect of their lives, women have been invaded, conquered, and colonized. But most women either won't admit that they're hostages of enemy forces or they go on believing that 'the battle' is a *joke*! A war is an armed conflict, yet women consciously, willingly, choose to live their lives *dis-armed* and 'disarming.'

In spite of such behaviors, Lesbians have provided, and continue to provide, much of the energy that has fueled a dwindling and sputtering WLM. In return for our care, our patience, and hard work, heterosexual feminists have claimed that Lesbians 'divide' wimmin when we demand all-wimmin spaces; they've called us 'extremists' when we refused to 'be nice' to their 'exceptional men'; they've accused us of 'heterophobia' when we objected to their insistence on male presence in wimmin's groups. This is patriarchal reversal. What continues to scatter and defuse the energies of WLM in this century is the central place in their lives heterosexual feminists continue to give to their 'exceptional men.'[11]

And, because so many women persist in believing that men can change, and delude themselves by thinking men *will* change, insisting that their own fate is inextricably bound up with that of men, a lot of Lesbian energy has gone into maintaining shelters for battered women (NOT spouses!), rape crisis lines, and rape patrols. In spite of the real and needed aid and solace such projects provide, they're nothing more than field hospitals for the wounded, the maimed, and the dead – the fatalities of the 'battle between the sexes.' And the war goes on. Denials of its existence don't stop it; refusals to name it for what it is don't make it any less real or dangerous.

Men rape women at will, beat up women when it pleases them to do so, murder their wives and daughters, rape their daughters, grand-daughters, nieces, sisters, cousins, use and abuse any and every woman to whom they have access. Rape and murder are the activities of WAR. Looting and destroying the possessions of the conquered are what war is all about. Does it improve our situation to point out that it's our MINDS and BODIES that are daily looted and destroyed? Is it not war because we have nothing of our own but our minds and bodies to protect? Yet, only a few hundred wimmin, at the most, will acknowledge that women are at war, and that we're losing, have lost. Only a few will name the enemy. Why?

The Sitting Ducks

If any group of wimmin has been hurt by the failure of 'sisterhood,' it's Separatists. We eagerly embraced the vision of a world of wimmin, free and unfettered by the rule of men. We made that vision the focus of our lives and energies. In return for our commitment, we demanded the same commitment to change and struggle from other wimmin.

When the WLM began to 'go bad' as we knew it would, Lesbians, Separatists in particular, became the scapegoats for the anger and frustration of the neo-humanist, reform feminists. How utterly, drearily predictable. We're much easier to get to because we're accessible: we chose wimmin. We're easier to hurt because we love wimmin; we're safer to attack because the only 'weapon' we have for our own defense is further withdrawal, retreat from our own commitment to wimmin. But we're not only more accessible for scape-goating than the men who run this world's governments, we have neither their power nor their will to hurt other wimmin. Separatists haven't simply been silenced, although it's true that we have. We've also consciously maintained our silence, refusing to respond every time we were attacked in print by other wimmin and Lesbians, because we didn't want to respond in kind; we didn't want to help perpetuate the horizontal hostility that keeps us from confronting and fighting our real enemies. Lacking the resources and having failed to adequately protect ourselves from the psychic pain inflicted by other wimmin, we have remained the sitting ducks of the WLM.

There's hardly an issue in this world or a type of oppression that Separatists haven't been blamed for, from racism to the sexual objectification of other Lesbians. On this, see, for example, Chapter 14, 'The Extremist Fringe,' in *Sunday's Women* by Sasha G. Lewis, where Separatism is called 'latter-day lesbian fascism,' and blamed for the 'coldness of instant anonymous sexuality that is more reminiscent of a large subgroup of the gay male culture than of lesbians' (pp. 174–81). The false attributions and mistaken identities of this chapter are too confused for adequate discussion here. It's so much easier to call Separatists names than it is to fight the power of the heteropatriarchy.

The idea that an autonomous 'wimmin's liberation movement' is somehow invalid or insignificant is the fundamental assumption of the essays in *Yours in Struggle* (*YIS*).[12] Barbara Smith, for example, extolling the usefulness of what she calls 'identity politics' (which she doesn't define) in the development of 'Third World feminism,' asserts that '[i]dentity politics has been much less effective when primary emphasis has been placed upon exploring and celebrating a *suppressed* identity within a women's movement context, rather than upon developing practical political solutions for confronting oppression in the society itself' (p. 84, my emphasis). In order to make this distinction between 'effective' and 'ineffective' uses of 'identity politics,' Smith must assume a dichotomy between 'political activism' and exploration/celebration 'within a women's movement context.' Whatever is identified as 'personal,' or focussed on wimmin's identity, is treated as politically irrelevant.[13]

It [identity politics] has undoubtedly been most clarify-

ing and catalytic when individuals do in fact have a
combination of non-mainstream identities as a result of
their race, class, ethnicity, sex, and sexuality; when
these identities make them direct targets of oppression;
and when they use their experiences of oppression as a
spur for activist political work (p. 84).

Although she's generously willing to grant that other oppressions do exist, and she implies that being a female and a Lesbian
might make one the 'direct target' of oppression, she conceptually
puts what she regards as valid 'political activism' in opposition to
'celebration' of a 'suppressed identity.' This convenient solipsism
ignores what oppression is and what it does to each of us as
individuals. It ignores the self-hatred not only of Lesbians but of
all other oppressed peoples, and it refuses to consider how that
ingrained self-hatred divides us and perpetuates horizontal
hostility. How, Barbara Smith, are we to engage in what you'd
consider 'political activism' if we don't confront our self-hatred, if
we don't work to eradicate the ways our self-hatred continues to
be used against us? How do we get from here to there without
first learning to respect and value ourselves?

The answer is that, in Smith's framework, we don't. Being
female or a Lesbian, according to her description, doesn't mean
that we're oppressed. It's only when 'these identities make them
[i.e., *us*] *direct targets of oppression*' that sex and sexuality are
valid to her. How many combinations of oppression does it take
before one can see herself as legitimately oppressed? How
DIRECT does the oppression have to be before it qualifies as
significant in Smith's framework? Clitoridectomy, infibulation,
coerced sterilization, daughter rape, and the bride slaughter going
on in India are **wimmin's** issues. Once we've said that women do
two-thirds of the world's work, get 10% of the wages paid for
work, and own only 1% of the world's property, we have
acknowledged that we are the largest, most exploited, most
impoverished class in the world.

And it is LEGITIMACY that's in question, for Smith goes on to
say this about Jewish 'identity politics':

When Jewish feminism has subscribed to or been
influenced by cultural feminism, separatism, or a
narrow version of identity politics, it has been limited
in both analysis and strategy, since, for example, anti-
Semitism does not manifest itself solely as attacks upon
individual's identities, nor does it only affect Jewish
women (p. 84).

'Limited,' 'narrow,' 'solely,' and 'only.' These words betray the real intention of Smith's 'analysis.' If we aren't working with men, if our attention is turned to women, it isn't 'politics.' Why has Smith persisted in attacking Separatist politics for the past decade? If we're so wrong-headed and irrelevant, why not ignore us and hope we'll go away? Perhaps she thinks that Separatists are simply 'perverse' or 'quirky' for refusing to allow men to have access to our energies, because she persists in saying that Separatists deny that some men are oppressed. We do not, and the statement that we do utterly devalues our decision to concentrate on fighting oppressions that make wimmin's lives miserable. That decision entails a commitment to eradicating *all* kinds of racism and classism, as they affect us as wimmin. It doesn't entail giving energy to men.

Smith's failure to grasp this point and her insistence on valuing men can only be understood by referring to her avowed Socialism. The hatred of wimmin, the more virulent hatred of Lesbians aren't grounded in the material causes which Socialists define. We must make a choice, one *forced* on us by male domination. WE MUST CHOOSE WIMMIN.

The utter devaluation of women, of Lesbians in particular, and the insistence on prioritizing men, has destroyed the very idea of a WOMEN'S LIBERATION MOVEMENT. Smith, for example, cites as a 'major misunderstanding within feminism as a whole . . . that it is politically viable to work on anti-Semitism, racism, or any other system of oppression solely within a women's movement context' (p. 84). I don't understand now why Barbara Smith calls herself a 'feminist,' since the 'women's movement context' is apparently insignificant to her.

No matter how oppressed a man is, he always has a woman somewhere who bears the brunt of his anger and frustrations. I cannot ignore the fact that men rape women, ALL MEN. Yet, Barbara Smith and Elly Bulkin would have me somehow 'forget' this. They would have me regard my oppression as a Lesbian as insignificant in order to concentrate my energies on what they consider 'real politics.' I'm asked to ignore sexism, heterosexism, and Lesbophobia. I'm asked to somehow be more noble or generous than my oppressors, MEN. I'm asked to tolerate their intolerance of me; in other words, Bulkin and Smith, like so many other segments of heteropatriarchal society, want me to devalue myself.

I'm tired of being told that I'm a 'bad person' because I'm a Separatist. I'm tired of being attacked because I choose to concentrate my energies on Lesbian oppression. Men of any and all groups not only don't believe that Lesbians are oppressed, which would be *something*; they regard us as sub-human, as bourgeois degenerates, as a 'dirty joke.' I'm sorry, I will not ignore the way I'm treated by men in order to qualify for Smith's validation. I won't work with men and endure their sexism and heterosexism in order to 'measure up' to Smith's definition of 'political activism.' I will not tolerate being ignored and demeaned, and that's exactly what Smith has done. I will not work side by side with anyone unless and until I believe that they are as committed to dealing with my issues as I am to dealing with theirs.

At the same time that she's busy telling me what's 'legitimate' and what isn't, Smith goes on, in the very next paragraph, to inform 'some Jewish feminists' that it's 'offensive' to 'Black and other women of color' to say that to be or to have been at any time a Christian 'is to be by definition anti-Semitic' (p. 77). In order to cover herself, in order to place Black xtians beyond political criticism, she distinguishes between what she calls 'institutionalized Christianity' and 'the mere practice of Christianity' (p. 77). What is xtianity if not anti-Semitic? How can one 'practice' xtianity without also being anti-Semitic? She doesn't attempt to answer these questions but, instead, asserts that Blacks have 'reshaped' xtianity 'into an entirely unique expression of Black spirituality and faith, . . . a major source of sustenance and survival for our people' (p. 78).[14]

That my questions indicate a contradiction in Smith's assertions becomes obvious when women and (invisibly) Lesbians are accused of 'limited' and 'narrow' 'cultural feminism for emphasizing the development of a distinct women's culture through such vehicles as music, art, and spirituality' (p. 84). Why does Smith place challenges to xtianity 'off limits' because Blacks practice it, but persist in demeaning the political significance of wimmin's/Lesbian's attempts to identify/create our own culture? Why is the xtian religious impulse among Blacks a 'survival' strategy, but the desire for a wimmin's culture and spirituality not? What is the difference we're being asked to acknowledge? Exactly **what** is being prioritized by this differential treatment?

Not surprisingly, as a result of the socialists' insistence that anything woman-centered is unimportant, *misogyny* is a word that has disappeared from the 'feminist' vocabulary, along with *sexism* and *heterosexism*. Reading *Yours in Struggle*, I could believe, if I wasn't aware of the continued rise in rape, battering and incest, that misogyny had ceased to be a problem. Whatever happened to *sexism* as a fundamental issue for feminists? It's virtually impossible now to mention *sexism* without a shuffling sort of embarrassment, and, when I do happen to hear it, it's usually a heterosexual woman accusing Lesbians of 'oppressing' some man. Feminists can see their way clear these days to saving anyone from 'sexism' if he's also, coincidentally, MALE.

Once feminists extended the range of 'sexist' oppression to include men, the word lost its meaning, and, although that extension required one of the most mind-boggling semantic tricks in recent history (Ronald Reagan and George Bush still have us beat, though), only Separatists objected. In order to believe that a male can be sexually oppressed, one must also posit that, at the same time that he's benefiting from oppressing women, it's his *benefits* that 'oppress' him!!! If I hear one more womon say, as an afterthought, that men and boys are 'raped, too,' I may turn in my 'feminist secret decoder ring' that so many Lesbians have demanded I relinquish. Gladly. Perhaps then I could watch the internal intrigues and hostilities and betrayals with some serenity; perhaps then I could turn my attention to more satisfying contemplations.

Ending sexism and its devastating effects in the lives of women has yielded to a dogmatic insistence on 'human beingism.' We wouldn't, after all, want to assert the unforgivable idea that we should, first and foremost, be committed to healing ourselves from the violence and battering and rape and incest perpetrated by men, and to making whatever lives we can for each other amidst the emotional devastation caused by male violence! Oh no! Feminists have tripped all over themselves, trampling many of us in the process, to reassure the timid and the reactionary that they're worried about *everyone*, and it's now taboo to suggest that we might be our own PRIORITY. How many other oppressed groups have been so willing and eager to make their oppressors' welfare their primary concern?

The authors of *YIS*, between their persistent refusal to identify Lesbian oppression as central in their political analysis and their perpetual demeaning of a wimmin-only politics, tacitly assume that heterosexual dominance is, has been, and will always be. Underneath that, I believe, is a fear of casting their lot with Lesbians. This fear isn't explicit, of course. It's to be found in what isn't said, in the silences and omissions. In her final chapter, 'Openings,' Bulkin, for example, says:

> I believe, for instance, that our choices both of political priorities and of strategies are influenced by our definitions of our community and our home, by the people we can trust are beside us and those we see only across the room or down the block (p. 191).

I agree. Choosing one's 'political priorities' entails hierarchizing oppressions. But how does Bulkin define her community? She doesn't say, but she doesn't name Lesbians as her political priority either. Being a Lesbian isn't Bulkin's priority, and I want to know why. Why do Lesbians have to wait until all the oppressed men are taken care of?

Two possible answers to my question can be found in Bulkin's article: (1) the 'scarcity' theory of political struggle, whose identification she attributes to Melanie Kaye/Kantrowitz (p. 139); and (2) the obvious warmth and safety she associates with the word *home* in the above quotation. I agree that feeling as though one must choose between one or more forms of oppression is disturbing, but we **do choose** those with whom we 'cast our lot,' and we make that choice on the basis of who we look to for 'community.' The way Bulkin uses the word *home* indicates that her model of community is based on the heteropatriarchal nuclear family, a mother and a father who make a 'home' in which their children are 'safe.' In contrast, for me the word *home* conjures violent nightmares, memories of the years I spent locked in my bedroom so my stepfather couldn't get to me. And I know I'm not alone in rejecting the nuclear family as a metaphor for community or 'haven.' For too many of us, the 'family' was an arena of on-going torment, torture, and pain. It was within the hetero-patriarchal family that we experienced, first-hand, the reality of male power and female powerlessness. While our 'fathers' raped us, our mothers stood by, silent and tearful. Socialists and reformists refuse to question their reliance on the nuclear family as a model of 'community.'

Both Bulkin and Smith look to constituencies other than Lesbians/wimmin for their support and validation, while, simul-taneously claiming the label 'feminist' for themselves. Why are they ignoring HETEROSEXUAL DOMINANCE? At what cost are they ignoring the political significance of their Lesbianism? Why have they gone to such lengths to rationalize their choices, over and over and over? Why don't they go off and be socialists and stop trying to discredit Separatism? What is their investment in casting Separatists as the 'enemy'? Why do they believe so strongly that Separatists are more 'dangerous' to them than either men or heterosexuals?

The fact of the matter is, as Mary Daly has said over and over again, **we aren't supposed to question the BACKGROUND.** We're expected to limit our analytical attention to the FORE-GROUND of heteropatriarchy, thereby limiting the potential of our insights and dis-coveries. By and large 'feminists' like Smith and Bulkin have dutifully stuck to the heteropatriarchal agenda, asking safe questions and intoning the predictably safe answers. For these reasons, although some Lesbians continue to call themselves 'radical' or 'Lesbian feminist,' trying, thereby, to keep alive the radical promise of WLM, many of us have ceased to call ourselves 'feminists.' Some now refuse any label for their politics, so tainted are the available options; others of us continue to wield the name 'Separatist,' as a reminder to 'feminists' that they might have made other choices than the ones they did.

As Sid Spinster pointed out in her excellent rebuttal of Adrienne Rich's confused 'Notes for a Magazine: What Does Separatism Mean?'[15]

> It's time for non-Separatist Lesbians to start explaining yourselves. What does it mean to not be a Separatist in 'our' movement? What is your strategy for the defeat of patriarchy over the long haul? Can you honor the choice of Separatist wimmin of color not to work with men? Is it racist *not* to be a Separatist; not to withdraw your support from patriarchy, not to fight for an anti-racist Lesbian-identified culture?

I have **yet** to hear even *attempted* answers to Sid's questions, which indicates two things to me: First, the neo-humanists among us didn't (and don't) take her questions seriously; second, they can't *afford* to take them seriously because they don't have answers to them. To date, neo-humanists have substituted Separatist-baiting and name-calling for outlining a viable, plausible political analysis of their own, thereby avoiding the unpleasant prospect of asking themselves questions they're afraid to answer. . . .

I want wimmin who choose men to take responsibility for that decision, because it's a choice that everything in our society encourages, urges, *man*dates, requires. **I live in a society that tells me every day to choose men.** When I turn on the radio or television, no one screams at me to choose Lesbians. No one tells me to buy Diet Pepsi because then I'll meet 'the Dyke of my dreams.' I'm not told to buy Hanes pantyhose because Dykes 'prefer' them! (Which is probably just as well for me!) In such a society, try to imagine the insult to my intelligence, my sensibilities, when Starhawk, who calls herself a 'feminist,' asserting that 'we need images of both genders to enable us to come into all of our powers' and that 'the part of us that feels free and autonomous, out of the realm of mother's control, comes to be identified with maleness,' LEAPS to the conclusion that, 'This might change, of course, if our childcare arrangements changed so that men as well as women become associated with the fears and pleasures of infancy . . .'[16]

What kind of 'political' analysis is this? It's pure heterosexualism.[17] When Starhawk asserts that 'we' need both sexes for role models, she blithely ignores those of us who were brought up by our mothers, liked it that way, and believe that our lives are better and stronger *because* we didn't have a male parent during our formative years. Some of us *have* managed to do well for ourselves, and, even though I agree with her claim that we associate freedom and independence with men, I can't conclude, with her, that allowing men access to babies and children will help to break that association. If anything, as an incest survivor, I believe that allowing men unlimited and unsupervised access to children is a stupid, dangerous idea, made to appear plausible in the context of a humanist framework that asks us to ignore real and provable differences between the behaviors and actions of women and men. If men get their way, and women let them participate in raising children, we'll very quickly notice a substantial increase in the numbers of incest victims. And I know too well the damaging extent and power of my past experiences as an incest victim, and how, without my being aware of it, those experiences controlled and poisoned my responses in intimate relationships.[18]

Finding My Way Back

As I sit here today, trying to trace the outlines of my pain and isolation, I see that I had to go back and touch the old pains I'd thought were 'behind' me, for the old and the new are the same knowledge: I don't 'belong' anywhere. But the new pain, now identified, hurts more because I believed, for a while, that I'd found a community among Lesbians, that I did belong somewhere. As painful as it is to realize that I don't belong in the WLM anymore, having been defined out of it, it's harder to admit that I have no place to go among Lesbians, either. Harder, because if I don't belong among Lesbians I have no other place to go. Because I'm a Lesbian, I've never had the 'option' of joining heterosexual society. They won't have me, and I won't have them. I can't delude myself with the possibility of assimilation, nor accept the humiliation of tolerance, as 'gay wimmin' can. Because I'm a Lesbian, and so obviously a Lesbian, many (but not all) of the privileges attached to my white skin aren't going to come my way. And so, I also say, any Lesbian who believes that skin privilege, class privilege, or any other privilege *over-rides* or *cancels* the social sanctions against Lesbians should look again. (Lesbians who pass as heterosexuals do, however, retain such privileges. That's why they consent to passing.)

Do I appear to now have some of the benefits usually associated with class or skin privilege? Then Lesbians who're fond of dismissing other Lesbians because of one -ism or another should admit that they're looking at us as 'products' and ignoring the processes and experiences in our lives that brought us where we are, and that isn't fair to us. You deny the reality of our lives. Class privilege? I had some, yes, for about six years, while I lived under the roof of my stepfather, but that brief respite from economic poverty was purchased at the cost of my sexual victimization. The 'exchange' was explicit: In return for a roof over my head and food in my belly, I was expected to tolerate his sexual abuse.

You say I have college degrees? Indeed, I do. But I didn't get them because of class or skin privilege. I was kicked out of TWO universities *because I was a Lesbian* and denied entrance to two others *because I was a Lesbian* and that fact was on my transcripts. Finally, I lied to get into City College of New York City. Why CCNY? Because the tuition was only $12 a semester, something I could afford while I worked full-time as a file clerk for $45 a week. I went through college on the 'beg, borrow, and steal' program, supplementing my income with the five-fingered discount. I won't allow anyone, Lesbian or otherwise, to dismiss the violence done to me because I am a Lesbian.

I'm tired of simple-minded assumptions about the life of one Lesbian being 'easier' than that of another. We have to stop using those assumptions, and the ways of talking to and about each other that follow from them in order to justify the hurt we're inflicting on each other. Even Barbara Smith admits to the pain she's experienced when other 'feminists' have attacked her (*YIS*, p. 76), yet she dismisses the ways we deal with each other as simply not worth our time (p. 85). If Lesbians/wimmin cannot find better and less hurtful ways of talking to each other, I, for one, cannot imagine what I'm supposed to expect from the men Smith and Bulkin insist I 'struggle with.'

Yes, so far I've 'survived.' Because of people who were in the right place at the right time and willing and able to protect me when my survival was threatened, and my own stubbornness and hard work. Yes, I've made choices, but if you want to talk about those choices then I want you to also know what my options were. At 18, I could've worked in a factory or driven a lunch truck in Hialeah, Florida; I could've gone into the military; or I could somehow get a college degree and try to survive in academia. Those are the traditional options available to Lesbians unwilling or unable to 'pass.' The military was 'out' for me because I was also fat and, therefore, more 'obvious' as a Lesbian. (Also, I understood, more likely to be kicked out, too, during one of the frequent purges.) Why did I choose academia over factory work? Because three Lesbians sat me down one night in a bar and told me I should go back to college if I could. They told me I could use my 'brains' to help other Lesbians like them. They believed our lives could be better and I believed them. Ridiculing the naive 'upward mobility' of working-class dykes in order to dismiss them and me is both cruel and unnecessary.

They had dreams, those Lesbians, and they passed them on to me. Now, though, the dreams are endangered. Many Lesbians, oppressed because of race and ethnic background as well as their Lesbianism, have chosen their heterosexual communities over the possibility of a Lesbian community. (See, for example, essays in *Nice Jewish Girls* and *This Bridge Called My Back*.) And I feel abandoned, and believe I deserve better from other Lesbians. Is this pain all I get for my work and energy? Is it impossible for Lesbians to make a community for ourselves? Do you think that Separatism is the 'threat'? It's not. Heterosexuality and the pull of heterosexual bonds is the danger. Those ties are pulling us away from each other, daily.

It's too easy to sit back and ridicule or trivialize another woman's efforts, to deflect our ancient anger against men and target other wimmin for its expression. It's called 'horizontal hostility' and is the behavior that most surely marks an oppressed group. We will, every time, turn our anger in on ourselves rather than direct it against the perpetrators of our oppression. I'm not advocating the kind of liberalism that urges uncritical support or validation for every impulse or idea of any womon. We need to be critical of each other, and it's easier to see the errors and misconceptions of someone else than it is to see them in ourselves. We need to remain aware of heteropatriarchal traps, to monitor ourselves as well as other wimmin, to question, question, question.

But we cannot go on as we are. We may have to consider the possibility that being Lesbians simply isn't 'enough' to enable us to create communities for ourselves. Perhaps because of my own experience, my necessary reliance on other Lesbians for community, and my lack of investment in any heterosexual group, I've believed that we, Lesbians, do need each other. The strongest, surest part of me cries out for a Lesbian community. Part of me says I'll take a scruffy, loud-mouthed, pushy dyke any day, **every**

day, because I'm a 'scruffy dyke.' A part of me is invested in the survival of every Lesbian, whether I like her or not. Maybe she's a vegetarian, an alcoholic, batterer or battered, sado-masochist, or hermit, but she's created herself, and every day she lives she's backed up against the same wall I am, the heteropatriarchy.

There's no retreat from that simple fact. I can't 'go back' to anywhere from here. Once I became conscious of my oppression and all that my life would never be because of it, I closed that door. Now, I must continue, somehow, to live the conceptual impossibility of being a Lesbian, of trying to make myself whole. That is my reality, my life. Now I re-member.

Can we call each other to being other than we are, for the sake of a vision we can live toward, at the same time remembering that we will continue to make mistakes, continue to hurt each other, continue to forget how serious our differences are? Can we be critical and remain kind, learn perhaps to disagree honestly without disowning each other? Can we value and respect each other's strengths, skills, and talents without devaluing ourselves? Can we learn to thank each other for time and effort? Can we stop taking each other for granted, and stay in touch with the miracle of self-realization that each of us is? Can we focus more on the good things we do without forgetting that we must continue the process of critical self-examination? Can we end the destructive effects of our victimization in the heteropatriarchy, distinguish the pain we bring with us into our communities, identify when our feelings arise out of past experiences and gradually learn to respond to our *present* context? Can we break the control that our past exercises over us in order to create a present context for survival? Can we unlearn the behaviors of victims and come to value ourselves as survivors? So far, our anger and frustrations, directed at each other rather than our real enemies, have worked to destroy us internally far more success-fully than any retaliatory actions undertaken by men. Can any one of us afford to do their work *for* them?

Can we go on *together*?

There are three possible answers to that question: yes, no, and maybe. I can't assume a positive answer, as much as I'd like to. We can no longer assume that 'being Lesbians' is 'enough' of a bond to enable us to put ourselves first. Maybe we can't go on together, and we need to look at this negative possibility now, acknowledge it, and talk about it. Perhaps only a few of us are, first and last, identified as Lesbians. If so, we need to find each other and work out ways of supporting our vision of a community where we can heal ourselves, or find satisfactory ways of reconciling ourselves to our isolation.

We're at 'maybe' now, and we must be honest with ourselves. If the answer is 'no,' then we can all 'go back' to whatever we were doing before the dream of a Lesbian movement called forth our best energies and commitment. I will not base my life on deluded expectations and false hopes. Easy affirmations won't do either. If the answer is 'yes,' then we have a lot of hard work to do as we renew our focus on creating a Lesbian **community**, and we'll have to begin by discovering values we share, values that will identify us to each other.

I suggest we begin with honesty, of the variety that originates in critical self-examination, each of us asking herself exactly what we want and expect from other Lesbians, and results in clarity. Whatever we do, we deserve honesty and clarity from each other. If we cannot go on together, as Lesbians, we need to say it now.

Notes

1. Lesbophobia in Mexico and South America is so severe and so overt that discovery of one's Lesbianism often has dire social consequences and can, too frequently, be fatal. I say this because the Lesbians who took me to the bar were being courageous in their gesture of sisterhood.
2. Lesbian bars (and gathering places) do vary according to the economic class of the clientele the owners seek. A middle-to-upperclass bar, for example, the old Sahara in NYC, had carpeting, potted palms and other greenery, and couches and easy chairs for customers to sit in. Googie's, in contrast, was much like other working-class bars: wooden stools, tables, and chairs, and a bare floor, covered with a thin spattering of sawdust. I'm also ignoring here the fact that most 'Lesbian' bars are owned by the Mafia, and it's the Mafia that profits from alcoholism among Lesbians. 'Comfortable,' then, is a relative term, and I use it here, without regard to what members of one class or another may find most 'comfortable' for themselves, to mean that *I* feel comfortable as long as I'm within a space occupied by Lesbians and permeated with the animation of Lesbian energies, period.
3. For my purposes here, I'll use a variety of spellings and terms for the female sex in an effort to signal the distinctions I wish to make among conflicting social/political categories as clearly and consistently as I can. Please bear with whatever discomfort you may experience as a result of such shuttling back and forth; the nature of this article requires some generalizing and, in an effort to avoid both overgeneralization and oversimplification, I decided to resort to these distinctions by using different terms and, in the case of wimmin/women, spellings to try and name, as specifically as I could, the groups to which I refer. I realize that

it's difficult to go back and forth with these words and different spellings for them, and hope that the following explanations will make that process somewhat easier.

SEPARATIST: A Lesbian (virtually always) who believes that men, individually and collectively, oppress women, that every man benefits directly and indirectly, from birth, from the oppression of women, that the rule of men, patriarchy, is a social structure designed to perpetuate the subjugation of women and the dominance of men, and that all females must withdraw their energies from men and cease to nurture and take care of them if women's oppression is to cease.

LESBIAN: A womon whose primary sexual and emotional intimacies are shared, in any of many ways, in relationships with wimmin. Alix Dobkin quotes the definition proposed by Mary E. Hunt, 'A Lesbian is a woman who is radically serious about loving women.' (Thank you, Alix, for taking the time between concert tours to sit down and send me Mary's name and the accurate version of her definition!) What is significant to me is a womon's decision to act on her deepest and best feelings for wimmin, whatever the rewards may be for denying those feelings.

FEMINIST: A womon, Lesbian or non-Lesbian, who calls herself such; frequently modified here by *heterosexual* to acknowledge that some Lesbians call themselves *lesbian-feminist*, as I have in the past, and to indicate in the context that I'm talking about non-Lesbians specifically.

WOMON/WIMMIN: Used here somewhat optimistically to talk about females generally, and to impute to those so named the *potential* for an unqualified political commitment to destroying the heteropatriarchy; a Lesbian spelling convention in the U.S.

FEMALE: In spite of the fact that this term is derived from the French *femelle*, it was reanalyzed in the 14th century by the Anglo-patriarchs so that it'd *look* as though it was derived from the base word *male*. I use it here as a generic term to refer to our biological sex and to distinguish between our biological sex, *female*, and the heteropatriarchal class, *woman*. For this essential insight, I'm indebted to the writings of Monique Wittig and to the arguments I've had with Ariane Brunet and Louise Turcotte, who maintain that going back to the early spellings of *woman* doesn't change its etymology (*wif* + *man*).

WOMAN/WOMEN: I use the heteropatriarchal spelling here, following Monique Wittig and other Radical Lesbians, to designate females whose primary (and secondary and tertiary) allegiances, sexual, emotional, intellectual, political, and social, are to men and to heteropatriarchal values. See, for example, Wittig's article, 'One is Not Born a Woman,' (*Feminist Issues*, vol. 1, no. 2, Winter 1981) in which she pursues the implications of de Beauvoir's observation that women are made, not born. I realize that, in the course of reading this article, you may feel my choices are sometimes inconsistent, and that my usage of one term or spelling rather than another may appear whimsical to some. I assure you, however, that every choice has been weighed and debated in my own mind.

4. The word *dyke* remains an insulting term to a majority of Lesbians in the U.S. because of the ways it has been used against us by men and women, but I've been called a 'dyke,' 'bulldyke,' and 'diesel dyke' since I

first started frequenting bars in Miami. Because I've never been able to 'pass,' *dyke* remains, for me, a primary term to name my strength and to congratulate myself for having lived so long. Rita Mae Brown, in *Sudden Death* (Beacon, 1984, p. 189) makes the following snide (and false) distinction between dykes and Lesbians: 'In this world there are Lesbians and dykes. The two have nothing in common. Lesbians are women who love women. Dykes are women who imitate men.' Is comment or analysis necessary?

5.   Throughout this article, I use the label 'Radical Feminist' to describe those feminists who were unwilling to settle for mere political reforms, who demanded a thorough restructuring of society, not just a handful of token women occupying positions in the male superstructure and acting like men, who identified the nuclear family as the essential cell in the heteropatriarchal body, and who sought, not just a piece of the pie for women, but an entirely different pie. The distinction I wish to suggest between 'radical feminists' and 'reform feminists' is similar to the detectable difference between meals cooked from scratch, in which only fresh ingredients are used, and those put together from frozen, or otherwise pre-packaged foodstuffs. Both methods of cooking will result in a meal, but the former requires time, care, watchfulness, and the expenditure of considerable energy, while the latter requires more money but less time, care, and energy. Which method produces the better meal? The answer depends on what we're willing to eat.

6.   I'd like to point out here that sexual behaviors involving sado-masochistic rituals, scat orgies, and golden showers have been around for a long time, and, although Lesbians didn't invent them, have been the common preference of a few Lesbians for as long as I know of. S&M among Lesbians isn't new, and would hardly deserve comment if its practitioners hadn't insisted upon also calling themselves 'feminists.' Sado-masochism provides another example of the ways feminist values have been eroded and diluted until it's embarrassing to try and talk about feminist 'values' in any context.

With only a few exceptions (to the best of my knowledge), those Lesbians who persist in identifying themselves as 'gay' do so for a good reason. Pat Califia, for example, prefers to call herself 'gay,' thereby making a political statement about the system of values she chooses to live by. Gayle Rubin, who also identifies as 'gay,' does so because she advocates pederasty as an expression of 'children's rights.' Lesbians who refuse to abandon xtianity and involve themselves in groups like MCC, Dignity, and the like appropriately prefer to call themselves 'gay.' The label 'gay' designates a Lesbian's decision to identify herself with male issues, male institutions, and male descriptions of the world. As long as we label ourselves honestly, in ways that accurately describe the values we choose to live by, we'll avoid a lot of misunderstanding and unnecessary pain.

7.   I've enjoyed sports ever since I can remember, and actively indulged myself in them whenever the opportunity appeared. When I was 9, 10, and 11 I believed I could grow up to play first base with the Brooklyn Dodgers or become a forward on a pro basketball team. (All of this was,

of course, before I'd realized what 'The Difference' would mean in terms of my career options.) But, in high school, something strange began to happen. In spite of my athletic ability, my 'letters,' and my membership in the Girl's Athletic Association (GAA), I found myself ostracized in subtle, yet painful, ways.

And I tried to 'fit in' because I wanted to so badly. I had what my coaches still called 'baby fat,' but several of the other women were 'large' so it wasn't my size *per se* that governed the way they treated me. I wore the conventional female jock uniform for 'passing,' a straight skirt (black or dark blue), a white Ship 'n' Shore blouse, low-heeled flats, and I carried the (also black or dark blue) small, rectangular purse that was supposed to signal my desire to be 'discreet.'

I must've stuck out in every crowd, in spite of my efforts to look, walk, talk, and act like the other women. I was, alas, 'too masculine,' as one after another of my P.E. acquaintances informed me. It wasn't 'safe' to be 'seen' with me. I had no female friends; I wasn't invited to 'slumber parties,' lest, I suppose, I lose control of myself and attack someone. Yet, several of those women *were* Lesbians as surely as I was then. Instead of that shared identity becoming a source of bonding among us, their fear of discovery and its consequences for them drove a wedge between us that it still hurts me to think about.

From high school, almost all of us entered Florida State University in Tallahassee, Florida; it'd been an all-woman school until recently at that time, and still retained some of the former attractions that would draw young Lesbians to it. Again, I went out for sports, intramural as well as intercollegiate, and tried to become active in the women's sports club. This time, my ostracism was complete and final. Not only was I told that I was barred from majoring in women's sports, but also that I wasn't to be anywhere around the women's gymnasium (except, of course, for my required four hours of P.E. classes).

Around campus, the other Lesbians I'd known as members of teams in and around Miami simply stopped speaking to me. My greetings went unacknowledged, and when 'seeing' me was unavoidable on the sidewalk those women looked through me. I became invisible and nonexistent as far as they were concerned. My 'indiscretion' meant that I was dangerous to them. I spent a lot of time crying in my room that first year.

Yes, that was all 28 years ago. Has women's athletics changed in its attitudes toward the Lesbians in its ranks? No. When Billie Jean King's ex-lover sued her, Billie Jean admitted that she'd had an affair with the woman, but I got tired very quickly of seeing pictures of her with her 'loving husband' in the popular magazines. When word got out about Martina Navratilova's relationship with Rita Mae Brown, Martina hastily retreated into what she called her 'bisexuality,' swearing that Nancy Lieberman was helping her to become heterosexual.

I know stories more devastating and cruel than those that've gotten media attention, but, to 'protect' the parties involved, I can't tell them here. I know enough stories about the persecution and maltreatment of Lesbians in women's P.E. in only the past five years to assert that women's athletics is NOT a safe place for Lesbians to be, in spite of the large numbers of Lesbians still active in athletics. Only those who can pass need apply. The cult of femininity remains unchallenged within women's P.E. departments, and it oppresses Lesbians.

8. In our society, we're taught the metaphorical concept ARGUMENT IS WAR. Consequently, when we talk about arguments, we say things like, 'I tried to *defend my position*, but she *outflanked* me,' 'I really *shot down* her objections,' 'her arguments were *right on target*.' No wonder we feel so good when we *win* arguments and so bad when we *lose* them. Our thought patterns mold our behaviors so that our arguments are 'dangerous,' 'threatening,' and 'risky' for us. Suppose, instead, that we came up with new ways of thinking about arguments, ways that helped us learn less painful and destructive ways of behaving during arguments. How about ARGUING IS A SCAVENGER HUNT, ARGUMENT IS QUILTING, ARGUING IS WORKING A PUZZLE, ARGUMENT IS DANCING, or ARGUMENT IS SURFING? If we don't teach ourselves new ways to argue with each other, the alternative is to learn to agree with whatever another womon says, regardless of what we really think. That's lying, and I think, still, that we deserve better from each other.

9. I'm grateful to Sarah Lucia Hoagland for passing on her observations about the frequent use of militaristic metaphors in the descriptions of events during the 1984 Olympics in Los Angeles.

10. During a conversation about this article on November 11, 1984.

11. For the dubious, those readers who don't believe that such ideas are the very essence of mainstream thinking, consider the TV series, 'V,' which features, among its regular characters, the 'exceptional lizard,' the 'good lizard.' In spite of the fact that his people, reptilian extraterrestrials, have invaded and conquered our planet, the 'exceptional lizard' belongs to a group of human resisters. In the latest (Feb. 15, 1985) episode, he told a human woman that he could never be 'family' to her in the way that her gang was, but she said, 'You're family to me in my heart!' and threw her arms around him. I have nothing against lizards, especially 'exceptional lizards,' but I wonder if it's merely coincidence that the 'exceptional lizard' is male, while two of the nastiest, cruellest lizards are females.

12. Elly Bulkin, Minnie Bruce Pratt and Barbara Smith, *Yours in Struggle* (Brooklyn: Long Haul Press, 1984). I am purposely ignoring Minnie Bruce Pratt's essay in *YIS* because she's made herself so vulnerable and abject that her essay won't stand a critical reading.

13. Ironically enough, Kim Painter came to the opposite conclusion in her recent review of *Yours in Struggle* (*Common Lives/Lesbian Lives* #14 [Winter 1984], p. 106), in which she lauds the authors for 'delineating [their] concerns in both personal and political terms.'

I think that Lesbians, myself among them, have been misguided when we recommend books like *Yours in Struggle* without mentioning their flaws, questioning dubious assertions, and pointing out errors in fact or internal contradictions in the development of arguments. I was, as I recall, reluctant to review Lesbian work critically because I believed strongly that we could resolve our differences without verbally hurting each other. Having been hurt once too often by things alleged about me in print, I've changed my mind.

14. The situation in which an oppressed group uses the oppressors'

religion or religious precepts is much more complicated than I've indicated in the main text of this essay, and I'd like to be more explicit here. Religion, of any kind, is often the only 'survival mechanism' available to oppressed people, and I include here both Lesbians and wimmin generally. Black slaves, for example, used xtian hymns as a code to signal that a clandestine meeting was about to occur. For centuries, xtian nunneries provided women with their only alternative to living in a father's house or to heterosexuality and marriage, and they continue to offer that kind of sanctuary, at a price. That women willingly surrender other freedoms (speech, self-chosen movement) for such sanctuary indicates their desperation more than it does the benevolence of the religious institution.

But these facts don't justify continuation of heteropatriarchal religious practices within oppressed groups. I don't understand how a socialist can reconcile her politics with becoming an apologist for xtianity, a religion that has systematically opposed social change for hundreds of years, persecuted Jews, Blacks, women, Lesbians, practiced ideological imperialism in every non-xtian culture by sending out 'missionaries' to 'convert' its people and subvert its mores, and supports, with its considerable wealth, white, male, heterosexual domination. For a Lesbian, I don't understand how there can be any 'compromise' with xtianity.

15. Adrienne Rich, 'Notes for a Magazine: What Does Separatism Mean?' *Sinister Wisdom* 18, Fall 1981, pp. 83–91. Sid Spinster, Letter to the Editors, *Sinister Wisdom* 20, Spring 1982, pp. 104–5.
16. Starhawk, *Dreaming the Dark* (Boston: Beacon, 1982), p. 86.
17. The word *heterosexualism*, as I use it here, was coined by Sarah Lucia Hoagland in her book, *Lesbian Ethics*, now in manuscript.
18. I describe the effects of incest with respect to my sexuality and emotional capabilities in '*Whose* Past Are We Reclaiming?,' *Common Lives/Lesbian Lives* 13, Autumn 1984, pp. 16–35.

Journal Entry

Elana Dykewomon
1981

'Journal Entry' was written about my feelings on including the short story 'The Fourth Daughter's Four Hundred Questions' in *Nice Jewish Girls, A Lesbian Anthology*, originally published by Persephone Press, and republished (without my consent) by Crossing Press. The question I had then, as I have now, is to what degree can we define our audiences, and what effect that has on our work, our ability to build community. The 'Journal Entry' represents a truth that I had never expressed to myself as clearly.

i start to have a vision of the thing i mean . . . yes, my jewish story
has stuff in it i dont want pricks to know or read/ and yes, i would
like it to be in the jewish lesbian anthology – i want to be counted
as a jewish lesbian among lesbians in the way i want and i want
jewish lesbians to hear what i have to say/ and i think and think
about all the questions – some of ego, some of advertisement – all
the contradictions

   but spacing out i thought i saw
 for a second a letter from the other alphabet
 the one i secretly dream i am participating in making
 all the english words of my jewish story boiling down
 into one flaming new letter
 (not unlike a letter from the hebrew alphabet – but
 totally changed)

– and i saw all the english words of my fat story boiling down into
one soft, round, folding letter –
 some day i will find the art to make those letters really be and
we, all of us who make the new letters from the language of our
lives, from the honesty, howl and longing that rise up from us –
we will recognize these letters instantly – begin to be able to
communicate with them – in a language which, when it is drawn,
changes the mind, and when it is spoken, changes the world
 – now how can you let go of the substance, the clay, the stories
from which you hope to squeeze that letter? let it be out and
accessible to the straight, the prick world? but the truth is yer
conception of that is extremely far-fetched, aint it? just a 'poetic
fantasy', as it were, shining off at the edge of yer mind – a time
when the spoken word had power to effect the physical universe
by the depth power sound shape creation of the word itself
      & the time when womyn could
find that word in themselves and each other – no one's gonna
believe that that quest is what motivates you in this yer 'cranky
didactic separatism that limits your ability to move and to move
towards even the women you say you want with you'
     and yet there is a way that it never
occurred to me that every womon wouldn't instinctively know,
understand, language that only women can find between us, bit by
bit, that that wasnt the only possible motivation for wanting so
much to keep it among us to try to get it clear

RESOURCING

A Beginning Bibliography on Lesbian Separatism Based on the Lesbian Herstory Archives Collection

Joan Nestle
1983

Introductory Notes

Since separatism is an evolving concept, it is hard to give a definitive listing of sources. For instance, some may feel that the Lavender Menace presence of the early seventies was its first expression while others may feel separatism has always been a part of Lesbian life. In this beginning attempt at a definitive Lesbian separatist bibliography, I have included background works, titles with the word 'separatism' in them, works by separatist authors and performers, special collections, a listing of separatist journals both in print and out of print as well as a listing of Lesbian and women's archives around the country. I have also included some articles critical of separatism to show the full scope of ideas connected to this topic. Doing a bibliography of this sort makes me appreciate even more the work of Clare Potter and the Circle of Lesbian Indexers; there are many Lesbian newspapers and newsletters as well as feminist periodicals that I did not have the time to go through. I apologize to any woman who searches for her work here and does not find it. Please write to me about what is missing and if the Archives has it, I will be sure to include it in an updated edition of the bibliography. If we do not have it, I will let you know and suggest you send copies of the material to one of the many Lesbian archives around the country.

One final thought: as I typed each entry, I experienced the wonder at what we have done in taking our lives seriously; I am still marked by the times of deviance and remember the shame that I had to work so hard to turn into a life. Now I can sit and type out bibliographies on the culture of my people.

Post script, 1988 Since 1983 many more materials on Lesbian Separatism have been added to the collection.

Bibliography

Adrienne Rich. 'Notes for a Magazine: What Does Separatism Mean?' *Sinister Wisdom* 18 (Fall 1981), 83–91.

Alice. 'Separatism,' *Women in Hartford* 5 (October 1982) 1.

Alice, Debbie, Gordon and Mary. *Lesbian Separatism: An Amazon Analysis.* July 4, 1973, Seattle, Washington. Also 'Addition to the 1st Printing of *Lesbian Separatism* . . .' March 18, 1974. Two-page statement.

Alice Molloy. *In Other Words: Notes on the Politics and Morale of Survival.* Oakland: The Women's Press Collective, 1971–73. An influential work.

'Alix' in *The New Lesbians: Interviews with Women Across the United States and Canada,* edd. Laurel Galana and Gina Covina. Berkeley: Moon Books 1977. Interview with Alix Dobkin.

Alix Dobkin. *Adventures in Women's Music.* New York: Tower Press, 1979.

——. Individual Collection. Memorabilia: tickets, programs, flyers, posters, clippings.

——. 'Lavender Jane Loves Women,' in *The Lesbian Path*, ed. Margaret Cruikshank. Monterey: Angel Press, 1980. Reprinted by Double Axe Books and distributed by Naiad Press, P.O. Box 10543, Tallahassee, Florida 32302.

——. 'Performers and Politics,' *The Lesbian Feminist* (June 1977) 7.

Recordings. *Lavender Jane Loves Women.* New York: Women's Wax Works, 1973. With Kay Gardner and Patches Attom.
Living With Lesbians. Preston Hollow: Women's Wax Works, 1976.
XX Alix. Preston Hollow: Women's Wax Works, 1980.

Almania Barbaour. 'Put the Cow Back in N.O.W. or Wow Sisters,' Six-page pamphlet written by 'a Black militant Woman in Philadelphia,' nd.

Amazons Then, Lesbians Now (Amazones d'hier, Lesbiennes d'aujourd'-Hui) English version of script for videotape. The Video-Amazone Collective. Quebec, Canada, 1981.

Amethyst/Artemis. 'Dyke Separatist/Amazon Magick Gloss Journal,' Berkeley: nd. Also correspondence.

Anna Lee. 'One Black Separatist,' *Innerviews* 5 (Sept. 1981) np.

Anne et Francine. 'Rapport D'Atelier: Réflexions sur l'atelier des Lesbiennes Radicalés,' *Amazones d'hier, Lesbiennes d'aujourd'Hui* 1 (Dec. 1982), 96–114.

'Anthology on Lesbian Separatism.' One-page flyer calling for contributions by Julia Penelope and Sarah Lucia Hoagland, nd.

Artemis March, Ellen Bedoz, Cynthia Funk, Rita Mae Brown, Lois Hart and Barbara Gladstone with other Radicalesbians. 'The Woman-Identified Woman.' May, 1970. Flyers, reprints. A beginning document.

Audre Lorde. 'Man Child: A Black Lesbian Feminist Response,' *Conditions* 4 (1979) 30–36.

'Battle Fatigue,' *Spectre* 4 (Sept.-Oct. 1971) 8–9.

Barbara Smith. 'Responses-Letter, Feb. 3, 1982.' *Sinister Wisdom* 20 (Spring 1982) 100–104. Response to Adrienne's article, 'Notes for a Magazine . . .'

Barbara Smith and Beverly Smith. 'Across the Kitchen Table, A Dialogue,' *Sinister Wisdom* 18 (1981) 63–75. Also in *This Bridge Called My*

Back: Writings by Radical Women of Color, edd. Cherríe Moraga and Gloria Anzaldúa. Watertown: Persephone Press, 1981. Includes a discussion of Lesbian separatism.

Betsy Rodgers. 'Separatism in Three Acts,' *The Lesbian Feminist* (Sept. 1977) 10–12.

Billie Lusisi Potts. 'Owning Jewish Separatism and Lesbian Separatism 9982,' *The Lesbian Insider/Insighter/Inciter*, no. 9 (Dec. 1982) 3+.

Billie Rensberger, 'Gay Separatism: Dead End,' *International Worker* (Dec. 13, 1975) 1.

Bonnie Zimmerman, 'The Politics of Separatism,' *Lavender Woman* 3 (March 1974) 11.

'Calling All Separatists.' One-page flyer announcing the birth of *Dyke* magazine. 1974. Liza Cowan, Penny House.

Carla, Donna, Kris. 'Separatists Speak Out,' *Sister* (Dec. 1978/Jan. 1979) 11. First of a series of writings by the Lesbian Separatists Study Group as presented to Lesbian Feminists of Los Angeles.

Carol Hardin. 'Record.' *Cowrie* 1 (Feb. 1974) 4–5. 'This is a record kept by a typical, everyday, extraordinary Dyke Separatist.'

Charlotte Bunch. 'Learning from Lesbian Separatism,' *Ms.* (Nov. 1976) 60+.

——. 'A Letter to the Staff,' *The Furies* 2 (May June 1973) 10. A response to a letter criticizing an earlier article on separatism.

——. 'Self Definition and Political Survival,' *Quest* 1 (Winter 1975) 2–15.

——. 'Perseverance Furthers: Separatism and Our Future,' *The Furies* 1 (Fall 1972) 3+. Continued in 2 (Feb. 1973).

Charoula. 'Dyke Separatist Womanifesto,' *Tribad* 1 (May 1977) 1–4.

——. 'Reforming the Road to Revolution: A Separatist Point of View,' *Tribad* 1 (March-April 1978) 7–8.

'Chasing Balls for Big Bucks,' *Womynlovers Separatists Newsletter* 1 (Summer 1981) 1+.

Clair. 'Coming Up for Air: A Lesbian Separatist Speaking,' *Lesbian Connection* 2 (March 1976) 12–13.

Claire Krulikowski and Jeanne Cordova. 'Perspectives: Feeling as a Dark Woman: Interview with Sirani Avedis,' *The Lesbian Tide* 9 (Jan.-Feb. 1980) 4–5.

Collective Lesbian International Terrors (C.L.I.T.) Statement #1 'The Divorce is Final,' *Majority Report* (1974). Also *Off Our Backs* (1974). Also *Dyke* 1 (Winter 1975–76) 6–8.

——. C.L.I.T. Collection 1, statement no. 2 *Off Our Backs* (July 1974) 11. Also *Dyke* 1 (Winter 1975–76).

——. C.L.I.T. Collection 11 statement no. 3 *Dyke* 1 (Spring 1976) 41+.

Combahee River Collective. 'A Black Feminist Statement,' in *This Bridge Called My Back: Writings by Radical Women of Color*, edd. Cherríe Moraga and Gloria Anzaldúa. Watertown: Persephone Press, 1981. Includes a discussion of Lesbian separatism.

Dana Morrison. 'Lesbian Mother: Presented at L.F.L. Panel Discussion On Lesbian Separatism,' *Cowrie* 1 (Feb. 1974) 16–18.

Dancin and Birdie. 'Young Lesbians: Future Tense,' *The Lesbian Tide* 6 (May-June 1977) 11. Discusses the problems of 'two young dyke separatists, ages 17 and 19.'

Diaspora Distribution. Organizational files. Brochures, flyers. 'Diaspora was formed in 1980 to distribute the work of Lesbians to Lesbians' by Elana and Dolphin. P.O. Box 272, Langlois, Oregon 97450.

Eileen Kane. 'Comparative Study of the Women's Movement,' *Tribad* 1 (May 1977) 5–7; *Tribad* 1 (July August 1977) 3–6.

Elana Dykewomon. *They Will Know Me By My Teeth*. Northampton: Megaera Press, 1976.

——. 'The Fourth Daughter's Four Hundred Questions,' in *Nice Jewish Girls: A Lesbian Anthology*, ed. Evelyn Torton Beck. Watertown: Persephone Press, 1982.

——. *Fragments from Lesbos*. Langlois: Diaspora Distribution, 1981.

——. 'Silencing Separatists,' *Lesbian Connection* 5 (Sept. 1980) 4–5. Responses to the article, *Lesbian Connection* 5 (Sept. 1981) 17–18.

——. Tape of reading at the Lesbian Herstory Archives, October 1, 1982.

——. 'XX Alix: Stand Up to Time,' *The Lesbian Insider/Insighter/Inciter* 3 (April 1981) 16.

Elana Dykewomon and Dolphin Waletzky. 'Diaspora Distribution: A Dyke Alternative,' *The Lesbian Insider/Insighter/Inciter* 2 (Jan. 1981) 7.

Elana Nachman (Dykewomon). *Riverfinger Woman*. Plainfield: Daughters, Inc., 1974.

Erika Munk. 'Outrage Department,' *Village Voice* (October 1–7, 1980) 114. Short statement by a straight woman about her anger at a women's only event.

Estelle Freedman. 'Separatism as Strategy: Female Institutional Building and American Feminism, 1870–1930,' Reprint from *Feminist Studies* 5 (Fall 1979) 512–529.

Flying Thunder Cloud RDOC. 'Adversity – a Poem,' *Feminary* 12 (1982) 106.

——. 'Fantastic 1700 Womon Light Years,' two page letter from Third World Lesbian mother separatist.

——. Special Collection. Correspondence.

Fort Dyke. Organizational File. Flyers, announcements, clippings about a Lesbian separatist space, New York City, 1977.

G. Kelley. 'Separatism/Building Alternatives,' *The Lesbian Tide* 5 (May 1976) 29.

Gahan Kelly. '*Dyke* Magazine Strikes Out,' *The Lesbian Tide* 5 (March April 1976) 16. In the next issue, Liza Cowan answers, '*Dyke* Editor Responds: "I Analyze the World Through Me." ' *The Lesbian Tide* 5 (May-June 1976) 28. *The Tide* responds in the same issue, 'Criticism: Whitewash or Portrait,' 29.

——. 'Review: Linda Shear: Modern Day Troubador,' *The Lesbian Tide* 5 (May June 1976) 24.

Gloria Z. Greenfield. 'Straight Talk About Lesbian Separatism,' *Sojourner* (Nov. 1978) 9+. Interview with Liza Cowan and Alix Dobkin.

Gudrun Fonfa and Janice Elsen. 'Alix Dobkin's New Album "Living with Lesbians," ' *The Lesbian Tide* 4 (May June 1976) 25.

Gutter Dyke Collective. 'Separatism,' *Dykes and Gorgons* 1 (May June 1973) 16–17.

Resourcing

'How We Stopped Choking – or Separatism,' *Spectre* 2 (May June 1971) 2+.

Jacqueline Elizabeth. 'Separatism,' *The Lesbian Insider/Insighter/Inciter* no. 5 (Nov. 1981) 17. A Poem.

Jan Oxenberg. 'Review of *Lesbian Nation*,' *The Lesbian Tide* 2 (May June 1973) 13.

Jean Sirius. *And Everyone of Us a Witch*. 1979. Originally published as *Womyn/Friends: A Book of Poems*. Brooklyn: Sirius Books, 1979.

——. *The Green Womon Poems*. Brooklyn: Sirius Books, 1980.

——. *Lesbian Love Poems: An Aid to the Inarticulate*. Brooklyn: Sirius Books, 1981. Drawings by Gaia.

Jean Sirius and Cara Vaughn. Special Collection. Oral herstory tapes, graphics, correspondence.

Jeanne Cordova. 'Radical Feminism? Dyke Separatism?' *The Lesbian Tide* 2 (May June 1973) 20–41.

Jil Clark. 'Alix Dobkin: Still a Separatist.' *Gay Community News* 7 (March 29, 1980) 8–9. Also 'Letter in Response – Allies,' *GCN* 7 (May 17, 1980) 4.

Jill Johnston. *Amazon Nation*. New York: Simon and Shuster, 1973. Background work.

——. 'Five Years Later,' *Gay Community News* 4 (April 30, 1977) 3.

——. Special Collection. A complete set of *Village Voice* columns, documenting Jill's coming out and the development of her ideas.

Jody. 'And Ain't I a Separatist?' A statement by 'a Lesbian Separatist Chicana Press member' of *Out and About* from Seattle, Washington, nd. Two-page article.

Joy Justice. 'Vision,' *Sinister Wisdom* 4 (Fall 1977) 66.

Joy Scorpio. 'What is Sisterhood?' *Coming Out Rage* 1 (May 1973) 6. *Coming Out Rage* was 'a feminist journal for Lesbians, produced by Lesbian Feminists/D.O.B. in New York City.' As far as we know, this is the only issue.

Juana Maria Paz. *The La Luz Journal*. Fayetteville, Arkansas, 1980.

Julia Penelope. 'A Cursory and Precursory History of Language....' *Sinister Wisdom* 1 (July 1976) 5–12.

——. 'Lesbian Relationships and the Vision of Community,' *Feminary* 9 (April 1978) 4–9.

——. 'Lesbian Separatism: The Linguistic and Social Sources of Separatist Politics,' in *The Gay Academic*, ed. Louie Crew. Palm Springs: ETC Publishers, 1976.

——. 'Mystery or Monster: The Lesbian in Heterosexual Fantasies,' *Sinister Wisdom* 15 (Fall 1980) 76–91.

——. 'Why Men Should Not be Allowed to Live With Wimmin,' in *Fight Back*, edd. Frédérique Delacoste and Felice Newman. Minn.: Cleis Press, 1982.

——. Special Collection. Includes manuscripts written with Susan Wolfe (Robbins). Fifty-four manuscripts on linguistics, Lesbian humor, aesthetics, gay slang, Lesbian novels, teaching, gay oppression, the prostitute as paradigmatic woman, revolution and coming out. Of special importance for this bibliography are: 'The Lesbian Perspective:

Pedagogy and the Structure of Human Knowledge.' Xerox copy of paper delivered at the National Council of Teachers of English, November 26–29, 1976, Chicago. 'Why Lesbian Separatism?' Prepared as part of the workshop on the topic of Lesbian Separatism at the Fourth Annual Conference of the Rutgers' Student Homophile League, Rutgers University, April 19–21, 1974.

Julie McCrossin. *Women Wimmin Womyn Womin Whippets.* nd. 10-page pamphlet printed in Australia 'to coincide with Mary Daly's visit.' Critical of Separatism.

Katharine Hess, Jean Langford, and Kathy Ross. *Feminismo Primero: Un Ensayo sobre Separatismo Lesbiano./Feminism First: An Essay on Lesbian Separatism,* 1981.

Land. Subject File Collection. Clippings, letters, articles, flyers documenting the struggle of women living on women only land communes.

Lee Schwing and Deborah George. 'Editorial,' *The Furies* 2 (March April 1973) 5–6. An editorial response to a debate over separatism that was going on in the pages of *The Furies.*

Leila Klasse. 'Interview with Sally Gearhart,' *The Lesbian Insider/ Insighter/Inciter* 1 (August 1980) 13.

'A Lesbian Nation Would Have to Deal With Tourists,' *Sister* (Feb.-March 1977) 2. Report on discussions of 'seventy five women or so' at Los Angeles Women's Forum on the topic of separatism.

'Lesbian Separatism,' *Lesbian Connection* 1 (May 1975) 16.

'Lesbian-Separatist Survival Gathering.' Announcement of separatist gathering, August 1981. One page.

Lesbian Separatist Study Group. 'Separatists Speak Out,' *Sister* (Dec. 1978/Jan. 1979) 11.

Lesbian Space. Subject File Collection. Flyers announcing events of New York's separatist space.

Lesbians International Satellite Tribadic Energy Network (L.I.S.T.E.N.) Press release 1, July 1980; Press release 2, October 1980, flyers.

——. Statement 2. October 1982. One-page article.

Linda Shear. Tape. 'A Lesbian Portrait.' Northampton: Old Lady Blue Jeans, 1975.

'Linda Shear: A Lesbian Portrait,' *The Leaping Lesbian* 1, no. 11 (1977) 23–24.

Lesbians in Voluntary Expatriation (L.I.V.E.) 'Dyke Separatism Lives.' Two-page flyer celebrating New York's nine years of Lesbian Separatism. New York, 1980.

Lois Anne Addison. 'Separatism Revisited,' *Sinister Wisdom* 21 (Fall 1982) 29–34.

Lucia Valeska. 'The Future of Female Separatism,' *Quest* 2 (Fall 1975) 2–16.

Margaret Sloan. 'The Issue is Woman Identification,' *Plexus* 3 (June 1976) 7.

Margy. 'The Myth of Lesbian Pride,' *Lesbian Connection* 4 (December 1978) 8. Article in support of Linda Shear and Sirani Avedis.

Maricla Moyano. 'The Amazons: The Original Lesbian Separatists,' *Tribad* 1 (Sept. Oct. 1977) 11–12. (See also *Tribad, Big Apple Dyke* in Journal listings.)

——. 'Dyke Separatism: A Personal Statement,' *Tribad* 1 (July August 1977) 1–2.

Marjorie Canton and Rogi A. Rubyfruit. 'Alix Dobkin and Liza Cowan on Money, Motherhood and Mutes,' *The Lesbian Tide* 7 (July August 1977) 12+.

Marilyn Frye. 'Lesbian Perspective on Women's Studies,' *Sinister Wisdom* 14 (1980) 3–8.

——. 'Some Thoughts on Separatism and Power,' *Sinister Wisdom* 6 (Summer 1978) 30–39. Reprinted in 1977 as a pamphlet by Tea Rose Press, East Lansing, Michigan.

——. 'To Be and Be Seen: Metaphysical Misogyny,' *Sinister Wisdom* 17 (Summer 1981) 57–70.

Marina Fairchild. 'Just What Can Feminists Afford? A Belated Lesbian Separatist Response to "Creating a Women's World" and Its Broader Political Implications.' Reprint, January 1978. Article appeared originally in *Big Mama Rag*, April 1978 and May 1978. A response to a *New York Times* article on Daughters, Inc., a Lesbian publishing house.

Mary Daly. *Gyn/Ecology: The Metaethics of Radical Feminism*. Boston: Beacon Press, 1978. Also in archive's collection, *The Church and The Second Sex*. New York: Harper Colophon Books, 1975 and *Beyond God the Father*, Boston: Beacon Press, 1977 and an individual file containing articles, clippings, flyers. An author who is important to many separatists.

Monique Wittig. *Les Guérillères*. New York: Avon Books, 1969.

——. *The Lesbian Body*. New York: William Morrow and Co., 1975.

——. 'One is Not Born a Woman,' *Feminist Issues* 1 (Winter 1981) 47–54.

Monique Wittig and Sande Zeig. *Lesbian Peoples: Material for a Dictionary*. New York: Avon Books, 1976.

Morgan Murielchild. 'Dyke Separatism,' *Coming Out Rage* 1 (May 1973) 8.

Nancy and Alice. 'Jill Johnston: Interview,' *The Lesbian Tide* 2 (July 1973) 5+. Includes her comments on separatism. The next issue of *The Tide* has a response by Nancy Robinson, 'Jill Johnston – Right on Feminist?' (August 1973) 6.

Nike. 'Offensive Offense and Lesbian Separatism,' *Tribad* 1 (May 1977) 11–12.

——. 'On the Straight Women and Straight Lesbian Dilemma in Relation to Dyke Separatism,' *Tribad* 1 (July-August 1977) 7–8.

Prairie Fire Organizing Committee of New York. 'Fort Dykes = Fascism in the Lesbian Movement.' Prepared for Lesbian Pride Week, 1977. Four-page article.

Radical Feminists 28. 'On Separatism,' Minn.: May, 1972. Two-page article.

'Responses.' *Lesbian Connection* 4 (May 1978) 12. Letters discussing Alix Dobkin's Women Only Concerts.

Rose Jordan. 'On Our Struggle . . . ,' *Coming Out Rage* 1 (May 1973) 9.

Rue Malloy. 'Understanding Separatism,' *Plexus* (May 1980) 5.

Sally Gearhart. *The Wanderground*. Watertown, Mass.: Persephone Press, 1978. An author important to many separatists.

Sally Gearhart. Individual File Collection. Clippings, articles, flyers.

Sally Gearhart, Lani Silver, Sue Talbot, Rita Mae Brown, Jeanne Cordova, Barbara McClean. 'A Kiss Does Not a Revolution Make,' *The Tide* 3 (June 1974) 3+. 'A round table discussion to develop a Lesbian Feminist ideology.' Includes a discussion of separatism. Continued in *The Tide* 3 (July 1974) 10+ and *The Tide* 4 (August 1974) 12.

Sarah Hoagland. 'Lesbian Ethics,' *The Lesbian Insider/Insighter/Inciter* 1 (Jan. 1981).

——. 'Re-membering Lesbian Lives,' *Sinister Wisdom* 14 (Summer 1980) 52–56.

——. Special Collection. Includes papers and tales written by Sarah's students in her Advanced Feminist Philosophy Course, 1981, correspondence with the University of Nebraska and nineteen manuscripts on linguistics, sociobiology, academia, rhetoric, science, reverse discrimination, Wittgenstein, book reviews and the following manuscripts:

'Femininity, Resistance and Sabotage,' September 1980.

'Sadism, Masochism and Power,' 1981.

'Violence, Victimization, Violation,' August, 1980. Also appeared in *Sinister Wisdom* 15 (Fall 1980) 70–74.

'Vulnerability and Power,' 1981. Also appeared in *Sinister Wisdom* 19 (Winter 1982) 13–23.

Tapes. At Home with the Archives, June 7, 1981. Reading and discussing 'Vulnerability and Power.'

At Home with the Archives, December 20, 1982. Reading and discussing 'Lesbian Ethics Part Two: Anger, Separatism, and Bearing Witness.'

Sarah Grace. 'Some Thoughts on Separatism,' *The Lesbian Insider/Insighter/Inciter* 5 (Nov. 1981) 3.

'Separatism and the Spirituality Movement.' One-page article from an unidentified periodical.

'Separatism . . . Overdose?' *Lesbian Connection* 2 (July 1976) 8–9.

Sharon McDonald. 'Profile: Ginny Berson: Burning Out Is Not An Option,' *The Lesbian Tide* 7 (Jan. Feb. 1978) 5+. Discusses her early days in *The Furies*.

——. 'Profile: Sally Piano: Political Musician,' *The Lesbian Tide* 6 (Jan. Feb. 1977) 2.

——. 'Transsexuals: The Woman Within or the Woman Without,' *The Lesbian Tide* 6 (May June 1977) 6–7. Includes the views of Alix Dobkin.

Sirani Avedis. Recording. *Tattoos*. Terrapin Records, 1980.

Sidney Spinster. Special Collection. Includes flyers, correspondence, photographs, academic papers, clippings and the following:

'The Evolution of Lesbian Separatist Consciousness,' September 1981. Also in *The Lesbian Insider/Insighter/Inciter* 7 (April 1982) 1+.

'Feminist Visions of a Nuclear Free Future,' 1979.

'May Twenty Second: Fight Fire with Water,' 1979.

'Response-Letter.' *Sinister Wisdom* 20 (Spring 1982) 104–105. Discusses Adrienne's article 'Notes for a magazine. . . '

'What is Women's Music?' 1979.

Tapes. *Dyke Pioneers: Lesbian Songs by Sidney Spinster.* Radical Rose Recordings SL 23, 1982.

(See also *Lunatic Fringe* in Journal listing.)

'Sober Separatist Delicious Dykes,' *Womynlovers Separatists Newsletter* 1 (Winter 1981) 1.

'Some Further Thoughts on Separatism,' *Lesbian Connection* 2 (March 1976) 10–11.

Study Group Northampton Mass. 'Analysis of a Lesbian Community, Part 1.' *Lesbian Connection* 3 (July 1977) 6–8. 'Part 11.' *Lesbian Connection* 3 (Sept. 1977) 9–10.

Susan Cavin. 'InternationaLesbian Separatists vs Male Machine Gun Governments a.k.a. Nationalist Military Divisions of World Patriarchy – Part 1.' *Tribad* 1 (July-August 1977) 9–11. 'Part 2' *Tribad* 1 (Sept.-Oct. 1977) 1–4.

——. 'A Lesbian Eye View of the Seventies,' *Tribad* 2 (Sept.-Oct. 1978) 8–10.

——. 'Lesbian Origins Sex Theory,' *Sinister Wisdom* 9 (Spring 1979) 14–19.

——. 'Lesbian Separatism in the World: Context of Waves of Succeeding Seceding Separatist Movements of the Seventies,' *Tribad* 1 (March-April 1978) 1–4.

——. 'Some Lesbian Separatist Solutions to Convert Late Patriarchy into Dead Matter,' *Tribad* 1 (Nov.-Dec. 1977) 2–4.

——. See also *Big Apple Dyke*, *Green Mountain Dyke* and *Tribad* in Journal listing.

Susan Leigh Star. 'The Politics of Wholeness,' *Sinister Wisdom* 5 (Winter 1978) 82–102.

Susan Silverwoman. 'Notes on Dyke Separatism.' 1972. Seven-page Xeroxed article.

Susan Silverwoman and Morgan Murielchild. 'Shuffle Your Ass and Say Lesbian,' *Come Out is Dead*, nd. Announces their decision not to work with men anymore.

Susan J. Wolfe. 'Amazon Etymology: Rooting for the Matriarchy,' *Sinister Wisdom* 12 (Winter 1980) 15–21.

Suzi Kehler. 'Why Separatism,' *Lesbian Connection* 3 (July 1977) 13–14.

Thrace. 'Action Proposals for a Lesbian Revolutionary Movement from a Lesbian Separatist Position,' *The Lesbian Insider/Insighter/Inciter* 3 (April 1981) 12.

Toni Chestnutt. 'Out of the Closet and Into the Ghetto,' *Plexus* 3 (June 1976) 7+.

Valerie Solanas. SCUM Manifesto. Self published, nd. Background work.

Journals of Special Interest to Separatists

Amazons d'hier, Lesbiennes d'aujourd'Hui. Vol. 1, nos. 2–3 (Dec. 1982), c.p. 1721, Succ. La Cité, Montreal. H2W2R7 Québec Canada.

Big Apple Dyke News. Vol. 1, no. 1 (March 1981); BAD News, 192 Spring Street, New York 10012.

Dyke. Vol. no. 1 (Summer 1981); no. 6 (Summer 1978). Complete run; out of print.

Dykes and Gorgons. Vol. 1, no. 1 (May-June 1973). The only issue we have, out of print.

The Furies. Vol. 1, no. 1 (January 1972); Vol. 2, no. 3 (May June 1973). Complete run; out of print.

Green Mountain Dyke News. Vol. 1, no. 1 (May 1980); Vol. 1, no. 6 (December 1980). Complete run; out of print.

The Lesbian Insider/Insighter/Inciter. Vol. 1, no. 1 (August 1980). P.O. Box 7038, Minneapolis MN 55407.

Lunatic Fringe. Issue 1 (July 1980, Hallomas 9981); Issue 9. Complete run; out of print.

Spectre. Issue 1 (March-April 1971); Issue Six (Jan.-Feb. 1972). Complete run; out of print.

Tribad. Vol. 1, no. 1 (May 1977); Vol. 2, no. 5 (March-April 1979). Complete run; out of print.

The Udder Side. Issue 1 (April 1973); *Cowrie* Issue 2 (June 1973); Vol. 2, no. 3 (October 1973). Complete run; out of print.

Women's Network (Dorothy Feola) Vol. 1, no. 1 (1977); 2137 Quimby Avenue, Bronx, New York 10473.

Womynlovers. Vol. 1, No. 1 (Summer 1982) – F.P.O. Box 10621, Oakland, CA 94610.

Archives

*Lesbian Herstory Archives, PO Box 1258, New York, NY 10116.

*Third World Womens Archives, PO Box 159, Bush Terminal Station, Brooklyn, NY 11232.

*West Coast Lesbian Collections, Box 23753, Oakland, CA 94623.

*The Florida Collection of Lesbian Herstory, PO Box 5605, Jacksonville, FL 32207.

New Alexandria Lesbian Library, PO Box 402, Florence, MA 01060.

Kentucky Collection of Lesbian Her-Story, PO Box 1701, Louisville, KY 40201.

Tennessee Lesbian Archives, Box 252, Lattrell, TN 37779 (address to Catherine Risingflame Moirai not TLA)

Lesbian Heritage/DC, 1519 P Street, NW, Washington, DC 20005.

International Gay History Archives, Box 2, Village Station, New York, NY 10014.

National Gay Archives, Box 38100, Los Angeles, CA 90038.

*Canadian Gay Archives, Box 639, Station A. Toronto, Ontario, Canada M5W 1G2.

Stonewall Library and Archives, PO Box 2084, Hollywood, FL 33022.
Southeastern Lesbian Archives: Atlanta Lesbian Feminist Alliance, Box 5502, Atlanta, GA 30307.
Gay and Lesbian Archives of Texas, PO Box 16041, c/o IH, Houston, TX 77222.
Homophile Research Library, c/o The Church of the Beloved Disciple, 348 W. 14th Street, New York 10014.
Lesbian and Gay Archives of Naiad Press, PO Box 10543, Tallahassee, FL 32302.
Southern Gay Archives, PO Box 2118, Boca Raton, FL 33432.
Midwest Gay and Lesbian Archives, c/o GAU, PO Box 60046, Chicago, IL 60046.
National Coalition of Black Gays Archives, PO Box 57236, Washington, D.C. 20037.
One Institute Library, 2256 Venice Blvd., Los Angeles, CA 90006.

publish Newsletters – a valuable source of information.

Bibliography on Lesbian Separatism

Clare Potter
1983

(From the *Lesbian Periodicals Index*, for the Circle of Lesbian Indexers)

Abbreviations used:

Ag	August	Ja	January
Ap	April	Je	June
COR	*Coming Out Rage*	Jl	July
CWR	*Cowrie*	LFem	*The Lesbian*
D	December		*Feminist*
DY	*Dyke*	LL	*The Leaping*
DYGN	*Dykes & Gorgons*		*Lesbian*
EOS	*Echo of Sappho*	LLp	*Lesbian Lipseri*
F	February	LT	*Lesbian Tide*
Fl	Fall	LW	*Lavender Wom*
FR	*The Furies*	LV	*Lesbian Voices*
il	Illustration	Mr	March

My	May	S	September
N	November	SIS	*Sisters*
(n)	notice, brief	Sm	Summer
	mention	SP	*Spectre*
O	October	Sp	Spring
OAA	*Out and About*	SYOL	*So's Your Old*
p.	page		*Lady*
por il	portrait illustration	W	Winter
(rpr)	reprint	WGIt	*We Got It*

About racism and what's been going on in OAA. (re: 'A criticism . . .') Janey [Meyerding] OAA S '77:5+

Alix Dobkin and Liza Cowan on money, motherhood, and mutes. Majorie Canton and Rogi A. Rubyfruit por il LT 7:1:12+ Jl/Ag '77

An analysis of the politics of separatists working with lesbian feminists. Separatist Gang OAA Jl '78:9+

And ain't I a separatist? (re: 'A criticism . . .') Jody OAA Ag '77:insert

(Anthology on separatism planned.) (n) OAA Ap '81:29

Battle fatigue. [Ann Arbor Revolutionary Lesbians] SP [1]:4:8+ S/O '71

(. . . best joke on political dogma; re: 'The switch . . .') Lotus OAA Mr '78:12

Big bad separatists rock G.A.U. conference (N.Y.C.) Roz Richter LFem D '75:3

C.L.I.T. papers (statement #1 and #2). Collective Lesbian International Terrors (rpr) DY 1:1:6+ W '75/'76

C.L.I.T. collections #II (statement #3). Collective Lesbian International Terrors (rpr) NY 1:2:41+ Sp '76

CSLD 76: to march or not to march. Josephine Kelly LFem [Je] '76:3+

Coalition politics, dialogue between Judy Freespirit, Ivy Bottini, Jeanne Cordova and Maria Ramos. por il LT 7:2:4+ S/O '77

A comment from the OAA Collective (responding to male privilege exercised by gay men). OAA S '80:16

Comments from Separatist Circle (on change of name). OAA O '81:11

Community of separatist women. [Ann Arbor Revolutionary Lesbians] SP [1]:4:3 S/O '71

A criticism of lesbian separatism. Rising Fire Study Collective OAA Je '77:4+; part 2, Jl '77:6+

A critique of separatism. Kris Melroe OAA O '81:22+

Letter. Thrace LW 3:7:2 D '74

(Letter asks lesbians to confront anti-separatist gossip.) Lakey LW 3:5:2 Jl '74

Letter, Gorgons speak for separatism. (re: book review published in LT, Mr/Ap '77:29+) Gorgons LT 6:6:27 My/Je '77

Letter in response. Linda Regnier SYOL 5:24+ Sm '74

Letter: patriarchy marches on. Amethyst LT 9:2:18 S/O '79

Letter. (re: 'A criticism . . .') Lois OAA Ag '77:7

A letter to staff. Charlotte Bunch FR 2:3:10 My/Je '73

Letters. (re: 'A criticism . . .') Sustana and Pud Street OAA Jl '77:8+

Madison: universal minutes on separatism. Kathy Gimbel LW 1:2:7+ D '71

Man hating reviewed. Roberta Dill SIS 4:7:23+ Jl '73

Men/media/terror. (re: 'A criticism . . .') Sinistra OAA S '77:14+

A minority opinion. Tayloe Ross LFem [Je] '76:5

More about the Cleveland conference. B[onnie] Z[immerman] LW 3:4:2 Je '74

More on the Cleveland conference. Karen LW 3:5:3 Jl '74

Movement notices: (lesbian separatists). (n) LFem Je '77:19

National women's music festival. Laura Sky Brown LL 2:5:3+ (see p. 4) My/Je '78

The need for change: ideas about separatism from a dyke separatist. EOS 1:4:22+ '73

OAA responds. (re: 'A critique . . .') OAA O '81:24+

OAA collective statement, a clarification. (re: 'Separatist corner . . .') OAA S '81:11

Open letter to Gorgons. (re: 'The switch . . .') It's About Time and Red and Black Bookstore Collectives OAA Mr '78:16

Over the walls. il DYGN 1:1:2 My/Je '73

Perseverence furthers: separatism and our future. Charlotte Bunch FR 1:7:3+ Fl '72

The politics of separatism. Bonnie Zimmerman LW 3:2:11 Mr '74

Radical feminism? dyke separatism? Jeanne Cordova LT 2:10/11:20+ My/Je '73

Reply to 'A criticism . . .' Separatist Gang OAA Jl '77:18+

Response (to 'An analysis . . .') Kristin OAA O '78:6

Response (to 'A critique . . .') Janey Meyerding OAA N '81:24+

(Response to 'Silencing separatists.') Joanna Russ OAA Ja '81:19+

Seattle needs lesbian space. Danielle Harway OAA My '80:9

Separatism. Gutter Dyke Collective il DYGN 1:1:16+ My/Je '73

Separatism. Kathleen Spikes LLp 1:7 :2 N '75

Separatism. Nancy Davis LW 3:4:14 Je '74

print anti-separatist articles.) (re: 'A criticism . . .') OAA S
'77:2

The writing on the (pink) wall – some reactions (to anti-male
graffiti.) OAA Ap '79:25

Z on separatists. Z Budapest OAA N '81:26

New Alexandria Lesbian Library
Holdings on Lesbian Separatism

Bet Power (Director),
Annie B. Susan and Liz Seaborn
1983

For more information, to visit the library, or to add your
contribution, call (413) 584–7616 or write to: New Alexandria
Lesbian Library, P.O. Box 402, Florence Station, Northampton,
MA 01060.

CLL (Chicago Lesbian Liberation) Archives – (Chicago, IL: 1971
to 1974)
> Includes the group's by-laws, board of directors, herstory
> and list of membership.

LFC (Lesbian-Feminist Center) Archives – (Chicago, IL:
1974–1977)
LFC-LWC (Lesbian Writers' Conference) CONTROVERSY

1. Roberts, JR (1976) WHY I CHOOSE ANGER: An Open
   Letter to the Lesbian Writers' Conference.
2. Jamie (October 8, 1976) To anyone and everyone.
   > on: LWC controversy (non-supportive) and resignation
   > from LFC Collective.
3. Roberts, JR to: Jamie
   > on: Response to Jamie's letter of October 8, 1976.

LFC 'NO BOY CHILDREN' POLICY

1. New LFC Policy Announcement (August 1, 1976), 'No boy
   children.'
2. Farrow, Sunny (August 18, 1976) to: Dear Sisters.

on: policy, non-supportive.
3. Murry, Bernice (September 2, 1976) to: LFC Collective
   on: policy, supportive.
4. Lesbian Ex-Mental Prisoners Group (September 7, 1976) to:
   CWLU (Chicago Women's Liberation Union).
   on: policy, censorship of LFC by CWLU.
5. Early, Cathy (September 1, 1976) to: Sisters.
   on: policy, supportive.
6. Francis, MJ (September 1, 1976) to: Sisters.
   on: policy, supportive.
7. Blazing Star (September 26, 1976) to: Sisters of the LFC.
   on: policy, non-supportive.
8. Bart, Pauline B. (September 9, 1976) to: CWLU Steering
   Committee.
   on: policy, non-supportive.
9. Dobkin, Alix (September 14, 1976) to: LFC.
   on: policy, supportive.
10. Brelinger, C. and Hoffa, N. (September 19, 1976) to: Dear
    Wimin.
    on: policy, non-supportive.
11. Wessel, Elaine (September 26, 1976) to: Pauline Bart.
    on: policy, supportive.
12. Bamonte, Tom (October 1, 1976) to: LFC.
    on: policy, non-supportive.

LFC AND LAVENDER WOMAN: CONTROVERSY ABOUT AN ANTI-SEPARATIST CARTOON
1. Cartoon (original sketch)
2. Letter from LFC Collective (names) (July 30, 1974) to: the
   members of the Chicago Lesbian Liberation
   on: censorship of LFC because of its position on the
   cartoon.

LFC INTERNAL MEMOS AND ORGANIZATIONAL STATEMENTS
1. photo of LFC storefront: poor quality
2. LFC brochure
3. THE LESBIAN FEMINIST CENTER, statement of birth.
4. Statement in response to Jacy, 'Rumor Has It,' *OOB*, Vol. 5,
   #6 (July, 1975) 22.
   on: alleged boycotting of Susan B. restaurant.
5. Kennedy, Leigh, 'Some Comments by Leigh to be shared
   with the LFC Collective.'
   on: policies, goals.
6. Staffing hours, LFC member names and phone numbers.
7. Staffing guidelines.

8. Trainees for staffing schedule.
9. Lesbian Feminist Periodical listing from Center Bookstore.
10. List of Committees and who will explain each at the meeting.
11. Memo on: Economic crisis at LFC (July 25, 1977).
12. New LFC Policy (August 1, 1976) 'No males, no boy children.'
13. LFC moving memo, re-opening of NAL (New Alexandria Library).
14. LFC Collective (February 28, 1978) to: Dear Womyn
    on: closing of LFC and Bookstore, intolerance for LFC's separatist political position.

LFC CORRESPONDENCE
1. Lee, Julie (April 25, 1975) to: JR Roberts.
    on: response to letter of April 21, 1975 (missing).
    Dialogue on separatism.
2. Roberts, JR (April 29, 1975) to: Julie Lee.
    on: NALLW (New Alexandria Library for Lesbian Women), separatism, ageism, personal politics.
3. Lee, Julie (May 1, 1975) to: JR Roberts.
    on: NALLW, separatism, ageism.
4. Stewart, Sally (June 13, 1975) to: Sisters.
    on: archiving, how to. Herstory of NALLW.
5. Roberts, JR (April 29, 1975) to: Sally Stewart.
    on: founding of NALLW.
6. Valeska, Lucia (April 26, 1975) to: Carolee Kamlager.
    on: separatism, research inquiry.
7. Kamlager, Carolee (May 24, 1975) to: Lucia Valeska.
    on: reply to April 26, 1975 letter.
8. Women's Press Collective, CA. (undated) to: Joan.
    on: separatism, Press Collective herstory.
9. Cohen, Judy (undated) to: Dear Sisters.
    on: separatism, Sagaris school for lesbians.
10. Pone, Nancy & Cohen, Jocey (June 21, 1974) to: Joan and sisters.
    on: Helaine Victoria Enterprises.
11. Gardner, Kay (January 16, 1974) to: Dear Joan.
    on: partnership with Alix Dobkin.
12. Berson, Ginny (undated) to: Dear Women.
    on: open house for Meg Christian concert
13. Gittings, Barbara, President of Gay Task Force of ALA (American Library Assn.) (April 26, 1974) to: unspecified.
    on: thank you for hospitality and support.
14. Spotts and Casse Culver (undated) to: LRC (Lesbian

567

> Resource Center – a counseling group within LFC)
>   on: Winter Solstice greetings.

15. Poore, Nancy & Cohen, Jocey (September 17, 1974) to: Joan Capra, Chicago Women's Center. postcard.
   on: HVE (Helaine Victoria Enterprises) business.
16. Paxton, Evan (undated) to: Joan.
   on: *Heart of the Matter*, performance details.
17. Heim, Reina (July, 1976) to: LFC.
   on: note to drop from mailing list.

FAMILY OF WOMAN SUBJECT FILE
1. 'A Family of Women' by Bonnie Taman, *Chicago Express*, June 27, 1973, p. 7.
2. Family of Woman collective statement.
   on: politics of the band, statement of principles.
3. Poster – Season of the Witch, A festival for and by Women featuring 'Family of Woman' Lesbian Feminist musicians.

POST-LFC (NEW LESBIAN CENTER DEVELOPMENT) NEWS-CLIPS
1. 'Lesbian Center Considered,' *Chicago Gaylife* April 14, 1978. Vol. 3, Number 31.
2. 'Planning Proceeds for Lesbian Center,' *Chicago Gaylife* April 21, 1978. Volume 3, Number 32.

LFC QUESTIONNAIRE
1. Five completed questionnaires on evaluation of LFC by women who used it.

LFC CALENDARS AND NEWSLETTERS
Collection of LFC calendars and newsletters dating from September, 1974 through June, 1975.

LFC POSTERS AND FLYERS
Collection of posters, flyers and notices from LFC, having to do with Center groups, wimmin's events and activities connected with the LFC.

UNPUBLISHED WRITINGS
Roberts, JR. Memoir: Chicago Lesbian Community, 1973–1977. A transcribed oral herstory interview between JR Roberts, founder of The New Alexandria Lesbian Library and Clare J. Potter.

LFC LOGS
1. April 1974 through June 13, 1974.
2. June 13, 1974 through August 29, 1974.
3. August 29, 1974 through September 26, 1974.
4. September 26, 1974 through December 30, 1974.
5. January 1, 1975 through June 19, 1975.
6. June 20, 1975 through December 31, 1975.
7. January 1, 1976 through May 30, 1976.
8. May 22, 1976 through November 23, 1976.
9. November 23, 1976 through February 25, 1977.

CASSETTES OF LFC COLLECTIVE PROCESS
1. Women's Center Meeting 5/13/74.
   on: name change to Lesbian Feminist Center.
2. LFC Collective Meeting 6/9/74.
   three tapes.

NALL Internal/Organizational Archives
CORRESPONDENCE
   Daly, Mary. Correspondence with NALL, 1979.
   Dobkin, Alix. Correspondence with New Alexandria Lesbian
      Library, 1978–79.
   Shear, Linda and Hope, Tryna. Correspondence with NALL,
      1979.
   Van Deurs, Kady. Correspondence with NALL, 1979.

In the General NALL COLLECTION
UNPUBLISHED SEPARATIST WRITINGS
   Anderson, Rosemary. Selection of Short Stories and Poetry,
      1966–1981.
   Birdfish, Bet. Poetry, 1966–present.
   Cavin, Susan. 'I Made it all Up – Lesbian Love and War
      Poems.'
   Dyke Separatists Gathering Subject File. A collection of
      written materials from the Dyke Separatists Gathering
      held at the San Francisco Women's Building on July 9,
      1983, sponsored by S.E.P.S. (Separatists Enraged, Proud
      and Strong) of Oakland, CA. Includes the following:
   Anonymous. 'Lesbians Against Families.' Eleven-page
      paper analyzing the family's negative impact on
      Lesbians. Includes 'Motherhood is Violent to Lesbians'
      section. First printed 6-16-77; reprinted 6-83 by S.E.P.S.
   Bev. 'Why I'm a Dyke Separatist.' Two-page paper

distributed at the Gathering.

Bev. 'Women Only.' Three-page paper distributed at the Gathering.

'Bibliography for a Dyke Separatist Gathering.' List of relevant books, periodicals, newspapers, articles, records and archives on Lesbian separatism.

'Dyke Separatists Gathering.' Information sheet about the event and schedule of workshops.

'Dyke Separatists Gathering: Feedback Sheets.' Thirteen completed questionnaires from workshop participants.

'Dyke Separatists Gathering: Who We Are.' Information sheet about the event's eight organizers.

Lee, Anna. 'One Black Separatist.' *Innerviews*, Vol. 5, Issue 3. reprint of article made available at the Gathering.

Linda (for S.E.P.S.). Letter to NALL on Dyke Separatists Gathering.

Marty (and S.E.P.S.). 'Relating to Dyke Separatists: Hints for the Non-Separatist Lesbian.' July, 1983.

'We Are Everywhere.' List of foreign Lesbian and Gay periodicals and foreign contact Lesbians.

'We, Seps.' Two-page explanation of S.E.P.S., a group of eight Lesbians in Oakland, CA.

Dykewomon, Elana. 'Speaking of Fat out Loud at Last,' 1980.

Dykewomon, Elana. 'The Fourth Daughter's Four Hundred Questions,' 10–11/1979.

Gesmer, Susan Lynn. Collection of Short Stories, Prose and Poetry, 1979–present.

Me, Shari. 'The Queendom of IX.'

——. 'Baffle and Baffoon.'

——. 'Gracias from Glorius.'

——. 'The Raisin of a Prune.'

——. 'Chapter 10: Life in Hyacinth Fields.'

——. 'A Strategy of Dyke Nation – Chapter 3: "One Way to Do It." '

——. 'Remains to be Scene.'

Peters, Betty. 'A Way to be Gay.'

——. 'Childrearing or . . . Who's In Charge Here: A History of Chicago Lesbian Liberation.'

——. *The Dyke in the Sea.*

Shelley, Martha. 'Stepin Fetchit Woman.'

Skinner, Sidney. 'May Twenty-Second: Fight Fire With Water.'

——. 'What is Women's Music,' April, 1979.

Wile, Debra. 'Balance between Individual and Community as seen in a Womyn's Farm Collective.' A thesis submitted to the Faculty of Wesleyan University, June, 1982.

REEL-TO-REEL TAPES
Rehearsal for 'Family of Woman' Band Concert. Chicago, IL. October 6, 1972. Includes Linda Shear, Ella Szekeley, Joan Capra. (2 tapes).

CASSETTE TAPES
1. Best of Mother Right: Mother Right Band. Chicago, IL. 1971.
2. Family of Woman Band. Madison, WI. March 8, 1974 (2 tapes).
3. Alix Dobkin Concert. Chicago, IL. April 30, 1976.
4. Alix Dobkin Concert, sponsored by NALL. Chicago, IL. April 13, 1979. (2 tapes) And flyer/statement.
5. Vernita Gray, Bet Birdfish: Poetry Reading at Mountain Moving Coffeehouse. Chicago, IL. November, 1978. Includes Bet reading from JR Roberts Memoir: on Separatism in the Chicago Lesbian Community, 1973–77. And flyer.
6. Linda Shear Concert. East Lansing, MI. June 9, 1979 (2 tapes).
7. VALLEY WOMEN'S VOICE interview with Bet Birdfish, Diane Sievers on move of NALL from Chicago to Crescent Moon Star Farm, Huntington, MA in 1979 (10 acres of lesbian land once owned by Jill Johnston), near Northampton, MA and herstory of NALL. Northampton, MA. March, 1980.
8. 'DYKE PIONEERS' – Sidney Spinster. Radical Rose Recordings, 1982.

VIDEO TAPES
National Lesbian Conference. Chicago, IL. April, 1973. by Vulva Video (2 tapes).

TAPE TRANSCRIPTIONS
1. Transcript of taped interview with Linda Shear by Marie Kuda, 1972.
2. Transcript of taped discussion between members of key Lesbian publications, Chicago, IL, June 30, 1973.
   Includes representatives from: *Lavender Woman, Focus, Whole Woman, Killer Dyke, St. Louis Lesbian Newsletter, Dykes and Gorgons, Lesbian Tide, Cries from Cassandra.*

Includes many Chicago separatists. Also discussion on Family of Woman Band, Jill Johnston, etc.

REPRINTS OF PUBLISHED SEPARATIST WRITINGS

Chaps. 'Separatism! Separatism? Separatism ... Separatism ... Separatism ...,' *Aurora: A Feminist Magazine* (Fall, 1981).

Dyke Salad. Production Statement (Lesbian Separatist NYC Radio program, 1975).

Dykewomon, Elana. 'An Interview or How I Learned to Masturbate Among Other Things,' *The Second Wave* 4, 3 (Spring, 1976).

Family of Womon Band. Letter 'Dear Sisters' and News clipping from *Chicago Express* (June 27, 1973).

Haggard J. and Spinster, Sidney. Radical Rose Recordings, 'Tape Information Sheet.' Minneapolis, MN. 1983.

Hoagland, Sarah. Collected Papers, 1976–1979. Especially:

——. Review of *Gyn/Ecology: The Metaethics of Radical Feminism*, by Mary Daly.

——. Review of *The Transsexual Empire: The Making of a She-Male*, by Janice Raymond.

Kearon, Pam. 'Man-Hating.'

——. 'Lesbian Center Considered,' *Gay Community News* 3, 31 (April 14, 1978).

Lesbian Separatist Group. 'Addition to the first printing of "Lesbian Separatism: An Amazon Analysis",' (March 18, 1974).

Lightfoot, Barbara and Tibby. 'Porcupines and Valentines: The True Story of Amazon Nation,' 1973.

Lindsey, Karen. 'Why are Men Excluded from Events Run by Women,' 1976.

New York Radical Lesbians. 'The Woman-Identified Woman.'

——. 'Planning Proceeds for Lesbian Center,' *Gay Community News* 3, 32 (April 21, 1978).

Penelope, Julia. Collected Papers, 1972–1977. Especially:

——. 'Lesbian Separatism: The Linguistic and Social Sources of Separatist Politics,' 1974.

Radical Feminists. 'On Separatism,' 1972.

Shelley, Martha. 'Gay is Good.'

Skinner, Sidney. Review of Trying to Survive, by The Berkeley Women's Music Collective.

——. Review of Songs of Fire: Songs of a Lesbian Anarchist, by Kathy Fire.

——. Review of *Magical Songs*, by Malvina Reynolds.

——. Letter to Editors. 'Undue Inconsistency,' *OOB*.

Wilson, Margaret. 'Lesbian Lore' Column in *Chicago Gay Crusader* (1973–1974). Member of Chicago Lesbian Liberation. Information on 'Lesbian Cultural Festival' sponsored by Amazon Nation in Chicago, Family of Womon Band Concerts, and plans for first Lesbian Center in Chicago.

SIGNIFICANT SEPARATIST ARTICLES IN PERIODICALS

Addison, Lois Anne. 'Separatism Revisted,' *Sinister Wisdom*, 21 (1982: 29).

Bethel, Lorraine. 'What chou mean we, white girl,' *Conditions 5* (July, 1979): 86.

Bev. 'Women only,' *Lesbian Insider/Insighter/Inciter* 3 (April, 1981): 1.

——. 'Why are lesbians passing for straight?' *Lesbian Insider/Insighter/Inciter* 2 (January 1981):

Collective Lesbian International Terrors. 'C.L.I.T. Papers,' *Off Our Backs* (July, 1974): 10.

——. 'C.L.I.T. #4.' *Green Mountain Dyke News*, part 1: vol. 1, no. 3 (September, 1980): 4; part 2: vol. 1, no. 4 (October, 1980): 4; part 3: vol. 1, no. 5 (November, 1980): 4.

Cordova, Jeanne. 'Radical Feminism? Dyke Separatism?' *The Lesbian Tide*, (May/June, 1973): 20.

Dobkin, Alix. 'Why Be a Separatist?' *Womanews* (April, 1983): 6.

Dykewomon, Elana. 'Silencing Separatists,' *Lesbian Connection 5*, 1 (September, 1980): 4.

——. 'The Survivor's Story,' *Lesbian Insider/Insighter/Inciter* 2 (January, 1981): 19.

Elizabeth, Jacqueline. 'Separatism,' *Lesbian Insider/Insighter/Inciter* 5 (November, 1981): 17.

Falcon, Naomi. 'Why a Dyke Newsletter?' *Dyke Undoings* 1. (May, 1980): 1–3.

Family of Woman. 'Family Statement,' *Lavender Woman* 2, 5 (August, 1973): 2.

Feinstein, Sally. Letter to editors. *Lesbian Insider/Insighter/Inciter* 2 (January, 1981): 4.

Feinstein, Sarah. 'It Has To Do with Apples,' *Lesbian Insider/Insighter/Inciter* 4 (July, 1981): 1.

Frye, Marilyn. 'Some Notes on Separatism and Power,' *Sinister Wisdom* 6, (Summer, 1978): 30.

Gearhart, Sally, Silver, Lani, Talbot, Sue, Brown, Rita Mae, Cordova, Jeanne and McLean, Barbara. 'A Kiss Does Not a Revolution Make – a Search for Ideology,' Parts 1–3. *The Lesbian Tide* (June, July, August, 1974): 3, 10, 12.

Grace, Sarah. 'Some Thoughts on Separatism,' *Lesbian Insider/Insighter/Inciter* 5 (November, 1981): 3.

Hoagland, Sarah. 'Vulnerability and Power,' *Sinister Wisdom* 19 (1982): 13.

'Jill Johnston – an Interview,' *The Lesbian Tide* (July, 1973): 5.

Kearse, Sharon. 'Like Separating Siamese Twins,' *Lesbian Connection* 2, 2 (May, 1976): 8.

Kehler, Suzi. 'Why Separatism?' *Lesbian Connection* 3, 3 (July 1977): 13.

L.I.S.T.E.N. 'L.I.S.T.E.N.' *Lesbian Insider/Insighter/Inciter* 3 (April, 1981): 13.

Morningmoon, Q. 'Letter to editors,' *Lesbian Insider/Insighter/ Inciter* 2 (January, 1981): 4.

Northampton Lesbian Study Group. 'Analysis of a Lesbian[1] Community.' Parts 1, 2. *Lesbian Connection* 3, 3, 4 (July, September, 1977): 6, 9.

Peters, Betty. 'Notes on Coming Out, i.e. They Mean to Kill Us All,' *Lavender Woman* 1, 3 (May, 1972): 3.

Potts, Billie. 'Owning Jewish Separatism and Lesbian Separatism 9982.' *Lesbian Connection* 9 (December, 1982): 3.

Responses to 'Silencing Separatism,' *Lesbian Connection* 5, 3 (September, 1981): 17.

Rich, Adrienne. 'Notes for a Magazine: What Does Separatism Mean?' *Sinister Wisdom* 18 (1981): 83.

'Separatism . . . overdose?!' *Lesbian Connection* 2, 3 (July, 1976): 8.

Shear, Linda. 'Politicalesbians,' *Lavender Woman* 1, 1 (November, 1971): 6.

Smith, Barbara. 'Response,' *Sinister Wisdom* 20. (1982): 100.

Spinster, Sidney. 'The Evolution of Lesbian Separatist Consciousness,' *Lesbian Insider/Insighter/Inciter* 7 (April, 1982): 1.

——. 'Response,' *Sinister Wisdom* 20 (1982): 104.

Stevens, Marie. 'On Being a Political Lesbian,' *Lesbian Insider/ Insighter/Inciter* 2 (January, 1981): 12.

Thrace. 'Action Proposal for Lesbian Revolutionary Movement from a Lesbian Separatist's Position,' *Lesbian Insider/Insighter/ Inciter* 3 (April, 1981): 12.

Thundercloud, Flying. 'Letter to Editors,' *Lesbian Insider/ Insighter/Inciter* 7 (April, 1982): 5.

Waletzky, Dolphin and Dykewomon, Elana. 'Diaspora Distribution – A Dyke Alternative,' *Lesbian Insider/Insighter/Inciter* 2, (January, 1982): 12.

Zimmerman, Bonnie. 'The Politics of Separatism,' *Lavender Woman* 3, 2 (March, 1974): 11.

LESBIAN SEPARATIST PERIODICALS
The Amazon Nation newsletter, vol. 1, no. 1.
Chicago, IL, vol. 1, no. 2.
daughtervisions – parthenogenesis newsletter, vol. 2, spring 1981.
vol. 3, summer, 1981.
vol. 4, lammas, 1981.

Dyke, winter, 1975–76
spring, 1976.
fall, 1976.
fall, 1977.
summer, 1978.
The Furies, vol. 1 (January, 1972).
vol. 2 (February, 1972).
vol. 1, issue 3 (March-April, 1972)
vol. 1, issue 4 (May, 1972).
vol. 1, issue 5 (June-July, 1972).
vol. 1, issue 6 (August, 1972).
vol. 1, issue 7 (Fall, 1972).
vol. 2, issue 1 (February, 1973).
vol. 2, issue 2 (March-April, 1973).
vol. 2, issue 3 (May-June, 1973).
The Killer Dyke, vol. 1, no. 1 (September, 1971).
vol. 1, no. 2 (October, 1971).
vo. 2, no. 1 (June, 1972).
Lesbian Feminist Center, Womanspace, news and calendar,
October-November, 1974 through November, 1976.
Lunatic Fringe, no. 1 (July, 1980).
no. 2 (post music festival).
no. 3 (September, 1980).
Tribad, vol. 1, no. 2 (July-August, 1977).
vol. 1, no. 3 (September-October, 1977).
vol. 1, no. 4 (November-December, 1977).
vol. 1, no. 6 (March-April, 1978).
vol. 2, no. 1 (May-June, 1978).
vol. 2, no. 2 (July-August, 1978).
vol. 2, no. 3 (September-October, 1978).
vol. 2, no. 4 (January-February, 1979).
Womynlovers Separatist Newsletter, vol. 1, no. 1 (Summer, 1981).
vol. 1, no. 2 (Autumn, 1981).
vol. 2, no. 1 (Spring, 1983).

BOOKS
– Non-Fiction

Bunch, Charlotte. 'Learning from Lesbian Separatism,' in *Lavender Culture*, edited by Karla Jay and Allen Young. NY: Jove, 1979.

'Can Men and Women Work Together? A Forum.' in *After You're Out*, edited by Karla Jay and Allen Young. NY: Pyramid Books, 1975.

Daly, Mary. *Gyn/Ecology*. Boston: Beacon Press, 1978.

Dobkin, Alix. *Alix Dobkin's Adventures in Women's Music*. Preston Hollow, NY: Tomato Publications, 1979.

Frye, Marilyn. *Some Reflections on Separatism and Power*. East Lansing, MI: Tea Rose Press, 1977.

Johnston, Jill. *Lesbian Nation*. NY: Simon and Schuster, 1974.

Martin, Del. 'If That's All There Is,' in *Lesbians Speak Out*. Oakland, CA: The Women's Press Collective, 1974.

Members of the Class Workshop. 'New York All Women's Dance,' in *Lesbians Speak Out*. Oakland, CA: The Women's Press Collective, 1974.

Myron, Nancy and Charlotte Bunch (eds). *Lesbianism and the Women's Movement*. Baltimore, MD: Diana Press, 1975.

Paxton, Evan (ed). '1971 L.A. Gay Women's Conference,' in *Lesbians Speak Out*. Oakland, CA: The Women's Press Collective, 1974.

Solanas, Valerie. *The S.C.U.M. Manifesto*. NY: The Olympia Press, 1968, 1970.

– Fiction

Charnas, Suzy McKee. *Motherlines*. NY: Berkeley, 1979.

Dykewomon, Elana. *They Will Know Me By My Teeth*. Northampton, MA: Megaera Press, 1974.

Gearhart, Sally. *Wanderground*. Watertown, MA: Persephone Press, 1978.

Russ, Joanna. 'When It Changed,' in *The New Women of Wonder*, edited by Pamela Sargent. NY: Vintage Books, 1978.

Wittig, Monique. *Les Guérillères*. NY: Avon, 1973.

——. *The Lesbian Body*. NY: Avon, 1976.

– Poetry

Bissert, Ellen Marie. *The Immaculate Conception of the Blessed Virgin Dyke*. NY: 13th Moon, 1972, 1977.

Cavin, Susan. *Me and Them Sirens Running All Night Long*. NY: self-published, 1973.

Dykewomon, Elana. *Fragments From Lesbos*. Langlois, OR: Diaspora Distribution, 1981.

——. *They Will Know Me By My Teeth*. Northampton, MA: Megaera Press, 1976.

Shelley, Martha. *Crossing the DMZ*. Oakland, CA: The Women's Press Collective, 1974.

Stevens, Wendy. *i am not a careful poet*. Washington, DC: self-published, 1975.

We Are All Lesbians: A Poetry Anthology. NY: Violet Press, 1973.

RECORD ALBUMS
Avedis, Sirani. *Tattoos*. Chicago: Terrapin Records, 1979.

Dobkin, Alix. *Lavender Jane Loves Women*. Preston Hollow, NY: Women's Wax Works, 1974.

Dobkin, Alix. *Living With Lesbians*. Preston Hollow, NY: Women's Wax Works, 1975.

Flying Lesbians. West Berlin: Frauenbuchvertrieb, 1975.

Shear, Linda. *A Lesbian Portrait*. Northampton, MA: Old Lady Blue Jeans, 1975.

ART
Anderson, Rosemary. 'Study of Hands' 1969; 'Rose Abstraction' 1977.

Deep Moss Liza. 'Breast form: Self Image,' no date; Logo for NALL buttons, 1982.

Gesmer, Susan. 'Torso' 1974; Untitled watercolor 1983.

Photos: Wendy Dragonfrye, Alix Dobkin, Kady VanDeurs, Michelle Brody. Photographs of various Lesbian Separatists in the Pioneer Valley Lesbian community taken at the Northampton Lesbian and Gay Pride March, May 14, 1983.

NORTHAMPTON LESBIAN COMMUNITY COLLECTION – FLYERS (Partial Listing)
1. Astrological Charts and tarot readings: Flash Silvermoon.
2. 'Ancient Cross Cultural Images of Woman and the Goddess,' Slide shown by Diane O. M. Davies, MA Common Womon Club, Northampton, MA. Friday, April 9, 9 pm.
3. Program for Alix Dobkin Concert. Northampton, MA. March 13, 1982.
4. Invitation: you are warmly invited to an open house at New Alexandria Lesbian Library. Sunday, September 19, 1982. Leeds, MA.
5. 'I LOVE THE LIBRARY PARTY' A celebration for Lesbians at the New Alexandria Lesbian Library, February 20, 1983. A support party in response to the threats to arson to NALL and threats to Bet Birdfish.
6. 'A reading of prose and poetry: Elana Dykewomon,' Smith College, Northampton, MA. Saturday, September 25, 1982.
7. 'Jeb: a Slide show,' Northampton, MA.
8. 'A Concert for Women – performed by Michelle Brody,'

Northampton, MA, 1979. (photos of concert)
9. Flyers of events for Lesbians at Lesbian Gardens, (mid-1970's) Northampton, MA.
10. 'A poetry Reading for Lesbians' – Vernita Gray, Bet Birdfish, Tryna Hope signing. Produced by Old Lady Blue Jeans, Northampton, MA.
11. 'Linda Shear,' Lesbian Musician in Concert, Tuesday, December 11, Hampshire College, Amherst, MA.
12. 'Linda Shear,' Winter Solstice Celebration, Sunday, December 17, Boston University, Boston, MA.
13. 'Marilyn Gayle,' Dyke Music – A Lesbian life in songs and drawings and music. (undated)

Lesbian Archives, Europe

Archives, Recherches et Cultures Lesbiennes
B.P. 662 75531 Paris Cedex II France

Les Lesbianaires
Centre for documentation and research on radical lesbianism c/o I. Dargent BP 2024 Bruxelles 1 1000 Bruxelles Belgium

Spinboden
Lesbian archive
Postfach 30 41 49 1000 Berlin 30 West Germany

Lesbisch Archief Amsterdam
Postbus 10870
1001 EW Amsterdam Netherlands

Lesbisch Archief Nijmegen
Postbus 1220 6501 BE Nijmegen Netherlands

Archivi Lesbici Italiani
Centro Femminista Separatista Via San Francesco di Sales 1A 00165 Roma Italy

The Lesbian Archive
BCM Box 7005 London WC1N 3XX England

CONTRIBUTORS' NOTES

Alice, Gordon, Debbie, and Mary formed a separatist group which existed in Seattle in the early 1970's.

Alix Dobkin I am a lesbian songwriter, singer and entertainer whose main purpose in life is to support lesbians and to help all women know that they can choose to love women.

Anita Cornwell is an essayist/fiction writer who finally turned playwright after thinking about it for nearly two decades. Her first book, *Black Lesbian in White America*, was published by Naiad Press.

Anna Lee I'm delighted that separatists resisted the trend towards the right. The number of years that it took to get this anthology published attests to the strength of conservatism and the degree that lesbians conformed to the white male heterosexual hegemony. I'm still a separatist and separatism is the only position that makes sense to me. It's been a long time since I've lived in the midwest but I'll shortly get a chance to find out if the conditions I deplored in 'A Black Separatist' have changed.

Anne E. Schulherr Waters is a poet, philosopher and Ph.D student at Purdue University (Philosophy Department), West Lafayette, Indiana, USA, 47907. She is published in areas of ethics and feminism, and holds degrees from The University of New Mexico, Washington University in St. Louis, Mo., and Purdue University. To understand her separatism, it is important to recognize she is American Indian and Jewish, and this heritage has challenged her to appreciate personal, social, and political aspects of separatism. Her recent research concerns feminist worldviews, global politics and reproductive technologies. Her activist interests are race, sex/gender, class, and children/future generation issues. She lives with her loving friend BJ and their cat Ziddi Ji.

Ariane Brunet I am a French speaking lesbian from Québec, active in the lesbian movement since 1976. A founding member of the magazine, *Amazones d'Hier, Lesbiennes d'Aujourd'hui*, I now continue to pursue and develop a lesbian radical political thought that is both lucid and aware of the questions that still need to be addressed with integrity and a clarity of vision. And I bring all of that to my work as one of the organizers of the Third International Feminist Book Fair in Montreal in 1988.

Baba Copper I am a Crone Futurist, a contemporary version of the honorable tradition of old wimmin who cultivate plant friends, wild birds and other willful searchers. I now live alone in a house by the sea, where I have written a book about ageism and am working on another about radical lesbian grandmothering.

Bet Power (formerly Bet Birdfish) has lived with and directed the New Alexandria Lesbian Library since 1977. A butch/Lesbian/transvestite/top/performance poet & dancer, Power has a Master of Arts degree in Women's Studies in Lesbian Literature and a career as a corporate advertising executive. An ex-'70's-Chicago-Lesbian separatist, Power is also the founding member of SHELIX, a Lesbian S/M and pro-sexuality support group which meets in Northampton.

Bette S. Tallen is a 37-year-old Jewish lesbian feminist, born in New York City and now living in Chicago where she teaches and coordinates the Women's Studies Program at Northeastern Illinois University. She dreams of a world where feminist process would not mean constant meetings.

Billie Potts I am a forty-eight year old lesbian feminist from a New York City, U.S.A. Jewish working-class background. I am a writer, herbalist, gardener, crystal-healer, tarot-reader, mother, potter, onetime goatkeeper (over 17 years), anti-discrimination, anti-war, anti-nuclear, anti-sexual exploitation, pro-lifeforce, pro-woman, activist. Currently I research and train in the field of health effects of computer-mediated work, particularly the effects on women, and VDT ergonomics. Since the writing of 'Jewish Separatism/Lesbian Separatism' I have survived the Reagan eighties, life, loss, and familial death in Miami, mainly through the help of womon-loving friends. I still attempt in my work to fertilize future revolutions by creating womon-magic, and juggling computer chips, healing plants, airport sojourns, and matrix crystals. My vision and politics are intact, my strategies changed. I am the author of *Potworks: A First Book of Clay*, *Small-scaled Goatkeeping*, *A New Women's Tarot*, *Witches Heal: Lesbian Herbal Self-sufficiency*, co-author of *Ergonomics: The Changing Office*, contributor and coordinator of the *Amazon Tarot* Decks. For information on these books and the tarot deck, write to Billie at Hecuba's Daughters, Box 488, Bearsville, N.Y. 12409.

Carol (Murf) Moorfield graduated as a Woman Studies Major from Towson State University in 1974, and received her formal initiation in Wicca in 1978. She and her partner, Barbara, have raised 3 young women, Maria, Carla, and Julie. They currently run Caldron Crafts, a wicca oriented craft and gemstone business (915 Montpelier St., Baltimore,, MD 21218). Murf's next project is a video entitled 'Legacy of the Matriarchy.'

Caryatis Cardea is happy to be celebrating, at this writing, her thirteenth year as a lesbian separatist, her first semester as a returning student majoring in history at UC-Berkeley, and the approach (a mere matter of days) of her 37th birthday. She is of the white working class (Irish/Québecoise), disabled, and chooses, for the time being, to wear her hair long – so there!

Clare Potter edited the *Lesbian Periodicals Index* (Naiad, 1986) and was a founding member of the West Coast Lesbian Collections, a community archives (now called the June L. Mazer Collection, 3271 N. Raymond Ave., Altadena, CA 91001).

Claudie Lesselier, Graziella Raso, Irene Bouaziz, Martine Laroche and Françoise Roux have been involved in the Lesbian Movement in France for several years and at the time when the texts were written, in the FLR (Front des lesbiennes radicales – Radical Lesbian Front). Since 1982, the FLR no longer exists. Claudie Lesselier is currently involved in the Lesbian Archives in Paris, created in 1983.

C.L.I.T. Collective:
> **Maricla Moyano** is an Argentine-American dyke-feminist-pacifist-democratic socialist waiting for anarchism. She is a contributing editor and copy editor of *Big Apple Dyke News* and author of *Beginning book*, a work of fiction, and *Burning Bright*, a work of fiction. She worked for 'Women Against Prison' and at Fort Dyke-*Tribad*.
> **Susan Cavin** has been a Lesbian Separatist since 1972, has been a member of the C.L.I.T. Collective, TRIBAD-FORT DYKE-, and is currently Editor-Publisher of *Big Apple Dyke News* (B.A.D. News). Author of *Lesbian Origins* (San Francisco, Calif.: ism press, 1985).
> **Marcia Segerberg** I became a separatist during the winter of 1970–71, as my friends Jill Johnston and her collaborator Jane O'Wyatt were putting together *Lesbian Nation*. After almost a decade as a 'professional' lesbian feminist, I made the decision to go back to school in order to avoid starvation

and other forms of personal destruction. I expect to receive my Ph.D. in neuroscience in the spring of 1988, at which time I will have become a vegetarian lesbian separatist neurophysiologist friend of a turkey-baster girl child, among other things.

Doreen Worden dreams of a gentler, more diverse society where women can worship the goddess and realize our strength and beauty together.

Elana Dykewomon is a Jew, a poet, a survivor of psychiatric assault, fat, a life-long lesbian, a separatist for 13 years, hip-deep in dyke community, author of *Riverfinger Women*, *Fragments from Lesbos* and *They Will Know Me By My Teeth* (the last still available from Diaspora Dist.). She is the current editor of *Sinister Wisdom*, a Journal for the Lesbian Imagination in the Arts and Politics. She loves to keep asking questions and turn somersaults in the water.

Emily Levine 31 year-old groundskeeper by profession, recently returned to college. Lives in Lincoln, Nebraska with her lover and three cats.

Flyin Thunda Cloud, RDOC is a 31-year-old dyke, who lives in a state where there is very little support 4 bein a separatist. she has an almost 9-year-old girlchild. she is native amerikan (mowhawk/cherokee & blackfoot), west indyan (jamaican) & afro amerikan. she loves *all* her sisters and sistahs.

Ginny Z. Berson was a founding member of The Furies newspaper and collective. The collective began in 1971, disbanded in 1972 (?) and the newspaper published into 1973. Other members included Coletta Reid, Charlotte Bunch, Rita Mae Brown, and Joan E. Biren (JEB). Ginny Berson was also a founding member of Olivia Records, which she left in 1980. For 6 years she was the Director of Women's Programming at KPFA-FM in Berkeley, California, where she is now the Program Director. Many of her beliefs have changed, but she still loves women, cats, and softball.

Gorgons was a separatist collective in Seattle in the late 1970's.

Gutter Dyke Collective published *Dykes and Gorgons* in May/June 1973. The collective existed in 1973 in Berkeley, California, and included Bev Jo (note separate listing here under S.E.P.S.), Anne, and Aida.

iandras moontree This piece was written several years ago and of course, reflects where I was at that time. Essentially, I feel the same but would express it in more specific terms now. Generally, I am less idealistic and more pessimistic. In my utopian fantasy, I would live within a culture of Lesbians in a slow-paced, closer-to-the-earth way. I believe that as long as so many men have so much power and control, it is impossible to co-exist in a peaceful, gentle way. This makes me very sad.

Isabel Andrews is a 56-year-old, rural working class, raging man-hating dyke separatist, who hopes that mainstream lesbians will soon stop selling us out.

Isabel Dargent Both 'How Gay to be Different' and the leaflet handed out on the abortion demonstration were signed and approved by 'Le Feminaire' (a Radical Lesbian Feminist Collective in Belgium) and by Des Lesbiennes Feministes Radicales. Both leaflets were later published in 'Le Feminaire' Number 4. They marked a decisive turning point in our strategy and political position: men were no longer allowed in our places of resistance; some lesbians became more radical, 'Le Feminaire', for example, became 'Le Lesbianaire' from issue 5 onwards. It's important that these leaflets be attributed to the collectives from which they emerged for historical accuracy, despite the current deep splits between lesbian feminists and radical lesbians. Nowadays I define myself as a radical lesbian and a Latina.

Jan Hardy generally has many more hopeful dreams about women than nightmares. She has published poetry in *Sinister Wisdom*, *off our backs*, *Black Maria*, and other journals. Her first chapbook, *out here flying* is available from Sidewalk Revolution Press, P.O. Box 9062, Pittsburgh, PA 15224.

Jean Langford, K. Hess, Kathy Ross 'FEMINISM FIRST' was an essay on lesbian separatism that grew out of our experience in the Seattle lesbian-feminist community during the 1970's. At the time of this printing we have varying levels of agreement with this paper ranging from virtually no agreement to partial agreement. We have consented to the reprinting of certain excerpts because we believe they have historical value. The original essay was published by Tsunami Press in both Spanish and English.

Jeffner Allen is the author of *Lesbian Philosophy: Explorations* (Institute of Lesbian Studies (1986); P.O. Box 60242, Palo Alto,

CA 94306). She is the editor of *Lesbian Philosophers and Culture*, a collection of essays by lesbian philosophers, which will be published by SUNY Press (Spring, 1989).

Joan Nestle is a forty-seven year-old Jewish Lesbian who came out as a fem in the late fifties. She is co-founder of the Lesbian Herstory Archives and the Lesbian Herstory Educational Foundation, Inc. She is also a writer of erotica or pornography, depending on who is doing the name calling. Her most recent book is *A Restricted Country* published by Firebrand Books, Ithaca, New York, 14850. She is not a Lesbian separatist; she does believe in an army of queers, whores, and workers.

Jorika Anna This is a dated piece for me – I now disagree with the nazi/true-to-yourself comment (the most), believing currently that you can't be both. Mainly, though, I'm happy to realize how much I've grown since, becoming positive and life-affirming; less reactive and more centered in my own power/spirit/soul. While moving from the word 'separatist' as it focuses on what we are separating from and not on what we are moving toward, I remain truly a radical 'biophilic lesbophilick' (life-loving, lesbian-lover) even in the hills of Vermont – which can be difficult. These same hills also reflect my spirit power back to me; for these paradoxes of life I am always wary and grateful.

Joyce Trebilcot The 1979 essay published here, 'Craziness as a Source of Separatism,' says that I maintain my separateness in order to resist rape. It does not address the question of why I resist 'unioning,' or merging with others, even on occasions when there seems to be no threat of rape. The answer is that I believe that there is ALWAYS a threat of rape, that is, of someone else controlling me. I believe further that ideas of open-mindedness, love, and ecstasy are used by men to make us vulnerable to their control. Adopting such values for lesbian communities is like dykes wearing high heels or getting married. For me, having learned the patriarchal lessons well, consciousness of perpetual metaphor, of always talking about what is going on, is like opening my legs to a man. Being physically surrounded by wimmin doesn't change that.

Juana María Paz is a N.Y. born Puerto Rican lesbian writer who has been widely published in the feminist and alternative press. She is also a waitress, playwright, radio & TV announcer, actress, singer/songwriter, welfare mother and welfare rights advocate. 'Atlantis' was produced by the Front Room Theater Guild in

Seattle, Washington in the spring of 1984. It and several other lesbian and feminist plays are available (free to non-profit theater groups) from the author, c/o Paz Press, P.O. Box 820, New Port Richey, Florida 34656-0820.

Julia Penelope After 46 years of living as a Lesbian, Julia Penelope still hasn't made any sort of 'peace with the world,' and rumors alleging that she's 'mellowed' are false. She finds 'peace' an illusive concept in a world where male violence, whether acted out or verbally threatened, keeps most women in bondage to men. In her work, she continues to identify and analyze language structures in English that limit the shape of our conceptual processes, and is working on a book about how women can use what she's found to show other women how we can learn to think *beyond* the limitations imposed by the categories and structures of patriarchal English (to be published in the Pergamon Athene Series).

Kathleen R. Valentine is an amateur archeologist who has been active in Lesbian and Gay politics. She has taught a number of courses on Women's and Gay History.

Kathy Munzer This story was written in the spirit of healing. It is dedicated to all womyn who have been battered. I am a Chicago separatist who has been doing production at Mountain Moving Coffeehouse for the past five years.

Lee Lynch lives in rural Southern Oregon with Tee Corinne, five cats and a dog. She has published two books of stories and three novels with Naiad Press, the latest of which is *Dusty's Queen of Hearts Dinner*. She believes it is essential that we have the right to choose with whom we mate, live, work and play.

Linda Shear I still believe strongly in our need to build, protect, and nurture our lesbian culture. As it became clear that the revolution was not happening next week, I found myself caught in the struggle of finding a position of balance in the world. Surviving as a lesbian in our culture while maintaining the dignity of a lesbian centered vision becomes increasingly complex. I have few answers – many, many questions. As I begin my 40's, I feel myself stretching to find pieces of my old songs to nurture my heart and spirit, and have learned to be compassionate with my present search for new ones.

Liza Cowan I live in Woodstock NY and in New York City. I still live with Alix, we've been family for sixteen years, and I'm still best friends with Penny. I call myself a separatist and continue to believe that separatism is an analysis, not a life 'style.' For the last two years I've been dedicating most of my time to studying Neuro-Linguistic Programming, which is a model of how our minds work, the study of subjective reality. It is a powerful tool for change, for both individuals and systems. I am an Assistant Trainer at the NY Training Institute For NLP. In 1989 I will be a certified Trainer. Now I am bringing Lesbian-ity to my school and my trainings. I'm working at bringing NLP to Lesbians.

Lola Lai Jong Nothing has touched me as deeply as when I can write about the lives of womyn – Chinese womyn – her mother – and ancestresses. As a Pacific/Asian Lesbian, I have found that Lesbian separatist politics afforded me a healthy way to define myself, which includes mothering a male chyld. As far as where my main focus and energies are – I love being with Lesbians in Lesbian space.

Louise Turcotte I am a French-speaking lesbian printer who came out in 1974 in the feminist movement. I have been politically active in Lesbians Only groups since 1976 and since 1979 I've been working with my video and magazine collective, *Amazones D'Hier, Lesbiennes D'Aujourd'hui* as well as other radical lesbians to form and develop a radical political thought of lesbianism.

Margaret Sloan-Hunter has been involved for the past 25 years in the liberation of oppressed people. At the age of 14 she was involved in tenant unions, rent strikes and campaigns against lead poisoning. At 17 she founded the Junior Catholic Inter-racial Council, a student group working against racism. She was involved in civil rights activities and attended Malcolm X Community College. In 1966 she participated in the Open Housing Marches with Dr Martin Luther King and SCLC and in Operation Breadbasket with Jesse Jackson. She is one of the founding editors of MS Magazine and has lectured with Gloria Steinem on Sexism and Racism throughout the U.S., Canada and Europe. In 1973 she founded and was the first Chairwoman of the National Black Feminist Organization. She has given over 400 lectures at such institutions as Harvard and Yale and to grassroots groups such as the National Welfare Rights Organization. A writer and poet, her articles have been published in numerous magazines and she has appeared on many television and radio programs. In 1975 she moved with her daughter to Oakland, California where she worked as an organizer for the Berkeley

Women's Center, the Feminist School for Girls and as a founder of the Women's Foundation. She is currently completing a book of poetry and prose entitled 'Black and Lavender'.

Marilyn Frye is a philosopher and writer. She has taught for many years at Michigan State University, both philosophy and women's studies, where she has all along been 'out' and is relatively notorious for being a separatist, whatever that means to those who 'note' it. She is of southwestern/midwestern U.S., middle class and protestant origins; she is white. She is involved in her local lesbian community and has worked off and on in lesbian and feminist publishing and bookselling. Her lover Carolyn Shafer (an artist) is often her philosophical collaborator and critic. She is the author of *The Politics of Reality: Essays in Feminist Theory* (Freedom, CA: The Crossing Press, 1983).

Marthe Rosenfeld Born in Antwerp in 1928, I grew up in Belgium and soon began to feel the effects of the rise of fascism and anti-Semitism in Europe. As a Jewish refugee of World War II, I was very fortunate at thirteen to be able to immigrate with my close relatives to the United States. In New York City where I lived from 1941 to 1959, I pursued my studies in French. Since the early 1970's I have been teaching both French and Women's Studies at Indiana University – Purdue University, Fort Wayne. A sabbatical leave in Paris during the academic year 1976–1977 enabled me to gain firsthand knowledge of the different factions of the women's liberation movement in France. My work on the writings of Monique Wittig have appeared in *Frontiers*, *Mosaic*, and *Vlasta*. I am currently a member of the Lesbian Archives of Paris and identify as a Jewish lesbian.

Mary Daly is a Positively Revolting Hag who teaches Feminist Ethics in the Department of Theology at Boston College. She is the author of *The Church and the Second Sex*, *Beyond God the Father*, *Gyn/Ecology*, and *Pure Lust* (all available from Beacon Press).

Micheline Grimard-Leduc teaches biochemistry and related sciences, but extends her personal research to cultural domains, hoping to promote our lesbian culture. The Mind-Drifting Islands is an excerpt from *L'île des amantes* which can be ordered from Productions MGL, 361 rue d'Orléans, St-Lambert, Québec, Canada J4S 1Y1. Prices, postage included, $8-Canadian in Canada and USA, $9-Canadian in other countries.

Monique Wittig is the author of *The Opoponax* (New York: Simon and Schuster, 1966); *Les Guérillères* (New York: Avon Books, 1973); *The Lesbian Body* (New York: Avon Books, 1976); *Lesbian Peoples: Material for a Dictionary*, co-authored with Sande Zeig; *Virgile, non* (Paris: Editions de Minuit, 1985), translated as *Across the Acheron* (London: Peter Owen, 1987). In addition she has translated several books, and is author of a number of short stories, critical essays, and plays, including *The Constant Journey*. *The Constant Journey* was first produced in the U.S. at Goddard College, Vermont, in 1984. It has toured cities in the U.S. Midwest including Madison, Minneapolis, and Chicago. It was produced in France as *Le Voyage sans fin* in 1985 at the Theatre du Rond-Point, Paris. Sande Zeig has been a co-director in these projects. A video of the play is distributed by the Centre audio-visual Simone de Beauvoir. Monique Wittig has been a Visiting Professor of French at the University of California at Berkeley and also at Davis. Currently, she is a Visiting Professor at Vassar College in Poughkeepsie, New York. 'The Straight Mind' was written in French, and 'One Is Not Born a Woman' was originally written in English.

Nancy Breeze is a 56-year-old white Florida crone, whose natural habitat is the sand dunes at sunset. She lives at Pagoda, a St. Augustine Lesbian community. A typesetter and a charter member of the Lesbian Grandmother's Association, she often can be found sunbathing, dancing, or reading.

Naomi Dykestein Since I wrote this article, my life has grown and changed in directions which would have surprised me then. I am almost two years clean and sober and in recovery; my marriage of 12 years is over (though my relationship with her is not). One of my most important relationships is with a 12-year-old boy, with whom I hope to continue to share my life. I work in the AIDS field, and care intimately for many of the men and women with whom I work – I credit this crisis with teaching me respect for the humanity and dignity of the various communities affected by the disease. I no longer believe – either as a Lesbian or as a Jew – that my only two options are assimilation or separatism. I have learned that I can share my life, my love, my energy, without risking losing my identity, culture, sexuality or power. About the same time I began to suspect that women weren't the perfect glorious creatures I'd always wanted us to be, I also began to suspect that then perhaps men weren't evil incarnate. My recovery has meant that I no longer have to (or am able to) perceive life in such alcoholic extremes. I work at being more at peace in my life, and I have no regrets for where I was or where I am now.

Naomi Littlebear Morena 'Coming Out' comes from a lesbian rock opera called *Survivors*, which I wrote and produced in 1980. The story was about a white middle-class incest survivor named Jane and her brown womon lover, Clara, survivor of rape and physical abuse. The story tells how class and race may have affected the way each womon dealt with her abuse and the psychological effects of abuse and heterosexual orientation. The musical among many things was an opportunity to speak out from the closet of my own repressed separatism. Even though I was raised in racial separatism and was at best reluctant to assimilate into white culture, my desire to choose a path that rejected compulsory heterosexuality and the almost infinite ways in which this empire of heterosexism manifests, was thwarted by the 'New Authority'* which proclaimed separatism as racist. I did not exist and if I did I was a racist or a deviant. The conflicts of all women of color are yet again increased when we are told, usually by white middle-class or the college educated, that we are invalid. First we share the great pain of leaving our cultures behind, usually to survive the racist institutions of learning, then again to survive outside of the ingrained sexist or homophobic traditions of our given culture. When I came out I knew no other brown women who were dykes, the ones I know now are precious to me for the like pains we may share. The pain increases when white wimmin tell me that only they can hate men and that only white men hurt wimmin and when a man of color has hurt me it was because the white man hurt him first. My color is the excuse ignorant whites use to keep me down, my sex is the excuse all men make to keep me down. Sadly enough it has been lesbian women who have policed my thoughts and kept my ideas at bay with guilt-inducing, man-serving propaganda. To all white sisters – let your sisters of colors breathe life into their thoughts, stop placing *all* our people into safe, compartmental categories. We are not children. There should be a safe place for wimmin of all colors who desire freedom from forced assimilation into white or hetero institutions.
* Quoting my lover, Helen's, term for the new laws & moralities being formed by conservative lesbian communities.

New Alexandria Lesbian Library is a national collection of Lesbian herstory for EveryLesbian, with regional, national and international archives, founded in 1974 and located in Northampton, Massachusetts. The Library documents with respect and honor the lives of all Lesbians and archives separatist Lesbian materials in the same way it archives materials on butch, fem and androgynous Lesbians, bar dykes, conservative Lesbians, leftist Lesbians, corporate Lesbians, Lesbian prostitutes, transvestite Lesbians, Third World Lesbians, S/M Lesbians, differently-abled dykes, older Lesbians, tomboys, Jewish Lesbians, radical lesbians, anti-porn Lesbians and pro-sex Lesbians, passing women and Lesbians who pass . . . and more. The Library is a passionate act of love performed by Lesbians today, powerful enough to travel through time to Lesbians of tomorrow, enacted again and again in a home for us all. 'Holdings on Lesbian Separatism' was compiled in 1983 by Bet Power (Director, NALL) (note separate listing above) and Annie B., Susan and Liz Seaborn. Since then, many more materials in this subject area have been added to the collection.

Penny House I was the co-founder and co-editor, with Liza Cowen, of *DYKE* magazine. Since I wrote this article in 1978, I've moved back and forth across the country, changed lovers, apartments, jobs, avocations and my appearance, but I remain a separatist in my heart and in my thinking. And I'm still amazed (and amused) by the horror and ignorance with which Lesbians react when confronted with a separatist.

Radicalesbians involved in the writing of 'The Woman-Identified Woman' include Rita Mae Brown, Ellen Bedoz, Cynthia Ellen, Lois Hart, March Hoffman, and Barbara XX. From **Rita Mae Brown**: The Radicalesbians were formed from existing women's groups at that time – late sixties, the beginning of the seventies. Unable to function in N.O.W., Redstockings, W.I.T.C.H., and the gay male groups we had little choice but to withdraw from those groups and form a separate one. The name lacks imagination but it was the best we could come up with at the time. The group numbered in the hundreds in New York City. It's probably hard for a young person today to realize how much pressure we were under. The women's movement not only pushed us back in the closet, they nailed the door shut. As for the gay men, they had no interest whatsoever in the issues central to lesbians and straight women. Lesbians and straight women might as well have been from another planet. The other important point is that most of us were in our early twenties. We had an excess of enthusiasm and a shortage of experience. I'm amazed that we accomplished as much as we did. Our message was simple: the freedom to be the individuals we truly were. How could straight women talk about men oppressing women and then turn around and do the same things to us? How could gay men talk about community and then be so unwilling to accept women as equals? The Radicalesbians didn't ask for special treatment. We asked to be part of the decision-making process. In the long run, the women's movement realized what it had done. As to the gay men's movement, I think the jury is still out. As for us, the work it took to fight for ourselves gave us dignity. Even if we didn't win full equality we came out of this time better off than we were before.

Rebecca Lillian I am a first generation American hoping to someday discover that I'm not the only generation of Lesbian in my Russian-Jewish family. I wrote 'My Poem' in 1981 and have since been fortunate to find work that is not so fragmenting. I was born (1–16–59) and raised in Chicago, now live in Northampton, Mass.

Redwomon Formerly a celibate lesbian, Redwomon is now a celibate heterosexual (?) Christian who still respects separatism. She is part white and part Cherokee. She avoids feminists and lesbians in general, finding such contact too often painful partly because of fascist and classist attitudes and games. She takes in stray cats, collects clothing for Indians and for runaway children, and is looking for an abandoned or cheap house. She wants to find caring, gentle people to be with who are activists in helping others and in changing the face of the world.

Revolutionary Lesbians was composed of two women in Ann Arbor, Michigan, who wrote the paper, *Spectre*, in 1971. There were six issues. These women (a couple) were separatists for nine years. One is now straight, the other is still a lesbian who no longer counts herself as a separatist. Unlike many former separatists, she feels good about those years and counts them as crucial in her life, and she still cares and struggles around the issues they wrote about. *Spectre*'s articles were unsigned because the authors wanted to break out of the private property of ideas. They saw themselves as part of a national process, even while separatists. One of the authors, Lois Addison, published an article in *Sinister Wisdom* #21, Fall 1982 entitled, 'Separatism Revisited.'

Sarah Grace is a 51-year-old Jewish lesbian who came out in 1979 after 24 years of marriage and six children, five of them male. 'Out there' she works with retarded adults, but her real work is the journey she's chosen to her own power and spiritual witchy center.

Sarah Lucia Hoagland is a philosopher and a Chicago dyke. She is 42, white, of upper and middle class values; she has been drug-dependent (cortisone) and has learned to manage her asthma through alternative healing methods. She rejected heaven and hell at age 6 upon being told that her recently deceased best friend (a cat) was in neither place. Her childhood was spent mostly by herself, though she played with animals and best girlfriends. Upon being assimilated, she lost her gift of communication with animals and became a womanhater. She has lived in Chile (1957–1959) and Panama (1959–1963), where she learned about U.S. imperialism, France (1967), and England (1973–1974). Affected by the Berkeley free speech movement in 1964, she began to address racism and anti-semitism. In 1971 she began to consider feminism. She came out in 1975, a year after being labeled p.d.o.f. (potential dyke on faculty) by her lesbian students, and she named herself 'separatist' in 1976. Her cats have been attempting to teach her to again communicate with animals. She has been teaching philosophy and women's studies at Northeastern Illinois University in Chicago since 1977, and has given talks around the U.S. for 14 years. She is author of *Lesbian Ethics: Toward New Value*, forthcoming from the Institute of Lesbian Studies (P.O. Box 60242, Palo Alto, CA 94306 USA).

Sarah Valentine hopes someday to build an expert system which can provide the snappy comeback within 30 nanoseconds. She still doesn't believe it's safe for Lesbians to work with breeders. Lesbian energy should belong to Lesbians – D^2.

S.E.P.S. (Separatists Enraged Proud and Strong) included:
   Bev Jo I came out before the Women's Liberation Movement and never was het. I was born in 1950 in a working-class family of Irish, English, French, and German ancestry in Cincinnati, Ohio, U.S.A. I am an ex-catholic. I have a chronic hidden disability which limits my work. I have been a Dyke Separatist activist since 1972. I was one of the writers and editors of *Dykes and Gorgons* in 1973, which was the first Dyke Separatist publication the collective knew about. I have written many Separatist articles and was part of the collective that planned the Dyke Separatist Gathering in San Francisco in 1983 and the Lesbian Forum on Separatism in Oakland in 1984. I taught self-defense in female-only classes for ten years. I am now writing a book with Linda Strega and Ruston, *Dykes-Loving-Dykes*, which is a Separatist analysis of strong dyke identity and how we can protect ourselves and our Dyke cultures from increasing heterosexism among Lesbians. My hope is to be part of a growing international Dyke Separatist community which

includes Separatists from all backgrounds.

Jamalia is Afrikan-American, radical, militant, lesbian, feminist, 40 years old. Lesbian rights activist, grass-roots organizer, activist in the feminist movement and Afrikan liberation struggles since 1968. Grew up extremely poor in the urban south. Agnostic, out as a Dyke since 1979, incest survivor, Pisces.

Linda Strega I'm a working class Italian-descent U.S. Dyke, ex-catholic, with a hidden disability, born in 1941. An ex-het who resisted marriage and motherhood, I came out through the Women's Liberation Movement in 1972 and have been a Dyke Separatist since 1973.

Marty came out as a Lesbian in 1975 and as a Separatist in 1981. As one year of right-wing backlash moves into another, she remains an undaunted radical dyke, still separatist after all these years!

Roxanna Fiamma is 44, Italian american of color, working class-upwardly mobile, able-bodied with hearing loss, urban/ Denver, recovering catholic, came out in winter of 1967, incest survivor, P.E. teacher.

Fran is 45, Western European American (ancestors from Ireland, Scotland, & England) grew up rural working class, able-bodied with recent stress/job related health problems, vegetarian, animal rights activist, former bulimic, elementary teacher for 25 years, came out in 1976.

Sidney Spinster Political ideals do not a movement make. Although I have many ideals in common with most other separatists, often the similarity ends there. Since 1981, when I wrote my contribution, I have found all sorts of verbal abuse of other Lesbians done in the name of 'defending' Separatism or Separatists. I've also shared deep love with many gentle and friendly Separatists. I want to be part of a strong *movement* of loving, nurturing, action-oriented Separatists who encourage each other as we find ways to increase Lesbian Freedom. But right now, I don't know how to get there from here.

Susan In the six years since I wrote this piece I have refined, deepened, and radically expanded my knowledge. Yet, because of my firmly rooted, absolutely essential belief in lesbian separatism I am choosing to publish. I want to stress the complexity with any parallel between lesbian separatism and Jewish cultures. Inquiry into such salient points as historical context, anti-Semitism, forced ghettoization, economic restrictions, class and race, etc. must be involved with any complete analysis. Re: part 13, I know men to be quite inferior to womyn and now believe that no womon needs a man for '. . . happiness and becoming.' Womyn are with men because of a purposefully intended all pervasive patriarchal plan which is a lethal denial, deadening, and/or literal rape and murder of most womyn's power, passion, and elemental force. In the event of a revolutionary return to matriarchy (which will and must occur) where men no longer have the power, we would perhaps be sexually gynandrous – tho never would men's simple bodies compare to the beauty and depths of womyn's. Excluded from my presentation of gynocidal patriarchy and my renderings of accountability are the surviving traditional gynocratic womon centered aboriginal and native tribal peoples of the world. This work was intended as my voice speaking from spirit and emotional intuitive experiences as well as linear thought. It does not attempt to encompass the whole of any of its threads. The writing in stanzas is prose set off spatially for distinction. Kindling in my present life is the radical feminist revolutionary and healing potential within shamonism, witchcraft, and magic. I make my home in Northampton, Massachusetts.

Sylvia Foley lives and works in Brooklyn, NY. Her work has appeared in *Sinister Wisdom*, *Conditions*, and *Other Voices*. She has recently completed her first novel, *Rooms*.

Vernita Gray still separate, separating myself, from bad vibes, mean men, and wilted roses, to be with other, blooming separatists.

Vivienne Louise is an African-American lesbian who has lived in the San Francisco Bay Area for ten years. She comes from a middle-class background in Washington DC, is partially disabled with one leg shorter than the other, and survived a 12-year span of incestual molestation by her father. She considers fear her most formidable internal demon and consistently resists his attempts to bind her being into stagnant and negative attitudes; dreaming instead of lesbian nations.

zana is 41, Jewish, disabled, living on lesbian land, helping weave a lesbian culture of joy and sharing. *herb womon*, a collection of her poetry and drawings, is available for $7 from her at 12150 w. calle seneca, tucson, az 85743.